Catholic Biblical Scholarship for the Third Millennium

John F. McCarthy

LORETO PUBLICATIONS

FITZWILLIAM NEW HAMPSHIRE 03447
AD 2017

DECLARATION:

In obedience to the Decrees of Pope UrbanVIII and other Pontiffs, we declare that we submit, without reserve, the entire contents of this book to the judgment of the Apostolic See of the Holy Roman Catholic Church.

2017 First Edition — Loreto Publications

ISBN 978-1-62292-121-8
All Rights Reserved
Layout and Cover Design by Michael Hamilton

Loreto Publications
P. O. Box 603
Fitzwilliam, New Hampshire 03447
603-239-6671
www.LoretoPubs.org

Printed and Bound in the USA

TABLE OF CONTENTS

Introduction

1. This volume is a collection of articles first published separately under my name in *Living Tradition* on the general subject of biblical interpretation. This book is aimed at bringing together localized ideas that fit into a larger picture suggesting answers to some long-standing problems in the field of biblical interpretation that are in urgent need of clarification. Of course, the book represents only my personal opinions and not the official teaching of the Church, except where the official teaching is quoted. And I am grateful for any improvements and corrections that competent readers may bring forward. This volume embodies an attempt to expand upon the call of Joseph Cardinal Ratzinger, in a seminal address delivered in New York City on January 27, 1988, for a synthesis of the historical critical method with the objects of Catholic faith – a goal, he said, that would require the efforts of an entire generation of biblical scholars and others. This book does not present a finished synthesis, but I hope that it offers enough facts and ideas to encourage many others over time to undertake and complete the task.

2. In a series of articles published over the years under my name in *Living Tradition,* beginning in 1979, I have supported the *neo-patristic approach* to the interpretation of Sacred Scripture, in contrast with that form of *historical criticism* which calls itself exclusively the "historical critical method," now in vogue also among Catholic Scripture scholars with the broad approval of the Roman Catholic Hierarchy. This form of historical criticism is an approach originally developed within the tradition of the eighteenth-century Enlightenment and is in its non-Catholic and native environment essentially reductive, naturalistic, rationalistic, and modernist. It is *reductionist,* because it regards as factual only the human element in the sacred writings and never the divine. It is *naturalistic,* because it admits only natural effects and never the supernatural. It is *rationalistic,* because it professes the superiority of human reason over divine revelation, and it does not accept divine inspiration as a certified source of factual knowledge. And it is *modernist,* inasmuch as it adheres to what mainline

historical critics call "the outlook of modern man." The condemnation of Modernism by Pope Pius X was aimed chiefly at the approach of certain Catholic critics of the Bible, but it came into the Church from writings of the Enlightenment tradition and of non-Catholic critics like Émile Durkheim and Hermann Gunkel. Catholic scholars who follow this historical critical method, as Catholic believers, do not profess any of these four anti-Catholic presuppositions, but the presuppositions always remain in the background, and, in the absence of any critical and thoroughgoing analysis of the historical critical method from the viewpoint of Catholic faith and tradition, each Catholic scholar has the responsibility to use the method without ending up in contradiction to his or her Catholic faith.

3. In chapter 1, we bring out the widespread confusion that exists today in the field of Catholic biblical interpretation, due mainly, it seems, to the chronic failure of many Catholic Scripture scholars and others to work in keeping with the "big picture" presented in the Bible and thus the failure to integrate adequately their exegetical work with the objects of Catholic faith. In the words of Pope Benedict XVI, spoken on October 14, 2008, to the constituents of the Fourteenth General Congregation of the Synod of Bishops, when "*the hermeneutic of faith is missing,*" then "*a deep chasm is created between scientific exegesis and lectio divina,*" and so, he continues, "*for the life and the mission of the Church, for the future of faith, this dualism between exegesis and theology must be overcome.*" Pope Benedict pointed out, quoting the words of *Dei Verbum* 12 of the Second Vatican Council, that what is "*almost absent*" but greatly needed by Catholic scholars in the interpretation of the biblical text is an awareness of "*the unity of the entire Scripture,*" and of "*the living tradition of the whole Church,*" together with attention to "*the analogy of faith.*"

4. While the Catholic Church has always been favorable to historical criticism in the sound and original application of the term, which is the use of critical thinking in the activity of any competent historical researcher, a form of biblical criticism which existed among some liberal non-Catholic interpreters under the name of "higher criticism" in the late nineteenth century was rejected by Pope Leo XIII in 1893 as an "inept method," [1] and after this method had appropriated exclusively to itself the name of "historical criticism" in the early twentieth century, it was refused again under this name as "the natural fruit" of modernist philosophical principles by Pope

---

1 Pope Leo XIII, *Providentissimus Deus,* no. 17. Passages from the papal encyclicals quoted in this book in English translation are taken from Claudia Carlen IHM, ed., *The Papal Encyclicals* 1740-1981, in five volumes (McGrath Publishing Company, 1981).

Pius X in 1907.[2] Thus, a confusion of terminology has arisen in the field of biblical studies, where "historical criticism" has become the watchword of a method that arose in rationalist circles and whose new cutting edge, under the name of "form-criticism" (literally, "form history"), has been greatly promoted by writers like Hermann Gunkel, Martin Dibelius, and Rudolf Bultmann. That confusion continues today. For instance, in his intervention of October 14, 2008, quoted in the paragraph above, Pope Benedict XVI notes that, in *Dei Verbum* 12, the Second Vatican Council "confirms the need to use the historical critical method," because, he says, "historical fact is a constitutive dimension of Christian faith," but the pope is not saying that the Council confirms the use of historical criticism in the exclusive sense promoted by Gunkel, Dibelius, and Bultmann, and so confusion has reigned in biblical studies as a result of the ambiguous use of this term. In the course of this book I shall use the term *historical criticism* to mean that "child of the Enlightenment" whose cutting edge since the beginning of the twentieth century has been the method of *form-criticism*.

5. Joseph Cardinal Ratzinger, then prefect of the Congregation for the Doctrine of the Church, surveyed the inadequacy of this method of historical criticism in a seminal address given in New York City on January 27, 1988, and widely published in several languages, titled *Biblical Interpretation in Crisis*, in which he reviewed some *"great errors"* maintained by modern exegetes over the previous century, due above all to *"the influence of Martin Dibelius and Rudolf Bultmann,"* called for *"a new and thorough reflection on exegetical method,"* and presented the basic elements of a needed *"new synthesis"* of biblical exegesis. For this effort, the cardinal said, it is essential to include in the desired new synthesis *"the great outlines of patristic and medieval thought."* In *Living Tradition* no. 9 (January 1987), the Roman Theological Forum welcomed the call of the Extraordinary Synod of Bishops of 1985 for *pluriformity without pluralism* within the Church, and we undertook to assist in the restoration of certain dogmatic, moral, and mystical traditions within the Church that were then being underemphasized. Of course, what we are referring to here is radical pluralism, in which basically contradictory theories of knowledge are held in the same mind or system. Also, one of the special aims expressed in that issue was to continue to promote the neo-patristic interpretation of Sacred Scripture.

6. Since the introduction of the use of the form-critical method of biblical interpretation among Catholic exegetes, the absence of any adequate

---

2 Pope Pius X, *Pascendi dominici gregis,* no. 30.

synthesis of the method with the principles and objects of Catholic faith has been a glaring handicap. An enduring and ever unfulfilled need of Catholic historical criticism has been a systematic separation of the positive elements in the historical critical method from its negative elements and a resulting synthesis of the positive remainder with the objects and spirit of Catholic faith, as called for in our time by then Cardinal Joseph Ratzinger in January 1988, and as concisely expressed later by him as Pope Benedict XVI in his appeal made to the Ordinary Synod of Bishops in 2008 (see nos. 3 and 5 above). This needed synthesis was never pursued by traditional Catholic thinkers, mainly because the claimed usefulness of the historical critical method had already been rejected by Popes Leo XIII and Pius X (see no. 4 above), and no Catholic historical critic has ever accomplished this task. However, Catholic and other historical critics of the form-critical type, in the unfortunate absence of a working framework of synthesis of their exegetical work with the objects of Catholic faith, have, nevertheless, made many contributions to the understanding of Sacred Scripture which deserve to be recognized. Joseph Ratzinger/Pope Benedict XVI, in his *Jesus of Nazareth*, points out that historical critical exegesis "has already yielded its essential fruit" and must now "take a methodological step forward and see itself once again as a theological discipline, without abandoning its historical character," in the course of which "it must recognize that a properly developed faith-hermeneutic is appropriate to the text and can be combined with a historical hermeneutic, aware of its limits, so as to form a methodological whole." It has been his hope that his undertaking in writing *Jesus of Nazareth* constitutes a significant step in that direction.[3]

7. Father Marie-Joseph Lagrange, OP, a loyal and talented Catholic exegete who wrote extensively at the turn of the twentieth century and beyond in promotion of the new historical critical method and who is regarded by many as the great pioneer of the historical critical movement

---

3 "One thing is clear to me: in two hundred years of exegetical work, historical critical exegesis has already yielded its essential fruit. If scholarly exegesis is not to exhaust itself in constantly new hypotheses, becoming theologically irrelevant, it must take a methodological step forward and see itself once again as a theological discipline, without abandoning its historical character. It must learn that the positivistic hermeneutic on which it has been based does not constitute the only valid and definitively evolved rational approach; rather, it constitutes a specific and historically conditioned form of rationality that is both open to correction and completion and in need of it. It must recognize that a properly developed faith-hermeneutic is appropriate to the text and can be combined with a historical hermeneutic, aware of its limits, so as to form a methodological whole" (Joseph Ratzinger, Pope Benedict XVI, *Jesus of Nazareth,* (Ignatius Press, 2011) part two, pages xiv-xv).

within the Catholic Church and even as the founder of modern Catholic biblical scholarship, saw also the need for a "fundamental reflection on the coherent status of truth" that a synthesis of the historical critical method with the common Catholic understanding of Sacred Scripture would entail, but he never undertook the task, regretting that he did not feel that he had "either the strength or the aptitude for that."[4] Believing Catholic historical critics basically follow a critical process beginning from the epistemology and world-view of Immanuel Kant and other exponents of the Enlightenment and at a certain point, where felt necessary, introduce loyally but also dualistically and from a distance the outlook of their Catholic faith.[5] They do this largely by individual initiative and in a non-systematic way in the absence of any adequate mental framework having the principles necessary to solidify their exegetical work with Catholic tradition.

8. Hermann Gunkel (1862–1932) formally initiated the exegetical method of form-criticism (*formgeschichte*: literally "form-history") with the publication in German in 1901 of his famous work *Genesis*, a commentary on the Book of Genesis. He was at the time a leading member of a group of Enlightenment scholars known as the "History of Religions School," who had already agreed among themselves that the Book of Genesis consisted largely of short passages of imaginary literature ("literary forms") later linked together by anonymous editors into a continuous narrative. Gunkel claimed that the right way for contemporary rationalists to understand this text from a rational historical point of view was to look into the historical development of each individual story, that is, into their "form-histories." Gunkel's book is a collection on virtually every page of outrageous attacks against belief in the inerrancy of Sacred Scripture. It has been countered by

---

4 "The true result of biblical revelation will not contradict the truth discovered by the historical critic. Father Lagrange regretted not being in a position to advance greatly this fundamental reflection on the coherent status of truth, learned from Thomas Aquinas. 'I truly wish that the good Lord had given me more genius to do the work that is necessary to be done in order to reconcile public opinion with modern criticism, but I do not feel that I have either the strength or the aptitude for that'" (Bernard Montagnes, OP, *The Story of Father Marie-Joseph Lagrange: Founder of Modern Catholic Biblical Study*, English translation by Benedict Viviano, OP, [Paulist Press, New York, 2006], p. 39).

5 "Finally, redaction criticism studies the modifications that these texts have undergone before being fixed in their final state; it also analyzes this final stage, trying as far as possible to identify the tendencies particularly characteristic of this concluding process. At this point one is in a position to consider the demands of the text from the point of view of action and life" [PBC, *The Interpretation of the Bible in the Church*, p. 38].

Catholic scholars in various details, but it has never been met by Catholic form-critics, as far as I know, with a substantial response to its denial of the truth of the Book of Genesis, and I attribute this failure to their lack of a mental framework of principles governing the answers to the specific questions that Gunkel and his colleagues have raised.

9. It is important to consider how historical criticism arose in the first place. It came from rationalist thinkers who wanted to disprove the Christian faith in general and in particular the historical truth of the Bible, and this was part of the movement known as the Enlightenment. In the 1890s a group of "enlightened" German scholars had formed a school which they called "higher criticism," based on the idea that the Bible was composed by writers who represented a sub-rational believing community and produced imaginary episodes and scenes for the use of their people. As a "scientific" basis of their stand they relied on the doctrine of (David) Émile Durkheim (1858–1917), who "is commonly regarded as a principal architect of modern social science and a father of the science of sociology." His *Elementary Forms of the Religious Life* (1912) presented a theory of religion which compared and contrasted the social and cultural lives of aboriginal societies with those of modern societies."[6]

10. Durkheim makes a radical distinction between "primitive societies" and "advanced societies." He holds that primitive societies tend to function on a sub-rational level, and he attributes the origin of religions in primitive societies to a felt need of security against uncontrolled threats (such as violent storms, floods, earthquakes, wars, diseases, famines, enemies, etc.) in answer to which they invented the existence of gods and sacred things and actions which they believed could help them to fend off these threats. Now, as regards his *Genesis* of 1901 and the method of form-criticism, Hermann Gunkel followed an earlier version of the theory of Durkheim in classifying the social background of the Old Testament, and in particular of the Book of Genesis, to be the product of a primitive society whose religion arose and functioned on the level of sub-rational emotion and instinct, and whose responses could even be predicted by rational investigators using sociological laws governing instinctive reactions of sub-rational groups to their respective situation in life (*Sitz im Leben*).

11. Rudolf Bultmann and about four other rationalist scholars founded the form-criticism of the New Testament around 1919–1921. Not surprisingly they immediately classified the Synoptic Gospels of Matthew, Mark, and Luke as products of a sub-rational religious society, the early

---

6 Cf. *Wikipedia* (January 2015), "David Émile Durkheim" with internet links.

Christian community, which, they claimed, generated anonymously many brief stories divided into several "literary genres," that is, imaginary stories about the teachings and deeds of Jesus of Nazareth. The best known founding books presenting the form-criticism of the New Testament are Martin Dibelius, *Die Formgeschichte des Evangeliums* (1919) (Eng. trans., *From Tradition to Gospel*) and Rudolf Bultmann, *History of the Synoptic Tradition* (1921). Traditionally, Catholics do not consider the beliefs of religions formed outside of the Judeo-Christian culture to reflect spiritual realities or to be of authentic divine origin. Hence, what Durkheim claimed to have ascertained in his study of the native religious beliefs of American Indian tribes and of groups of Australian aborigines has no impact upon Catholic belief in the existence and providence of the one true God. It is rather the unfounded assumption of mainline (non-Catholic) form-critics that the religious belief recorded in the Old and the New Testaments arose from an instinctive and sub-rational religious community, a presupposition which, I maintain, offends against scientific procedure.

12. In chapter 2, part I, we review some points made in the widely published address given in New York City in 1988 by then Joseph Cardinal Ratzinger (quoted above), in which he pointed out that the *"historical critical method" is neither historical nor sufficiently critical of itself.* Rather, he said, *it is reductive and limited to the Kantian philosophical categories.* He examined some Rationalist presuppositions of the historical critical method, as inherited from the liberal Protestant school of "higher criticism" and from the form-criticism of Hermann Gunkel, Martin Dibelius, Rudolf Bultmann, and others. According to Cardinal Ratzinger, the main philosophical presupposition underlying modern historical criticism lies *"in the philosophic turning point proposed by Immanuel Kant which limits human intellectual life to the realm of the Kantian 'categories,' and, by very definition, excludes interventions of God as well as any new initiative from another plane."*[7] What Cardinal Ratzinger calls the Kantian "philosophical turning point" or the "Kantian split," according to which human intellectual life is considered to be limited to the realm of the Kantian categories, effectively serves the anti-Christian project of viewing all religion as a merely subjective state of mind. The cardinal outlines a number of ways in contemporary use of the historical critical method which he claims are unscientific, such as that historical criticism on fuller investigation turns out to be neither truly historical nor sufficiently critical of its own

---

7 Joseph Cardinal Ratzinger, in Richard J. Neuhaus, ed., *Biblical Interpretation* in Crisis (Grand Rapids: Eerdmans, 1989), pp. 14-15).

mistakes, and that it has an inability to distinguish between hypotheses that are helpful and those which are not. The cardinal expresses his hope that in a new study of exegetical method *"scientific exegesis"* would come to recognize *"the philosophic element present in a great number of its ground rules,"* such as the influence of Kantian philosophy upon its approach and the use of techniques based upon questionable presuppositions of the so-called "modern point of view."

13. Non-believers in general consider the objects of Christian faith to be religious fantasies, over and above the Kantian conclusion that all non-empirical knowledge is mere opinion and not certified truth. What Kant did was to give some intellectual justification to the rationalist supposition that every account of supernatural being or activity is a product of human fantasy. In other words, Kant proposed some seeming arguments to back up an anti-supernatural bias which form-critical Scripture scholars and others often nurture even apart from any awareness on their part of the Kantian categories. In this and the following chapter we shall begin to consider whether the method of historical criticism is truly historical and truly scientific.

14. In chapter 2, part II, we present a critical examination of the philosophy of Immanuel Kant as lying in the background of the modern historical critical approach to Sacred Scripture. Kant presents what he calls "transcendental idealism," the viewpoint that the subjective reality of conscious objects is more real than the seeming reality of external material objects, and that sense perception of seeming external objects outranks the objects of mental speculation. This is a reductive approach which downgrades historical realities and attacks the moderate realism of Aristotelian/Thomist philosophy as well as sheer common sense generating the "Kantian split" in which all divinely inspired thinking is branded as "fanciful." In the Kantian perspective, the ideas of God, immortality, and the human soul survive, not as reflecting reality, but only as subjective aesthetic pursuits. In Chapter 1 it was noted that the empiricism of Immanuel Kant, like all empiricism, has a reductive approach to reality. This reductive view of reality might be called "scientific" by a certain class of thinkers, but it is actually a violation both of reason and of common sense. Kant's error here lies in making the proximate object of human knowledge (the mirror-like image) into the only accessible object, and thus in obscuring the real remote objects of human knowledge. While the Aristotelian/Thomist theory of proximate-versus-remote objects of knowledge opens the way to a better understanding of the human mind, Kant bases his stand on

wrong definitions of knowledge, reason, understanding, and even of reality itself. The way to liberation from these epistemological errors is open through an application of the principles and teaching of Thomas Aquinas and other great thinkers of the Catholic tradition. It is a pity that Kant chose a sweeping rejection of Aristotelian/Thomist epistemology rather than a serious study of it. The philosophy of Immanuel Kant embodies a frontal attack against Christian faith that needs to be refuted point by point, as has, unfortunately, not been adequately done over the years, even by Catholic philosophers and theologians, although summary replies have not been lacking.

15. Accordingly, in chapter 2, part III, the pervading influence of the anti-Christian philosophy of the Enlightenment and especially of Kant's philosophy upon the historical critical method is taken up. Kant's uniting of European materialism with European idealism is a synthesis that falls short of and negates the moderate realism of Aristotelian/Thomist philosophy and which also provides the background for his subjectivist and reductive attack on the objects and worldview of Christian faith. "Many of the characteristics of the positions of those who deny authoritative and inerrant revelation are drawn directly from Kant" (David Beck). The "criticism" in these methods bears a relationship to Kant's critical approach, even though Kant did not originate the term,[8] and all of these forms of biblical exegesis are naturalistic in the sense that they do not allow for the possibility of any supernatural influence or activity in the "modern" understanding of the Bible." Kant's blending of David Hume's empiricism with his own conception of "transcendental ideas" reduces the importance of testimony in the acquisition of knowledge. The form-criticism of Gunkel and Bultmann is a critical approach to the interpretation of Sacred Scripture in the sense that it sets aside Christian faith and concentrates exclusively upon critical reason in the Kantian sense in order to critique the Bible. It does not consider at all the use of proper historical reasoning in biblical interpretation, in the sense that properly based critical reasoning can also be used to certify and to defend the historical truth of the Sacred Scriptures, to probe their historicity, and to achieve a fuller understanding of them.

---

8 The so-called "critical" approach to the interpretation of Sacred Scripture, now known as "historical criticism," was brought into focus in 1678 by Richard Simon, a convert and Catholic priest, when he published what he called a "critical history" of the Old Testament. He called his work a "critical history," because he subjected the text of the Old Testament to what he considered to be the "critical judgment" of his human reason.

16. Also, in chapter 2, Part III, are listed several unscientific procedures of the form-critical method of Rudolf Bultmann. These include viewing the sacred text always from an exclusively rationalist point of view, using false historical method, using circular argumentation, drawing conclusions from internal indications alone, using poorly defined terms, assuming that simpler statements are therefore older. In addition, Bultmann claims to use the form-critical method in order to "go back historically" behind the text of the Gospels into their formative history. To do this, for instance, he uses his naturalistic presupposition that the supernatural does not really exist in order to assume that Jesus was not really the Son of God and could not even have been thought of by early Jewish Christians as the Son of God before Christianity had expanded into the Greco-pagan world, where the idea of a god-man was imaginable. Thus, he excludes all references to Jesus the God-Man from what he considers to be the earlier Christian kerygma, deletes conceptually these references from the text of the Gospels, and then calls this a step backward into the history of the Gospel tradition. But this is not a historical step backward; it is only an application of the false philosophical presupposition that nothing supernatural can happen or exist. The fact is that Bultmann's "earlier version" of the kerygma is not an earlier version; it is just an impoverished remnant of the final text. In addition, his method is anti-historical, because it proceeds from so-called internal evidence alone, while ignoring external historical evidence, such as the testimony of witnesses.

17. In chapter 3, we review and expand upon the call of then Joseph Cardinal Ratzinger in 1988 for "a better synthesis between historical and theological methods," between criticism and dogma by means of self-criticism of the "historical method" being used by exegetes today. He traces the need for this revision today to the abiding influence of Martin Dibelius and Rudolf Bultmann "whose methodological orientations determine even to this day the methodology and course of modern exegesis." Cardinal Ratzinger proposes some "basic elements for a new synthesis," and he notes that the time is ripe for a "radical new reflection on exegetical method." Central to this whole discussion about historical science is the question of the meaning and function of the concept of reality, which Bultmann treats at length for his own purposes. Secondly comes the question of the meaning and function of historical science. Out of a critical analysis of the techniques of historical criticism today hopefully will come what I call "the science of historical theology."

18. The exegetical framework to be developed will be an analytical refinement of the approach that is implicit in the exegesis of the Fathers of the Church. St. Thomas Aquinas has given a valuable explanation of the four senses of Sacred Scripture. He points out that the spiritual enlightenment derived from reading the Scriptures is scientific because it is knowledge of God, who is real and is the consummation of all that is real. St. Thomas uses the example of the use of the word "light" in Genesis 1:3 to illustrate how the method of the four senses opens up whole new vistas of insight into the meaning of the sacred text. In this chapter as a more detailed example we present the exegesis of St. Thomas on the allegory of the Old and New Testaments in Galatians 4:21–31.

19. In chapter 4, part I, we examine in some detail the difference between the neo-patristic method and historical criticism of the form-critical type. The reconstituted Pontifical Biblical Commission, in its 1993 document, *The Interpretation of the Bible in the Church* (IBC), declares that the historical critical method is "indispensable" for the "scientific study of the meaning of ancient texts," including Sacred Scripture, seeing that the Bible is the "word of God in human language." We have noted above in the introduction that, in this document of the PBC, the expression "historical critical method" is identified with that "child of the Enlightenment" whose cutting edge since 1901 has been the method of form-criticism, initiated by Hermann Gunkel and extended by Rudolf Bultmann and many others, and we have reason to question whether this historical critical method is basically a scientific study at all, even though it is widely called "scientific exegesis" in Catholic academia. Nevertheless, as Joseph Cardinal Ratzinger points out in his preface to the *Interpretation of the Bible in the Church,* the reconstituted Pontifical Biblical Commission is "not an organ of the teaching Church." Hence, it is not an expression of the magisterium of the Church and should not be treated as such, for instance, by being included in the *Enchiridion Biblicum, Documents of the Church on Sacred Scripture,* and in many other ways as well. This reconstitution of the Pontifical Biblical Commission by Pope Paul VI in his motu proprio, *Sedula cura,* of 27 June 1971, marked a kind of historical vindication of the cause of this kind of historical criticism within the Catholic Church after a struggle for acceptance of over seven decades. It was the judgment of Pope Paul, following upon desires expressed earlier by Pope Pius XII in his encyclical letter *Divino afflante Spiritu,* that Catholic scholars of liberal bent be respected and treated with charity by those who were more attached to traditional Catholic exegesis. The original Pontifical Biblical Commission,

founded by Pope Leo XIII with his apostolic letter, *Vigilantiae,* of 30 October 1902, was composed of a group of voting cardinals aided by other persons learned in biblical studies and in sacred theology and was an organ of the teaching Church. Now the reconstituted PBC is composed of a group of no more than twenty Scripture scholars, mostly historical critics of the form-critical type, presided over *ex officio* by one cardinal, the prefect of the Congregation for the Doctrine of the Faith. They are "a commission of scholars who, in their scientific and ecclesial responsibility as believing exegetes, take positions on important problems of scriptural interpretation, and they know that for this task they enjoy the confidence of the teaching office" (Card. Ratzinger, in his Preface to the Document, quoting from the founding decree of the reconstituted Commission).

20. Contrary to the opinions of most non-Catholic form-critics, the believing exegetes of the PBC agree that the spiritual sense of the biblical text, so central to the teaching of the Fathers of the Church and of medieval exegetes, "when read under the influence of the Holy Spirit in the context of the paschal mystery of Christ and of the new life which flows from it, ... truly exists" (*IBC,* II.B). This statement implies that the so-called "higher criticism" of human reason alone is not really higher than the viewpoint of Christian faith. The scholars recall in regard to the multiplicity of senses in the biblical text that for many years, historical critical exegesis followed the principle of one single meaning for every segment of the biblical text, but, they commendably say, they are "now open to a multi-sense approach." The Commission notes also for good reason in the same place that the spiritual sense represents "a transition to a higher level of reality" and results from setting the text of the paschal event "in relation to real events which are not foreign to it."

21. However, Catholic form-critics in a growing number of instances deny absolutely the historical reality of some biblical events, and they also call some other biblical episodes non-historical, while continuing to believe them as objects of faith. While mainline form-critics like Hermann Gunkel and Rudolf Bultmann clearly, although unreasonably, take for granted that all of the remarkable episodes recorded in the Scriptures are products of make-believe, Catholic form-critics seldom address directly the problem that this presupposition raises for believers, seemingly because their minds are not clearly focused on the questioning that historical criticism tends to raise regarding the reality of the objects of faith. A Catholic form-critic may say, for instance, that there was no real, historical appearance of the Angel Gabriel to the Blessed Virgin Mary, while then continuing to believe

in this appearance as an act of faith, but where does that put the reality of the objects of faith? The same form-critic may continue to recite the *Angelus* and to say in prayer, "The Angel of the Lord declared unto Mary, and she conceived of the Holy Spirit," and go on to add, "that we to whom the Incarnation of Christ thy Son was made known by the message of an angel," but how strongly in this case is his response keeping this object of faith within the continuum of external reality, considering that an object cannot both be and not be true at the same time and in the same way (using the basic logical principle of non-contradiction)? A form-critic may have a response to this, but I wonder what this kind of radical dualism does to the unity of truth. It is true that, in order to keep objects of Catholic faith within one's continuum of reality, it is not necessary to have thought reflectively about this problem, but the critical questioning lies implicitly within the presuppositions of the historical critical method, and every Catholic historical critic has to face this problem on his own, without the availability of any standard set of principles relating the method to Catholic faith except very general principles of traditional Catholic theology and philosophy that are not specifically tuned to many of the problems that historical criticism raises, so that wrong conclusions may easily be drawn. Hence, Catholic historical critics should welcome the preparation of the new synthesis of exegetical method called for by then Cardinal Ratzinger, in which the false presuppositions of mainline form-criticism will be handled in a truly scientific manner within the fuller proportions of the science of historical theology. Similarly, where discoveries of empirical science raise serious problems about a traditional reading of a passage of Sacred Scripture, believers, without necessarily having to find the inspired text to be erroneous, have a right and a reason, as St. Augustine of Hippo pointed out sixteen centuries ago, to examine the interpretation that has been traditionally given to the questioned passage, and to see if, perhaps, there is a better interpretation that will resolve the difficulty See, for example, in the Appendix my suggested interpretation of the "days of creation" in Genesis one.

22. In its 1993 document, *The Interpretation of the Bible in the Church*, the reconstituted Pontifical Biblical Commission finds that the historical critical approach "is a method which, when used in an objective manner, implies of itself no *a priori*," and that "for a long time now scholars have ceased combining the method with a philosophical system" (*IBC*, 1A.4). But actually, according to the exposition of then Joseph Cardinal Ratzinger, the historical critical method is in itself so

saturated with philosophy that its notion of objectivity is completely out of focus. Believing Catholic historical critics do not intentionally profess the philosophy of Immanuel Kant or of other spokesmen of the Enlightenment, but in using the historical critical method, they use also at least unawarely its presuppositions, and thus they tend to lose focus on the mental framework that they would need to be aware of in order to get completely away from the reductionism, naturalism, rationalism, and modernism currently in practice within the system."

23. In Chapter 4, part II, I introduce some features that should be present in a new synthesis of exegetical method. The first step is to realize that the new framework must begin from the viewpoint of Catholic faith and not from the secularized approach that Hermann Gunkel and Rudolf Bultmann call "the outlook of modern man." The new synthesis must begin from an openness of mind and heart to the God-related reality of the message of the sacred text and not to the reductive, naturalistic, and rationalistic purview of the Enlightenment. Therefore, the new synthesis must become both a treasury of theological insight into the spiritual wealth of the inspired word of God and a grand defense of the historical and objective truth of what is said in the Bible.

24. The second step in creating the new synthesis of Catholic biblical exegesis is the development of a mental framework of exegetical presuppositions that are compatible with Catholic faith and theology. This could begin with an epistemology based upon Aristotelian/Thomist moderate realism in place of the Kantian "transcendental idealism" that cuts off the historical critical exegete from contact with the external world. The third step could well be the use of a better concept of science. Historical critics often refer to their method as "scientific exegesis," but they show little reflection on the meaning of this term. Probably they derive this from the fact that, in its native environment, historical critical study focuses only on the human and natural side of the text of the Bible, but this usage of the word "science" is reductive in the sense that it seems to ignore the other dimensions of the sacred text, as outlined, for instance, in the *Catechism of the Catholic Church.*

25. A fuller and more precise concept of science is present in the Catholic philosophical tradition, such as, for example, in the philosophical writings of Thomas Aquinas. In our time, a good reference may be had in Anthony Rizzi's *The Science before Science.*[9] Rizzi starts out with the fact that, in contemporary Western culture, only "scientific conclusions" are

---

9 See my review of Rizzi's book in *Living Tradition* 123 (May 2006).

considered to be unquestionably true knowledge, while all other ideas are taken to be mere opinion. And by "scientific conclusions" people usually mean the results of empirical science alone (Rizzi, p. xv). But the empirical sciences are not the only fields that offer certified knowledge. We can have proper knowledge from the direct experience of our sensory faculties as well as from correct reasoning from facts and principles that we have personally "seen" and recognized to be true. The trouble is that those who refuse to recognize any sound philosophical principles in their thinking about empirical science become the victims of blind religious, or more often anti-religious, opinion (Rizzi, p. 19). He shows throughout his book that the knowledge particular to the empirical sciences must logically be rooted in objective reality, and he shows that all physical scientists do in fact maintain a working assumption that they are dealing with objective reality even though they may claim otherwise. He adds that "Our proof that something is true comes from conformity with reality, not from systems of ideas" (Rizzi, pp. xvi and 57). Rizzi concentrates his argument upon the pure sciences in a sustained effort to show that the physical and mathematical sciences become false guides if they are not underpinned by the higher principles of metaphysics (Rizzi, pp. 55–60).

26. Rizzi goes on to note that Immanuel Kant (1724–1804), for instance, has had great influence over the thinking of many modern physical scientists. Kant, following in the subjectivist line of thinking of René Descartes (1596–1650), made empiriometric (formally mathematical and materially physical) science the ground of his philosophy and thus, for certified knowledge, gave beings of reason priority over what exists in objective reality (p. 169). Rizzi's point is that empirical science can go astray if it neglects the insights of the higher science of metaphysics, such as the fact that all true science must be based upon objective reality, and that attitudes of scientists that offend against these more evident insights are anti-scientific. Kant and many others like him have produced systems of thought that are highly organized and consistent with their own defined principles, but which are inconsistent with more fundamental principles that stand outside of and above their system. Rizzi points out that "To the degree [that] we leave (objective) Being out, even implicitly, that is the degree [to which] we allow irrationality to reign" (p. 344), and again, "Knowledge is about reality, not about knowledge" (p. 351). That is why metaphysics is the science that comes before all other sciences. Rizzi locates the valid set of metaphysical principles needed for the pursuit of all other sciences in the philosophy of Aristotle, especially as interpreted by Thomas Aquinas (p. 185).

27. In chapter 5, on the nature of the science of historical theology, we begin by asking ourselves what "science" is, and we arrive at the conclusion that "science is the knowledge of reality as such." So the concept of reality plays a great role in discussions about the nature of science. We then consider two levels of science: common sense (common science) and specialized science. Important for the study of historical science is the distinction between the use of logical universals and syllogisms in classical science and the use of singular objects and intuitive reasoning in historical science. We question whether the knowledge of science requires the reduction of all of its conclusions to the level of sensory experience, as Immanuel Kant claimed. We ask where the concept of intellectual intuition of singular objects fits into the cognitive theory of Aristotle and Thomas Aquinas. Then we take a look at the task of formulating a theory of history that is compatible with Catholic faith and tradition, using mainly the speculation of William H. Walsh as a beginning. Now, "reasoning" is the human intellect in operation, and we ask ourselves what historical reasoning is like. We shall discover that human reasoning may be either horizontal or vertical.

28. With regard to the historical inerrancy of the biblical text, in this book I treat of several instances of seemingly subtle historical meanings. A notable example of a possible subtle historical meaning would be the question of the claimed "erroneous" and "non-historical" six "days" of creation in Genesis 1, where in the Appendix of this book I have suggested an updated alternative solution to the problem in keeping with the original thinking of St. Augustine of Hippo. Another example is the supposed irreconcilable conflict of the two genealogies of Jesus in Matthew 1 and Luke 3, for which I propose a historically based solution in chapter 15 (no. 14), in keeping with the suggestions of Urban Holtzmeister and others. A third example is the claimed mistaken mathematics in Matthew 1:17 regarding the three sets of "fourteen" generations in the genealogy of Jesus. I find Matthew's counting not only to be correct, but possibly also by a mathematical trick to indicate (cryptically) the exact day, month, and year of the birth of Jesus in Bethlehem (see chapter 14). A fourth example is the supposedly mistaken reference in Matt. 2:23 to "the prophets'" as having called Jesus a Nazarene (answered in chapter 15). A fifth example is the play on words in the calling of Nathaniel (John 1:45–51), which is proposed in chapter 17.

29. In chapter 6, part I, regarding historical criticism of the form-critical type as a critical method, we shall examine how the presuppositions of this method affect the conclusions that are drawn from it. Just prior

to the birth of form-criticism in 1901, Pope Leo XIII claimed that the "higher criticism" from which it sprang was *"tainted with false philosophy and rationalism"* and would *"lead to the elimination from the sacred writings of all prophecy and miracle and of everything else that is outside of the natural order."*[10] This statement does not presume that any Catholic biblical scholars were engaged in this worldly activity, but neo-patristic researchers also question whether Catholic historical critics have defined their science with the needed clarity of concepts. Although René Descartes excluded (dualistically) from his universal methodic doubt all matters pertaining to faith and morals, a wide spectrum of his followers did not. Similarly, while Catholic historical critics distinguish between the historical critical method and the rationalist philosophy in which its founders encased it, they do not identify clearly the rationalist biases upon which the method itself is based. Many Catholic historical critics, dualistically and without a working framework of synthesis with the objects of Catholic faith, begin their approach to passages of the sacred text of the Bible from the viewpoint of a non-believer, and all that they can reasonably hope to derive from this activity are the conclusions of a non-believer.

30. In chapter 6, part II, regarding historical criticism as a historical method, we consider whether there is true history in the narrative of events in the biblical text. We take a look at the "central issue" in the discussion of neo-patristic scholars with form-critics like Hermann Gunkel, and we take as an example the origin of Abraham and Sarah as reported in Genesis 11:26–29. Catholic form-critics like Richard Clifford, Bruce Vawter, Alexa Suelzer, John Kselman, and others, in the absence of a sufficiently differentiated mental frame of reference, do not profess the rationalist presuppositions of mainline non-Catholic form-critics, but they rather tend more to ignore these presuppositions than to refute them. However, since to understand means to know a reality in relation to some previously known reality, no Catholic can adequately understand the text of Sacred Scripture who cannot focus what is written in the sacred text within the purview of the Catholic Faith, every exegetical method whose basic approach rules out the real effects of God's presence will tend to diminish rather than to increase the biblical interpreter's understanding of Sacred Scripture.

31. Chapter 7, regarding a neo-patristic approach to the inerrancy of the inspired word of God, begins with a survey of quotations from six sources of the authentic teaching of the Church, telling us that a) the one

---

10 *Providentissimus Deus, EB* 119.

true God is the Author of both the Old Testament and the New Testament; b) that the sacred books have God as their primary Author; c) that all of the parts of Sacred Scripture have been completely inspired by the Holy Spirit; d) that the traditional teaching of the Church regarding the complete inerrancy of Sacred Scripture is to be defended by commentators; e) that the immunity from errors of Sacred Writ is not limited to those things which are conveyed concerning God and moral and religious matters; f) and that the books of Scripture, firmly, faithfully, and without error teach the truth as God, for the sake of our salvation, wished to see recorded in the form of Sacred Writings.

32. We then consider critically the teaching of some Catholic historical critics like Lionel Swain and Raymond Collins. Swain has many good things to say, but he also has a tendency to identify "rationalism" with sound human reasoning, whereas there is an essential difference between the two, since rationalism is reasoning from false philosophical principles, especially from the false presupposition that miraculous events are historically impossible. And he tends also to identify reasonable arguments in defense of the historical truth of the Scriptures with "a negative, defensive attitude" and with unreasonable opposition to what he considers to be "scientific and historical accuracy." Collins also presents a historical critical view of biblical inspiration where he says that objections to the "theory of verbal inspiration" have led most critical scholars to abandon it, and he maintains that "the inerrant 'truth' of the Bible was deemed all-important," but this approach, he says, has changed since Vatican II. Collins is referring to his translation of *Dei Verbum* 11, which is highly questionable. Collins points out that increased data (available to historical critical scholars) regarding the origins of the earth and of the human race "led to incompatibility between scientific knowledge and a naïve, literal reading of the creation narratives." I wonder how hard he tried to solve these two problems. The original Pontifical Biblical Commission, in a response to the problem of the six "days" of creation in Genesis 1, dated June 30, 1909, declared that the word *yom* (day), as used for the six days of creation, "may be taken in its strict sense as the natural day, or in a less strict sense as signifying a certain space of time" (*EB* 1961, no. 331). In the Appendix of this book, I present a contemporary development of the powerful solution to the same question published by St. Augustine of Hippo early in the fifth century A.D.

33. In chapter 8 we critically review Father Jean Levie's *The Bible, Word of God in Words of Men*, a book published originally in French in

1958 and in English translation in 1961, which was very influential just before and during the Second Vatican Council. Father Levie, a Catholic historical critical Scripture scholar and then professor of Sacred Scripture at the Theological College of St. Albert in Louvain, presents a history and defense of the historical critical method of the form-critical type from its introduction into Catholic biblical studies until what he calls its acceptance by Pope Pius XII in his encyclical letter *Divino afflante Spiritu* of 1943. Levie argues from the position that Catholic biblical scholars before the acceptance of historical criticism never appreciated sufficiently the role of the human side of biblical authorship, and it is this side of the coin that he develops in his book. However, one notes that it is only the human side that he expounds, and the reason is that he is using no synthesis of the form-critical method with the objects of Catholic faith, no mental framework in which the form-critical method is reconciled to the vital functioning of Catholic belief, and so he uses, somewhat unwittingly, the philosophical principles of the Enlightenment from which the historical critical method has sprung. The conclusions of this kind of historical critical reasoning were highly contested by traditional-minded Catholic scholars and also in papal encyclicals and by the Supreme Sacred Congregation of the Holy Office before and after *Divine Afflante Spiritu*, and this contention goes on. In the words of Cardinal Joseph Ratzinger, then Prefect of the Congregation for the Doctrine of the Faith and President of the Pontifical Biblical Commission, in his Preface to the document of 1993 of the (reconstituted) Pontifical Biblical Commission, *The Interpretation of the Bible in the Church*: "The emergence of the historical critical method set in motion at the same time a struggle over its scope and over its proper configuration which is by no means finished as yet."

34. In Chapter 9 we present a critical review of the Rationalism in the form-critical method of Herman Gunkel, founder of the form-criticism of the Old Testament. Form-criticism (*Formgeschichte*) purports to be a scientific search into the historical development of the literary forms used in the Bible, but Gunkel's *Genesis* (1901) is not a true historical exercise in comparison with the work of a historian like William Foxwell Albright, who later covered the same biblical period in his *From the Stone Age to Christianity* (1957). Albright's historical work can be taken as a corrective of Gunkel's form-critical work, also in the sense that the thinking in Gunkel's *Genesis* seems to be an application of four or more presuppositions and a set of hypotheses that control his research. Gunkel's thinking is *reductive* in the sense that he excludes *a priori* any real act of God in the narrative

of the Bible. Consequently, his thinking is *naturalistic* in the sense that he allows only natural happenings to be able to belong to the real world. His thinking is rationalistic in the sense that it places private reason over the teaching of the Bible and of the Church and *a priori* does not allow the Bible to be a source of independent real facts. And his thinking is modernistic in the sense that he believes in the so-called "outlook of modern man," which considers miracles to be absolutely impossible. Historical science has presuppositions, but not the presuppositions of form-criticism, and the characteristic reasoning of historical science is not so much the deductive or inductive reasoning typical of classical science as it is *abductive reasoning* in detecting the causes and meanings of real events.

35. Historical science depends much upon the testimony of reliable witnesses, while the form-critical method depends almost exclusively upon the plausibility of working hypotheses that do not provide solid evidence. First among these hypotheses is the speculation that the Sacred Scriptures are not divinely inspired, but are only the instinctive product of a subrational religious society (the early Christian Community) which, he says, anonymously invented stories to satisfy its felt needs and concerns. Obviously implausible form-critical hypotheses could be rejected by the form-critical originator himself or by his peers, while acceptance of an argument by some others of his fellow historical critical workers could make his hypothesis "established" for the historical critical community even though it never had any actual historical proof.

36. In chapter 10 we review seven Catholic responses to the demythologizing program of Rudolf Bultmann. The first five listed responses are attempts to provide a fair appraisal of Bultmann's program while giving a defense of Catholic belief, and these replies contain many good ideas, but, due to the absence of an adequate mental framework, their responses appear also to be somewhat confused. The last two articles, those of Anton Vögtle and Ugo Lattanzi, are strong attempts to visualize a proper mental framework of response to the destructive work of Rudolf Bultmann.

37. In chapter 11 we return to the Catholic responses of the preceding chapter in a search for a more complete Catholic frame of reference able to refute the outrageous conclusions of Rudolf Bultmann and his colleagues. The first requirement is a heart and mind on fire with love for God and strengthened by firm conviction that the objects of faith really exist in the continuum of reality that is external to the subjectivity of the believer, and, therefore, whose reality needs to be affirmed and defended from the attacks

of non-believers. In these attacks I am referring, not only to the existentialism of Martin Heidegger, which came later into Bultmann's theology, but also and especially to the anti-Christian philosophies of rationalism, naturalism, and modernism that saturate his form-critical method itself. Needed for this response is a return to the moderate realism of Aristotle as proclaimed by Thomas Aquinas. Hovering over Bultmann's theology is his belief in the radical separation of faith and reason and the consequent setting up of an alternate world of religious belief, which Bultmann conceives of as "non-world." As Michael Waldstein incisefully points out: "At the very foundations of Bultmann's thought, which was complete in its essential outlines before his encounter with Martin Heidegger, there lies the philosophical thesis that being human in the authentic sense does not mean being an object in the cosmos with a certain nature or essence; it means 'existing'; and existing means being a historical possibility which continually realizes itself through decision."[11] In Bultmann's: own words: "*The free deed is the expression of our existence; in fact, only in the free deed, and nowhere else, do we exist in the authentic sense, since the free deed is nothing but our existence itself....*"[12] This idea needs better formulation than that of Rudolf Bultmann. In fact, the framework capable of refuting Bultmann's errors must restore, where needed, Catholic confidence in the harmony of authentic Catholic faith with the results of right reason, including the findings of natural science and solid history.

38. In chapter 12 we review a widely circulated form-critical interpretation of the first chapter of the Gospel of Matthew by then Father Jean Daniélou, having of necessity to use the form-critical method without the benefit of a synthesis of this method with Catholic faith and tradition. Daniélou maintains that the message of Matthew 1 is not about the virginal conception of Mary or the appearance of an angel to Joseph, but is only about the human natural event of Joseph having adopted Jesus as his foster son. In spite of his best intentions, obvious contradictions of logic and common sense appear in the course of his analysis, due to his lack of a mental framework that could do justice to the rest of what the text of Matthew is obviously saying.

39. In chapter 13 we discuss the problem of the genealogy of Jesus in Matthew 1, relative to the fact that many form-critical scholars consider this genealogy and the genealogy of Jesus in Luke 3 to be in no way accurate

---

11 Michael M. Waldstein, "Analogia Verbi: The Truth of Scripture in Rudolf Bultmann and Raymond Brown," in Scott W. Hahn, Editor, *For the Sake of Our Salvation*, p. 98.

12 Waldstein, ibid. with references.

records of the ancestry of Jesus. In defense of the inerrancy of Sacred Scripture I present in this chapter six possible solutions to this problem, while granting further on that more positive work needs to be done by scholars in this area, especially regarding the origin of the genealogies and the meaning of the patterns of the names.

40. In chapter 14 we discuss the literal and historical meaning of the forty-two generations enumerated in Matthew 1:17, while facing the contemporary question: Could Matthew even count correctly to fourteen? First we review some of the arguments made in past times to establish Matthew's count of 14 x 3 generations. Then we examine the accuracy of some ancient calendars at the time of the composition of the Gospel according to Matthew in the search for a possible subtle literal meaning of Matt. 1:17. Finally, we arrive at a tentative conclusion that in the arithmetic of this verse divine inspiration may have left a clue to those who find it of the exact day, month, and year of the birth of Jesus in Bethlehem. I don't claim that this clue is there, but I leave the question to the study of any competent researchers who might take the time to ponder it.

41. In chapter 15, part I, we examine the long-debated reference in Matthew 2:23 to *"the prophets,"* where it says: *"And he went and dwelt in a city called Nazareth that what was spoken by the prophets might be fulfilled that he would be called a Nazorean."* Our study begins with the etymology (origin) of the name "Nazareth," following the answer of Thomas Aquinas and many other writers. We look at three possible Hebrew words of origin and their occurrence in the Old Testament and also at the probable origin of Matthew's Infancy Narrative.

42. In chapter 15, part II, regarding Matt. 2:23, a critical response is given to the form-critical analyses of Martin Dibelius and Rudolf Bultmann. Looking into the background of their approach we find that their conclusions stem as logical conclusions from a set of presuppositions and a number of postulates that serve as accepted hypotheses. The form-critical arguments are not based upon historical evidence but only on what appear to them to be plausible conclusions. A second basic error of their method is the lack of precise definitions of terms and the absence of genuine historical evidence for what they conclude.

43. In chapter 15, part III, we critically examine Father Raymond Brown's form-critical interpretation of Matt. 2:23, which he presents as a good example of how form-critical research proceeds. We consider some seeming flaws in the form-critical process, including the function of such presuppositions as rationalism and modernism and the unwitting use of anachronism.

44. In chapter 16 we present a brief commentary on the second chapter of the Gospel according to St. Matthew, using the method of the Four Senses of Sacred Scripture. This is a line-by-line commentary in which I treat in order first the literal sense and then possible spiritual senses of the text. What seems to come through is the richness of the interpretations of the Fathers of the Church and the precision of medieval theologians, led by St. Thomas Aquinas. Here and there I add some ideas of my own, especially as regards questions raised by modern scholars.

45. In chapter 17, the concluding essay of this book, I treat of the calling of Nathaniel in John 1:45–51, beginning with an analysis of form-critical interpretations by Rudolf Bultmann and Raymond Brown. This analysis leads to some questions about John's report that suggest the presence under the plain literal reading of the text of a possible subtle historical meaning which may be uncovered by studying the etymology (origin) of the words. This study appears to me to bring to light another genre of meaning of the conversation between Jesus and Nathaniel.

Chapter 1

Regarding Pope Benedict XVI's Address on Biblical Exegesis and Theology of 14 October 2008

Living Tradition 143 (November 2009)

1. In his address of October 14, 2008, to the constituents of the Fourteenth General Congregation of the Synod of Bishops, Pope Benedict XVI commented on the need that critical analysis of the biblical text be thoroughly informed by the hermeneutics of faith, as called for in *Dei Verbum* of the Second Vatican Council. The text of this address, as released in an unofficial English translation on the Vatican web site, is as follows.

"Dear Brothers and Sisters, the work for my book on Jesus offers ample occasion to see all the good that can come from modern exegesis, but also to recognize the problems and risks in it. *Dei Verbum* 12 offers two methodological indications for suitable exegetic work. In the first place, it confirms the need to use the historical critical method, briefly describing the essential elements. This need is the consequence of the Christian principle formulated in John 1:14, Verbum caro factum est [the Word was made flesh]. The historical fact is a constitutive dimension of Christian faith. The history of salvation is not a myth, but a true story and therefore to be studied with the same methods as serious historical research.

However, this history has another dimension, that of divine action. Because of this *Dei Verbum* mentions a second methodological level necessary for the correct interpretation of the words, which are at the same time human words and divine Word. The Council says, following a fundamental rule for any interpretation of a literary text, that Scripture must be interpreted in the same spirit in which it was written and thereby indicates three fundamental methodological elements to bear in mind the divine dimension, the pneumatology of the Bible: one must, that is, 1) interpret the text bearing in mind the unity of the entire Scripture; today this is called canonical exegesis; at the time of the Council this term had not been created, but the Council says the same thing: one must bear in mind the unity of all of Scripture; 2) one must then bear in mind the living tradition of the whole Church, and finally 3) observe the analogy of faith.

Only where the two methodological levels, the historical critical and the theological one, are observed, can one speak about theological exegesis — of an exegesis suitable for this Book. While at the first level, today's academic exegesis works on a very high level and truly gives us help, the same cannot be said about the other level. Often this second level, the level constituted of the three theological elements indicated by *Dei Verbum* seems to be almost absent. And this has rather serious consequences.

The first consequence of the absence of this second methodological level is that the Bible becomes a book only about the past. Moral consequences can be drawn from it, one can learn about history, but the Book only speaks about the past and its exegesis is no longer truly theological, becoming historiography, the history of literature. This is the first consequence: the Bible remains in the past, speaks only of the past.

There is also a second even more serious consequence: where the hermeneutics of faith, indicated by *Dei Verbum*, disappear, another type of hermeneutics appears of necessity, a secularized, positivistic hermeneutics, whose fundamental key is the certitude that the Divine does not appear in human history. According to this hermeneutic, when there seems to be a divine element, one must explain where it came from and bring it to the human element completely. Because of this, interpretations that deny the historicity of divine elements emerge. Today, the so-called "mainstream" of exegesis in Germany denies, for example, that the Lord instituted the Holy Eucharist and says that Jesus' corpse stayed in the tomb. The Resurrection would not be a historical event, but a theological vision. This occurs because the hermeneutic of faith is missing: therefore, a profane philosophical hermeneutic is stated, which denies the possibility both of the entrance and the real presence of the Divine in history. The consequence of the absence of the second methodological level is that a deep chasm was created between scientific exegesis and lectio divina. This, at times, gives rise to a form of perplexity even in the preparation of homilies.

Where exegesis is not theology, Scripture cannot be the soul of theology and, vice versa, when theology is not essentially the interpretation of the Scripture in the Church, this theology has no foundation anymore. Therefore for the life and the mission of the Church, for the future of faith, this dualism between exegesis and theology must be overcome. Biblical theology and systematic theology are two dimensions of the one reality, what we call Theology.

Due to this, I would hope that in one of the propositions the need to bear in mind the two methodological levels indicated in *Dei Verbum* 12 be mentioned, where the need to develop an exegesis not only on the historical level, but also on the theological level is needed. Therefore, widening the formation of future exegetes in this sense is necessary, to truly open the treasures of the Scripture to today's world and to all of us."

Some Reflections on this Papal Address of 14 October 2008

2. Pope Benedict XVI begins by noting both the good that can come from modern exegesis and the problems and risks that it contains. By "modern exegesis" he is referring mainly to the "historical critical method" of biblical interpretation, and he bases the need for this modern approach on the fact that Christianity is a historical religion rooted in true historical events, such as the real historical incarnation of the divine Son of God in the humanity of Jesus of Nazareth and his real historical resurrection from the dead. This observation of the Pope needs to be understood correctly. He is pointing out that, while many religious faiths present mythical and imaginary objects of belief, the objects of Christian faith, and in particular the objects of Catholic Christian faith, are real and are part of the context of historical fact.

3. Let it be noted that the expression "historical critical method," as used here by Pope Benedict XVI, and as generally used today in ecclesiastical parlance, is ambiguous. Pope Benedict is referring to this method as it is characterized in its essentials in the Second Vatican Council document, *Dei Verbum*, no. 12. What are these essential elements? In the first place, according to *Dei Verbum*, the interpreter of Sacred Scripture "*should carefully search out the meaning which the sacred writers really had in mind, that meaning which God had thought well to manifest through the medium of their words.*" And so, "*attention must be paid, among other things, to 'literary forms', for the fact is that truth is differently presented and expressed in the various types of historical writing, in prophetic and poetical texts, and in other forms of literary expression.*" And so, the biblical interpreter" *must look for that meaning which the sacred writer, in a determined situation and given*

the circumstances of his time and culture, intended to express and did, in fact, express, through the medium of a contemporary literary form."

4. Note that the examples of literary forms mentioned in *Dei Verbum* are the classical categories of historical, prophetic, and poetic, with an added general reference to certain other unnamed forms of literary expression, and the reference given by the Council document to this whole sentence is Saint Augustine's *De doctrina Christiana.* But the way in which the expression "historical critical method" is commonly understood today even within ecclesiastical circles is the method characterized by the use of the "form-criticism" introduced into biblical interpretation by Hermann Gunkel, Rudolf Bultmann, and others of the liberal Protestant tradition. This method uses a framework of novel literary forms, such as "myth," "legend," "saga," "prophecies after the fact," "miracle stories," "I-sayings of Jesus," "*midrash*," and other avenues of literary fiction in no way consonant with the teaching of Saint Augustine, of *Dei Verbum*, or of Catholic biblical tradition. In fact, this method was condemned as a pseudo-science by Pope Leo XIII and as a product of Modernism by Pope Pius X.[1] And the truth is that, while the non-Catholic founders of this method were self-professed Modernists, whereas Catholic form-critics do not consciously subscribe to the principles of Modernism, neither have Catholic form-critics ever properly sorted out the problem of philosophy that underlies this method.

5. Pope Benedict XVI then referred to another dimension, or methodological level, of history, namely, the "divine action" which is "necessary" for the correct interpretation of the inspired words of Scripture, because the sacred text "must be interpreted in the same spirit in which it was written." And for this, he said, there are three fundamental elements: the unity of the entire Scripture, the living tradition of the whole Church, and the analogy of faith. This second level, he added, is almost entirely absent in contemporary exegetical interpretation. As a result, he continued, the Bible has come to be understood merely as a book of the past, as a part of the history of literature. Also, the "hermeneutics of faith" disappears, and there appears "a secularized, positivistic hermeneutics," based on the

---

1 To quote the exact words of Pope Pius X: *"Some Modernists, devoted to historical studies, seem to be greatly afraid of being taken for philosophers. About philosophy, they tell you, they know nothing whatever – and in this they display remarkable astuteness, for they are particularly anxious not to be suspected of being prejudiced in favor of philosophical theories which would lay them open to the charge of not being objective, to use the word in vogue. And yet the truth is that their history and their criticism are saturated with their philosophy, and that their historico-critical conclusions are the natural fruit of their philosophical principles"* (*Pascendi dominici gregis*, no. 30).

conviction that divine interventions do not occur in human history, but can always be reduced to human acts. Thus, he said, for this approach, the Resurrection of Jesus from the dead was not a real historical event, but is only a theological vision. Thus also, there results a "deep chasm" between what is called "scientific exegesis" and *lectio divina*. And so, theology loses its foundation in historical reality.

6. It is important to understand properly these thoughts of Pope Benedict XVI. Form-criticism functions on the presupposition that, except for very limited exceptions, the so-called historical events recorded in Sacred Scripture are actually forms of literary fiction presenting products of religious imagination. While the expression "literary forms" as mentioned in *Dei Verbum* 12 and in other magisterial documents of the Church represents a larger category which includes every kind of written expression, such as real history, legal documents, prophecies, poetry, books of mathematics, maps, etc., according to the method of form-criticism, anything written in the Bible under the guise of history is assumed to be actually fictitious unless there is solid evidence that it is not. This assumption is clearly expressed in the writings of Gunkel, Bultmann, and other founders and mainline promoters of form-criticism, but it is often covered in the writings of Catholic form-critics.

7. Thus, for instance, Hermann Gunkel (1862–1932) assumes that many of the stories narrated in the final text of Genesis were taken originally from imaginary stories about pagan gods that were gradually transformed by Hebrew poets into their own imaginary stories about the Hebrew God, fictitiously acting in relation to fictitious patriarchs whom they projected as founders of their nation. Gunkel says that he doesn't understand why believing Christians should be shocked by such an idea, since for him it is only a matter of understanding the fictitious literary genres of the stories.[2] Of course, the problem is that Catholic faith is based upon an affirmation of the reality of the objects of faith, not upon their being "understood" as embodied in fictitious literary forms.

8. And Modernism is functional in the form-criticism of Hermann Gunkel. Contrary to the viewpoint depicted in the Book of Genesis and underlying the traditional outlook of Catholic faith and Catholic exegetical tradition, Hermann Gunkel avers: *"Following our modern historical world-view, truly not an imaginative construct but based on the observation of facts, we consider the other view entirely impossible."* As a modern man, he feels that the extraordinary events recounted in Genesis *"contradict our advanced*

---

2 See *Living Tradition 77*, paragraph 19.

knowledge," to the extent that it would be doing an "*injustice*" to the text of Genesis if we were to "*incorporate it into sober reality*."[3] It is clear from these words that Gunkel's judgment is based upon the rationalist presupposition that miracles and divine interventions could not have happened. This rationalist premise is confirmed when he says that God *never appears to us as an active agent alongside others, but always as the ultimate cause of all*."[4]

9. Gunkel went on to say that Jesus and his Apostles *thought* that the accounts of Genesis were historical events of the real world, but "they shared the opinions of their time," and so "we may not, therefore, seek information in the New Testament concerning questions of the history of the Old Testament literature." Gunkel was convinced that he, as a modern man, had a viewpoint superior to the "primitive" viewpoint of Jesus and his contemporaries.[5]

10. The basis of this judgment is Gunkel's adherence to what is called the "modern historical world-view," an outlook which has its origins in the presuppositions of Deism, Naturalism, Rationalism, and Modernism, attitudes that are simply assumed without proof. According to the presupposition of the Deist, God cannot intervene in the world of created nature, and, therefore, the preternatural events described in Genesis are deemed impossible. According to the presupposition of the Naturalist in religion, nature is a closed system that does not admit of outside interference, and, therefore, many of the accounts of Genesis are incredible. According to the presupposition of the Rationalist, nothing is accepted as real that cannot be demonstrated from natural reason, and, therefore, many of the accounts of Genesis are automatically assumed to be unreal. According to the presupposition of the Modernist, the marvelous accounts of Genesis are constructs deriving from religious imagination, and, therefore, are unacceptable to the belief of modern man.

11. Gunkel subscribed to all of these presuppositions, and they led him to assume without sufficient reason that the accounts of Genesis are legends, not history. For Gunkel, the one true God does not *really* act in history, and this view is Deism. Gunkel's method also reflects Naturalism where he tells us that "a series of myths can be understood in terms of a natural event often or regularly occurring in the real world which provided the palette

---

3 Gunkel, *Genesis*, p. x.

4 Gunkel, *Genesis*, ibid. See *Living Tradition* 111, paragraph 38.

5 Gunkel, *Genesis* p. viii. See chapter 2, part 3 paragraph 42 below. For a detailed analysis of Gunkel's approach to form-criticism see chapter 9 below.

for an account of such an event in the primordium."[6] This means that, for Gunkel, alleged acts of God are not located "in the real world." But Gunkel is also a rationalist, as he tells us himself. "In many cases, we too, whose worship withstood a powerful purification in the Reformation and again in Rationalism, do not, or only partially, understand the original meaning of what we see and hear in our churches."[7] How much of Christian worship did manage to survive the "purification" of Rationalism in Gunkel's mind is a big question, but it is obvious that the action of God in the reality of this world did not. And Modernism reigns also behind his "modern historical point of view." He finds that those legends of Genesis created out of a desire "to explain something" are characteristic of the childish mode of thinking and reasoning,[8] while others arose as "pure products of the imagination," in a manner that he calls "novelistic," or even "fairy-tale-like."[9] Yet, he explains, the originators of these legends did not deliberately intend to deceive. "Legend stems from times and circles which did not yet have the intellectual ability to distinguish between fiction and reality."[10]

12. Somewhat later, when the form-criticism of the Gospels arose in the early 1920s, the accounts in the Gospels were also assumed to be "fiction, not history." Catholic faith, while it is primarily and *per se* an affirmation of the dogmas of Catholic faith, is also, secondarily and *per accidens*, an affirmation of the reality of what is stated in Sacred Scripture rightly understood. Central to this whole discussion is the notion of historical reality. I contend that science is science only to the extent that its medium of thought is recognized and defined, and, therefore, that historical science is historical science only to the extent that the historical medium of thought is recognized and defined in the mind of the historian. The frame of reference in the mind of the historian is his historical present. I contend that the awareness in the mind of the biblical scholar of the presence of the one true God, of the God who presents Himself in the Sacred Scriptures, is necessary for the scientific interpretation of the Scriptures.[11]

13, Gunkel sees in the "primal legends" of Genesis both the presence of "weakened myths" and "a quiet aversion to mythology." By a "myth" he

---

6 Gunkel, ibid., p. xiii.

7 Gunkel, ibid. p. .

8 Gunkel, ibid., xxi. Cf. ibid., lxvii, lxix.

9 Gunkel, ibid., xxiii.

10 Gunkel, ibid., xxvi. See *Living Tradition* 77, paragraph 21.

11 See chapter 6, part 1, paragraph 22 above,.

means "a story of the gods." Israel's strong emphasis upon monotheism would tolerate only "myths in which God acts alone, as in the creation narrative," or myths "in which the story takes place between God and people."[12] But these "myths," as so identified by Gunkel, are obviously seen to be merely fictitious stories, since (the one true) God is for Gunkel always and only "the ultimate cause of all" and never plays any role in human history or the history of the world. In this description Gunkel may be retaining a residual belief in the existence of the one true God, but as far as his interpretation of Genesis is concerned, what comes out in the "primal myths" is the fictitious god of Israel, who is depicted as acting either alone or with people. In this interpretation there is no real connection between the god of Israel and the one true God of authentic Christian belief.[13]

14. According to Hermann Gunkel, the patriarchal accounts of Genesis are legends, that is, they are poetic recastings of vague historical memories, into which later popular elements and even whole other figures have been interwoven.[14] He sees these accounts as constructs fashioned from imaginary thinking, such as, for example, from the idea that every different nation was descended exclusively from a different remote ancestor, in such wise that two closely related nations would be imagined to have descended exclusively from brothers or from the same mother. He thinks that Abraham, Isaac, and Jacob probably never existed, but, even if they did, what they were like could not have been remembered, because over a period of so many centuries the personal characters of these persons could not have been preserved.[15] To conclude this, he had to assume that no handwriting was available to these shrewd traders and their successors, that an oral account could not be preserved intact by narrators with good memories, and that there could have been no divine inspiration or help of divine providence. But he had no external evidence to back up these assumptions.

15. Does Gunkel's analysis of the separate accounts in Genesis really stand up under truly scientific criticism? I think that it does not, but it is amazing that, over more than a century of use of his book by Catholic form-critics, there has been practically no searching criticism of his method. Gunkel's method presumes that everything miraculous narrated in the

---

12 Gunkel, *Genesis,* pp. xii–xiii.

13 See *Living Tradition* 108, paragraph 12.

14 Gunkel, *Genesis,* p. xvi.

15 Gunkel, *Genesis,* p. lxviii. See chapter 9, paragraph 15 below.

Genesis accounts and every intervention on the part of the one true God are historically non-factual and need to be given a natural explanation. Is this presumption in keeping with historical science? I would say that it is not. *Natural science* is limited to the observation of natural facts and occurrences, but *historical science* is not. A natural scientist as such cannot recognize the occurrence of a miracle or of any divine intervention in the world of physical reality, but he is obliged to accept the results of those higher sciences that can observe supernatural occurrences, and historical science is one of these, because *historical science* observes whatever has taken place in the past and must accept these occurrences without excluding in advance what exceeds the workings of physical nature. Therefore, the evidence for a happening is what concerns the historian and not whether or not the happening is within the bounds of a natural occurrence. But Gunkel's method, because it is governed by the false principle of Naturalism, excludes in advance, even without any evidence, the recorded reality of every happening that exceeded the workings of physical nature, and, therefore, Gunkel's method is not historically scientific.[16]

16. Rudolf Bultmann (1884–1976) was the most celebrated of five principal founders of the form-criticism of the New Testament. His *History of the Synoptic Tradition* (1921) was an exegetical work in which he employed form-criticism seemingly to the almost total elimination of the historicity of the Synoptic Gospels of Matthew, Mark, and Luke, leaving as a residue not much more than the man Jesus of Nazareth, who did exist, was, indeed, probably crucified, and did quite possibly enunciate a few identifiable sayings that are attributed to him in the Synoptic Gospels.

17. Joseph Cardinal Ratzinger, in a widely circulated lecture, titled "Biblical Interpretation in Crisis," delivered in New York City on January 27, 1988, and published soon afterwards in English and in other languages,[17] observed that over the past hundred years biblical exegesis has made some great errors and these errors "have in some measure grown to the stature of academic dogmas."[18] He traced this problem to the influence of Martin Dibelius and Rudolf Bultmann, whose "basic methodological approaches continue even today to determine

---

16 See chapter 9, paragraph 27 below.

17 Joseph Cardinal Ratzinger, in Richard J. Neuhaus, ed., *Biblical Interpretation in Crisis* (Grand Rapids: Eerdmans, 1989), pp. 1–23).

18 Ratzinger, ibid., p. 21. For more on this discussion, see *Living Tradition*, issues 41 and 137.

the methods and procedures of modern exegesis."[19] Ratzinger found it imperative at this juncture of time to challenge the fundamental ideas behind the method of Dibelius and Bultmann, such as the carrying over of the evolutionist model of natural science into the history and life-processes of the spirit.[20]

18. "The real philosophic presupposition of the whole system," he said, seems to be situated "in the philosophic turning-point proposed by Immanuel Kant," according to which "the voice of being-in-itself cannot be heard by human beings."[21] "In theological terms," said the Cardinal, "this means that revelation must recede into the pure formality of the eschatological stance, which corresponds to the Kantian split," and to this extent, for Bultmann and for the majority of modern exegetes, "there lies in modern exegesis a reduction of history into philosophy, a revision of history by means of philosophy."[22]

19. The Cardinal proposed some "basic elements for a new synthesis," which will require the attentive and critical commitment of a whole generation.[23] On the level of the integration of the biblical texts into their historical context, said the Cardinal, the time is ripe for a " new and thorough reflection on exegetical method," also in the sense that "scientific exegesis must recognize the philosophic element present in a great number of its ground rules, and it must then reconsider the results which are based on these rules." To achieve this task he saw the need to introduce into the discussion "the great outlines of patristic and medieval thought."[24]

20. Regarding philosophical systems, the Cardinal affirmed: "At its core, the debate about modern exegesis is not a dispute among historians; it is rather a philosophical debate."[25] As to the "scientific" and "historical" character of the historical critical method, the Cardinal remarked: "Now, at a certain distance, the observer determines to his surprise that these interpretations, which were supposed to be so strictly scientific and purely 'historical,' reflect their own overriding spirit, rather than the spirit of times long ago. This insight should not lead us to skepticism about the method,

---

19 Ratzinger, ibid., p. 9.

20 Ratzinger, ibid., pp. 10, 14–15.

21 Ratzinger, ibid., p. 15.

22 Ratzinger, ibid., p. 16.

23 Ratzinger, ibid., pp. 16 and 17–23.

24 Ratzinger, ibid., pp. 21–22.

25 Ratzinger, ibid.

but rather to an honest recognition of what its limits are, and perhaps how it might be purified."[26]

21, Both Bultmann and Gunkel based their idea of modern man, at least implicitly, upon Kant's thoroughgoing distinction between factual *knowledge*, as gained from empirical observation, and metaphysical and religious *opinion*, which is postulated but not known. The form-criticism of Gunkel and Bultmann is *a critical approach* to the interpretation of Sacred Scripture in the sense that it sets aside Christian faith and concentrates exclusively upon critical reason in the Kantian sense in order to critique the Bible. It does not consider at all the critical reasoning of traditional biblical interpretation in which the *ars critica* of conventional historical research is used also to certify and defend the Scriptures as well as to achieve a fuller understanding of them. The method of Gunkel and Bultmann is *a modernist method* in the sense that it unreasonably extols the reasoning of so-called "modern man" over the supposedly inferior thinking presented in the sacred writings. The form-criticism of Gunkel and Bultmann is also *a reductive method* in that it focuses exclusively upon the human side of the Bible and rules out *a priori* in its reasoning any divine and supernatural influence in the writing of the sacred books. It is reductive also to the extent that it puts aside the use of sound metaphysics and thus falls repeatedly into philosophical errors that only sound philosophy can adequately ascertain.

22. To be sure, Gunkel and Bultmann do not follow Kant in explicitly assuming that the things we see do not exist outside of our own minds, but they and their followers do fall into the consequent error of using a defective subject-object model of reasoning that overlooks the formal object of human understanding and thus puts out of critical focus the very mental framework that they are using in the course of their reasoning. Finally, the "Kantian split" is functional in this form-critical method, because the aura of reality is given only to their own critical thinking, while the teaching and historical episodes of the Bible are consigned arbitrarily to a religious dream-world of myth and fancy. So why was the Bible relevant at all for Gunkel and Bultmann? They studied it, I think, not only to critique it in the Kantian sense, but also with the idea that its fiction retains an underlying existential meaning for modern Christians that is to be found on the other side of the "Kantian split."[27]

23. Rudolf Bultmann often raised the question of "reality" in relation to Christian faith and the contents of the New Testament Scriptures.

---

26 Ratzinger, ibid., p. 8.

27 See chapter 2, paragraph 44.

To resolve the dilemma that the question of reality raised for him, he divided the concept of reality into two and proposed a novel meaning of *Wirklichkeit*, the German word for reality: a) the reality that is known by sense experience and constitutes the real world of empirical science he called, not *Wirklichkeit*, but *Realität*, and this is the objective representation of the world in which man finds himself; b) and he called *Wirklichkeit* "the reality of the historically existing man."[28] This distinction enabled Bultmann to predicate reality in relation to a certain understanding of the object of faith without predicating reality in the commonly understood sense to the object of faith itself. This was a wrong answer to the question of reality, but it did address a question that for too long has escaped the critical attention of modern exegetes of the prevailing school.

24. Modern historical critical exegetes, to the extent that they uncritically follow the method of Bultmann and make use of his presuppositions, actually cut themselves off from the reality that is objectively presented in the Scriptures along the lines of Bultmann's exclusion of *Realität* in the objects presented by the biblical narrative. Catholic form-critics seldom raise the question of reality at all, and one of the unanswered questions throughout almost the whole of their discourse is whether in their judgment the biblical events which they are interpreting really happened or did not.

25. In his speculation, Rudolf Bultmann often raised the question of "history" in relation to Christian faith and the contents of the New Testament Scriptures. Again he proposed a double meaning of the German word for history, *Geschichte*, and he set up a radical distinction between history as *Historie*, which, he said, is composed of causally connected events and relationships between facts which are objectively verifiable and chronologically determinable,[29] and history as *Geschichte*, which consists of the encounters of the "genuinely" existing human being, whose "existential constitution" ultimately signifies "to exist, to be confronted with non-being, to be able to be and ever to decide anew." Thus, for Bultmann, the question of the "historicity" of the Gospels was subjectivized into the possession by the contemporary thinker of what he called "true historicity," which was "the existential constitution of the being which necessarily exists

---

28 R. Bultmann, "Zum Problem der Entmythologisierung," in H. W. Bartsch et al., *Kerygma und Mythos* (Hamburg: Evan-gelischer Verlag), vol. VI-1: a) "...die ein objektivierenden Sehen vorgestellte Wirklichkeit der Welt, innerhalb deren sich der Mensch vorfindet..." (p. 20); b) "... als die Wirklichkeit des geschlichtlich existierenden Menschen" (p. 21).

29 R. Bultmann, *History and Eschatology* (New York: Harper and Row, 1957), pp. 143–144.

in history."[30] While these definitions of reality and of history are proper to Bultmann, they are derived from the "Kantian split" between empirical "reality" and the "fictitious" nature of all other forms of thought.

26. Finally, in his address of 14 October to the Fourteenth General Congregation of the Synod of Bishops, Pope Benedict XVI concludes that, *"for the life and the mission of the Church, for the future of faith, this dualism between exegesis and theology must be overcome."* This dualism is the simultaneous presence in the minds of Catholic exegetes and theologians of two opposing systems of thought, namely, the framework of form-critical thinking and the framework of Catholic belief. And it is really a dualism, because the framework of form-criticism being used has never been synthesized with the outlook of Catholic faith or with the corpus of Catholic theology. Catholic form-critics do not deny their faith; they simply do not use their faith when they are doing their form-critical thinking. Often they strive to put their form-criticism aside when they are saying their prayers, but they also often preach and think about results of this method which tend to call into question the theology that they have learned. And that is a big reason why this dualism of exegesis and theology must be overcome, in the words of Pope Benedict XVI, "for the life and the mission of the Church, for the future of faith."

---

30 Cf. R. Bultmann, in H. W. Bartsch ed., *Kerygma and Myth: A Theological Debate,* vol. I (London: SPCK, 1953), pp.191–193, and 200.

Chapter 2

Some Rationalist Presuppositions of the Historical Critical Method

Part I. Regarding the Testimony of Joseph Cardinal Ratzinger

Living Tradition 137 (September 2008)

1. According to the 1993 document of the (reconstituted) Pontifical Biblical Commission, titled *The Interpretation of the Bible in the Church* (*IBC*), the historical critical method "is the indispensable method for the scientific study of the meaning of ancient texts" (p. 34).[1] It is "*a historical method*," says the Commission, not only because it studies the significance of ancient texts "from a historical point of view," but also and especially "because it seeks to shed light upon the historical processes which gave rise to biblical texts." According to this same document, the historical critical method "is *a critical method*, because in each of its steps (from textual criticism to redaction-criticism) "it operates with the help of scientific criteria that seek to be as objective as possible." Hence, "as an analytical method, it studies the biblical text in the same fashion as it would study any other ancient text and comments upon it as an expression of human discourse" (*IBC*, p. 37). In the following reflection I shall maintain that the historical critical method, as it is intended by the Pontifical Biblical Commission in the above-described document (*IBC*), especially as regards the phases of

---

1 Pontifical Biblical Commission, *The Interpretation of the Bible in the Church* (Vatican City State: Libreria Editrice Vaticana, 1993).

literary criticism and form-criticism (genre-criticism), *is neither scientific nor historical,* and its constant use of rationalist presuppositions *rules out any real objectivity* in its conclusions. The Commission claims that the historical critical method, as outlined in its document of 1993, "when used in an objective manner, implies of itself no *a priori,* to the effect that any concomitant *a priori* principles would not pertain to the method itself, but rather "to certain hermeneutical choices which govern the interpretation and can be tendentious." And so, continues the Commission, "for a long time now scholars have ceased combining the method with a philosophical system" (*IBC,* p. 40). On the contrary, it will be my contention that Catholic historical critical scholars have never ceased combining their method with a philosophical system, and, moreover, that in most cases these scholars have not even clearly recognized the philosophical systems that they are using.

2. As authoritative evidence for my claims, I submit some statements of Joseph Cardinal Ratzinger, made in a widely circulated lecture titled "Biblical Interpretation in Crisis" (*BIC*), delivered in New York City on January 27, 1988, and published soon afterwards in English and in other languages.[2] Regarding philosophical systems, the Cardinal affirms: "At its core, the debate about modern exegesis is not a dispute among historians; it is rather a philosophical debate" (*BIC,* p. 16). Again he observes: "In the diachronic reading of an exegesis, its philosophic presuppositions become quite apparent" (*BIC,* p. 8). As to the "scientific" and "historical" character of the historical critical method (as defined in the *IBC* document), the Cardinal remarks: "Now, at a certain distance, the observer determines to his surprise that these interpretations, which were supposed to be so strictly scientific and purely 'historical,' reflect their own overriding spirit, rather than the spirit of times long ago. This insight should not lead us to skepticism about the method, but rather to an honest recognition of what its limits are, and perhaps how it might be purified" (*BIC,* p. 8). What historical criticism needs at this point, said the Cardinal, is "a criticism of criticism ... based on the inherent potential of all critical thought to analyze itself," and this implies "a self-criticism of the historical method, which can expand to an analysis of historical reason itself, in continuity with and in development of the famous critique of reason by Immanuel Kant" (*BIC,* p. 6). Ratzinger maintained that exegesis depends upon its own history,

---

2 Joseph Cardinal Ratzinger, in Richard J. Neuhaus, gen. ed., *Biblical Interpretation in Crisis* (Grand Rapids: Eerdmans, 1989), pp. 1–23.

and, therefore, it needs "a critical arrangement of its respective positions within the totality of its own history," in order to be able to recognize "the relativity of its own judgments" and "the errors which may have crept in," and in order to be able to "distinguish between those hypotheses which are helpful and those which are not" (*BIC*, p. 22). The Cardinal thus expressed the hope for a new and thorough reflection on exegetical method in which "scientific exegesis" would recognize "the philosophic element present in a great number of its ground rules," and then begin to "reconsider the results which are based on those rules" (*BIC*, p. 21).

3. The Cardinal does not subscribe to Kant's critique of reason. It seems rather to him that the main philosophical presupposition underlying the exegetical system of form-criticism developed by Hermann Gunkel, Martin Dibelius, and Rudolf Bultmann seems to lie "in the philosophic turning point proposed by Immanuel Kant, which limits human intellectual life to the realm of the Kantian "categories," and, by very definition, excludes interventions of God as well as any new initiative from another plane (*BIC*, pp. 14–15). In this view, he adds, "revelation must recede into the pure formality of the eschatological stance, which corresponds to the Kantian split" (*BIC*, p. 16). What Cardinal Ratzinger was proposing was the need to begin joining the tools of "historical method" with a "better philosophy which would entail fewer drawbacks foreign to the text, which would be less arbitrary, and which would offer greater possibilities for a true listening to the text itself" (*BIC*, p. 17). He challenged the current use by form-critical scholars of the rule that what appears to be simpler in the biblical text is more original, and what seems to be more complex is taken to be a later development. Behind this approach he espied "a simplistic transferal of science's evolutionary model to spiritual history" (*BIC*, p. 10), brought into the method by the history-of-religions school (*BIC*, p. 14). Thus, he said, "modern exegesis," has adopted the dictates of the so-called "modern world-view'" of natural science by which the biblical text is treated as a reality completely of this world and has thus "relegated God to the incomprehensible, the otherworldly, and the inexpressible" (*BIC*, pp. 17, 19). He noted that, in searching for the immediate historical context of biblical presentations, modern exegetes have lost sight of the total movement of history and the light that is shed on it by the central event of all history, which is Jesus Christ (*BIC*, p. 20). Again, he noted that, for the use by historical critics of philological and scientific literary methods, "an understanding of the philosophic implications of the interpretative process is required" (*BIC*, p. 22), [and this understanding seems to me to

be singularly absent from the PBC's document of 1993 (*IBC*, p. 40), seeing that it sees no *a priori* in the standard interpretative process of the historical critical method].

4–5. Cardinal Ratzinger pointed out in his address of 1988 that the concerted efforts of a whole generation of scholars would be needed to weed out the limitations of the existing historical method from its "undeniable insights" (*BIC*, pp. 5–6). [And this task, I would add, would necessarily include distinguishing the true criticism of serious historical science from the criticism promoted by Hermann Gunkel, Martin Dibelius, Rudolf Bultmann, and their followers, which has become the kind of "historical critical method" most in use among Catholic biblical scholars today. Pope Leo XIII called this historical method a "pseudo-science," and Pope Pius X called it the logical fruit of Modernism.] Thus, the Cardinal observes that the basic methodological approaches of Dibelius and Bultmann "continue even today to determine the methods and procedures of modern exegesis," to the extent that their essential elements "have widely achieved an authority like unto dogma." Among these basic elements is the presupposition that "everything in the Bible develops from the Christian proclamation," to the extent that, for Bultmann, the proclaimed word generates the scene, while all of the events presented are assumed to be secondary and mythological (*BIC*, p. 9). Again, it is presupposed in the methodology of both Dibelius and Bultmann that there is no continuity between the historical Jesus and the Jesus of faith (cf. *BIC*, pp. 9–10). Then there is the assumption of a "creative Christian community," concerning which "the works of Gunkel and Bousset exerted decisive influence" (*BIC*, p. 13). Thus, says the Cardinal, we need to investigate, not just into Bultmann the existentialist theologian, but also into "Bultmann the exegete, who is responsible for an ever more solid consensus regarding the methodology of scientific exegesis" (*BIC*, p. 14).[3]

6. According to Cardinal Ratzinger, contemporary debate about biblical hermeneutics suffers from a reductive approach in which the exegesis of the Fathers of the Church is dismissed as mere "allegory," and the Scholastic philosophy of the middle ages is branded as "precritical" (*BIC*, p. 16). Again he notes that historical criticism replaces the organic continuity of the Old and New Testaments with a principle of discontinuity and leaves out both the analogy of Scripture and the purpose that it contains (*BIC*, p. 20). To correct this imbalance, he continues, "exegesis must recognize itself as a historical discipline." For this work, he adds, "the great outlines of patristic

---

3 Cf. *Living Tradition* 136 (July 2008), no. 16.

and medieval thought must be brought into the discussion," as well as the "fundamental judgments made by the Reformers" (*BIC*, p. 22). Finally, he remarks, exegetes must be aware that, in their exegetical work, they do not "stand in some neutral area, above and outside of history and the Church," as though faith itself were not a hermeneutic (*BIC*, pp. 22–23).

Comments on the teaching of Cardinal Ratzinger and of the reconstituted Pontifical Biblical Commission.

7. From these citations it is clear that, according to the view of Cardinal Ratzinger in 1988, the historical critical method, proposed as "indispensable" by the (reconstituted) Pontifical Biblical Commission, and now characterized by the use of the form-critical method of Hermann Gunkel, Martin Dibelius, and Rudolf Bultmann, is neither scientific nor historical, but is rather an uncritical application of the subjectivist philosophy of Immanuel Kant. In this form-critical expression of historical method, philosophical presuppositions are of the very essence, inasmuch as the Kantian split rules out *a priori* all real divine interventions in the writing of Sacred Scripture, and the biblical text is treated as a merely human product. Strangely, the PBC called its form-critical version of the historical critical method "indispensable," while at the same time admitting that the value and validity of this kind of historical method is under serious attack from many directions by competent scholars (*IBC*, pp. 29–32). In his Preface to this 1993 document, Cardinal Ratzinger, then President of the Commission, expresses the opinion that the document will be "very helpful for the important questions about the right way of understanding Holy Scripture," as it "takes up the paths of the encyclicals of 1893 and 1943," but he also points out that "the Pontifical Biblical Commission, in its new form after the Second Vatican Council, is not an organ of the teaching office, but rather a commission of scholars who, in their scientific and ecclesial responsibility as believing exegetes, take positions on important problems of scriptural interpretation and know that for this task they enjoy the confidence of the teaching office" (*BIC*, pp. 26–27).

8. Since the term "historical criticism" has become somewhat ambiguous in common Catholic parlance, I am taking the name here according to the description given in the 1993 document of the Pontifical Biblical Commission, and, therefore, as the method inherited from the "higher criticism" of the nineteenth century and refined according to the form-criticism of the twentieth century. This is how the 1993 document

of the PBC defines the term (cf. *IBC,* pp. 34–36). While the reconstituted Pontifical Biblical Commission claims that the classic historical critical method, including the essential elements of higher criticism and the form-critical developments of Hermann Gunkel, Martin Dibelius, and Rudolf Bultmann, "when used objectively" (cf. *IBC,* p. 39), is a truly historical method and a truly critical method, operating with the help of scientific criteria (*IBC,* p. 37), Cardinal Ratzinger avers that the results of this kind of historical criticism are not very scientific or historical, but rather are "an expression of their own overriding spirit" (cf. no. 2 above). The *IBC* notes that, while nineteenth century higher critics "expressed highly negative judgments against the Bible," nevertheless, "for a long time now scholars have ceased combining the method with a philosophical system" (*IBC,* p. 40), although, it says, some writers like Rudolf Bultmann "combined form-critical studies with a biblical hermeneutic inspired by the existentialist philosophy of Martin Heidegger" (*IBC,* p. 36). Now, this is a misleading statement, because Bultmann published his classic form-critical work, *The History of the Synoptic Tradition,* in 1921, basing his conclusions on the rationalist presuppositions of the method, and it was only many years after this that he began to use the existentialist philosophy of Martin Heidegger to argue that a "demythologized" Christian faith could still, (to a minimal extent), survive the wreckage of the Synoptic Gospels that his form-critical method had produced. The writers of the 1993 document of the PBC seem to be totally unaware of the rationalist presuppositions of their method. More correctly, Cardinal Ratzinger has pointed out the need to look into, "not just Bultmann the existentialist theologian, but also Bultmann the exegete" (*BIC,* p. 14).

9. Is the form-critical method recommended by the PBC in 1993 a truly historical method, as it sets out, using internal indications alone, to determine "the historical processes which gave rise to (the) biblical texts" (*IBC,* p. 37)? William Foxwell Albright, one of the most renowned archaeologists of the twentieth century, didn't think so. He had the following to say about this method: "From the standpoint of the objective historian data cannot be disproved by criticism of the accidental literary framework in which they occur, unless there are solid independent reasons for rejecting the historicity of an appreciable number of other data found in the same framework."[4] And again: "However, only modern scholars who lack both historical method and perspective can spin such a web of

---

4 William F. Albright, *From the Stone Age to Christianity* (2nd ed., Baltimore: Johns Hopkins Press, 1957), pp. 381–382.

speculation as that with which form-critics have surrounded the Gospel tradition."[5] Cardinal Ratzinger has pointed out (see no. 2 above) that the debate about modern exegesis is a philosophical, not a historical, one, as becomes apparent in the diachronic reading of examples of the exegesis. In other words, when the history of the development of modern form-critical exegesis is looked into, its rationalist presuppositions come to light. Ratzinger concentrates by way of example on the pervasive influence of the critical philosophy of Immanuel Kant. Is the form-critical method truly scientific? Cardinal Ratzinger points out that, from a distance, this kind of historical criticism is not very historical or scientific (cf. no. 2 above). In other words, its results do not represent historical science. And the Cardinal joins Albright in pointing out that various rules of the form-critical method are unscientific and unhistorical, such as consistently arguing in a circle,[6] assuming in the absence of outside evidence that what seems to be simpler is, therefore, earlier, and what seems to be more complex is, therefore, a later development, as well as presupposing that the Jesus of the Gospels is mostly a product of religious fantasy and is not the Jesus of history. Cardinal Ratzinger saw in this approach, not only some false philosophies of the past, but even an attempt to transfer the model of biological evolution to the supposed evolution of ideas in Sacred Scripture (cf. no. 4 above).

10. The 1993 document claims that its form of historical criticism is a *critical method* inasmuch as "it operates with the help of scientific criteria that seek to be as objective as possible" (*IBC*, p. 37). I have quoted Cardinal Ratzinger above to the effect that the historical critical method, as it is practiced today also by Catholic exegetes, is neither historical nor scientific, and is not even critical, in that it is largely uncritical of its own method and history. The term "historical criticism" is derived historically from the fact that its users took an unbelieving approach to the Bible and treated it as a purely human work. In this sense, this historical criticism is *critical* in that it does not accept the "word of God" as being actually the word of God, and this kind of criticism betrays the rationalism at its foundations. More specifically, the word "critical" in "historical criticism" refers back to the "critical" approach of Immanuel Kant and the use of his "scientific criteria," which may not be as scientific as its adherents claim. We shall undertake to examine what Kant claimed to be the criteria of science and how they pertain to the historical criticism that takes its origin from him. Following

---

5 Albright, op. cit., p. 387.

6 Albright, op. cit., p. 382.

the lead of Cardinal Ratzinger, I intend to examine whether this historical criticism is a) truly historical, b) truly critical, and c) truly analytical, and d) truly scientific.

11. Among the things that are needed in this discussion are clear concepts of science and history. As regards the definition of science, what seems to be lurking behind this kind of historical critical approach is the Transcendental Aesthetic of Immanuel Kant, which limits the term "science" to phenomena bounded by space and time along the lines of empiricist philosophy. These phenomena become "objective," while the other objects of historical science as well as of traditional philosophy and theology are relegated to the subjective and ultimately non-real. Hence, the function of the notion of reality is crucial in the whole question of science. We shall have to concentrate some attention upon the function of the notion of reality in the definition of science as we go along with this study and analyze what the 1993 document of the PBC claims to be "the scientific study of the meaning of ancient texts" (cf. no. 1 above). Also the definition of history must be clarified in relation to the notion of reality.

12. Cardinal Ratzinger notes that historical criticism is not a body of scientific knowledge that applies universally in the here and now, but is rather a controversial approach containing, not only some undeniable insights, but also errors that remain out of sight when the past of this higher criticism is kept out of focus. So the Cardinal called for "a new and thorough reflection on exegetical method," and presented some basic elements of a new synthesis which will require "the attentive and critical commitment of an entire generation."[7] Neo-patristic scholars implement this advice in the sense that they have undertaken a process of criticism of the historical critical method while attempting to formulate more clearly the principles of historical method itself. In this endeavor they distinguish between the valid and the invalid principles of contemporary historical criticism, especially as it is characterized by form-criticism, and they analyze historical critical conclusions for insights that they may suggest. In this work they carry out the 1964 injunction of the original Pontifical Biblical Commission. "*As occasion warrants, the exegete may look for what sound elements there may be in the 'method of form-criticism,' that could aptly be used for a fuller understanding of the Gospels. However, he must move with caution in this*

---

7 Ratzinger, *Biblical Interpretation in Crisis.*, pp. 16–17. Cf. *Living Tradition* 136 (July 2008), nos. 16–17.

area, because the method is often interlaced with inadmissible philosophical and theological principles which frequently vitiate both the method itself and its judgments on literary questions."[8]

13. Neo-patristic scholars are undertaking to implement this needed program of Cardinal Ratzinger and the original PBC. They begin their study of the sacred text from two departure points: from a critical reading of modern historical critical interpretations in the light of Catholic exegetical tradition and from a critical examination of their own frame of reference and medium of thought. The conclusions of form-critical exegetes often suggest ideas that can become real insights by formulating correctly presuppositions that are often either non-formulated or incorrectly formulated and are, therefore, out of context in a fuller view of historical reality. This requires a clear formulation of principles of historical method in the neo-patristic scholar's own frame of reference, which he takes especially from the Fathers and Doctors of the Church, as well as from an updated expression of modern historical method. As Cardinal Ratzinger says, it will take the work of at least one whole generation of scholars to bring about this change (cf. no. 6 above). In pursuing this study, neo-patristic scholars must systematically refute the outrageous conclusions of writers like Hermann Gunkel and Rudolf Bultmann, as they reformulate the existing principles of the form-critical method, fit it into the bigger picture of the neo-patristic method, and replace the so-called "world-view of modern man," as promoted by writers like Hermann Gunkel and Rudolf Bultmann, with the world-view of the Sacred Scripture, as revealed by God.

14. It is interesting to note that, among the ten or so approaches mentioned in *The Interpretation of the Bible in the Church* as possible ways to supplement its brand of historical criticism in our time, the method of the Four Senses of the Fathers of the Church is not included. Rather it says that "the allegorical interpretation of Scripture so characteristic of patristic exegesis runs the risk of being something of an embarrassment to people today" (*IBC*, p. 97). But Cardinal Ratzinger says in his Preface to the same document: "On the other hand, there are also new attempts to recover patristic exegesis and to include renewed forms of a spiritual interpretation of Scripture" (*IBC*, p. 26). And the *Catechism of the Catholic Church*, which appeared in the year previous to that of the *IBC*, presents the method of the Four Senses as the basic way to interpret Sacred Scripture (*CCC*, nos. 115–119). An issue at hand is this, that all of the Fathers and Doctors of

---

8 *EB* 647. ET: Cf. [1964] Instruction of the Pontifical Biblical Commission, *The Historicity of the Gospels* (Boston, MA: St. Paul Editions), pp. 4–5.

the Church upheld the historical truth and inerrancy of Sacred Scripture, as do all of the pertinent papal encyclicals from 1893 to 1950.

15. What Cardinal Ratzinger calls the Kantian "philosophical turning point" of the "Kantian split," according to which human intellectual life is considered to be limited to the realm of the Kantian categories, fits into the larger anti-Christian project of viewing all religion as a merely subjective product. Non-believers in general consider the objects of Christian faith to be religious fantasies, over and above the Kantian conclusion that all non-empirical "knowledge" is merely subjective. What Kant did was to give some intellectual justification to the rationalist supposition that every account of supernatural being or activity is a product of human fantasy. In other words, Kant gave seeming arguments to back up an anti-supernatural bias which Scripture scholars and others can nurture apart from any awareness of the Kantian categories.

16. In an analysis of the influence of the philosophy of Immanuel Kant upon the approach of contemporary scholars to biblical inerrancy, David Beck observes that most historians regard Kant as "one of the most important framers of the modern mind," especially because he synthesized empiricism and rationalism into an integrated whole, and this has caused his influence upon theology to become "unparalleled."[9] He adds that many of the arguments of those who deny the inerrancy of Sacred Scripture are drawn directly from the reasoning of Immanuel Kant.[10] Beck quotes Bultmannian scholar Schubert Ogden to the effect that Kant's thoroughgoing separation of "pure" from "practical" reason is comparable in impact to St. Thomas Aquinas's distinction between faith and reason, and Beck points out that any theology of inerrant biblical inspiration must refute two basic tenets of Kant's epistemology: a) that reason and sense perception are entirely separate in operation; and b) that space, time, causality, etc., are solely functions of the mind and are not in the sense data.[11] This isolation of metaphysics from factual knowledge split knowledge into two unrelated parts and placed religion in the realm of the *postulated* but not *known*, setting up autonomous man as the one who determines for himself what he will believe about God,[12] as an opinion "which each man is free to hold

---

9 W. David Beck, "Agnosticism: Kant," in Norman L. Geisler, ed., *Biblical Errancy* (Grand Rapids, MI: Zondervan, 1981), p. 53.

10 Beck, ibid., p. 72.

11 Beck, ibid., pp. 76–77.

12 Beck, ibid., p. 54. Cf. Immanuel Kant, *Religion within the Limits of Reason Alone* (New York: Harper and Row, 1960), p. 39.

as he finds edifying."[13] And for Kant, human freedom is a postulate of practical reason, not an objective truth known from pure reason.[14] This leads Beck to conclude that the task of constructing a better epistemology than that of Kant "is extremely crucial."[15] We shall be considering in this study how the philosophy of Immanuel Kant underlies historical criticism of the form-critical school and how it influences the use of historical criticism by Catholic biblical scholars and theologians.

17. Hence, what David Beck says here about Protestant theology applies also, to a large extent, to contemporary Catholic theology and Scripture scholarship. When Catholic biblical scholars took up historical criticism, "child of the Enlightenment," as their approach to the interpretation of the Bible, they implicitly turned away from the epistemology of St. Thomas Aquinas and of the Scholastic tradition in general, and they adopted, often unwittingly, the epistemology of Immanuel Kant and of the Enlightenment in general. In the absence of the moderate realism of the Thomist tradition, they became open to the false distinction between the *factual* knowledge given by sense perception alone, and metaphysical or religious *opinion*. Beck points out that, for many contemporary (Protestant) theologians, "the source of science is different from the source of values," to the extent that facts are taken to be known, while metaphysical or religious values are not considered items of real knowledge, "even though they may be considered important."[16] Similarly, when Catholic theologians and biblical scholars call form-criticism "scientific exegesis," are they not implying that the events narrated in Sacred Scripture are in the category of "values" that are not scientifically, and, therefore, not objectively, certified in themselves, and so that, as "critical historians," they are seeking to discover only how these allegedly fictitious ideas and events arose in the human and social consciousness of the biblical writers? What Cardinal Ratzinger has with reason recommended is that exegetes and theologians today, in the name of biblical and theological science, re-examine from where the method of form-criticism has arisen in the minds of the form-critics.

18. An important issue is the mental frame of reference being used. Neo-patristic interpreters use and defend the great framework of the Four Senses

---

13 I. Kant, *Religion Within the Limits of Reason Alone*, p. 39. Cf. Beck, op. cit., p. 63.

14 Immanuel Kant, *Critique of Practical Reason* (Indianapolis: Bobbs-Merrill, 1949), p. 132. Cf. Beck, ibid., p. 61.

15 Beck, ibid., p. 78.

16 Cf. Beck, ibid., p. 73.

of Sacred Scripture and the approach implied in the Bible itself. Form-critics, in their reflections about the "subject-object relationship," usually seem to ignore their own mental frame of reference, whereas, in the moderate realism of St. Thomas Aquinas, neo-patristic exegetes examine their own thoughts and images as the proximate object of their knowledge, and they know external things as the remote object of their knowledge. And so, contrary to the Kantian model, neo-patristic thinkers, confident that human minds do know external things in themselves, just as mirrors really depict external things as they are in themselves, try to be critically aware of the principles that they are using in the exegesis of Sacred Scripture. As a special task, they analyze the corpus of form-critical writings to identify the principles that form-critics are using there, in order to recognize insights and to sift out the errors that have logically followed from false or poorly defined presuppositions. They examine also and try to update the principles used in the historical and exegetical writings of the great Scholastic thinkers, especially those of St. Thomas Aquinas, whose reasoning is rock-solid for the most part, but whose data obviously need to be revised in some areas, such as those of history and natural science. As Cardinal Ratzinger points out, Immanuel Kant was certainly right in calling upon thinkers to examine and clarify the principles of their own thought (*BIC*, p. 6), but this project in our day must include a critical examination of Kant's own reasoning. And so, in the next part I shall try to present a more detailed study of the validity of Kant's approach and the impact of his philosophy upon the historical critical method as it is presently being practiced by form-critics.

Part II. The Critical Philosophy of Immanuel Kant in the Background

A. Some Basic Elements of The Critical Approach of Immanuel Kant

Living Tradition 139 (January 2009)

19. A subjectivist philosophy: Many historians have characterized the philosophy of Immanuel Kant (1724–1804) to be a forging of British empiricism and continental idealism into a higher synthesis which

Frederick Copleston, in his *History of Philosophy*, calls "a triumph" over both.[17] Kant began with a critique of the materialism of David Hume (1711–1776) and added to it another critique of the idealist tradition of René Descartes (1596–1650), Gottfried Wilhelm von Leibnitz (1646–1716), and Christian von Wolff (1679–1754). In this way Kant undertook to bring together, on the one hand, the mechanism and determinism of the empiricist approach, based on the model of Newtonian physics, and, on the other hand, the theories of freedom and deduced ideas, developed by Descartes, Leibnitz and other idealist philosophers, into one contrasting system of thought which Kant labeled "*transcendental idealism.*" Agreeing with Hume that whatever we know must be given in sensory experience, Kant reasoned that knowledge must also be somehow constructed by and within the mind of the knower, because strict universality cannot be derived from items of sense experience in themselves, so he postulated the function of *a priori* forms in human consciousness, the first of them being the forms of space and time.[18] This idea allowed him to retain the empiricist practice of regarding the impressions of sensory data as the only objects of scientific knowledge, while seeming to open the way also in human consciousness for a rationally legitimate but scientifically indemonstrable belief in freedom, God, and the immortality of the soul (*KC,* p. 455). Kant did not deny the empiricist idea that true science deals only with observations of the material world, but he enclosed these observations of the material world within what to him are the merely subjective forms of space and time and then other *a priori* forms said to exist only within the consciousness of the individual thinker. This gave to Kant a subjectivist philosophy of the material world.

20. Kantian terminology: Hume had assumed that the real constituents of human experience are only discrete, atomic perceptions, and that the human self is just a bundle of these perceptions having no essential unity (*CHP,* p. 199). Kant added to this outlook the transcendental unity of human apperception (consciousness) as a basic condition of human experience (*KC,* pp. 94–95), noting that Hume had granted it to be necessary that sensory conceptions have an *a priori,* but it had never occurred to him that the understanding itself might be the author of the experience in which these objects were presented to it (*KC,* p. 92). Kant agrees that empirical

---

17 Frederick Copleston, *History of Philosophy,* vol. 6, *Modern Philosophy,* Part II, *Kant* (Image Books: Garden City, NY, 1964) [hereinafter referred to as CHP], p. 218.

18 Cf. Immanuel Kant, *Critique of Pure Reason* (English translation of the second edition, 1787: New York: Dutton and Co., 1934 [hereinafter referred to as KC]) pp. 102 and 413.

cognitions alone are items of real knowledge (*KC*, p. 102), but human knowledge springs also from two main sources *entirely within the mind*: the power to receive sensory impressions, which he calls *intuition*, and the power to produce mental conceptions from these impressions, which he terms *understanding*, and, he adds, no knowledge is possible without the simultaneous action of the two (*KC*, p. 62).[19] In Kantian theory, the undetermined object of an empirical intuition is called a *phenomenon*, while the form, or determination, of the phenomenon lies ready, *a priori*, in the mind and is distinct from all sensation. Thus, extension and shape are not objects of sensation but are merely internal powers that form the objects of sensation (*KC*, pp. 41–42). *Reason*, on the other hand, never applies directly to experience or to any sensory object; it applies to the understanding of the manifold of cognition (*KC*, p. 213). The particular function of reason is to arrange transcendental ideas into a *system*, that is, to give them connection according to a principle (*KC*, p. 374). Kant applies the term *transcendental* to all knowledge which is occupied with the mode of our knowledge of objects, rather than with objects themselves (*KC*, p. 38). Reasoning about objects or ideas not directly derived from sensory experience is always fictitious (*KC*, p. 373).

21. Transcendental idealism: Kant advocates what he calls *transcendental idealism*, according to which it is assumed that all things intuited in space and time and presented to us as extended bodies or series of changes have no self-subsistent existence apart from human thought. In other words, transcendental idealism holds that mental phenomena are not things in themselves; they are mere representations which, apart from their being perceived, are non-existent (*KC*, pp. 296–297). And even the whole world is not a whole existing in itself (*KC*, p. 304). In Kant's view, the only *a priori* intuition is that of the pure forms of phenomena, which are space and time ((*KC*, p. 413). What we see as the extension and shape of bodies does not actually belong to external things themselves, because what seems to be external space is just the result of our own subjective disposition that enables us to have intuitions of these objects. *Space* does not exist, because, if the objects in space are subtracted, all that remains is a pure internal intuition,

---

19 In Kant's terminology, an *intuition* clings singularly to the sensory perception, while a *conception* has a mediate relation to the sensory perception and may be common to several things. A *pure conception*, having its origin in the understanding alone, and, therefore, not in a sensory perception, he calls a *notion*. A representation formed from notions, and, therefore, transcending the possibility of sensory experience, he calls an *idea*, or a *conception of reason* (KC, p. 222).

and this is the "empirical reality" of space (*KC*, p. 46). *Time* is simply "the form of the internal sense," that is, "the form of the intuitions of self and of our internal state." While space is the pure form of the intuition of external phenomena, time is the formal condition *a priori* of all phenomena, because all phenomena are in time, and this is the "empirical reality" of time (*KC*, p. 50).[20] "The schema of *substance* is the permanence of the real in time" (*KC*, p. 120). This idea of permanence does not come from any external experience; it is rather "an *a priori* necessary condition of all determination of time," including also of the internal sense with reference to our own existence, and thence to the existence of external things (*KC*, p. 172).

---

20 Problematical idealism: In refutation of Descartes' "problematical idealism," Kant defends the following theorem: *"The simple but empirically determined consciousness of my own existence proves the existence of external objects in space."* His proof goes like this. I am conscious of my own existence as determined in time. The consciousness of my own existence is at the same time an immediate consciousness of the existence of other things without me. Our proof shows that external experience is properly immediate, that only by virtue of it – not, indeed, the consciousness of our own existence, but certainly the determination of our existence in time – is possible. In (the representation *I am*) we cannot find any knowledge of the subject, and therefore, also no empirical knowledge, that is, experience. For experience contains, in addition to the thought of something existing, intuition, and in this case it must be internal intuition, that is, time in relation to which the subject must be determined. But the existence of external things is absolutely requisite for this purpose, so that it follows that internal experience is itself possible only mediately and through external experience (KC, pp. 170–172). And we are obliged to employ external intuition to be able to represent the successive existence of ourselves in different states (KC, p. 179). Probably not a contradiction. Some writers, including Frederick Copleston, have seen the above-quoted theorem as being in contradiction to Kant's basic principle that the external world and the things in it do not really exist. But I think that a closer look reveals some consistency in Kant's reasoning. Descartes' opening statement was *Cogito, ergo sum* ("I am thinking, therefore, I am"). Kant counters that the fact that I am thinking does not prove that I am, if, by "I am" is intended anything about me except the mere existence of a knowing subject as such, because this factor of consciousness is absolutely empty and has no content. And this seems to be true. But the consciousness that I am thinking can exist only in coincidence with an object that I am observing, and so the reasoning of Descartes, inasmuch as he holds rational substances to be conscious independently of external things (KC, p. 242) and tries to derive all philosophy subjectively from his *Cogito, ergo sum,* does not stand up. There seems to be no contradiction in this point of Kant's reasoning, if we consider that he is here using the word "external," not as meaning external to human consciousness, but rather as external only to what Kant calls the "internal sense " and the subjectivity of Descartes' *cogito.* It remains that for Kant the object being sensorially observed is always within the mind and never outside of the mind. Thus, he does not seem here to contradict his total subjectivism, although his claim that the thinking self can never establish himself reflexively as an object appears to me to be gratuitous and without foundation.

22. Only phenomena are real: Kant avers that everything real is presented to us as a *phenomenon*, never as a *noumenon*, or thing in itself (*KC*, p. 199). The conception of a physical *noumenon* is not an arbitrary or fictitious notion, but it is incapable of presenting us with any positive data from beyond the field of conscious phenomena. A physical *noumenon* is, at best, a not-to-be-excluded notion of an unknown something (*KC*, pp. 188–189). In the epistemology of Immanuel Kant, "*reality*, in the pure conception of the understanding, is that which corresponds to a sensation in general; [it is] that, consequently, the conception of which indicates a being (in time)" (*KC*, p. 120), or, in other words, "that which coheres with the material conditions of experience (sensation) is *real*" (*KC*, p. 166; cf. p. 410). "Reality is concerned only with sensation, as the matter of experience, and not with the form of thought, with which we can no doubt indulge in shaping fancies. ... It is perception which presents matter to the conception that is the sole criterion of reality" (*KC*, pp. 168–169). "The conceptions of reality, substance, causality, nay, even of the necessity of existence, have no significance out of the sphere of empirical cognition, and cannot, beyond that sphere, determine any object" (*KC*, p. 391). The intelligible object of transcendent ideas may be called a "transcendental object," but, since such an object has no connection with empirical conceptions, we may not affirm its existence (*KC*, p. 333). "Transcendental ideas...cannot be conceptions of objects, and, when thus considered, they assume a fallacious and dialectical character" (*KC*, p. 374).

23. Transcendental ideas: For Kant the critique of reason "forms part of the native rights of human reason, which recognizes no other judge than the universal reason of humanity; and as this reason is the source of all progress and improvement, such a privilege is to be held sacred and inviolable" (*KC*, p. 430). And so, in metaphysics mistakes can be avoided "if we are sufficiently cautious in the construction of our fictions, which are not the less fictions on that account" (*KC*, p. 29). The pure conceptions of reason are *transcendental ideas*. From the cognition of self to the cognition of the world, and through these to the supreme being, the progression is so natural that it seems to resemble the logical march of reason from the premises to the conclusion (*KC*, p. 231). The first transcendental idea of pure reason is the ego, considered merely as a thinking nature or soul. The second transcendental idea is the conception of the universe. The third transcendental idea, containing the hypothesis of a being which is valid merely as a relative hypothesis, is that of the one and all-sufficient cause of all cosmological series, in other words, the idea of God (*KC*, pp. 395–396).

Of these three, only the transcendental unity of apperception is objectively valid (*KC*, p. 98). But to show reasons why, for instance, we are endowed with precisely so many functions of judgment and no more, or why time and space are the only forms of our intuition, is impossible to explain (*KC*, p. 101), and the intuition of self does lie in the original constitution of the mind (*KC*, p. 59). But our awareness of ourselves as knowing subjects is only as a phenomenon, and not as we actually are in ourselves (*KC*, p. 107).

24. The transcendental speculation of reason: Kant goes on to say that we are inclined to assume the existence of "a wise and omnipotent author of the world," not as having absolute and objective reality, but merely as an ideal being that we think about (*KC*, p. 402). Kant's "transcendental speculation of reason" relates to three things: the freedom of the will, the immortality of the soul, and the existence of God (*KC*, p. 453). Kant is certain that we shall never see sufficient demonstrations of the two cardinal propositions of pure reason, namely, the existence of a Supreme Being and the immortality of the soul. We need not, then, he says, have recourse to invalid scholastic arguments, because we have on our side the support of the subjective maxim of reason, and we can, therefore, look upon all the existing sophistical "proofs" with calm indifference (*KC*, pp. 423–425). Reason does not assure us of the objective validity of the conception of God; it merely gives us the idea of something on which the supreme and necessary unity of all experience is based (*KC*, p. 390). This world is, it is true, an intelligible world; for of such a systematic unity of ends as it requires, the world of sense gives us no hint. But the reality of this world can be based on nothing else than the hypothesis of a supreme original good (*KC*, p. 462). In Kant's "transcendental metaphysics," the ideas of the soul, of freedom, and of the existence of God become objects of faith rather than of knowledge (*CHP*, pp. 27–28). In the Idea of God we think the totality of supersensible or noumenal reality, and in the idea of the world we think the totality of sensible reality (*CHP*, p. 174). God and the world are not "substances outside my ideas but the thinking whereby we make for ourselves objects through synthetic *a priori* cognitions, and are, subjectively, self-creators of the objects we think" (*CHP*, pp. 174–175).

25. Practical knowledge: In Kant's terminology, theoretical knowledge is knowledge of *what is*, and practical knowledge is knowledge of *what ought to be* (*KC*, p. 368). Theoretical knowledge is *speculative* when it relates to an object which is not given in and cannot be discovered by means of experience (*KC*, p. 369). Kant maintains that no speculative "metaphysics" that tries to use pure concepts of the mind (soul, substance, etc.) in order

to transcend sense experience and envision so-called realities going beyond the senses can legitimately be called a science or is even anything more than fiction (*KC*, p. 29). To Kant it is evident that the ultimate intention of nature, in the constitution of our reason, has been directed to the *moral* alone (*KC*, p. 455). The faculty of reason, accordingly, enunciates laws which are imperative, or objective, *laws of freedom*, and which tell us what *ought to take place*, thus distinguishing themselves from the *laws of nature*, which relate to that which *does take place*. The laws of freedom, or of free will, are hence termed practical laws (*KC*, p. 456). Kant says that he is "morally certain" that there is a God and another world, but only because these beliefs are interwoven with his moral nature (*KC*, p. 469). To view ourselves called, as Leibnitz does, to a kingdom of grace, in which all happiness awaits us, is a practically necessary idea of reason (*KC*, p. 461). The moral law in us, "this mighty, irresistible proof," accompanied by an ever-increasing knowledge of the purposive finality in everything we see around us, does still remain to humanity (*KC*, p. 246).

26. Freedom of the will: Kant assumes that there are pure moral laws which prescribe the use that the rational being should make of his freedom, and it is, then, in their moral use that the principles of pure reason possess objective reality (*KC*, p. 458). Copleston sees this as meaning that practical reason produces its objects and makes them real (*CHP*, p. 103). The whole interest of reason, speculative as well as practical, is centered on the three following questions: 1) What can I know? 2) What ought I to do? 3) What may I hope (*KC*, p. 457)? The human will is a faculty of self-determination existing in man independently of all sensuous coercion (*KC*, p. 317). The idea of a moral world has, therefore, objective reality, conceived, however, only as an object of pure reason in its practical use (*KC*, p, 459). So far as relates to the empirical character of the world there can be no freedom (*KC*, p. 325), since the principle of an unbroken connection between all events in the phenomenal world, in accordance with the unchangeable laws of nature, is "a well-established principle which admits of no exception," so that, if phenomena were absolutely real things in themselves, freedom would be impossible. Certain effects may, therefore, be considered to be free in relation to their intelligible cause and necessary in relation to the phenomena of which they are a necessary consequence (*KC*, pp. 318–319).

27. The "categorical imperative": Regarding Kant's teaching on free will and religion, Copleston makes some further observations along the following lines. Kant postulates that man is an end in himself, and that the will of man, taken as a rational being, must be regarded as the source

of the moral law which he recognizes as universally binding. This is the principle of the autonomy of the human will. And to say that the moral will is autonomous is to say that it gives itself the law which it obeys (*CHP*, pp. 120–121). As belonging to an intelligible world, man finds himself under moral laws which have their foundation in reason alone. The idea of freedom makes each human thinker a member of an intelligible world to which his actions should conform, and this is the categorical imperative. No human reason can ever discern how this imperative is possible, but it is a necessary consequence of the presupposition that the will of an intelligence is free, and, in Kant's view, the practical necessity of this moral agency is sufficient for the laws of morality (*CHP*, p. 125). The categorical imperative implies a call to a moral perfection that cannot actually be attained in the time allotted, and thus emerges the idea of the immortality of the human soul, which, again, is not demonstrable by reason in its theoretical use (*CHP*, p. 130). The same moral law leads us, on a practical level, to postulate the existence of God, and theoretical reason should try to conform to this belief (*CHP*, p. 134). Thus, "morality leads inevitably to religion" (quoting Kant), but Kant rejects any idea of unique divine revelation or the legitimacy of an authoritarian Church (*CHP*, p. 136). He claims that natural scientists should see a purposive unity in physical nature that could imply the work of a divine hand, but as a conclusion having only subjective validity (*CHP*, p. 144).

B. Some Critical Remarks Regarding Kant's Critical Approach

28. The reductive approach: The empiricism of Immanuel Kant, like all empiricism, has a reductive approach to reality. This reductive approach can be illustrated by the following hypothetical example. Michelangelo's painting of the Last Judgment on the front wall of the Sistine Chapel has been viewed by millions and often photographically reproduced. But suppose that a scientific study of this wall were undertaken by scientists always holding their eyes close to the wall and using magnifying glasses and microscopes as technical instruments. And let us suppose that every square centimeter of the wall was precisely measured and chemically analyzed so that what seemed to be, for instance, smooth and even lines turned out under scientific examination to be jagged and uneven, with the colors overlapping, and other results of this kind. It could happen that those responsible for this scientific study might begin to declare that there is no

picture at all on the wall and to affirm that those who claim to see a picture there are obstructing the progress of science. This reductive view of the wall might be called "scientific" by a certain class of thinkers, especially if they disagreed with the message of the painting, but it would actually be a violation both of reason and of common sense.

29. Kant's reductive approach: Now, Kant's assumption that we cannot know what exists outside of our mind, because all that our senses receive are "atomic impressions" coming from sources to which we have no immediate access (no. 20 above), is a violation both of reason and of common sense. It is a violation of reason, because it can easily be shown that mirrors, even though they receive only "atomic impressions" of external things, nevertheless reproduce those things as they are, and so also with our human sensory perception. And it is a violation of common sense, because everyone knows that we are immersed in an external world of material things that are spatially spread out in a sequence of time. In a football game, for instance, each of the players knows that the bodies of twenty-two players are spread out there, that there is a real football, a real line of scrimmage, two goal-lines a hundred yards apart, and a definite length of time until the end of the game. This whole scenario could not really be situated only within the minds of the players, and it is difficult to believe that Kant, as he took his daily afternoon walk, did not realize that he was passing through real and extra-mental space and time. In fact, he admitted that no one can really help thinking that these objects are extra-mental, and he had to constantly force his mind into conformity with his theory. And this gave rise for Kant and for many of his followers to a confused understanding of the function of common sense.[21]

30. Common sense: Thus, Kant attacks the "Naturalists of pure reason" who claim that common sense without the aid of science or of metaphysical speculation can provide better answers to the great questions of life, and who maintain that the neglect of all scientific means is the right way to advance our knowledge. And he notes the absurdity of such a stand (KC, p. 483), but this depiction is largely a caricature of the question at hand. Of course, opposition to all technical science and metaphysical speculation is absurd. And there was, indeed, in Kant's time a "school of common sense"

---

21 "(Kant) maintained that we must refrain from asserting dogmatically the existence of the thing-in-itself, though we cannot help thinking it. It is clear that Kant thought it absurd to reduce reality to a mere construction of the subject, and that he therefore looked on the retention of the concept of the thing-in-itself as a matter of common sense... In (Fichte's) opinion, Kant was a man who tried to have things both ways at once, and who therefore involved himself in hopeless inconsistencies" (CHP, p. 221).

that arose in Scotland and did excessively oppose metaphysical speculation, basing its approach upon the conviction that "philosophy has no other root but the principles of common sense; it grows out of them and draws its nourishment from them."[22] It carried its opposition to metaphysical speculation too far, but it was mainly opposed to the empiricism of David Hume and the subjectivist speculation of the continental idealists,[23] and its stand was basically correct in the sense that both natural science and sound metaphysics do grow out of common sense, which is just another name for common science, and which arises from a number of self-evident principles "which are the foundation of all reasoning and which neither admit of direct proof nor need it."[24] Actually, all *sound* physical science and philosophy, so it seems, are based upon that realism of common sense that is characteristic of adults of balanced mind. It is, indeed, a function of technical science to correct the illusions to which common sense is sometimes subject, but most of what common sense sees is not illusionary, and, to the extent that technical science does not convincingly correct occasional misreadings of reality performed by common sense, it is logically bound to adhere to what common sense presents. Even natural scientists working in a laboratory have to use common sense in carrying out their experiments. What exactly Immanuel Kant meant by his idea of "transcendental idealism" has been in constant debate since the first edition of his *Critique of Pure Reason* in 1781, mainly over whether it is just a version of George Berkeley's phenomenalist conception of objects in space. Kant forcefully maintained that it is not, but in either case it seems that Kant's theory is a direct violation of common sense as explained in this essay.

31. Moderate realism: In the present reflection, Thomist philosophy and theology, vis-à-vis empirical science, are approaches plainly based upon a technical development of common sense. It is a pity that Kant limited his critical philosophy to the parameters of British empiricism and continental subjectivism, while he ignored the wide expanses of Thomist reasoning. In the moderate realism of Thomas Aquinas, as a technical development of common sense, the reality of things outside of the mind constitutes the remote object of human knowledge, while the conscious perception of these things constitutes the proximate object

---

22 Thomas Reid (1710-1796), *Works* (1863 edition), p. 101 (quoted in William Turner, *History of Philosophy* [Boston: Ginn and Co., 1929], p. 593).

23 Cf. F. Copleston, *History of Philosophy* (Garden City, NY: Image Books, 1963), vol. 4, p. 49.

24 Copleston, ibid., p. 49.

of human knowledge. Kant's error here lies in making the proximate object of human knowledge (the mirror-like image) into the remote object and thence in obscuring the very existence of the remote object of human knowledge. For Kant, space and time belong only to human consciousness and have no reality apart from it (*KC*, p. 102); they are for him the necessary internal forms for the assembly of all sense perceptions into phenomena of the imagination. On the contrary, in Thomist philosophy, space and time are beings of the mind with a foundation in external reality. This means that space *as a relation* of distance and time *as a measurement* of motion exist only in the mind, but they are based upon real external extension and real external motion or change.[25]

32. The common-sense concept of reality: But what is *reality*? For Kantian subjectivism, reality is constituted by and limited to the conscious objects of sensory perception, and not by anything outside of the mind. Kant maintains this position in sheer opposition to common sense and common experience, even though the very idea of reality is rooted in common sense, and it consists in the distinction that is made early in life between truth and falsehood, between truth and error, and between what is real and what is non-real inasmuch as it is either a deception, an illusion, a lie, or a fantasy. Hence, the correction of illusions is also a function of common sense, and here technical science comes to its aid by the use of precise instruments and methods, but never by ignoring observations of common sense and simply saying "yes, this looks obvious, but here you must ignore the obvious," as many empiricists and all subjectivists do.

33. Intellectual consciousness: The Aristotelian/Thomist theory of proximate versus remote objects of knowledge opens the way to a better understanding of the human mind. Within human consciousness lies human intelligence, the proper function of the rational intellect with which man is endowed, essentially divided in its function between a knowing subject and the object of his knowledge. Whenever a human being is conscious and thinking, he is a knowing subject viewing objects. Thus, the unity of the perception of one's own existence is given in consciousness and is a spontaneous awareness, contrary to the claims of empiricists, mechanists, and all other materialists. Kant agrees basically with this, but only reductively, because for him there is no independent intuition of the knowing subject apart from its connection to the act of *sense* perception. Now, awareness of self as a knowing subject is a characteristic of all higher

---

25 Cf. R.P. Phillips, *Modern Thomistic Philosophy* (Westminster, Maryland: Newman Press, 1950), vol. I, pp. 96 and 123.

animals, because the act of all finite knowing is made up of an object of knowledge and of a knowing subject of that knowledge. But, while animal knowing contains a merely spontaneous knowing subject, intelligent human knowing contains the power of reflective awareness within the unity of apperception. It is true that the unity of this intelligent apperception has no content of its own, since it is an empty factor of finite intelligence as such, but it has the ability to discover constituents lying behind this awareness by seeing them as objects.[26] As far as mental objects go that are not perceptions of the senses, he accords a kind of validity, that is, a kind of reality, also to the mental objects of time, space, and "the transcendental unity of apperception," but why these mental objects alone, in addition to phenomena of the sensory imagination, are real he cannot explain; nor can he produce any proof from his power of reason to show why the mind is constructed as it is—as far as logical categories and functions of judgment go (cf. no. 23 above). Hence, much of Kant's critical epistemology is based on what he simply assumes and takes for granted.

34. The "Kantian split": In Kant's terminology, transcendental philosophy is the idea of a science which is the system of all the principles of pure reason (KC, p. 39). He says that the critique of reason leads to science, while the "dogmatic" use of reason without this criticism leads to gratuitous assertions and equally gratuitous counter-assertions (KC, p. 422). As Copleston puts it, Kant "affirms the value of metaphysics considered as a natural disposition but denies its claim to constitute a true science which gives us theoretical knowledge of purely intelligible reality" (CHP, p. 27). Kant cautiously affirms the three "transcendental ideas" mentioned above (no. 23), while sweepingly excluding as confusion in which "all insight and knowledge cease to exist" (KC, p. 285), most of the ideas presented hitherto by other philosophers, not only by the continental idealists, but also (without a fair hearing) by the philosophy and theology of Thomas Aquinas and his peers. But even the few transcendental ideas that Kant retains are to him "fictions" that are always to be recognized as such (no. 23 above). And here appears the "Kantian split" mentioned by Cardinal Ratzinger as a defect of modern thought that needs to be remedied (no. 3 above). For Kant, only the intra-mental objects of sensory perception and things closely tied to it, such as time and space, are "real," while all other objects are lacking in reality, and all of the transcendental

---

26 Cf. my treatment of "Intellectual Consciousness" and "The Discovery of Truth" in *The Science of Historical Theology* (2nd printing, Rockford: TAN, 1991), [now Saint Benedict Press, LLC, 13315 Carowinds Blvd. Suite Q, Charlotte, NC 28273] pp. 15–25.

ideas of conventional metaphysics are thus to be recognized as fictitious (no. 22 above). Now, if we define "science" as "certified knowledge of the real as such," in Kant's "critical" view, all of the objects of conventional philosophy and theology are unscientific. Kant avers that intellectual hypotheses and faith should not be called into the service of our practical interests; nor should we present them under "the pompous titles of science and insight," for speculative knowledge cannot find any other objective basis than sensory experience (*KC*, p. 286). Now, sensory experience does have general rules of unity in the synthesis of phenomena, but, he adds, the objective reality of these rules can always be shown from sense experience itself (*KC*, p. 127*)*.

35. Kant's critical philosophy as "permissible fiction": Kant tells us that there is a natural tendency to philosophize, but for him this tendency, apart from his own reductive permissions, has no basis in or logical connection with science and objective reality; it is a universe of discourse unto itself. Kant allows himself to venture a little into "critical philosophy," but with the proviso that such thinking is only permissible fiction at best (no. 23 above). He claims that science and reality pertain only to thoughts directly connected with sense experience, but he offers no convincing arguments for this opinion. The fact is that most of the things that people really know are learned from others. Not even most of the specialized knowledge of empirical scientists is known from their own personal sense experience. Knowledge of history and the majority of what people know about real things depend on the testimony of others, and there are common-sense rules, as well as further technical rules, for judging whether such testimony is reliable. But Kant rules out *a priori* all such testimony on the ground that "the only true teacher" is sensory experience (*KC*, p. 285). Kant's limited notion of "the only true teacher," sets up an inadequate idea of historical fact and historical knowledge. Applying his notion that all phenomena "are not given as things in themselves, but in experience alone," he says that "things that really existed in past time" are to him "real objects only in so far as I can represent to my own mind that a regressive series of possible perceptions ... conducts us to an elapsed series of time as the condition of the present time." When Kant says that objects existed prior to his experience: "this means only that I must begin with the perception present to me, and follow the track indicated, until I discover them in some part or region of experience" (*KC*, p. 298). Here, as elsewhere, Kant is in violation of that common experience which recognizes the external reality of historical events and the value of testimony in the acquisition of

knowledge of the past. Certainly past events do not have present existence, but Kant's approach takes the documented facts of history entirely out of the realm of external reality and reduces them to some kind of fiction.

36. Kant's "universal reason" as the supreme judge: Kant holds as a fundamental principle that the "critique of reason" is a native right of man that is subject to no other judge but itself (no. 23 above). Unfortunately, this is the basic presupposition of all rationalism. He considers "universal reason" to have a "sacred and inviolable" right to judgment that is not subject to any external authority, (not even to the authority of God), and on this "sacred" ground, he sweeps away all appeals to divine revelation and all claims of a divinely established Church (no. 27 above). Moral conscience he acknowledges, but he makes it totally subject to a use of reason that is not grounded in objective truth. This is an egoist worldview that Kant has constructed around his own unaided reason. Yes, man has a tendency to think, whether wholesomely or perversely, but man also has an obligation to conform his reason to objective truth, and this includes conformity to historical reality and to common sense, while Kant's unrealistic and arbitrary definition of reality puts out of focus, not only the validity of historical testimony, but even the very basis in common experience of the concept itself of reality. Kant views the physical world as a totally closed system of causality with which free human acts cannot in any way interfere (no. 26 above). With this doctrine the effects of Kant's "free acts" are presented as a purely aesthetic illusion, and this stand is counter to common sense, for it is easy to demonstrate at any time that free human acts really can have an intervening effect upon the physical operation of Nature. Hence, Kant's appeal to "universal reason" is actually only an appeal to his own fallible reason.

37. Kant's idea of subjective reason: Kant characterizes all speculation about supersensible things in themselves as mere objects of faith that do not exist outside of ourselves, but are self-created by us (no. 24 above) except as limited to what *ought to be* in the view of moral reasoning (no. 25 above). Thus, he sets up a real world of empirical science and a totally separate and non-real world of moral tendency and obligation. While he says that he is "morally certain" that there is a God, and that it is perfectly permissible to use faith-based language, he requires a prior recognition that these objects of practical reason and of faith do not in any way constitute real knowledge ((KC, p. 426). So, by "morally certain" he means acceptable to a tendency of one's critically disciplined mind to entertain the unreal idea of God, but with the proviso that such reasonings are fictitious at

best. For the existence of God and the immortality of the human soul, Kant favors pure subjective reason over objective proof (no. 24 above). Obviously, of course, to favor subjective reason over objective proof is the flimsiest of arguments, and the mere inclination of people to assume the existence of a wise and omnipotent Author of the world is not a sufficient argument in itself. Skeptics and free-thinkers have often said things like this: "Some people like music, some like sports, some like narcotics, some like drama, and some like religion." In other words, Kant reduces religion to an aesthetic preference whose conclusions have for him no certitude in objective reality.

38. A Thomist approach to reason and understanding: Kant bases his stand on wrong definitions of knowledge, reason, understanding, and reality itself. The way to liberation from these epistemological errors is open through an application of the principles and teaching of Thomas Aquinas. The word *science* is commonly understood to mean "certified knowledge." Kant holds that only knowledge certified by sensory experience is scientific, while all other claims to knowledge are at best just faith or opinion (*KC*, p. 466). This brings up the question of how knowledge and understanding arise. Knowledge of concrete, individual, material things arises from sense perception, while what these things mean pertains to understanding. Simply put, *understanding* is the knowledge of one thing, or truth, in relation to a previously known thing, or truth. This relation, or inference, can be immediate or mediate. In the first case, there is a mere juxtaposition of the new thing, the remote object, to the previously known thing, the proximate object in the comparison. In the second case, a logical process is involved. Aristotelian/Thomist theory postulates that there are innate principles in human intelligence. From these beginning principles the rest of logic can be deduced. All people of sound mind think according to these principles, and thus science arises. There first arises common science, otherwise known as common sense. This has been developed into technical science, which uses precise methods and technical terms. In the Thomist synthesis, the word *scientia* means both "knowledge" and "science," and this is reasonable, because science is certified knowledge, and knowledge that is not certified is not really knowledge; rather it is error or mere opinion. But scientific knowledge, that is, real knowledge, is not limited to one's own sensory experience; it includes the certified testimony of others and validly reasoned conclusions regarding these objects. Kant unreasonably makes a nonfunctional separation of reason and understanding in the sense that he calls the perception of material objects *understanding* and logical reflection

about non-material mental objects *reason*. This division is false, because even empirical scientists reason about material objects in order to obtain an understanding of them, and there is a treasury of understanding in logical reflection about non-material objects, as Thomism bring out so effectively. Kant writes off this treasury of understanding, but only on the basis of false definitions of knowledge, reason and understanding.

39. The name of science: From the Thomist point of view, not only documented history, but also sound philosophy and sound theology deserve the name of science, because they produce knowledge and understanding of reality. We may define *history* as "the knowledge of past reality as such," including in its content all verified events of the past. Philosophy is "the science in which natural reason, apart from divine revelation, seeks to understand all things by a knowledge of their first causes."[27] Finally, sacred theology is the science of revealed reality as such, and it applies to "the whole study of revealed truth"[28] Each of these three sciences is a technical development of common science, as also is natural science. And each of these sciences has its own mental frame of reference. The science of history is organized around the concept of "the past as such," and it reaches back from known developments to the origins of these developments. It is essentially a backward view. The science of philosophy deals on the level of natural reason with knowledge that extends beyond the purview of the natural sciences. And the science of sacred theology develops from knowledge of revealed truth through the use of logic and natural reason.

40. Conclusion: The philosophy of Immanuel Kant has been too influential to be summarily dismissed, but the thought of the Fathers of the Church and of Catholic philosophers and theologians over the centuries has been even more influential, and so neither should their thought be summarily dismissed, as Kant clearly does. For instance, it is a pity that Kant chose a sweeping rejection of Thomist epistemology rather than a serious study of it. Contrary to the valid insight of common sense, Kant based his philosophy upon the reductionist approaches of British empiricism and European continental idealism, out of which he constructed a dualism that denies the reality of philosophical and theological truth. This dualism enabled Kant to provide some standing for the ideas of human freedom, God, and the immortality of the human soul, but only as permissible aesthetic pursuits. There is no reason why scientific thinking has to be limited to methodical

---

27 John A. Hardon, "Philosophy," in his *Modern Catholic Dictionary* (2nd printing, Bardstown, KY: Eternal Life, 2001).

28 Hardon, "Theology," op. cit.

conclusions from sensory observations. In fact, logical thinking and verified testimony can be the basis of true sciences. Nor is there any reason why scientific knowledge cannot arise from supersensible realities revealed by God. Faith begins from hearing, and most of what we know about natural things we have learned from others. Sense knowledge is not the only certified knowledge. The objects of Christian faith are also sources of valid knowledge. But philosophical conclusions that are based on a denial of common sense have no claim to validity. The aim of philosophy is the understanding of truth, but Kant's limitation of understanding to the perception of sensory images is off the track. So also is his definition of reason, and the making of his approach to reason the supreme judge of all values. Actually, the Aristotelian/Thomist use of criticism is more refined and more serviceable for correct thinking than is Kant's critique of reason. The philosophy of Immanuel Kant is a frontal attack against Christian faith that needs to be refuted point by point, as has, unfortunately, not been adequately done over the years even by Catholic philosophers and theologians, although summary replies, such as that of Frederick Copleston frequently referred to in this discussion, have not been lacking. Much work remains to be done, and, in the next part of this presentation, I hope to bring out in particular how the influence of Kantian thinking has influenced and continues to influence the exegetical thinking of Catholic Scripture scholars and theologians.

Part III. The Influence of Kantian Philosophy Upon Historical Criticism

Living Tradition 140 (March 2009)

41. The Kantian approach: Immanuel Kant has often been acclaimed as a "creative genius" and as "one of the most important framers of the contemporary mind."[29] His influence upon the development of modern thought "can hardly be overestimated."[30] However, that this influence has been basically positive and helpful is highly questionable. For one thing, Kant's approach is fully empirical, and thus it presents a reductive view that puts out of focus a large part of reality (no. 28 above), and it plainly

---

29 W. David Beck, "Agnosticism: Kant," in Norman L. Geisler, Ed., Biblical Errancy (Grand Rapids, Michigan: Zondervan, 1981), p. 53.

30 William Turner, *History of Philosophy* (Boston: Ginn and Company, 1903), p. 547.

violates common sense in claiming that there are no perceivable things outside of the human mind (nos. 29–30 above). Aristotelian/Thomist epistemology has a much more realistic and satisfying approach in that it identifies extra-mental things as the remote object of human knowledge and the intra-mental representation of these things as the proximate object of its knowledge (nos. 31–32 above). Kant combines the materialism and mechanism of his empirical approach with an idealism centered upon the unity of the knowing subject of consciousness, from which radiates outward his whole parallel world of transcendental objects of thought that do not have reality but may be humanly important. For him some of these objects, namely, the objects of his "critical thought," have a kind of "fictional reality" to the extent that they are not pure fantasies like what he judges the teachings of classical philosophy and traditional religion to be, since they are related in some way to the reality of sensory experience (nos. 33 and 35 above). And thus appears the "Kantian split" mentioned by Cardinal Ratzinger as the bane of modern philosophy, in particular as used in the historical critical method (nos. 3 and 7 above).

42. Historical criticism and its 20th century development, form-criticism: The "higher criticism" of the late nineteenth century and its continuation in the "historical criticism" of the twentieth century, characterized especially by the "form-criticism" of Hermann Gunkel, Martin Dibelius, and Rudolf Bultmann, is "a child of the Enlightenment" of the eighteenth century, to which Kant gave considerable contributions. As David Beck observes: "Many of the characteristics of the positions of those who deny authoritative and inerrant revelation are drawn directly from Kant. In many cases the reliance on Kant is explicit and admitted. And, while it is true that some elements of this position are prior to Kant, it seems evident that it was Kant who first put them into a coherent whole and introduced them into the mainstream of Christian (particularly German) theology."[31] And he adds (quoting Schubert Ogden) that, as far as the authority of Sacred Scripture is concerned, Kant's fundamental distinction between theoretical and practical reason has a prominence among Protestant theologians comparable to the effect of Thomas Aquinas' distinction between faith and reason.[32] The "criticism" in these methods bears a relationship to Kant's critical approach, even though Kant did not originate the term,[33] and all

---

31 Beck, ibid., p. 72.

32 Beck, ibid., p. 76.

33 The so-called "critical" approach to the interpretation of Sacred Scripture, now known as "historical criticism," was brought into focus in 1678 by Richard Simon, a converted

of these forms of biblical exegesis are rationalistic in the sense that they do not allow for the possibility of any supernatural influence or activity in the modern understanding of the Bible.[34] Hermann Gunkel, founder of the form-critical method of historical criticism, in his celebrated work, *Genesis* (first German edition, 1901), concentrated his attention on the history of what he saw to be the fictional forms, or literary genres (*Gattungen*), that constituted the text of Genesis. In this way was born the method of *Formgeschichte* (literally, "form-history," but called "form-criticism" in English). Gunkel pointed out that, once one has accepted the total separation between the alternate world of faith and the real world of reason, one only needs to "understand" that the legends of Genesis belong to that alternate world. He went on to say that Jesus and his Apostles *thought* that the accounts of Genesis were historical events of the real world, but "they shared the opinions of their time," and so "we may not, therefore, seek information in the New Testament concerning questions of the history of the Old Testament literature."[35] Gunkel was convinced that he, as a "modern man," has of necessity a viewpoint that is superior to the primitive viewpoint of Jesus and his contemporaries. Pope Leo XIII, in his encyclical letter of November 18, 1893, had called upon Catholic scholars to rise to the defense of the truth of the Sacred Scriptures in opposition to the rationalist exegetes, "who, trusting in their turn in their own way of thinking, have rejected even the scraps and remnants of Christian belief which had been handed down to them."[36] Rudolf Bultmann (1884–1976) was the most celebrated of five principal founders of the form-criticism of the New

---

Catholic priest, when he published what he called a "critical history" of the Old Testament. He called his work a "critical history," because he subjected the text of the Old Testament to what he considered to be the "critical judgment" of his human reason.

34 The word *rationalism* has as a secondary meaning "the doctrine that knowledge comes from the intellect in itself without aid from the senses." But I am using the word here as meaning "the principle or practice of accepting reason as the only authority in determining one's opinions or course of action" *Webster's New College Dictionary* (2007). The German Illuminist H.S. Reimarus (died 1768), was the founder of rationalism as an explicit and self-styled approach to the systematic interpretation of Sacred Scripture with his *Apologia for the Rational Worshippers of God*.

35 Hermann Gunkel, *Genesis* (English trans.: Macon Georgia: Mercer University Press, 1997), p. viii. For a detailed analysis of Gunkel's approach to form-criticism see J.F. McCarthy, "Rationalism in the Historical-Criticism of Hermann Gunkel," at chapter 9 below.

36 Pope Leo XIII, *Providentissimus Deus,* no. 2, in Claudia Carlen ed., *The Papal Encyclicals* (McGrath Publishing Co.), vol. 2, p. 326.

Testament. His *History of the Synoptic Tradition* (1921) was an exegetical work in which he employed form-criticism seemingly to the almost total elimination of the historicity of the Synoptic Gospels of Matthew, Mark, and Luke, leaving as a residue not much more than the man Jesus of Nazareth, who did exist, was, indeed, probably crucified, and did quite possibly enunciate a few identifiable sayings that are attributed to him in the Synoptic Gospels. Both of these founders of the form-critical method based their idea of modern man upon Kant's thoroughgoing distinction between factual *knowledge*, as gained from empirical observation, and metaphysical and religious *opinion*, which is postulated but not known.[37]

43. Kant's reductive view of history: Kant's blending of David Hume's empiricism with his own conception of "transcendental ideas" reduces the importance of testimony in the acquisition of knowledge. In fact, for Kant knowledge that is not acquired from experience of the senses is not knowledge at all (no. 22 above), although even in the natural sciences most of what people know is learned from the testimony of others, and most of those who follow his philosophy do so because they *believe* his teaching to be correct. And yet, according to Kant's teaching, anything that does not represent the knowledge of sensory phenomena is only one's own opinion or human faith in the opinions of others, and both of these have for him at best only subjective validity. (Hence, in this regard Kant seems implicitly to admit that his own critical philosophy has only subjective validity and does not constitute real knowledge.) He even claims that, since historical knowledge has no intrinsic relationship to the moral improvement of everyone, it belongs to the class of *adiaphora* (things neither helpful nor hurtful), which each man is free to hold as he finds edifying.[38] Moreover, his reductive view of history not only excludes the reality of all external historical facts, but also leaves no room for reliable witness of historical events and the testimony thereof (no. 35 above). And this impoverished conception of history applies above all to the testimony of miracles on the part of witnesses who perceived them by sensory experience, because Kant affirms an absolutely closed system of material causation that excludes *a priori* any possible divine intervention into his notion of the world (no. 26 above). Hence, Kant's system of thought rules out *a priori* the authority of the Bible as a record of historical facts as well as its divine inspiration and inerrancy. But this mechanistic presupposition is based upon confused notions of history and of objectivity.

---

37 Cf. Beck, ibid. p. 54.

38 I. Kant, *Religion within the Boundaries of Mere Religion* (English trans.: New York: Cambridge University Press, 1998), p. 65, footnote.

44. Influence of Kantian thinking upon the form-critical method of Gunkel and Bultmann: The form-criticism of Gunkel and Bultmann is *a critical approach* to the interpretation of Sacred Scripture in the sense that it sets aside Christian faith and concentrates exclusively upon critical reason in the Kantian sense in order to critique the Bible. It does not consider at all the critical reasoning of traditional biblical interpretation in which the *ars critica* of conventional historical research is used also to certify and defend the Scriptures as well as to achieve a fuller understanding of them. The method of Gunkel and Bultmann is *a modernist method* in the sense that it unreasonably extols the reasoning of so-called "modern man" over the supposedly inferior thinking presented in the sacred writings. The form-criticism of Gunkel and Bultmann is also *a reductive method* in that it focuses exclusively upon the human side of the Bible and rules out *a priori* in its reasoning any divine and supernatural influence in the writing of the sacred books. It is reductive also to the extent that it puts aside the use of sound metaphysics and thus falls repeatedly into philosophical errors that only sound philosophy can adequately ascertain. To be sure, Gunkel and Bultmann do not follow Kant in explicitly assuming that the things we see do not exist outside of our own minds, but they and their followers do fall into the consequent error of using a defective subject-object model of reasoning that overlooks the formal object of human understanding and thus puts out of critical focus the very mental framework that they are using in the course of their reasoning. Finally, the "Kantian split" is functional in this form-critical method, because the aura of reality is given only to their own critical thinking, while the teaching and historical episodes of the Bible are consigned arbitrarily to a religious dream-world of myth and fancy. So why was the Bible relevant at all for Gunkel and Bultmann? They studied it, I think, not only to critique it in the Kantian sense, but also with the idea that its fiction retains an underlying existential meaning for modern Christians that is to be found on the other side of the "Kantian split" (no. 23 above).

45. The historical critical method of Catholic form-critics: Catholic historical critics hold that "the historical critical method is the indispensable method for the scientific study of the meaning of ancient texts,[39] and they

---

39 Pontifical Biblical Commission, the *Interpretation of the Bible in the Church* (Rome: Libreria Editrice Vaticana, 1993), p. 34. Note that the term "historical criticism" has become somewhat ambiguous inasmuch as, while it applies originally to the successors of the "higher criticism" of the 19th century, it is being used sometimes to mean in general the critical method of all sound historical research. For this reason I have concentrated this discussion on the form-critical phase of historical criticism as it is being practiced by

see form-criticism as an essential phase of the historical criticism that they practice.[40] The 1993 document of the reconstituted Pontifical Biblical Commission praises Hermann Gunkel, founder of form-criticism, for bringing higher criticism out of the ghetto of a literary criticism aimed simply at the dissecting and dismantling of the text of the Bible (especially the Old Testament) by his concentrating attention upon the previous history of the "fanciful" literary forms that he and other historical critics claimed to see there, while the same document gives credit to Martin Dibelius and Rudolf Bultmann for bringing Gunkel's form-critical method to the Synoptic Gospels (and onward to the rest of the New Testament). The 1993 document describes the process of historical criticism as proceeding from textual criticism through form-criticism and tradition-criticism to redaction-criticism, and it avers that this type of criticism is *a historical method*, above all "because it seeks to shed light upon the historical processes which gave rise to the biblical text," and it is also *a critical method*, "because in each of its steps it operates with the help of scientific criteria that seek to be as objective as possible."[41] At the same time Catholic form-critics have striven to lessen the negative impact of mainline form-criticism upon Catholic belief in the Sacred Scriptures by stressing the importance of editors in the Gospel tradition.

46. From another perspective: The form-criticism characteristic of Catholic historical critics is *a reductive method* (nos. 28–29 above) in the sense that in its earlier stages it prescinds from the realities of Catholic faith to focus exclusively upon a four-step rationalistic process, and also inasmuch as it ignores the theological and philosophical implications of its approach to concentrate exclusively upon the phenomenological level of the inspired writings. Thus, in its 1993 document, the Pontifical Biblical Commission, regarding the historic role of Gunkel and Bultmann, focuses entirely upon the supposed knowledge of the Scriptures that they gained through the application of their rationalistic form-critical method, without adverting to the devastating impact of their exegetical work upon the objects of Catholic faith. The Commission does point out that, at the stage of redaction-criticism, the sacred text is explained with an eye to the character of the sacred text "as a message communicated by the author to his contemporaries" and to the demands of the text "from the point of

---

Catholic historical critics.

40 Pontifical Biblical Commission, the *Interpretation of the Bible in the Church*, pp. 37–38.

41 Pontifical Biblical Commission, the *Interpretation of the Bible in the Church*, pp. 36–37.

view of action and life,"[42] but this is aimed at the human authors alone and does not even attempt to retrieve the supernatural objects of Catholic faith from the trash-heap to which they have been consigned in the preceding stages. For instance, both Gunkel and Bultmann based their form-critical reasoning upon the presupposition that the supernatural episodes and events narrated in Sacred Scripture are merely religious fantasies resembling fairy tales for adults, and when this approach is used by Catholic exegetes, the supernatural objects of Catholic faith have been implicitly reduced to a kind of second-class reality that is not reality at all, unless the Catholic exegetes explicitly address this problem, which they seldom do. Since the act of Catholic faith is an affirmation of the reality of the objects of faith, including the historical truth of the events recorded in Sacred Scripture, exegetes have an inherent obligation from their faith, which pertains to their common sense in this situation, to defend this truth, as the Magisterium of the Church has often pointed out. But Catholic form-critics have characteristically shown a painful lack of aptitude or even of desire to defend this truth, and have rather coined words like "concordism" to show contempt for this needed apologetic exercise. The extensive confusion in the Catholic Church today over the meaning of Sacred Scripture is largely due to the ongoing failure of many Catholic form-critics to defend the historical truth of the divinely inspired Scriptures, which is being under-mined by the rationalistic presuppositions of their method.

47. Some philosophical and theological implications: What about the philosophical and theological implications of form-criticism? Gunkel, Bultmann, and their colleagues impressed upon the form-critical method a conception of the subject-object relationship inherited from the anti-Christian Enlightenment of the eighteenth century, and particularly from the thinking of Immanuel Kant. An element of this false conception is a lack of attention to the formal object of human intelligence which constitutes the frame of reference of scientific thinking (nos. 31 and 33 above). In the natural sciences, for instance, mathematics provides an explicit mental frame of reference that enables reasoned thinking, and Kant allowed for some use of pure mathematics in the natural sciences (*KC* pp. 415 and 416), as well as for the use of logic in thinking about what he called "transcendental ideas," but he turned the material objects of human knowledge into the formal objects, thus putting the intellectual medium, or frame of reference, out of focus and folding into subjectivity those external realities in conformity with which all truth consists. In other words, Kant limited both knowledge

---

42 Pontifical Biblical Commission, the *Interpretation of the Bible in the Church*, p. 38.

and understanding to the mental construction of material phenomena and thus excluded the formal principles upon which all real understanding depends. This Kantian epistemological model appears in the form-criticism of Gunkel and Bultmann as follows. They both base their critiques upon Kant's empirical approach as they extol "the outlook of modern scientific man" over the supposedly "primitive" and "pre-scientific" thinking of the human authors of the Bible. This supposed "modern outlook" is barren, not only of needed philosophical and theological principles, but even of common sense. For Gunkel and Bultmann, "biblical science" is located in the results of their reductive criticism, except that, whereas rationalists in general reject the Bible outright as a product of superstition, Gunkel and Bultmann see a valid reason for Christians to study the Bible, and this is the "permissible fiction" that survives the Kantian critique (no. 35 above). Kant rejected the Bible as such, but he allowed for some subjective religious thinking, and this opened the door to empiricists like Gunkel and Bultmann to take it up from there, as they attempt to "save" Christian faith by reducing its meaning to the subjective experience of modern man. For them, modern thinking is empirical thinking with allowance for some subjective religious thinking along Kantian lines, so that some thoroughly critiqued religious thoughts are allowed to survive subjectively as a human aspiration, although they always remain fictitious and unscientific. For Bultmann, this permissible subjective experience is existential in the sense that it is devoid of all formal objectivity and all truth, being limited to the self-consciousness of the knowing subject as such, but, in the operation of his form-criticism, this subjective experience is a resort that is out of sight and merely potential.

48. Reality and Catholic faith: Kant distinguished between sensory *reality* as immediately perceived and reasoned non-reality, which he characterized as a kind of reduced and fictional *validity* of reason to the extent that it was critical enough for him. Bultmann, over and beyond his form-critical work, used this same idea of the Kantian split, but he used it in a somewhat different way: he distinguished between the *objective reality* of empirical science and the *subjective reality* of "the authentically existing man." To express this distinction, he used two German words: *Realität* for the objects of empirical science, and *Wirklichkeit* for the "authentic" consciousness of self. On the contrary, for a Thomist, to think scientifically means to have a univocal and clearly defined concept of the one univocal reality into which the various objects of thought either fit or do not fit. The essential concept of all valid science is the continuum of

reality, as it is first recognized by common sense, or common science, and then refined by technical science. The supernatural gift of faith infused at baptism provides an intuition of the reality of the objects of faith as they are situated within this one continuum of reality, in such wise that to doubt the univocal reality of these objects of faith is a sin against faith. The objects of Catholic faith include things like the physical resurrection of Jesus from the dead and the reality of Heaven and Hell, of the human rational soul, of sanctifying grace as an entitative quality of the soul, and of many other things, including the historical reality of the events recorded in the Bible. Catholics believe that the historical facts recorded in the Bible cannot conflict with facts established by the natural sciences, but, where an apparent conflict occurs, Catholics do have an obligation to ascertain whether or not the affirmed fact of natural science is based upon solid proof, and to defend the truths of their faith against the frequently biased thinking of natural scientists and historians. This has been the constant tradition of the Catholic Church from the time of her founding. Now, since science can be defined as "certified knowledge of real things," to believe the objects of Catholic faith is to have common *scientific knowledge* in the fuller meaning of the term, whereas the presuppositions of Kant's critical method, by his very definition of terms, take the objects of Catholic faith and the teaching of the Bible out of the category of certified knowledge, so as to leave them in the realm of subjectivity and of merely aesthetic value. But the rationalist presuppositions of the form-critical method of Gunkel and Bultmann do the very same thing. To achieve this, they rule out the "big picture" of science in favor of a reductive approach that reflects the mechanism and empiricism of Kant. Now, Catholic form-critics, in using this method, do not characteristically deny the objects of Catholic faith; they keep them in mind, not functionally, but only through a dualism of two opposing systems, of which the form-criticism is in focus and the Catholic teaching is in the background. Their form-criticism they call "scientific exegesis," while Catholic faith and traditional Catholic philosophy and theology are reductively excluded from the status of being "scientific."[43] But, since Catholic faith pertains to the common sense underpinning the "big picture" of historical reality (no. 32 above),

---

43   The same reductive notion of science has overflown even into official Catholic magisterial statements, in which a contrast is sometimes made between faith and science, philosophy and science, or theology and science. The correct distinction should be between these other sciences and *empirical* science.

Catholic biblical interpretation should be synthesized with this and with the established principles of Catholic philosophy and theology, but form-critics have never carried out this task.

49. Is form-criticism scientific and objective?: Catholic form-critics maintain that form-criticism is a *critical method*, because "it operates with the help of scientific criteria that seek to be as objective as possible" (no. 45 above). But what do they mean by "scientific," and what do they mean by "objective?" It seems that by "scientific" they mean reduced to the level of phenomena only, where the text of Sacred Scripture is viewed as a mere phenomenon, and its divine and supernatural characteristics are kept non-functional and out of view. And by "historical" they seem to mean the assumption that the historical testimony in the sacred text is basically fictitious (with some underlying historicity) and the result of religious fantasy, as Gunkel and Bultmann presuppose in keeping with the rationalism of their approach. But this is not a historical approach in the true sense of the word. For instance, when some Catholic form-critics aver that there was no miraculous holding back of the waters of the Red Sea, as reported in Exodus, or that Jesus did not miraculously multiply the loaves and the fishes, they are shocking the faith of Christian believers without any historical proof, because the only evidence that they have for these assertions is the rationalist presupposition that these nature-miracles could not have occurred. And this is turning historical science into unscientific philosophy. Thus William Foxwell Albright, a competent historian, observed in 1957 that form-critics "have pushed their research out in increasingly subjective directions" and that "vicious circles are evident throughout their work," and he went on to point out that "from the standpoint of the objective historian data cannot be disproved by criticism of the accidental literary framework in which they occur, unless there are solid independent reasons for rejecting the historicity of an appreciable number of other data found in the same framework."[44] By way of summary, he remarked: "Only modern scholars who lack both historical method and perspective can spin such a web of speculation as that with which form-critics have surrounded the Gospel tradition."[45] Similarly, the original Pontifical Biblical Commission, in an instruction of 21 April 1964, invited Catholic exegetes to investigate *what sound elements there might be in the form-critical method* amidst the *unacceptable philosophical and theological principles* that it contains (*EB* 647).

---

44 W.F. Albright, *From the Stone Age to Christianity* (Baltimore, MD: John Hopkins Press, 1957), pp. 381–382.

45 Albright, ibid., p.387.

50. Some presuppositions of the form-critical method itself: The 1993 document of the reconstituted Pontifical Biblical Commission avers that the historical critical method (including form-criticism) "is a method which, when used in an objective manner, implies of itself no *a priori*," although, when used together with some *a priori* principles not pertaining to the method itself but to certain hermeneutical choices governing the interpretation, this can be "tendentious."[46] The example given of such tendentious interpretation is that of Rudolf Bultmann, who "combined form-critical studies with a biblical hermeneutic inspired by the existentialist philosophy of Martin Heidegger."[47] In saying this, the PBC overlooks two things. The first is that Bultmann did not use the existentialism of Heidegger in his classic *History of the Synoptic Tradition* (1921), with which he brought form-criticism to the interpretation of the Gospels. It was about twenty years later, in an effort to provide some justification for Christian belief in the wake of the devastation that his form-criticism had produced, that he used the existentialist philosophy of Heidegger. And the second thing is that Bultmann did in his pre-Heideggerian form-critical work, and all other form-critics do now, use philosophical and method-ological presuppositions in their form-critical reasoning, some of which are the following:

Rationalism: Sound epistemology and the supernatural realities of Christian faith are excluded from the method.

False historical method: Historical science deals with what has taken place, not with what the historian presupposes could or could not have taken place. Form-criticism presupposes that no miraculous events have ever taken place. Catholic form-critics do not affirm that no miracles have ever happened; they dualistically let their faith restrain them from drawing some of the conclusions to which form-criticism naturally leads. Bultmann has taunted believing form-critics about this, saying: "Once you begin to use the method, where can you draw the line?" Catholic form-critics have never presented a worthy answer to this challenge.

Circular argumentation: Form-critics draw conclusions that are already presupposed in their thinking. For instance, their conclusions that Jesus did not really work this or that miracle are based only on the presupposition that miracles do not occur. Bultmann admits this where he says: "It is essential to realize that form-criticism is fundamentally indistinguishable from all historical work in this, that it has to move

---

46 Pontifical Biblical Commission, the *Interpretation of the Bible in the Church*, p. 39.

47 PBC, ibid., p. 36.

in a circle. The forms of the literary tradition must be used to establish the influences operating in the life of the community, and the life of the community must be used to render the forms themselves intelligible."[48] Bultmann shows here a false concept of historical method, inasmuch as he tries to derive historical facts from a sociological concept (the Sitz-im-Leben of Hermann Gunkel).

Drawing conclusions from internal indications alone: Form-critics can argue forever about what they conclude from the comparison of texts of Sacred Scripture, while ignoring possibilities, or even likelihoods, when these indications do not lead in the direction that they have chosen.

A double concept of reality: What is the purpose of form-criticism to begin with? Non-believers can debunk the Scriptures in the name of "science" just for their own amusement, but the ultimate alleged purpose of form-criticism is to help Christian believers to discover some value for them in a debunked Bible, and the concept that its founders chose for this purpose was Kant's idea of "permissible fiction." Without this dualism, form-criticism would be totally destructive, seeing that throughout its development every new "discovery" of a seeming error or contradiction in the Scriptures has been considered a step forward for the method, and every case where the historicity survived has been viewed as a temporary snag waiting to be overcome. Form-criticism aims to help the Christian believer to discover, not only that the episodes of the Scriptures are fictitious, but also that his own Christian illusions, even though they are not real in a univocal sense, still have some value.

Use of poorly defined terms: The vagueness of terms among the founders of form-criticism is redoubled among Catholic form-critics. Words like *scientific, historical, objective,* and *literary form* are immersed in ambiguity, while analysis of the word *reality,* which is the central concept of all science, hardly occurs at all.

Other presuppositions: Catholic form-critics use other unhistorical presuppositions, such as presuming that simpler descriptions in the sacred text are older and that biblical episodes or locutions repeated in the text with some contrasting differences could not actually have occurred more than once.

51. Defense of the inerrancy of Sacred Scripture: The 1964 instruction of the original Pontifical Biblical Commission implies that Catholic exegetes are obliged to remain aware in their mental frame of reference, not only

---

48 R. Bultmann, *History of the Synoptic Tradition* (English trans. of the 3rd German ed., 1958: Oxford, England: Basil Blackwell, 1963), p. 5.

of the objects of Catholic faith, but also of sound Catholic philosophical and theological principles, things which the form-critical method systematically excludes. Pope Pius XII had pointed out in 1943 in *Divino afflante Spiritu*, in reaffirming the perennial teaching of the Church, that Catholic interpreters should strive to "refute the objections of adversaries" and seek regarding difficult problems "a satisfactory solution which will be in full accord with the doctrine of the Church, in particular with the traditional teaching regarding the inerrancy of Sacred Scripture, and which will at the same time satisfy in a fitting way the certain conclusions of the profane disciplines" *(EB 564)*.

52. Jean Levie: As a group, Catholic form-critics have not fully lived up to these requirements. For instance, Jean Levie, in his well-known book of 1958 on the rise of the form-critical method, develops the idea that the Bible is "the word of God *in the words of men*."[49] To present this development he takes the usual reductive approach of form-criticism in the sense that he presents the interpretation of the Bible *only* as the words of men without ever getting around to the Bible *as the word of God*, which is presumed but is totally non-functional. Levie brings out the dualism employed by Catholic form-critics where he conjectures that the encyclical letter *Divino afflante Spiritu* of Pope Pius XII did not stress the condemnation of the "theory of the two-fold truth" (relative, not absolute) of Sacred Scripture as much as the preceding encyclical *Spiritus Paraclitus* of Pope Benedict XV did, and this, he says, seemed to open the way to the theory of fictional genres of form-criticism, that is, to an interpretation in which biblical accounts are expounded "in keeping not with the reality of the facts, but with what popular contemporary opinion said on a subject."[50] Levie goes on to say: "God speaks to us through a real man, as he was in his world and in his own age. Any literary form, as long as it is intrinsically moral, can convey the divine message."[51] So a myth or a fictitious story, presented as a historical account, can convey a divine message which is morally true, and this is precisely the idea of the merely relative truth whose standing condemnation had, in fact, been repeated in 1950 by Pius XII in his encyclical letter *Humani generis*, where he says: "They even wrongly speak of the human sense of the Scriptures, beneath which a divine sense, which

---

49 J. Levie, *La Bible, parole humaine et message de Dieu* (Paris-Louvaine, 1958); English translation: *The Bible, Word of God in Words of Men* (London: Geoffrey Chapman, 1961).

50 Levie, ibid., p. 146, note 7.

51 Levie, ibid., p. 167.

they say is the only infallible meaning, lies hidden" (*EB* 612). In other words, Catholic form-critics maintain that the historical truth regarding these biblical accounts resides, not in the accounts themselves, but rather in the conclusions of form-criticism.

53. The divine message: Now, rationalist form-critics like Gunkel and Bultmann deny that there is any real divine message in the Bible, while Catholic form-critics do believe, in accordance with the teaching of the Catholic Church, that there is a divine message, although they do not find this message in their form-critical work as such (no. 45 above), and their aversion to philosophizing about their method is universal enough that I have never seen an example where a form-critic attempted to show how the objects of Catholic faith share a univocal reality with the conclusions of their form-critical system. In fact, the Kantian split is evident in their work, as they call "scientific" the human and natural objects of their thought, while the objects of faith are left in the twilight zone of an official but, nevertheless, prescientific doctrine different, but not clearly distinct, from the fancy that they attribute to the biblical narratives themselves. What I am saying is that whatever degree of reality is left in the form-critical process to the supernatural objects of faith has never been an object of concerted apologetic defense on the part of Catholic form-critics, and they have never, to my knowledge, presented a tenable answer to the rationalism inherent in their system. And so they are left with a radical dualism of "scientific" form-critical reality and aesthetically appealing but prescientific religious belief.

54. Jean Daniélou on the Virginal Conception: Catholic form-critics can make into objects of prayer and belief the very scenes that they have "scientifically" eliminated from historical reality. For instance, Jean Daniélou, following form-critical reasoning, claims that the scenes in the Infancy Narratives of Matthew and Luke are fabrications built mainly on sayings and scenes of the Old Testament. Thus, for example, he avers that angels are imaginary literary devices of the Old Testament, and the annunciation of the Angel Gabriel to the Virgin Mary is an imaginary *midrash* on Isaiah 9 in which, for instance, the expression, "Hail, full of grace…" is a phrase borrowed from Zeph. 3:14–17, or Dan. 9:21–27, and placed on the lips of this imaginary angel. Similarly taken from different places in the Old Testament are the words depicted as having been spoken by the angel, namely, "fear not, Mary…," and "and the Lord God will give to him the throne of David his father…," and "the Holy Spirit will come upon you," and "the power of the most High

will overshadow you," while two other phrases in the angel's discourse were invented by Luke himself or by the Christian circles of his time to express their belief in the divinity of Jesus, namely, "He will be great and will be called the Son of the most High" and "therefore, the child to be born will be called holy, the Son of God."[52] Now, having totally destroyed the historicity of the biblical account of the annunciation to Mary, Daniélou goes on to affirm that the Virginal Conception of Mary in this story, as also in the episode of the appearance of an angel to Joseph in Matt. 1:20, "rests on a historical basis," and "is a historical account which takes (the Virginal Conception) for granted," because it "is an element in a tradition that antedates them both."[53] But this resort to the historical reality of a prior tradition has no evidence of historicity apart from the episodes claimed by Daniélou to be fictions produced by a story-making Christian community, and so Daniélou's claim that the Virginal Conception of Mary is "historical" only reveals the dualism in his approach, whereby one can *believe* a historical event to be true as long as he does not oppose the form-critical conclusion that it is not. And this is how Catholic form-critics can deny "scientifically" the historical truth upon which this object of faith is based, and even denounce as "concordists" those who defend its historicity, and still, for example, pray the Angelus and the joyful mysteries of the Rosary, repeating over and over again in devout reverence the very scenes and words whose historical truth they have eliminated in their form-critical work. There are numerous other examples of this resort, which illustrates the fact that Catholic form-critics need to revise a confused epistemology which transcendentally unites the supposed form-critical reality with a form of pseudo-Christian make-believe.

55. Raymond Brown on the Virginal Conception: In his widely circulated book, *The Virginal Conception & Bodily Resurrection of Jesus*,[54] Father Raymond Brown has written many true things about the Scriptures, but, as a form-critical biblical scholar, he also questionably concludes that the Gospels; "are not simply factual reporting of what

---

52 J. Daniélou, *The Infancy Narratives*, translated by Rosemary Sheed (New York: Herder and Herder, 1968) – (original edition: *Les Evangiles de l'Enfance* (Paris: Editions de Seuil, 1967), pp. 33–37. For a fuller review, see chapter 8 below.

53 Daniélou, op. cit., pp. 41–42.

54 R. Brown, *Virginal Conception and Bodily Resurrection of Jesus* (London: Geoffrey Chapman, 1973). For a fuller review, see *Living Tradition* 133 (January 2008).

happened in Jesus' ministry, but they are documents of faith written to show the significance of those events as seen with hindsight."[55] He affirms that "the presence of the Virginal Conception in the infancy narratives of two Gospels carries no absolute guarantee of historicity,"[56] considering also that "modern Protestant and Catholic scholars are in surprising agreement on the generally figurative and non-historical character of the infancy narratives."[57] As a believing Catholic, Brown accepts the Virginal Conception of Jesus as an object of faith, but, as a form-critic, he doubts whether the Virginal Conception is a *biological* fact.[58] Brown admits that "if the Christology associated with Virginal Conception was known [by Jesus, by the Virgin Mary, and by others] from the first moments of Jesus' earthly career, the whole critical theory falls apart." It is Brown's opinion that Matthew's infancy narrative "is redolent of the folkloric and imaginative," while Luke's narrative does not reflect "the atmosphere of purely historical reporting."[59] This judgment is guided by the naturalism of the form-critical school and by the Kantian split. It is only on the basis of an *a priori* exclusion of real divine interventions that Matthew's narrative seems folkloric and imaginative, and it is only on the basis of an *a priori* exclusion of divinely inspired writing that goes beyond the capabilities of contemporary human historians that Luke's account does not seem to reflect "the atmosphere of purely historical reporting." Regarding the Virginal Conception of Jesus as a biological fact, it is Brown's studied conclusion that "the totality of the *scientifically controllable* evidence leaves an unresolved problem."[60] This brings up a bigger unresolved problem. What is "scientifically controllable evidence," and what is "purely historical reporting"? Catholic form-critics like to call their work "scientific," but

---

55 Brown, *Virginal Conception*, p. 17.

56 Brown, *Virginal Conception*, p. 32.

57 Brown, *Virginal Conception*, p. 52.

58 Brown, *Virginal Conception*, p. 37.

59 Brown, *Virginal Conception*, pp. 53–54.

60 Brown, *Virginal Conception*, p. 66. Brown affirms the doctrine where he says: "In Roman Catholic theology, according to the usual criteria, the Virginal Conception would be classified as a doctrine infallibly taught by the ordinary magisterium," but he questions the doctrine where he goes on to say: "The Virginal Conception under its creedal title of 'virgin birth' is not primarily a biological statement, and therefore one must make a judgment about the extent to which the creedal affirmation is inextricably attached to the biological presupposition" (R. Brown, *Birth of the Messiah* [Garden City: Doubleday, 1977], p. 529).

they do not seem to be working with an adequate concept either of science or of historical method (see no. 49 above). All true science is organized around a clear and highly differentiated concept of reality, whereas, in the dualism of Catholic form-criticism, the objects of Catholic faith are left in an undefined real or unreal world of religious belief, and what does this *belief* have to do with biological *fact*? Similarly, true historians deal with everything that has happened; they do not, like Bultmann and his school, *presuppose* that much of what is reported in the infancy narratives and in the rest of the Gospels could not really have happened. The assumption that the perception of miraculous facts having a supernatural meaning has to be imaginary or folkloristic is contrary to the fundamental principles of historical science, for historical science knows that historical meaning, while it is conceptually *distinct* from bare historical fact, is not *separate* from it. Brown's separation of Gospel doctrine from the historical facts in which it is embedded is, therefore, unscientific. Hence, when he wonders how the Church's connatural insight into divine revelation could apply to "a question of *biological* fact," he is separating this dogma from historical fact and unscientifically reducing it to the level of a *theologoumenon*. Brown maintains, as do Daniélou and virtually all form-critics, that the appearances of an angel to Mary in Luke 1 and to Joseph in Matt. 1 are mere literary forms developed to convey the underlying idea of a Virginal Conception.[61] This means that there were no real appearances of an angel and there were no historical annunciations at all, but the idea of a Virginal Conception did arise, and this, he says, needs to be accounted for. He reasons that the idea was probably not derived from pagan religious beliefs or from Old Testament stories, but he fails to consider and refute the resultant implication in the form-critical method that the early Christians could simply have made up the story on their own with no basis in historical reality and without any suggestion from other traditions, and so he actually gives no effective defense of this belief. I do not doubt the integrity of Father Brown's Catholic faith, but I do question the objective validity of his dualistic separation of Catholic beliefs from historical facts.

56. A few general conclusions: Among others, the following general conclusions may be drawn concerning the use by Catholic Scripture scholars of the form-critical method.

As Joseph Cardinal Ratzinger observed in 1988, historical criticism uses the philosophy of Immanuel Kant.

Catholic form-critics are largely unaware of the philosophical presup-

---

61 Brown, *Birth of the Messiah,* pp. 521–522.

positions of their method.

Catholic form-critics do not consciously subscribe to the anti-religious outlook of the Enlightenment or the anti-Christian outlook of Immanuel Kant, enshrined in his *Critique of Pure Reason* and even more explicitly in his *Religion within the Boundaries of Mere Reason*, but Catholic form-critics do dualistically (even if unwittingly) subscribe to Kant's reductive definition of science, as limited to the phenomenal level of objectivity and to the human level of Sacred Scripture, which they hold in tandem with but not synthesized with the teaching of the Catholic Church.

Catholic form-critics follow the epistemology of Immanuel Kant in the sense that they use a concept of the subject-object relationship in which the formal object, which includes the objects of faith on the level of common science and Catholic philosophy and theology on the level of technical science, has been put out of focus. As a result, in their use of the form-critical method, as Cardinal Ratzinger pointed out in 1988, they do not pay sufficient attention to the established principles of Catholic philosophy and theology, nor are they sufficiently critical of their own mental frame of reference.

The technical terms and historical techniques used by Catholic form-critics are imprecise and inaccurate.

The rationalist flavor of the form-critical method inhibits Catholic form-critics from trying hard enough to preserve the historicity of biblical accounts or to understand the deeper meanings of the sacred text.

The moralizing goal which constitutes a claimed positive purpose of form-critical interpretation is based on the subjectivist and existentialist side of the Kantian split.

Chapter 3

Neo-Patristic Exegesis to the Rescue

Living Tradition 41 (May 1992)

1. A needed new approach: Joseph Cardinal Ratzinger, in an important lecture and subsequent article published originally in German in 1989, then in English, and then in Italian and other languages,[1] has called for a better synthesis between historical and theological methods and between criticism and dogma in the interpretation of Sacred Scripture, to be arrived at by means of self-criticism of the historical method being used today by exegetes and by the use of a less arbitrary philosophy which offers a greater number of presuppositions favoring a true hearing of the text.[2] Cardinal Ratzinger observes that over the past hundred years biblical exegesis has made some great errors "and these errors have become virtually academic dogmas."[3] He traces this problem to the influence of Martin Dibelius and Rudolf Bultmann, whose basic methodological orientations determine even to this day the methodology and course of modern exegesis. Ratzinger finds it imperative at this juncture of time to challenge the fundamental ideas behind the method of Dibelius and Bultmann, such as the carrying over of the evolutionist model of natural science into the history and life processes of the spirit. Bultmann the exegete, he avers, represents a background consensus of the scientific exegesis dominant today, and yet Bultmann was not so much a scientific as a systematic worker, whose exegetical conclusions are not the result of historical findings but emerge from a framework of systematic presuppositions.[4] Why, Ratzinger asks, are

---

1 Joseph Cardinal Ratzinger, in Richard J. Neuhaus, ed., *Biblical Interpretation in Crisis* (Grand Rapids: Eerdmans, 1989), pp. 1–23.

2 Ratzinger, ibid., p. 17.

3 Ratzinger, ibid., p. 21.

4 Ratzinger, ibid., pp. 8–9.

these broad explanatory principles of Bultmann and Dibelius taken for granted and used unquestioningly by exegetes even to this day as though they were self-authenticating by the very obviousness of their application? The method seems to be situated, he says, in the philosophical twist taken by Kant according to which the voice of being in itself cannot be heard by man . At this level modern exegesis admits of a reduction of history to philosophy.[5]

2. To resolve this problem, Cardinal Ratzinger proposes some basic elements for a new synthesis,[6] which will require the attentive and critical commitment of a whole generation.[7] The process of biblical interpretation must be seen as having two steps: integration of the biblical texts into their historical context and then their location in the totality of their historical unfolding, beginning from the central event, which is Christ.[8] On the level of integration into the historical context, the time is ripe for a radical new reflection on exegetical method. Scientific exegesis must recognize that in a good number of its fundamental axioms the philosophical element is present, and it must therefore critically reconsider the results based upon these axioms. Ratzinger affirms that biblical exegesis must come to recognize itself as a historical discipline, also in the sense that its own history is part of what it is, and it needs to acquire knowledge of how the philosophical element influences the process of interpretation. On the second level, which is that of total meaning, the texts must be integrated into a theological vision in the strict sense, based upon the experience of Revelation. To achieve this task it will be necessary to introduce into the discussion the great proposals of patristic and medieval thought, with reflection also upon the fundamental options of the Reformation and on the choices it involved in the history of interpretation.[9]

3. The call of Cardinal Ratzinger for a new synthesis of historical and theological methods in the process of biblical interpretation, involving a critique of biblical criticism and a reintegration of patristic and medieval insights, comes at a time, not only when a better methodology is urgently needed, but also when the elements of a new synthesis are more available than they have ever been before. On the one hand, new and largely untried techniques of historical method can now be used for critically analyzing

---

5 Ratzinger, ibid., pp. 15–16.

6 Ratzinger, ibid., pp. 17–23.

7 Ratzinger, ibid., pp. 6, 16.

8 Ratzinger, ibid., p. 20.

9 Ratzinger, ibid., pp. 21–22.

the literature of form-critics and other so-called "historians," while, on the other hand, the principal elements of a comprehensive framework of interpretation on both the merely historical and the mystical levels of Sacred Scripture are waiting to be used. Serious students of the Scriptures now have more reason than ever to be dissatisfied with a self-characterized "historical method" that leaves confused and undefined even such all-pervasive terms as "history," "historical," and "method." They are more prone than ever to reject the conclusions of a "scientific exegesis" that has never defined for itself or for its audience what the word "science" means or how its labors can seriously be called "scientific." Cardinal Ratzinger, in the article I have quoted, makes the telling observation that modern exegetes of the prevailing school are working from questionable presuppositions that they have never adequately analyzed or integrated into a method that deep thinkers can readily accept. But modern exegetes, among whom Rudolf Bultmann stands out as the supreme example, have raised epistemological questions which draw our attention to the need of a better and more complete biblical hermeneutic, and it is to the task of building such a hermeneutic that we must now dedicate ourselves.

4. Scientific exegesis at last: Cardinal Ratzinger recommends what he calls a "diachronic approach"[10] to the results of historical critical exegesis, by which he means, not simply taking these conclusions as timeless data, but rather seeing them in the perspective of their own history, and he notes that in historical perspective these interpretations, which seemed so scientific and purely historical, "reflect in reality the spirit of their authors rather than the spirit of the past ages." Let us concentrate briefly on the thought that to view the conclusions of historical critical exegesis "in the perspective of their own history" is to see them "in reality." The word "reality" must have a very important role to play in the construction of the new biblical hermeneutic.

5. Rudolf Bultmann often raised the question of "reality" in relation to Christian faith and the contents of the New Testament Scriptures. To resolve the dilemma that the question of reality raised for him, he proposed a novel meaning of *Wirklichkeit*, the German word for reality: a) the reality that is known by sense experience and constitutes the real world of empirical science he called, not *Wirklichkeit*, but *Realität*, and this is the objective representation of the world in which man finds himself; b) and he called *Wirklichkeit* "the reality of the historically existing man."[11] This distinction

---

10 Ratzinger, ibid.,p. 6.

11 R. Bultmann, "Zum Problem der Entmythologisierung," in H. W. Bartsch et

enabled Bultmann to predicate reality in relation to a certain understanding of the object of faith without predicating reality in the commonly understood sense of the object of faith itself. This was a wrong answer to the question of reality, but it did address a question that for too long has escaped the critical attention of modern exegetes of the prevailing school.[12] Modern historical critical exegetes, to the extent that they uncritically follow the method of Bultmann and make use of his presuppositions, actually cut themselves off from the reality that is objectively presented in the Scriptures along the lines of Bultmann's exclusion of *Realität* in the objects presented by the biblical narrative. Such exegetes, whom for the sake of brevity I shall henceforth call "form-critics,"[13] seldom raise the question of reality at all, and one of the unanswered questions throughout almost the whole of their discourse is whether the biblical events which they are interpreting are real or not.

6. In his speculation Rudolf Bultmann often raised the question of "history" in relation to Christian faith and the contents of the New Testament Scriptures. Again he proposed a double meaning of the German word for history, *Geschichte*, and he set up a radical distinction between history as *Historie*, which, he said, is composed of causally connected events and relationships between facts which are objectively verifiable and chronologically determinable,[14] and history as *Geschichte*, which consists of the encounters of the "genuinely" existing human being, whose "existential constitution" ultimately signifies "to exist, to be confronted with non-being, to be able to be and ever to decide anew." Thus, for Bultmann, the question of the "historicity" of the Gospels was subjectivized into the possession by the contemporary thinker of what he called "true historicity," which was "the existential constitution of the being which necessarily exists

---

al., *Kerygma und Mythos* (Hamburg: Evangelischer Verlag), vol. VI-1: a) "…die ein objektivierenden Sehen vorgestellte Wirklichkeit der Welt, innerhalb deren sich der Mensch vorfindet…" (p. 20); b) "…als die Wirklichkeit des geschlichtlich existierenden Menschen" (p. 21).

12 I have treated Bultmann's notion of reality at length in J. F. McCarthy, *The Science of Historical Theology* (reprinted by TAN Books and Publishers, Rockford, Illinois, 1991), [now Saint Benedict Press, LLC, 13315 Carowinds Blvd, Suite Q, Charlotte, NC 28273] pp. 13–14; 106–113.

13   The "form-criticism" (*Formgeschichte:* literally, "form-history") of the Gospels emerged in Germany among liberal Protestant scholars between 1919 and 1922 through the publications of Martin Dibelius, Karl Ludwig Schmidt, Rudolf Bultmann, M. Albertz, and G. Bertram.

14 R. Bultmann, *History and Eschatology* (New York: Harper and Row, 1957), pp. 143–144.

in history."[15] Bultmann based his presuppositions regarding history and historicity upon the existentialism of Martin Heidegger and the idealism of Robin G. Collingwood. Thus, he did not hesitate to affirm: "I think I may take for granted that the right question to frame with regard to the Bible—at any rate within the Church—is the question of human existence. I am driven to that by the urge to inquire existentially about my own existence. But this is a question which at bottom determines our approach to and interpretation of all historical documents. For the ultimate purpose in the study of history is to realize consciously the possibility it affords for the understanding of human existence."[16] Bultmann was challenging in the questions he asked and in the answers he suggested, even though his questions were deceiving and his answers were wrong. The question of human existence is one of the right questions to frame with regard to the Bible, but it is not the first question, and to place it first is to put the Bible out of its proper perspective, because the first question that has to be asked is the question regarding reality. It is a matter of observation that the first and all-pervading question that science asks about anything is the question of its reality. The fact is that the concept of reality is the general medium of all true science, so that only what is real is the object of science, and even the imaginary is studied by science under the aspect of its reality. Science arises from the moment that the knowing subject begins to realize the difference between the real and the unreal among the objects of his knowledge, and science grows as the knowing subject concentrates upon the real and excludes the unreal from his field of vision.[17] Reflection upon the role of the concept of reality as the general medium of all true science leads to the following set of definitions, which are important for the elaboration of a better method of Scriptural interpretation:

Science is the knowledge of reality as such.

History is the knowledge of the past as such.

Historical science is the knowledge of past reality as such.

Theological science is the knowledge of revealed reality as such.

The science of historical theology is the knowledge of past revealed reality as such.[18]

---

15 Cf. R. Bultmann, in H. W. Bartsch ed., *Kerygma and Myth: A Theological Debate*, vol. I (London: SPCK, 1953), pp. 191–193 and 200.

16 R. Bultmann, ibid., p. 191. I have analyzed Bultmann's theory of history in *The Science of Historical Theology*, pp. 7–9 and 113–119.

17 See McCarthy, *The Science of Historical Theology*, pp. 34–56.

18 These five definitions are presented on page 100 of *The Science of Historical*

These five definitions presuppose that there is one continuum of reality which reaches to everything that is real. When Bultmann proposed a double meaning of reality, he was either denying this continuum or making it irrelevant for theology, but, in doing so, he took his speculation out of the realm of science. Bultmann's thought, the entire system of his conclusions, belongs to the realm of fiction, not of fact, and, because he speculates in his thought about reality and uses an elaborate method and terminology, the exact genre of his writings is that of pseudo-science, which looks like science but is imaginary."[19]

7. True historical science: Since history is the past as such, it can be divided into fictional history and real history. Imaginary stories, for instance, belong to fictional history. In ordinary parlance, we tend to reserve the term *history* for real events of the past, and we call unreal events *stories*. What people usually mean by *history* is historical science. But, when Catholic form-critics interpret the Gospels, we have difficulty in determining whether they are talking about real events or stories, because form-critics as such do not use a differentiated concept of reality—they are not scientists at work. Bultmann, on the other hand, openly considered the Gospel narratives to be fictional stories, and he sought reality in the presuppositions of his method, but, because his presuppositions were false, his conclusions were not real, and his recourse to history as "existential encounter" made him a writer of fiction.[20]

8. Scientifically speaking, to ask questions about a text or object of some sort means to place that text or object within the focus of a mental framework and seek to draw conclusions by means of a valid logical process. An indication of the unscientific character of the form-critical method is the general lack of awareness in its practitioners of the mental framework that they are using. Bultmann's success with the method lay in his ability to manipulate unformulated principles of method and to express them in a twisted or inverted fashion. Thus, his classic work of exegesis of the Synoptic Gospels, which he entitled *The History of the Synoptic Tradition*,[21]

Theology, and the reasoning leading to their formulation is given in the preceding eighty-five pages.

19 The pseudoscientific and fictional character of Bultmann's theological production is analyzed in *The Science of Historical Theology,* pp. 155–164.

20 Bultmann's notion of theological understanding as being basically and exclusively self-understanding is analyzed in *The Science of Historical Theology,* pp. 141–155.

21 R. Bultmann, *Die Geschichte der synoptischen Tradition* (1st ed., 1921; 8th rev. ed.: Gottingen, 1970); Eng. trans. by John Marsh, *The History of the Synoptic Tradition*

is actually a masterpiece of false principles and fallacious arguments which new-wave Catholic exegetes have been unable to refute, principally because they do not have the technical apparatus that is needed to analyze Bultmann's arguments.

9. For instance, with regard to historical matters relating to philosophy and theology, Bultmann proposed that the terms subjective and objective be eliminated from discussion,[22] and this fit his double notion of reality, but it also destroyed the notion of theology as a science. Now, the answer to this proposal depends upon the recognition that the human mind is itself a medium between the knowing subject and the object of his knowledge, so that science in the mind is the proximate object of theology, while the concrete objects of faith are its remote object. New-wave exegetes, especially of a form-critical bent, are typically not methodologically aware of their minds as proximate objects, and thus they can easily be confused by a writer like Bultmann concerning the subject-object relationship and its particular use in Scriptural exegesis.

10. Hence, the "critique of criticism" must begin from an analysis of the mental framework that form-critics use and of the kind of arguments that they construct. Cardinal Ratzinger notes that "from a distance the observer becomes aware with surprise that these interpretations (of critical exegetes), which were taken to be so rigorously scientific and purely 'historical,' reflect in reality the spirit of their authors rather than the spirit of ages gone by."[23] I understand this to mean that the critical exegetes in point had not adequately examined their own minds as the medium of their thought and were, therefore, not equipped to examine the mentalities of other thinkers. The medium of thought for the historical scientist is the general medium of his own intellectual present plus the special medium of the past as an intellectual concept with the methodology that this implies.[24] Until critical exegetes become aware of this historical medium, they will never be historical scientists or scientific exegetes.

11. Two basic ways of developing a scientific method of exegesis are available. One way is the "critique of critical exegesis," whereby, with the

---

(Oxford: Basil Blackwell, 1963).

22 R. Bultmann, *Essays Philosophical and Theological* (trans. by J. C. Greig: London, 1955), p. 287.

23 Joseph Ratzinger, *"L'interpretazione della Bibbia in conflitto,"* loc. cit., p. 103.

24 See J.F. McCarthy, "The Relationship of Past and Present in Historical Science," in *The Science of Historical Theology,* pp. 64–72.

use of at least a minimal scientific framework, the mis-formulated general historical principles and logical fallacies of critical exegetes are put straight and true formulations come to light. There is abundant literature at hand for this work, beginning, logically, with the writings of Bultmann and Dibelius. The other way is to analyze directly the medium of both historical and theological science and to test this analysis on the text of the Scriptures. Out of this work will come the discipline that is so badly needed to answer the Scriptural problems of today. I call it "the science of historical theology."

12. An analytical exegetic framework: The exegetical framework to be developed must be an analytical refinement of the framework that is implicit in the exegesis of the Fathers of the Church and was partly formulated by medieval exegetes. This approach is patristic in its origin and in its general outlook, and yet, because it needs to be organized in a more systematic manner, using also recent scientific and historical insights, it is properly called the "neo-patristic method."

13. From the approach begun by the Fathers of the Church, early medieval exegetes developed a method known as the "four senses of Sacred Scripture." The use of this method opened the door to many insights into the meaning of the inspired word, but the elaboration of the mental framework underlying the method was not carried very far before the time of St. Thomas Aquinas. There is, however, an abundant literature of medieval writings on the "four senses," which are the literal and historical, the allegorical, the tropological (or moral), and the anagogical (or final) senses of Sacred Scripture.[25]

14. St. Thomas reflected on this method and gave a valuable explanation of the four senses in addition to expounding them in his commentaries on the Scriptures.[26] His teaching can serve as the starting point for a more extended and differentiated exposition of this method, beginning with the first big distinction between the literal sense and the spiritual, or mystical, sense. For St. Thomas, this distinction arises from the fact that the rightly understood meaning of *the words themselves* of Sacred Scripture pertains to the literal, or historical, sense, while the fact that the things expressed

---

25 See, e.g., Henri de Lubac, *Exégèse médiévale. Les quatre sens de l'Ecriture* (Paris: Aubier, 1959). This work is remarkable for the copiousness of the sources cited.

26 See especially Aquinas, *Summa Theologiae,* part I, quest. 1, art. 10; *Quodlibet Seven,* quest. 6; and *Commentary on the Epistle of St. Paul to the Galatians* (infra, note 43). For a brief summary of St. Thomas's teaching on the four senses of Sacred Scripture, see Thomas Kuffel, "St. Thomas's Method of Biblical Exegesis," in *Living Tradition,* No. 38 (November 1991).

by the words signify other things produces the spiritual sense. Thus, the spiritual sense is understood to be a typical, or figurative, sense which is based upon the literal sense and presupposes it.[27] This basic double sense is possible because God, who is the principal Author of Sacred Scripture, has brought it about that things and events having their own historical meaning are used also to signify other things. But the central thing signified by these pre-figurements is Jesus Christ Himself, who as the God-Man is the central focus of the spiritual sense and the subject of an extended symbolism which is known as the allegory of Christ.

15. The distinction between the literal and the spiritual senses of Sacred Scripture is analytical, even though spiritual realities are often the primary meaning of a text, because a certain interaction of faith and reason is implied in this division. The original meaning of words can be examined by unaided reason, as can the unfolding of visible happenings, but the spiritual meaning of words and events can be seen only by the light of faith. In Part I, Question I of the *Summa Theologiae*, St. Thomas points out that revealed teaching is *necessary* for man (article 1), that this teaching is a *science* based upon revealed truths that are visible under the light of faith (article 2), and that *God* is the subject of this science (article 7). Approaching, then, the distinction between the literal and the spiritual senses from an analytical point of view, I would say that the literal sense tends to be exclusively seen by the unaided human reason, while the spiritual sense is penetrated by theological reason aided by the light of faith. Where the text is speaking literally about spiritual realities, and above all about supernatural realities, the unaided reason can see the statement in a flattened and unmeaningful way, but it cannot "understand" the statement. Where the text contains spiritual meanings beneath the literal sense, the unaided reason can see these meanings at best in a flattened and unmeaningful way, while reason enlightened by faith can both see the spiritual meanings in a meaningful way and see the literal meaning in a more complete way—provided that it has the appropriate theological framework at its command.

16. Looking, then, at sacred teaching as presented by the text of Sacred Scripture, and reasoning along the lines of St. Thomas, we can justifiably say that the inspired writings are *necessary*, not only because what is contained in them spiritually could not be figured out by man on his own, but also because the poor, fallen reason of man tends away from the spiritual truth and towards his own self-gratification. Men without grace do not want to know the spiritual truth, and they endeavor to rub it out where it is written.

---

27 Cf. Aquinas, *Summa Theologiae*, I, q. 1, art. 10 corp.

But men possessed of faith and sanctifying grace will discover the truth and understand it. Again, the spiritual truth derived from the Scriptures is a *science*, because the remote object of this knowledge is God, who is real and is the consummation of all that is real. The reality of God is the summit of the one continuum of reality. The light of infused faith is an intellectual light having for its object the reality of God and elevating within it the concept of reality that is given by natural reason to the level of a higher science. Sacred theology is the knowledge of revealed reality as such, and it is developed principally by taking the supernatural dimension of reality that is revealed in the text of the Bible and comprehending its meaning in terms of a valid process of reasoning and intuition. The reality that sacred theology knows is in the one continuum of reality that natural reason knows on its own level, and these two levels of reality are synthesized in the mind of the theological thinker.[28]

17. The light of Christian faith enables its possessor to perceive the reality of God in a higher and more concrete way than is open to unaided human reason. The more proximate object of Christian faith is the teaching of the Church, but more remotely it is the words of Scripture upon which most of this teaching is based. The ultimate object of faith is God Himself and those things which relate to God. God as an object of the human intelligence is in this life always obscure and never clearly seen, but the understanding of the spiritual sense of the words of Sacred Scripture actuates a much clearer and more concrete perception of God than is possible without their help. The New Testament and the Fathers of the Church explain to us that God is more clearly and more concretely revealed in the figure of Jesus Christ, who is God as well as He is man. The Sacred Scriptures were written to tell us about God in Jesus Christ, and this is true to such a degree that the central event and the key to the spiritual understanding of the entire Bible is the Incarnation of God in the human nature of Jesus Christ. The event of Christ unifies the Old Testament and the New, the letter and the spirit, the historical and the mystical, the visible and the invisible, the natural and the supernatural. The pattern in which this unification has been set down in the Scriptures is known as the allegory of Christ and His Church.

18. Four distinct senses: St. Thomas answers affirmatively to the question "whether there ought to be distinguished four senses of Sacred

---

28 The notion of Christian faith as an affirmation of the reality of revealed objects and as a perception of this reality is expounded in *The Science of Historical Theology*, pp. 87–100.

Scripture,"[29] basing his response upon the authority of St. Augustine of Hippo and of Venerable Bede. St. Augustine observed: "In all the holy books it is behooving to discern the eternal things to be seen there, the deeds that are there narrated, the future things that are predicted, the things that are commanded to be done."[30] St. Thomas sees these four things to refer respectively to the anagogical, the historical, the allegorical, and the tropological senses of Sacred Scripture.

19. St. Thomas also quotes Venerable Bede as saying: "There are four senses of Sacred Scripture: history, which narrates things done; allegory, in which one thing is understood from another; tropology (that is, moral discourse), in which the ordering of habits is treated; and anagogy, by which we are led upward to treat of highest and heavenly things."[31] St. Thomas identifies the "historical sense" of Bede with the *literal* sense presented by the words themselves, and he makes an analytical division of the spiritual sense into allegory, tropology, and anagogy. "The *spiritual* sense," he says, "is taken to be or consists in this that certain things are expressed through the figure of other things, since visible things are accustomed to be figures of invisible things, as Denis says," and that is why it is called the "spiritual" sense. "But," he continues, "the truth which Sacred Scripture presents through the figures of things is aimed at two things, namely, at rightly believing and at rightly doing. If at rightly doing, we have the moral sense, which is also called the tropological sense; but if at rightly believing, it behooves to distinguish according to the order of believable things, since as Denis says in the fourth chapter of the *Heavenly Hierarchies*, the state of the Church is midway between the state of the Synagogue and the state of the triumphant Church. Therefore, the Old Testament was a figure of the New, while the Old and New Testaments together are a figure of heavenly things. Therefore, the spiritual sense ordered to rightly believing can be based upon that manner of figuration in which the Old Testament figures the New, and this is the allegorical, or typical, sense according to this that the things which happened in the Old Testament are expounded of Christ and the Church; or it can be based upon that manner of figuration in which the New and the Old Testaments together signify the Church Triumphant, and this is the anagogical sense."[32]

---

29 Cf. Aquinas, *Quaestiones Quodlibetales, quest. 6, art. 2.*

30 Augustine, *Commentary on Genesis,* bk. I.

31 Bede, *Commentary on Genesis.*

32 Cf. Aquinas, *Quaestiones Quodlibetales, ques. 6, art. 2.*

To clarify these distinctions, St. Thomas notes in the first place that things which actually happened can refer to Christ and his members as shadows of the truth, and this is what produces the allegorical sense, while other comparisons, being imaginary rather than real, whether in Sacred Scripture or in other literature, do not stand outside of the literal sense. Hence, the allegorical sense of Sacred Scripture is not imaginary and is not a genre of human inventiveness.[33]

It might seem in the second place that the tropological sense should not be distinguished from the allegorical, since there is one Church of the Head and the members, and the allegorical sense seems to pertain to the Head of the Church, i.e., to Christ, while the tropological sense seems to pertain to its members, i.e., to the faithful. To this difficulty St. Thomas replies that "the allegorical sense pertains to Christ not only under the aspect of the Head but also under the aspect of his members, just as by the twelve stones picked from the Jordan (Joshua 4:3) are signified the Twelve Apostles. But the moral sense pertains to the members of Christ with regard to their own acts and not insofar as they are considered as members."[34]

It might seem in the third place that the moral sense should not be distinguished from the literal, because in several places Sacred Scripture gives moral instructions according to the literal sense. To this St. Thomas replies that "the moral sense is not every sense by which morals are taught, but (that sense) through which the teaching of morals is taken from a likeness to things done, and thus the moral sense is the spiritual side, because the moral is never the same sense as the literal."[35]

It might seem in the fourth place that, since Christ is the Head of the triumphant as well as of the militant Church, the anagogical sense should not be different from the allegorical. To this St. Thomas responds that "just as the allegorical sense pertains to Christ according as He is the Head of the Church Militant, justifying it and infusing grace, so also the anagogical sense pertains to Him according as He is the Head of the Church Triumphant, glorifying it."[36]

Finally, it might seem that, if these four senses were necessary for Sacred Scripture, each and every part of Sacred Scripture would have to have these

---

33 Ibid., to the first objection.

34 Ibid., to the second objection.

35 Ibid., to the third objection.

36 Ibid., to the fourth objection.

four senses, but, as Augustine says in his commentary on Genesis, "in some parts the literal sense alone is to be sought." To this St. Thomas replies that various parts of Scripture have four, three, two, or only one of these senses. Thus, the literal events of the Old Testament can be expounded in the four senses. The things spoken literally of Christ as the Head of the New Testament Church can also be expounded according to the four senses, because the historical Body of Christ can be expounded allegorically of the Mystical Body of Christ, and tropologically of the acts of the faithful to be modeled after the example of Christ, and anagogically inasmuch as Christ is the way to glory that has been shown to us. The things spoken literally of the Church of the New Testament can be expounded in three senses, because they can also be expounded tropologically and anagogically, but not allegorically, except that things mentioned literally regarding the primitive Church may have allegorical meaning regarding the later Church of the New Testament. The things of moral import in the literal sense can be expounded only literally and allegorically. And, finally, the things spoken literally regarding the state of glory cannot be expounded in any other sense.[37]

20. A wide application: These principles of interpretation given by St. Thomas in regard to the four senses of Sacred Scripture have a much wider application than has been supposed in modern times, even by traditional Catholic exegetes. Let it become our purpose to discover some new dimensions of their application, and let us begin by looking briefly at St. Thomas's own application of these principles in his commentary on the Epistle to the Galatians, chapter 4, verses 21 to 31, where St. Paul says that "Abraham had two sons" (v. 22) and that "these things are said by allegory" (v. 24).[38] Commenting on Galatians 4:24, St. Thomas avers that "allegory is a manner of speaking by which one thing is said and another thing is meant." Thus, he says, "the word allegory comes from alos (alien) and gogé (a leading)" because it leads, as it were, "to a different understanding." St. Thomas makes clear that allegory in the sense used here is not imaginary and is not within the power of merely human authors to create, because by merely human means only words can be used to signify, but God can use real events to signify other things. Thus God in the Sacred Scriptures has made things of the Old Law to signify

---

37 Ibid., to the fifth objection. Cf. Kuffel, op. cit., p. 7.

38 T. Aquinas, *Super Epistolas S. Pauli Lectura* (Turin-Rome: Marietti, 1953), pp. 619–624; Eng. trans. by F. R. Larcher, *Commentary on St. Paul's Epistle to the Galatians* (Magi Books: 33 Buckingham Dr., Albany, N.Y., 1966), pp. 134-149.

the New Law and things of the New Law to signify future glory. And he gives a general example.

21. In Genesis 1:3 it is written: "God said, 'Let there be light,' and light was made." Taken literally, "Let there be light" refers to physical light; allegorically, it refers to the birth of Christ in the Church; tropologically, it refers to the illumination of our intellects and the inflammation of our wills through Christ; anagogically, it refers to our being brought into the light of glory through Christ.[39]

22. In this example we see a wide application of the word "light" in the Scriptures, not merely to physical light, but by way of allegory to the light that is Christ, the light of Christian faith and charity, and the light of eternal glory. Such a perspective transcends the narrow horizon of the form-critic and opens up whole new vistas of insight into the Scriptures. If in the beginning God actually said, "Let Christ be born in the Church," and "Let the light of Christ arise in the minds and hearts of the children of God," and "Let the light of eternal glory shine forth in the minds of the blessed in heaven"—then there is more written in the Bible than form-critics perceive or even dream of.

23. The proper disposition: A lesson concerning the proper disposition for the interpretation of the inspired Word of God can be taken from the commentary of St. Thomas on Jn. 1:26–27.[40] John the Baptist replied: "…but in your midst there has stood one whom you do not recognize, …the strap of whose sandal I am not worthy to loosen." How is Christ standing in the midst of form-critical exegetes like Bultmann and his followers? Historically, according to Gregory the Great, Chrysostom, and Augustine, Christ is presented in His human nature in the Gospels, "taking the form of a servant and being made like unto men" (Phil. 2:7), so that He could say, "I am in your midst as one who serves" (Lk. 22:27). But form-critics like Bultmann cannot either grasp the fact that God was made man or recognize how great Jesus is according to the divine nature that is concealed in Him.

24. According to Origen, Christ the God-Man stands in the midst of all creation, because, being the Person of the Word, He has filled heaven and earth from the beginning (Jer. 23:24). But form-critics like Bultmann do not recognize Him, because "He was in the world, but the world knew him not" (Jn. 1:10).

---

39 Cf. Aquinas, commentary on Galatians 4:24a (ibid.).

40 Cf. Aquinas, *Super Evangelium S. Ioannis Lectura* (Turin-Rome; Marietti, 1952), p. 49; Eng. trans. by J. A. Weisheipl and F. R. Larcher, *Commentary on the Gospel of St. John* (Magi Books: 33 Buckingham Dr., Albany, N.Y., 1980).

25. Tropologically, according to St. Thomas, Christ (as the Word of God) "shines in everyone's understanding, because whatever light and whatever wisdom (natural or supernatural) exists in men has come to them from participating in the Word," and, thus, Christ "enlightens every man coming into this world" (Jn. 1:9). But form-critics like Bultmann do not recognize Christ, because the light of wisdom is not in them. The Pharisees were Scripture scholars too, but they did not recognize Christ as the Messiah, because, according to the Evangelists, their hearts were hardened by unbelief and their eyes were blinded so that they did not recognize to be present the One whom they were expecting to come. Similarly, form-critics like Bultmann in their blindness do not recognize the God-Man who has come and who is revealed in the inspired Word of Scripture.

26. Allegorically, according to Gregory the Great (cited here by St. Thomas), since sandals are made from the skin of dead animals, the sandal of Christ signifies the mortal human nature which He has assumed to his divine Person, and the strap is the hypostatic union of the divine and human natures, which, as the mystery of the Incarnation, no man can "loosen," that is, explain adequately, although Christian preachers can open up this mystery to some extent.

27. But form-critics like Bultmann use a false and rationalistic distinction between the "Jesus of history" and the "Christ of faith," whereby they empty the reality of the Incarnation of its objective meaning and subjectively reduce the divinity of Christ to a function of their own pride as "modern men."[41] Thus they do not succeed in perceiving the reality behind the mystery, as John the Baptist was able to do by counteracting pride with humility.

28. The allegory of the two testaments: In commenting on the allegory of the Two Testaments in Gal. 4:21–31, St. Thomas points out that, according to St. Paul, Sarah, the free woman, signifies allegorically the Church of the New Testament, even though she was historically the physical mother of the Chosen People of the Old Testament, while Hagar, the bondwoman, signifies the Synagogue of the Old Testament, even though historically she was the Egyptian mother of the Ishmaelites. The physical descendants of Sarah as such are the original "children of the promise," but that promise regarded temporal rewards. The descendants of Sarah according to the spirit are the inheritors of a new testament in

---

41 For an analysis of the error involved in the notion of "modern man" as used in form-critical reasoning, see *The Science of Historical Theology*, articles 8.4 and 8.5 (pp. 119–128).

the Blood of Christ and the children of a new promise which regards eternal life.

29. St. Thomas, following the reasoning of St. Paul, explains in the first place that Hagar, the bondwoman, signifies the Old Testament, which promised temporal, earthly rewards, but gave birth unto slavery as regards feeling, understanding, and result: as regards feeling, because those of the Old Testament were motivated to obey God out of fear rather than out of love (Rom. 8:15); as regards understanding, because they knew only the figures of revealed things and not what the figures represent (2Cor. 3:14); and as regards result, because the Old Testament bestowed at best the small gifts that were due to servants bound to the goods of this world. Similarly, Sarah, the free woman, signifies the New Testament, the law to be written by God in the hearts of the people of the new Israel (Jer. 31:31–33), which gives birth unto freedom: as regards feeling, because those of the New Covenant are motivated by love; as regards understanding, because its children know the truth about God revealed in Jesus Christ (Jn. 8:32); and as regards result, because those of the New Testament receive the divine inheritance of eternal happiness owing to the adopted children of God (Rom 8:15–17).

30. St. Thomas explains in the second place that Hagar and Sarah are figures also of the two Jerusalems. Hagar, who is a figure of the earthly Jerusalem, and is thus the figurative mother of the earthly community of the Jews,[42] "is in bondage with her children" (Gal. 4:24–25), because Mount Sinai (where the Law of Moses was given) "is in line with the Jerusalem that now exists" (Gal. 4:24–25). Mount Sinai is in line with the earthly Jerusalem geographically in the sense that it was on the route of the Hebrew people as they migrated from Egypt to the earthly Promised Land of Canaan (St. Thomas), or, more broadly, because it is on the same existential plane, namely the plane of this visible world, and it gave birth unto bondage, because the Law of Moses did not provide the means to escape from the bondage of Original Sin (Jn. 8:34).

31. But Sarah is a figure of "that Jerusalem which is above," which is free (Gal. 4:26), because it has been "delivered from the servitude of corruption into the liberty of the glory of the children of God" (Rom. 8:21). The name Jerusalem, according to conventional etymology, means "vision of peace," and it is to the beatific vision of eternal peace that St. Paul is referring when he speaks of "that Jerusalem which is above" (cf. Heb. 11:16), that is, which is above the plane of the natural world. St. Thomas

---

42 Cf. Aquinas, *Commentary on St. Paul's Epistle to the Galatians* 4:23.

explains that this heavenly city has an initial phase in the present life and a final phase in the next. The children of God are engendered in this life by the Church Militant (Jn. 3:5) and are resurrected after death into the Church Triumphant (1 Pet. 1:3). The members of the City of God in this life have the "vision of peace" by means of the supernatural virtue of faith, which gives them a partial view of the divine realities that they will see clearly in the next life. This partial view is unfolded in the allegory of Christ and His Church that has been impressed by God upon the Sacred Scriptures. Faith supported by hope and charity can enable the faithful to raise their minds to see not only this lower allegory but also the higher allegorical pattern of the "anagogy" of the heavenly Jerusalem, which has also been impressed by the divine author upon the pages of Holy Writ (Col. 3:1–2).

32. The heavenly Jerusalem is a reality on a higher plane than the earthly Jerusalem. The allegorical casting out of Hagar by Sarah represents a reality that is on a higher level than the historical episode itself. Allegorically, the episode means that the children of this world who persecute Christ and his followers in this life will be cast out of the inheritance of eternal happiness in the next and are even in large part excluded from membership in the Kingdom of God of the present time. But Hagar and Ishmael as historical persons, apart from the drama of the allegory in which they are actors, are not understood to have incurred the disfavor of God. The divine command, "Cast out the bondwoman and her son: for the son of the bondwoman shall not be heir with my son Isaac" (Gen. 21:10) refers allegorically to Christ, of whom Isaac is a prototype, but the episode is explained differently on the historical level.

33. St. Paul tells us: "But as then he that was born according to the flesh persecuted him that was according to the spirit; so also, it is now" (Gal. 4:29). St. Thomas suggests that, since Ishmael was older than Isaac, he may sometimes have made sport of the younger boy when they were playing together. But this would have been a minor offense at worst. The historical reality goes deeper. The Scriptures tell us that Sarah was a good woman (1 Pet. 3:6) who by faith, "being barren, received strength to conceive seed, even past the time of age, because she believed that he was faithful who had promised" (Heb. 11:11). And Hagar, who had conceived earlier according to the ordinary law of nature, when she had realized that she was with child, "despised her mistress" (Gen. 16:4). But, because of this, it was Sarah who persecuted Hagar, so that she ran away (Gen. 16:6). And it was Sarah who, for seemingly selfish reasons, became, if not the cause, at least the occasion

of the "carnal theory of salvation," that is, that membership in the People of God lies in mere blood descent from her. It is to the carnal descendants of Sarah that St. Paul is referring when he says that those born "according to the flesh," even now persecute those (Christians) who have been born "according to the spirit."

34. Therefore, it must be admitted that, in the historical sense of St. Paul's teaching, Hagar and Ishmael were good persons. To have been a slave or the son of a slave is a disgrace in the eyes of men of this world, but not in the eyes of God (Phil. 2:7). Hagar, in obedience to the command of God, returned to the service of Sarah and humbled herself under Sarah's hand (Gen. 16:9). Ishmael was also a son of divine promise (Gen. 21:13); God heard his prayers (Gen. 21:17), and God was with him (Gen. 21:20). And so, historically speaking, who was good and who may have been discardable by God depends basically, not on the role he or she played in the allegory, but on the way each one responded to the grace of God in real life and on how each one rose above merely carnal relationships to live according to the spirit. This seems to be the interpretation given by Our Lord Himself in Lk. 11:28.

35. Allegorically, the sacrificial lamb of the Old Testament prefigures Christ, the Lamb of God, by whose Blood the New Testament has been ratified. The people of the New Testament are sanctified by the Blood of Christ, and they too, in following Christ, must sacrifice themselves and be sacrificed.

36. The idea of the people of God as a people of sacrifice is a tropological dimension of the allegory of the two testaments. St. Paul tells us that the Old Testament is "from Mount Sinai, engendering unto bondage" (Gal 4:24b). St. Thomas comments that Mount Sinai signifies pride: "Give glory to the Lord your God before it be dark, and before your feet stumble upon the dark mountains" (Jer. 13:16). This would indicate that a tropology of sin was involved in that the journey from the figurative Mount Sinai to the earthly Jerusalem, that is, toward the vision of peace which this world promises but cannot give, was made by stumbling over the mountains of pride and self-aggrandizement, and this led only to enslavement. But, we might add, the tropological journey from Mount Calvary to the heavenly Jerusalem is liberating, because it frees us from self-love and opens our minds and hearts to the knowledge and love of God. Christians "cast out the bondwoman" (Gal. 40:30) by casting out the sin of pride from their hearts, and thus they achieve the freedom of the children of God.

Chapter 4

Neo-Patristic Exegesis: Its Approach and Method

by John F. McCarthy

The following is the text of an address delivered in Rome on 6 June 1998 at a convocation sponsored by the Roman Theological Forum.

Part I. The State of the Question

Living Tradition 75 (May 1998)

1. The reformed Pontifical Biblical Commission, in its document of 23 April 1993, *The Interpretation of the Bible in the Church* (henceforth to be referred to also as *IBC*), presents the historical critical method as "indispensable" for the proper understanding of Sacred Scripture:[1] Nevertheless, the Commission points out already in its Introduction to the document that "at the very time when the most prevalent scientific method—the historical critical method—is freely practiced in exegesis, it is itself brought into question," to some extent among scholars through the rise of alternative approaches and methods, but also " through the criticism of many members of the faithful," some of whom maintain that "nothing is gained by submitting biblical texts to the demands of scientific method," and who insist that "the result of scientific exegesis is only to provoke perplexity and doubt upon numerous points which hitherto had been accepted without difficulty."

2. The document of the Commission summarizes the series of stages characteristic of the historical critical method, which are: the movement

---

1 Pontifical Biblical Commission, Eng. ed. (Libreria Editrice Vaticana: Nov. 1993), the opening words of ch. I.

from textual criticism to literary criticism, then to a critical study of forms, and finally to an analysis of the editorial process. In fine, the document avers: "*All this has made it possible to understand far more accurately the intention of the authors and editors of the Bible, as well as the message which they addressed to their first readers. The achievement of these results has lent the historical critical method an importance of the highest order*" (*IBC*, IA.1).

3. As an overall evaluation, the Commission finds that the historical critical method "*is a method which, when used in an objective manner, implies of itself no a priori. ... Oriented, in its origins, towards source criticism and the history of religions, the method has managed to provide fresh access to the Bible. ... This method has contributed to the production of works of exegesis and of biblical theology which are of great value. For a long time now scholars have ceased combining the method with a philosophical system. ... We must take care not to replace the historicizing tendency, for which the older historical critical exegesis is open to criticism, with the opposite excess, that of neglecting history in favor of an exegesis which would be exclusively synchronic. To sum up, the goal of the historical critical method is to determine, particularly in a diachronic manner, the meaning expressed by the biblical authors and editors. Along with other methods and approaches, the historical critical method opens up to the modern reader a path to the meaning of the biblical text, such as we have it today*" (*IBC*, IA.4).

4. In its document of 1993, the reconstituted Pontifical Biblical Commission notes that the Fathers of the Church "*have a foundational role in relation to the living tradition which unceasingly accompanies and guides the Church's reading and interpretation of Scripture.*" The Fathers, it points out, "*look upon the Bible above all as the Book of God, the single work of a single author,*" although they do not "*reduce the human authors to nothing more than passive instruments,*" because "*they are quite capable, also, of according to a particular book its own specific purpose.*" Nevertheless, "*their type of approach pays scant attention to the historical development of revelation.*" The Fathers, it goes on to say, "*had recourse fairly frequently to the allegorical method. But they rarely abandoned the literalness and historicity of texts. ... In principle, there is nothing in it which is to be set aside as out of date or completely lacking in meaning.*" In conclusion, "*The allegorical interpretation of Scripture so characteristic of patristic exegesis runs the risk of being something of an embarrassment to people today. But the experience of the Church expressed in this exegesis makes a contribution that is always useful*" (*IBC*, IIIB.2).

5. The document of 1993 defines the spiritual sense of Sacred Scripture as "*the meaning expressed by the biblical texts when read, under the influence of the Holy Spirit, in the context of the paschal mystery of Christ and of the new life which flows from it,*" and the Commission avers that "*this context truly exists.*" (*IBC*, IIB).

6. Joseph Cardinal Ratzinger, in his Preface to the PBC's document of 1993, points out that "*there are also new attempts to recover patristic exegesis and to include renewed forms of a spiritual interpretation of Scripture.*" And Pope John Paul II, in his address of acceptance of this document of the Pontifical Biblical Commission, avers that "*The Catholic exegete does not entertain the individualist illusion leading to the belief that one can better understand the biblical texts outside the community of believers,*" and he goes on to say: "*It is comforting to note that recent studies in hermeneutical philosophy have confirmed this point of view and that exegetes of various confessions have worked from similar perspectives by stressing, for example, the need to interpret each biblical text as part of the scriptural canon recognized by the Church, or by being more attentive to the contributions of patristic exegesis.*"[2]

7. The Second Vatican Council reminds us that "*since Sacred Scripture is also to be read and interpreted in the same Spirit by whom it was written, in order correctly to derive the meaning of the sacred texts, no less diligently must attention be given to the content and unity of the whole of Scripture, account having been taken of the living Tradition of the entire Church and of the analogy of faith*" (*DV*, 12). The *Catechism of the Catholic Church*, in expounding these three rules of the Council for the correct interpretation of Sacred Scripture—attention to the content and unity of the whole of Scripture, to living Tradition, and to the analogy of faith—defines the 'analogy of faith' as "*the coherence of the truths of faith among themselves and within the whole plan of Revelation*" (*CCC*, 114), and the *Catechism* adds in this place, by way of explanation of these three rules, a brief exposition of the four-senses approach to the interpretation of Sacred Scripture. It says: "*According to an ancient tradition, one can distinguish between two senses of Scripture: the literal and the spiritual, the latter being subdivided into the allegorical, moral, and anagogical senses. The profound concordance of the four senses guarantees all its richness to the living reading of Scripture in the Church*" (*CCC*, 115). After briefly describing and summarizing these four senses, the *Catechism* immediately cites the same paragraph 12 of *Dei Verbum*

---

2 Pope John Paul II, Address of 23 April 1993 to the members of the Pontifical Biblical Commission, no. 10.

to the effect that "*It is the task of exegetes to work, according to these rules, towards a better understanding and explanation of the meaning of Sacred Scripture in order that their research may help the Church to form a firmer judgment*" (*CCC*, 119).

8. The neo-patristic approach to the interpretation of Sacred Scripture is based upon the tradition of the four senses, initiated by the Fathers of the Church, developed systematically to a degree by medieval exegetes and theologians, and now on the threshold of its full flowering after centuries of neglect in modern times. And neo-patristic exegetes and theologians take this teaching of the *Catechism of the Catholic Church*, together with various other statements of the Magisterium of the Church, not only as an encouragement, but even as a mandate to work toward a fuller expression of this approach for the greater utility of the Church and the needs of the times, keeping always in mind that all of the things said by the Second Vatican Council and reported in the *Catechism of the Catholic Church* regarding the proper manner of interpreting Sacred Scripture "*are ultimately subject to the judgment of the Church*" (*DV*, 12). In the act of approving the *Catechism of the Catholic Church*, Pope John Paul II proclaimed that it "*is a statement of the Church's faith and of Catholic doctrine, attested to or illumined by Sacred Scripture, the Apostolic Tradition and the Church's Magisterium*," and he declared it to be "*a sure norm for teaching the faith and thus a valid and legitimate instrument for ecclesial communion.*"[3] The Biblical Commission's 1993 document on *The Interpretation of the Bible in the Church* is a far-reaching study that was joyfully accepted by Pope John Paul II as the fruit of a collegial work undertaken at the initiative of Cardinal Ratzinger[4] and constitutes a very useful source for understanding what many Catholic exegetes think today about their specialized work. However, as Cardinal Ratzinger points out in his Preface to this document, "*The Pontifical Biblical Commission, in its new form after the Second Vatican Council, is not an organ of the teaching office, but rather a commission of scholars who, in their scientific and ecclesial responsibility as believing exegetes, take positions on important problems of scriptural interpretation and know that for this task they enjoy the confidence of the teaching office.*" We may say that the document represents an imperfect consensus of the scholars who composed it regarding the state of Catholic exegesis today, emphasizing what they consider to be the supreme importance of the historical critical

---

3 Pope John Paul II, Apostolic Constitution *Fidei depositum*, 11 October 1992 (reprinted at the beginning of the CCC).

4 Ibid, no. 1.

method while attempting to be as open as possible to other methods and approaches, and it is with this understanding that I shall continue to cite the document in this essay.

9. Literary genres. The Second Vatican Council speaks of the importance of recognizing literary genres: *"In finding out the intention of the sacred writers, among other things literary genres must also be taken into account, because truth is set forth and expressed in different ways in texts distinctly historical, or prophetic, or poetic, or in other forms of speaking. Furthermore, it is needful that the interpreter seek out the meaning which the sacred writer, in the concrete circumstances and conditions of his time and culture, with the aid of the literary genres used at that time, intended to express and did express"* (*DV*, 12). Both the papal address of acceptance and the PBC document itself refer back to the teaching of *Divino afflante Spiritu* in this regard. As the Biblical Commission puts it: "According to *Divino afflante Spiritu*, the search for the literal sense of Scripture is an essential task of exegesis and, in order to fulfill this task, it is necessary to determine the literary genre of texts (cf. EB, 560), something which the historical critical method helps to achieve" (*IBC*, IA.4).

10. The neo-patristic method, in contrast with the historical critical method, takes note that the literary genres mentioned in such documents of the Magisterium as *Divino afflante Spiritu* and *Dei Verbum* endorse expressly only the presence in the Scriptures of such analytical literary genres as those historical, juridical, poetic, didactic, prophetic, and, therefore, takes the time and effort to reexamine in the light of Catholic exegetical tradition and in terms of an adequate critical apparatus the novel and unorthodox approach to literary genres taken by such founders of the historical critical method as Johannes Weiss, Julius Wellhausen, Hermann Gunkel, Karl Ludwig Schmidt, Martin Dibelius, Rudolf Bultmann, M. Albertz, and G. Bertram, because neo-patristic exegetes are convinced that the critical writings of these liberal Protestant exegetes have not been properly analyzed up to now. For example, Rudolf Bultmann, in his *History of the Synoptic Tradition* (*HST*), which has been probably the most influential contribution to the historical critical method in the entire twentieth century,[5] through a form-critical analysis of what he calls literary genres, arrives at seven stages in the rise of the "gospel genre": the story of the death and resurrection of Jesus, the addition of the passion and Easter

---

5   R. Bultmann, *Die Geschichte der synoptischen Tradition* (1st ed., 1921; 8th rev. ed., Gottingen, 1970); Eng. trans. by J. Marsh, *The History of the Synoptic Tradition* (Oxford: Basil Blackwell, 1963) hereafter to be referred to as HST.

narratives; the introduction of sacraments; the creation of miracle-stories; the elaboration of apophthegms and other sayings of Jesus; the combining of the sayings with the kerygma to form a unity; and the insertion of exhortations and congregational regulations (*HST*, 348–350). The neo-patristic method critically examines the analytical validity and historical use of these form-critical genres.

11. Bultmann uses the word '*apophthegms*' to mean "sayings of Jesus set in a brief context" (*HST*, 11), and he divides them into 'controversy dialogues,' 'scholastic dialogues,' and 'biographical apophthegms' (*HST*, 12–39). He concludes that "controversy dialogues are all of them imaginary scenes" (*HST*, 40), having their *Sitz im Leben*, not in the life of Jesus, but "in the discussions the Church had with its opponents, and as certainly within itself, on questions of law" (*HST*, 41). Again, he finds that "the outlook of the early Church could be clothed in the form of a scholastic dialogue as easily as in the form of a controversy dialogue" (*HST*, 54). The '*biographical apophthegms*' are for Bultmann "narrative scenes in which the hero makes a statement especially revealing his character," [6] and he concludes that "finally we may say quite generally: a biographical apophthegm from its very nature is not a historical report—and that applies to Jesus as much as to any other historical personality" (*HST*, 57). He lists about a hundred shorter passages in the Synoptic Gospels which embody '*logia*,' that is, 'wisdom-sayings,' placed on the lips of Jesus (*HST*, 73–79). He grants that "here if anywhere we can find what is characteristic of the preaching of Jesus," but he cautions as well that "it must also be seen that many a saying owes its reception into the tradition only to its suitability for a specific sphere of the Church's interests," and, therefore, "it will only be in very few cases that one of the logia can be ascribed to Jesus with any measure of confidence" (*HST*, 105). '*Prophetic sayings*' are "those in which Jesus announces the coming of the Kingdom of God," [7] and they include the genres of 'preaching about salvation,' 'minatory sayings,' 'admonitions,' and 'apocalyptic predictions' (*HST*, 108–125). Bultmann questions "whether it was originally intended to ascribe such prophetic sayings to Jesus," since "they could very easily have gained currency at first as utterances of the Spirit in the Church," and "the Church drew no distinction between such utterances by Christian prophets and the sayings of Jesus in the tradition"

---

6 R. Bultmann, "The New Approach to the Synoptic Problem," in *Existence and Faith*, (Cleveland: World Publishing Company, 1960), p. 47. The essay was first published in 1926.

7 Bultmann, "The New Approach to the Synoptic Problem," loc. cit., 51.

HST, 127–128). The '*I-sayings*' are sayings "where the person of Jesus plays a substantial part" (*HST*, 152). It is Bultmann's conclusion that "the 'I-sayings' were predominantly the work of the *Hellenistic Churches*, though a beginning had already been made in the *Palestinian Church*. Here too Christian prophets filled by the Spirit spoke in the name of the ascended Lord sayings like Rev. 16:15" (*HST*, 163).

12. Apart from 'apophthegms' and 'dominical sayings,' a third great category of Bultmann's investigations regards '*miracle stories*.' He acknowledges that "miracles were certainly ascribed to Jesus in the Palestinian Church," but "the Hellenistic miracle stories offer such a wealth of parallels to the Synoptic, particularly in style, as to create a prejudice in favor of supposing that the Synoptic miracle stories grew up on Hellenistic ground" (*HST*, 239–240). By *legends* are meant "those parts of the tradition which are not miracle stories in the proper sense, but instead of being historical in character are religious and edifying." Bultmann does not deny that historical happenings may underlie legends," but they are "unhistorical" in the sense that "they are not, in the modern sense, historical accounts at all" (*HST*, 244). He finds that their 'literary character' is such that "one has to assume their formation in a more developed form of Christianity than the Palestinian Church attained—apart, that is, from Q's narrative of the Temptation" (*HST*, 303). It seems clear to him that the legend of the "Virgin Birth" [Virginal Conception] must be assumed to have been derived from the pagan Hellenistic environment (*HST*, 304), but other legends, such as the Easter stories, "have grown up within the Christian tradition itself," and their origin is to be sought "in Christian faith and Christian worship, or alternatively in the unconscious tendency to depict the life of Jesus from the standpoint of faith and of cultic ideas" (*HST*, 305). As an overall conclusion, Bultmann points out that, after the "traditional picture of Jesus has been dissolved, principally by the investigations of Wrede and Wellhausen," form-critical analysis continues the process and "comes at first to the negative conclusion that the outline of the gospels does not enable us to know either the outer course of the life of Jesus or his inner development." Bultmann frankly confesses that "the character of Jesus as a human personality cannot be recovered by us."[8] Consequently, "the Christ who is preached is not the historic Jesus, but the Christ of the faith and the cult," while "the kerygma of Christ is cultic legend and the Gospels are expanded cult legends." Furthermore, he concludes, the "Christ myth" gives to the Gospel of Mark "a unity based upon the myth of the kerygma,"

---

8 Bultmann, "New Approach," loc. cit., 52.

while in the Gospel of John "the myth has completely violated the historical tradition" (*HST*, 370–371).

13. Presuppositions. The form-critical analysis of Rudolf Bultmann, as cited in the previous three paragraphs, has been and remains shattering to Catholic belief in the Gospels. While Catholic form-critical exegetes from 1921 onwards reacted against the anti-dogmatic aspects of Bultmann's conclusions, they were not able to produce a systematic refutation of his highly technical and superbly organized presentation, and so they began to emphasize the role of the "editors" of the "final redaction" of the Gospels, thus relying upon 'redaction-criticism' to save the doctrinal beliefs of Catholic faith, while accepting a certain basic validity of Bultmann's form-critical method. Catholic exegetes and theologians also wrote against Bultmann's "philosophical presuppositions." As the 1993 document of the PBC points out: "*Conscious of the cultural distance between the world of the first century and that of the twentieth, Bultmann was particularly anxious to make the reality of which the Bible treats speak to his contemporaries. He insisted upon the 'pre-understanding' necessary for all understanding and elaborated the theory of the existential interpretation of the New Testament writings. Relying on the thinking of Heidegger, Bultmann insisted that it is not possible to have an exegesis of a biblical text without presuppositions which guide comprehension. ... To avoid subjectivism, however, one must allow pre-understanding to be deepened and enriched—even to be modified and corrected—by the reality of the text*" (*IBC*, IIA:1). The Commission believes that the historical critical method, of which form-criticism is an initial step, "*when used objectively, implies of itself no a priori,*" and "*if its use is accompanied by a priori principles, that is not something pertaining to the method itself, but to certain hermeneutical choices which govern the interpretation and can be tendentious*" (*IBC*, IA:4). And the Commission cautions against "*the temptation to apply to the study of the Bible the purely objective criteria used in the natural sciences. On the one hand,*" it continues, "*all events reported in the Bible are interpreted events. On the other, all exegesis of the accounts of these events necessarily involves the exegete's own subjectivity. Access to a proper understanding of biblical texts is only granted to the person who has an affinity with what the text is saying on the basis of life experience. The question which faces every exegete is this: which hermeneutical theory best enables a proper grasp of the profound reality of which Scripture speaks and its meaningful expression for people today?*" (*IBC*, IIA: 2).

14. These citations from the PBC's document regarding 'pre-understanding' illustrate the extent to which the thinking of Bultmann

has influenced historical critical discussion during the twentieth century. With attention drawn away from the presuppositions of the historical critical method itself, and especially of the form-critical method, which is assumed to imply "*no a priori*" when it is used objectively, the discussion of presuppositions is centered around the acceptance or rejection of Martin Heidegger's existentialist philosophy, as applied by Bultmann to the interpretation of Sacred Scripture, and the Biblical Commission opts for an alternative view of existence, namely, a hermeneutical theory which makes the profound reality of Scripture a "meaningful expression for people today." In contrast, the neo-patristic method, having distinguished Bultmann's form-critical presuppositions from his supervenient existentialist meditations, critically examines both levels of his thought. The logic of his writing career is simple: having 'eliminated' in his *History of the Synoptic Tradition* everything miraculous, everything supernatural, almost everything historical from the life of Jesus as depicted in the four Gospels, his subsequent discourse was aimed at suggesting from a philosophical point of view why anyone should be a Christian at all, and so he presented his minimal idea of Christianity in a series of works over the following years.[9] But most important of all was his famous essay, "*Neues Testament und Mythologie*," published in Munich in 1941, which touched off the "demythologizing debate" that embroiled liberal Protestant exegesis for decades thereafter.[10] Since 1941 much of the discussion regarding 'pre-understanding' in the interpretation of the Bible has centered around the demythologizing debate as a sequel to the devastating results of form-critical analysis of the New Testament.[11]

15. With respect to the devastating use of form-criticism by Bultmann and other liberal Protestant exegetes, Catholic exegetes gave partial responses, especially in their oral teaching, but, to my knowledge, nothing very thoroughgoing and systematic ever appeared in print. It

---

9 Among Bultmann's significant post-exegetical works are to be included his *Jesus* (Tübingen, 1926), *Glauben und Verstehen* (4 vols.: Tübingen, 1933–1965), and many others. Among English-language editions of his writings which illustrate his 'pre-understanding' may be included *History and Eschatology* (1955), *Jesus and the Word* (1958), *Jesus Christ and Mythology* (1958), *Existence and Faith* (1960), and *Faith and Understanding* (1969).

10 R. Bultmann, "Neues Testament und Mythologie," in *Offenbarung und Heilsgeschehen: Beiträge zur evangelischen Theologie*, vol. VII/2 (Munich, 1941); republished in English as "New Testament and Mythology," in Hans Werner Bartsch ed., *Kerygma and Myth: a Theological Debate*, vol. 1 (London, 1953).

11 See chapters 10 and 11 below.

does not seem an exaggeration to say that *The History of the Synoptic Tradition* has sat poorly digested in the belly of Catholic historical critical scholarship from 1921 to the present day. When articles regarding Bultmann's form-critical work began to appear in Catholic periodicals after 1945, they were mostly expository of what he himself maintained, with a paragraph or two added at the end cautioning that certain of his conclusions were unacceptable to Catholic faith. Some Catholic theologians undertook to refute the presuppositions of Bultmann's 'demythologizing,' but for the most part did not directly examine their use in his exegetical method as such. In the meanwhile, more and more Catholic exegetes were attempting to make prudent use of Bultmann's exegetical method, seeking at the same time not very successfully to exclude his anti-dogmatic assumptions and conclusions. Thus a state of tension arose between Catholic followers of the new exegesis and adherents to traditional Catholic exegesis. This tension is alluded to in a document put out by the International Theological Commission in 1988, which recalls that "the conflict between exegesis and dogmatic theology is a modern phenomenon."[12] The 1993 Biblical Commission's document remarks that "there was no conflict in a generalized sense between Catholic exegesis and dogmatic theology but only some instances of strong tension" (*IBC*, IIID.4). It seems that, on the one hand, some Catholic followers of the historical critical school were presenting results of their technical procedures that reflected anti-dogmatic premises, while, on the other hand, traditional theologians were objecting on grounds of purely dogmatic reasoning to the anti-dogmatic appearance of some of these results without taking the time to analyze the exegetical procedure itself. Looking at this controversy from a contemporary neo-patristic point of view, one is able to say that the Catholic form-critical exegetes had recognized in the exegetical procedures of Bultmann *et. al.* the raising of problems whose explanation could serve for a development of the Catholic interpretation of the Bible, but they did not have the technical apparatus needed to purify the method sufficiently of its deleterious presuppositions and procedures. At the same time, the dogmatic theologians who reacted against the historical critical method did so for the most part on dogmatic grounds without making the needed effort to analyze the procedures of the method itself.

---

12 International Theological Commission, Eng. trans., "On the Interpretation of Dogmas," in Origins 20 (1990–1991).

16. A call for a new approach to exegesis. Joseph Cardinal Ratzinger, in a programmatic article published originally in German in 1989, and subsequently in English and then in Italian,[13] called for a better synthesis between historical and theological methods, between criticism and dogma in the exegesis of Sacred Scripture through self-criticism by exegetes of the historical method in use, and by the employment of a less arbitrary philosophy which offers a greater number of presuppositions favoring a true hearing of the text.[14] The Cardinal observed that errors made in biblical exegesis over the preceding century have virtually become academic dogmas,[15] owing especially to the influence of Martin Dibelius and Rudolf Bultmann, whose basic methodological orientations determine even to this day the methodology and course of modern exegesis, and he found it imperative at this juncture of time to challenge the fundamental ideas of their method. Bultmann the exegete, he said, "represents a background consensus of the scientific exegesis dominant today," even though Bultmann was not so much a scientific as a systematic worker, whose exegetical conclusions are not the result of historical findings, but emerge from a framework of systematic presuppositions.[16] Noting that, in the form-criticism of Bultmann and Dibelius, through the influence of Immanuel Kant, modern exegesis reduces history to philosophy, the Cardinal proposed some basic elements for a new synthesis,[17] which will require "the attentive and critical commitment of a whole generation."[18] On the level of the integration of the biblical texts into their historical context, said the Cardinal, the time is ripe for a radical new reflection on exegetical method, also in the sense that biblical exegesis must come to recognize its own history as part of what it is and to learn how the philosophical element influences the process of interpretation.[19] And, on the level of their location "in the totality of their historical unfolding," that is, of their total meaning, he said, the biblical texts "must be integrated into a theological vision in the strict sense, based upon the experience of Revelation." To achieve this task he saw the need "to introduce into the discussion the

---

13 Joseph Cardinal Ratzinger, in Richard J. Neuhaus, ed., (Grand Rapids: Eerdmans, 1989), pp. 1–23).

14 Ibid, p. 17.

15 Ibid., p. 21.

16 Ibid., pp. 9–10.

17 Ibid., pp. 17–23.

18 Ibid., pp. 6 and 16.

19 Ibid., p. 21.

great proposals of patristic and medieval thought," as well as reflection upon "the fundamental options of the Reformation and on the choices it involved in the history of interpretation." [20]

17. The four senses. The neo-patristic approach is rooted in a radical and pervasive distinction between the literal and the spiritual sense of the inspired text and it proceeds by the use of an explicit framework of the traditional four senses, namely, the literal sense, the allegorical sense, the tropological, or moral, sense, and the anagogical, or eschatological, sense of the sacred text.[21] The neo-patristic method makes use of the insights of the Fathers of the Church, and of other early ecclesiastical writers, as well as the insights of medieval, modern, and contemporary exegetes and theologians, in the construction and use of a scientific framework of thought that is deemed adequate both on the level of faith and on the level of reason. The neo-patristic approach arises from two general observations: a) the problems raised by historical critical exegetes regarding the interpretation of Sacred Scripture, if resolved in a different mental framework, could occasion a positive development of Catholic exegesis; and b) the exegetical tradition of the Fathers of the Church, together with its elaboration in medieval and modern times, is the key to the synthesizing or rejecting of particular results of historical criticism. The neo-patristic exegete finds material for his study in the historical critical literature, and he finds the formality of his study in the Patristic literature, as expanded also into the commentaries of Catholic biblical scholars over the centuries, together with the input of contemporary neo-patristic scholarship. The overall framework of the neo-patristic approach is constructed according to the Patristic notion of the four senses of the inspired text of Sacred Scripture. The Fathers actually varied in their notion of the number and names of the senses of Sacred Scripture, and they often used the notion without speculating on this question. St. Augustine alludes to four senses of Sacred Scripture at the beginning of his *De Genesi ad litteram*, where he says: "In all the sacred books, we should consider the eternal truths that are taught, the facts that are narrated, the future events that are predicted, and the precepts or counsels that are given."[22] St. Thomas Aquinas greatly developed the theory of the four senses and speculated on their relation to

---

20 Ibid., pp. 22–23.

21 There is an abundant literature of medieval writings regarding the four senses. See, e.g., H. de Lubac, *Exégèse medievale. Les quatre sens de l'Ecriture* (Paris: Aubier, 1959).

22 A. Augustine, *The Literal Meaning of Genesis* (trans. by J.H. Taylor, New York: Newman Press, 1982), bk. 1, ch. 1 (*Ancient Christian Writers,* vol. 41, p. 19).

one another, and, for this reason, he could be considered to be the founder of the neo-patristic approach.[23] His teaching serves as a starting point for a more differentiated exposition of the method, beginning from the first big distinction between the literal sense and the spiritual sense. For St. Thomas this distinction arises from the fact that the rightly understood meaning of the words themselves is embodied in the literal sense, while the fact that the things expressed by the words signify other things produces the spiritual sense. But the central thing signified by these prefigurements is Jesus Christ Himself, who, as the God-Man, is the central focus of the spiritual sense and the subject of an extended symbolism which is known as the allegory of Christ and his Church.

18. History and reality. There is reason to be dissatisfied with a self-characterized 'historical method' which leaves undefined such all-pervasive terms as 'historical,' 'scientific,' and 'real.' Let us reflect briefly on the thought that to view the conclusions of historical critical exegesis "in the perspective of their own history," as Cardinal Ratzinger put it, means to view them in the context of 'reality.' Bultmann, in order to provide some verbal plausibility for the object of Christian faith as stripped of its historical reality through form-critical analysis, proposed a double meaning of 'history' and a double meaning of 'reality.' In his terminology, history as *Historie* is composed of causally connected events and of relationships between facts which are objectively verifiable and chronologically determinable,[24] while history as *Geschichte* consists of the encounters of the "genuinely existing" human being, whose "existential constitution" ultimately signifies "to exist, to be confronted with non-being, to be able to be and ever to decide anew." By the use of this existentialist distinction, Bultmann subjectivized the question of the historicity of the Gospels and of the object of Christian faith into the possession by the contemporary thinker of what he called "true historicity," that is, "the existential constitution of the being which necessarily exists in history."[25] Bultmann did not hesitate to proclaim that "the right question to frame with regard to the Bible—at any rate within the Church—is the question of human existence," and he saw this as "a question which at bottom determines our approach to and interpretation of

---

23 See especially Aquinas, S.Th., I, q. 1, art. 10; *Quodlibetalis VII*, q. 6; *In epist. S. Pauli ad Galatas*. Cf. T. Kuffel, "St. Thomas' Method of Biblical Exegesis," in *Living Tradition* 38 (Nov. 1991).

24 Bultmann, *History and Eschatology*, 143–144.

25 Bultmann, in *Kerygma and Myth*, loc. cit., vol. 1, 191–193 and 200.

all historical documents."[26] But for the neo-patristic exegete this principle of Bultmann puts out of focus all truly scientific study of the Bible or of any historical document, because the first question that has to be asked is the question of reality: Did what is recounted in the historical books of the Bible, and above all in the Gospels, *really* take place as described or not? Bultmann did ask this question, and, in order to reassure his audience of believing Christians, he presented a convenient distinction between reality as *Realität,* which is what he calls the reality that is known through sense experience and constitutes the objectively existing world in which man finds himself, and reality as *Wirklichkeit,* which for Bultmann is the reality of "historically existing men," as described above.[27] This distinction, using a play upon the subject-object relationship in human understanding, enabled Bultmann to predicate the word 'reality' of the post-form-critical imaginary object of Christian faith, while at the same time excluding the reality of the object of faith in the spontaneous meaning of the word 'reality.' But the double meaning of 'history' and of 'reality' in the teaching of Bultmann does not stand up under neo-patristic analysis.

19. Neo-patristic exegesis seeks to clarify the definitions of such terms as *'scientific,' 'historical,' 'critical,' 'real,' 'literal,' 'spiritual,' 'literary form,' 'historical reality,' 'level of meaning,' 'context,'* and many others. The neo-patristic method highlights the *concept of reality* in the definition of science, taking the term *'science'* to mean "the knowledge of reality as such," *'historical science'* to mean "the knowledge of past reality as such, and *'theological science'* to mean "the knowledge of revealed reality as such."[28] These definitions of terms lead to the concept of the *'science of historical theology,'* as "the knowledge of past revealed reality as such," and these concepts are elements in the scientific medium of the neo-patristic interpreter which, in my opinion, he should use, not only in examining the inspired text, but also in examining the writings of other interpreters. For instance, in approaching a biblical passage, the neo-patristic exegete will

---

26 Bultmann, Ibid., p. 191. An analysis and answer to Bultmann's theory of history is given in J.F. McCarthy, *The Science of Historical Theology* (2nd printing, Rockford, Ill.: TAN, 1991), pp. 7–9 and 113–119.

27 Cf. R. Bultmann, *"Zum Problem der Entmythologisierung,* in H.W. Bartsch et al., *Kerygma und Mythos* (Hamburg: Evangelischer Verlag), vol. VI–1: a) "… die ein objektivierenden Sehen vergestellte Wirklichkeit der Welt, innerhalb deren sich der Mensch verfindet…" (p. 20); b) "… als die Wirklichkeit des geschlichtlich existierenden Menschen" (p. 21).

28 See McCarthy, *The Science of Historical Theology,* pp. 34–42, 60–63, and 97–100.

include the processing of prominent interpretations given also by followers of the historical critical method, and, in fact, he will find that historical critical literature is an important source of material, keeping clearly in mind his own scientific medium of thought in the realization that science is science only to the extent that it is aware of its own medium of thought and knowing that the primary question in all instances is the reality of its object of thought. Thus, in examining the reasoning of historical critical writers as of all other exegetes and theologians, the neo-patristic researcher will carefully consider how they handle the concept of reality and how clearly they are aware of their own medium of thought. Cardinal Ratzinger notes that "from a distance the observer becomes aware with surprise that these interpretations [of historical critical exegetes], which were taken to be so rigorously scientific and purely 'historical,' reflect in reality the spirit of their authors rather than the spirit of ages gone by."[29] We take Cardinal Ratzinger's expression "in reality" to mean "in the concept of reality as an explicitly recognized and differentiated medium of one's own thought.

20. The literal sense. In keeping with the teaching of the Church on the fundamental character of the literal sense, the neo-patristic method begins with the literal sense and never contradicts it, but it views the literal sense in the framework of the four senses, as did Aquinas. It is interesting to note that St. Thomas, while he collected many of the insights of the Fathers of the Church into his presentation of the spiritual senses of the inspired text, at the same time did such an excellent job for his time in interpreting the literal sense in his commentaries that he greatly expedited the tendency among Catholic exegetes over the subsequent centuries to emphasize the literal meaning to the extent of virtually abandoning the pursuit of the spiritual meanings objectively inherent in the text. The neo-patristic method begins with and maintains the literal sense of the sacred text, which it also assumes to be inerrant, and it seeks to use precisely defined literary genres in the way requested by Pope Pius XII in *Divino afflante Spiritu* to explain instances in which critics claim to find historical errors in the inspired text (see no. 9 above). There is a strong tendency among contemporary exegetes to base their reasonings upon many supposed contradictions in the inspired text which prove under fuller analysis not to be contradictions at all. Hence, a prime activity of neo-patristic exegetes is to eliminate non-factual contradictions from scientific consideration, and they find that the resolving of many of these apparent contradictions leads to new insights into the text. They use the best techniques of textual

---

29 Ratzinger, *Biblical Interpretation in Crisis,* p. 8.

criticism to determine the exact wording of the text, and they look for sources behind the text, not excluding by any means divine inspiration as the primary source. They do not claim to know the solution to all of the historical problems surrounding contemporary study of the biblical text, but they are confident that the answers are objectively there to be found.

21. The historical sense. In neo-patristic exegesis, the historical sense of the text is on the level of the literal sense and may be defined as "that sense which is the direct object of historical science." By 'historical science' is meant "the knowledge of past reality as past reality." Thus the formality of historical science in the neo-patristic framework is the concept of the past within the general concept of reality, and this approach enables the neo-patristic researcher to distinguish sharply between historical fiction and historical reality, so that whether the biblical text is presenting fact or fiction in its literal sense is the first question to be resolved. Bultmann claims that the entire text of the Gospels is presented in a fictional genre, and neo-patristic scholars undertake to refute this claim, not only in general but also verse by verse. In doing so they first eliminate the presuppositions of Bultmann's method and then eliminate his use of these presuppositions in his exegetical works. It is interesting to note that this work of sifting and rejecting is not purely negative, because Bultmann has challenged Catholic exegetes to look more deeply into their own exegetical methods, he has misformulated historical principles that are still waiting to be formulated correctly, and he has called attention to aspects of meaning in the sacred text that are still waiting to be expressed correctly. An example of this is Bultmann's use of the subject-object relationship, which for New Testament purposes he reduces to the sheer subjectivity of the Heideggerian existential moment. By this maneuver he challenges exegetes to formulate a correct expression of the subject-object relationship with respect to historical understanding. The neo-patristic method responds to this challenge by first distinguishing two phases of objectivity: the remote objectivity of extra-mental reality and the proximate objectivity of mental reality. Within the mental concept of reality it locates its knowledge of the real past as its scientific historical medium, and it concentrates on and develops this historical medium as a tool for examining the historical sense of Sacred Scripture. On this point, the difference is that the neo-patristic is consciously aware of his intellectual historical medium, whereas the Bultmannian is not. As a result, Bultmannians waste a lot of time supposing what was the mentality or point of view of the New Testament writers without having performed the prior task of formulating clearly their own mentality or point of view.

Part II. A Neo-Patristic Reply to the Historical Critical Question

Living Tradition 76 (July 1998)

22. In the course of the demythologizing debate following the publication of Bultmann's famous essay in 1941, responses more or less incomplete were eventually given by Catholic theologians to the presuppositions involved.[30] Some Catholic theologians published replies that appear to be completely inadequate, as though the writers did not understand the true dimensions of the problem. Others presented some good elements of a response together with some statements that caused them to fall partly into Bultmann's hands, because they did not have a sufficiently precise terminology to address the problems adequately. Thus, for example, Leopold Malevez, in an impressive book on the subject of demythologizing published in 1954, eloquently points out why Bultmann's idea of the kerygma cannot replace the mystery of the God-Man, that Bultmann, in his denial of the possibility of divine miracles or of any divine intervention, including, of course, the Incarnation, does not really speak in the name of modern science, and that Bultmann/Heidegger have not validly disproved the self-standing objectivity which traditional Christianity has always attributed to the objects of faith. Again, René Marlé, in two books and two articles published between 1953 and 1967, pointed out, among other things, that the Word of God is not merely an act or an event but is a divine Person, that the Christian message is a real witness to a real Resurrection of Jesus, that Bultmann does not correctly describe the world-view of the ancients or the fallen nature of man, and that a world of extra-conceptual realities is contained in the Christian religion.

23. A third group of Catholic theologians put the problems of Bultmannian interpretation into proper context on the level of principles, so as to make at least a beginning of an adequate response to the demythologizing of the New Testament, without, however, undertaking a systematic refutation of Bultmann's exegesis. Thus, in a lengthy article published in 1957, Anton Vögtle noted that Bultmann, in his demythologizing, uses presuppositions of differing kinds and varying provenance, taking them, not only from historical criticism and the history of religions school, but also from rationalist liberalism with its view of man, of the modern world, and of

---

30 See chapters 10 and 11 below.

reality itself, as also from the teachings of Martin Luther, from dialectical theology and existentialist philosophy, "bringing them finally together into a compact unity which is so imposing that to some critics it seems almost terrifying."[31] From these presuppositions he singled out four systematic and three historical premises. The four systematic premises are said to be: his radical dualism between 'non-world' and world; a double concept of history and of historical knowledge; the hermeneutical principle of 'pre-understanding' (*Vorverständnis*); and a double concept of time. In addition, Vögtle identified in Bultmann's program three basic historical premises: an extremely negative picture of the origin of Christianity; the life of Jesus as being non-messianic; and Christian faith as being not based upon real objective facts. In 1963 Ugo Lattanzi[32] followed the path laid out by Vögtle, but he distinguished at the basis of Bultmann's thought three postulates and two presuppositions which he described as follows: a) Bultmann's theological postulate of radical opposition between world and 'non-world' excludes any reasonable doctrine about God and any doctrine revealed by God. b) Bultmann's exegetical postulate that the message of Jesus was only eschatological allows him to consider as authentic words of Jesus only those which depict the early Church as having no interest in history properly so called (*Historie*). c) Bultmann's sociological postulate that an anonymous Christian community created the kerygma allows him to exclude the input of eye-witnesses. Lattanzi lists two presuppositions of Bultmann's thought: the spontaneous generation of the Church, which seems to him to have been suggested to Bultmann by the modernist teachings of Alfred Loisy (although it is expressed in general in the philosophy of Émil Durkheim); and the later transformation of the Church into a historical community.

24. Reviewing in summary fashion the earlier responses by Catholic theologians to the demythologizing of Rudolf Bultmann in terms of the neo-patristic approach, we find that they are implicit elements of a framework that neo-patristic thinking makes explicit. The "radical dualism of world and 'non-world' "shows up on opposite sides of the concept of reality in the subject-object relationship, and the mystery of 'non-world,' that is, the 'total otherness' which Bultmann attributes to any idea of God or of divine action becomes plainly and simply an unjustified recourse to the genre of religious fiction, so that it devolves upon neo-patristic exegesis

---

31 A. Vögtle, *"Rivelazione e mito,"* in *Problemi e orientamenti di teologia dogmatica,* vol. I (Milan, 1957), 832.

32 U. Lattanzi, *"I Sinnottici e la Chiesa secondo R. Bultmann,"* in *Miscellanea Antonio Piolanti,* vol. I (Rome, 1963) [*Lateranum,* new series, 29th year], 141–169.

to defend consistently the reality of the object of Christian faith and its validity as an object. To accomplish this, neo-Patristic exegesis distinguishes the proximate objectivity of its scientific medium from the remote objectivity of the real things to which faith refers. These considerations may seem obvious, but they do not have an established place in historical critical exegesis. In the light of the neo-patristic framework, Bultmann's existentialist reasonings fall to the ground, because he does not recognize the role of the scientific medium which must exist between the knowing subject as such and the remote object of his knowledge. In order properly to defend a reasonable doctrine about God and the existence of divine revelation and inspiration, the spiritual character of Christian faith and the spiritual sense of the inspired Scriptures, both of which are elements of the neo-patristic framework, have to be kept in view. The neo-patristic approach assumes at all times that, over and above the literal sense, there is impressed upon the Scriptures a portrait of Christ which belongs to their overall literary genre. Thus, to explain what is meant when one says that "the kerygma cannot replace the mystery of the God-Man," we need to distinguish systematically between the literal sense and the spiritual sense of the object of our faith. Bultmann and his predecessors in the 'history of religions' school have wreaked havoc with their distinction between the 'historical Jesus' and the 'Christ of faith,' by placing out of focus a distinction that really exists, not in the Person of Jesus Christ, but in the two levels of meaning in the Scriptures. The mystery that surrounds the spiritual sense could indeed be described as a "world of extra-conceptual realities," but always keeping in mind that they *are* realities and that they are to a degree extra-conceptual, not because they are pre-conceptual as Bultmann maintains, but because the essence of God exceeds any conceptual ability of the human mind.

25. At this point, we must note the importance of the *continuum of extra-mental reality*, by which we mean that the supernatural realities that constitute the object of Christian faith must be recognized to be in *the same continuum of reality* as are the realities known from natural experience. Certainly supernatural realities are in a higher order of reality, and the reality of God is infinitely above any created reality, but they are in the same continuum of reality in the sense that they come within a univocal concept of reality and within a single universe of discourse. The neo-patristic exegete knows that, in his scientific awareness, he stands face to face with the reality of God and of the entire supernatural order, and this awareness of God and of the supernatural as real objects in a univocal sense has its

role in the scientific historical medium of thought with which he studies the biblical text. Just as Catholic faith is a belief in the reality of its object, so does neo-patristic exegesis presuppose in faith that the "Gospel genre" is a reality-genre, not a genre of religious fiction. Consequently, whatever is recounted in the Gospels is assumed to be historically true unless in particular cases it can seriously be demonstrated that a passage does not report historical fact. Moreover, neo-patristic exegesis does not uncritically accept such methodological presuppositions of Bultmann and others as: that none of our four Gospels reports eye-witness accounts of the deeds and teaching of Jesus; that our four Gospels arose directly out of Greek Christianity; that the 'essential historicity' of the four Gospels cannot be assumed by the exegete. Neo-patristic exegesis goes back to study how these assumptions are thought to have been demonstrated, and it looks for mistakes and unwarranted assumptions in the reasoning process that brought them into vogue. Another unfounded assumption of Bultmann that is sometimes used unwittingly even by Catholic form-critics is that the kind of literary form found in the Gospels "is a sociological concept and not an aesthetic one," inasmuch as, he says in agreement with Dibelius, the literature of primitive Christianity is "essentially 'popular,'"since it had not reached the intellectual level of an aesthetic medium. Looking at this assumption in the neo-patristic framework, we find that Bultmann is basically attributing what he has identified as units or forms in the Gospel narratives to the action of a religious instinct that is pre-conceptual in its nature and therefore predictable according to some psychological law that the form-critic utilizes. As Bultmann puts it, "every literary category has its *Sitz im Leben* (Gunkel), whether it be worship in its different forms, or work, or hunting, or war. The *Sitz im Leben* is not, however, an individual historical event, but a typical situation or occupation in the life of the community" (*HST*, 4). This outrageous assumption, which traces back to the philosophy of Émile Durkheim, is refuted on a theoretical level in the neo-patristic hermeneutical framework and on a practical level in the neo-patristic exegesis of the Gospels. Rudolf Bultmann was a total modernist in his idea of "modern man," and Ugo Lattanzi claimed that Bultmann's notion of the creative Christian community was owing in part to Alfred Loisy's modernist attribution of the Gospels ultimately to the unfolding of a blind religious instinct.

26. It is also to be noted that Bultmann openly uses circular reasoning in his form-critical analyses. He declares: "It is essential to realize that form-criticism is fundamentally indistinguishable from all historical work in this,

that it has to move in a circle. The forms of the literary tradition must be used to establish the influences operating in the life of the community, and the life of the community must be used to render the forms themselves intelligible. There is no method of regulating or even prescribing the necessary and mutual relationships of both these processes, no rule to say where the start must be made." But, for neo-patristic research, this assumption of Bultmann is contrary to correct historical methodology, since Bultmann thus ends up time and again in seeming to prove what he has merely assumed, and falsely assumed. Thus, having merely assumed, on the basis of an *a priori* exclusion of everything supernatural, that Jesus could not have had any real divine power, he reasons that the 'miracle stories' are all imaginary inventions attributable to the felt needs of the religious instinct. Having merely assumed that there cannot be any real prophecy of future events, he concludes that the prophecies of Jesus were formulated after the event by the Christian community and placed on the lips of Jesus. Having merely assumed that no man can ever rise from the dead, he concludes that the Resurrection of Jesus was invented by his followers after his death. The root of Bultmann's error lies in an illicit transfer of statistical laws of natural science to the realm of history, where they do not apply, at least by way of exclusion of the unusual or of the supernatural. The neo-patristic approach seeks to formulate and use the rules of valid historical method, in the realization, however, that no adequate theory of history has ever been published, and that, consequently, Catholic exegetes are operating without a fully formulated set of principles of historical method.[33] Neo-patristic interpreters are aware of this need and are ready to join with others in developing a full-blown science of history which will serve as a basis for a more correct understanding of the historical sense of the Sacred Scriptures.

---

33 Father Marie-Joseph Lagrange, founder of the École Biblique of Jerusalem in 1890, was the first to make a notable attempt to bring the historical critical method into use by Catholic exegetes. In his *La méthode historique surtout à propos de l'Ancien Testament* (Paris, 1903) he attempted to show "how the historical critical method could be used in biblical interpretation without any detriment to Christian faith and Catholic life" (J.A. Fitzmyer, *The Biblical Commission's Document "The Interpretation of the Bible in the Church,"* (Pontifical Biblical Institute: Rome, 1995), 154. In this and other works, Father Lagrange used with a certain moderation and in avoidance of the violation of Catholic doctrine the method of Hermann Gunkel and other historical critics. However, in this work of "historical method," he did not undertake the preliminary task of determining from a Catholic point of view what exactly is history and what is historical method, and so he used the method of Gunkel and others without the benefit of a clear idea of what he was doing, and this has been largely the case with Catholic historical critical exegetes ever since.

27. Looking more closely at the scientific medium of the neo-patristic method, we find a two-tiered structure, made up of objects of faith and objects of reason. On the level of faith there are the revealed truths of Christianity which enable the perception of the spiritual sense of the Scriptures, visible, at least inchoatively, from the first moment of observation, and not merely after the Scriptures have already been processed and interpreted by source-criticism and form-criticism. Historically, source-criticism and form-criticism came out of the minds of liberal exegetes who had inherited the tradition of an absolute separation of faith from reason and of a subsequent usurpation of the realm of faith by falsely based reason. In neo-patristic exegesis, the reality of the objects of faith in univocal continuity with the reality of the objects of reason is a prime feature of the hermeneutic framework of thought, and it is of supreme importance to the neo-patristic interpreter to refute any assumption that the genuine objects of faith are not real in a univocal sense. Just as reality is the all-embracing concept of the neo-patristic approach as a scientific method, so the real past and the real present are its universal objects as a method of historical science. As a historical approach, the real present through which and in terms of which the neo-patristic interpreter views the past is generically his entire apparatus of understanding and specifically is his knowledge of how the real past has become the real present. Thus, the scientific medium in which the neo-patristic interpreter views the historical narratives of the Scriptures is the historical present, which is an objective framework, and not the mere experience of a knowing subject. And so, with respect to Bultmann's synthesis of presuppositions, in the neo-patristic hermeneutic framework, 'time as flux' vs. 'time as now' become the historical past vs. the historical present; the assumed pre-conceptual mentality of the New Testament writers becomes the un-self-criticized mentality of the Bultmannian form-critic, which in turn is critically reformulated in the consciously self-appropriated scientific medium of the neo-patristic approach; the *Historie* of Bultmann becomes the remote historical objects under study, while the *Geschichte* of Bultmann becomes the historical medium of thought as historical; the *Realität* of Bultmann becomes the reality presented in the historical accounts of Sacred Scripture, while his *Wirklichkeit* becomes the understanding of that reality in its relation to the notion of reality in the mind of the interpreter, including his knowledge of present and of supra-temporal realities and his patristic and neo-patristic frame of reference. The neo-patristic interpreter is aware that he is face-to-face with the effects of God's presence, and he knows that this presence is real; the neo-patristic

interpreter knows that God has acted in human history, that He continues to act, and that He will act even more dramatically in the future. The neo-Patristic interpreter does not and will not prescind from this awareness in some prior phase of examining the text of Sacred Scripture.

28. Neo-patristic exegesis allows for all of the refinements of valid textual criticism. It also allows for study into the diachronic formation of the biblical accounts, and it can gain insights from this study, but it opposes the stripping method of form-criticism whereby the form-critic seems to go back into earlier stages of the Gospel tradition by simply stripping away elements that do not meet the criteria of unproved *a priori* presuppositions, such as: to start out from the assumption that the accounts in the Scriptures are not historical; or to strip away miracles and prophecies as being not original in the life of Jesus on the ground that they could not really have happened; to end up with certain verses or phrases that are called an "earlier stage" of the accounts, whereas they are actually present in the "final stage." In brief, any source-critic who disregards the serious historical intent of the Gospel writers, the divine activity in the life of Jesus, and the inspiration of the Holy Spirit in the writing of the inspired text is not working with a full bag of tools.

29. The spiritual sense. The PBC's document of 1993 defines the spiritual sense as "the meaning expressed by the biblical texts when read, under the influence of the Holy Spirit, in the context of the paschal mystery of Christ and of the new life which flows from it," and, the document avers, "this context truly exists" (*IBC*, IIB.2). And, with reference to the spiritual sense, the *Catechism of the Catholic Church* says: "Thanks to the unity of God's plan, not only the text of Scripture, but also the realities and events about which it speaks can be signs" (*CCC*, 117). Neo-patristic exegesis sees both historical and meta-historical aspects in the relationship between the Old Testament and the New Testament. On the historical level, the New Testament can be viewed as a kind of relative historical present through which the events of the Old Testament can be viewed. But the Bible contains also moral and prophetic aspects that transcend the historical arena. The Fathers of the Church, along with other early ecclesiastical writers and medieval theologians, saw meanings and patterns of meaning in the text of the Bible that illustrate in various ways what is called the allegory of Christ and of his Church. This pattern of meaning is taken to be intended by the Holy Spirit and to be really and objectively in the text, even though it does not add any essential element that is not expressed somewhere in the literal sense of the Scriptures. It is an allegory

inasmuch as it is a communication of meaning that results from an extended metaphorical use of words, but it is not fictional. Neo-patristic exegesis seeks to clarify the kinds of meaning that are represented in the inspired text and their precise relationship to one another, in continuance of the work begun especially by Thomas Aquinas. The false distinction between the 'Jesus of history' vs. the 'Christ of faith' which is fundamental to liberal form-critical analysis of the Gospels, appears in another way in the neo-patristic framework as the distinction between the history of Jesus and the allegory of Christ. The literal sense of the biblical text is written partly in the historical genre and partly in other genres, all of which are considered capable of having both a literal meaning and an additional spiritual meaning by way of prefigurement or metaphor. The central figure of the spiritual sense is the allegory of Christ and of his Church, which is known essentially from its expression in the literal sense of the sacred text and is discovered by relating this to what is said in other passages. Thus, there is found to be impressed upon the bare literal expression of the text a portrait of Christ and of his Church, in which the divinity of Christ stands out in a way that is not visible to mere natural perception.

30. The neo-patristic exegete can start almost anywhere in his search for meanings on the level of the four senses of the sacred text. Examples are abundant in the writings of the Fathers and of the medieval theologians, but they often need to be rediscovered to the extent that either they have been buried by the neglect of exegetes over recent centuries or they have been undermined by incorrect expositions of the literal sense. A good place to begin is in the text of the Gospels, upon which commentaries of the Fathers exist, whose spiritual exegesis is collected in works such as the *Catena aurea* of Thomas Aquinas along with his commentaries on Sacred Scripture. But the neo-patristic study of medieval commentaries does not take place apart from a prior or simultaneous analysis of the commentaries of modern biblical scholars. Having presented elsewhere some examples of neo-patristic exegesis,[34] as a new example I shall make here a comparison of the statements of Jesus in John 14:6 and 10:7. The three main steps in the process will be: on the level of the literal sense, to examine two celebrated historical critical interpretations; then on the level of the spiritual sense to examine the interpretations of the Fathers of the Church, and, finally, to locate these interpretations in the framework of the neo-patristic approach.

---

34 Cf. J.F. McCarthy, "A Neo-patristic Return to the First Four Days of Creation," in *Living Tradition,* numbers 45–50 (March 1993 to January 1994).

31. In John 14:6, Jesus says: "I am the way and the truth and the life." Rudolf Bultmann[35] interprets these words in keeping with his own Heideggerian understanding of existence and faith, and of the mythology which he thinks is at the root of John's Gospel, and this interpretation can be dealt with on the level of Bultmann's presuppositions. But let us look briefly at what Bultmann says. He sees this statement about the way, the truth, and the life as having been placed on the lips of Jesus by the Hellenistic Christian community in order to demythologize to an extent the question of Thomas in the preceding verse: "Lord, we do not know where you are going: how can we know the way?" To Bultmann this question is typical of the mythological outlook, "which can only conceive of the goal and the way as things within the world."[36] We have shown above that by "the world" he means things that are in the continuum of reality that is first recognized through the senses and is distinguished from dream worlds. Bultmann sees this statement in verse 6 as declaring that "the way and the goal are not to be separated as they are in mythological thinking," and he adds: "In the myth the redemption has become embodied in a cosmic event, and therefore—contrary to the intention of the myth—it is conceived as an intra-mundane event, as a divine history, which takes place apart from the existence of man, who is referred to it as the guarantee of his future."[37] Hence, for Bultmann, "just as Jesus is the way, in that he is the goal, so he is also the goal, in that he is the way." And again, "The discovery of this truth is not something established once and for all, at men's disposal, such as could be communicated in 'condensed form' like a truth of science," since "this truth does not exist as a doctrine. ..."[38] From a neo-patristic standpoint, here as elsewhere Bultmann artfully eliminates all self-standing objectivity from the words of Jesus and he even eliminates the historical truth of the words themselves.

32. As a Catholic historical critic, Father Raymond Brown, regarding John 14:6, traces "the background from which this concept of Jesus as 'the way' was drawn" to a chain of usage, and as his studied answer he says: "We suggest that John 14:6 reflects this whole chain of usage of imagery of 'the way' originating in the Old Testament, modified by sectarian Jewish

35 Bultmann, *The Gospel of John* (Oxford: Basil Blackwell, 1971), 604–607 (translated from the 1964 printing of *Das Evangelium des Johannes* with the Supplement of 1966).

36 Bultmann, *The Gospel of John*, 603.

37 Bultmann, *The Gospel of John*, 605.

38 Bultmann, *The Gospel of John*, 606.

thought illustrated at Qumran, and finally adopted by the Christian community as a self-designation. It is not unusual for the Johannine Jesus to take terminology once applied to Israel (and subsequently adopted by the Christian community) and to apply it to himself. ... The imagery of the sheepfold and vineyard, applied in the Old Testament to Israel and in the Synoptic Gospels to the kingdom of God, is applied in John to Jesus, the shepherd and the vine. The same process seems to be at work in calling Jesus rather than the Christian community 'the way.'"[39] In his exegesis, Brown finds that the Christian community here has Jesus presenting Himself, not as "a moral guide," but as "the only avenue of salvation," inasmuch as Jesus is *the truth*, the only revelation of the Father who is the goal of the journey, and He is also the way "in the sense that he is *the life*," and "life comes through the truth," because "those who believe in Jesus as the incarnate revelation of the Father (and that is what 'truth' means) receive the gift of life." Brown thus concludes: "Bultmann is correct in insisting that when a person comes to Jesus for the truth, it is not simply a matter of learning and going away. Rather, one must belong to the truth. Thus, not only at the moment of first belief but always Jesus remains the way." [40]

33. The neo-patristic source-seeker, in looking for the sources, not only of the New Testament preaching, but also of historical critical teaching, will find the thinking of Bultmann to be one source of Brown's thinking in his exposition of John 14:6, and Catholic faith to be another. Assuredly, Brown does not accept Bultmann's conclusions indiscriminately, but neither does he counteract effectively the deleterious implications of Bultmann's methodological presuppositions. For Bultmann, Jesus could not have said that He is "the way, the truth, and the life," because Jesus was only a man, and a very naive and uneducated man at that, whose sociological environment would not have enabled Him to say such a thing. But since, for Brown, Jesus is both God and man, why does he have to search for a source of these words apart from Jesus Himself? There seems to be an unresolved conflict of methodology here that prevents Brown from arriving at a clear exposition of the text. For Bultmann, as we have just seen, to imagine, as Brown does, that the Father is "the goal of the journey" is purely mythological thinking, as is the belief that "Jesus is the incarnate revelation of the Father." Hence, Brown, in not defending the full historical truth of the words of Jesus and in agreeing that "Bultmann is

---

39 R. Brown, *The Gospel According to John* (New York: Doubleday, 1970 [*The Anchor Bible*, vols. 29 and 29A]), 628–629.

40 Brown, *The Gospel According to John*, 630–631.

correct" in how to come to Jesus for the truth, is not facing the devastating import of Bultmann's reasoning. From the neo-patristic viewpoint, Jesus is the Word of God Incarnate, the Second Person of the Blessed Trinity, and "the truth" means to recognize this. For Bultmann, a person "comes to Jesus for the truth," to use Brown's phraseology, when a person has his own purely subjective experience of existential self-authenticity, so that to "belong to the truth" means to have gained possession of oneself in an existential moment that must be "repeated and ever repeated again." Brown is assuredly not agreeing with this, but neither does he seem to be able to handle in a sufficiently independent manner Bultmann's teaching on the subject.

34. The neo-patristic interpreter looks for light in the patristic exegetical tradition. Thomas Aquinas, at John 14:6 in his *Catena aurea*, quotes Augustine as saying: "The Word of God, who with the Father is truth and life, in assuming (the nature of) man, became the way. Walk through the man and you will arrive at God." And he quotes John Chrysostom to the effect that, in saying that 'no one can come to the Father except through me,' Jesus "makes Himself equal to the One who begot Him." St. Thomas, in his commentary at John 14:6, goes to the heart of our discussion where he says that truth is the *adaequatio rei ad intellectum* (the conformity of what is conceived in the mind with what actually exists outside the mind), and the divine Word of God is truth itself, to whom everything created, in order to be true, must conform. Thus, says St. Thomas, Christ is the way according to his humanity and both the truth and the life according to his divinity, and he quotes several verses of Sacred Scripture to confirm this. The central issue for us in this discussion on the level of the literal sense is whether one realizes that the idea of Jesus being both God and man conforms to external reality univocally understood. Bultmann's opinion completely fails this test, because he does not see the reality of what is being said about Jesus in the Gospel of John; for Bultmann the divinity of Jesus is a pure figment of the imagination. Hence, Bultmann's approach does not enable any real understanding of the verse. The teaching implied in this verse about the way, the truth, and the life is that the followers of Jesus are called by God to move along a real path toward a real destination in the next life, a real future life that will be a continuation of this life in the same continuum of reality, even though the circumstances will be different. Christian faith requires us to believe in this reality.

35. Neo-patristic exegesis is interested also in examining this verse in the framework of the four senses. It appears that, beyond the question of

reality that is resolved on the level of the literal sense, the three spiritual senses can also be discerned. The "truth" relates to the allegory of Christ and his Church; the "way" relates to the tropology of the soul and its virtues; and the "life" pertains to the anagogy of the Most Holy Trinity and the future life. St. Thomas in the same place quotes Theophylact in this regard: "And so, when you are being active, Christ becomes your way; when you persist in contemplation, Christ is made your truth. Life is attached to action and to contemplation, for it is fitting to be on the move and to preach about the world to come." For the neo-patristic exegete, once the role and mission of Jesus Christ have been established in the literal sense, Jesus the truth reflects the allegorical sense, Jesus the way reflects the tropological sense, and Jesus the life reflects the anagogical sense. These are three patterns that appear over and over again in the Scriptures and which, in being related to themselves and to one another, produce understanding in the believer. To learn the metaphors by which the divinity of Christ is presented in the Scriptures is to come to know Jesus better. To perceive the way in which these metaphors impact upon the soul of the believer by an extension of the allegory to the powers of the soul, is to know better how to walk toward Jesus. To perceive how eternal life and the vision of the Blessed Trinity are presented in the Scriptures by an extension of the allegory of Christ and his Church is to make use of the beginning of infused contemplation that is instilled in the soul at Baptism.

36. One procedure of the neo-patristic method is to compare words, verses, and passages of Sacred Scripture with one another. In John 10:7–10 Jesus presents himself as "the *door* of the sheep. "Jesus, therefore, said to them again, 'Amen, amen, I say to you, I am the door of the sheep (v. 7). All who came before me are thieves and robbers, but the sheep did not heed them (v. 8). I am the door: if anyone enters through me, he will be saved, and he will go in and go out and will find pasture (v. 9). The thief comes only to steal and to kill and to destroy; I have come that they may have life and may have it abundantly (v. 10).'" Rudolf Bultmann sees no logical homogeneity in this passage or in the entire narrative of the Good Shepherd (verses 1–39), which he reorganizes in accordance with his studied conclusion that verses 1–5, 8 and 10, 11–15a, and 27–30 comprised "the source on which the complex is based," while the remaining verses were composed by the unknown person whom he calls the "evangelist" or by the "editor" who finished the passage.[41] He sees a certain inconsistency in the presentation of Jesus as being "the door

---

41 Cf. Bultmann, *The Gospel of John*, 360.

of the sheep," since, in the parable in verses 1–5, Jesus is the *shepherd* who goes in and out of the door together with his sheep. In his view, verses 7–10 "give the impression of being an explanatory gloss" placed on the lips of the Johannine Jesus by the (unidentified) evangelist, who was using a Gnostic source for his discourse about the Good Shepherd).[42] Characteristic of his style, Bultmann gives no credence to the possibility of allegory in the passage, even though he is aware that others have explained the order of the passage in terms of allegory.[43]

37. Raymond Brown finds that the metaphorical use of the word *gate* can be interpreted either as the gate through which the shepherd approaches the sheep (verse 8) or as Jesus being the gate through which the sheep pass to salvation.[44] According to his opinion, the material in John 10:7–30 "consists of allegorical explanations," some of which "may represent a later expansion of Jesus' remarks." As with the explanations of certain parables in the Synoptic Gospels, he says, "So too in John 10, while not all the explanations of 7 ff. need come from the one time or the one situation, there is no reason to rule out the possibility that we may find among them the traces of Jesus' own simple allegorical explanation of the parables in 10: 1–5."[45] And he agrees with Johannes Schneider that the explanations of three terms, *gate, shepherd,* and *sheep* accounts for the structure of this entire passage.[46] With reference to verses 7–10, Brown does not refute Bultmann's reasoning that "I am the door of the sheep" is a gloss on an original (Gnostic) parable," but instead he adds a doubt of his own as to whether the "thieves" in verse 8 are to be placed in the same category as the "thief" in verse 10, since the latter thief "is an instance of the tendency of the historical enemies of Jesus' ministry to become more general figures of evil as the gospel message is preached in a later period on a worldwide scale."[47] Finally, Brown contrasts the simple allegory of these Gospel explanations with "the elaborate patristic allegories built around John 10," regarding which he notes that "Cornelius aLapide, that 17th century mirror of patristic exegesis, tells us that *the flock* is the Church, *the owner* of the flock is the Father, *the gatekeeper* is the Holy Spirit, etc."

---

42 Cf. Bultmann, *The Gospel of John,* 359.

43 Cf. Bultmann, *The Gospel of John,* 360, note 2.

44 Brown, *The Gospel According to John,* 393–394.

45 Brown, *The Gospel According to John,* 391.

46 Brown, ibid.

47 Brown, *The Gospel According to John,* 395.

And Brown concludes: "It is this type of developed allegory that is an anachronism on Jesus' lips."[48]

38. For the neo-patristic interpreter, putting words on the lips of Jesus is a serious matter. In his exegesis of the parable of the Good Shepherd, Bultmann allows not even a trace of origin in the teaching of Jesus, because he believes that Jesus was too simple and too uneducated a man to have thought up such an idea, especially as regards the divinity which is contained in it, and he sees nothing in the sociological environment (*Sitz im Leben*) of the life of Jesus which might have drawn it forth. Therefore, he ascribes the origin of the parable to a Gnostic milieu in the later Hellenistic world, and he conjectures the source of this parable, as of much of St. John's Gospel, to have been a Gnostic document expounding the myth of a divine redeemer. Bultmann assigns the 'I-saying' in John 10:7–10 to an evangelist who was "demythologizing" the Gnostic myth. Brown, as a Roman Catholic, knows that Jesus was and is the God-Man, but he does not use this knowledge effectively in his exegesis of this passage, nor does he undertake an explicit refutation of Bultmann's exegesis. Instead, Brown leaves the question open by vaguely attributing the Gospel explanations of the parable to the "time" and the "situation" (*Sitz im Leben*), and by merely allowing for the "possibility that we may find among (the explanations in John 10:7 ff.) the traces of Jesus' own simple allegorical explanation of the parables in 10:1–5." Bultmann, on the basis of his unbelief in the divinity of Jesus, has a logical reason for excluding the factual historicity of the words of Jesus in this passage, but Brown shows no logical reason for his doubting that Jesus spoke all of these words as they read. Brown, of course, does not accept Bultmann's theory of a supposed "Gnostic Revelatory Discourse" portraying a Gnostic "redeemer myth" as being the original source of many of the discourses of Jesus in St. John's Gospel; he looks rather for the source in "Old Testament speculation about personified Wisdom" or in the thinking of sectarian Judaism; but why should there be any other ultimate source than the lips of Jesus Himself? Brown does not find that the dependence of St. John's Gospel on a "postulated early Oriental Gnosticism" has been disproved,[49] and he defends Bultmann's conclusions about a dependence

---

48 Brown, *The Gospel According to John*, 390–391.

49 "In summation, one cannot claim that the dependence of John on a postulated early Oriental Gnosticism has been disproved, but the hypothesis remains very tenuous and in many ways unnecessary. We hope to show below that OT speculation about personified Wisdom and the vocabulary and thought patterns of sectarian Judaism, like the Qumran community, go a long way toward filling in the background of Johannine

of St. John's Gospel upon an alleged "redeemer myth" against the charge of circular reasoning. Thus, in speaking of "Jesus' own simple allegorical explanation," Brown does not establish a sufficiently clear difference of his view from Bultmann's methodological presupposition that Jesus was too 'simple' a man to have been able to give such an elaborate explanation. And Bultmann's circular reasoning needs to be refuted, not defended. To the neo-patristic interpreter, it is absolutely essential not to leave Bultmann's "redeemer myth" theory hanging around as a possibility in the background of St. John's Gospel or of any of the Gospels, because it is a false accusation against the reality of the object of faith and against the historical truth of Christianity. I think that Bultmann's Gnostic myth theory is disproved by the fact that there was no such myth before the time of Jesus. This kind of Gnosticism is a heresy corrupting the teaching of Jesus.

39. The neo-patristic exegete, like the Patristic exegete, has in his hermeneutical framework an active awareness that Jesus is the God-Man who speaks in his own name and who is described and quoted in the Gospels by evangelists writing under the inspiration of the Holy Spirit. Thomas Aquinas, in the *Catena aurea* and in his commentary on the Gospel according to St. John, relying on the preceding commentaries of the Fathers of the Church, provides the basis of a neo-patristic explanation of the teaching of Jesus about the Good Shepherd and about the "door of the sheep." As to why Jesus used metaphors and spoke in parables, he gives two reasons: so that the mysteries of the Kingdom of God would remain unknown to the unworthy and so that the worthy would be drawn to seek an understanding of them. Aquinas points out that the passage about the Good Shepherd is logically constructed in this way: it explains the three elements that are presented in the opening two verses of the parable: the door of the sheepfold, the thieves who do not enter through the door, and the good shepherd. Thus, on the level of sources, Raymond Brown credits Johannes Schneider, writing in 1947, with an explanation that was clearly given by Thomas Aquinas in the thirteenth century and even earlier than that by the Fathers of the Church. Aquinas quotes several interpretations of the "door of the sheepfold" given by the Fathers. John Chrysostom says that the door represents Sacred Scripture (Col. 4:3), because through the Sacred Scriptures the faithful have access

---

theological vocabulary and expression. Since these proposed sources of influence are known to have existed, and the existence of Bultmann's proto-Mandean Gnostic source remains dubious, we have every reason to give them preference" (Brown, *The Gospel according to John*, p. LVI).

to the knowledge of God (Rom. 1:2), because Sacred Scripture protects the spiritual life of the faithful (Jn. 5:39), and because the truth of Scripture keeps heresies away from the faithful (2Tim. 3:16). On the other hand, Augustine says that the door is Jesus Christ (Apoc. 4:1; Rom. 5:1; Acts 4:12), which can be entered only by putting away pride and imitating the humility of Jesus (Matt. 11:29). Hence, Jesus is both the Shepherd and the Door, and He enters through Himself in the sense that He is truth itself, so that as man he enters through Himself as God. Gregory the Great distinguishes, in the metaphor of the door, between those going into the Church on earth and those exiting the Church on earth to enter the Church triumphant in Heaven.

40. Contemporary neo-patristic exegesis builds on the commentaries of Thomas Aquinas and others, utilizing a more differentiated hermeneutical framework and a more fully systematic approach. It asks what are the elements of the allegorical framework and how they relate to the literal sense and to each other. The neo-patristic method does not look for subjectively based spiritual meanings, but rather for spiritual meanings that are rooted objectively in the inspired text and are discernible objectively in the neo-patristic exegetical framework. Accordingly, in briefly surveying the exegesis of the Fathers cited in the preceding paragraph, I make the following observations. The bare meaning of the words of the parable is its literal sense, while the application of the words is the spiritual sense. Jesus Himself gives us the basic spiritual meaning of the parable in verses 1–5 by his explanation in verses 7 and 9 ("I am the door of the sheep") and in verse 11 ("I am the good shepherd"). Thus, as Aquinas points out, Jesus is the Good Shepherd, the sheep are the faithful who live in the grace of God (Ps. 94 [95] 7, and the sheepfold is the congregation of the faithful (Mich. 2:12). The explanation of these elements in the literal sense of verses 7, 9, and 10 is a Scriptural basis of the allegory of Christ and his Church which afterwards can be discovered as a pattern in other places in Sacred Scripture. It is only by seeing Jesus as the shepherd and his followers as the sheep that one can understand this parable at all. Only by knowing who Jesus really is, namely, the Second Person of the Blessed Trinity having become incarnate in this man Jesus in order to lead his sheep through the present life and into the next life, can anyone really "understand" the parable. In the parable, Jesus, the Good Shepherd of the sheep, "goes before them, and the sheep follow Him, because they know his voice" (verse 4). Thus, the first and most essential response to Rudolf Bultmann is that, when Jesus says "I

am the door of the sheep" (verse 7), his sheep recognize that this really
is his voice and not a voice invented by some merely human member
of a later Christian community and fictitiously placed on his lips, for
whatever religious purpose such a member might have had. Bultmann's
theory of 'knee-jerk' responses to a religious instinct, responses that are
characterized as too pre-conceptual to be accused of dishonesty, does not
stand up under objective criticism.

41. In the neo-patristic framework, one can discern a parallel between
the explanation by Jesus of the elements in the parable of the Good
Shepherd and the teaching of Jesus that He is "the way and the truth
and the life" (Jn. 14:6). When John Chrysostom sees the "door of the
sheepfold" (verse 1) as representing Sacred Scripture, he is alluding to
an extension of the allegory of Christ in the form of the allegory of the
word, a metaphorical pattern spread out on two levels: the lower allegory
of the revealed word and of the two Testaments, and the higher allegory
of the uncreated Word who is consubstantial with the Father. Jesus
Christ, in his humanity as presented in Sacred Scripture, leads people
into the fold of the Church on earth, and, in his divinity, he receives
them into the happiness of the Beatific Vision. In the allegory of Christ,
as Augustine remarks, Jesus Himself is also the doorkeeper, because Jesus
is the dispenser of his grace (Eph. 2:5). But, according to the allegory of
the word, as Chrysostom tells us, first Moses and then the other inspired
writers can be considered doorkeepers in that they announce Christ and
open the minds of their readers to Christ. Yet even more, says Augustine,
is the Holy Spirit the doorkeeper, because it is by the infused virtue of
faith and the gifts of knowledge and understanding of the Holy Spirit
that minds are opened to Christ, and, we might add, because the Holy
Spirit is also the principal Author of the whole of Sacred Scripture.

42. As Cornelius aLapide brings out in his great commentary,[50] the
true shepherd is the one who is indicated by the authority of the Scriptures,
namely Jesus, and Jesus presents Himself in the Scriptures by his own divine
authority as well. That Jesus presents Himself also as "the door of the sheep"
(verse 7) introduces a tropological aspect to the parable, inasmuch as the
movements of the sheep in and out of the doorway are implied, because

---

50 Cornelius aLapide, *Commentarii in Scripturam sacram*, vol. 8, *Expositio in quatuor
Evangelia* (Lyons, 1864); Eng. trans., *The Great Commentary of Cornelius aLapide* (John
Hodges: London, 1887), at John 10. The quotations and references given in paragraphs
39–42 of this essay are taken from the commentaries of Thomas Aquinas and Cornelius
aLapide, as indicated.

tropology regards the response of the believing subject to objective revealed truth. Augustine speculates that to go in through the doorway means to do well in one's spirit according to the inner man, while to go out through the doorway means to do well in one's exterior actions, and that is to enter the sheepfold through contemplation and to exit through good actions. John Chrysostom sees the door as providing safety and freedom for those who adhere to Christ or preaching the good news of the Gospel to those inside the Church and those outside, or joy both in conversion of heart to Christ and in suffering persecution. The neo-patristic exegete interests himself in finding how tropological interpretations like this fit into the framework of the four senses and in sifting out applications that are not objectively implied in the inspired text. This research requires a differentiated idea of what is meant, for instance in the present case, by the contrast between the inner man and the outer man, between contemplative prayer and good exterior actions, between communion with others in the Church and dialogue with those outside the Church. But the tropology of the individual soul is based upon the allegory of Christ and his Church, since every true follower is a member of the Mystical Body of Christ. Cornelius aLapide sees that Gregory the Great's explanation of the "door of the sheep" as the entering of people first into the Church on earth and then going out of the same into the bliss of Heaven is a transition to the anagogy of the Four Last Things (Jn. 10:10b). Augustine also, on the level of anagogy, sees Jesus, the Good Shepherd, going ahead of his sheep by rising from the dead as the firstborn of the resurrected. The insight underlying these explanations of the Fathers is that to understand the parable means to see how the elements in it apply to the Kingdom of God. In the words of St. Augustine: "He enters the sheepfold through the door who enters through Christ. And he enters through Christ who thinks and preaches the truth about Him who is at one and the same time the Creator and the Redeemer of the human race, and who keeps what he preaches." In conclusion, if modern Scripture scholars will look more attentively at their own mental framework of interpretation and then at the framework used implicitly by the Fathers of the Church, they will understand better, not only the allegorical, tropological, and anagogical senses of the inspired text, but its literal sense as well.

Chapter 5

Timely Reflections on the Science of Historical Theology

Part I: The Nature and Meaning of Science

1. In 1976 I published a book entitled *The Science of Historical Theology: Elements of a Definition*, as the principal part of a doctoral thesis in biblical theology. The purpose of that study was to determine whether there is a science of historical theology and what would be its function. The study revolved around the nature and meaning of the three elements of this discipline: science, history, and sacred theology. A second aim was to show that the form-critical method of Rudolf Bultmann is not a scientific procedure. In the meanwhile, there have been two outstanding developments toward the advancement of the science of historical theology: a published lecture given by Joseph Cardinal Ratzinger in 1988 in New York City, titled "Biblical Interpretation in Crisis," and an outstanding intervention by Joseph Ratzinger as Pope Benedict XVI at the Synod of Bishops of 2008 on the dualism prevalent in Catholic scholarship. The following article presents an updated review of my thesis originally published in 1976.

2. Science in general. The question immediately arises as to whether there is or could be any such thing as a "science of historical theology." To answer this question, let us begin by asking ourselves what science is. Empirical scientists commonly have difficulty in providing a precise definition of their discipline. But *Webster's New College Dictionary* (2007) defines "science" as "systematized knowledge derived from observation, study, and experimentation, carried on in order to determine the nature

or principles of what is being studied," especially as "concerned with establishing and systematizing facts, principles, and methods, as by experiments and hypotheses," or as "the systematized knowledge of nature and the physical world." Note that this definition of science does not include as sciences the areas of philosophy and theology as they were so understood in earlier times. According to *Wikipedia* (A.D., 2015): "In modern usage however, 'science' most often refers to a way of pursuing knowledge, rather than the knowledge itself. It is also often restricted to those branches of study that seek to explain the phenomena of the material universe." *Wikipedia* notes also that, since the nineteenth century the word "science" has become increasingly associated with the scientific method itself, "as a disciplined way to study the natural world," and "it has also continued to be used in a broad sense to denote reliable and teachable knowledge about a topic" such as social science and political science. In these definitions it is always implied that scientific knowledge is certified knowledge, that is, knowledge that we can depend on to be factual and true, but the scope of its knowledge is now very much restricted from what it included in earlier times and what is still included in Catholic philosophical and theological tradition.

3. Let me begin my explanation by giving a more comprehensive definition of "science" as "the knowledge of reality as such," or as "the knowledge of the real as real ."[1] This definition recognizes that science is an expression of knowledge within human consciousness and that science is in some way knowledge of reality. It also brings out that the door to science is opened by the recognition within human consciousness of the notion of reality, leading normally to an ever deeper understanding of the meaning of reality. It follows that science is mediate knowledge in that scientific thinkers, inasmuch as they are thinking scientifically, do not admit into their thinking anything that they know is not contained within the focus of reality.[2] Even the bare notion of reality on the level of common sense provides a viewpoint for the recognition of truth. From this approach it seems obvious that knowledge acquired by the use of the

---

1 In the standard terminology of Scholastic philosophy, "science" is defined as "a system of demonstrated conclusions," but these definitions assume that the things are real things and that the causes are real causes and also that its conclusions are derived from solid reasoning. Therefore, the concept of reality plays in science a fundamental role (cf. Vincent Edward Smith, *The General Science of Nature* [Bruce Publishing Company, Milwaukee, WI, 1958]), pp. 3–7.

2 See McCarthy, *The Science...*, pp. 34–36.

"scientific method" must have some identity and meaning of its own, and that any textbook of empirical science embodies a doctrine, whether its writers call it that or not.

4. Common Sense. In contemporary parlance the expression "common sense" is used negatively by some to denote a naïve point of view as contrasted with the outlook of empirical science, and it is used positively by others to represent "a set of attitudes and assumptions presumed to be held by plain men who are untutored in a conscious philosophy."[3] In its essence I would define common sense as "the right reason of sound judgment not involving technical concepts."[4] By this concept, common sense, or "common science," is the general and initial phase from which technical science springs; it is the source of self-evident and incontrovertible truths and the rough instrument of realistic thinking. The basic principles of common sense are intrinsic to all science; they cannot be flatly contradicted or substantially left behind by any truly valid science. Specialized science, in its specialization, tends to lose sight of the total picture which common sense retains. What is lost from the field of view by closed specialized science includes those areas of realistic thought which are capable of developing into other specialized sciences as well as the area which is the ground of that wisdom which is the power of the disciplined mind to keep in check functions of consciousness occupied by emotion, volition, and the subjectivity of the self. It is a mistake to define common sense by its defects alone, because its correct use by the specialist will keep him from exaggerating the importance of his specialized conclusions and keep his mind open to the reality of truth transcending his specialized field. Somewhat surprisingly, even so prominent a modern Catholic philosopher and theologian as Bernard Lonergan reduces common sense to mostly "common nonsense" and denies any logical connection between common sense and technical science,[5] even overlooking the fact that Catholic faith

---

3 Arthur Danto, "Common Sense," in *Encyclopedia Americana* (1967), Vol. VII, p. 415

4 Compare with the definition that "common sense" is "ordinary good sense or sound practical judgment" *Webster's New College Dictionary* [2007].

5 Bernard Lonergan maintains that the correct meaning of such terms as *reality, knowledge,* and *objectivity* cannot be attained by appealing to what common sense finds obvious (B. Lonergan, *Insight: A Study of Human Understanding* [London/New York: Longmans, 1958²] pp. 419-421). While Lonergan's observations about the limitations and characteristic dangers of common sense contain an amount of truth, his description of common sense almost entirely in terms of its negative and imperfect features is more a caricature than a factual description, for instance, where he says that common sense is "almost invariably" associated with an admixture of bias and "common nonsense" (p.

is part of the "common sense" that underlies all technical science. Genuine common sense will present within an intelligible focus the moral priority of the ethical mind over the remote reasoning of the empirical mind, and it will preserve specialized science from idealistic fantasy. Solid common sense will remain open to the possibility of recognizing in other traditions forms of specialized science distinct from what modern empirical scientists are usually prepared to recognize as science. Having at hand a fund of past experience, it will view with healthy distrust the fatal tendency of undisciplined reason to dissolve its integrity into irrational pluralism. This common level of science will not be persuaded by false argumentation that its primary grasp of the world of reality is but a "cosmological myth" needing to be burst open into two totally exclusive universes of discourse as soon as the "outlook of modern man" has been ripened by the growth of empirical science. It is the fundamental conservatism of common sense which provides the basis for a unified concept of science and the possible unification of the conclusions of the specialized sciences with all of the data of consciousness in terms of intelligible principles.[6]

5. Specialized Science. But what is "reality"? According to Webster's New College Dictionary (2007), the adjective "real" means "existing or happening as or in fact; actual, true, etc.; not merely seeming, pretended, imagined, fictitious, nominal, or ostensible." Essentially reality is the object of a concept that comes to every normal individual early in childhood as at least in some way distinguished from the illusory, the deceptive, the imaginary, the aesthetic, and the satisfaction of non-intellectual appetite, and it implies at least vaguely conscious recourse to verification in experience. The earliest tendency of a science-oriented consciousness is toward verification merely by the senses, but the normal human mind has a natural tendency to admit concepts that are not included in matter and to derive conclusions by way of reasoning which are removed from

---

53). He declares the independence of "scientific thinking" from the "naïve realism" of the "familiar world of poetry and common sense" in that it constitutes an entirely distinct and separate universe of discourse (*Insight*, pp. 297-298). However, since common sense contains the "empirical residue" of his basic dichotomy, it includes, not only the imperfection left behind by the empirical focus of mind, but also every other science that is not included in this focus. Lonergan has uncritically adopted Kant's absolute division of human knowledge into empirical knowledge, which he calls "scientific," and all other knowledge, which is characterized as "unscientific." For a more detailed critique of Lonergan's position on common sense, see J.F. McCarthy, *The Science of Historical Theology* (2nd printing, Rockford: TAN, 1991), pp. 43–45.

6 Cf. McCarthy, *The Science...*, pp. 42–46.

matter as such. For instance, even rigid empiricists generally admit the generalizations of mathematical principles and the use of mathematical deduction.[7] One may go on to say that the component which gives to science its depth and proper character is the developed recognition of the intellectual dimension of reality.[8] Hence, reality may be considered to be a kind of mental continuum whose solidity provides the firmness of scientific knowledge, whose base is the verity of the world known to sense experience, and the line of whose altitude is solidified by the verity of the reasoning process, divided into steps of graduated intelligibility by the separated and ordered identity of particular insights.[9]

6. It follows that the supposition in some empirical-science circles that the need of science to verify all of its conclusions requires, therefore, the reduction of all of its conclusions to the level of sensory experience has no basis in the fuller picture of reality, because the fully scientific picture of reality is like a "solid" figure that comes into its own as it emerges from the "flat" figure of sense phenomena and begins to manifest the qualities proper to its intellectual state of being.[10] The recognition of the intellectual dimension of reality is the condition of advancement to a fuller understanding of the meaning of science. But whoever seeks to survey even the face of reality must attend also to the medium of his knowledge.[11] The idea of meaning is a mental event, and the notion of reality contains an implicit awareness that the universe of objects presented by the external senses is a meaningful whole.[12] We call an "insight" any act of recognition in the knowing subject by which his intelligence sees a new comprehensive meaning in the relevant data being considered. An insight is, therefore, an act of intellectual intuition which is possible because of the intelligibility residing within the thing being considered and the vitality residing within the intellect of the knowing subject. Intelligence, as the power of intellectual intuition, is called reason, and the process of transition from one insight to another is called reasoning. The abiding element of reason is called understanding. Understanding is the pervasive aspect of human intelligence. It

---

7 Ibid., p. 37.

8 Ibid., p. 47. Cf. H. Margenau, *The Nature of Physical Reality* (New York: McGraw-Hill, 1950, pp. 19 and 450).

9 Ibid., p. 48.

10 Ibid., p. 48.

11 Ibid., p. 51.

12 Ibid., p. 39.

precedes, accompanies, and succeeds the reasoning process. The power of intelligibility underlying real objects produces intellectual vision of the kind of object that exists only in intelligence. Hence, a meaning is a unit of reasoned conclusions, and understanding is the structural medium between the insight of a knowing subject and the meaning which he apprehends. The difference between science and pseudo-science lies materially in the truth or falsity of the respective conclusions, but formally in the truth or falsity of the medium of thought.[13] This medium of thought first appears under the name of presuppositions, that is, of elements of thought antecedently required in order that conclusions can be reached.

7. In my opinion the presupposition essential to all true science is the proper use of the concept of reality. In its subjective aspect, science is real knowledge of things, and in its objective aspect, science is knowledge of things in their reality; it is, therefore, the ordered totality of real things as they are known and understood by qualified thinkers. The phenomenal aspect of science is a concentration upon the data of sense, and the rational aspect is a correlative concentration upon the understanding of the data.[14] After the mind has become sufficiently differentiated to be able to examine its reason as an object, the organization of such disciplines as logic and theory of knowledge becomes possible. Theory is necessary for any specialized science, to the extent that "To deny the presence, indeed, the necessary presence of metaphysical elements in any successful science is to be blind to the obvious, although to foster such blindness has become a highly sophisticated endeavor in our time."[15]

8. The fact of intellectual intuition is basic to the cognitive theory of Aristotle/Aquinas and to the whole process of Scholastic philosophy. In this view, intellectual development may be described as the deepening of intuition, which grows by a process of comparing and contrasting ideas and by the analysis and synthesis of mental objects. The use of direct comparison is called "intuitive reasoning," while indirect comparison is called "syllogistic reasoning." An adequate grasp of the nature and meaning of science must take both of these forms of reasoning into account. Syllogistic reasoning with the use of logical universals has served as a powerful instrument of science to the extent that the importance of

---

13 Cf. Aquinas, *Post. Analyt.*, bk. I, Lect. XLI, numbers 6–16.

14 Cf. Aquinas, *Post. Analyt.*, bk. I, Lect. XVIII, number 9.

15 H. Margenau, *The Nature of Physical Reality* (New York: McGraw-Hill, 1950), p. 12).

intuitive reasoning has sometimes been eclipsed to the point of neglect. A good example of such neglect may be seen in the search for a valid theory of history.

9. Historical Science. In the secular area of studies from near the end of the nineteenth century philosophers have tended to see history as a form of knowledge that is concrete and individual, as opposed to the abstract and general knowledge offered by the natural sciences.[16] While many empirical scientists and others do not consider any historical work to be scientific, the fact that most historians strive to produce a "significant account" of why events took place and how successive events were linked to one another indicates to them that historical thinking may be a science which differs in an intellectual way from the intellectuality of the classical sciences.[17]

10. A useful preparation for the task of formulating a theory of history has been performed in our time by William Walsh in his *Introduction to Philosophy of History*.[18] Walsh defines "science" as "a body of knowledge acquired as the result of an attempt to study a certain subject-matter in a methodical way, following a determinate set of presuppositions," and he maintains that "the scientist asks questions from a definite set of presuppositions, and his answers are connected just because of that."[19] But in order to exclude from the definition of science the presence of pseudo-science, I would add that the function of the concept of reality must also be included in the definition of any true science. He notes that, not only is historical evidence presupposed for historical reproduction, but also "the general framework of questions inside which we seek to exploit both it and the conclusions we draw from it" (*IPH*, 195). As noted in the preceding paragraph, the conclusions drawn by the historian are characteristically conclusions of the concrete and particular type. Walsh points out that differences between historians are mainly differences between philosophies, that is, "differences between moral and metaphysical beliefs" (*IPH*, 103). And so, in my view, history remains a hitherto unexploited science whose contradictory expressions are attributable to the prescientific thinking of historians. It is the unfulfilled task of historians to isolate and study their medium of thought and draw from it objective conclusions upon which

---

16 Cf. W.H. Walsh, *An Introduction to Philosophy of History*, 3d rev. ed. (London: Hutchinson and Co., 1970), pp. 14–15.

17 Cf. ibid., p. 18.

18 W. H. Walsh, *An Introduction to Philosophy of History* (Hutchinson and Co., 3rd [revised] edition, 1967).

19 Cf. ibid., p. 35.

they can all agree. Walsh expresses the recognition that "colligation" under general terms in historical study is a different form of thought from the application of universal laws to individual cases, as is done in classical science (*IPH*, 25). He also brings out the insight that explanation of events by tracing their intrinsic relations to each other within a context of development is a procedure distinctive of historians, and he admits cases in which a frankly teleological explanation is justified (*IPH*, 61). Perhaps most important of all is his drawing attention to the "conceptual structure of historical knowledge" (*IPH*, 70–71), a notion placing the focus of attention upon the historical medium and opening the door to one's entry into historical science of the advanced and genuine type. Walsh notes that historians have not been prone to speculate much on the nature of their study, while natural scientists are notoriously amateurish when it comes to defining clearly what science is.[20] What I call historical science as such consists, not simply in recounting the precise course of individual past events, which is the material object of historical study, but also in the recognition of historical meaning in the course of those individual past events, which is the formal object of historical study. Hence, historical insight is a species of understanding that is recognizably different from the kind of understanding that characterizes classical science.

11. Empirical scientists commonly believe that historical study is not a science. Historians in general are themselves confused as to whether or not historical study is a science, but some aver that historical work is a science, but is not an exact science, since its approach is not based characteristically on mathematics. Stephen Meyer points out, however, that among secular historians William Whewell, in his *History of the Inductive Sciences* (1837) and in his *Philosophy of the Inductive Sciences* (1840), raised the argument that historical sciences differ from empirical sciences such as physics and chemistry by having as their aim the "study of past causes," as opposed to the establishing of universal laws governing the operation of physical nature, and by finding the explanation of later phenomena from the causation of past events, as well as in the characteristic use of a different mode of reasoning whereby they infer retrospectively past conditions and causes from "manifest effects." In other words, "Whewell realized that historical sciences do not study 'forces that are permanent causes of motion, such as gravitational action,' but 'causes that have worked their effects in temporal succession.'" This type of reasoning is called

---

20 Cf. ibid., pp. 11–15.

"abduction." Abductive reasoning infers unseen facts, events, or causes in the past from clues or facts in the present."[21] Regarding abductive reasoning, historical scientists have elaborated some convincing methods of determining the causes of particular events, such as, for instance, "inference to the best explanation" (Peter Lipton). Michael Scriven and others describe this historical method of "retrospective causal analysis" as a simple three-part analysis of evaluating proposed causal explanations. [22]

12. Apart from the flight of empirical scientists from any exact definition of science, Meyer points out that philosophers and historians of science do not agree about how to define science, and many doubt that there is any single definition that can characterize all of its different kinds of science, as well as distinguish them from every pseudo-science, considering also the fact that scientists in different fields use different methods.[23] This situation emphasizes the need being proposed in this article of a broader definition of science covering a more precise differentiation of its various divisions and subdivisions and the exclusion of all pseudo-sciences.

13. There is no unified philosophy of history or theory of historical interpretation. In the midst of fundamental ambiguities, by the early twentieth century secular historians were described in the synthesis of Harry Elmer Barnes as divided into eight principal schools of interpretation, each seeking the meaning of history in an area contrasting with the older theory of political causation.[24] But in my estimation, consciousness of the past, real or unreal, is the distinguishing feature of all history, and so history in its widest sense may be defined as "knowledge of the past as such," whereas real history is rather defined as "knowledge of the real past as such." Real history arises as the mind of the historian concentrates upon real events of the past and qualifies or excludes from his narrative any events that he has found to be unreal.[25] This concentration upon the quality of being real produces historical science, which can be expressed either on the level of common sense or on the level of technical historical science. Most contemporary historians regard historical

---

21 Cf. Stephen C. Meyer, *Signature in the Cell: DNA and the Evidence for Intelligent Design* (HarperCollins, 10 East 53rd St., New York, NY 10022), pp. 152–153.

22 See Meyer, op. cit., pp. 154–159 and 167–168.

23 Cf. Meyer, op. cit., p. 400.

24 See H. E. Barnes, *New History and the Social Studies*.

25 The scientifically focused mnd can attend indirectly to imaginary forms of history, but only as known to be imaginary.

study as focused upon the human past only and upon the events with which that past is embodied.[26] The lack of an adequate theory of history has led a large percentage of empirical scientists to deny any serious and scientific validity to the affirmations of historians, and it has led most professional historians to ignore problems emerging in the field of "natural history," which they consider to be a province of "natural science" alone, even though natural scientists are usually studying these events without the benefit of principles applying to events as such.[27]

14. Common-sense historiography makes many distinctions and creates many historical terms, but it does not characteristically ask itself such questions as how or why it makes these distinctions or how historical knowledge can be justified in relation to the other sciences, but these and other epistemological questions are important, because it is in the area of epistemology that the greatest confusion exists, seeing that the inability to make epistemological distinctions makes historiography vulnerable to the introduction of false and inept forms of historical work.

15. The present of historical science. The presence of one's own mental activity is a general present common to history and to the other sciences. The historian makes use of his general mental equipment, above all of the understanding which he has derived from every kind of genuine mental growth, as his generic present, while his special present is the historical present. The special present of historical science may be absolute or relative. Either one is concrete, mobile, and tied to a vision of the past. Historical vision is necessarily retrospective, and it is the retrospective gaze from the present at the remembered absent that brings the past to mind. Very often the images that the historian chooses to consider are contained in a record or account, which has itself a formal medium, but the direct formal medium of the historian is the understanding of his own mind against the background of everything that he himself knows and understands about everything. This is his absolute present. The ultimate aim of the historical scientist should be an ever fuller and deeper understanding of events inasmuch as the facts have been verified in sensory experience.

16. The historical understanding to be derived from the contemplation of past events, as regards the distinctiveness of its approach, is centered upon concrete and particular objects, whether they are as singular as the biography of one individual person or as broad as events in the history of a nation, within a background of universal concepts as secondary equipment.

---

26 Cf. Walsh, op. cit., pp. 16, 21.

27 See McCarthy, *The Science*, pp. 60–62.

The past of historical science is the visibility of remembered objects as they are observed through the absolute or relative present in the mind of the historian. The outcome of any event in a narrative of the past can be used as a relative present looking back to the causal relationship to what came before. The fuller intelligibility of any past event is dependent upon further knowledge of the results and deeper insight into them. The fuller meaning sought by the historical scientist requires greater abstraction from the strictly material circumstances of the events. It involves the abstraction of concrete intuition. The account of events in terms of their historical reasons is known as historical explanation. But historical explanation cannot exist in valid form without a precise knowledge of past events and without a certain abstraction from the historical details by seeing the details in relation to the bigger picture that is there.

17. The present can be considered as an object of cognitive awareness. Historical science arises as the thinker begins to see that he is actually looking at the past in terms of certain preconceptions constituting his viewpoint, and his historical science increases as he brings these preconceptions into view and isolates their objective elements from the part that remains subjective and unintelligible, thus eliminating such things as bias, emotion, ignorance, and other factors that distort his viewpoint and falsify his judgment As the level of historical knowledge increases, more and more of the historian's absolute present must be brought into use. At this point historical evaluations can become falsified if they are not expressed by a mind that is fully honest and fully informed also and especially about its absolute present. Many of the general judgments about the past have been defective because they have proceeded from oversights and biases that should have been eliminated, but which escaped the process of scientific analysis.

18. The past of historical science. The historical past is the remembered absent as extended in time. The absolute past may be divided by an indefinite number of relative presents into an equal number of relative pasts. The relative present is in this sense a point having no dimension or content of its own but is merely the principle of the division into past and future. The intellectual medium of historical science is present in the understanding of the historian. The origin of historical science as historical is the distinction between relative past and relative future, while the origin of historical science as science is the perception of past objects in the medium of reality. Historical science grows by the progressive discovery of the meaning of past reality in the presence

of the understanding of the historian. Through the knowledge of his own absolute present, the historian maintains a certain awareness of the direction which the developments of the past have assumed and of their results. It is this awareness of directions and results which gives intelligibility to the past as such. [28]

19. The form of historical reasoning. Reasoning is the human intellect in operation. This activity of the human intellect can be considered either horizontally or vertically. The horizontal development is the application of acquired understanding to the acquisition of greater knowledge about things apart from a concomitant deepening of the understanding of things, while the vertical development is the process of deepening the understanding and the acquisition of deeper insight into things. Historical reasoning is horizontal inasmuch as the historian can simply increase his knowledge of historical facts, and it is vertical to the extent that he can arrive at a deeper grasp of reality as a result of his study. Historical thinking as such is distinct from the characteristic reasoning of classical science in that it reasons in terms of individual things or at least in terms of classes of things that are not "open".[29] Classical science and historical science are alike in the fact that they both require a general mental framework of principles that must be operative in the mind of the thinker, if the characteristic type of conclusion is to be reached, but the distinctive presuppositions of the classical scientist are principles of the general type, while the distinctive presuppositions of the historical scientist are principles of the concrete type, even though the historian is constantly also using universal concepts in his thinking,

20. St. Thomas Aquinas, at the very beginning of his *Summa Theologiae,* among the many objections and answers that he raises in the course of his work, mentions the following: *No science deals with individual facts. But the text of Sacred Scripture treats of individual facts, such as the deeds of Abraham, Isaac, and Jacob. Therefore, the teaching of Sacred Scripture is not a science.* In reply to this St. Thomas says: *Individual facts are treated of in Sacred Scripture, not because it deals with them principally, but to present them as examples to be followed in our lives and to establish the authority of those men through whom the divine revelation, on which this sacred writing, or teaching, is based, has come down to us.* [30]

---

28 For a more detailed exposition of the preceding three paragraphs see McCarthy, *The Science,* pp. 64–71.

29 See McCarthy, *The Science,* p. 74.

30 Cf. Aquinas, *S. Th.,* I, q. 1, art. 2, obj. 2.

21. In this response Aquinas does not dispute the claim that "no science deals with individual facts," but he points out that individual facts can be examples to be followed in our lives and that they can establish the historical truth of what is written in Sacred Scripture. It is my contention that there is or can be a science of history in its own right and a science of historical theology dealing with the historical truth and meaning of individual facts and events reported in the Bible, in contrast with the historical critical method that some form-critics call "scientific exegesis." In the Aristotelian approach "science" is certified knowledge of things in their causes, which is proven by syllogistic reasoning from universal principles. The causes referred to in this Aristotelian definition of science are the material cause, the formal cause, the efficient cause, and the final cause. In this response Aquinas implies the function of the final cause operating in the lessons given in Sacred Scripture for our instruction, and, therefore, the meaning of these historical examples.

22. In my estimation the common assumption of Scholastic philosophy that "intelligence is (only) in the universal," that is, in open concepts, is not a proven fact. Rather, we can also know individual things intelligently. For instance, the universe itself is a set of concrete objects, while judgments made about any thing or situation in the universe can be based upon intelligence, and it is my contention that any serious investigation on the level of logic and of theory of science will show that immediate historical inferences are intellectual as well and can be as abstract as are judgments of the classical type.[31] Indeed, Thomas Aquinas, in speaking of what he calls the "cogitative power," admits that the "particular reason" that is exercised by humans is higher than the merely instinctive discourse of brute animals,[32] and he adds that from repeated memories of the same sense image, as it is presented by different individuals of the same class of things, by a kind of reasoning in which one particular thing is related to another particular thing, human beings are able to grasp something common in the many individual things remembered, and this (intuitive) reasoning about sense experiences provides the condition in which human experience can know universals, and so there is in some way sense knowledge of universals.[33] It is my contention that human intelligence and understanding begins from the ever-present division in human consciousness into a knowing subject

31 See ibid., p. 178.

32 Cf. Aquinas, *De Anima*, bk. II, lesson XIII, nos. 395-398. See McCarthy, The Science..., 2, 3:18a (pp. 32–33, footnote).

33 Cf. Aquinas, *Post. Analyt.*, bk. 2, lect. 20, nos. 11–14.

and the object of his knowledge. Science begins with the distinction by the knowing subject between objects that are real and those that are not. The first level of science is that of common sense, or common science, the level on which the discourse of the Bible is usually presented. In the history of Western thought, science has developed from common science largely into two areas: first, into deductive science, and later, into inductive science. But common science could also develop along the lines of what is now often referred to as "abductive science," which uses the "intuitive reasoning" of direct comparison of objects rather than mediate comparison through syllogisms or mathematics. The science of history uses abductive reasoning, for instance, by directly comparing and contrasting diachronically different states in the development of an individual object to find the meaning of the development and the meaning of events.

23. Celestine Bittle expresses the common approach of Scholastic philosophers where he shows that the grounds or logical reasons upon which the inductive method of investigation is based are the principle of causality and the principle of the uniformity of nature.[34] He notes that these presuppositions of the inductive method are based upon the self-evident principle of identity—"a thing is what it is and can be nothing other"—and upon the self-evident principle of (non)—contradiction—"a thing cannot both be and not be at the same time and in the same way," as well as upon the principle of sufficient reason, namely, that "a thing must have a sufficient reason to be what it is." Bittle notes that only God has sufficient reason in Himself to exist and that all other existing beings depend upon the causality of some other thing for their existence. Bittle cites the principle of causality as stating that every effect has a cause, and this presupposition is necessarily functional for all contingent beings that undergo change. The causality of natural objects is always the same, because their natures are always the same, and they always function in a uniform way, due to the fact that "God the Creator has endowed them with definite powers and tendencies which they, being non-free agencies, necessarily strive to realize."[35]

24. The knowing subject. What is characteristic of man in that vital act of awareness called consciousness is the power of intelligence. The normal person in his waking consciousness is immediately and continuously

---

34 Celestine N. Bittle, O.F.M. Cap., *The Science of Correct Thinking* (Bruce Publishing Company, Fourteenth Printing, Milwaukee, 1948) p. 279.

35 See Celestine N. Bittle, O.F.M. Cap., *The Science of Correct Thinking* (Bruce, Milwaukee, 1937), chapter XVIII.

aware of himself as conscious and of the reality by which his conscious self is surrounded. Human consciousness is always thus divided into a knowing subject and the object of his knowledge, and it pertains to human consciousness for the knowing self to know that he knows. The reason for this characteristic division of human consciousness into a subjective and an objective area lies in the nature of human intelligence.[36]

25. It is an interesting and verifiable fact that, although the knowing self and the object of his knowledge are essential components of consciousness, the mind can move by concentrating attention upon one component or the other, in such wise as to put its counterpart out of focus while not forgetting it entirely. Such concentration brings into focus new areas and new dichotomies. It is the gradual bringing into intelligible focus of new objects and new areas by means of these dichotomies that constitutes one principal factor in the dynamism of the mind. The other principal factor is the activity of reuniting in mental unity the extra-mental being that it has brought into focus by its act of division. This work of organization and unification is called synthesis; it is joined to its counterpart, analysis, in dynamic and dialectical union as the reciprocal components and mutual contributors to that process which we call learning. The synthesis of the two parts of the fundamental dichotomy of intellectual consciousness (the subjective and the objective areas) yields the notion of the mind.

26. The discovery of truth. Behind the knowing self in the darkness of the unintelligible lie the driving forces of human nature, the appetitive faculties.[37] In the intellectual dichotomy into cognitive and appetitive functions, the appetitive drives are represented in intellectual consciousness by the intellectual self, which is directly experienced as the knower, but is not subject to direct examination as the known.[38] The knowing self can admit the meaning of reality into his consciousness, or he can block its access by those acts of his free will which we call acts of pride. By the word "truth" is meant the conformity of a judgment with the way the thing really is.[39] Truth offers pure and rational satisfaction to the will in the fulfillment

---

36 See McCarthy, The Science, pp. 15–17, cf. Aquinas, De Anima, bk. 3, lesson XI); L.S. Kubie, "Psychiatric and Psychoanalytic Considerations of the Problem of Consciousness," in J.F. Delafresnaye, ed., Brain Mechanisms and Consciousness (Oxford, 1954), 1954), p. 454.

37 Cf. T. V. Moore, The Driving Forces of Human Nature (London: Heinemann, 1948), diffused.

38 Cf. F. H. Bradley, Appearance and Reality (Oxford, 1897), pp. 81, 93–96).

39 Cf. Aquinas, Truth (Chicago, 1953), q, 1, art. 1.

of its nature, while pride offers impure and irrational gratification to the will in the frustration of its nature. If truth prevails, the region of objectivity develops, and the self withdraws into that tiny area within consciousness called humility. The acceptance of the truth is the truest act of freedom, for it is the truth which truly makes one free (John 8:31–32).[40]

27. As the mind concentrates upon particular fields of objectivity, its attention is focused on particular material things, that is, the mind isolates things in their individuality and sees them as meaningful wholes, which is to say that the "synthetic sense" constructs the meaningless sensory impressions into pre-intellectual things that have meaning on a level common with the higher animals, and then the human intelligence seeks rational meaning from these sensible images in keeping with its characteristic mode of operation. The human mind does this by a process of intellectual analysis and synthesis[41] in which the mind advances from the fundamental division of knower and object to a series of subsequent dichotomies by which the object becomes intellectually known and understood. Thus, the object may be hot or cold, heavy or light, bright or dark, hard or soft, moving or still, or have many other features that may enable the knowing self gradually to establish its identity, to locate it within a category, and to give it a general name. It is interesting to note that the primordial dichotomy between the knowing subject and the object of his knowledge can play a role in the determination of "viewpoints." We may define a "viewpoint" as a concentration of the mind upon one side or the other of a dichotomy that it has already realized.[42] I look for the continuity of function of the knowing self, not only in the operation of consciousness as a psychological whole, but also and especially in the way in which the knowing subject, the "intellectual self," allows his mind to develop through the conscious use of his will. If he uses his freedom to concentrate his mind upon the intelligibility of objects in such wise that his understanding may develop in the pursuit of truth, then his "intellectual self" will be fully engrossed in the sight of pure, self-appropriated objectivity.

28. The simple awareness of self-evident truths. When the mind begins to concentrate within the area of objectivity, it brings with its concentration the simple (non-reflexive) awareness of some self-evident principles, such

---

40 For a more detailed presentation see McCarthy, *The Science*, pp. 21–25.

41 Cf. Aquinas, S. Th., I, q. 78, art. 4; plus I, q. 79, art. 3, and Moore, *Cognitive Psychology* (Chicago, Lippincott, 1939), p. 241–242).

42 The application of dichotomy to form and privation is shown by Thomas Aquinas in his *De Anima*, bk. III, lesson 11, no. 759.

as the principle of identity: that "a thing is its self," and the principle of non-contradiction: that "a thing cannot both be and not be at the same time and in the same way." This function of the intelligence is only implicit within the state of consciousness until the mind has developed to the point at which it can distinguish between the act of knowing and its content, and at that point the act of knowing becomes in a secondary way an object of knowledge, entering "visibly" into the area of objectivity. Thus, the act of knowing becomes the subject of such disciplines as logic and epistemology.

29. St. Thomas did not devote much time to the search for the intellectuality of concrete meanings. Rather, he took as his working principal the proposition that human understanding is of universals, and he stayed in large part within the limits of this principle. But in speaking of what he calls the "cogitative power," he admits that the "particular reason" that is exercised by it is human and higher than the merely instinctive discourse of brute animals.[43] According to the theory of Aristotle, the awareness of self-evident first principles arises in human consciousness with the knowledge of universals, which in turn are non-moving objects standing outside of the flow of inductive experience. From repeated memories of the same kind of image, he says, man is able by a kind of reasoning in which one particular thing is related to another to grasp something common in the many individuals remembered. And this inductive reasoning of experience provides the condition in which intelligence can know universals. But, he continues, this would not be possible if there were not in some way sense knowledge of universals.[44] Now, this explanation does not seem to fully resolve the issue. Since Aristotle's theory is based upon the principle that understanding is exclusively of universals, he is constrained to posit a kind of sense-knowledge of universals together with a type of reasoning which he calls "inductive" and which is neither intellectual nor sensitive but belongs somehow to man. Furthermore, the process by which intellectual knowledge arises in human consciousness is not explained, except as the emerging of quiescent universals in the soul, while the relation of *per se* evident principles to the emerging of universals is not clarified.

30. Now, I believe that these lacunae in Aristotle's explanation of the origin of *per se* evident principles can be filled from the notion of intellectual consciousness as described above. A puppy can recognize its mother and some milk, and a human infant can recognize his mother and some milk.

---

43 Cf. Aquinas, *De Anima*, bk. II, lesson XIII, nos. 395–398. See McCarthy, *The Science* ..., 2, 3:18a (pp. 32–33, footnote).

44 Cf. Aquinas, *Posterior Analytics*, bk. II, lesson 20, no. 14.

But of these two, only the human infant can *know* that this is his mother and some milk. As intellectually conscious, the infant is spontaneously aware of himself as distinct from the sensory object confronting him at the given moment, that is to say, he knows himself subjectively as a concrete and distinct identity, and from this awareness arises the knowledge that the object with which he is confronted is distinct from his own identity. This division of human intellectual consciousness seems to me to be the first of all self-evident principles, and it contains under it every succeeding object of intellectual knowledge. Furthermore, by a transfer of this spontaneous knowledge that his identity is distinct from the object of his experience, he distinguishes the identity of his mother from her sensible form as well as the identities of all other objects that come before his mind from their sensible forms. In other words, he recognizes the "self" in the object, and implicit in this process is the self-evident first principle that "a thing is its self." But because this dichotomic theory of human intellectual consciousness does not posit the awareness of Aristotelian universals as the essential feature of human intelligence, it leaves room for the possibility of intellectual knowledge of particular objects.

31. A universe of selves. As the undeveloped mind begins to discover the world of objects, the self-evident world of the original self yields the center of focus to a universe filled with other selves. There are the table itself, the chair itself, the room itself, the house itself; there are warmth itself and coldness itself, the inside itself and the outside itself, truth itself and goodness itself; there are objectivity itself, non-selfhood itself, and even nothingness itself. What is the credibility of the "self" residing in other things? When the mind looks at an object like a table or a chair, it looks "beyond" the impressions of sense for a particular identity which will characterize the thing and set it apart from everything else. This identity is called the self. We know that the mind ascribes identity to things, and we know that the mind can err in this operation. The fact that the morning star and the evening star are always seen at opposite ends of the sky could lead one to believe that they are different stars, while a closer look will show that they are the one planet Venus. It is a natural function of the mind to seek identities and then to proceed by a process of precision from what seems to be to what becomes known to be.

32. Human knowledge. Human knowledge is "the consciousness of objects present or remembered," and it is distinguished from pure experience, which is its source."[45] And there is the whole world of fanciful

---

45 T. V. Moore, *Cognitive Psychology* (Chicago, Lippincott, 1939), pp. 237–238

objects, derived from the consciousness of man, having no authentic counterpart in the real world. Thus, the knowledge of the knowing subject is cleanly divided, at least in concept, between the world of reality and the world of imagination, although the borderline may be indistinct and one can be deceived into placing in the realm of the real what is actually imaginary and vice versa.

33. Part of the reason for contemporary confusion about historical method is lack of understanding about the role of its use of immediate inference. Change and development in individual things can be and are perceived by historians often in a direct and extra-syllogistic way, and this is an intelligent process. We need to keep in mind that the first principles of human reasoning, some of which are listed in the preceding paragraph, are of the concrete type, and, therefore, it is not absurd to suspect that non-classical sciences could be developed from these same first principles. Some insight can be gained from the famous argument of René Descartes: *Cogito, ergo sum*, that is, "I am thinking, therefore, I am." This is a valid inference of intuitive reasoning involving the particular notions of me and my existence, which are the two components in all human thinking, namely, a knowing subject and the object of the knowing subject's thinking. This conclusion could be considered another innate and self-evident principle of human reasoning that is prior to the use of universal terms and syllogistic reasoning. Descartes claimed that this is the first and most fundamental truth that cannot be doubted, and he saw this as the ultimate foundation of trustworthy knowledge in the face of radical doubt. A fuller form of this claim, Descartes wrote, is to say: "I doubt, therefore, I am thinking, therefore, I am."[46] Actually several well-known philosophers prior to Descartes made this claim. For instance, Aristotle wrote that "whenever we perceive, we are conscious that we perceive, and whenever we think, we are conscious that we think, and to be conscious that we are perceiving or thinking is to be conscious that we exist" (Nicomachean Ethics 1170a25). And Augustine of Hippo wrote: "If I am mistaken, I am." (City of God, XI, 26).

34. Anthony Rizzi, an accomplished physicist and Aristotelian/Thomist philosopher, in his book, *The Science Before Science*,[47] clearly presents the need of valid philosophical principles for correct scientific thinking at all levels. He starts with the fact that in contemporary Western culture the

---

46 R. Descartes, *Principles of Philosophy* [1644], Part I, art. 7.

47 Anthony Rizzi, *The Science Before Science* (Baton Rouge, LA: IAP Press, 2004, xx plus 390 pages—available from IAPpress@iapweb.org.

conclusions of only the empirical sciences are considered by many to be certified facts, while all other ideas are taken to be mere opinion at best, and the dominant theme of his book is that sound philosophy, the study of the first principles of all things, is a science on a par with the empirical sciences and is helpful rather than harmful to the empirical fields of study (p. 9). The trouble actually is, he notes, that those who will not give due recognition to sound philosophical knowledge often become themselves victims of blind religious, or more often anti-religious, opinion (p. 19).

35. Rizzi uses the moderate realism of Aristotle and Thomas Aquinas to develop a mental structure that begins from one's sense knowledge and personal experience and extends through the physical sciences to the ontological analysis of being considered in itself. He shows throughout his book that the knowledge particular to the empirical sciences must logically be rooted in objective reality, and he shows that all physical scientists do in fact maintain a working assumption that they are dealing with objective reality, even though subjectivist philosophers over the ages have "fashioned great systems of clarity and force that, nevertheless, crashed against the rock of reality" (p. 11). Rizzi concentrates his argument upon what are known today as the "pure sciences" in a sustained effort to show that the physical and mathematical sciences become false guides if they are not underpinned by the higher principles of metaphysics (p. 23). In *The Science Before Science*, the reader is led methodically to an awareness of the metaphysical principles needed to understand the mathematical findings of empirical science in the fuller context of the world of objective reality. For instance, Immanuel Kant (1724–1804) gave beings of reason priority over what exists in objective reality (p. 169) and thus went astray through neglect of the higher science of metaphysics and of the awareness that all true science must be based upon objective morality. Rizzi observes that Kant and many others like him have produced systems of thought that are highly organized and consistent with their own defined principles, but which are inconsistent with more fundamental principles that stand outside of and above their system (p. 344). Rizzi notes that "Knowledge is about reality, not about knowledge" (p. 351), and that is why metaphysics is the science that comes before all other sciences.

36. Rizzi stresses in his book the academic need today among educated Catholics to bring back the use of Scholastic philosophy, including the updating of Aristotelian/Thomist cosmology, noting that in general whole new vistas of knowledge are waiting to be discovered through

a metaphysical processing of the data of modern empirical science (p. 261). Since empirical scientists who neglect the truths of ontology are impelled by ignorance to make absurd statements (p. 341), they need the broadening influence of correct philosophical principles to escape the false philosophies that otherwise will stand implicitly in their place (p. 346). In *The Science Before Science*, Anthony Rizzi invites empirical scientists to open their eyes to the whole of science, and he also invites Aristotelian philosophers to reaffirm the validity of their field vis-à-vis the findings of modern empirical science. The time is long overdue when the Aristotelian theory of matter and form should once again take its rightful place that is winnable today in the totality of certified knowledge, so that the materialistic, mechanistic, subjectivistic world-view that has come to be identified with contemporary scientific knowledge will at last be replaced by the fuller view that is the heritage of the Western world through Greco-Roman philosophical insight and the intellectual accomplishments of the best medieval thought.

Part II. Regarding the Locus of the Science of Historical Theology in Human Consciousness

37. The act of Catholic faith is an affirmation that the objects of Catholic faith are real, that is, that they are in the same universe of discourse, the same continuum of reality, as are the other real things that we know. This means that we acknowledge to ourselves that Jesus of Nazareth really died and really rose from the dead, that God really exists and has providence over our lives, and that He hears us when we pray. In brief, it means for this discussion that the acts of God recounted in the Old and New Testaments are not in a literary genre of mythology resembling "fairy-tales for adults," as the founders of form-criticism, such as Hermann Gunkel and Rudolf Bultmann, maintained. Catholics approach the objects of faith in a spirit of devotion. Their minds and hearts are open to these truths, as they keep in mind that the true meaning of what is said in Sacred Scripture is not available to those whose minds and hearts are closed. In the words of Jesus: *"This is why I speak to them in parables, because seeing they do not see, and hearing they do not hear, nor do they understand. With them indeed is fulfilled the prophecy of Isaiah which says: 'You shall indeed hear but never understand, and you shall indeed see but never perceive. For this people's heart have grown dull and their ears are heavy of hearing, and their eyes they have closed, lest they*

should perceive with their eyes, and hear with their ears, and understand with their heart, and turn for me to heal them'" (Matt. 13:13–15).

38. In his celebrated lecture given in New York City in 1988, Joseph Cardinal Ratzinger pointed out that *"scientific exegesis must recognize the philosophic element present in a great number of its ground rules, and it must then reconsider the results which are based on these rules."* He went on to say: *"Exegesis can no longer be studied in a unilinear, synchronic fashion, as is the case with scientific findings which do not depend upon their history, but only upon the precision of their data. Exegesis must recognize itself as a historical discipline. Its history belongs to itself. In a critical arrangement of its respective positions within the totality of its own history, it will be able, on one hand, to recognize the relativity of its own judgments (where, for example, errors may have crept in). On the other hand, it will be in a better position to achieve an insight into our real, if always imperfect, comprehension of the biblical word."* As a matter of fact, the form-critical method of Hermann Gunkel and Rudolf Bultmann stems from the anti-Christian movement of the eighteenth century Enlightenment and is aimed principally at finding defects and errors in the Sacred Scriptures. Its immediate cradle was the "higher criticism" pursued in the 1990s History-of-Religions School in Germany, from which Hermann Gunkel and several other rationalist scholars sought the psychological origins of all religions in the supposed sub-rational instincts of primitive people. Various hypotheses were proposed whose plausibility was evaluated by one another, and those conclusions, once they were deemed to be quite plausible, became in their eyes settled science. Thus, for instance, Bultmann recalls the conclusive impact of ideas studied by William Wrede on the "Messianic Secret," by Johannes Weiss on *The Earliest Gospel*, and others like Julius Wellhausen, who "stated very clearly the fundamental assumption that the [Gospel] tradition consists of individual stories or groups of stories joined together in the Gospels by the work of the editors."[48]

39. The form-criticism (literally, "form-history") movement is a scholarly effort to find cracks and logical contradictions in the text of Sacred Scripture, wherein the founders and their mainstream (non-Catholic) successors have found joy and encouragement in every "verified" contradiction of historical fact in the biblical text in keeping with their general presupposition that the episodes presented, for instance, in the Book of Genesis and later in the four Gospels are predominantly products

---

48   Rudolf Bultmann, *History of the Synoptic Tradition* (Oxford: Basil Blackwell, 1963), pp. 1–2.

of religious fantasy. Conclusions drawn from this presupposition are neither in keeping with historical fact nor with historical method. In the words of Pope Leo XIII (Nov. 18, 1893): "*There has arisen, to the great detriment of religion, an inept method, dignified by the name of the 'higher criticism,' which pretends to judge the origin, integrity and authority of each Book from internal indications alone. It is clear, on the other hand, that in historical questions, such as the origin and the handing down of writings, the witness of history is of primary importance, and that historical investigation should be made with utmost care; and that in this matter internal evidence is seldom of great value, except as confirmation. To look upon it in any other light will be to open the door to many evil consequences.*"[49] Dampers were on published participation in the method by Catholic scholars until Pope Pius XII's encyclical letter *Divino afflante Spiritu* of 1943, and it now enjoys the favor of the Catholic hierarchy. Spokesmen for the method claim amazingly that the philosophical excesses of the higher-critical movement of the 1890s have in the meanwhile been ironed out to the extent that the historical critical method now has no such presuppositions or, in fact, any presuppositions at all. Believing Catholic form-critical exegetes, of course, do not accept the presupposition that the miracles of Jesus recounted in the Gospels are all products of religious fantasy, but in the absence of any available synthesis of their form-critical investigations with the common understanding of their Catholic faith, it is left to the resourcefulness of each individual Catholic form-critic to individually try to reconcile the two fields and thus avoid falling into sheer dualism.

40. I believe that what Pope Benedict XVI calls the need for a "properly developed faith hermeneutic" in contemporary biblical exegesis (quoted above) is fulfilled in the interpretation of Sacred Scripture according to the neo-patristic method. In this emerging new synthesis of exegetical method, a beginning of this improvement must include the realism of humble Christian prayer, direct and indirect, to the one true God, seeing that the meaning of Sacred Scripture cannot be understood by anyone whose mind and heart are not open to the existence and presence of God. In part I of this article attention was drawn to the fundamental division of human intellectual consciousness into a knowing subject and the object of his knowledge. The message of the Bible is personally addressed to every reader, but the knowledge of the meaning of Sacred Scripture requires a knowing subject who is humbly postured with reference to God and who believes

---

49 Pope Leo XIII, Encyclical Letter *Providentissimus Deus,* no. 17, in Claudia Carlen IHM, *The Papal Encyclicals,* vol. II, p. 334.

what God is telling him through the words of the Bible. In addition, any sincere student of the Bible needs to pray to God to give him knowledge of its meaning. These techniques of humble prayer should be an integral part of the exegetical method itself.

41. Most working historians, including many Catholic historians, are known for their aversion to philosophical analysis of their subject by way of what some call "idle speculation" about the nature and function of history. As a result, there is no developed theory of history that is adequate for Catholic faith and theology, and so a second element in the needed synthesis of modern biblical exegesis with Catholic faith and theology is a developed theory of history that serves the needs of Catholic believers in defending their Catholic outlook from the misuse of historical principles by critics of biblical truth. A useful preparation for the task of formulating a suitable theory of history has been performed in our time by writers like William Walsh in his *Introduction to the Philosophy of History* (*IPH*).[50] He notes that, not only is historical evidence presupposed for historical reproduction, but also "the general framework of questions inside which we seek to exploit both it and the conclusions we draw from it" (*IPH*, 195). As noted above in part I, the conclusions drawn by the historian are characteristically conclusions of the concrete and particular type. Walsh points out that differences between historians are mainly differences between philosophies, that is, "differences between moral and metaphysical beliefs" (*IPH*, 103). And so, in my view, history remains a hitherto unexploited science whose contradictory expressions are attributable to the prescientific thinking of historians. It is the unfulfilled task of historians to isolate and study their medium of thought and draw from it objective conclusions upon which they can all agree. Walsh expresses the recognition that "colligation" under general terms in historical study is a different form of thought from the application of universal laws to individual cases, as is done in classical science (*IPH*, 25), he brings out the insight that explanation of events by tracing their intrinsic relations to each other within a context of development is a procedure distinctive of historians, and he knows of some historical events in which a frankly teleological explanation is justified (*IPH*, 61). Perhaps most important of all is his drawing attention to the "conceptual structure of historical knowledge" (*IPH*, 70–71, a notion placing the focus of attention upon the historical medium and opening the door to entry into historical science of the advanced and genuine type.

---

50 W. H. Walsh, *An Introduction to Philosophy of History* (Hutchinson and Co., 3rd [revised] edition, 1967).

42. The needed theory of history should focus also upon the nature and origin of historical knowledge and understanding. The claimed historical understanding of the Scriptures upon which the mainline form-critical method is based comes from the philosophy of the Enlightenment and of modern empiricism, and it is reductionist, naturalistic, and rationalistic in its approach, inasmuch as it ignores true historical evidence in favor of the biases of what it calls "the outlook of modern man;" it relegates to the area of fantasy any described event that exceeds the known powers of created nature; and it does not consider the Bible to be an independent source of verified facts. On the other hand, the neo-patristic method uses a theory of historical understanding that does not exclude *a priori* the presence and activity of the one true God; it accepts as historical any event that biblical witnesses say actually took place, whether or not it happened within the known powers of created things, and it accepts as true what the Bible says without needing first to verify the claims of the Bible by subjecting them to the scrutiny of biased human reason. Regarding the origin of historical understanding, we may begin by examining from the origin of all human understanding how historical understanding arises. In part I of this article I noted how René Descartes famously traced the origin of human understanding to the expression "*Cogito, ergo sum.*" Now, thinkers of the Enlightenment utilized this expression and other elements of Cartesian philosophy to develop what they call "the outlook of modern man," but it need not have developed in this way, because Descartes' "I am thinking, therefore I exist" is a logically intuitive conclusion that other contemporary Catholic philosophers, such as the teachers at the College of Paris, need not have rejected out of hand. In fact, this same self-evident principle was taught earlier in their own way by Aristotle and by St. Augustine of Hippo (see above), and this is a good place to begin challenging the subjectivism and materialism of the so-called "outlook of modern man." I have noted in Part I of this essay how the presence of this fundamental dichotomy of human intellectual consciousness can be used to produce insights into other dichotomies, such as the self-evident distinctions of such self-principles, as that "a thing is its self," "a thing either is or is not," and "a thing cannot exist and not exist at the same time and in the same way." These are fundamental insights upon which all other human understanding is based, and they are potential universals, but they first involve immediate intuition into concrete, individual things. For instance, the awareness of "I" or "me" can, it is true, also be treated as a universal, such as, in speaking of the

"human ego," but it is primarily a concrete and individual idea from which do come other universal ideas, such as in the distinction between essence and existence, or between matter and form, or between substance and accident, which arise from the insight given first in the immediate and self-evident intuition of "I am thinking, therefore I am," where there is nothing more singular and concrete than "I am." A point to be made here is that the jump from this concrete innate idea "me" to the universal ideas of deductive and inductive science, for all the undeniable value that it represents, does not necessarily exclude jumps to intelligent insights of common sense and other intelligent uses of intuitive reasoning based upon simple comparison of objects of thought, such as, in our case, upon stages of a concrete historical development or upon mystical insight.

43. In the Aristotelian tradition *science* may be defined as "the knowledge of things in their causes," and this kind of science reaches verified conclusions by way of syllogistic reasoning. As Celestine Bittle puts it, "The universals lie at the very foundation of scientific knowledge," and "the validity of science (and of philosophy, the super-science) stands and falls with the validity of the universals."[51] This exclusion of singular and individual terms from the notion of scientific thinking may be at least part of the reason for which Catholic scholars have never developed a full-fledged theory of history, even though they have written many excellent works of history through the careful use of common sense. Historians make constant use of universal terms, but the reasoning that is characteristic of historical study involves intuitive reasoning about developments of individual things, whether they be of something as limited as the biography of one person or as extensive as the changes within a whole nation. It is for this reason that I have dwelt in part I on the singularity of the first self-evident truths upon which all scientific thinking is based and the possibility of a science in which intuitive (non-syllogistic) thinking is characteristic.

44. Since I have claimed that "science" is "the knowledge of reality as such," it might seem that I should consider the form-critical approach of Hermann Gunkel and Rudolf Bultmann to the interpretation of Sacred Scripture to be clearly scientific, since it distinguishes clearly between their own critical reasoning and the fanciful content of biblical religious thinking. But the fanciful character of the biblical text is not a proven feature of the Bible; it is just an unproven presupposition of their method. Joseph Cardinal Ratzinger famously remarked that the "historical method" of form-criticism (literally, "form-history"—*Formgeschichte*) is not a

---

51 C. Bittle, *The Science of Correct Thinking*, pp. 44–45.

historical method at all, but is only an application of the philosophy of Immanuel Kant.[52] For example, the philosophy of Kant assumes that religious thinking is fanciful thinking and that miraculous events in the Bible are fictitious events, but this is not a historical conclusion. Rather, historical research begins from the concrete evidence of whether an event took place or not, and it is not limited by the *a priori* assumption that no claimed miracle could ever have actually taken place. The fact is that form-criticism is limited by the (false) principles of naturalism, rationalism, and modernism, and is not, therefore, true historical research. Form-criticism never shows historical evidence that the miraculous events reported in the Bible never took place; it only presumes this. Thus, a priest in a homily once made the claim that the ancient Hebrews never walked dry-foot across the Red Sea, and a lady in the congregation justifiably asked him, "Were you there, Father?" Oftentimes form-critical teachers will deny a miracle of Jesus, by saying, for instance, that Jesus never miraculously multiplied loaves and fishes, but if asked to show historical evidence for this claim, they do not produce historical evidence but rather resort to *ad hominem* arguments, such as "Who are you to challenge what biblical science has determined?" Actually, the common sense of Catholic faith is reason enough to challenge it. There is no good reason for which a Christian believer should put his or her private judgment above the historical truth of the Bible, in spite of the massive assault upon its historicity that has been made over the past century and more. Catholic form-critics have introduced some good arguments in defense of biblical truth, but for the most part there has been an impulsive readiness to accept critical hypotheses and a certain reluctance to try very hard to solve the emerging doubts. As a result, the large mass of form-critical interpretations now at hand provides abundant material for neo-patristic analysis with the goal, not only of solving the doubts, but also of finding in the process new insights into the treasury of truth present in the biblical text. The neo-patristic method follows the approach of the Fathers of the Church and of the great medieval theologians, especially of St. Thomas Aquinas. The Fathers did not use an expressly formulated theory of history, but they were extraordinarily accurate on a common-sense level in quoting sources and in reporting the insights that they had received. The neo-patristic method seeks to add to their insights an expressly formulated theory of history in the synthesis of exegetical method that it is proposing.

---

52 Joseph Cardinal Ratzinger, in Richard J. Neuhaus, ed., *Biblical Interpretation in Crisis* (Grand Rapids: Eerdmans, 1989).

45. Thomas Aquinas teaches that *sacred theology* ("sacred doctrine") is a science in its own right, truly scientific and truly distinct from philosophy and from natural science, and that its formal viewpoint is God as He has revealed Himself.[53] Aquinas says that the principles of sacred science are those articles of faith which are about God or at least are seen in their relationship to God. The theologian does not know directly what God is, but he demonstrates things about the divine Cause in terms of God's effects.[54] For Thomas Aquinas to believe means "to think with assent," and he adds that no man can attain his destiny of knowing God (in the Beatific Vision) without believing in (the real existence of) God.[55] In relation to what many mainline form-critics say about the act of faith, St. Thomas explains that it is the conscious deliberation of universal meanings that belongs to the intellectual realm, while deliberation about particular meanings belongs to the sensitive realm of consciousness. He goes on, nevertheless, to say that human persons do see particular meanings by some sort of comparison made by particular reasoning.[56] In these latter considerations St. Thomas follows the idea that intelligence is (only) through universal ideas, but he also shows openness to the notion of a certain potential of intelligence in human concrete ideas, and it is from here that the thought of a science of history arises.

46. In the exposition of St. Thomas, Christian faith is a virtue perfecting human understanding.[57] The *gift of supernatural understanding* instilled by God is an imperfect insight into facts such as that external appearances do not contradict the truths believed by faith.[58] The *gift of knowledge* is the possession of correct judgment concerning what is to be believed and what is not to be believed.[59]

47. Sacred theology is based upon the extra-mental existence of revealed things. Corresponding to the extra-mental meaning of revealed things is the power of supernatural faith in the knowing subject, and the existence of the object of faith is evident only to those who have the power of faith. The objects of faith form a continuum with the reality of the rationally

---

53 Cf. Aquinas, S. Th. I, q. 1, art. 2.

54 Cf. Aquinas, S. Th., I, q. 1, art. 7.

55 Cf. Aquinas, S. Th., II-II, q. 2, art. 1.

56 Cf. Aquinas, S. Th., I, q. 78, art. 4.

57 Cf. Aquinas, S. Th., II-II, q. 1, art. 3.

58 Cf. Aquinas, S. Th., II-II, q. 8, art. 2.

59 Cf. Aquinas, S. Th., II-II, q. 9, art. 1.

conscious subject as such to the extent that the unity of consciousness in the believing subject is the origin of sacred theology. Therefore, personal comprehension has the same degree of necessity as has divine revelation, for individual understanding is the formal actuation of a revelation that would otherwise remain useless. [60] (The charity of supernatural love is higher than faith, but in this exercise we are primarily trying to know and to understand what these cognitive objects *mean*.) The ultimate material reality for faith is the observable signs and symbols containing divine revelation. They are the material substratum of a realm of meaning which transcends the meaning of the natural world. Graduated meaning is contained "objectively" and extra-mentally in the revealed sentences, the comprehension of whose meaning is an ascent into objectivity, not into subjectivity. The believer sees the simple credibility of what is materially signified by the signs and symbols of revelation and by acts of faith affirms the reality of these supernatural phenomena. He uses his natural understanding positively to make the judgment that this divine intervention is *real* and negatively to exclude doubts as to the reality of these divine interventions of God. This use of natural understanding resolves itself into special problems, questions, and situations, and thus develops into sacred theology as a "rational" science. The awareness that belief is meaningful and reasonable (not absurd) is the formal element of the act of supernatural understanding in its minimum degree. That is what is meant by the saying that the conscious life of the believer unfolds under the light of faith.

48. It is my impression that the object of Catholic faith is not only the perfections of God as seen in open classes, but also God Himself as concretely known in these classes. Similarly, more proximate concrete objects of faith include Our Lord and Savior Jesus Christ, the Real Presence of Jesus in the Holy Eucharist, the presence of sanctifying grace in one's own soul, the character of the priesthood in a validly ordained priest, and other things of this sort. The intellectual consciousness springing from nature must seek to conform itself and develop itself according to the higher norm of faith, while the higher consciousness of supernatural understanding must tend to penetrate and transform every facet of natural intellectual consciousness. These two tendencies of conformity and transformation are the true basis of the dynamism which underlies the process of sacred theology. This supernaturalized state of mind and heart is known as the "interior life," and it is much needed for a correct interpretation of the sacred text of the Bible.

---

60 See McCarthy, *The Science*, pp. 90–91.

49. The "outlook of modern man," as visualized by mainline form-critics, obscures the vision of Catholic Christian belief, inasmuch as it reduces *a priori* the objects of Christian faith to beings of the imagination. If we add to that reductionism the scenario of Kantian idealism, then within the scenario of the subject-object relationship, the objects of faith presented in Sacred Scripture are given purely mental existence, and the knowing subject, who in this case is the reasoning subject, could even be tempted to regard himself as the "supreme being" within his purely subjective world that is cut off from any demonstrated contact with the extra-mental world.

50. For matters of historical theology, the historical events recorded in Sacred Scripture are accepted as independent sources of factual knowledge, and their historical truth is considered worthy of apologetic defense. Where attendible problems are raised, believing interpreters should examine the problems raised and consider, first, whether the problems are based upon solid historical evidence, and secondly, whether there may be a more subtle literal interpretation of the text that careful study may bring out, especially through the use of solid historical methodology and in view of possible spiritual meanings beneath the literal sense of the text. Let us consider in passing, for example, the problem of the historicity of the days of creation in Genesis 1 (considered at greater length in the Appendix of this book) in relation to the idea of a possible subtle meaning in the reality of the text. We know that John 1 contains commentary on the text of Genesis 1 in which Jesus as the divine Word of God and as the human Savior of the world is presented as the key to a fuller and deeper understanding of the Old Testament in general and in particular to the narrative of the creation of the world in Genesis 1. John 1 tells us that "*all things were made by Him*" and that "*without Him was made nothing that was made*" (verse 3). John 1 tells us also that "*in Him was life, and the life was the light of men*" (verse 4). Let us suppose that these words in John relate to the creation of man as a creature having the light of intelligence and stressing the importance of this light in the creation of the world. This awareness could help us to suspect that the constant repetition of the expression "*evening and morning*" in the six days of creation could be a definition of the word "*day*" to mean a transition from a state of darkness to a state of light rather than simply the course of a natural day. And so on for other problems.

51. The theology of concrete meanings. The historical theology emerging in our era arises from the recognition also on the part of Catholic

thinkers that concrete objects of the mind can be viewed and reasoned about in an intellectual way. The aim of historical theology is to provide a theoretical basis for the overcoming of problems and doubts arising from the failure of deductive reasoning to provide thorough answers in areas standing outside of the limits of that approach. Thus, the thrust of historical theology is positive and expansive, realistic and spiritually sensitive. Historical theology has for its proper and precise object that portion of the formal meaning of revealed truth and divine inspired truth that is historical in character. According to formal theory, the supernatural gift of knowledge has for its minimum content the articles of Catholic faith and the divinely inspired text of Sacred Scripture. The supernatural gift of wisdom is the increase of supernatural understanding as viewed on the level of supernaturalized consciousness. In the real world any outlook or attitude violating the supernatural insight of Catholic teaching and infused contemplation cannot be considered a true insight. The science of historical theology is a science, and, therefore, its focus is upon reality as such. But it also presupposes that events presented in Sacred Scripture as historically true did really happen, and could this presupposition be really scientific? The answer is that no convincing proof that these biblical events are a genre of religious fantasy has ever been presented, and so the historical truth of these events can in general be assumed and deserves to be studied and defended in particular instances. The science of historical theology must refute and eliminate the pseudo-theologies that have arisen in the area of concrete meaning and have flourished on fallacies because of the absence of proper methods to discover and refute them. In a general way the methods of historical theology do exist in the apologetics of the Fathers of the Church and of the great Catholic theologians, but not as precisely formulated to apply to the problems raised in our time by historical critics of the form-critical type and by many other critics. But this branch of theology can advance only in the presence of cleanness of heart, and there is no formal step forward towards greater understanding and love for God that does not include a step backward from personal pride. The specific locus of the science of historical theology in human consciousness is that area of knowledge which is historical, scientific, and supernatural; it is the awareness of that scientific objectivity which is brought into view when the historical medium as such is interposed between the knowing subject and the objects of his faith.[61]

---

61 For a more detailed exposition of this paragraph, see J. F. McCarthy, *The Science*, pp. 96–100.

Part III. The Four Senses of Sacred Scripture

52. The science of history, as historical, regards the past, not the future. The science of history regards everything that has happened, and is not necessarily limited by what some historians think could never have happened. Those who believe in the consistent truth of the Bible accept as literally true what the Bible says has happened, and this is logical as long as the understanding of what the Bible says has happened is correct. Hence, it is very important for a believer to understand correctly what the Bible actually says has happened. Form-critics like Hermann Gunkel and Rudolf Bultmann have written that many events described in the Bible, such as in the Book of Genesis and in the four Gospels, never actually occurred, but rather are examples of imaginary literary genres which they classify as fanciful, not on the basis of historical evidence, but rather on the reductive basis of general presuppositions contained in the philosophical approaches of naturalism, rationalism, and what they call "the outlook of modern man." As far as apologetics and the science of historical theology are concerned, it is important to realize that most of the claims of biblical errors can rather easily be refuted, while some others of the supposed errors may be based upon faulty interpretations of the biblical text, but this does not mean, as Gunkel, Bultmann, and so many of their followers aver, that to brand those "unbelievable" biblical episodes as myths and legends is a correct solution. The fact is that those true believers who take the time to study critically the objections of form-critics and others to the constant historical truth of the Bible are usually rewarded with greater insight into what the Bible is saying.

53. The science of historical theology is aimed at using technical means to refute baseless objections to the historical truth of Sacred Scripture where it speaks of real events, and part of its mission is to distinguish where the Bible is speaking about real events and where it is not. For instance, parables are not literally intended to be descriptions of real historical events. A prime object of historical theology is to observe the present but false presuppositions in the conclusions of many mainline form-critics, and to supply the needed but missing true presuppositions. Into this study comes the use of a valid epistemology of historical thinking, such as has been described in the first part of this essay. For instance, every reader of the Bible is the knowing subject of the objects of thought presented therein, and the words of Sacred Scripture are addressed both in their literal and in

their spiritual senses to each individual thinker. Rationalist (non-Catholic) form-critics customarily see themselves as uninvolved observers using their power of reason to judge the truth or falsity of what they are reading in the biblical text, but they are in fact not just uninvolved thinkers, because the word of God is speaking to them, but to understand this the reader must know that it is the one true God who is really speaking to them. It is important how the reasoning subject views one's self, whether with pride or with humility, with love for or with rejection of the existence and presence of God. Studied awareness of the presence of God is not always necessary to understand the Scriptures, but studied rejection of the presence of God shuts off all understanding of what the Scriptures are telling us. This is where the realism of the science of historical theology first comes in. What believers know from sacred theology comes secondarily from the innate principles of human reason, beginning from the fundamental dichotomy of the knowing subject and the objects of his knowledge, but it comes primarily from faith in the revealed and inspired truth of the sacred Scriptures. The reductive approach of Kantian philosophy, as it cuts off any intuitive awareness of the external existence and presence of God, leaves the knowing and reasoning subject of consciousness as the presumed supreme existent within its little subjective theater of human conscious-ness and obscures the need of mental acts of humility before the one true God and the God-Man Jesus of Nazareth. It is, therefore, difficult for a Kantian to understand the point of departure in the exclamation of Mary, the mother of Jesus: "*My soul does magnify the Lord, and my spirit rejoices in God my Savior* (Luke 1:46–47).

54. The theology of history is conventionally centered upon predictions regarding the unfolding and meaning of history in the sense of where the history of mankind and of the natural world are finally heading. A prime example of this is St. Augustine's *City of God*. However, the science of historical theology is aimed, not so much at future events, as rather at what has already taken place, and only by default is the science of historical theology also interested in the anagogical, that is, the eschatological, sense of Sacred Scripture. The science of historical theology is mainly interested in the truth and meaning of past events, especially as reported in Sacred Scripture and in the history of Christendom, and it provides a framework of principles for studying claimed errors in these fields.

55. The literal and historical sense. The neo-patristic approach makes a minor distinction between the literal and the historical meaning of Sacred Scripture in that every text of Scripture has a literal sense, but only certain

texts, although being many, have a historical sense. Neo-patristic study uses theory of history to examine historical texts in a truly diachronic way. Solutions to problems raised about the historicity of some passages sometimes involve the discernment of the presence in the scriptural text of a seemingly plain literal sense with a true but subtle literal and historical sense lying underneath. A plain example of a subtle literal and historical meaning is given in John 2:19–21, where Jesus says: "*Destroy this temple, and in three days I will raise it up*," and the text goes on to say: "*But he spoke of the temple of his body.*" Now, this saying was a puzzle spoken by Jesus which was solved on the basis of the later historical information of the resurrection of Jesus from the dead. The identifying of subtle historical meanings can solve apparent errors and contradictions in the text of the Bible, and they often remain somewhat ambiguous, but they can give new insights into the meaning of the text. Other passages where I have seen subtle but convincing historical meanings include the six "days" of creation in Genesis 1, the seeming conflict between the two genealogies of Jesus in Matthew 1 and Luke 3, the 42 generations in Matthew 1, the calling of Nathaniel in John 1, and the need to eat the flesh and drink the blood of Jesus in John 6, a puzzle which was solved by the institution of the Sacrament of the Holy Eucharist.

56. The three spiritual senses of Sacred Scripture. There are three spiritual senses of Sacred Scripture, as described by St. Thomas Aquinas and as listed in the *Catechism of the Catholic Church* (numbers 115–119). They are all based upon the method of allegory relating to the figure of Jesus Christ, of the moral and intellectual virtues, and of prophecy regarding the future of mankind and of the world. The literal sense can be seen also by the unaided human reason, while the spiritual sense is penetrated mainly by theological reason aided by the light of faith. Through the science of historical theology the way is open to a thoroughgoing and systematic arrangement of spiritual meanings in the sacred text in proportion to the insight of individual writers. The neo-patristic method enables the bringing of the literal and the spiritual senses into a single mental framework, centered upon the allegory of Christ and of his Church.

57. The allegory of Christ and of his Church. The spiritual meaning of words and events presented in the Bible can be seen and understood only by the light of faith. Thomas Aquinas very well points out that the presuppositions of the science of sacred theology are based, not upon what is self-evident to natural human reason, but rather upon what is evident by the light of a higher science, namely, by the knowledge and wisdom of

God. Now, regarding the spiritual senses of Sacred Scripture, St. Thomas, quoting Pope Gregory the Great, observes that Sacred Scripture surpasses every other science, because, while it describes a literal fact, it reveals also a mystery.[62] The neo-patristic method begins from examples of the allegory of Christ and of his Church and seeks to build upon these examples in keeping with the enlightenment given by God through prayer and study. Since historical meaning is retrospective, the science of historical theology can help a researcher to perceive where the New Testament enlightens one to see spiritual and historical meanings in the Old Testament. From within a correct framework of moral virtues, the moral allegory comes to light, and, with the help of biblical prophecy, the anagogical meaning can be perceived, even though prophecies are often obscure.

58. An allegory is a sustained metaphor whose meaning differs from the literal, or surface, meaning of a text. The allegory of Christ and of his Church is a sustained metaphor set down literally in the historical development especially from the Mosaic covenant between God and the chosen people of Israel to the covenant between God and the members of the Mystical Body of Christ. This allegory is based upon a sequence of events as narrated in the Bible that prefigure Jesus Christ and his Church and upon the etymology of names.[63]

59. The historical critical method of the form-critical type, at least in its original and mainline form, both presupposes and concludes that the "seemingly historical events" narrated, for instance, in the Book of Genesis and in the Gospels, are products of religious imagination created by sub-rational religious dreamers. It is a task of historical theologians to show that this presupposition is not based upon historical fact. Similarly, the presupposition based upon the similarity of Gospel events to various Old Testament happenings that the marvelous actions of Jesus of Nazareth in the four Gospels are largely re-workings of Old Testament events used to enhance the image of Jesus, has also no basis in historical fact. The science of historical theology, as a science, maintains its focus upon reality in keeping with the belief that the objects of faith are real. Claims that the objects of Christian faith are not real, but are really fictitious and mythological, are based upon unscientific hypotheses and theories of knowledge. The answer to these claims is first of all to resist such temptations by making acts of love for God and for the objects of faith under attack and then to

---

62 Cf. Aquinas, *Summa Theologiae*, part I, q. 1, art. 10.

63 Cf. Peter A. Kwasniewski, "A Brief Introduction to the Literal and Allegorical Senses of Scripture," in *The Latin Mass (Magazine)*, vol. 25, no. 2, Summer 2016, pp. 6–9.

use sound theories of knowledge in general and of historical knowledge in particular to refute them. For this reason a wide effort of apologetic study to embrace and refute these attacks is urgently needed, and those believing individuals who have the capability of engaging in this effort are cordially invited to do so. In our favor is the fact that, in the midst of the immense assault upon the historical truth of the Bible that we have seen in our time, the text of Sacred Scripture has for the most part solidly held its ground and only needs for our benefit and especially for the benefit of those who are being drawn away from their faith some urgently needed polishing up of Christian apologetics.

Chapter 6

Two Views of Historical Criticism

Part I. Historical Criticism as a Critical Method

Living Tradition 77 (September 1998)

1. In this chapter two viewpoints and two key terms will be examined. The two viewpoints are the historical critical method versus the neo-patristic method in the interpretation of Sacred Scripture, and the two key terms are the words "critical" and "historical." The definition and division of "biblical criticism" leads to the questions of the literary analysis of the inspired word and of historical method. Connected with these two questions is the problem of presuppositions in the minds of modern interpreters of the sacred text and, in particular, of how these presuppositions relate to "scientific historical method." The notion of "scientific method" itself is crucial in this regard. In general, then, this article deals with the importance of using clearly defined terms in the process of making judgments about what is said in Sacred Scripture, and, therefore, of having an adequate mental apparatus, or mental framework, for all valid scientific interpretation, including, not only the interpretation of the canonical books of the Bible, but also the interpretation of statements made by the Magisterium of the Church regarding the interpretation of the Bible. The present article is critical of the "historical critical method," as this term is commonly understood today, but it is aimed only at technical aspects of the method itself and does not question the good faith or loyal intentions of the Catholic historical critics whom it quotes for the sake of example.

2. A great issue within Catholic Scripture scholarship throughout the entire twentieth century has been how to reconcile certain results of historical critical research into the human aspects of the inspired text with

the supernatural character and inerrancy with which this text is endowed. Scholars of the historical critical school profess that, in traditional Catholic exegesis up to and often including the twentieth century, the limitations of the human authorship of the sacred books were systematically overlooked or underestimated, while scholars of the traditional school maintain that historical critics downplay the divine authorship and the supernatural effects of divine inspiration. In this article, by the "historical critical school" is meant those writers who follow the method of biblical criticism initiated by Richard Simon in 1678, developed over the intervening years by Albert Eichhorn, Hermann Gunkel, Martin Dibelius, Rudolf Bultmann, and a host of other writers, and now in use among Catholic exegetes with various modifications of their own choosing. The name "historical criticism" is used in this article to distinguish writers of what is commonly referred to today as the "historical critical school" from writers who use other methods of historical criticism. The two Catholic schools of interpretation agree that "the inspired books teach the truth," but they disagree over the extent of that truth and the manner in which it is conveyed, as well as over what the human authors truly wanted to affirm and what God intended to say to us through their words. This discussion revolves largely around the question of the literary genres used by the inspired writers, whether they are the standard genres of history, poetry, prophecy, legal norms, wisdom sayings etc., and their sub-genres, or the special genres of the historical critical school, such as apophthegms, logia, I-sayings, miracle stories, legends, and midrash. The neo-patristic approach stands within the perennial tradition of Catholic interpretation, taking its inspiration from the writings of the Fathers and Doctors of the Church and seeking to make a fresh start in addressing this important issue through the use of a more fully developed critical and hermeneutical apparatus. This project involves a critical reexamination of the concepts and distinctions used by historical critics in arriving at their conclusions. The subject of the present article is the notion of historical criticism itself.

3. *Webster's Dictionary* defines "criticism," in the sense that we are discussing here, as "the scientific investigation of literary documents (as the Bible) in regard to such matters as origin, text, composition, character, or history."[1] Along the same lines, a Catholic historical critic defines *criticism* as "the art of distinguishing the true from the false," which, as applied to a literary work, "proposes to establish the authenticity (who the author is), the integrity, the genre of truth which fits it, etc.," so that the Bible, while it

---

1 "Criticism," in *Webster's Third New International Dictionary* (1996).

is exempt from all error, "in the exact measure in which it is a human work, is subject to the criteria with which other human works are judged."[2] This definition places full emphasis upon the literary texts themselves, and, in the case of the inspired books of the Bible, places the sacred writers on the defensive. From a different perspective Louis Bouyer says that "criticism" means in particular "the systematic activity of verifying the grounds for our various judgments," and he divides the term in this way: "Textual criticism endeavors to verify the authenticity of the texts in question, and historical criticism to verify the authenticity of generally admitted facts. In the same way, philosophical or theological criticism is legitimately practiced in verifying the arguments by which we attempt to establish or justify our beliefs."[3] This second definition places emphasis upon the verification of the mental processes used by the critic in passing judgments upon written texts, and thus it also brings under examination the thinking of the critic himself and the mental apparatus that he is using. In the rise of modern biblical exegesis, historical critics have been powerfully on the offensive in their criticism of the inspired texts and of traditional interpretations of them, but they have been weak in examining the thought-processes by means of which they arrive at their conclusions.

4. Textual criticism searches for changes that may have occurred in the transmission of the text in order to restore it to its original state. Neo-patristic exegetes are in agreement over the need and usefulness of textual criticism, as brought out by Pope Pius XII in his great encyclical letter *Divino afflante Spiritu*, where he calls upon the exegete of today to imitate St. Jerome, "as far as the science of his time permitted," and "not a few" of the great [Catholic] exegetes of the sixteenth and seventeenth centuries in striving "to acquire daily a greater facility in biblical as well as in other oriental languages and to support his interpretation by the aids which all branches of philology supply," so as to be able to explain the original wording of the text, "and this can be done all the more easily and fruitfully, if to the knowledge of languages be joined solid skill in the art of criticism (*solida criticae artis peritia*) of the same text,"[4] which art he identifies with textual criticism in the following words:

The great importance which should be attached to this kind of criticism was aptly pointed out by Augustine, when, among the precepts

---

2 S. Lyonnet, "Critica biblica," in the *Enciclopedia cattolica*, vol. 4 (Sansoni: Florence, 1950), 928–929.

3 "Criticism," in L. Bouyer, *Dictionary of Theology*, (Eng. ed., Desclée: New York, 1965).

4 *Cf. Divino afflante Spiritu*, no. 16 (EB 547).

to be recommended to the student of the Sacred Books, he put in the first place the care to possess a corrected text. ... In the present day, indeed, this art, which is called textual criticism and which is used with great and praiseworthy results in the editions of profane writings, is also quite rightly employed in the case of the Sacred Books, because of that very reverence which is due to the Divine Oracles. For its very purpose is to insure that the sacred text be restored, as perfectly as possible, be purified from the corruptions due to the carelessness of copyists and be freed, as far as may be done, from glosses and omissions, from the interchange and repetition of words and from all other kinds of mistakes which are wont to make their way gradually into writings handed down through many centuries.[5]

5. The historical critic uses literary criticism to examine the content of the sacred books "under the triple aspect of language, composition, and origin," and this includes philological study of the text, detailed analysis of its content, investigation of the sources used, determining the literary genre of particular passages, and drawing judicious conclusions regarding the authorship of each respective book.[6] In the common denotation of these words, literary criticism was also practiced by such early ecclesiastical writers and Fathers of the Church as Origen, Hesychius, Jerome, and Augustine, in that they developed and applied rules for discerning the truth and meaning of the Scriptures, which rules have been further refined and used by Medieval scholars and Catholic exegetes down to the present time, but historical critics have special meanings for expressions like "investigation of the sources," and "determining the literary genre," and "drawing judicious conclusions." Dyson and MacKenzie associate the term "literary criticism" with that "higher criticism" which has the task of determining the "origin and mode of composition" of a text, an activity which, "with its refined scientific methods, is chiefly a 19th century development," regarding which "the first name to be mentioned of a critic in the modern sense of the word is that of the French Catholic priest Richard Simon (1638–1712), justly called 'the father of biblical criticism.'" They note that "He saw and formulated the major problems that have occupied criticism since his day, and boldly applied scientific methods for their solution."[7]

---

5 *Divino afflante Spiritu,* no. 17 (EB 548).

6 Cf. L. Vaganay, "Catholic Exegesis," in A. Robert, A. Tricot, *Guide to the Bible* (Desclée: New York, 1960), 738–743.

7 R.A. Dyson and R.F. MacKenzie, "Higher Criticism," in *A Catholic Commentary on Holy Scripture* (Thomas Nelson and Sons: London, 1953), nos. 43d and 43f. Cf. R. Simon, *Histoire critique du Vieux Testament* (Paris, 1678), and his other writings.

But the works of Father Simon were placed on the Index of Prohibited Books, and "further Catholic work on these lines was discouraged," with the result that "the critical analysis of the Bible, when it came, was entirely non-Catholic—indeed anti-Catholic—and vastly more irresponsible and destructive than it need have been."[8] In the opinion of another historical critic, "notwithstanding certain rash opinions [of Father Richard Simon] and certain statements at least not very opportune, his principles are still those of modern critics," [but] "unfortunately, in the eighteenth and nineteenth centuries, rationalism took possession of the arms which the new discipline was furnishing in order to undermine the authority of the Holy Books and to construct anew a history of Israel, rather a history of Christian origins, in which every supernatural intervention disappears and the principal personages, not excluding even Jesus Christ, end up having a very secondary role, when even their very existence does not get denied, as has happened more than once."[9]

6. Neo-patristic researchers recognize a certain fundament of truth in these and similar judgments of Catholic historical critics about the origin of their method, but it questions the technical precision of many of these judgments. What exactly is "higher" about "higher criticism"? If higher-criticism is "higher" because it assumes the superiority of its "refined scientific methods" over a postulated naivety of the inspired text, then this approach needs to keep clearly in view how it is distinguished from the "higher criticism" rejected by Pope Leo XIII in *Providentissimus Deus* in the following words:

"These latter [professors of Sacred Scripture, etc.], with a similar object in view, should make themselves well and thoroughly acquainted with the art of true criticism. There has arisen, to the great detriment of religion, an inept method, dignified by the name of "higher criticism," which pretends to judge the origin, integrity, and authority of each book from internal indications alone. It is clear, on the other hand, that in historical questions, such as the origin and handing down of writings, the witness of history is of primary importance, and that historical investigation should be made with the utmost care; and that in this manner internal evidence is seldom of great value, except as confirmation. To look upon it in any other light will be to open the door to many evil consequences. It will make the enemies of religion much more bold and confident in attacking and mangling the sacred books; and this vaunted "higher criticism" will

---

8 Dyson and MacKenzie, ibid., no. 43f.

9 S. Lyonnet, *"Critica biblica,"* loc. cit., 929.

resolve itself into the reflection of the bias and the prejudice of the critics. It will not throw on the Scripture the light which is sought, or prove of any advantage to doctrine; it will only give rise to disagreement and dissension, those sure notes of error which the critics in question so plentifully exhibit in their own persons; and seeing that most of them are tainted with false philosophy and rationalism, it must lead to the elimination from the sacred writings of all prophecy and miracle, and of everything else that is outside the natural order."[10]

7. Neo-patristic interpretation presumes the loyalty to the Magisterium of the Church of those Catholic historical critics whose explanations it examines, and it excludes from them the personal bias and prejudice which Pope Leo XIII attributes to the users of higher-criticism in the passage of *Providentissimus Deus* quoted just above, in keeping with the following directive of Pope Pius XII in *Divino afflante Spiritu* regarding the freedom of exegetes to probe the problems raised by the teaching of the Church about the inerrancy of Sacred Scripture:

Let all the other children of the Church bear in mind that the efforts of these resolute laborers in the vineyard of the Lord should be judged, not only with equity and justice, but also with the greatest charity; all, moreover, should abhor that intemperate zeal which imagines that whatever is new should for that very reason be opposed or suspected. ... This true liberty of the children of God, which adheres faithfully to the teaching of the Church and accepts and uses gratefully the contributions of profane science, this liberty, upheld and sustained in every way by the confidence of all, is the condition and source of all lasting fruit and of all solid progress in Catholic doctrine, as our predecessor of happy memory Leo XIII rightly observes, when he says: 'Unless harmony of mind be maintained and principles safeguarded, no progress can be expected in this matter from the varied studies of many.'[11]

8. The neo-patristic method presumes that Catholic historical critics, in their judgments and in their expositions, aim to avoid the rationalism inherent in classical higher-criticism, but it also questions whether there has been sufficient precision in the adaptations that they have made. Have Catholic historical critics defined their science with the needed clarity of concepts? Have they reached a sufficiently scientific level of historical investigation? One of the steps in the neo-patristic method is to examine

---

10 *Providentissimus Deus*, EB 119.

11 *Divino afflante Spiritu*, nos. 47–48 (EB 564–565), quoting Leo XIII, apostolic letter *Vigilantiae* (EB 143).

relevant historical critical interpretations in terms of the presuppositions and logical method underlying their conclusions, seeking to incorporate whatever is found to be scientifically solid, in the realization that an adequate historical method will, indeed, lead to certain new discoveries. In doing this, neo-patristic interpreters follow the advice of Pope Benedict XV, where he says: "*We warmly commend, of course, those who, with the assistance of critical methods, seek to discover new ways of explaining the difficulties in Holy Scripture, whether for their own guidance or to help others. But we remind them that they will only come to miserable grief, if they neglect our predecessor's injunctions and overstep the limits set by the Fathers.*"[12] Historical critics, while admitting that Richard Simon had "many errors in his works," nevertheless maintain that he "laid the foundations of Catholic critico-historical study of the Bible."[13] Neo-patristic thinkers are interested in determining how these "foundations of critico-historical study" fit in with the deeper principles of human thought in general, and how they stand up under logical analysis.

9. Modern *rationalism* has well been defined as "the view that the human reason, or understanding, is the sole source and final test of all truth," and it is often associated with a certain shallow and misleading philosophy, "frequently put forward in the name of science," by which "questionable philosophical speculations are taken for scientific facts, and science is falsely supposed to be in opposition to religion."[14] Rationalism acquired its modern meaning in 1637 with the publication of the *Discourse on Method* of René Descartes (1596–1650), in which he declared that there are in man certain innate, self-evident principles from which all true knowledge must necessarily flow. In the winter of 1619–1620, Descartes conceived his method of "universal methodic doubt," which he began to apply systematically to all branches of knowledge as a quasi-mathematical process which begins from natural human intuition and moves forward by deduction. The system he devised was presented in finished form in his *Discourse on Method* (1637) and in his *Meditations on First Philosophy* (1641). Descartes' exclusively deductive method sharply contrasts with what is known today as the "scientific method," and yet he has been hailed as the "Socrates of modern thought," in that he drew the attention of modern thinkers to the nature of thought and the conditions of certified

---

12 *Spiritus Paraclitus* (EB 453).

13 W. Leon and B. Orchard, "The Place of the Bible in the Church," in *A Catholic Commentary on Holy Scripture*, no. 3j.

14 F. Aveling, "Rationalism," in *The Catholic Encyclopedia*, vol.12, 652.

knowledge, but his approach to human understanding "was vitiated by his preconceived doctrine of the absolute antithesis of mind and matter, a doctrine which, by creating an imaginary chasm between subject and object, undid all that Socrates, Aristotle, and the Schoolmen had accomplished," with the unfortunate result that how to bridge this imaginary mental chasm "came to be the problem which almost every great philosopher since Descartes' time has striven in vain to solve."[15]

10. The critical method of Descartes was later modified by Immanuel Kant (1724–1804), so as to admit sense-experience as a factor of rational knowledge, and afterwards by Georg Wilhelm Hegel (1770–1831) and others. These rationalist methods of human reasoning have had enormous influence over modern thought, and there is need carefully to consider how elements of their methods can be incorporated within the great synthesis of Thomas Aquinas, but what is of direct concern in this article is the danger, in the use of the historical critical method by Catholic interpreters of Sacred Scripture, of defective Cartesian, Kantian, and Hegelian thinking inherent in the method. Although Descartes excluded from his universal methodic doubt matters pertaining to faith and morals,[16] this exclusion was rejected

---

15 W. Turner, *History of Philosophy* (Ginn: Boston, 1929), 461. Cf. ibid., 447–451, 460–461.

16 Consider the following statements of Descartes: "Now, as to the fact that in the Fourth Meditation I treated only of the mistakes made in distinguishing between the true and the false, but not of the error that occurs in the pursuit of good and evil, and touching the fact that I always excluded those things that concern our faith and the conduct of life, when I asserted that we should assent only to what we clearly and distinctly know; with these two facts the whole context of my works manifests agreement" (Descartes, "Reply to the Fourth Set of Objections," in R.M Hutchins et al., *Great Books of the Western World*, vol. 31, p. 162). "For although the things are dark of which our faith is said to treat, yet the grounds on which we embrace it are not obscure, but clearer than any natural light. Nay, we must distinguish between the matter or fact to which we assent, and the formal reason that constrains our will to assent to that. For it is in this reason alone that we require clearness. ... Further, it should be noted that the clearness or evidence by which our will can be constrained to assent, is twofold, one sort proceeding from our natural light, the other from divine grace. But though the matters be obscure with which our faith is said to deal, nevertheless, this is understood to hold only of the fact or matter of which it treats, and it is not meant that at the formal reason on account of which we assent to matters of faith is obscure; for, on the other hand, this formal reason consists in a certain internal light, and it is when God supernaturally fills us with this illumination that we are confident that what is proposed for our belief has been revealed by Him Himself, and that is clearly impossible that He should lie: a fact more certain than any natural light and often indeed more evident than it on account of the light of grace" (Descartes. "Reply to the Second Set of Objections," loc. cit., p. 125). "For the same thing which might possibly seem very imperfect with some semblance of reason if regarded by itself, is found to be

by a wide spectrum of his followers, so that there arose a historic effort on the part of critical thinkers, especially of those interested in questions of faith and reason, gradually and as a spontaneous tendency of their method, to reject all religious tenets that cannot be justified by reason alone. In the late eighteenth century two prominent schools of "rationalism in religion" took form, one in England and the other in Germany. English deism arose to proclaim a viewpoint which, while accepting the fact of the creation of the world by God, rejected on principle any subsequent intervention of God and admitted religious truths only to the extent that they could be understood and verified by reason alone, thereby reducing the revealed doctrines of Christianity to an inferior level of thought. For its rationale, deism depended upon the naturalism of Herbert of Cherbury (1581–1648), a contemporary of Descartes, and the empiricism[17] of Isaac Newton (1642–1727). Herbert of Cherbury had advocated the principle of naturalism, according to which there was said to be a universal natural religion whose principal tenet is "Believe in God and do your duty," and having the negative doctrine that all official religion is just an artifice of cunning rulers and priests.[18] Then, by the early eighteenth century, wide acceptance had been given to Newton's theory that physical nature is a closed mechanical system governed by unbreakable physical laws. Hence deists, while accepting the idea of creation of the universe by God, found it more and more difficult to accept any intervention of God in the natural world, whether in the form of alleged miracles or relating to any other supernatural claim, such as the divinity of Christ, the marvelous events recorded in Sacred Scripture, and the idea of divine inspiration.

11. Partly in opposition to the writings of British Naturalists, there arose the German school of rationalism in religion, originating from the philosophical system of Christian Wolff (1679–1754). Wolff produced arguments intended to provide rational proof for supernatural truths presented in Sacred Scripture, in opposition to the anti-supernaturalism of

---

very perfect if regarded as part of the whole universe; and although, since I resolved to doubt all things, I as yet have only known certainly my own existence and that of God, nevertheless, since I have recognized the infinite power of God, I cannot deny that He may have produced many other things, or at least that He has the power of producing them, so that I may obtain a place as a part of a great universe" (Descartes, "Meditation IV," loc. cit., p. 90).

17 While rationalism is based essentially upon the idea that certified knowledge results only from logical deductions from innate principles of the human mind, empiricism holds that all certified knowledge is based upon sense perception.

18 Cf. Turner, op. cit., 494–495.

the Naturalists, but his method "turned out to be strongly in favor of the naturalism that he wished to condemn," because he made natural human reason the ultimate judge of both natural and revealed religion. Thus, as time went on, German rationalists mounted an ever-growing offensive against the miracles and other extraordinary events recorded in the Bible. Before the end of the eighteenth century, Semler, Teller, and others claimed to have shown the merely local and time-conditioned character of the biblical records, ostensibly in order "to safeguard the deeper revelation, while sacrificing to the critics its superficial vehicle."[19] Early in the nineteenth century there arose in Germany a "second wave" of religious rationalism, spearheaded by G.W. Hegel, under whose influence David Friedrich Strauss (1808–1874), Ferdinand Christian Baur (1792–1860), and others developed the "higher criticism" of Sacred Scripture, by the use of which "its supernatural elements were systematically explained away as products of mythology." Then came forward the theory that religion arises from a religious sense in man that is distinct from the faculty of reason, to the effect that revelation is not to be attributed to an exterior and objective speaking of God, but only to an interior and subjective personal experience. Thus, Ludwig Feuerbach (1804–1872) "explained the very idea of God as a projection of man's desire and need."[20] And so, early attempts by the German rationalist school to defend a consistent message of truth in the biblical accounts soon gave way to the acceptance of "undeniable errors," and to the admission that the outlook of even the New Testament biblical writers was simply "not up to the requirements of modern man." This development of critical outlook in the German school of rationalism in religion was expressed over a span of a century and a half from about 1768 to 1914 in a long series of critical works,[21] towards the end of which arose,

---

19 Aveling, ibid.

20   B. Blanshard, "Rationalism," in the *Encyclopedia Americana* (1967 international edition), vol. 23, p. 230c.

21   Among the most significant German rationalist critiques of this period were the following: H.S. Reimarus, *Apologia for the Rational Worshippers of God* (1768); H.E.G. Paulus, *Commentary on the First Three Gospels* (1800–1804), and *Manual of Exegesis* (1830); D.G. Strauss, *Life of Jesus* (1835–1836); B. Bauer, (writings from 1840); F.C. Baur, *Paul the Apostle of Jesus Christ* (1845); F. Schleiermacher, *Life of Jesus* 1864); J. Weiss, *The Preaching of Jesus on the Kingdom of God* (1892); W. Wrede, *The Messianic Secret in the Gospels* (1901); A. von Harnack, various works, including *The Essence of Christianity* (1900), and *The Gospel and the Church* (1902); and A. Schweitzer, *Sketch of the Life of Jesus* (1901), and *The Quest of the Historical Jesus* (1906). An extended critique of these and other rationalist works of the same period may be seen in G. Ricciotti, Eng. trans., *The Life of Christ* (unabridged edition,

on the basis of selected previous positions of the same school of thought, the method of form-criticism, which first attracted the positive interest of the Catholic exegete, Marie-Joseph Lagrange, in the early 1890s and has now become the dominant approach among Catholic Scripture scholars.

12. The method known as form-criticism dates back to the work of Hermann Gunkel (1862–1932), with his commentary on Genesis, first published in 1901.[22] Gunkel built upon the Documentary Theory of the origin of the Pentateuch elaborated by Julius Wellhausen in the 1870s, in which literary-criticism and source-criticism had been used in such a way that "the different sources (J, E, D, P) of the Pentateuch and the redactional material that now unites them were separated from each other on grounds of style, vocabulary, and the like, as well as the distinctive theological and religious outlook and interest that could be discovered in each source."[23] But Gunkel added a new methodology. In the final years of the nineteenth century, there had emerged the history of religions school, which directed its attention to the development of the traditions behind the biblical text. Hermann Gunkel had "pioneered these new ideas" with the publication in 1895 of his *Creation and Chaos in the Beginning and at the End of Time*, which surveyed "the biblical creation myths from Genesis 1 to Revelation 12."[24] In his book *Genesis*, Gunkel then concentrated his attention on the "literary forms" of Hebrew literature and on the "literary history" behind them, on the assumption that each form belonged to "a quite definite 'setting in life' (*Sitz im Leben*); that is, the particular literary form in which a subject matter found expression was itself dictated by the particular setting in life to which it was addressed."[25]

13. Suelzer and Kselman relate that, for the most part, nineteenth-century Catholic exegetes, often also as a result of pressure from the authorities of the Church, rejected the new exegetical approach being fostered by these rationalist researchers, and they made "no distinction between the methods

---

Bruce: Milwaukee, 1947), pp. 179–216).

22 H. Gunkel, *Genesis* (Göttingen, 1901); Eng. trans. of the 3d revised edition (1910), *Genesis* (Mercer: Macon, Georgia, 1997).

23 E.W. Nicholson, "Foreword to the English Translation" of H. Gunkel, *Genesis*, p. [3].

24 Nicholson, ibid., [4]–[5].

25 Nicholson, ibid., [6]–[7]. Gunkel named this method *Formgeschichte*, that is, "form-history," but it is usually called in English "form-criticism," just as the German *Redaktionsgeschichte*, that is, "redaction-history," is usually translated as "redaction-criticism." It would be interesting to review the historical reasons for this twist of terminology.

and conclusions of the new criticism and the rationalist philosophy upon which the system was based."[26] But, beginning in 1897, Marie-Joseph Lagrange publicly "championed a positive response to the challenges of higher criticism." He urged "that critics replace their modern Western concepts with a Semitic view of authorship and historicity," and, regarding the testimony of Mosaic authorship of the Pentateuch, "distinguish between the literary and the historical testimony." Then, in 1905, in his *Historical Criticism and the Old Testament*, "he demonstrated the application of such a procedure to the besetting problems of Catholic exegesis: the relation of criticism to dogma, to science, and to history," and he pointed out that, to trace the observed fact of the development of dogmas, "one must employ the historical method in the study of Scripture." With reference to critical attacks on the historicity of the Scriptural accounts, "Lagrange insisted that the first task in assessing the value of portions having the appearance of history is to analyze their literary genres."[27]

14. With regard to this adoption, as cautious as it may have been, by a Catholic exegete of the critical methods in use by rationalists, the first question before the eyes of a neo-patristic researcher is whether a sufficient distinction was made, not only between the new critical method itself and the rationalist philosophy upon which it was based, but also between the presuppositions of the new critical method itself and the elements of valid historical science that it might contain. It seems that Lagrange, in preparing his book on historical criticism, foresaw the need of a preliminary analysis of the concepts of history and historical method, but he, nevertheless, plunged into the method without performing this task. How "scientific" is the form-criticism of Hermann Gunkel? To approach that question properly we must first define exactly what is meant by science, especially in the area of historical science. But one can spot chinks in the structure even prior to that. The Catholic exegete should, perhaps, separate the methods and conclusions of the new criticism from the rationalist philosophy upon which it is based, but what if the rationalist philosophy is part of the method? Gunkel's painstaking analyses of "style, vocabulary, and the like" need, of course, to be looked at carefully and in detail before any judgment can be made, but his method also involves evaluations on grounds of "the distinctive theological and religious outlook and interest that could be discerned in each source."[28] How much

---

26 A. Suelzer and J. Kselman, "Modern Old Testament Criticism," in *The New Jerome Biblical Commentary* (1990), p. 1121, no. 33.

27 A. Suelzer—J. Kselman, ibid., no. 35.

28 See paragraph #12 above.

confidence can a Catholic have in the ability of a rationalist to make such judgments? How objective will these judgments be? Gunkel's *Creation and Chaos* undertakes to trace the history of the "biblical creation myths," but, in order to carry out this study, he first had to *presume* that these creation accounts are myths, and he never proved this presupposition. Again, in his *Genesis*, Gunkel distinguished different literary genres on the presumption that each genre arose from "a quite definite *Sitz im Leben*," and was "dictated by the particular setting in life to which it was addressed." Now, neo-patristic exegetes allow that the life-setting (properly defined) played a role in what the sacred writers wrote, but it also allows for the influence of human intelligence on the one hand and of divine inspiration on the other. What room does Gunkel's method leave either for the exercise of human intelligence in the origin of the biblical accounts or for a formal and discernible role of the divine Holy Spirit in the composition of the biblical texts? A full answer to this question requires a detailed examination of Gunkel's conclusions, but his evident bias against the very possibility of supernatural happenings as well as his exclusion on principle of any real supernatural illumination or guidance of the sacred writers would seem from the start to have prevented him from seeing the whole reality, even of the smaller passages that he picked out as literary units.

15. The neo-patristic method posits divine inspiration as a source of all that is written in the canonical books of Sacred Scripture in keeping with the following teaching of *Providentissimus Deus*: "For all the books which the Church receives as sacred and canonical are written wholly and entirely, with all their parts, at the dictation of the Holy Spirit; and so far is it from being possible that any error can coexist with inspiration, that inspiration not only is essentially incompatible with error, but excludes and rejects it as absolutely and necessarily as it is impossible that God Himself, the supreme Truth, can utter that which is not true. This is the ancient and unchanging faith of the Church, solemnly defined in the Councils of Florence and Trent, and finally and more expressly formulated by the [First] Council of the Vatican."[29] All Catholic Scripture scholars accept this teaching in some way, but Catholic historical critics tend, in view of the conclusions of their method, to believe that the scope of this definition of biblical inspiration has been restricted by later documents of the Magisterium, especially by the encyclical *Divino afflante Spiritu*, by the *Instruction of the Pontifical Biblical Commission* of 1964, and by the constitution *Dei Verbum* of the Second Vatican Council, proclaimed in 1965. Neo-patristic exegetes attend also to

---

29 Pope Leo XIII, *Providentissimus Deus*, 18 November 1893—EB 124–125.

these later declarations, but they interpret them to have stressed different aspects of biblical exegesis without limiting the scope of divine inspiration as defined in the above quotation from *Providentissimus Deus*, and they find that the interpretations given to these later documents by historical critics show an evident ambiguity and lack of scientific precision.

16. Historical critics believe that the widespread, almost continuous inconsistencies, conflicts, awkward constructions, and non-factual statements, especially as regards seemingly historical accounts, which they claim to have discovered in the inspired text give credibility to the historical critical interpretation of Sacred Scripture. Historical critics do go back over these claimed discoveries, so as to reject some and reorganize others, but it is the overall increase in the number of cracks thought to have been discovered in the text that has made their field advance. On the contrary, neo-patristic exegetes presuppose the historical inerrancy of the inspired text, and so, while they are quite interested in probing the literary forms used, they, nevertheless, undertake to defend the text from alleged historical errors and contradictions between one passage and another, just as did the Fathers of the Church. Catholic historical critics are prone easily to accept incongruities in the biblical text and to catalogue them neatly in categories of their own creation. Neo-patristic interpreters are often amazed at the readiness of historical critics to see conflicts even where the apparent problems can be resolved without much effort. This does not mean that neo-patristic scholars claim that they can resolve every conflict that has been raised, or that historical criticism has not opened up a challenging new field of study, but it does underscore a radical difference of approach. For the historical critic, whatever in the biblical text has so far revealed no inconsistencies to their critical gaze stands as a kind of residue not exempt from continuing study, while, for the neo-patristic researcher, the biblical text is basically consistent, and whatever problems of consistency have not been resolved stand as a residue that continues to be worked on, realizing, as St. Augustine pointed out long ago, that no one can expect to resolve all the problems, seeing that some of them have been deliberately planted by the Holy Spirit in the biblical text in order to incite the study of them.

17. Catholic historical critics think that concerted efforts to defend the historical consistency of the biblical text represent, not a scientific approach, but rather the outlook of biblical "fundamentalism." Thus, e.g., David Stanley avers: "If we are to avoid the fundamentalist mentality, we must be on our guard against the superficial conclusion that, because one is forced to admit that certain details in an Evangelist's narrative (or even its general

framework) are due to the literary form used or to his specific purpose, the whole story has been invented. Such a 'black-or-white' attitude is simply due to the failure of a modern, Occidental mind to comprehend the Semitic view evinced by the Evangelist. Finally, it will not infrequently happen that, after the most patient analysis, we cannot decide with any certainty *what actually happened*, and we must content ourselves with such imprecision."[30] Or again: "The problem posed by certain literary forms in our Gospels is in no sense to be regarded as one of reconciling the 'history' with the Christology. Once we grant the supreme truth of the Incarnation with all its consequences, the Christology *is* the history."[31] The short answers to these statements are as follows. In the first place, opposition to Stanley's notion of the literary form of Gospel history has been part of the Catholic exegetical tradition for nineteen centuries, while "fundamentalism" has its origins in the Protestant Reformation and dates, as a term, only from the American Biblical Congress which was held in Niagara, New York, in 1895. In the second place, it is not a question of a "'black-or-white' attitude"; it is rather a question of whether David Stanley understood what history is and what history is not. An imaginary scene, such as form-critics project, is not an account of reality, even if it was occasioned by a real event. In the third place, even the most patient analysis is not conclusive if it is not correctly carried out. In the fourth place, Catholic Christology is based upon real history. If the historical reality of the Incarnation, as it is described in Matthew and Luke, is taken away, there is no way to replace the Incarnation as a real happening and as a real object of Christian faith. Again we come back to the question of what is real history and of how Catholic faith is based upon historical reality.

18. Descartes was correct in excluding from his method of universal methodic doubt "those things that concern our faith and the conduct of life," and when he allowed that "the same thing which might possibly seem very imperfect with some semblance of reason if regarded by itself, is found to be very perfect if regarded as part of the whole universe." He acknowledged a certitude of Christian faith made possible through the infusion by God of "a certain internal light" by which what He has revealed can be perceived, and he saw this as knowledge that is certified, because "it is clearly impossible that He should lie: a fact more certain than any natural light and often indeed more evident than it on account of the

---

30 D. Stanley, "The Conception of Our Gospels as Salvation History," in *Theological Studies,* vol. 20 (1959), p. 577.

31 Stanley, ibid., 584.

light of grace."[32] If Descartes' followers had understood these two insights, perhaps there would not have arisen the naturalism that has so narrowed the vision of empirical scientists and the rationalism that has spawned such a long series of attacks on the truth of Sacred Scripture. Descartes saw a place in the real world for supernatural phenomena that do not fit into what rationalists call the "world-view of modern man," an outlook that came to be enshrined in the 1890s in the method of the history of religions school, from which have sprung the Old Testament form-criticism of Hermann Gunkel with his Genesis (1901) and the New Testament form-criticism of, among others, Rudolf Bultmann with his *Die Geschichte der synoptischen Tradition* (1921). Both of these works and many like them have been acclaimed as representing the "modern scientific approach" to biblical interpretation, but are they really scientific?

19. Hermann Gunkel declared in 1901 that, for the modern historian, the book of Genesis is legend, not history.[33] By legend he understands "a popular, long-transmitted, poetic account dealing with past persons or events."[34] Legend, he notes, is not real history. "The most obvious characteristic of legend is that it frequently reports extraordinary things incredible to us. The reality of this poetry differs from the reality pertinent to prosaic life and ancient Israel also considered many things possible that seem impossible to us. Thus, Genesis reports many things that contradict our advanced knowledge."[35] And so he states his principle: "Following our modern historical world-view, truly not an imaginative construct but based on the observation of facts, we consider the other view entirely impossible."[36] He does not feel that his modern world-view of the accounts in Genesis to be detrimental to Christian faith. First of all, because of the nature of legend: "Legend is not a lie. Instead it is a specific genre of

---

32 See note on Descartes' "universal methodic doubt" in paragraph 10 above.

33 "Does Genesis recount history or legend? This is no longer a question for the modern historian. ... Uncivilized people do not write history. Incapable of objectively interpreting their experiences, they have no interest in reliably transmitting the events of their time to posterity. Their experiences become discolored under their hand; experience and imagination intermingle. They are able to present historical events only in poetic form, in songs and legends. Only at a certain stage of culture does objectivity mature to the point and the drive to communicate one's own experiences to posterity becomes so great that historiography can arise" (H. Gunkel, *Genesis* (English edition), vii.

34 Gunkel, ibid., viii.

35 Gunkel, ibid., ix.

36 Gunkel, ibid., x.

literature."[37] He cannot understand why any Christian should be hesitant to accept the existence of legends in the book of Genesis. "The question of whether the accounts of Genesis are history or legend does not involve belief or unbelief, but simply better understanding. It has been objected that Jesus and the apostles apparently regarded these accounts as reality and not poetry. Certainly. But NT figures had no particular stance regarding such questions. Instead, they shared the opinions of their time. We may not, therefore, seek information in the NT concerning questions of the history of OT literature."[38]

20. Contemporary scientists have difficulty in providing an exact definition of what they mean by "*science*," but they do stress that the word signifies "knowledge obtained and tested through the use of the scientific method" (*Webster's*). Thus, for instance, Fergus Wood observes: "In a general sense, the term scientific method may be applied to processes of establishing the truth of widely diverse propositions of seemingly unscientific nature by resort to the demonstrative methods of science. In general, scientific method entails those processes of logical reasoning by which the aggregate of all truth is rigorously established."[39] Has the form-criticism of Hermann Gunkel and his followers added to the aggregate of all truth regarding the Bible? Is it really and objectively true, as he says, that the book of Genesis is legend, not history? Does it really not make any difference to Christian faith whether Genesis is history or legend? Is it true that the belief of Jesus in the historical reality of the Genesis accounts was an error due to the limitations of his time and culture? The question of reality is central to the whole issue of whether the form-critical method is scientific or not, and the principal reason for which modern scientists have difficulty in defining the word "science" is that they tend to leave the concept of reality out of the definition. On an analytical level, "science" can be properly defined as "the knowledge of reality as such."[40] While the common, ordinary use of human intelligence in addressing reality is already common sense, that is, "common science," the knowledge of reality arrived at through the use of precise distinctions and a rigorous reasoning method is the "technical science" to which

---

37 Gunkel, ibid., vii.

38 Gunkel, ibid., viii.

39 F.J. Wood, "Scientific Method," in the *Encyclopedia Americana* (1967), p. 418A.

40 This precise definition is analyzed at length in J.F. McCarthy, The Science of Historical Theology, pp. 34–56.

the word "science" usually refers. And it is its precise adherence to the concept of reality that protects science from straying into such non-scientific realms of thought as fantasy, illusion, bias, and pseudo-science.

21. Gunkel is touching on the notion of reality where he classifies the accounts in the book of Genesis to be legend, not history, and where he says that many of the events recounted in Genesis are "entirely impossible" (no. 19 above). The basis of this judgment is his adherence to what he calls the "modern historical world-view," an outlook which has its origins in the presuppositions of deism, naturalism, rationalism, and modernism, attitudes that are simply assumed without proof. According to the presupposition of the deist, God cannot intervene in the world of created nature, and, therefore, the preternatural events described in Genesis are deemed impossible. According to the presupposition of the naturalist in religion, nature is a closed system that does not admit of outside interference, and, therefore, many of the accounts of Genesis are incredible. According to the presupposition of the rationalist, nothing is accepted as real that cannot be demonstrated from natural reason, and, therefore, many of the accounts of Genesis are automatically assumed to be unreal. According to the presupposition of the modernist, the marvelous accounts of Genesis are constructs deriving from the religious imagination, and, therefore, are unacceptable to the belief of modern man. Gunkel subscribed to all of these presuppositions, and they led him to assume without sufficient reason that the accounts of Genesis are legends, not history. For Gunkel a myth is simply "a story of the gods." He finds that myths appear in Genesis only "in faded colors" for the reason that they have been reduced by Israel's monotheism to events "in which God acts alone" or "in which the story takes place between God and people."[41] For Gunkel, the one true God does not *really* act in history, and this view is deism. Gunkel's method also reflects naturalism where he tells us that "a series of myths can be understood in terms of a natural event often or regularly occurring in the real world which provided the palette for an account of such an event in the primordium."[42] This means that, for Gunkel, alleged acts of God are not located "in the real world." But Gunkel is also a rationalist, as he tells us himself. "In many cases, we too, whose worship withstood a powerful purification in the Reformation and again in Rationalism, do not, or only partially, understand the original meaning of what we see and

---

41 Gunkel, ibid., xii-xiii.

42 Gunkel, ibid.

hear in our churches."[43] How much of Christian worship did manage to survive the "purification" of rationalism in Gunkel's mind is a big question, but it is obvious that the action of God in the reality of this world did not. And modernism reigns also behind his "modern historical point of view." He finds that those legends of Genesis created out of a desire "to explain something" are characteristic of the childish mode of thinking and reasoning,[44] while others arose as "pure products of the imagination," in a manner that he calls "novelistic," or even "fairy-tale-like."[45] Yet, he explains, the originators of these legends did not deliberately intend to deceive. "Legend stems from times and circles which did not yet have the intellectual ability to distinguish between fiction and reality."[46]

22. In the Old Testament form-criticism of Hermann Gunkel the accounts in the book of Genesis are legends, not history. Somewhat later, when the form-criticism of the Gospels arose in the early 1920s, the accounts in the Gospels were also assumed to be "fiction, not history." These form-critical assumptions are opposed by neo-patristic researchers on the basis of nineteen centuries of Catholic biblical scholarship. The most basic issue is the question of reality. Catholic faith is an affirmation of the reality of its object. This means that Catholic faith, while it is primarily and *per se* an affirmation of the dogmas of Catholic faith, is also, secondarily and *per accidens*, an affirmation of the reality of what is stated in Sacred Scripture rightly understood. Therefore, what seem to be presented in Sacred Scripture as historical accounts are to be defended as historical accounts unless the contrary is proved to be true, both because of the presence of divine inspiration and because what is contained in the biblical accounts is recognized to be in the one continuum of reality that is first known from natural awareness and experience. Central to this whole discussion is the notion of historical reality. We contend that science is science only to the extent that its medium of thought is recognized and defined, and, therefore, that historical science is historical science only to the extent that the historical medium of thought is recognized and defined in the mind of the historian. The frame of reference in the mind of the historian is his historical present. Neo-patristic exegetes contend that the awareness in the mind of the biblical scholar of the presence of the one

---

43 Gunkel, ibid., xx.

44 Gunkel, ibid., xxi. Cf. ibid., lxvii, lxix.

45 Gunkel, ibid., xxiii.

46 Gunkel, ibid., xxvi.

true God, of the God who presents Himself in the Sacred Scriptures, is necessary for the scientific interpretation of the Scriptures. Gunkel makes a patronizing reference to the "providence of God" in the final sentence of his Introduction without endorsing the idea, and in his form-criticism every mention of the action of God in history is deemed "mythical." Patristic exegesis, on the contrary, is built upon the awareness of the presence of God, now and in the past. And neo-patristic exegesis critically examines and rejects evidences of deism, naturalism, rationalism, and modernism in the mental frameworks of form-critics. Thus, for neo-patristic researchers, the "criticism" in historical criticism, taken as an acceptable approach, requires study of mental frameworks as well as of biblical texts. Especially to be criticized is the form-critical assumption that supernatural events are "unscientific." We shall examine whether this presupposition of naturalism is not a confusion of historical method with the special methods of the natural sciences. In the historical rise of the historical critical school, literary-criticism led to form-criticism through the influence of Hermann Gunkel and others. In the rise of the neo-patristic school, it is hoped that a healthy criticism of the historical critical method will lead to a broad acceptance of the traditional Four Senses of Sacred Scripture, with special emphasis on the historical sense. The great thrust of neo-patristic exegesis derives from the greatly expanded horizon of historical research and methodology, with all of the challenges that this brings to the patristic approach, and thus, in the opening up of new dimensions of meaning in the sacred text to traditionally oriented exegetes as they meet the challenges presented by modern biblical scholarship.

Part II. Historical Criticism as A Historical Method

Living Tradition 78 (November 1998)

23. The definition of history. *Webster's Third New International Dictionary* gives three relevant definitions of the word "history": a)"a narrative of events connected with a real or imaginary object, person, or career"; b)"the events that form the subject matter of a history"; c)"a systematic written account comprising a chronological record of events and usually including a philosophical explanation of the cause and origin of such events." We note from these three descriptive definitions

that the word "history" can mean either a record of events or the events themselves and it can also mean a narrative of real events or of imaginary events. All of these meanings of history enter into the present discussion in ways that can only be recognized clearly on a more analytical level. Analytically speaking, history is "the past as such." The past does not have any ontological existence in itself; it is rather an idea in the mind of a thinker who, from the viewpoint of some chronological present is regarding objects in a real or imaginary chronological past. Thus, "the events that form the subject matter of a history" are objects that were first in the mind of an observer and then consigned to a record. Recorded events have existence always in relation to the mind of the one who recognized them, with the result that the outlook of the viewer has a formal effect upon how what was viewed has been understood by the viewer. History can be a narrative of real events or of imaginary events, and this is the great watershed of all history. Many people think of history as referring only to real events and of stories or tales as referring to imaginary events, but usage among modern biblical scholars has greatly obscured this distinction, especially because they have not included the concept of reality in their definition of science. The analytical difference between these two kinds of history, real and unreal, arises from the use or non-use of the idea of reality. "Science," in its most comprehensive sense, must be defined as "the knowledge of the real as such." This knowledge of the real as real can occur on a popular level or on a technical level. Accounts of past events recorded on a popular level reflect historical science on a popular level, if the observer and the writer adhered constantly to the concept of reality while avoiding digression into fancy or illusion motivated by a lack of common sense or by emotional involvements. On the other hand, accounts of past events that follow a disciplined and systematic adherence to the concept of reality reflect historical science on a technical level. It is our position that what constitutes the beginning of historical science is *the intent to describe the facts as they really took place*, and common-sense observers can succeed in this objective, even though they may not be able to recognize certain technical aspects of the events that they describe or be able to describe these events on the level of technical historical narrative. For instance, a good common-sense observer could accurately describe on a popular level how a serious automobile accident took place, even though he might not have recognized aspects of the happening that a policeman, a lawyer, a medical doctor, or a mechanic might have noticed.

24. A fundamental question of the present discussion is whether there is true history, that is, narration of real events, in the inspired text of Sacred Scripture. Did the writer of Genesis, did the writers of the Four Gospels, write historical science in that they narrated events as they really took place? We disagree with Louis Bouyer where he says that "only with the Renaissance" did "a real science of history based on criticism of documents and facts take shape," both because the common-sense narration of real events is already historical science on a popular level and because the criticism of documents and facts existed long before the Renaissance and even in ancient times. Still, we agree with Louis Bouyer as he goes on to say: "But history, as a critical science, can establish, on the one hand, the inadequacy of historical explanations that would eliminate the data of faith; and, on the other, the accord between what faith tells us and what we can know with certainty about the facts accessible to science."[47] It is true that serious historians in ancient times did not have access to all of the facts or all of the methods that are available today, but neither were some of them, in particular the sacred writers and the historians of the Patristic era, impeded by certain rationalistic prejudices that tend to falsify the judgments of many modern historians.

25. Henry Elmer Barnes, in a standard reference article, tells us this about patristic historiography: "The Christian 'literati' set out to produce a synthesis of the past which would give due weight to the alleged glories of Hebrew antiquity and would, at the same time, show why the Jews were no longer worthy of their heritage, which had now passed to the Christians. ...The central actor was Jehovah, now the God of all the earth. ...Man's career on earth became a fall. ...In this Christian synthesis of world history, aside from the artificiality of its chronology and synchronisms, two characteristics are noteworthy, namely, the absurd relative importance attached to Hebrew history and the serious bias against pagan civilization which made an objective historical narrative well nigh impossible."[48] This judgment is not as neutral as it purports to be. The Fathers of the Church did not "produce" the idea that the heritage of the Jews "passed to the Christians"; this fact is clearly imprinted upon the New Testament itself. That man's career on earth became a fall is equally impressed upon the opening chapters of Genesis. If the one true God exists, as every true Christian believes

---

47 L. Bouyer, *Dictionary of Theology*, p. 205.

48 H.E. Barnes, "History, Its Rise and Development," in the *Encyclopedia Americana*, vol. 14, p. 210.

and knows, then "Jehovah" is certainly the central actor of all real history, as the entire Bible makes clear, and, therefore, Hebrew history, as narrated in the Bible, is unquestionably special in contrast with the infidelity of pagan civilizations, not as civilizations but as pagan.

26. Since the mental framework of the historian influences his judgments about historical facts, the judgment that Barnes makes here about the historical outlook of the Fathers of the Church raises the question of what he thinks about the existence of the one true God. It seems that it is his rationalist bias against possible divine interventions that makes for him an objective historical judgment about patristic historical method "well nigh impossible." He faults the early Christian writers with refusing to "assume towards the Hebrew creation tales" the critical attitude of Hecataeus toward Greek mythology, as though there were not an immense difference between the two, whence he concludes that for the Fathers, "if the obvious content of the inspired statement was preposterous and unbelievable, some hidden or inner meaning must be found, and, in response to this necessity, allegory and symbolism replaced candor and critical analysis as the foundations of historical method."[49] In this quotation Barnes simply assumes on rationalistic grounds that the inspired accounts are on a par with the dreams of pagan poets. A closer look at what the Fathers wrote would have shown him that they did not transpose into allegory what he calls preposterous and unbelievable. They accepted and defended the literal sense of the text, but without rationalistically presupposing that God could not have intervened in human history, and then they went on to expound the deeper sense of the same events.

27. Of course, rationalists deem miraculous interventions of the one true God to be unbelievable on the ground that such interventions are not in accord with the outlook of modern science. In assuming this attitude, they are failing to recognize an important distinction. The purpose of natural science is to study physical and biological nature in terms of laws and theories which cannot go beyond the limits of created nature itself, so that, by very definition, divine interventions are beyond the bounds of its purview. Hence, natural science, as natural science, cannot recognize the past or present occurrence of divine interventions. But natural science is obliged to recognize the valid conclusions of other sciences, and historical science can recognize the supernatural and the miraculous. Why? The reason is that historical science has for its object whatever has really taken place; its method is not limited to the bounds

49 Barnes, ibid., p. 211.

of the natural. And it is the purpose of historical method to ascertain what has really taken place, whether or not it can be explained according to the laws of nature.[50]

28. Historical method basically involves four things: a) a technique of investigation; b) an ability to identify what really took place; c) knowledge of what others are affirming in one's own field, in cognate fields, and in allied disciplines; d) an ability to express correctly what one has ascertained. Historical critics place much emphasis upon their techniques of investigation, but they are usually not well informed on what non-rationalist exegetes and theologians have said or are saying about their area of research. Cecil Slade observes that the historian should give credence to what experts are saying in allied disciplines and presume their technical skill and intellectual honesty "unless there is strong evidence to the contrary."[51] And, he continues, as regards research into what actually happened, the historian's knowledge "is entirely dependent on the transmission of information from those living at the time, and this information forms what is known as the source material for the particular period or topic," or else he has access to "something, be it verbal, written or material that is the end product of an occurrence." Such traces are the facts of history, while "the actual occurrences are deductions from the facts."[52] He points out that "comparison with parallel source material and knowledge of current interpretation will normally show the historian whether his particular source can be presumed true, partially true or faked," but this supposes that the compared sources are truly parallel, which we deny in the case of Sacred Scripture. And he goes on to say that it is mainly in the forming of hypotheses and in the establishing of relationships that intellectual error can occur, because "the subjective element of the historian's personality" plays a role.[53] It is important in this study to determine more precisely what is meant by "the subjective element" of the historian, and we locate it in his mental framework, which is the proximate object of his knowledge and understanding, or in his emotional attachments.

29. The determining of what really took place is often a matter of controversy, and we must keep in mind that elaborate techniques of

---

50 Cf. McCarthy, The Science of Historical Theology, p. 117.

51 Cf. C.F. Slade, "History: Methodology," in the Encyclopaedia Britannica, vol. 11, pp. 541–542.

52 Ibid., p. 541.

53 Ibid., p. 542.

investigation are used both by historians and by pseudo-historians. Form-critics like Hermann Gunkel and Rudolf Bultmann had elaborate techniques of investigation and marked ability to express their outrageous theories in a manner that appears plausible and well organized, with the result that many secular historians accept the validity of their conclusions, also because these secular historians share the same rationalistic presuppositions.[54] Once the conclusions of a form-critic like Gunkel or Bultmann have been accepted by their colleagues in the same field, in this case by their fellow rationalist exegetes, and even more so when sympathetic secular historians have begun to accept them also, they become part of "accepted history," and are given an objective validity in the minds of the public at large. For Bultmann the general results of Gunkel's reasoning were already "accepted history," and for Gunkel the reasonings of Julius Wellhausen and of his predecessors in the liberal Protestant school were accepted as well. The overall result is that, in picking up the exegetical writings of Gunkel or Bultmann or of others in their school, one finds himself in the midst of a tangle of already accepted conclusions, and this makes rational analysis of their exegesis very complicated. Gunkel begins from the historical fact, supposed to have been demonstrated by Wellhausen, that Genesis is composed of bits of three earlier documents crudely sewn together. Similarly, Bultmann accepts as established fact, not only Wellhausen's documentary theory, but also Gunkel's theory that each of the units of Wellhausen's mosaic has a long prehistory of its own. These form-critics disagree among themselves on many minor issues, but they are uncritical of each other's work in the larger issues, because they all have an emotional commitment to the same rationalist presuppositions. These presuppositions pertain to "the subjective element of the historian's personality," and it is from them that there arises the likelihood of error both in their hypotheses and in their conclusions.

30. Acceptance or non-acceptance of the real existence of the one true God is the central issue of the whole discussion between neo-patristic interpreters and historical critics like Gunkel and Bultmann. Neo-patristic exegetes recognize the past and present action of God in human history. This means that the awareness of the power of God is present in the neo-patristic frame of reference, and this awareness enables neo-patristic exegetes to study Sacred Scripture from a more realistic viewpoint than can those who have closed their eyes to this reality. And the eyes of neo-patristic exegetes

---

54 Since form-criticism is the most common contemporary expression of historical-criticism and has inherited all of the former methods of higher-criticism, in this study I have concentrated attention upon the form-critical method.

are open to the miraculous character of the Bible. The imposing array of form-critical demolitions of the inspired accounts falls away before the eyes of those who criticize form-critical reasoning with their eyes open to the full reality of the text. Form-critical reasonings do provide something: they provide a challenge to find answers, and, as answers are found, progress is made in the understanding of the Bible. Defense of the historicity of the biblical accounts is a challenge, and the discovery throughout the text of answers to the "unanswerable" objections of form-critics is a reward in itself, leading to the perception of new meanings in the Bible.

31. The form-criticism (*Formgeschichte*: literally "form history") of Gunkel and Bultmann is a theory according to which the small units in the biblical crazy-quilt postulated by Wellhausen are each supposed to have had a long history of development that can be unearthed by means of critical comparisons. Since these postulated units as well as the "legends" that were formed out of them are assumed to be imaginary stories, the real history that is thought to compose the object of "form-history" is not any true history presented by the sacred writers but is only the history of the development of the small units of imaginary history and the process by which they were sewn together into larger units and books[55] (see no. 21 above). Thus, Gunkel along with others of the "history of religions" school assumes that many of the stories narrated in the final text of Genesis were taken originally from imaginary stories about pagan gods and were gradually transformed by Hebrew poets into imaginary stories about an imaginary Hebrew God in relation

---

[55] "The literary collection of legends was not accomplished by one hand or in one period, but by several or even many in a very long process. We distinguish two periods in this process: the earlier for which we thank the collections of the Yahwist (J) and the Elohist (E), then a later, comprehensive reworking by the so-called priestly codex (P). ... The distinction of these three 'documentary sources' of Genesis is a common result of a century and a half of Old Testament scholarship.... The final decisive turn in the history of Genesis criticism was the work of Wellhausen, who taught us in his masterpiece *Prolegomena zur Geschichte* Israels to determine the sources of Genesis chronologically and to locate them in the total course of the history of Israel's religion" (Gunkel, Genesis, p. lxix).

"The most important and far-reaching work in the field of synoptic research since Wrede has been done by Wellhausen. ... Wellhausen stated very clearly the fundamental assumption that the tradition consists of individual stories or groups of stories joined together in the Gospels by the work of the editors. ... In these circumstances it was inevitable that the analysis of the synoptics into literary sources should give way to an attempt to apply to them the methods of form-criticism which H. Gunkel and his disciples had already applied to the Old Testament" (Bultmann, *History of the Synoptic Tradition*, p. 2).

to imaginary patriarchs who were projected as founders of the nation. Gunkel doesn't understand why believing Christians should be shocked by such an idea, since for him it is only a matter of understanding the literary genres of the stories, and he does offer the redeeming feature of an ongoing purification away from pure paganism in the biblical tradition, an intellectual ascent from belief in a plurality of imaginary gods to belief in a single imaginary God,[56] and of a gradual movement away from the basest pagan religious practices to higher moral ideals that appeal to people of our time and culture.

32. Let us take as a random example the origin of Abraham and Sarah as reported in Genesis 11:26–29, which reads as follows:

And Terah (Thare) lived seventy years and begot Abram and Nahor (Nachor) and Haran (Aran). 27And these are the generations of Terah: Terah begot Abram, Nahor, and Haran. And Haran begot Lot. 28And Haran died before the face of Terah his father in the land of his nativity in Ur of the Chaldees. 29And Abram and Nahor took wives to themselves: the name of Abram's wife (was) Sarai; and the name of Nahor's wife, Milcah (Melcha), daughter of Haran, father of Milcah and father of Iscah (Jescha).

33. Gunkel distinguishes a "difficulty" in the passage in this that Abram, "the first-born and honored patriarch" of the Israelites, is presented as having married Sarai, whose name in Hebrew means "princess," while Nahor, who is secondary and outside of the Israelite tradition, is said to have taken to wife Milcah, whose name in Hebrew means "queen." The Hebrew poets who fashioned this account would hardly have imagined their patriarch as married to the lesser woman or to be lesser in station himself. Gunkel suggests that this problem would be resolved "if one were to assume the Babylonian origin of the names," inasmuch as the Hebrew name Sarah ("princess") resembles the Babylonian word *šarratu* ("queen"), while the Hebrew name Milcah ("queen") resembles the Babylonian word *malkatu* ("princess"). Gunkel notes that in Babylonian mythology *Šarratu* is the goddess-wife of Sin, the moon-god of the city of Haran, while *Malkatu* is the name of his daughter. Hence, reasons Gunkel, a story about the Babylonian gods may have been turned by Hebrew poets into a story about the founding of the Israelite people, with Abram substituting for the moon-god Sin. Gunkel eases the shock

---

56 In studying the literary genre of form-critical exposition, one should not make the mistake of assuming that, because form-critics follow the literary convention of using a capital letter in referring to the Hebrew and Christian God, they are necessarily implying that the Hebrew and Christian God really exists.

of this astounding revelation by assuring Christian and Jewish believers that the pagan origin of the story "would have been long forgotten in the current tradition."[57]

34. Gunkel's reasoning appears to be weak. We are told in Joshua 24:2–14 that the persons mentioned in this passage were born in a pagan culture and served Mesopotamian gods. As real historical persons, they could easily have been given names relating to pagan gods, but, nevertheless, to match two-syllable combinations with two- or three-syllable combinations of a cognate language can be an extremely tendentious process leading wherever a researcher wants to go. (If the name Hermann superficially resembles the name of the pagan Greek god Hermes, does this give any grounds for suspecting that Hermann Gunkel may never have existed?) But *Šarratu* is not the name of the mythological queen-goddess of Haran; it is Nin-gal, while *šarratu* and *malkatu* are generic designations that could apply to any queen or princess. It is interesting also that Gunkel found no match in the Babylonian pantheon for Abram, who is the principal actor and center of the entire story. In fact, he admits elsewhere that the name Abram was not originally a divine name but was always a "simple personal name."[58]

35. If one wishes to speculate on the origin of these names in relation to Genesis 11, a better hypothesis can be derived from the traditional reading of the passage, granted that some obscurity surrounds it, especially as regards the origin of Sarai, whose paternity seems to have been deliberately omitted. According to an ancient rabbinical tradition, recorded by the Jewish historian Josephus and based upon a comparison with Gen. 20:12, Iscah and Sarai were the same person.[59] In Gen. 20:12 Abraham says to Abimelech regarding Sarah: Besides, she is indeed my sister, the daughter of my father but not the daughter of my mother; and she became my wife." Now, this is understood to mean that Abram and Haran were born of the same father but of different mothers, and Abram later married the daughter of Haran, namely Iscah, who was Abram's half-niece, and whom in this episode he called "my sister" according to Semitic usage. Haran seems to have been rather young when he died (Gen. 1:28), and he left

---

57 Cf. Gunkel, *Genesis*, p. 162.

58 Gunkel, *Genesis*, p. 157.

59 "Aran left a son Lot and daughters Sarra and Melcha … Nachor married his niece Melcha, and Abraham his niece Sarra" (Josephus, *Jewish Antiquities,* in *Josephus* [Harvard Univ. Press: Cambridge, Mass., 1930], vol. 4, p. 75. "… for she was his brother's child" (ibid., p. 105).

two unmarried daughters whom Nahor and Abram took to wife, probably also out of family concern. But Abram appears to have been self-conscious of the fact that he had married his half-niece Iscah, and there is reason to conjecture that he may have preferred from the start to call her by the affectionate name "my princess," with the result that in the passage of time her original name was forgotten. Gen. 17:15–16 tells us that the Lord God changed the name of Sarai to Sarah because from her son "kings of people shall spring." Gunkel seldom, if ever, consulted the Fathers of the Church, but Cornelius aLapide, following the indications of Jerome, Ambrose, and others, explains this to mean that Abram's merely affectionate name for his wife, "my princess," was changed by God in view of the fact that royalty was being bestowed upon her blood.[60] Furthermore, Gunkel's reading that Abram was recorded as Terah's first-born son does not seem to be justified. We are told in Gen 17:17 that Sarah was ten years younger than Abraham. Comparing these verses, if Abraham had been the first-born son, Haran would need to have been no older than nine when he begot Sarah. It is more reasonable to conclude that Haran was older than Abram and, therefore, to read Gen. 1:26 as making the point that Terah was seventy years old when he begot Abram (only), and stating in addition that he had already begotten Nahor and Aram. In this reading, Abram is mentioned first because he was to become the Patriarch of the Jews, and because he is the central human figure of the following account. That the three sons are not listed in descending chronological order is unusual, but the reason for this is implied in the text. In conclusion, the more likely origin of the name Sarai in the marital affection of Abram removes the "difficulty" upon which Gunkel based his imaginary existence of Abraham and Sarah. Gunkel pretended to be speaking in the name of historical science, but archaeological discoveries in the twentieth century have confirmed the real historical existence of Abraham and of the other Hebrew patriarchs.[61]

36. Catholic historical critics do not profess the rationalist presuppositions of Gunkel, Bultmann, and other representatives of the history-of-religions school, but they tend more to overlook these presuppositions than to

---

60 Cf. aLapide, *Great Commentary*, at Gen. 17:15.

61 "Who were the Hebrew Patriarchs? … Some formerly held that the Patriarchs were really de-potentized gods who were transformed by legend into human beings and lost their divine characteristics. Others have thought that, in the course of many centuries of story-telling, the Hebrew Patriarchs came to reflect early ethnic movements. Thanks to our present evidence [1967], it is certain today that the Patriarchs were indeed human beings who were the heroes of stories handed down from the Patriarchal Age" (W.F. Albright, [Athlone: London, 1968], p. 56).

refute them. Thus Richard Clifford, writing in the *New Jerome Biblical Commentary*, neither defends nor denies the real historical existence of Abraham, Isaac, and Jacob, nor does he challenge unequivocally Gunkel's theory of the mythical origin of the patriarchal accounts. His overview is as follows: "Genesis is concerned with origins—of the world of human beings, of Israel in its ancestors. The time of the origin of a reality is a privileged moment in the ancient Near East; the original intention of Fate and the gods is clearer than at other times. In the beginning the impress of the creating gods upon a thing is still fresh and discernible."[62] We might ask ourselves as Catholics what "the intention of Fate and the gods" has to do with origins in the Book of Genesis, unless Clifford is simply unequipped to declare his independence from the theory of the pagan origins of these biblical accounts. Clifford goes on to say: "The second half of Genesis, 11:27–50:26, tells of Israel's origins in its ancestors. Abraham and Sarah labor under the same divine imperatives as the nations—to continue in existence through their progeny and to possess their land. Their way is different, however: by direct relationship to their God in trust." In this view Abraham and Sarah are like another example of pagan literature except that they have a "direct relationship to their God in trust." But trust is a subjective state of mind, and, in this ambiguous, if not tendentious, wording, the God of Abraham and Sarah could be just the imaginary national god of the Israelites as distinct from the imaginary gods of the nations. Clifford tells us that he doesn't know what Genesis authentically has to say: "The position taken in this commentary is that authentic stories of 2nd millennium ancestors have been revised and added to in the long course of their transmission; recovery of the 'original' stories is impossible because of the lack of extra-biblical sources."[63] Predictably, Clifford takes no stand against the alleged "mythical" origin of Abraham and Sarah.[64]

37. Bruce Vawter, in his reference article on Genesis in the *New Catholic Commentary on Holy Scripture*, does venture to take a stand on the question of the real historical existence of Abraham, Isaac, and Jacob. He says: "Genesis is presented by its author as a history, not simply as a collection of religious truths in narrative form. ...Recognition of the author's historical purpose must be our first principle of the interpretation of Genesis, a principle that applies, even though in different ways, to the

---

62 J. Clifford, "Genesis," in *The New Jerome Biblical Commentary*, p. 8A.

63 Clifford, ibid., p. 9A.

64 Cf. Clifford, ibid., p. 19A–B.

history of origins in Gen. 1–11 as well as to the Patriarchal History. ...What is certain is that older opinions that regarded the stories of the Patriarchs as disguised myths or the fictitious accounts of eponymous ancestors can no longer be critically held."[65] However, as a historical critic, Vawter wavers between history and mythology in his explanations of the text of Genesis.

38. Catholic historical critics have tended to accept many of the conclusions of the rationalist founders of form-criticism in the absence of a scientific apparatus for critically examining the presuppositions of the method. Thus, for example, Alexa Suelzer, in a reference article in the *Jerome Biblical Commentary*, reprinted with some modifications by John Kselman in the *New Jerome Biblical Commentary*, identifies the rationalism of the history-of-religions school (notably Gunkel) with scientific method where she says: "For the most part the new discipline was conducted on positivist principles, i.e., principles subject to scientific verification. The goal of its research was fact uncolored by philosophical or theological interpretation. Biblical religion, consequently, was investigated on the same plane as other religions, for all religions were conceived to be a product of human culture."[66] In truth, the presuppositions of this school were contrary to historical fact, as we have illustrated above; the research of this school was colored by the philosophical principle of rationalism; and its investigation was guided by the false idea that the narratives of Genesis were the product of sheer religious imagination, proceeding from a subrational instinct prevailing in pre-modern man and copied essentially from the religious fantasies of the surrounding pagan cultures. Suelzer does not see any of these deficiencies in the history-of-religions methodology. In her evaluation of the form-critical method, Suelzer goes on to say: "By emphasis on oral tradition and by the utilization of the archaeological and literary materials of the Near East, it approached closer to the life situation that produced the biblical writings than did static literary criticism."[67] The truth is completely otherwise. Not only have archaeological studies negated the suppositions of form-criticism, but Gunkel and his colleagues, misled by the modernist idea that religion proceeds from a subrational religious instinct, entirely missed the life-

---

65 B. Vawter, "Genesis," in the *New Catholic Commentary on Holy Scripture,*" p. 168. An "eponym" is "a real or imaginary person for whom something is named," so that "eponymous" means "giving one's name to a place, institution, syndrome, or disease" (Webster's).

66 A. Suelzer, "Modern Old Testament Criticism," in the *Jerome Biblical Commentary* (1968), p. 596B; in *The New Jerome Biblical Commentary* (1990), p. 1120A.

67 Suelzer, in the *JBC*, p. 599B; in the *NJBC*, p. 1123A.

situation of the biblical writers. For authentic form-critics, the events recounted in the Scriptures represent a copying with adaptations of earlier purely imaginary events conceived by the religious imagination. The life-situation from which the accounts in Genesis originated was supposed to be a state of mind of Hebrew folk-tellers so primitive that they could not even have made up the stories themselves but had to depend on adapting pagan stories. This notion of the "history" of the forms of the biblical narratives is itself a product of the imagination of its form-critical originators; it certainly does not represent what Suelzer calls "sober investigation."[68]

39. In the parallel article on New Testament criticism, first published in the *Jerome Biblical Commentary* and republished with some modifications in the *New Jerome Biblical Commentary*, John Kselman shows the same inability of Catholic historical critics to identify the deficiencies of the form-criticism of the Gospels, as exemplified by its originators, K.L. Schmidt, Martin Dibelius, and, above all, Rudolf Bultmann. After an introductory tribute to "the great Old Testament scholar H. Gunkel," Kselman notes that Bultmann and other form-critics assumed that "the early Christians were not at all interested in history," and that, consequently, "the Gospels are not biographies, giving us a consistent historical picture of the life of Jesus, but reflections of the faith and life of the early church." Continuing to report what these form-critics assumed, Kselman goes on to say: "In fact, history was of so little concern to the early Christian community that they made no great distinction between the earthly history of Jesus and his post-resurrectional history and presence with the church, to whom he still spoke by the Spirit. Without the strictures of history and with its assurance of Jesus' presence, the early church could freely adapt and even creatively add to the tradition, if the needs of the church for preaching, apologetics, worship, etc., so required."[69] Kselman sees a pronounced skepticism in Bultmann's method "in that he assigns most of the tradition to the creative imagination of the early Christian communities."[70] That Bultmann and his colleagues took this outrageous position is known to many, but what is striking about Kselman's resume is the absence of any effective criticism of this stance. For Bultmann and others, the "post-resurrectional history of Jesus" is sheer religious fantasy, and this anti-Christian assumption should

---

68 Suelzer, in the *JBC*, p. 597A); in the *NJBC*, p. 1120A.

69 J.S. Kselman, "Modern New Testament Criticism," in *The Jerome Biblical Commentary*, p. 14; in *The New Jerome Biblical Commentary*, p. 1137.

70 Kselman, in the *JBC*, p. 15A; in the *NJBC*, p. 1138B.

not go uncorrected. To allege that the early Christian church, with naive credulity in the "presence" of a factually dead Jesus and of an imaginary "Spirit," took upon itself to invent stories in order to accommodate its message to its preaching and apologetic needs is a calumny that cannot be accepted. Bultmann excuses the early Christians for these alleged lies on the ground that they were too intellectually immature to be able to lie, but this also is a calumny having no basis in historical fact. In this regard we might well attend to the words of William Foxwell Albright, one of the most renowned archaeologists of the twentieth century, where he says: "Only modern scholars who lack both historical method and perspective can spin such a web of speculation as that with which form-critics have surrounded the Gospel tradition. ...In dealing with the Gospels the historian cannot but see a profound difference between their contents and typical examples elsewhere of matter which has been long transmitted by oral tradition. What we have in them is rather a reflection of reports of eye-witnesses who were overwhelmed by the profound experiences and the extreme tension of mind and body through which they had passed. Men who see the boundary between conventional experience and the transcendental world dissolving before their very eyes are not going to distinguish clearly between things seen in the plane of nature and things seen in the world of spirit. To speak of the latter as 'hallucinations' is quite misleading, since nothing like them is otherwise known to historians or to psychologists. Here the historian has no right to deny what he cannot disprove. He has a perfect right to unveil clear examples of charlatanry, of credulity, or of folklore, but in the presence of authentic mysteries his duty is to stop and not attempt to cross the threshold into a world where he has no right of citizenship."[71] In *A Catholic Commentary on Holy Scripture*, Gutwenger summarizes the situation in the following words: "In the description of the literary form of the gospel units the form-critics have shown much shrewdness. But in their conclusions they are as arbitrary as possible. The whole theory of Dibelius and Bultmann is built on the supposition that the early Christians had no biographical interest in the life of Jesus and that a strange transformation of the portrait of Jesus occurred at a time when plenty of eye-witnesses were still alive. *Sic volo. Sic jubeo.* External evidence is absolutely neglected by the form-critics. Instead we meet with a welter of unfounded hypotheses put down as facts with a breath-taking naivety."[72]

---

71 W.F. Albright, *From the Stone Age to Christianity* (Johns Hopkins Press: Baltimore, 1957), pp. 387 and 390.

72 E. Gutwenger, "The Gospels and Non-Catholic Higher Criticism," in *A Catholic*

40. Kselman praises Bultmann for "combining immense erudition and scholarship with a profoundly pastoral desire to preach a meaningful and relevant message to his contemporaries in a world where faith is no longer easy."[73] This is a very superficial judgment for a Catholic exegete. Bultmann's "immense erudition and scholarship" fall away to nothing as one falsity after another is unearthed throughout his writings, and his "profoundly pastoral desire" is hardly pastoral when viewed in its full reality. In fact, Bultmann's pastoral situation was as follows. After claiming to have eliminated almost all of the historical reality from the Gospel accounts, and to have exposed the literal teaching of the Gospels as primitive religious fantasy unacceptable to modern man, he had to find some excuse for contemporary Christians to believe and for contemporary preachers to preach. He claimed to have discovered this reason in the philosophy of Martin Heidegger, according to which a Christian could exercise his faith by using the message of the Gospels as an occasion to repeatedly choose his own self-authenticity, to seek over and over again "in the existential moment" and to grasp his own "authentic self" as a goal which he can never expect actually to achieve. This deceptive double-talk cannot be called pastoral in any meaningful sense; it is merely an excuse for having taken away by specious reasoning the real message of the Gospels. Hence, the only truly pastoral response to Bultmann is to refute every premise and conclusion of his biblical interpretation. Bultmann took the Lutheran notion of the radical separation of faith and reason to be an absolute separation of faith and reason, and he used this principle to negate the entire object of Christian faith. Believing Lutherans opposed this teaching of Bultmann in his day and they continue to oppose it today. On the Catholic side, an adequate response to Bultmann must include a clear demonstration that there is no such thing as the absolute separation of faith and reason.

41. One reason for which Catholic form-critics cannot adequately identify and refute the deficiencies of Bultmann's exegetical method is that they lack a sufficiently differentiated mental framework. Among the false principles underlying Bultmann's method are those of deism, naturalism, rationalism, and modernism. Bultmann absorbed these principles from the tradition in which he was educated and from his personal study, and they are expressed systematically in his various writings.[74] Catholic form-critics

---

Commentary on Holy Scripture (1953), p. 759B.

73 Kselman, "Modern New Testament Criticism," in the *JBC*, p. 14B; in the *NJBC*, p. 1137B.

74 A notable expression of the ideology inspiring Bultmann's exegetical work is his essay,

tend to ignore the influence of these principles and simply work with texts on a more superficial level, an activity which inevitably raises unanswered questions. For instance, Catholic form-critics halt their dissolving of the historical truth of the biblical text where a dogma of the Church would otherwise be attacked, not because their exegetical method calls for them to halt, but because the discipline of faith demands it. Bultmann has asked: "Once you have begun to demythologize the text, where can you draw the line?" Catholic form-critics have no good answer to that question; either they resign themselves to being inconsistent with the presuppositions of the method or they are tempted to begin thinking that perhaps the dogmas should be adjusted to fit the results of the method.

42. Catholic form-critics are for the most part, not sufficiently aware of their own framework of thought. Their borrowed method has been heavily influenced by the Kantian theory of knowledge, according to which the human mind knows only its own mental objects (*phenomena*) and cannot know extra-mental objects in themselves (*noumena*). In keeping with this philosophy, Catholic form-critics work, for the most part unreflectively, with what many modern thinkers call the "subject-object relationship," wherein the object is considered to be purely mental and only seems to reproduce extra-mental reality. Gunkel, Bultmann, Dibelius, and their colleagues worked within a mental atmosphere of shared rationalist presuppositions, and their goal was to produce from these presuppositions conjectures that would be deemed plausible enough to merit common agreement. Whether or not their conclusions corresponded with what non-Kantians call external reality made little difference to them, and, unfortunately, to one extent or another, Catholic form-critics often let themselves be drawn into that same Kantian atmosphere.

43. Neo-patristic interpreters follow a theory of moderate realism, according to which the human mind does know external reality, but in terms of reconstructions within the mind itself, just as a telescope reproduces within itself an image of its object. They sharpen as best they can their mental images in order to be able to see the external objects more exactly. One important mental object is the very concept itself of reality, by which a thinker is able to adhere intentionally to external reality

---

"*Neues Testament und Mythologie,*" first published in German in 1941, and republished in English as "*New Testament and Mythology*" in H.W. Bartsch, ed., Kerygma and Myth: A Theological Debate (vol. 1, SPCK: London, 1953). For a brief exposition of Bultmann's overall plan, see "*The Goal of Demythologizing,*" in J.F. McCarthy, *The Science of Historical Theology,* pp. 5–9 and 101–102). For a critique of this plan see McCarthy, ibid., pp. 102–140.

and to avoid conscious deviations into error or fantasy. We maintain that the biblical writers kept strict adherence to the concept of reality as they wrote their accounts. Bultmann's "literary forms" of the Gospels all pertain to the realm of fantasy; they are "literary" in the sense of "fictional." Catholic form-critics do try to distinguish a "historical base" for some of the Bultmannian forms, especially in the case of Gospel events related to dogmas of the Church, but the method does not allow these exceptions to look very convincing. When Catholic form-critics present their version of literary forms in the Gospels, they can never give a confident and decisive answer in the affirmative to the all-pervading question: "Are we dealing here with historical reality?" The presuppositions of the method simply do not permit a definitive answer in the affirmative. A better approach is to start with the patristic division of literary genres into the historical, the poetic, the didactic, and the prophetic with their subdivisions. This division brings immediately into consideration the use or non-use of the concept of reality, not only in the text under study, but also in the mind of the scholar making the study. The historical genre, in this Patristic division of literary forms, has to do with what really took place both outside of the mind of the sacred writer and outside of the mind of the biblical scholar.

44. With reference to our experimental definitions of "history" (no. 23 above), we have concluded that the history which is the direct object of biblical research is not merely "the past," but is rather "the real past." Form-critics characteristically disregard this proper object and assume that Gospel history is, for the most part, a history of imaginary episodes or imaginary elaborations of purely natural events, as they really developed in the minds of successive narrators. This form-critical "history of imaginary events and invented sayings" has no justification in historical science, defined as "the knowledge of the real past as such." Certainly there is a history of the narration of the real events and real discourses recorded in the text of the Gospels and in the whole of Sacred Scripture, and there is need to study this history, but the creative fantasy attributed to the sacred text exists only in the minds of the critics. The Gospels are chronological records of real events, systematically written, even though not according to the technical conventions of modern historians. One unique systematic feature of biblical historiography is the simultaneous exposition of a literal sense and of a spiritual sense portraying figures and analogies of various kinds. To ignore this feature is to misconstrue the biblical genre. The Gospels are scientific writings on the level of common science, that is, of common sense, and they contain true representations of the events that

they describe, even though they even deliberately refrain at times from the kind of material accuracy required of modern historians. While the sacred writers of both Testaments did not use all of the techniques of modern historical method, they did test their sources and they were aided in their writing by the inspiration of the Holy Spirit. Their awareness of the real existence and activity of God, which was far superior to the mundane awareness of later critics, gave them an advantage in the writing of history that has never been equaled or surpassed. Since *to understand* means to know a reality in terms of some other reality, no one can understand a text of Sacred Scripture who cannot relate what is written in the text to his own awareness of the presence of God. Every man, at every waking moment of his life, is interfacing with the real effects of God's presence, whether or not he is able to reflect on this fact. Hence, every exegetical method whose approach rules out the real effects of God's presence, not only as known to the mind of the sacred writer, writing under the influence of divine inspiration, but also as known or knowable to the mind of man, will tend to diminish rather than increase the biblical interpreter's understanding of Sacred Scripture.

Chapter 7

A Neo-Patristic Approach to Biblical Inspiration

Living Tradition 129 (May 2007)

1. The neo-patristic approach represents a continuation of the Catholic exegetical tradition and at the same time undertakes a comprehensive correction of the current historical critical approach to the interpretation of Sacred Scripture. The neo-patristic approach is based upon the method of the Fathers of the Church, amplified by the great Catholic theologians of medieval and modern times, and developed according to the mental framework of the Four Senses as elaborated by St. Thomas Aquinas. The neo-patristic method makes use of the valid techniques of modern historical science while it critically examines historical critical reasonings. For the purposes of the present article, I set out to present a neo-patristic understanding of the divine inspiration of Sacred Scripture together with a critical examination of Catholic historical critical ideas of the same. I have taken as historical critical examples the essays, "The Inspiration of Scripture," by Lionel Swain in *A New Catholic Commentary on Holy Scripture* (1969), and "Inspiration," by Raymond F. Collins in *The New Jerome Biblical Commentary* (1990). While these two monographs are not totally up-to-date, they are peer-reviewed by their historical critical editors and they are typical examples of the historical critical approach. I fully acknowledge that much valuable information is presented in these two essays, but I shall concentrate especially on some of their differences from the neo-patristic approach in order to bring out the urgent need for their replacement.

2. Divine Inspiration of the Scriptures as expressed in the authentic teaching of the Church.

2A. The Council of Trent: "The sacred and holy ecumenical and general Synod of Trent...clearly perceiving that [the aforementioned saving] truth and moral standards are contained in the written books and in unwritten traditions which have been received by the apostles from the mouth of Christ Himself, or from the apostles themselves under the dictation of the Holy Spirit, have come down to us, transmitted as it were from hand to hand, following the example of the fathers of the true faith, receives and venerates with equal devotion and reverence all of the books both of the Old and of the New Testaments, since God is the author of both, and also the traditions themselves, those that appertain both to faith and to morals, as having been dictated either by Christ's own word of mouth, or by the Holy Spirit, and preserved in the Catholic Church by a continuous succession (EB 57)."

2B. The First Vatican Council (1870): "But the Church holds these books as sacred and canonical, not because, having been put together by human industry alone, they were then approved by her authority; nor precisely because they contain revelation without error; but on account of this that, having been written by the inspiration of the Holy Spirit, they have God as their author and, as such, they have been handed down to the Church herself. Can. 4: If anyone shall not have accepted the entire books of Sacred Scripture with all their parts, just as the sacred Synod of Trent has enumerated them, as canonical and sacred, or shall have denied that they have been divinely inspired: let him be anathema (EB 77, 79)."

2C. Pope Leo XIII, Encyclical Letter *Providentissimus Deus* (1893): "For all the books which the Church receives as sacred and canonical are written wholly and entirely, with all their parts, at the dictation of the Holy Spirit; and so far is it from being possible that any error can coexist with divine inspiration that of itself it not only excludes all error, but also excludes and rejects it as necessarily as it is necessary that God, the supreme Truth, cannot be the author of any error whatsoever. This is the ancient and constant faith of the Church, defined by solemn judgment in the Councils of Florence and Trent, and finally and more expressly formulated by the [First] Vatican Council (EB 124–125)."

"Hence, it makes no difference at all that it was men whom the Holy Spirit took up as his instruments for writing, as though something false could have gotten away, not, indeed, from the primary author, but from the inspired writers. For, by supernatural power, He so moved and impelled them to write—He so assisted them when writing—that all of the things which He ordered, and these only, they first rightly understood, then willed faithfully to write down, and finally expressed aptly and with infallible truth. Otherwise, He would not be the author of all Sacred Scripture. Such has always been the persuasion of the Fathers (EB 125)."

2D. Pope Pius XII, Encyclical Letter *Divino afflante Spiritu* (1943): " ...(that the Catholic commentator) not only may refute the objections of the adversaries, but also may attempt to find a solid solution which will be in full accord with the doctrine of the Church, in particular with the traditional teaching regarding the inerrancy of Sacred Scripture, and which will at the same time satisfy the certain conclusions of the profane sciences (EB 564)."

2E. Pope Pius XII, Encyclical Letter *Humani generis* (1950): "For some audaciously pervert the sense of the [First] Vatican Council's definition that God is the author of Holy Scripture, and they put forward again the opinion, already several times condemned, according to which the immunity from errors of Sacred Writ extends only to those things which are conveyed concerning God and moral and religious matters. They even wrongly speak of a human meaning of the Sacred Books, beneath which lies hidden a divine meaning, which they declare to be the only infallible meaning. In interpreting Sacred Scripture, they will take no account of the analogy of faith and the 'tradition' of the Church. Thus they judge that the teaching of the Fathers and of the sacred Magisterium is to be put back on the scale of Sacred Scripture, as explained by the purely human reasoning of exegetes, instead of expounding Holy Scripture according to the mind of the Church which Christ Our Lord has set up as guardian and interpreter of the whole deposit of divinely revealed truth. ...There is no one who should not see how foreign all this is to the principles and norms of interpretation rightly fixed by Our Predecessors of happy memory, Leo XIII in his encyclical *Providentissimus*, and Benedict XV in the encyclical *Spiritus Paraclitus,* and also by Ourselves in the encyclical *Divino afflante Spiritu* (EB 612–613)."

2F. The Second Vatican Council, Constitution *Dei Verbum* (1965): "For Holy Mother Church, relying on the faith of the apostolic age, accepts as sacred and canonical the books of the Old and the New Testaments, whole and entire, with all their parts, on the grounds that, written under the inspiration of the Holy Spirit, they have God as their author, and have been handed on as such to the Church herself. To compose the sacred books, God chose certain men who, all the while he employed them in this task, made full use of their powers and faculties so that, though he acted in them and by them, it was as true authors that they consigned to writing whatever he wanted written, and no more. Since, therefore, all that the inspired authors, or sacred writers, affirm should be regarded as affirmed by the Holy Spirit, we must acknowledge that the books of Scripture, firmly, faithfully, and without error, teach that truth which God, for the sake of our salvation, wished to see confided to the sacred Scriptures (Flannery translation, no. 11)."

3. Speaking from the viewpoint of a modern historical critic, Lionel Swain avers that with the advancements of textual criticism in the sixteenth century, of literary criticism in the seventeenth century, of rationalism in the eighteenth century, and of archaeology, the natural sciences, and the more scientific study of history in the nineteenth century, "it had become increasingly evident that the assertions of the Bible could no longer be taken simply at their face value." What he means is that many believers now saw Sacred Scripture as being erroneous in many places, and others sought to cover over "the obvious discrepancies between the discoveries of the human reason and the Bible," or tried to reconcile various errors with its overall historicity, or just "buried their heads in the biblical sands."[1] There are problems with Swain's historical overview. It was, in fact, not at all evident that, by the late nineteenth century, statements in the Bible "could not be taken at their face value." In 1893 Pope Leo XIII declared it to be *the ancient and constant faith of the Church* that divine inspiration of itself excludes and rejects all error (no. 2C above). Swain here makes a kind of identification of rationalism with human reason, whereas there is an essential difference between the two. Rationalism is reasoning from false principles, especially from the false assumption that miracles and the miraculous cannot exist, and it was on the basis of this erroneous presupposition that errors and "discrepancies" were being ascribed to the Bible. Catholic exegetes and theologians were still defending the historical inerrancy of Sacred Scripture, but the historical critical view was just beginning to creep in whereby it was assumed to be "scientifically" mistaken even to try to reconcile the apparent contradictions with one another, although good science always makes this attempt. The techniques of form-criticism, initiated by Hermann Gunkel, were arising, according to which every plausible crack in the biblical fabric was accorded an advance of the historical method and every truly historical vestige remaining in the Bible was deemed a snag possibly to be overcome.

4. Swain goes on to affirm that the new historical criticism was combating "a negative, defensive attitude" which implicitly identified biblical truth with "scientific and historical accuracy." And, he continues, it was in this context that various documents of the Magisterium (such as

---

1 L. Swain, "The Inspiration of Scripture," in R.C. Fuller et al., editors, *A New Catholic Commentary on Holy Scripture* (Nashville: Thomas Nelson, 1969), p. 55, col. B.

those listed in nos. 2B-2C above and others by Pope Pius X, the Pontifical Biblical Commission, and Pope Benedict XV) "saw the necessity of affirming that the sacred books contained 'revelation without error.'"[2] But there is an equivocation in Swain's use of the expression "scientific and historical accuracy." The replies of the Pontifical Biblical Commission and other documents of the Magisterium had made clear that the biblical genre (even of its very nature) was not limited to the material precision that modern historians often set for themselves, but here we are not dealing with a question of precision. The question is rather of historical and scientific truth or error. The Magisterium has clearly and consistently taught over the centuries that the sacred text contains no scientific or historical errors, and Swain is trying to get around that. The "negative, defensive attitude" that he mentions is a feature of Catholic apologetics that has always been functional in the Church, but which has been greatly weakened in recent times, due largely to the failure of Catholic historical critics to recognize the fallacies in the attacks made against the truth of the Scriptures in the name of history and science.

5. Raymond Collins also presents a historical critical view of biblical inspiration where he says that objections to the "theory of verbal inspiration" have led most critical scholars to abandon it.[3] While this statement refers directly to what he calls the "prophetic model of inspiration," it has impact on the traditional Catholic approach. The words of Sacred Scripture are verbal expressions, and it is the traditional teaching of the Church that these words are inspired (see no. 2C above). The inspiration of Sacred Scripture refers, not to the events themselves, but to their verbal expression. And, even though "human writing processes were at work," a discernible supernatural process was also at work, and it is plainly evident both in the rapport of faith to the teaching of Scripture and in the inerrancy of the text. The non-Catholic originators of historical criticism and of the form-critical method, such as Hermann Gunkel and Rudolf Bultmann, openly excluded any real divine action underlying the writing of the Scriptures, and Catholic historical critics like Raymond Collins and Lionel Swain have the burden of clearly showing how their stand significantly differs from the original rationalist position, which is plainly contrary to the perennial teaching of the Church. But no clear Catholic position emerges here. While acknowledging that the historical critical method was "the

---

2 Swain, op. cit., p. 59, col. A.

3 Cf. R.F. Collins, "Inspiration," in *The New Jerome Biblical Commentary,* R.E. Brown et al., editors (Englewood Cliffs: Prentice Hall, 1990), p. 1028, col. B.

child of the Enlightenment," Collins points out that it brought about "the modification of traditional formulations by many Roman Catholics." The Magisterium intervened to correct these "modifications" (see nos. 2A–2E above), but, according to Collins, "in somewhat negative fashion."[4] Thus, Collins continues, "the inerrant 'truth' of the Bible was deemed all-important," but this approach, he says, has changed since Vatican II. However, Collins and other Catholic historical critics are simply exploiting an ambiguity in the wording of *Dei Verbum*, regarding *"the truth which God, for the sake of our salvation, wished to see confided to the sacred Scriptures."* These scholars read the text as though it means *only* that truth which is aimed at our salvation, but this reading is contrary to the intention of the Council, as is clearly indicated in the footnotes that the Council itself appended to these words. In fact, the footnotes of the conciliar document include references to *Providentissimus Deus,* exactly where it says that divine inspiration absolutely excludes any error (*EB* 124: see no. 2B above) and that error cannot be ascribed to the human authors as distinct from the divine author (*EB* 125: see again no. 2B above.) And the same footnote references include the following judgment from *Providentissimus Deus*: *"It follows that those who maintain that an error is possible in any genuine passage of the sacred writings either pervert the Catholic notion of inspiration or make God the author of such error."* Hence, the opinion that biblical inerrancy covers only that truth which pertains to our salvation cannot be sustained, as is brought out in the encyclical *Humani generis* of Pope Pius XII (1950), where he excludes once again *"the opinion, already several times condemned, according to which the immunity from errors of Sacred Writ extends only to those things which are conveyed concerning God and moral and religious matters"* (see no. 2E above).

6. Collins points out that increased data (available to historical critical scholars) regarding the origins of the earth and of the human race "led to incompatibility between scientific knowledge and a naïve, literal reading of the creation narratives."[5] Here Collins makes almost synonymous the adjectives *naïve* and *literal,* but there is a big difference between the two. While the Galileo case is usually the grand exhibit of secular humanists on this question, the fact is that Catholic exegetical tradition has regularly cautioned against naïve readings of the Scriptures, while upholding the literal reading of the same. Modern empirical science has raised serious questions regarding the reading of the "days" of creation in Genesis 1, but

---

4 Collins, op. cit., p. 1029, col. A.

5 Collins, op. cit., p. 1029, col. A.

the Magisterium, in the replies of the Pontifical Biblical Commission of June 30, 1909 (*EB* 324–331), has also clarified this in a very satisfying way, and it is by no means clear that the six creative interventions of God described in the first chapter of Genesis are at all incompatible with the findings of modern empirical science.[6] Similarly, the reduction by historical critics of the story of Adam and Eve in Gen 2–3 to the level of religious fiction is not based upon solid historical reasoning. While Catholic form-critics, in using the method of Gunkel and Bultmann, do not necessarily accept all of Gunkel's and Bultmann's outrageous conclusions, they have been notably inept at refuting them. As far as the needed refutation of errors is concerned, the multitude of fallacies in Gunkel's *Genesis* (1901) and Bultmann's *History of the Synoptic Tradition* (1921) have now lain undigested in the belly of Catholic historical criticism in the first case for well over a century and in the other almost a century. Gunkel's *Genesis* and Bultmann's *History of the Synoptic Tradition* are insults to Catholic belief, but no Catholic historical critic has ever written a worthy response to either of them. The English translation of the third edition (1910) of Gunkel's *Genesis*, published in 1997, can even be found on sale in many Catholic book stores mixed indiscriminately with works by solidly Catholic authors, and Bultmann is often quoted favorably in Catholic historical critical commentaries.

7. Collins maintains that "form-criticism has demonstrated that to a large extent the books of the Bible are products of faith communities,"[7] but he and other Catholic form-critics do not distinguish adequately how their notion of "creative faith communities" differs significantly from the rationalist notion of Bultmann, whose use of the term is earlier and "in possession." Bultmann reasoned from the rationalist social theories of Émil Durkheim to his pseudoscientific idea of the "creative Christian community," whose religious fantasy supposedly created most of the fictitious stories that he says constitute the Gospels, but this idea has no basis in objective history. Catholics who use the Bultmannian theory of the creative Christian community have actually imported into their work a rationalist presupposition about faith communities that does great injustice to the human writers and to the text of the Bible. Émile Durkheim (1858–1917), a French agnostic writer and teacher

---

6 For a study of this question and a literal defense of the days of creation see J.F. McCarthy, "A Neo-Patristic Return to the First Four Days of Creation, in *Living Tradition* 45–50 (March 1993 to January 1994), on the Internet at www.rtforum.org., archive of articles.

7 Collins, op. cit., p. 1032, col. A.

who was very influential, for weal and for woe, in the rise of modern sociology, contrasted two basic types of society: primitive and modern. *Primitive society*, he said, is "mechanically" organized and depends for its cohesion on the pressure of a collective conscience, presenting "collective representations" that are independent of individual consciousness. Of these pre-conceptual forms, religion is said to be the clearest expression.[8] In his final major work, *The Elementary Forms of Religious Life* (1912), using the presupposition that society is anterior to the individual together with data collected from observations of the habits of Australian aborigines, Durkheim maintained that the most fundamental ideas of religion are distillations of social experience. He held that the basic and universal distinction between the sacred and the profane arises instinctively in society, and that from the felt power of the community primitive man derived gradually his sense of deity and of the binding nature of the sacred. Relative to Immanuel Kant's theory of knowledge, he held that the basic categories of thought arose from the pressure of primitive community practices.[9] Durkheim's theory, however much it might apply to Australian aborigines, when it was applied by Bultmann to the early Christian Church, contradicted all historical experience and all Jewish and Christian religious belief. That Bultmann's idea does not concur with historical science can be shown by a detailed analysis of his exegesis of the Gospels, but Catholic form-critics have not done this. When we see them explaining the origin of supposedly fictitious stories and statements in the Gospels as having arisen because of dogmatic, apologetic, or polemic needs, and other purposes of this sort, we do not, indeed, hear them claiming to be promoting the Durkheimian paradigm of the primitive and pre-rational religious community, but neither do we find them giving clear evidence that they are opposing this rationalist structure. And it is this same irrational idea that is rejected in the encyclical *Pascendi dominici gregis* of Pope Pius X, where it rules out the modernist notion that belief in the objects of Christian faith is based ultimately upon a subjective feeling that arose instinctively in the subconscious of the primitive Christian community (*Pascendi*, no. 7). Hence, it is not that Catholic form-critics profess this error, but rather that they are so remiss in excluding it from their interpretations.

---

8 Cf. John M. Goering, "Durkheim, Émil," in the *Encyclopedia Americana*, vol. 9 (Danbury: Americana Corp., 1980), p. 494.

9 Cf. R.A. Nisbet, "Durkheim, Émil," in the *New Catholic Encyclopedia*, vol. 4 (New York: McGraw-Hill, 1967), pp. 1121–1122.

8. Collins downplays the perennial teaching of the Church as he affirms that, since the Second Vatican Council, "inerrant Scriptural 'truth'" has not received "primary emphasis in Roman Catholic circles," because of "a more adequate understanding of the nature of the Scriptures," namely that they are "not *primarily* a source for doctrine."[10] One can well wonder at the word-manipulations and mental gymnastics that it took these "Roman Catholic circles" to arrive at this conclusion, which directly and flatly contradicts the quotations from the Magisterium that are given in number 2 above. Collins goes on to assert that concentration on the inspiration of individual sentences and isolated biblical texts "can produce a type of fundamentalism."[11] The word *fundamentalism* applies to a group of American Protestant communities which adopted in the 1890s a brief set of propositions that they considered to be fundamental to all Christian belief, but Collins extends it here to embrace the whole traditional Catholic approach to the inerrancy of the sacred text, including that of the Fathers of the Church, the great medieval theologians, most Catholic commentators up to the end of the nineteenth century, and the traditional teachings of the Church as quoted above. Collins uses the new form-critical idea of literary forms to emphasize the "salvific truth" of the Bible, which, he says, "lies not so much in that its passages are without error, but in that through them God manifests his fidelity to his people, bringing them into loving union with himself."[12] Thus, biblical inerrancy recedes to a vague general theme hypothesized by the interpreter to ride above a biblical text believed to be composed mostly of fictitious stories and historical errors, but how this presupposed divine underlying sense, which alone is given the character of inerrancy, can escape the strictures of *Humani generis* as quoted above at no. 2E is a mystery to me.

9. Under the title of "Inspiration Today," Swain presents a similar position to that of Collins as he explains his understanding of the idea that "the Bible is entirely man's work and entirely God's work." The concept of "God's transcendent causality" is "truly liberating," because "it facilitates the dissociation of the notion of inspiration from any one of its preconceived modes" [such as, let us say, the modes defined by the Magisterium of the Church as quoted in no. 2 above], because, he continues, "revelation affirms the fact of inspiration, but it is left for human research [for us, the exegetes],

---

10 Collins, op. cit., p. 1030, col. B.

11 Collins, op. cit., p. 1032, col. B.

12 Collins, op. cit., p. 1033, col. B.

based on the data of the Scriptures themselves [which only we the exegetes can identify] to describe exactly *how* the Holy Spirit inspired the sacred writers."[13] Note how Pope Pius XII comments on this idea in number 2E above. But what is meant by "God's transcendent causality"? Swain explains by drawing a parallel with the doctrine of creation, "particularly in the light of the last century's evolutionary theories." I think that he is referring to the theories of certain theistic evolutionists who maintain that God created the original state of the universe and then left it to evolve on its own, which is a new form of Deism. According to this parallel, God would be seen to have allowed the Scriptures to be composed and written entirely by the natural forces of human activity, but "transcendentally" they would be God's Scriptures as well, even though there would be no discernible divine factor apart from the natural human endeavor. This idea is "truly liberating," not only from the traditional teaching of the Church, but also from the need to defend the divine element against non-believing critics who don't believe in it, such as the mainstream, non-Catholic historical critics of today. In other words, while Swain allows that "the actual Scriptures were written under a specific motion of the Holy Spirit related to certain charismatic functions within the people and at the service both of God and of the people,"[14] he does not explain how this motion of the Holy Spirit could appear and be identified in the actual exegesis of the text, and how, therefore, it is a real element at all.

A Neo-Patristic Understanding of Biblical Inspiration

10. The neo-patristic approach follows the traditional teaching of the Church regarding the divine inspiration of Sacred Scripture, as expressed in the decrees of the ecumenical councils, in the papal encyclicals, and in other documents of the Magisterium, as summarized in the *Catechism of the Catholic Church*. It maintains that the divinely revealed realities that are presented in it have been written down under the inspiration of the Holy Spirit, that God is the Author of Sacred Scripture, and that the canonical books of the Old and New Testaments have been written, whole and entire, with all their parts, under the inspiration of the Holy Spirit (cf. *Dei Verbum* 11; *CCC* 105). The neo-patristic approach holds that God used the sacred writers in such a way that they made full use of their own faculties and

---

13 Swain, op. cit., p. 57, col. A.

14 Swain, op. cit., p. 58, col. A.

powers so as to be true authors, but also in such a manner that they wrote whatever He wanted written and no more (cf. *Dei Verbum 11*; *CCC* 106). This means that they were preserved from writing any historical or natural errors, either because God willed that they write such errors or that they added them on their own. Thus, the books of Sacred Scripture "firmly, faithfully, and without error teach that truth which God, for the sake of our salvation, wished to see confided to the Sacred Scriptures" (*Dei Verbum* 11; *CCC* 107). Since it is the teaching of the Church that biblical inspiration absolutely excludes and rejects any error (*Prov. Deus,* 2C above), and since it is an obligation of interpreters to refute the objections of those who deny the inerrancy of the Scriptures (*Divino afflante Spiritu,* 2D above), neo-patristic exegesis undertakes the time-honored task of defending biblical inerrancy in the face of difficulties raised, not only by non-believers but also by believing historical critics. Therefore, it rejects the approach which casts biblical apologetics under the name of "concordism" and "fundamentalism" and seeks to show the methodological mistakes of those who attribute errors to the sacred text. While neo-patristic scholars cannot claim to have a ready answer to every difficulty that has been or could be raised, the number of superficially presented "discrepancies" is so great at the present time that the field of correction is wide open.

11. Lionel Swain's affirmation that in recent centuries it became increasingly evident that statements of Sacred Scripture "could no longer be taken simply at their face value," appears to be valid only to the extent that Catholic theologians and exegetes were neglecting their duty to solve the problems raised by some modern empirical scientists and by historians, especially of the historical critical school. It must be kept in mind that Catholic historical critical exegetes have no intellectual tradition of their own, and they tend to look back historically, not through Catholic intellectual tradition, but through the liberal Protestant tradition, with the result that they tend to accept many of the claims made against the Catholic tradition by influential thinkers of the "Enlightenment" of the seventeenth century, of the rationalism of the eighteenth century, and of the liberal Protestant exegetes of the nineteenth and twentieth centuries. Neo-patristic researchers keep this in mind as they examine the mental framework used by historical critical writers. Catholic historical critics have, for the most part, rejected the mental framework used traditionally by the Fathers and Doctors of the Church and by most Catholic theologians and exegetes over the centuries, with the result that they are left methodically with a largely implicit Protestant framework which, as Catholics, they can use

only partially. As a result, many of the principles that they use are not well-formulated in their minds and often function in an incorrect or twisted manner. They use terms that are poorly defined, they set up conclusions that they do not clearly express, and they ignore answers that were given long ago by writers of Catholic tradition. Thus Joseph Cardinal Ratzinger, in a widely circulated article published originally in 1989, called upon historical critical exegetes to employ "a less arbitrary philosophy which offers greater possibilities for a true hearing of the text."[15] He pointed out that it has become imperative at this juncture of time to build a new and better synthesis of exegetical method,[16] to challenge the framework of systematic presuppositions underlying the exegesis of writers like Rudolf Bultmann,[17] and to get modern exegesis away from the influence of Immanuel Kant, which has reduced history to philosophy.[18] It is a task of the neo-patristic method, in its critical review of the historical critical method, to formulate and correct the poorly formulated or incorrect principles of the historical critical method, to work with more clearly defined terms, and to recast the vague and largely implicit mental framework of Catholic form-criticism into an explicit framework of historical science.

12. In addition to the framework of the Four Senses, neo-patristic exegetes use the mental framework of Scholastic philosophy and theology, with which they conjoin the principles of a truly historical method, all of which provide for them precise definitions of terms. A methodological error characteristic of the approach of Catholic form-critics is the use of improperly defined terms, such as the words *scientific, historical, critical, real,* and *literary form.* For example, Catholic form-critics often refer to their method as being "scientific," but they ignore the essential element of all science, which is functional adherence to the concept of reality. Catholic form-critics expound at length the "meaning" of biblical passages, but usually without any reference to whether the events they are explaining really took place or not. On the other hand, Gunkel and Bultmann clearly affirm that most of the literary forms presenting biblical events are fictional and that all of the miraculous events are simply products of religious fantasy. In many instances, and especially in the case of biblical accounts

---

15 J. Cardinal Ratzinger, "Biblical Interpretation in Crisis," in Richard John Newhaus, ed., *Biblical Interpretation in Crisis: The Ratzinger Conference on Bible and Church* (Grand Rapids: Eerdmans, 1989), p.17.

16 Ratzinger, op. cit., p. 21.

17 Ratzinger, op. cit., p. 19.

18 Ratzinger, op. cit., p. 16.

reporting dogmas of the Church, the best that Catholic form-critics can do is to be silent, but to be silent about this matter is to be unscientific in one's approach.

13. In his encyclical letter on the interpretation of Sacred Scripture, *Divino afflante Spiritu* (1943), Pope Pius XII refers to such analytical and clearly distinguishable literary forms of Catholic exegetical tradition as *the historical, the juridical, the poetic, the didactic, and the prophetic*, while form-critics introduce novel and non-analytical forms that they claim to have discovered in Sacred Scripture, such as *apothegms, dominical sayings, miracle stories, legends, and myths*, all of them assumed to be fictitious. These novel forms are shattering to Catholic belief in the reality of the objects of faith and of the divine inspiration of Sacred Scripture. It was for this reason that then Cardinal Ratzinger, in his article of 1988, challenged the fundamental ideas of the form-critical method, called for a "radical new reflection on exegetical method,"[19] and proposed some "basic elements of a new synthesis."[20] This would require, he said, a return to "the insights of the great believers of the past."[21] What we need today, he explained, is "a self-criticism of the historical method which can expand to an analysis of historical reason itself."[22] Neo-patristic scholars implement this advice in the sense that they have undertaken a process of criticism of the historical critical method while attempting to formulate more clearly the principles of historical method itself. In this endeavor they distinguish between the valid principles of historical method in general and the many invalid principles of the "historical critical school." Catholic historical critics often call their method *historical* and *scientific* without defining what these words mean. In his essay quoted above, then Cardinal Ratzinger notes that "at a certain distance the observer determines to his surprise that these interpretations, which were supposed to be so strictly scientific and purely 'historical,' reflect their own overriding spirit, rather than the spirit of times long ago."[23] On the contrary, neo-patristic researchers seek clearly to define their terms. For instance, in my estimation, an exact definition of *science* is "the knowledge of reality as such," and an

---

19 Ratzinger, op. cit., p. 21.

20 Ratzinger, op. cit., p. 17.

21 Ratzinger, op. cit., p. 16.

22 Ratzinger, op. cit., p. 6.

23 Ratzinger, op. cit., p. 8.

exact definition of *historical science* is "the knowledge of past reality as such."[24] These definitions bring to the fore the essential importance of the concept of reality in all scientific thought. In this view, historical thinking is scientific only to the extent that the historical scientist is aware of his own scientific medium of thought, including the concept of reality. Bultmann, in his own way, understood this fact, and he resorted to an equivocal use of the idea of reality by excluding all of the objects of faith from the sphere of objective reality (*Realität*) and leaving to religious experience only what he called the "reality" (*Wirklichkeit*) of the "authentically existing man." Catholic form-critics usually do not accept this distinction, but neither do they characteristically address the problem for the Christian preacher who has eliminated everything supernatural from his faith that Bultmann, the form-critic, was facing. Neo-patristic exegetes, on the other hand, in their examination of form-critical writings, carefully consider how the writer handles the concept of reality in relation to the objects of faith and how clearly he seems to be aware of his own medium of thought.

14. The neo-patristic method is an old approach in the sense that it retains and uses the method of the Fathers and Doctors of the Church and of Catholic exegetical tradition, but it is also a new approach in that it uses the techniques of historical science to process historical critical literature and to solve the problems that historical criticism raises against the inerrancy of Sacred Scripture. The proof of the pudding is in the tasting, that is, in a neo-patristic, line-by-line commentary on the text of Scripture, in a more exact determination of its literal sense, and in a systematic search for the spiritual senses of the same. The allegorical sense reveals spiritual aspects of Christ that are otherwise hidden behind the literal sense; the tropological sense presents a pattern of application of the objective meaning to the subjective receptivity of the believer; and the anagogical sense unveils in many ways the hallmark of the divine Author of sacred writ in his three divine Persons, as well as insights into the four last things of death, judgment, Heaven, and Hell. The neo-patristic adventure is not a negative undertaking; it is filled with new insights, and it gives a feeling of exhilaration to those who have not been content with the destructive results of a historical criticism that often claims for itself the name of "modern Scripture scholarship."

---

24 See McCarthy, *The Science of Historical Theology* pp., 34–63.

Chapter 8

Jean Levie and the Biblical Movement

Part I. A Form-Critic as a Historian

Living Tradition 31 (September 1990)

1. Bultmann's publication in 1941 of his celebrated essay on the "demythologizing" of the New Testament did not pass unnoticed by the community of Catholic exegetes, who were soon aware of the presence of Bultmann's program at the center of debate in Protestant theological circles, just as they had been aware for two decades of Bultmann's *History of the Synoptic Tradition* (1st ed., 1921) and would be aware of his equally epochal *Theology of the New Testament* (1st ed., 1948), all of which, together with his (commentary on) *The Gospel of John* (1941) and a fairly constant production of shorter books and articles were turning Bultmann's works and ideas into "Germany's dominant theological export throughout the world."

2. Bultmann's proposal to "demythologize" the New Testament is articulated in terms of a particular notion of the historicity of the New Testament message. It may be useful to consider how a prominent Catholic exegete has interpreted the mind of the Church in matters touching upon this question. Jean Levie, professor of Sacred Scripture at the Theological College of St. Albert in Louvain, published in 1958 his studied opinion concerning the outlook of religious authority in the Church upon the Biblical Movement and how that outlook has developed.[1] Of particular

---

1 Jean.Levie, *La Bible, parole humaine et message de Dieu* (Paris-Louvaine, 1958); English translation: *The Bible, Word of God in Words of Men* (London: Geoffrey Chapman, 1961, henceforth to be referred to as *BWG*).

interest for the present article is the bearing of that outlook upon the question of "demythologizing."

3. Levie notes that until about 1890 Catholic exegesis remained for the most part in the "severely traditional" climate of the preceding periods, but, in France, Renan's *Vie de Jésus*, by its deleterious influence, had already clearly shown "the need for the renewal of Catholic biblical studies." Then, between 1890 and 1914, there arose in Catholic exegesis a great effort of "scientific work," provoked by the impact of "recent archaeological and historical discoveries" and by the "undoubted advances and unjustifiable deviations of nineteenth-century liberal exegesis." What made this period of history "especially distressing" was the "incapacity" of most conservatives to distinguish between the "sound and necessary" progress attempted by some exegetes and the imprudent daring of others, although, on the other hand, "no less blameworthy" were the "deceitful methods" of some of the progressives, their anonymous articles, and "their external attitude of fidelity to the Church, while estrangement from the faith had for long past existed in their heart."[2] It has often and rightly been said that certain Catholic exegetes of the period between 1890 and 1914 failed to appreciate the "theological implications" of the problems raised; they often "made into a principle" the separation of exegesis and theology. This "lack of theological and philosophical training" was one of the causes leading up to the Modernism professed by several Catholic Scripture scholars of that time. One of the "clear gains" of religious history and exegesis, both Catholic and Protestant, ever since has been "that Christian theology has once more found its way into the interpretation of Christian events."[3]

4. Levie recounts that Pope Benedict XV, in his encyclical *Spiritus Paraclitus* (1920), had repeated Leo XIII's teaching in *Providentissimus Deus* (1893) that the same principles which hold good for science can apply to history and cognate subjects, in the sense that one can apply a like line of argument when refuting the fallacies of adversaries and defending the historical truth of Scripture from their assaults, but Pius XII in his encyclical *Divino afflante Spiritu* (1943) "did not repeat the whole section" of *Spiritus Paraclitus* in which these words are found. Levie points out that Pius XII's omission of Benedict XV's explicit rejection of the theory of a twofold truth, absolute and relative attracted some notice and provoked considerable commentary after *Divino afflante Spiritu* appeared. Levie suggests in a footnote what turns out to be a basic premise of his book,

---

2 *BWG*, 41–43.

3 *BWG*, 52.

namely, that Pope Pius XII may have interpreted the "idea of two kinds of truth" to mean that the phrase "relative truth" qualifies a biblical exposition "in keeping not with the reality of the facts but with what popular contemporary opinion said on a subject," an approach which "is in practice echoed in the theory of literary form."[4]

5. (What Benedict XV actually said is that "those, too, who hold that the historical portions of Scripture do not rest on the absolute truth of the facts but merely upon what they are pleased to term their relative truth, namely, what people then commonly thought, are out of harmony with the Church's teaching." These exegetes, continues Benedict XV, maintain that "precisely as the sacred writers spoke of physical things according to appearance, so, too, while ignorant of the facts, they narrated them in accordance with general opinion or even on baseless evidence; neither do they tell us the sources whence they derived their knowledge, nor do they make other people's narrative their own." The exegetes in question claimed to deduce their approach from the teaching of *Providentissimus Deus*. "Such views are clearly false," says Benedict XV, "and constitute a calumny of our predecessor.")[5]

6. The encyclical *Divino afflante Spiritu*, observes Levie, seems to have spoken "the last word" regarding the principles of an "authentic historical criticism" reconcilable with the standards of inspiration. This final decision is "that God speaks to us through human beings, and that it is through this human language, in all its diverse forms, and within its inescapable limitations, that the divine message must be grasped, understood and accepted as infallible." The "persevering work" of Catholic exegetes, "momentarily halted" after the publication of *Pascendi* and *Lamentabili* in 1907, with regard to the theory of literary forms, but encouraged by a "more explicit acceptance of the principle of literary forms in historical narratives" in Benedict XV's Encyclical of 1920, led these exegetes ever more clearly to postulate it "as absolutely necessary for the true interpretation of many of the historical narratives in the Old Testament." This "long evolutionary process" was "successfully concluded" by the decision of *Divino afflante Spiritu*.[6]

7. Levie maintains that the principle underlying the method of distinguishing between literary forms in the historical narratives of the

---

4 *BWG*, 145–146.

5 *Spiritus Paraclitus*, no. 22.

6 *BWG*, 161–162.

Bible "is indisputable." It is the "guiding principle of profane historical criticism," and at the same time it is a "legitimate extension" of the Thomist idea of biblical inspiration "as it is universally understood today."

8. "Any literary form," he says, "as long as it is intrinsically moral," can convey the message which "God speaks to us through a real man, as he was in his world and in his own age." But the application of this principle is "singularly difficult." The fact that it can occasion "all sorts of capricious and reckless mistakes" is what undoubtedly persuaded the retention of "a certain obscurity" of expression even in *Divino afflante Spiritu*. Levie is sorry to note that "at this point in the Encyclical" there is "a marked lack of proportion" between the breadth of the principles laid down and "the simplicity, indeed the banality, of the examples occasionally brought forward." The problem raised in the light of former controversies certainly goes far beyond the kind of examples actually given to illustrate the teaching. While there is no intention of giving exegetes a free hand in the unlimited use of this method, it is left to Catholic exegetes themselves "to steer a course that is so straight, true and right that it will never need correction."[7]

9. In Levie's view, the Encyclical concludes that, because Catholic exegesis no longer restricts its endeavors to the refutation of opponents, but strives now to work "constructively," confidence in the authority and historical truth of the Bible, which, in the face of so many attacks, had in some minds been partially shaken, "has now among Catholics been wholly restored."[8]

10. Levie assures his readers that Pius XII's encyclical *Humani Generis* of 1950 has "only a few passages" concerned with Sacred Scripture, and they merely recall the directives restated in *Divino afflante Spiritu*. Four errors regarding the interpretation of Scripture are listed and forbidden: a) the limitation of Scriptural inerrancy to the truths of morality and religion; b) the illegitimate distinction between the divine meaning, hidden in Scripture and said to be alone infallible, and the human meaning; c) failure to interpret the Scriptures according to the mind of the Church by not taking into account either the analogy of faith or the tradition of the Church; and d) replacing the literal interpretation with a symbolic and spiritual exegesis.[9]

---

7 *BWG* 167–168.

8 *BWG*, 171–173.

9 *BWG*, 184–185.

11. Levie concludes his account of the progress of Catholic exegesis with the expression of three "apparently essential conditions" for the preservation of the modern Catholic Biblical Movement in its pristine purity within the framework of the faith. The first condition is that attempts at synthesis be loyally and increasingly continued. The second condition is that the Movement show an enlightened understanding of and profound respect for Catholic doctrine. The third condition is trust in the Church, in the instructions of the Church, and in the general movement of thought and faith in the Church. What is essential and fundamental for Catholic theologians and exegetes is that, as a visible society, under the invisible guidance of Christ, the Church alone is authorized to bring the teaching message of Christ to its true fulfillment as foreseen and willed by God. Only in unity with the Church can theological or exegetical science enjoy intellectual security and the guarantee of reaching the whole truth.[10]

Part II. The Problem of Levie's Account

12. Levie's review of the progress of Catholic exegesis in the twentieth century may be summarized under the following points.

A) Between 1890 and 1914 there arose in Catholic exegesis a great effort of scientific work, based upon the need for renewal in Catholic biblical studies shown by the deleterious influence of Renan's *Vie de Jésus* and stimulated by the impact of recent historical discoveries as well as by certain undeniable advances of nineteenth-century liberal exegesis. The task was to show in the presence of increasing denial the supernatural character of the work of Christ and of the origin of Christianity.[11]

B) Certain Catholic exegetes of the period between 1890 and 1914 failed to appreciate the theological implications of the problems raised; they often made into a principle the separation of exegesis and theology. One of the clear gains of both Catholic and Protestant exegesis since then has been that Christian theology has once more found its way into the interpretation of Christian events.[12]

C) In order that Catholic exegetes could honestly, in accordance with their conscience as sincere historians, solve the strictly historical

---

10 *BWG*, 195–199.

11 *BWG*, 41–43, 60.

12 *BWG*, 52.

problem of the narratives of the earlier books of the Bible, from about 1900 on there gradually emerged the principle of 'literary forms'; this long evolutionary process was successfully concluded by the decision in 1943 of *Divino afflante Spiritu* that it is through the language of human beings, in all its diverse forms, and within its inescapable limitations, that the divine message must be grasped, understood, and accepted as infallible.[13]

D) *Divino afflante Spiritu* expresses the law of unity of the faith: God, the principal Author of the Scriptures and of the definitive teaching of the Church, cannot contradict Himself; there are not two Christian doctrines.[14]

E) *Divino afflante Spiritu* does not present a doctrinal warning against any error or grave danger for the Church and for souls that certain persons were falsely alleging to be menacing from the historical critical exegesis of Sacred Scripture; the Encyclical is entirely positive in its approach; it is an optimistic and trusting exhortation to exegetes to work freely and fruitfully, and it stems from the awareness of Pope Pius XII that the numerous groups of Catholic research scholars would not distort the mind of the Church either by daring excess or by narrowness.[15]

13. Levie, however, makes other assertions which indicate respectively the problematic character of these five points.

A) Progress in Scripture studies in the twentieth century has consisted in a better understanding of the part played by the concrete man in his actual environment and era in the expression of God's message; the notion of inspiration as "dictation" by God did not sufficiently recognize the real, complete causality of the human author, as the free instrumental cause, under the action of God as the principal cause.[16]

B) *Providentissimus Deus* was more dogmatic than exegetical, just as Catholic exegesis of its time tended to be more dogmatic and theological than critically historical.[17]

C) The principle underlying the theory of literary forms is the guiding principle of profane historical criticism, and it is at the same time a legitimate extension of the Thomist idea of inspiration as it is universally

---

13 *BWG*, 161–162.

14 *BWG*, 156–157.

15 *BWG*, 142.

16 *BWG*, 163–164, 65–66.

17 *BWG*, 68–69.

understood today; any intrinsically moral literary form can convey the message which God speaks to us through a real man as he was in his world and in his own age.[18]

D) Benedict XV exposed the dishonesty of those exegetes who were falsely claiming a foundation in papal teaching for the theory that the sacred writers sometimes narrate untrue things because they were limited by the general opinion of their time; Benedict XV rejected the theory of a twofold truth, absolute and relative, in the Scriptures, but *Divino afflante Spiritu* conspicuously avoids any such rejection; Pius XII may have left out the affirmation that there is a twofold truth in the Scriptures for the reason that it could have been confused with Loisy's theory, but he does admit the principle of the twofold truth in the sense that there are expositions in the Scriptures which are in keeping, not with the reality of the facts, but with what popular contemporary opinion said on the subject.[19] A distinction must be made between the general spirit of scriptural interpretation and the interpretation of definite and specific passages. The argument from Patristic unanimity ought not to be invoked in purely historical or literary questions, but only where the discussion is concerned with doctrine concerning faith and morals.[20] Exegetes are striving for perfect sincerity both as historians and as believers.[21] Because Catholic exegesis is now working "constructively," the confidence of Catholics in the historical truth of the Bible, badly shaken before the turn of the century, has now been fully restored.[22]

E) Since 1918 many Christian people want to make a careful and personal study of contemporary exegesis and of the thought of contemporary minds, and Protestant exegesis has been showing a greater concern for living theology; this has transformed the atmosphere in Catholic exegetical circles from one of fear to one of joy.[23]

14. In making these assertions Levie weakens his position and plays into Bultmann's hands.

A) It is contradictory to say that the task of showing the supernatural character of the work of Christ and of the origin of Christianity was

---

18 *BWG*, 167.

19 *BWG*, 145–146.

20 *BWG*, 175–176.

21 *BWG*, 157.

22 *BWG*, 172–173.

23 *BWG*, 126–127.

fulfilled precisely by this, that there emerged a better understanding of the part played by the *concrete man* in his actual environment and era in the expression of God's message. Only paradoxically could increased knowledge of the *natural* causes show the *supernatural* character of the work of Christ and of the Word of God. Nowhere does Levie succeed in showing that exegetes have reinforced our knowledge of the *supernatural* character of the Bible, except as the postulated antithesis to the natural element. Nowhere does Levie suggest any defense worked out by new-wave exegetes against Bultmann's arguments excluding the role of God in the writing of the Bible.

Bultmann was as fully (even though distortedly) aware, as is any Catholic exegete, of the *natural* causes at work in the formation of the Bible. Because of his awareness only of the natural element, Bultmann has diminished the supernatural element to the point of extinction. To maintain the opposite position, Levie would have to show that Catholic exegesis has recognized, elaborated, and reinforced aspects of the *supernatural* character of the work of Christ that were not known prior to the year 1900. Levie does not do so.

B) Levie admits that it is an error to make into a principle the separation of exegesis and theology, yet in an important sense he uses this principle, for he accuses *Providentissimus Deus* of being more dogmatic than exegetical, just as the exegesis of its time was "more dogmatic and theological than critically historical."[24] He is therefore opposing the (preferred) exegetical approach to the (dogmatic and) theological approach. But Levie is using the word *theology* equivocally. While exegesis prior to 1914 was too "dogmatic and theological," he says, a clear gain since then has been that "Christian theology" has once more found its way back into the interpretation of Christian events. Obviously, Levie has never defined clearly in his mind what he means by "theology." What he seems to be saying is that a fusion of theology and exegesis has been taking place with the rise since 1918 of the existentialist approach and the decline of what Gogarten calls the "medieval metaphysical approach." But, if this is what Levie means, he is playing into Bultmann's hands, for Bultmann is *the* theologian of the Bultmannian era. There are enormous implications in the suggestion that Christian theology was not very operative in the interpretation of Christian events prior to 1914, and these implications are entirely consonant with Bultmann's position.

C) Bultmann, one of the founders of the form-critical method, holds that what he sees as the "mythology" of the New Testament conveys a message spoken to us through *real men* as they were in their world and

---

24 *BWG*, 68–69.

in their own age. The principle which Levie says was finally decided by *Divino afflante Spiritu* in 1943 fits perfectly the theology of Bultmann as enunciated two years earlier in his essay on "demythologizing" and in his commentary on the Gospel of John, viz.: "through this human language, in all its diverse forms, and within its inescapable limitations, the divine message must be grasped, understood, and accepted as infallible."[25] Catholic form-critics will protest that they do not mean this in the Bultmannian sense, but Catholic form-critics like Levie have never presented the technical and historical refutation of Bultmann's conclusions that would be necessary to give them a viable alternative position. On the grounds proposed by Levie, Bultmann wins. Catholic form-critics like Levie may say, "We *believe* that *God* is speaking," but Bultmann will reply that God and all the dogmas of the Church are mythological, and you Catholic form-critics, with your principle of literary forms, can point to no historical proof that they are not.

If Levie's principle of literary forms were true and had been properly formulated, it would not have been the occasion of "all sorts of capricious and reckless mistakes." Why would it have been so difficult for Pius XII to formulate it properly? Is a principle occasioning all sorts of capricious and reckless mistakes operative in profane historical studies as well? Levie claims that the breadth of this principle laid down by Pius XII is matched by the banality of the examples used. Is it not rather that the examples of Pius XII are aptly illustrating a principle diverse from the one that Levie is superimposing upon the Encyclical?

D) The question has never been whether there are two Christian doctrines, but whether an infallible Christian doctrine has been set down in a pattern of human errors. The principle of the unity of truth is that God cannot contradict Himself by saying in the Word of Scripture what is contradicted by the verifiable facts of nature and history. In upholding the principle of the twofold truth, Levie interprets *Divino afflante Spiritu* as saying the opposite of *Spiritus Paraclitus* and *Providentissimus Deus* on this issue. But in doing so he paraphrases the words of the Encyclical, draws his clear formula out of the "deliberate obscurity" of the Encyclical, and then reproves the Encyclical for not using examples that apply to his formula. Is this a sample of contemporary exegesis?

Furthermore, Levie distinguishes between purely historical or literary questions and doctrine concerning faith and morals. Is there such a thing as a purely historical or literary question about the Bible that is not in

---

25 *BWG*, 161.

some way concerned with faith or morals? Those who have followed the demythologizing debate will tend to think there is not. In addition, only specific passages are ever of immediate, concrete interest in any discussion about the truth of the Bible. Levie's distinction between the general spirit of interpretation and the interpretation of specific passages could ultimately relegate the teaching of the Church and of the Fathers to the "obsolete realm" of "medieval metaphysical interpretation."

E) It would seem from Levie's presentation that the demythologizing debate had never occurred, that the attack of liberal thought upon Christian faith was no longer operative, that Catholic believers of the non-exegete class could never be confronted with troublesome doubts from ideas in circulation as long as they maintained their trust in the exegetes. Can the intelligent Catholic reader be so sure that Catholic exegetes have solved these problems; will they never have reason to examine the problems for themselves? What kind of "careful and personal study" would that be? Levie's review of the history of Catholic exegesis in the earlier twentieth century does not present to the reader all of the significant facts. It seems rather to be a one-sided selection of items intended to illustrate his assumption that progress in Catholic thinking means becoming less dogmatic and more "historical."

III. Levie's Form-Critical Approach

15. While Levie favors form-criticism to the extent that it makes people realize that the Bible is the Word of God in words of *men*,[26] it is interesting to note the ways in which some of the original principles and presuppositions of the form-criticism of Bultmann and Dibelius, as summarized by Levie, are adapted to his purpose.

A) "The material found in our synoptic Gospels is essentially communal popular literature which originated and developed in a collective source (the early Church) and in response to the religious needs of this collectivity."[27] Hence, "The Church, so closely linked to the past through her Scripture and her tradition, is perpetually obliged to rethink her dogma, to reread her holy Scripture in terms of the present. ...New Testament Scripture is never for the Church the book of a past that has gone and which can only be reached through history."[28]

---

26 *BWG*, 214.

27 *BWG*, 120.

28 *BWG*, 300.

B) These narratives are now presented in a framework which is not historical in the modern sense: "Holy Scripture contains different literary forms to be interpreted according to the norms of the period in which these books appeared and not according to *a priori* norms drawn up in our own times. ...In the first place, there may be fictional historical forms whose sole aim in the mind of the inspired writer is to supply moral or didactic teaching and not to provide an account of real events in the past.[29] Jean Levie and other Catholic exegetes "were overjoyed to find the principle of 'literary forms' in holy Scripture clearly established and formally approved in the encyclical *Divino afflante Spiritu*," as well as that books of Scripture which are apparently historical in form seem in fact to be didactic writings, philosophical and religious discussions, theses, or haggadic midrash.[30]

C) We must study the evolution of the tradition in order to discover the concrete historical and social situation which gave rise to the literary forms: As with the Old Testament, "we must distinguish between what is contingent and what is definitive in a New Testament assertion."[31] "Therefore: "We have to take the Gospel narratives and think them out again in terms of the *religious needs* of the early Church and not in terms of an overriding preoccupation with historical truth."[32]

IV. A Brief Critique of Levie's Form-Criticism

16. Form-criticism begins and ends with the biblical writings as the *words of men* limited by the cultural possibilities of their own time and place. To a form-critic like Rudolf Bultmann, "God's message" is a mythological notion—an imaginary object of pre-conceptual belief. To a form-critic like Jean Levie, "God's message" is not defined as mythological; it becomes a "mystery," assumed to have valid meaning, but out of the reach of historical criticism. This "mystery" is thought to reside in the dogma and doctrine of the Church, whose credentials are unrecognized by form-criticism as such, but which can be accepted by the form-critic as a believer. The Catholic form-critic continues to believe what his form-critical conclusions have not eliminated, but he strives as well to update the dogmas and doctrines of the Church in keeping with what he has concluded as a "critical historian."

---

29 *BWG*, 222–223.

30 *BWG*, 224–227.

31 *BWG*, 280.

32 *BWG*, 299–301.

17. It is not necessarily a mistake in scientific method to undertake an interpretation of the Gospels beginning from what is presented on the human level and progressing from there to a penetration of God's message on the divine and mystical level. The great Catholic exegetes of the past have done that. But to limit the power of inspiration to the human powers of the inspired writers and of the primitive Christian community is a mistake in historical method for two reasons:

A) Inspired writing means that the writers present a viewpoint that is above and superior to the merely human outlook, and they were protected from errors that they might otherwise have made. Levie is impressed by the limitations that the inspired writings seem to show, but he forgets that these writings do not show such limitations except to those who have not studied them in depth or who began by assuming the limitations that they afterwards thought they had observed. It is the presuppositions of form-criticism that are especially deadly, and the presupposition here in point is that there was no supernatural cause active on the level of inspired historical writing.

B) Scientific conclusions are limited to the boundaries of the scientific medium of thought that is being used. To approach divine inspiration on the human level alone means to limit one's conclusions to the human level alone, and the subsequent 'understanding' of God's message derived from these conclusions cannot be anything higher than a merely natural understanding. It is standard exegetical procedure to examine first the literal and historical level of the Gospels and then the mystical level. Yet without an awareness of the supernatural dimension of biblical inspiration, not even the literal and historical level of the Gospels can be completely investigated by historical science.

18. There is no valid opposition between the historical and the theological approach to Sacred Scripture. When the medium of historical understanding is *subjoined* to the medium of theological understanding, the conclusions derived are an expression of the science of historical theology. When the medium of historical understanding is separated from the medium of theological understanding, the conclusions derived are usually distorted and always incomplete. While this is true of all history, it is especially true of biblical history. What is proposed by the historical narratives of Sacred Scripture is a series of humanly observable, or at least humanly perceivable, events whose meaning cannot be fully perceived on a merely human level, because their historical meaning, and therefore their complete historical being,

has a divine dimension. This meaning is historically final in the sense that the words of Sacred Scripture are endowed both with theological meaning that is eternally true and with historically theological meaning that is encased forever in the events that it narrates. The words of biblical history present objective reality supporting a structure of objective meaning that is as solid as the Rock of Gibraltar and which can never be dissolved as historically non-factual.

19. No type of philology will ever adequately distinguish the historical content of the Scriptures from the context in which it is presented; only historical science can do it. And the first task of historical science is to distinguish its own historical medium from the context in which it is presented. It is equally true that no un-elevated historical science will ever adequately distinguish the "religious" context of the Scriptures from the context in which it is presented; only theological science can do it. And the first task of theological science is to distinguish its own theological medium from the context in which it is presented. It follows that only the science of historical theology can resolve the problems presented by Jean Levie.

20. To the historical scientist the invitation to reread Sacred Scripture in terms of the present can mean nothing else than to read Sacred Scripture in terms of the explicit and objective theological and historical medium which is his own scientific present.[33] The result will be the objective historical truth of what the Scriptures say. The historical content of the New Testament is a past that can only be understood through historical science; to reduce this content to a pre-conceptual awareness of mystery is unhistorical and unscientific.

21. By reason of its inspired character, Sacred Scripture claims a special charismatic gift in the field of history. While the Scriptures do contain poetic and didactic as well as historical literary forms, these forms must be analyzed according to the objective norms of historical science. Without a grasp of these norms it is certainly impossible to determine *scientifically* which are the "fictional historical forms" in Scripture "whose sole aim in the mind of the inspired writer is to supply moral or didactic teaching and not to provide an account of real events in the past."[34]

22. One thing that *Divino afflante Spiritu* did not say is that some books of the Bible which are apparently historical in form seem in fact to be haggadic midrash. While Levie claims that this encyclical approved the

---

33 For details on the historical-theological medium see McCarthy, *The Science of Historical Theology*, pp. 63 and 92–100.

34 *BWG*, 222–223.

idea that in the Scriptures "any literary form as long as it is intrinsically moral can convey the divine message." he admits that "there is at this point in the Encyclical a marked lack of proportion between the breadth of the principles laid down and the simplicity, indeed the banality, of the examples occasionally brought forward."[35] The reason is that the examples given in *Divino afflante Spiritu* apply to other principles than those claimed by Catholic form-critics to be there. In conclusion I would like to make clear that, while my criticism of Father Jean Levie's method of interpreting Sacred Scripture embodies some disagreement with his form-critical approach, it is not intended to question in any way his loyal adherence to the Catholic Church and to the Catholic Faith.

---

35 *BWG*, 167–168

Chapter 9

Rationalism in the Historical Criticism of Hermann Gunkel

Living Tradition 108 (November 2003)

1. Hermann Gunkel was born in Springe, Germany, in 1862. His life of study and teaching was spent in Germany, and he died there in 1932. He is known as the founder of the form-critical approach to the interpretation of Sacred Scripture. His work and writings were mainly concerned with the Old Testament, and he was without doubt one of the most influential Scripture scholars of the twentieth century. In his famous commentary on the Book of Genesis, published in German in 1901, he took all of the results of the historical critical scholarship of his day and forged them into a method of research that went beyond the literary analysis of the text itself to the creative work of the authors of the individual units which were supposed to have anteceded the work of the editors of the final product. Gunkel's *Genesis* had a profound effect upon twentieth-century historical critical scholars, directly upon those who could read German and indirectly upon those who could not. Moreover, the publication in 1997 of the first English translation of Gunkel's commentary has aroused renewed interest among English-speaking scholars and thus gives us a timely occasion for a critical review of his famous work.

2. The Rationalism in the historical critical method of Hermann Gunkel stems from a tradition of rationalistic thinkers who had built up and diversified their "critical" approach to the interpretation of Sacred Scripture over a period of more than two hundred years. The so-called "critical" approach to the interpretation of Sacred Scripture, now known as "historical criticism," was brought into focus in 1678, when Richard

Simon, a converted Catholic priest, published what he called a "critical history" of the Old Testament. His book was rejected by the Holy See and placed on the *Index of Prohibited Books* in 1682. Simon called his work a "critical history," for the reason that he subjected the text of the Old Testament to what he considered to be the "critical judgment" of his human reason, and he thus placed himself within the category of writers who are characterized as Rationalists. Like all of the historical critical thinkers that succeeded him, he believed that he was using sound historical method to produce the results of his reasoning. Simon's work was not accepted into Catholic exegesis, but it was quickly taken up by liberal Protestant scholars, and it has grown now over a span of more than three centuries into the vast biblical movement that today calls itself "modern biblical scholarship." In the course of this article I shall contend that the historical criticism of Hermann Gunkel and other historical critics, while it is immensely critical of the text of Sacred Scripture, is extremely uncritical of its own method, and that it does not characteristically use sound methods of historical research.

3. The critical element in Simon's "critical history" and in the long series of historical critical works that have succeeded it consists in the exclusion of biblical faith, and especially of Christian faith, from its set of presuppositions and from its technical frame of reference. In doing this it places human reason above Christian faith, and it subjects the objects of Christian faith, as they appear in the Bible, to a reasoning process that depends upon this set of false assumptions. Traditional Catholic exegesis, on the contrary, while it makes an exquisite use of human reason in its thinking about the text of Sacred Scripture, does not subject the text of Sacred Scripture to the judgment of a reasoning process depending upon a set of false presuppositions. From a viewpoint of faith and reason, traditional Catholic interpretation regards the Bible as a unified whole, written ultimately by God as its principal Author, and it, therefore, gives the benefit of the doubt to the text of Scripture, whereas historical criticism tends of its very nature to arrive at a position in which it places the burden of proof on the Scriptures and gives the benefit of the doubt to the "critical" reasoning of the critics.

4. Traditional Catholic interpretation of the Scriptures begins from an attitude of faith in the truth of the sacred text and uses human reason to analyze that text. This approach means that what the sacred text narrates is presumed to be true, and that this presumption of truth will be defended, unless there is *proof* (not mere plausibility) that there is some falsehood or

contradiction in the narration. Rationalist interpretation, on the contrary, does not presume the truth of what is narrated in the sacred text, but rather presumes that any accounts of supernatural events are historically false, and so it searches for natural reasons underlying these alleged supernatural happenings. If rationalist exegesis could *prove* that the supernatural events recorded in Sacred Scripture did not really happen, its point would be made, but the rationalist reasoning process is not made up of proofs; it rather consists of strings of plausibility that tantalize the mind but do not have a solid basis in reality.

5. The Rationalism in the historical critical approach of Hermann Gunkel derives ultimately from the absolute separation of faith and reason that sprang from the Protestant Reformation of the sixteenth century. This unreasonable separation of the objects of Christian faith from the objects of human reason tended to place the objects of faith in an "alternate world" from the world of reality that presents itself to sense perception and natural reason. On the basis of this false principle of separation, liberal Protestant thinkers felt invited to reduce the world of Sacred Scripture with all of its details to a fictitious world whose historicity was just waiting to be debunked. Richard Simon, the Catholic convert, was not a self-styled Rationalist, but he exaggerated the role of unaided human reason in his study of the Old Testament. He just thought his unaided reasoning was more solid than it was. The German Illuminist H.S. Reimarus (died 1768), was the founder of Rationalism as an explicit and self-styled approach to the systematic interpretation of Sacred Scripture with his *Apologia for the Rational Worshippers of God*.[1] In his work Reimarus launched a total attack against belief in the existence of any supernatural happenings, such as in divine Revelation and in the divinity of Jesus.

6. This general attack, on an even more thoroughgoing level, had already been made more than a century earlier by the Englishman Thomas Hobbes in his notorious work *Leviathan* (1651). Hobbes was a complete materialist who denied the possibility of anything supernatural and even the existence of the human soul. It was his teaching that miracles do not take place, and so he reduced the reports of miracles recounted in Sacred Scripture to mere misinterpretations of natural events traceable to the gullibility of the onlookers. In fine, Hobbes characterized the New Testament teaching of Jesus about the Kingdom of Heaven to be simply

---

1 Reimarus finished this 4,000 page work shortly before his death in 1768 but did not have the courage to publish it. Lessing published seven extensive extracts of it between 1774 and 1778 under the title of *Anonymous Fragments*.

a misunderstanding of the Kingdom of God on earth portrayed in the Old Testament. But Hobbes did not have any sound historical evidence for his theory.

7. By the mid-eighteenth century biblical scholarship had begun more sharply to distinguish itself into the fields of Old Testament and New Testament interpretation, but with the findings of each field having a strong influence upon those of the other.[2] The attack of Reimarus provoked a strong reaction from other Protestant writers, among whom was the philologist J.S. Semler (1725–1791), who, however, sought to "save" the Gospels by giving natural explanations for the miracles recounted therein. He organized his approach under the name of "historical criticism." In his work he was inspired by the philosophy of Deism, according to which God is said to have created the universe in the first instant of time and then left it to run by itself. This theory enabled the Christian interpreter to avoid denying the existence of God while excluding any intervention of God into time-related events. It was used to justify the denial of the Providence of God, the existence of the supernatural, the possibility of miracles, and the divine inspiration of the Sacred Scriptures. H.E.G. Paulus between 1800 and 1830 followed the lead of Semler by accepting the fact that the "miraculous" events recounted in the Gospels as events really took place, while seeking to give a non-miraculous and merely natural explanation for each one of them. He claimed that it was the false opinion of the Evangelists that these events had happened miraculously. Paulus felt that he was thus giving a "rational explanation" of what the Evangelists present as miracles. D.G. Strauss felt that the rationalist explanations presented by Semler and Paulus were inept, and so, in his *Life of Christ* (1835–1836), he had recourse rather to the rationalist theory of "myth," inspired ultimately by the philosophy of G.W. Hegel. According to Strauss, myth is presented in the Gospels in the form of symbolic stories representing timeless ideas that constitute their true message, and it was to be the task of the critical Scripture scholar to identify these stories as myths and then interpret their message. Of course, Strauss took for granted in his reasoning that anything smacking of the miraculous never really could have happened, because

---

2 A good introduction to the background and development of the historical critical school of biblical research (especially with regard to the Gospels) is given by Giuseppe Ricciotti in chapter 13 of the Critical Introduction to his *Life of Christ* (1941; English translation, unabridged edition, Bruce Publishing, 1944), titled "The Rationalist Interpretations of the Life of Jesus." In this Introduction Ricciotti expresses another kind of historical criticism, not so much of the Scriptures as of the history of the method of the historical-critics.

miracles are ruled out by what he believed to be the "laws of historical development." Strauss' theory had a lasting impact upon historical criticism, especially for his false distinction between the "Jesus of history" and the "myth of Christ." Soon after this came the widespread acceptance of Charles Darwin's theory of evolution, which attributed all things to random occurrences and put man at the top of a self-made biological transformation of species. Evolution was seen to be both the evidence that modern man and modern technology were at the summit of all being and the confirmation of the idea that Modernism is the way of the present and of the future.

8. From about 1885 onward, the cutting edge of historical critical scholarship in Germany was merging into what soon became known as the History of Religions School, led by Albert Eichhorn, professor of church history at Halle. Adding something new to the already existing historical critical method of isolating and analyzing the "myths" and "legends" in the Bible, Eichhorn maintained that any valid interpretation of a biblical "myth" or "legend" must take into consideration the origin and development of that myth or legend. Thus was born the "tradition-historical method of biblical research." Hermann Gunkel became the leading pioneer of this new method, which he embodied in his first major work, *Creation and Chaos in the Beginning and at the End of Time. A Religio-historical Investigation of Genesis I and Revelation 12* (in German, 1895). In this work Gunkel's attention was focused upon what he considered to be the history of the tradition behind the text of these two chapters of the sacred text. When he later came out with his famous work, *Genesis* (first German edition, 1901),[3] his attention was now concentrated on the history of what he saw to be the fictional "forms," or "literary genres" (*Gattungen*), that constituted the text. Thus was born the method of *Formgeschichte* (literally, "form-history," but which has always been called "form-criticism" in English). Take, for instance, the story of the creation of the world in Genesis 1. Historical critics were already convinced that they knew that this story is a myth, for the reason that any depiction of the intervention of a god in this world is assumed by Rationalism to be mythological. But this myth is expressed in a literary form, and it was Gunkel's point that the myth could only be understood by tracing the development of the biblical literary form back to the pagan mythologies from which it was derived.

---

3 Hermann Gunkel, *Genesis* (Göttingen: Vandenhoeck & Ruprecht, first edition, 1901). The references in this article are to the English translation from the third German edition, 1910. Hermann Gunkel, Genesis (Macon Georgia: Mercer University Press, 1997).

9. The literary forms identified in the sacred text by the form-criticism of Hermann Gunkel are not the literary forms which Catholic Scripture scholars have distinguished over the ages, such as the historical, the poetic, the prophetic, and the judicial. They are all assumed to be poetic in the sense of fictitious. For Gunkel "Genesis is a collection of legends," and a legend is "a popular, long-transmitted, poetic account dealing with past persons or events." Regarding the shock to believers in hearing that Genesis presents fiction and not historical reality, Gunkel explains that this revelation "does not involve belief or unbelief, but simply better understanding."[4] This judgment depends upon the acceptance of Rationalism and Modernism. Yes, once one has accepted the total separation between the "alternate world" of faith and the real world of reason, one only needs to "understand" that the legends of Genesis belong to that alternate world. Gunkel avers that Jesus and his Apostles *thought* that the accounts of Genesis were historical events of the real world, but "they shared the opinions of their time," and so "we may not, therefore, seek information in the New Testament concerning questions of the history of the Old Testament literature."[5] Gunkel assures us that he, as a "modern man," has of necessity a viewpoint that is superior to the primitive viewpoint of Jesus and his contemporaries. Of course, many highly educated contemporaries of Gunkel and of his successors did not and do not agree that the accounts of Genesis are fictitious, but from the viewpoint of Hermann Gunkel and, in general, of all rationalist historical critics, these modern men *are not modern men.*

10. Gunkel seems to be speaking for modern man where he says: "Following our modern historical world-view, truly not an imaginative construct but based on the observation of facts, we consider the other view entirely impossible." The legends of Genesis, he says, frequently relate extraordinary events "that contradict our advanced knowledge," and the tellers of these stories are not even aware of the great unlikeliness of what they recount. And so we would actually be doing "injustice to this naiveté," if we were to "incorporate it into sober reality."[6] As a modern man he sees the outlandishness of such Genesis accounts as the Serpent speaking to Eve, Noah bringing every species of animal into the ark, and God walking in the Garden of Paradise, and he feels that the representatives in his time of the Evangelical Church in Germany would, therefore, do well to give

---

4 Gunkel, *Genesis*, pp. vii–viii (both quotations).

5 Gunkel, *Genesis*, p. viii.

6 Gunkel, *Genesis*, p. x.

up their refusal to see the first book of the Bible as a collection of fictitious legends in order to make possible for them "a historical understanding of Genesis."[7] What Gunkel does not suspect is that his "modern viewpoint" is probably a mere construction of his own subjectivity that does not correspond to objective reality. Many great thinkers of his time and of ours, be they natural scientists, historians, philosophers, technicians, teachers, statesmen, or whatever, have a modern viewpoint that accepts the fact of miracles in the Bible. These thinkers are not wedded to Deism, to Rationalism, or to Modernism as a philosophy, nor does reason require them to be so wedded, for Modernism is not based upon chronological fact; it's just an unsubstantiated belief of its own. Modern, non-modernist, men of Gunkel's time and of our time have reason to accept that the fallen angel Satan could speak to a woman from the form of a serpent, that Genesis is not saying that Noah took two of every species of animals on earth into the ark, and that, when Genesis says that God "walked" in the Garden of Paradise, it is using an obvious anthropomorphism.

11. Gunkel shows that he is a Deist where he says: "We believe God works in the world as the quiet, hidden basis of all things. [...] But he never appears to us as an active agent alongside others, but always as the ultimate cause of all."[8] On what does he base this belief apart from his prior belief in himself as a "modern man." Where there is no belief in the role of divine Providence, in divine interventions, in divine revelation, in divine inspiration, there is from our viewpoint no Christian faith. And there is always the *great temptation* to reject Christian faith, wholly or in part, in favor of the self-satisfaction to be had from thinking of oneself as a "modern man" whose own superiority of view overrides any and every suggestion of the supernatural, notwithstanding all evidence to the contrary.

12. Gunkel sees in the "primal legends" of Genesis both the presence of "weakened myths" and "a quiet aversion to mythology." By a "myth" he means "a story of the gods." Israel's strong emphasis upon monotheism would tolerate only "myths in which God acts alone, as in the creation narrative," or myths "in which the story takes place between God and people."[9] But these "myths," as so identified by Gunkel, are obviously seen to be merely fictitious stories, since (the one true) God is for Gunkel always and only "the ultimate cause of all" and never plays any role in human

---

7 Gunkel, *Genesis*, p. xi.

8 Gunkel, *Genesis*, p. x.

9 Gunkel, *Genesis*, pp. xii–xiii.

history or the history of the world. In this description Gunkel may be retaining a residual belief in the existence of the one true God, but as far as his interpretation of Genesis is concerned, what comes out in the "primal myths" is the fictitious god of Israel, who is depicted as acting either alone or with people. In this interpretation there is no real connection between the god of Israel and the one true God of Christian belief. Gunkel finds that Israel's notion of its one god was derived from various pagan sources. He assumes a Babylonian influence for the primal legends (which he also calls "primal myths"), since, for early Genesis, Babel was the oldest city in the world, and he surmises that these legends came first into Canaan and were from there passed to Israel at the time "when it [Israel] was grafted into the Canaanite culture."[10]

13. Viewed in the objectivity of an adequate mental framework, the writings of Hermann Gunkel and other historical critics provide a fertile source of material for the understanding of many texts of Sacred Scripture, not because their historical critical conclusions are correct, but because they challenge the traditional thinker to find correct solutions to the problems that they raise. The works of Hermann Gunkel and other notable historical critics deserve to be studied carefully and methodically, not according to their own method, but in a way such as to formulate correctly the principles of historical method and to separate the facts from a mere fascination for false ideas. It is important to have general observations about the reasoning and conclusions of historical criticism, but it is necessary also to delve into the concrete expressions of its reasoning, after first having identified its governing principles.

14. We might begin in a general way by asking again whether Gunkel's "modern historical world-view" is really modern or is only modernist. We might ask whether Gunkel's "modern historical world-view" is really historical or is only pseudo-historical. In the third place, we might ask whether Gunkel's "modern historical world-view" is truly "based on the observation of facts," or is only a biased view based on rationalist presuppositions that do not coincide with the historical facts. These questions should always be in the mind of the critical reader. Do what Gunkel calls the "legends of Genesis" really "contradict our advanced knowledge"? To answer this question one needs to look carefully at what these "legends" are saying to us in a context of understanding that is in keeping with historical science, properly defined, and is, therefore, free of unproven pre-suppositions....

---

10 Gunkel, *Genesis*, p. 1 (p. 50).

15. According to Hermann Gunkel the patriarchal accounts of Genesis are legends, that is, they are poetic recastings of vague historical memories, into which later popular elements and even whole other figures have been interwoven (p. xvi). He sees these accounts as constructs fashioned from imaginary thinking, such as, from the idea that every different nation was descended exclusively from a different remote ancestor, in such wise that two closely related nations would be imagined to have descended exclusively from brothers or from the same mother. Thus, the close relationship of the Israelites, the Moabites, and the Ammonites would be explained in the popular imagination by their having descended from the imaginary brothers Abraham and Lot. How can Gunkel say that Abraham and Lot are mere figments of the imagination? He contrasts two ways of thinking. He says that *mythical thinking* sees all tribes and nations, "as having resulted through reproduction," whereas "we know" (*in our modern historical thinking*) that peoples form in quite different ways, "perhaps through the incorporation of foreign clans" or "perhaps through fusion of immigrants and natives" (p. xv). He believes that the writers of Genesis couldn't have known anything about what Abraham, Isaac, and Jacob were like, even if they had really existed, because "everyone who knows the history of legends" is aware that, at a distance of so many centuries, the personal characters of these persons could not have been preserved (p. lxviii). So, in any case, they remain mere "literary figures" (p. lxix).

16. Gunkel's kind of modern historical thinking does not appear to be scientific thinking, since scientific thinking depends upon facts and makes clear distinctions as it proceeds. *Perhaps* the incorporation or *perhaps* the fusion of extraneous persons does not constitute a clear exclusion of blood descent, and, in fact, the Genesis account makes explicit provision for and gives many examples of the incorporation of extraneous persons into the nation of Israel. And it is clear from the entire Pentateuch that the Israelites lived under a severe prohibition of intermarriage with other peoples. Gunkel undertakes to erase the patriarchs from historical reality, not by means of historical evidence, but by deduction from such unproved general principles as that accounts like those of Genesis are necessarily a product of mythical thinking. Actually his conclusion is a product of unscientific thinking, for he here simply assumes without any historical evidence that the accounts of Genesis could not have proceeded from actual historical observation and experience, that orally narrated but real historical happenings could not have been preserved intact over centuries by human endeavor and by the help of divine Providence, that the writers

could not have been guided by divine inspiration. These assumptions are unscientific in that historical science has as its object whatever happened and does not decide in advance what could or could not have happened.

17. Gunkel observes in broad perspective that the "primal legend" (the story of creation) is essentially of Babylonian origin, while the "patriarchal legends" are "essentially of ancient Hebrew origin" (p. liii). Yet, he also holds that these patriarchal accounts are not of Hebrew origin but pre-existed elsewhere as stories that "wander from people to people, from land to land, and from religion to religion" (p. xlvii). They are stories, he says, that originated somewhere as "pure products of the imagination," and were much later "given new meaning on Israel's lips" (p. xxiii). What historical evidence is there that the stories of Abraham, Isaac, and Jacob were earlier floating around on the lips of other tribes and peoples? None. Gunkel is merely deducing from his idea of certain "epic laws" (p. xlii) that he feels are common to all folk literature. There are no such laws that would determine fictitious responses from individuals who we know were endowed with intelligence and free will nor laws that would exclude any divine inspiration and guidance. Gunkel assumes a virtual absence of free will where he says: "In addition the imagination powerfully excited by these accounts continued to work almost involuntarily." He readily admits that the narrators and hearers of these biblical stories believed that they were true, but, he maintains, they didn't have the intellectual capacity to distinguish fact from fiction (p. xxvi). And this is a gratuitous assertion. The Israelites were practical people; they were shrewd traders and realists. They called a spade a spade, a lie a lie, and a miracle a miracle. It is Hermann Gunkel who here seems to be laboring under a studied inability to distinguish the truth of Genesis from the fiction of the surrounding pagan literature.

18. Gunkel acknowledges that the text of Genesis speaks always of one god (the god of Israel), but he also sees here and there an "earlier polytheism" echoing through, such as in the "Let us" of Gen. 1:26, in the "Come, let us go down" of Gen 11:7, in the appearance of the Lord to Abraham as three men in Gen. 18, and in other places. He concludes that "all this cannot be based on one and the same God figure" (read "god-figure") (p. xlix). He maintains that a whole variety of god-concepts was transmitted in the legend material, and that Israel's Yahweh-figure was subsequently imprinted upon them all, thus elevating them to a mono-theistic level (p. lviii). According to an ancient viewpoint that Gunkel thinks he sees in the text, Yahweh himself moves around during the time

of the plagues in Egypt (Exod. 11–12), while in a later view his messenger does this (2Kgs. 19:35). In an earlier view Yahweh inspired the prophets, while in a later view an angel did this. In an earlier view Yahweh conducted the Israelites through the desert (Exod. 34:11), while in a later view an angel did this (Exod. 20:16). In an earlier version Yahweh appeared to Hagar at the well (Gen. 16:13), while in the later text it was the angel of the Lord (Gen. 16:7). But in an even earlier version it was the pagan god of the place that appeared to her, and his name was "el roi" (p. 186). Thus, by using his method of form-criticism, Gunkel thinks that he sees behind the text of Genesis a primitive mythology moving through many intermediate stages to a final belief in divine providence and in the one god of Israel (p. lix).

19. It is interesting to note that all of the things that Gunkel thinks he sees behind the text of Genesis are only questionable detractions from what is already plainly written in the text of Genesis itself. There is no independent documentation of earlier stages to back up his theory. We know from the plain text of Sacred Scripture that Abraham's belief in the one true God replaced the belief of his ancestors in many false gods, but Gunkel's conclusion that the interventions of the one true God described in the text of Genesis are fictional renditions of older stories about local pagan gods is not evident at all; it seems to depend mainly upon his own rationalist presupposition that there could have been no real interventions of the real God. The stories of the patriarchs in the text of Genesis look very real to those who examine them without recourse to the rationalist presuppositions of Gunkel's method. There are those Catholic scholars who say that these rationalist presuppositions do not necessarily govern the method and that Gunkel's form-critical conclusions have merit in themselves. They quote and recommend rationalist books with a certain abandon. I purchased a copy of the English edition of his *Genesis* as it was prominently displayed together with various Catholic commentaries in a large Catholic bookstore in Rome. Is this book as innocuous as some Catholic scholars seem to think?

20. The dangers of Rationalism have often been remarked in the teachings of the Popes. Back in 1832, Pope Gregory XVI pointed out the harmful element of pride in the "critical approach" to Catholic faith where he said: *"It is the proud, or rather foolish, men who examine the mysteries of faith which surpass all understanding with the faculties of the human mind, and rely on human reason, which by the condition of man's*

nature is weak and infirm." [11] In this statement, Pope Gregory XVI is not speaking against the use of human reason in studying the mysteries of faith, and even more so in examining Sacred Scripture, but he is rather warning against relying on human reason motivated by an attitude of pride which actually obscures the mind and closes it to the light of objective truth. And this is the thinking of the Modernist who places himself and his mind over all that comes from the distant past on the ground that his modern mind is superior just because it is modern.

21. In his encyclical letter *Providentissimus Deus* of November 18, 1893, published at the very time that Hermann Gunkel and other members of the School of the History of Religions were refining the methods of historical criticism, Pope Leo XIII called upon Catholic scholars to rise to the defense of the truth of the Sacred Scriptures and to oppose the rationalist exegetes, "who, trusting in their turn in their own way of thinking, have rejected even the scraps and remnants of Christian belief which had been handed down to them." [12] Pope Leo proceeded to summarize their rationalist approach by pointing out that they *"deny that there is any such thing as revelation, or inspiration, or Holy Scripture at all; they see instead only the forgeries and the falsehoods of men; they set down the Scripture narratives as stupid fables and lying stories; the prophecies and the oracles of God are to them either predictions made up after the event or forecasts formed by the light of nature; the miracles and the wonders of God's power are not what they are said to be, but the startling effects of natural law, or else mere tricks and myths; and the Apostolic Gospels and writings are not the work of the Apostles at all."* Then the Pope calls upon scholars and all true shepherds of souls to let their hearts be stirred up so that this rationalist "pseudo-knowledge" (1 Tim. 6:20) may be opposed with "the ancient and true knowledge which the Church, through the Apostles, has received from Christ, and that Holy Scripture may find the champions that are needed in so momentous a battle." [13]

22. Leo XIII went on to characterize the method of historical criticism, then known especially under the name of "higher criticism," as it was being proclaimed by Hermann Gunkel and his colleagues, in the following words: *"There has arisen, to the great detriment of religion, an inept method,*

---

11 Pope Gregory XVI, *Mirari vos*, no. 22, in Claudia Carlen ed., *The Papal Encyclicals* (McGrath Publishing Co.), vol. 1 p. 240.

12 Pope Leo XIII, *Providentissimus Deus*, no. 2, in Claudia Carlen ed., op. cit., vol. 2, p. 326.

13 Pope Leo XIII, *Providentissimus Deus*, no. 10, in Claudia Carlen ed., op. cit., vol. 2, pp. 329–330 (*Enchiridion Biblicum*, no. 100).

dignified by the name of 'higher criticism,' which pretends to judge of the origin, integrity, and authority of each Book from internal indications alone. It is clear, on the other hand, that in historical questions, such as the origin and handing down of writings, the witness of history is of primary importance, and that historical investigation should be made with the utmost care; and that in this matter internal evidence is seldom of great value, except in confirmation." [Otherwise], *"this vaunted 'higher criticism' will resolve itself into the reflection of the bias and the prejudice of the critics, […] and seeing that most of them are tainted with false philosophy and Rationalism, it must lead to the elimination from the sacred writings of all prophecy and miracle, and of everything else that is outside the natural order."*[14]

23. Well over a century has passed since Pope Leo XIII published his condemnation of the method of historical criticism, and during the intervening time there have occurred, among other things, various documents and decisions of the original Pontifical Biblical Commission, the condemnation of Modernism by Pope Pius X, an encyclical on Sacred Scripture by Pope Benedict XV, another encyclical on Sacred Scripture by Pope Pius XII, a document of the Second Vatican Ecumenical Council treating of divine revelation, and the reconstitution by Pope Paul VI of the PBC in favor of Catholic historical critics in such wise as to effect a somewhat ambiguous acceptance by the hierarchy of the Church of the method of historical criticism. In 1993 the reconstituted PBC published a document entitled *The Interpretation of the Bible in the Church*. In this document the PBC fully endorsed the historical critical method as "the indispensable method for the scientific study of the meaning of ancient texts."[15] Nevertheless, as the Commission pointed out in the Introduction to this document, "at the very time when the most prevalent scientific method—the 'historical critical method'—is freely practiced in exegesis, it is itself brought into question, to some extent through the rise of "alternative approaches and methods," but also "through the criticisms of many members of the faithful, who judge the method deficient from the point of view of faith," some of whom maintain that "nothing is gained by submitting biblical texts to the demands of scientific method," and who insist that "the result of scientific exegesis is only to provoke perplexity and doubt upon numerous points which hitherto had been accepted without

---

14 Pope Leo XIII, *Providentissimus Deus*, no. 17, in Claudia Carlen ed., op. cit., vol. 2, p. 334 (EB no. 119).

15 Pontifical Biblical Commission, *The Interpretation of the Bible in the Church* (Libreria Editrice Vaticana, 1993), opening words of chapter I.

difficulty." The purpose of the present study is to propose the neo-patristic method of biblical interpretation in place of what the PBC document of 1993 calls the "scientific method" of historical criticism, and, by the way, to raise the question of whether the "scientific method" of historical criticism is really scientific at all.

24. As noted above, the founder of the dominant approach of historical criticism known as form-criticism is Hermann Gunkel with his celebrated commentary on the Book of Genesis. In this commentary he notes that through form-criticism one can discern the whole literary development of this book, precisely because its passages were never fused into a smooth literary whole, but rather that the cracks are visible to skilled "legend scholars," and, therefore, that "theologians should learn that without legend research, and especially without legend analysis, Genesis cannot be understood."[16] In question here is what it means to "understand" the Book of Genesis. Does it mean to realize that the spiritual message of Genesis, such as it may be, is presented in fictitious stories resembling fairy-tales? Gunkel observes that "scholars have begun to see the basic form of account in the fairy-tale that focuses on people."[17] Or does it rather mean to comprehend that deep and imposing realities are expressed in these biblical narratives, in historically true episodes that carry a supernatural dimension unrecognized by historical critics? Historically and theologically valid analysis may reveal the answer.

25. First some general definitions. It is necessary to begin from an adequate concept of historical science. In its most general denotation, *science* is *"the knowledge of the real as such."* This means that science is the knowledge of what is real under the aspect of its reality. The notion of reality is the defining characteristic of all science. There are two basic levels of science: *common science*, also called *common sense*, and technical science. The difference is that *technical science* uses precisely defined terms and reasons with rigorous logic, while *common science* uses loosely defined terms and sometimes less rigorous logic. In ordinary parlance, when people use the word "science," they are referring to technical science, but technical science itself can be one of two kinds: *genuine science*, which presents reality as it is; and *pseudo-science*, which may have precisely defined terms and may use rigorous logic, but which reasons from one or more false governing principles with the result that it does not present reality as it is.

---

16 Gunkel, *Genesis*, p. lxxxvi.

17 Gunkel, *Genesis*, p. lxvii.

26. We take *history* to be "*the knowledge of the past as such.*" The defining characteristic of all history is the past seen under the aspect of its being past. Within this category, *historical science* is "*the knowledge of the real past as such,*" while *fiction* is *the knowledge of the unreal past as such.*" Included within the category of fiction is *historical pseudo-science*, which pretends to be technically scientific, but which may use terms that are not precisely defined and always reasons from one or more false principles.

27. In the present discussion, it would seem at first that Hermann Gunkel's historical criticism is a historically scientific way of analyzing the text of the Book of Genesis. He distinguishes the legendary accounts of Genesis from modern scientific historical accounts and divides them into fictional literary genres. Hence, he is working under the concept of reality and analyzing the Genesis accounts, not in terms of their fictional elements, nor by taking the stories as narratives of historical reality, but by uncovering the real historical processes according to which the original stories developed into the stories of the final text. But did such a historical development really take place? Does Gunkel's analysis of the separate accounts in Genesis really stand up under scientific historical criticism? It is amazing to learn that over more than a century of use of his book there has been practically no searching criticism of his method, even on the part of Catholic exegetes who have followed this method. Gunkel's method presumes that everything miraculous narrated in the Genesis accounts and every intervention on the part of the one true God are historically non-factual and need to be given a natural explanation. Is this presumption in keeping with historical science? I would say that it is not. *Natural science* is limited to the observation of natural facts and occurrences, but *historical science* is not. A natural scientist as such cannot record the occurrence of a miracle or of any divine intervention in the world of physical reality, but he is obliged to accept the results of those higher sciences that can observe supernatural occurrences, and historical science is one of these, because *historical science* observes whatever has taken place in the past and must accept these occurrences without excluding in advance what exceeds the workings of physical nature. Therefore, the evidence for a happening is what concerns the historian and not whether or not the happening is within the bounds of a natural occurrence. But Gunkel's method, because it is governed by the false principle of Naturalism, excludes in advance even without any evidence the recorded reality of every happening that exceeded the

workings of physical nature, and, therefore, Gunkel's method is not historically scientific.

28. The plain text of Genesis shows a studied intent to record real history as it really took place. Gunkel assumes without good evidence that the writer of Genesis was not able to distinguish fact from fiction and so wrote falsehoods without clearly realizing that he was doing so. Gunkel's method places the burden of proof for historical truth on the text of Genesis, not on the critic of Genesis. This means that everything recounted in Genesis is assumed to be non-factual or to be on the verge of being assumed non-factual according to the latest accepted opinion of historical critics. Any other plausible explanation is deemed better than acceptance of the supernatural, and the only criterion of judgment is whose explanation is the most plausible. But plausibility is not proof, and its strength lies largely in the bias of the critic as he reviews the strings of plausibility that he and other historical critics have provided. Thus, the entire system stands on weak and shifting grounds (cf. no.4 above).

29. The traditional Catholic approach assumes the historical truth of the accounts in Genesis unless there is solid evidence to the contrary. While Hermann Gunkel and other historical critics would have us believe that the text of Genesis presents historical contradictions from beginning to end, these so-called contradictions tend to dissolve one by one as the reasonings of the historical critics are carefully examined. What needs to be done in the case of Hermann Gunkel and of the many historical critics of Genesis who have succeeded him is to systematically examine and refute their analyses of Genesis on a line-by-line basis and thus restore the historical integrity of the sacred text. It is unfortunate that this work has not been done up to now. Historical critical commentaries on the text of Genesis present a great challenge to traditional exegesis, which, if effectively taken up, will enable impressive advances in the understanding of the text, since the critics are raising new questions that need to be addressed.

30. Gunkel's historical critical approach to Genesis is not a Christian approach. The first few chapters of Genesis, narrating the creation of the world and the creation and fall of man, provide the world-view of Christianity. To exclude the interventions of the one true God recorded in the Book of Genesis and throughout the Bible on the ground that there could be no divine interventions is to exclude Christian faith. Traditional Catholic Christian faith accepts and affirms these divine interventions as having taken place within the one external continuum of reality known

to human reason and rejects the idea of an alternate world of Christian belief that would not have place in the same univocal realm of reality. Gunkel's approach fails to recognize that the presence and activity of the one true God as recorded in the Sacred Scriptures is contained within the one continuum of reality known to science and thus misrepresents the sacred text.

31. Hermann Gunkel distinguishes between legend and history in this; that legend usually originates as an oral tradition, while history generally appears in written form and presumes the practice of writing. Again, Gunkel finds that history deals with great public events, while legend treats of personal and private matters dear to the people.[18] These distinctions display an imperfect conception of history. What eventually appears as history in written form can have earlier existed in memorized form. And history doesn't just deal with great public events; it deals with any event of the real past. Thus, biography pertains to history. The *Gulag Archipelago* of Alexander Solzenitzen is a work of history, even though for years before it was finally written down it was history only in memorized form. And many narrators in ancient times had marvelously accurate memories. Gunkel's method assumes that writing was totally unavailable to the traditions of the Hebrew Patriarchs until rather late in Hebrew history, even though writing existed all around them. What real evidence does he have that these shrewd traders were totally unable to read and write? And his method of biblical interpretation completely denies the possibility that a true account of past historical events could have been preserved intact over a long period of time in an oral tradition even through the aid of divine Providence. It also excludes the possibility that the sacred history of the past could have been revealed wholly or in part to the sacred writers through divine inspiration. Again, his method does not consider or even suspect that the events recorded in the first eleven chapters of Genesis could embody the true historical tradition of early human history as it was handed down possibly even from the time of Adam and Eve and their early descendants through the various peoples, a historical tradition which was transformed by pagan poets in the surrounding cultures into the distorted versions so well known to and exploited by historical critics, but which may appear intact in the biblical accounts or which may have been revealed to Moses. In Gunkel's historical critical analyses the pagan accounts are always considered to be older and more authentic than the biblical accounts, but what real evidence is there that the biblical accounts do not represent the older tradition?

---

18 Gunkel, *Genesis*, p. viii.

Gunkel thinks that his view is based upon "the observation of facts," but what modernist thinker, what modern astronomer, what natural scientist has observed the forming of the universe, the rise of vegetative and animal life on earth, or the emergence of man on the face of the earth? Only God and the angels observed these things as they took place, and only they could have communicated these facts to the tradition behind the biblical accounts. So the inspired world-view given in the first chapters of Genesis is actually more based upon the observation of facts than is the "modern world-view" proposed by Hermann Gunkel.

Chapter 10

The Incomplete Response of Catholic Theologians to the Demythologizing Method of Rudolf Bultmann

Part I. Leopold Malevez And Heinrich Fries

Living Tradition 80 (March 1999)

Introduction. When Rudolf Bultmann published his well-known essay of 1941 in which he called for the "demythologizing" of the Gospels and of the New Testament as a whole, he stirred up a response that became perhaps the greatest theological debate of the twentieth century. It had its first impact within German Lutheran theological circles, but it soon spread to other Protestant thinkers. Many liberal Protestant theologians were positively impressed by Bultmann's appeal and began to argue its details. On the other hand, many traditional Protestants saw it as a menace to their faith and wrote articles against it. Thus arose what came to be called the "demythologizing debate," a discussion that continued with high interest for more than twenty years. Almost immediately after the end of the Second World War it attracted the attention of some Catholic theologians, first with the publication of shorter articles that continued to appear for decades, and then with the production of longer articles and books. A growing number of Catholic theologians found Bultmann's proposal to be interesting, and the surprising thing was that they raised no great cry of alarm about its implications. Rather, the typical article by Catholic theologians would describe in summary the contents of Bultmann's essay, often make approving remarks about various aspects of the proposal, but including no refutation except for a concluding paragraph which would point out that much of what Bultmann was affirming could not, of course, be accepted by Catholics. In the meanwhile, especially in the 1950s and 1960s, some studies by Catholic theologians appeared in the form of longer articles and books. It is these studies that concern us here. Some Catholics have the impression that the negative aspects of demythologizing no longer have any great relevance, but others have strong suspicions that the reasoning behind Bultmann's program was never adequately countered by Catholic theologians and, therefore, remains to this day an approach waiting to be systematically refuted. In fact, more and more of the ideas of Rudolf Bultmann have crept into Catholic discourse as the years have gone by, and that is all the more reason why, in an important sense, the question of demythologizing is still current today and is asking for complete rebuttal. The "demythologizing debate" as such is now past, but its negative effects are still present. It is the purpose of the following review to examine a series of typical responses given by Catholic theologians in the 1950s and 1960s, to bring out some seeming inadequacies in the approach that they took, and also to suggest some ways in which the Catholic response can be brought to completion.[1]

The Response of Leopold Malevez

1. Exposition. One of the earliest book-length studies of Bultmann's program of "demythologizing" by a Catholic writer was Leopold Malevez's *Christian Message and Myth*, published in the original French edition in 1954.[2] The book consists of two things: a protracted attempt to describe the issues presented by Bultmann as impartially as possible and a much shorter attempt to reply to Bultmann from the viewpoint of tradition. In

---

1   For the essay which touched off the "demythologizing debate" see Rudolf Bultmann, "Neues Testament und Mythologie," in *Offenbarung und Heilsgeschehen*: Beiträge zur evangelischen Theologie, VII/2 (Munich, 1941); reprinted in H.W. Bartsch, ed., *Kerygma und Mythos* (Hamburg, 1948 [henceforth referred to as *KuM*]; Engl. trans., H.W. Bartsch, ed., *Kerygma and Myth: A Theological Debate*, vol. I (London: SPCK, 1962 [henceforth referred to as *KaM*]. For a brief summary of the demythologizing debate, especially among Protestant theologians, with the relevant bibliography, see J.F. McCarthy, *The Science of Historical Theology* (2nd printing, Rockford: TAN, 1991), pp. 1–5. For a brief presentation of the meaning and goal of the program of demythologizing, see McCarthy, ibid., pp. 5–14.

2   L. Malevez, *Le message chrétien et le mythe. La théologie de Rudolf Bultmann* (Brussels-Bruges-Paris, 1954 [henceforth referred to as *MCM*]); Engl. trans., *The Christian Message and Myth: The Theology of Rudolf Bultmann* (London: SCM Press, 1958 [henceforth referred to as *CMM*).

his reply, Malevez lists some positive features of Bultmann's approach and then criticizes its negative aspects. On the positive side, Malevez notes that Bultmann's essay of 1941 "has at least the merit of drawing the Christian's attention to the very heart of a central theme, the theme of revelation and of the Word of God, and of its incorporation into history."[3] He observes that Bultmann's concern for the reformulation of the Christian message in terms more meaningful to modern man confronts all theologians with a task they must not evade.[4] He points out that Bultmann's theology correctly emphasizes the principle of the existential interpretation of the Christian message, in the sense that the Christian message has to show its affinity with certain basic human hopes and longings brought to light by existential analysis, but he disagrees that such analysis need necessarily have anything to do with the philosophy of Martin Heidegger.[5] As a positive reaction against Liberalism, Malevez feels, Bultmann's program succeeds in retaining the elements in the theology of Karl Barth which emphasize the objective act of God in Jesus Christ while eliminating the weaknesses of Barth's absolute fideism, so as to bring the Christian message into relation with man—in his situation—and faith into relation with reason. But, in the ultimate analysis, Bultmann's insistence upon demythologizing and on a completely existential interpretation of the Christian message overreaches itself in such wise as to become a menace to the very truth that it sets out to defend.[6]

2. Remarks. In my opinion, Bultmann's theology does not correctly emphasize "the principle of the existential interpretation of the Christian message," for the simple reason that there is no such principle. The "basic hopes and longings" of modern man are brought to light, not by existential analysis, but by the teaching of the Gospel, by Christian prayer, and by searching out the objective moral sense of the inspired Word of God. Since Bultmann's program of demythologizing assumes that everything supernatural in the Gospel message is fictitious, a mere figment of the primitive religious imagination, and since Bultmann limits authentic Christian faith to the subjective experience of the believer, he can in no way be said to emphasize "the objective act of God in Jesus Christ." Thus, Bultmann's demythologizing is more than "a menace to the truth that he sets out to defend"; it is actually a total elimination of the objective truth contained in the biblical figure

---

3 Malevez, *MCM*, 115 (*CMM*, 118).

4 Malevez, *MCM*, 116 (*CMM*, 119).

5 Malevez, *MCM*, 118-119 (*CMM*, 120–121).

6 Malevez, *MCM*, 119-120 (*CMM*, 122–123).

of the God-Man Jesus Christ. Hence, Bultmann does not really "draw the Christian's attention" to the theme of revelation except in the act of mentally dissolving that revelation into a studied focus upon one's own unenlightened subjectivity.

3. Exposition. The first charge that Malevez as a Christian brings against Bultmann's program is that it "has taken away his Lord," for the *kerygma* cannot replace the mystery of the God-Man, as Bultmann would have it do.[7] Bultmann relegates the Incarnation to the realm of the mythological, but "the fact remains that Christians have always regarded it as essential to their faith. ...This is a new religion which is being proclaimed to us, which represents a break with the past, and this religion has the purely human authority of its author."[8] With regard to science, Malevez maintains that Bultmann does not really speak in the name of modern science, because modern science is now aware that it cannot draw a "picture" of everything in the world. Since the competence of modern science is restricted to the definition of order in the sequence of phenomena, it cannot exclude *a priori* a supernatural intervention of God by which there would be visible consequences of a divine intervention which in itself would remain invisible, e.g., in the assumption of a human nature by a divine Person or in the transubstantiation of the Eucharist.[9]

4. Remarks. Malevez is basically correct in declaring that Bultmann's program proclaims "a new religion," but it does even worse than that: it proclaims an anti-religion, as all rationalist systems do, and its only act is the imaginary existentialist act of an ever-repeated "choosing of one's own self-authenticity," devoid of all objective content. A "religion" with no objective content is no religion at all. And Malevez is absolutely correct in stating that Bultmann's program has taken away the Lord, but in 1941 only as a presupposition. Bultmann had already taken away the Lord in 1921, when he published his *History of the Synoptic Tradition*, introducing the form-criticism of the Gospels and pretending to have eliminated the objective historical truth of every supernatural fact and event recorded in the Synoptic Gospels, including, of course, the Incarnation, the Resurrection, and the Ascension into Heaven of the God-Man Jesus Christ. Catholic historical critics have never undertaken a systematic refutation of the fallacies embodied in Bultmann's book,

---

7 Malevez, *MCM*, 121 (*CMM*, 123–124).

8 Malevez, *MCM*, 122 (*CMM*, 125).

9 Malevez, *MCM*, 122-129 (*CMM*, 127–131).

especially because, having put their feet into the murky waters of the form-critical method, they lacked the will and the way.

5. Exposition. With regard to divine interventions in the sense of nature-miracles properly so-called, Malevez points out Bultmann's failure to see that science has no authority to set up the principle of determinism as a necessary principle of physical reality, and he corrects Bultmann's oversight with the observation that the order of nature, studied by science, has been integrated by God into another order which transcends it by encompassing it, *viz.*, "the order of those free supernatural relations which form the link between God and the universe of spirits."[10] Malevez sees the difficulty in claiming to be able to recognize exceptions to the laws of nature, when we admittedly do not even know with complete certitude what the laws of nature are. The Christian, he says, will have to concede that certain surprising events which appear to be veritable breaches in the laws of nature cannot logically be assumed to be miracles in the proper sense on those grounds alone, but, in the eyes of the Christian, they will, nevertheless, be attributed the value of authentic miracles, because from their religious context it would be seen that latent forces in nature are acting instrumentally through the action of God in response to prayers. Furthermore, according to Malevez, Bultmann's philosophical reason for excluding any intervention of God in the world is that the only kind of "objectivity" to which the philosopher as such has access is the objectivity of the existential encounter. This view limits divine action to the sphere of the existential encounter in faith, to the exclusion of any vision of "supernatural physical realities." In his philosophy, Bultmann rules out the self-standing exterior objectivity which traditional Christology has always attributed to the union of God and man. But, says Malevez, Bultmann and Heidegger have not disproved the essentialist ontology which they oppose. Malevez does not feel constrained to accept the nihilistic interpretation of Heidegger's *Sein und Zeit*.[11]

6. Exposition. Malevez finds that Bultmann's theological reason for excluding any divine intervention is based upon a misunderstanding of what the traditional theology of the Spirit actually holds. The traditional theology affirms that the Spirit, while being the source of divine movements and interior graces, does not disclose Himself to our methods of experimentation: the effects of His power are seen in our lives, but His actual power is still hidden from our eyes, so that only in faith can we recognize His work. The moment Bultmann admits a "presence" and a "statement" of the event to the mind

---

10 Malevez, *MCM*, 129–135 (*CMM*, 133–137).

11 Malevez, *MCM*, 139–145 (*CMM*, 142–147).

and heart of the believer, he is attributing to this event the same objectivity that is accorded by traditional theology to the Master of our inward life.[12] Bultmann, says Malevez, is basing his separation of God from the world of man upon an interpretation of Protestant faith which sees God as so high and humanity as fallen so low that there can be no revelation of God in our world of objects. It is an interpretation which leaves the reason of man in such shadows that faith can be founded on nothing outside of itself. But Bultmann's admission[13] that sinful man is tormented by the desire for God implies that God is already present to him to some extent. Malevez advances that this immanence of God as the end of human aspirations makes possible the interior action of the Spirit. In the sinner moving towards conversion God by grace creates light for the conscience and strength for the will which are not derived from any prior phenomenon and, therefore, do represent a break in the psychological determinism of the man, but not a break in every respect, for the God from whom they proceed is antecedently installed at the heart of being, and He has created this mysterious relationship with Himself. Hence, the interior grace of the Spirit actually gives us our authentic liberty, our true personality; it gives us back to ourselves. "In truth, God enters only those in whom He dwells."[14]

7. Remarks. The primary issue is not whether Bultmann understands the traditional theology of the Holy Spirit, since Bultmann denies the objective existence of the Holy Spirit, of the Holy Trinity, and of God as an extra-mental object. It is true that only living faith wants to recognize the work of the Holy Spirit, but the visible effects of miracles are there, even for those non-believers who do not want to recognize them. Bultmann attributes only imaginary and pre-conceptual objectivity to the "presence" of the Holy Spirit. Again, Bultmann's theology does have a point of departure from a conception of the total separation of faith and reason, but to the detriment of faith inasmuch as this separation comes out as pure rationalism, that is, as total confidence in human reason to the extent of relegating the object of faith to the realm of the merely imaginary. And that sinful man is tormented by the desire for God does not imply for his theology any real presence of an objectively existing God, but only as an imaginary object which is not a true element of faith and, therefore, can be dispensed with (*KaM*, 183).

---

12 Malevez, *MCM*, 145–146 (*CMM*, 148).

13 Bultmann, in KuM II, 192.

14 Malevez, *MCM*, 149–152 (*CMM*, 151–153).

8. Exposition. Bultmann's act of demythologizing faith, says Malevez, is very much like a mythological act of faith, and its impoverished kerygma (proclamation) is destined to frustration, for it has not enough intrinsic richness of content to evoke loyalty or even interest in any school of thought, whether ancient or modern. What Bultmann forgets is that our "objective ideas" about God are the fruit of intelligence in love with God; they indicate and signify with truth the transcendent Being.[15]

9. Remarks. Malevez rightly observes that Bultmann's act of demythologizing has no intrinsic richness of content, but it does have, unfortunately, the attractiveness of sin and error to the extent that it has, in fact, attracted an enormous amount of interest and a huge crowd of full or partial followers, not only among Protestant but also among Catholic scholars. And, in the absence (in 1999) over a span now of seventy-eight years of any substantial refutation of Bultmann's form-critical conclusions, in the absence over a span of fifty-eight years of a thoroughgoing rebuttal of Bultmann's theology, the dissolving power of his demythologizing has continued to wreak havoc in Catholic intellectual circles. Intelligence in love with God is an intelligence which spontaneously rejects the entire corpus of Bultmann's literary production and which works to produce a detailed and point-by-point refutation of his arguments. It is this task that the present generation of theologians is challenged to undertake and bring to completion, but this will not be accomplished without recourse to the patristic and the neo-patristic methods of Scriptural interpretation.

10. Conclusion. As the "verdict of tradition" Leopold Malevez advances four main points against the demythologizing of Bultmann:

a) On the level of simple belief, Bultmann has taken away the Christian's Lord, for the kerygma cannot replace the mystery of the God-Man.

b) On the level of science, Bultmann does not really speak in the name of modern science, for science is now aware that it cannot draw a picture of the world, and the profound mystery of being eludes it entirely; science has no authority to set up the principle of determinism as a necessary principle of physical reality; the order of nature has been integrated by God into the encompassing order of those free supernatural relations which form the link between God and the universe of spirits.

c) On the level of philosophy, Bultmann rules out the self-standing exterior objectivity which traditional Christology has always attributed to the union of God and man; Bultmann and Heidegger have not disproved the essentialist ontology which they oppose.

---

15 Malevez, *MCM*, 153–156 (*CMM*, 155–158).

d) On the level of theology, Bultmann misunderstands what the traditional theology of the Spirit actually holds.

11. But Malevez makes another series of statements which weaken these points:

a) Christians have always regarded the mystery of the God-Man as essential to their faith; this is a new religion, breaking with the past and having the purely human authority of its author.

b) We do not know with complete certitude what the laws of nature are; certain surprising events which appear to be veritable breaches in the laws of nature cannot logically be assumed to be miracles on those grounds alone, but in the eyes of the Christian they will be attributed the value of authentic miracles, because from their religious context it would be seen that latent forces in nature are acting instrumentally through the action of God in response to prayers.

c) Bultmann's theology correctly emphasizes the principle of the existential interpretation of the Christian message, in the sense that the Christian message has to show its affinity with certain basic human hopes and longings brought to light by existential analysis; Bultmann succeeds in retaining the elements in the theology of Karl Barth which emphasize the objective act of God in Jesus Christ and in bringing faith into relation with reason, although his insistence upon a complete existential interpretation overreaches itself so as to become a menace to the very truth that he sets out to defend.

d) Traditional theology affirms that the effects of the Spirit are seen in our lives, but his actual power is hidden from our eyes, so that only in faith can we recognize his work; God enters only those in whom He dwells.

12. In making these second assertions Malevez plays into Bultmann's hands.

a) Bultmann holds that the faithful have not always believed in the mystery of the God-Man. He has concluded from his form-critical research that this idea was introduced into Christian belief in the post-Palestinian era. It is Bultmann's contention that those believers who are modern men have advanced sufficiently beyond the stage of naive simplicity that they can no longer believe this dogma. But simple believers do not regard this mystery as essential to their faith, because their *existentiell* (I-thou) belief is concerned with something much more concrete and genuine; considering something as "essential to one's faith" is not an act of simple belief, but a theological reflection based on the philosophical concept of "essence." Bultmann retains the mystery of the God-Man in its demythologized form; this means that he accepts it as an *existentiell* point of departure for theological reflection, but this reflection consists in eliminating the mythological fabrication in terms of which the existential meaning of the myth is presented. Malevez does not exclude either dogmatic development or theological reflection. Therefore, an appeal to what Christians have always believed is not sufficient. Bultmann has reflected long on what is essential and what is dispensable. Malevez himself presents a notion of miracle which breaks with what the simple faithful have always believed in the past, derives from his own modern reflection, and has the purely human authority of its author. Yet, he does not accuse himself of proposing a new religion. As long as Malevez accepts in principle the validity of theological reflection that modifies what the naive believer takes for granted, he cannot on sheer principle reprove Bultmann for carrying out such a reflection.

b) It is Bultmann's contention that what cannot be distinguished as a miracle on the level of nature is regarded in the context of belief as the act of God. What Bultmann excludes is nature-miracles. Malevez concedes the basic point by his definition of miracles. From then on the burden of proof is on Malevez to show that his idea of miracle is significantly different from that of Bultmann. Malevez, under the heading of "the verdict of tradition" ("*Le jugement de la Tradition*") says that Bultmann does not speak in the name of modern science. But tradition and modernity are the opposite poles of a distinction. How, then, can tradition decide what modern science is or is not? Malevez claims to be speaking in the name of tradition, but is actually speaking in the name of his own modern reflection. The fact is that Malevez has taken almost without modification the argument of Karl Jaspers, who could hardly be considered a spokesman of tradition.

c) Once Malevez has admitted that Bultmann correctly emphasizes the principle of the existential interpretation of the Christian message, he takes upon himself the burden of showing that Bultmann and Heidegger have not disproved the essentialist ontology which they oppose. Malevez does not bring forth clear evidence to show that Bultmann's existentialist interpretation overreaches itself. The mere fact that Bultmann goes beyond Malevez is no more a proof than is the fact of Malevez's going beyond someone else a proof that Malevez' interpretation has overreached itself. Furthermore, Bultmann's principle of the existential interpretation of the Christian message is the antithesis of the traditional interpretation. How, then, can Malevez make this judgment in the name of tradition? What is this tradition to which Malevez refers? How can he be said to speak in its name? If tradition is dogma, he does not cite it. If tradition is philosophy, he himself calls it into question. If tradition is simply his viewpoint as a Catholic, how can it be called tradition? If Bultmann's existentialist approach is basically correct, has not the essentialist ontology been disproved? Malevez's argument is that Bultmann misunderstands the principles of Bultmann's theology and Heidegger misunderstands the principles of Heidegger's philosophy, but the presumption is in their favor. Does Malevez understand the principles of his own philosophy?

d) The traditional theology of the Spirit is based on the dogma of the Blessed Trinity, which Bultmann denies. The traditional Christian affirms the existence of the Holy Spirit as a living divine Person, acting within our souls. To deny that faith *sees* the Holy Spirit in the sense of affirming his presence would be to concede to Bultmann. The statement "God enters only those in whom He dwells," is a vague poetic paradox which, in its ambiguity, favors the kind of reflection that Bultmann advocates.

The Response of Heinrich Fries

13. Exposition. In 1955 Heinrich Fries published a study of Rudolf Bultmann's approach in which he compared and contrasted the theology of Bultmann with that of Karl Barth and then added an evaluation from the viewpoint of Catholic theology.[16] In formulating his response to Bultmann's challenge, he relied heavily upon the arguments of Barth, but he also used arguments of Geiselmann, Malevez, and other Catholic writers, as well as his own theological reasoning. His criticism takes the form of a rather lengthy list of short arguments against features of Bultmann's program. On the positive side, he notes that Catholic theologians cannot be grateful enough for the impetus that theology has received from Bultmann's emphasis upon its existential character. Statements about the understanding and attainment of authentic existence are made in the message of God's self-revelation in Christ, and, therefore, Bultmann's invitation to work out a process of thought which views man in the light of revelation and revelation in the light of human existence could lead to new and effective forms of confrontation between man and the word of God.[17]

14. Exposition. Fries is, however, of the opinion that, notwithstanding Bultmann's worthy intention, there are serious defects in his program, the first and most fundamental of which is what Karl Barth calls his "pre-Copernican"

---

16 H. Fries, *Bultmann-Barth und die katholische Theologie* (Stuttgart, 1955 [henceforth referred to as *BBKT*); Engl. trans., *Bultmann-Barth and Catholic Theology* (Pittsburgh: Duquesne Univ. Press, 1967 [henceforth referred to as *BBCT*).

17 Fries, *BBKT*, 137–138 (*BBCT*, 149–150).

attitude. Bultmann would make man and man's "pre-understanding" the measure of all understanding, including the understanding of revelation and the word of God, and this is the minus sign standing in front of the whole structure of Bultmann's theology.[18] And Fries agrees with Barth in asking whether Bultmann's "act of God" is not, therefore, better designated as an "act of man,"[19] for by limiting the understanding of God to the measure and belief of man, Bultmann seems to be cutting the dimensions of God down to the size of man.[20] Such a turning of theology into anthropology needs to be avoided, as it can be, if it is realized that existential statements are but one factor of theology. Theology is focused on the Person of Christ, and the question of man should stand within this larger and more basic framework.[21] Furthermore, Bultmann's stand on the viewpoint of modern science is less than critical in the sense that he says little about the dangers arising from modern science itself and from the self-understanding of modern man.[22]

15. Remarks. In my opinion, Catholic theology has been hurt by the subtleties of Bultmann's theology, but his outrageous ideas do constitute a serious challenge to Catholic theologians to produce the full Catholic response which, after the greater part of a century, is still being awaited. While the Catholic intellectual tradition has been maintaining for almost two millennia "a process of thought which views man in the light of revelation and revelation in the light of human existence," Bultmann has contributed nothing to this process except to pose problems whose correct solution could result in an expansion of Catholic theology, not in existentialist terms, but on the basis of Catholic theological tradition. An example of Bultmann's challenge is his use of the idea of pre-understanding. To make pre-understanding "the measure of all understanding" is not a minus sign in every sense. In the context of the existentialism of Martin Heidegger or the idealism of Robin Collingwood it leads to no insight, but it does invite Catholic theologians and exegetes to pay more attention to the mental frameworks that they use in arriving at conclusions. If we define "understanding" as "the knowledge of something true in terms of something else that is true," it is obvious that all understanding does derive in some sense from pre-understanding. Contemporary Catholic

---

18 Fries, *BBKT*, 129 (*BBCT*, 141–142).

19 Fries, *BBKT*, 136 (*BBCT*, 148).

20 Fries, *BBKT*, 139 (*BBCT*, 150).

21 Fries, *BBKT*, 140–141 (*BBCT*, 152).

22 Fries, *BBKT*, 157–158 (*BBCT*, 167–168).

theologians and exegetes, especially historical critics, have not been paying enough attention to the presuppositions of their own thinking. Christian theology is indeed focused on the Person of Christ, both in his divinity and in his humanity. Therefore, the "question of man" stands in the context of the Church as the Mystical Body of Christ and the human soul as recipient of the grace of Christ.

16. Exposition. Fries takes note that, from the viewpoint of Catholic theology, Bultmann overlooks two decisive factors, the one being the Bible as a self-interpreter (*sui ipsius interpres*) and the other being the analogy of faith (*analogia fidei*) contained within this self-interpretation. Bultmann completely ignores the fact that the Bible is above all a book of the Church; he does not realize that for the understanding of the Bible the interpretation and experience of the living Church is of the greatest importance.[23] The Church's understanding of the Scriptures recognizes a multiple level in their meaning: behind the direct literal meaning it sees a deeper spiritual meaning.[24] This obvious meaning of the New Testament is reflected in the Catholic theological concept of the "supernatural," which identifies "grace" as a new qualitative condition over against the natural and historical existence of man; it is an elevation and new creation, a participation in and partaking of the divine nature. As a supernatural quality and reality, as a free gift of the self-giving love of God, grace is not an *existential*, and its existential interpretation destroys it inwardly, relinquishing what is distinctively Christian in favor of merely human existence. The Catholic concept of the supernatural contains what is lacking in Bultmann's interpretation of grace, redemption, and salvation.[25]

17. Remarks. As Fries here points out, the Bible is a self-interpreter, and, to a great extent, its meaning is spontaneously grasped by the faith of the believer. Yet, to understand the Bible perfectly, and not to go astray, the guidance of the teaching Church is also needed, as well as a correct method of interpretation, such as is offered by the patristic and the neo-patristic approaches. On the other hand, the methods of historical criticism tend to impede a true understanding of the inspired word.

18. Exposition. Fries observes that the demythologizing of Bultmann is an attempt to carry the application of the Reformation principle of "justification by faith alone" even into the sphere of knowledge.

---

23 Fries, *BBKT*, 142–143 (*BBCT*, 153–154).

24 Fries, *BBKT*, 144 (*BBCT*, 155).

25 Fries, *BBKT*, 149–150 (*BBCT*, 160–161).

Bultmann's notion of "non-world" is an untenable point of departure for the development of a theory of myth, because, while there is no greater disparity and contrast than between God and creatures, there is also no greater proximity, community, and immanence than between God the Creator and the creature, man, in his world. Man is still an image and likeness of God. By not taking account of this relationship, Bultmann has omitted an essential element both in the reality of God and in the reality of the world.[26] The authentic act of faith is, indeed, a personal one, but a sufficiency of grounds of credibility is necessary in order that the act of faith in Christ may be justified in the eyes of reason and thus become genuinely personal.[27] Bultmann's demythologizing, by attempting to recast into purely existential significance everything given in the New Testament, tends to impoverish the content of faith and leads ever more towards the unreal (*ins Wesenlose*)—an aimless (*wesenlose*) existence which actually nullifies itself for the reason that it can no longer be fulfilled in itself and it can no longer fulfill anything else. This choice for or against authentic existence is based on a false alternative; the "either-or" of Bultmann is a dualism whose poles are not mutually exclusive.[28]

19. Remarks. The choice for or against "authentic existence" in the Bultmannian sense is a dualism whose poles are mutually exclusive inasmuch as the choice consists in rejecting the entire object of Christian faith as fictitious and, therefore, transferring the meaning of the act of faith to an affirmation of one's own "authentic existence" in the Heideggerian sense. The "either-or" of this false dichotomy is between believing what one does not realize to be fictitious and refusing to believe what one has discovered to be fictitious.

20. Exposition. Fries finds Bultmann's interpretation of the Reformation principle of the total fall of man to be contradictory. If man is that totally corrupt, as Bultmann maintains, how can so much be made to depend upon the response of man and his comprehending decision?[29] The fact of the Resurrection is the center of the apostolic kerygma, and an apostle is an eminently qualified witness to the Resurrection. Bultmann's interpretation of the Resurrection stands in irreducible contradiction to the witness of Paul the Apostle, for whom the fact of the Resurrection is the clear content

---

26 Fries, *BBKT*, 158–160 (*BBCT*, 168–170).

27 Fries, *BBKT*, 163 (*BBCT*, 172–173).

28 Fries, *BBKT*, 141 (*BBCT*, 152–153).

29 Fries, *BBKT*, 150–152 (*BBCT*, 161–162).

and object of the Easter faith.[30] The New Testament presents salvation-history as a complex reality (*Wirklichkeit*) within whose several dimensions the "contradictions" espied by Bultmann in the text of the New Testament are completely reconcilable.[31] The resolving of these alleged contradictions does not require a flight from *Historie* into *Geschichte*, for these two phenomena are not separable. It is specifically characteristic of revelation, of the saving-event and the Christ-event, that the "what-is-meaningful-for-me" in the *Geschichte* is so inextricably bound up with the "what-really-took place" in the *Historie* that the former cannot stand independently. By stressing the exclusivity of the present tense in the kerygma to the detriment of the past and the future, which have their own obvious and necessary function, by making relevant the proclaimed Christ, but not the historical Christ, Bultmann upsets the proper sequence, as Barth has pointed out, placing the "for me" in front of the "in itself" and calling the "in itself" into question. This is contrary to the obvious meaning of the text of the New Testament, the substance and center of whose Christian kerygma is the Person of Jesus Christ, his life, his death, his glorification, his mediation. These things do not derive their significance from faith and the kerygma; they receive their content and power from what is objective and what actually (*tatsächlich*) took place, and, therefore, their primary significance is what they are in themselves.[32]

21. Remarks. Bultmann's interpretation of the Reformation principle of the total fall of man is located on the fictitious side of the object of faith and, therefore, does not interfere with his rationalist belief in the soundness of human reason. While the "contradictions" that Bultmann claims to see in the text of the New Testament can indeed be reconciled, Catholic exegetes have not done the work required to refute the voluminous evidence that he pretends to have compiled in his exegetical works. That work remains to be accomplished. The reason why Bultmann proposed a flight in faith from the *Historie* of real history into the *Geschichte* of existentialist historicity was his contention that the real history claimed by the apostolic witness had been eliminated by historical criticism.

22. Exposition. Fries concludes that Biblical revelation does not present unhistorical ideas in the guise of history, but is rather

---

30 Fries, *BBKT*, 164 (*BBCT*, 173–174).

31 Fries, *BBKT*, 142–143 (*BBCT*, 154).

32 Fries, *BBKT*, 133–135 (*BBCT*, 145–147).

concerned specifically with the historical as what factually (*faktisch*) took place: the kerygma and faith of the New Testament spring from and are grounded in what factually happened. But Biblical revelation does present, and perhaps deliberately, what is historical, intensified by a supra-historical dimension in the clothing of mythical images and representations. Where myth is taken to mean the language of images, parables, and symbols, it abides together with the abstract language of conceptual science as a legitimate form of expressing what is. Myth has its rightful place at the meeting-point of man with the world and of man with the word of God.[33]

23. Remarks. Biblical revelation certainly recounts what factually took place. It is the task of this generation of theologians to restore the historical meaning of the inspired text and in the process to discover the depth of spiritual meaning that lies behind it. But myth is not just "the language of images, parables, and symbols;" it is poetic fantasy, and, as such, it has nothing to do with the Gospels.

24. Conclusion. Heinrich Fries' book presents a long list of short and undeveloped arguments against the theology of demythologizing. If developed, they could be formidable, but they are fragile in their undeveloped form. Fries says, for instance, that Bultmann's interpretation of grace, redemption, and salvation lacks the Catholic concept of the supernatural. But, in fact, Bultmann has *eliminated* the Catholic concept of the supernatural in his process of thought. Hence, Fries' needs to attack Bultmann's process of thought. Again, Fries says that Bultmann does not *take into account* that man is an image and likeness of God, that Bultmann has *omitted* an essential element in the reality of God and in the reality of the world. But Bultmann *does* take this into account in terms of his own carefully thought out idea of analogy and of the "twofold reality" by which man and the world are distinct. Fries does not attack Bultmann's idea of the "twofold reality" or his concept of analogy. Fries says that the "either-or" of Bultmann is a dualism whose poles are not mutually exclusive, but Fries should have developed this argument further. In the absence of specific refutation, Bultmann's dualism seems to stand. Furthermore, Fries' theory of history admits of conflicting statements. On the one hand, he holds that biblical revelation is concerned specifically with the historical as "what factually took place" and that the *Geschichte* is so inextricably bound up with what actually took place in the *Historie* that the former cannot stand

---

33 Fries, *BBKT*, 133–135 (*BBCT*, 145–147).

independently. But, on the other hand, he says that biblical revelation presents the historical intensified by a supra-historical dimension in the clothing of mythical images and representations. Once he admits that biblical revelation contains a supra-historical dimension in the clothing of mythical images and representations, it becomes his burden to prove that Bultmann's fuller sighting of myths is an unreasonable excess.

Part II. René Marlé and Joseph Cahill

Living Tradition 81 (May 1999)

The Response of René Marlé

25. Exposition. In pursuance of a shorter article on Bultmann, published in 1953, René Marlé presented a lengthier study of the same in 1956.[34] The principle upon which especially he bases his critique of demythologizing is clearly enunciated towards the end of this latter work. He says that, for the Catholic theologian, the Word of God is a manifold of signs having their focus, not merely in an act or in an event, but also and essentially in a Person: the Person of the Word Incarnate in the act of the gift of Himself that He has given to us on the Cross. Our encounter in faith is, therefore, an encounter with a Person. The paradox, which becomes in effect a *skandalon* for fleshly eyes, is that this Person is at one and the same time truly God and truly man.[35] Marlé observes that the theology of Bultmann, even though it has often been assessed as being basically destructive, aims to be constructive, and its guiding viewpoint is that of a resolute believer. The negative phase of Bultmann's demythologizing is intended only to clear the way for his very pure and very demanding "theology of paradox." Nevertheless, the idols of New Testament mythology that he has marked out for destruction do seem artificial and contrived.[36]

26. Remarks. While Bultmann claims that his theology is based upon paradox, a careful reading of his theological production reveals no positive content that could be called Christian theology.

---

34 Marlé René, *Bultmann et l'interprétation du Nouveau Testament* (Paris, 1956 [herein referred to as *MBI*).

35 Marlé, *MBI*, 179.

36 Marlé, *MBI*, 174–175.

27. Exposition. Another criticism is that for Bultmann the "eschatological" intervention of God in the ever-recurring "now" ends up having no more than a purely accidental connection with history, in the absence of any privileged moment. The consensus of Christian tradition has never hesitated regarding the essentials of the apostolic witness to the corporal Resurrection of Jesus. In order to be faithful to this witness in all its realism, we must not begin to accuse it of myths and thus reject all of the objective reality and all of the intrinsic meaning in the narratives by which the first disciples attempted to communicate to us their extraordinary experience of the Risen One. The Ascension and the gift of the Spirit have also an essential significance for our faith.[37] Marlé doubts whether the vague and obscure notion presented by Bultmann as the world-view underlying the New Testament narratives actually coincides with what the ancients thought. One reason for this doubt is that attempts at constructing world-views are a phenomenon of modern times.[38] Another reason is that the contrast between the ancient and the modern views of the world does not seem to be as clear-cut or as complete as Bultmann supposes.[39]

28. Remarks. Marlé is absolutely right in observing that the realism of Christian faith does not allow of its being accused of fabricating myths. Nor does Bultmann's notion of the biblical world-view coincide with what a careful study of the wording of Sacred Scripture can ascertain. Bultmann is blind to the way in which figures and symbols are used in the Scriptures, and he has no awareness of the way in which allegory is fitted into the real historical sense of the biblical accounts.

29. Exposition. Elements rejected by Bultmann as depending upon the mythical world-view may fit the viewpoint of modern man, for it is not to be excluded that there may be a world of realities not accessible to conceptual thought, and it is such a world of extra-conceptual realities that is expressed in religion. Thus, the imaged and symbolic language of myth could be the proper language of religion, in which case Bultmann, in eliminating the mythical form of the New Testament description, could be eliminating its content as well.[40] Marlé says that what Bultmann calls "myth" we call "mystery," for this is what Tradition has handed down to us,

---

37 Marlé, *MBI*, 171–172.

38 Marlé, *MBI*, 62–63.

39 Marlé, *MBI*, 64.

40 Marlé, *MBI*, 66–69. Cf. *MBI*, 63.

and we are convinced that outside of Tradition the fullness of revelation contained in the New Testament cannot be adequately safeguarded, that, in fact, the entire Christian faith would be gravely menaced. Whatever may be the theories that can be constructed to account for the singular reality of the glorified body of Christ, whatever may be the obscurity in which the Resurrection is enwrapped in the New Testament narratives, we do not fear to reiterate that it is *the very same* Jesus whom the disciples followed during his earthly life and whom they saw living after his death. The "humanity" of Our Lord and Savior is not for us merely the expression of a speculation concerning the metaphysical nature of Christ.[41]

30. Remarks. Bultmann maintains that the New Testament presents extra-conceptual ideas in the sense of pre-conceptual fantasies produced by primitive religious dreamers. Hence, his attack on the truth and reality of the New Testament accounts must be refuted.

31. Exposition. Marlé notes that Bultmann's reduction of the relevant history in the New Testament to *my* history, that is, to the historical "moments" constituting my individual existential "decisions," does not seem to be adequate, not only on the level of faith, but even on the level of philosophy, for it tends towards a radical individualism in which society and community, development and tradition lose all of their genuine value.[42] While Bultmann wishes to leave a place for the interpersonal and social dimension of man, he speaks of this communal aspect only occasionally, and then only with reference to limited topics. Bultmann places the ultimate value of history in the uncovering of the possibilities of my own existence, but he does not provide sufficiently for the possibility that my discovery of my own potentiality may be connected with an eschatological purpose which concerns more than just myself.[43]

32. Exposition. Marlé asks whether Bultmann's rejection of all positive value in philosophical undertakings as such apart from purely formal inquiries is justified. Bultmann bases this rejection upon his affirmation that the fall of man is total. Marlé is not convinced that it is impossible to believe in the intelligibility of being. He suspects that to negate our being's fundamental aspiration to complete light and fullness of life is to give vent to a violent decision. Has man no longer any trace of the image of God in

---

41 Marlé, *MBI*, 180–181.

42 Marlé, *MBI*, 99.

43 Marlé, *MBI*, 101–103.

him? Bultmann does not deny the presence in man of this basic aspiration, but he says that it is immediately and totally perverted.[44]

33. Exposition. In an article published in 1961 for the English-speaking world,[45] Marlé points out the strongly subjective character of Bultmann's notion of faith. In his work of 1956, Marlé had restated Barth's criticism of Bultmann's exposition of faith that the salvific meaning of the Cross is no longer to be sought within the process of time, but only beyond time, and that the Resurrection, as being the salvific meaning of the Cross, is not seen as an event in time, with the result that the object of the faith of the believer is not considered to have any reality outside of the reality of the believer himself.[46] In his article of 1961, Marlé affirms that it is certain that Bultmann's "leap of faith" is purely subjective in character and hence does not support the thesis that Christianity is the only true religion. Referring to John Macquarrie's conjecture that Catholic theologians would have gone much further in agreeing with Bultmann, if the Magisterium of the Church had not clamped down on any such tendency, Marlé observes that Macquarrie is without doubt not entirely wrong on this point, but "there has never in fact been a need to await the intervention of the *Magisterium* to denounce the fatal outcome to which Bultmann's premises would normally lead." It is to Bultmann's premises that Catholic theologians object first and foremost, and when they refer to the weakness or hollowness of his conclusions, it is only to bring more into the foreground the fundamental weaknesses contained in these premises.[47]

34. Exposition. Marlé avers that the historical character of Christian revelation must be preserved in order that faith may retain, not only its

---

44 Marlé, *MBI*, 135.

45 Marlé, "Demythologizing Assessed," in *The Heythrop Journal* (1961), 42–47.

46 Marlé, *MBI*, 169–170.

47 Marlé, "Demythologizing Assessed," 45-46. "Catholic theologians object first and foremost to his premises, and if they point out the weakness, or hollowness, of his conclusions, it is only to bring more into the foreground the fundamental weaknesses contained in these premises. In this connection, some insist on his narrow philosophical anthropology, others on the indefensible assumptions of his exegesis, others on his Lutheran premises whose full danger is eminently clear in his system. It is indeed possible to show how all these different factors are not unconnected" (ibid., 46). However, in *MBI*, 176, note 5 (to which he here refers the reader), Marlé seems to admit an inability to distinguish with any degree of success which are Bultmann's premises and which are his conclusions: "Il nous semble assez vain de nous demander si la position de Bultmann dépend de la manière dont il pose son problème initial, des catégories qu'il utilise, de la philosophie dont il se réclame, ou de la foi qu'il confesse. Tout, peut-on dire, est a la fois chez lui cause, conséquence, symptôme…"

content, but also all of its reality. Bultmann's method is to reduce the content of faith to a "minimal core of factuality" (Macquarrie), whose emptiness will make it invulnerable to critical attacks, but it is useless to uphold any claims to the historical aspect of Christianity unless one is ready to admit that it prolongs itself in an Institution, in a Tradition, by establishing itself in a Dogma.[48]

35. Exposition. In a work on Bultmann published in 1966,[49] Marlé expresses himself more favorably with regard to Bultmann's basic purpose. He still maintains that Bultmann's conceptual instruments are much too rigid to support a true theology or to appreciate the value of all of the New Testament revelation. Moreover, the "kerygmatic concentration" of Bultmann's preaching and the "narrowly practical" character of his spirituality provoke a feeling of stiffness and monotony. Bultmann, it is true, does not equate myth with fable, he recognizes that myth has a positive meaning, but the very general meaning which he ascribes to it keeps him from exploring all of the power to reveal which contemporary philosophy and anthropology have discovered in myth.[50]

36. Remarks. For Bultmann, the difference between myths and fables is that myths are imaginary stories about gods, while fables are imaginary stories about animals. One cannot defend the reality of the object of faith by talking about the revelatory power of myths.

37. Exposition. Marlé is of the opinion that Bultmann's use of the philosophy of Heidegger consists mainly in the borrowing of certain distinctions, with total neglect of what Heidegger has to say about the "poetic" sense of mystery, for Heidegger, while not exceeding the bounds of philosophy, tended more and more towards the use of symbolic language. The intense fear of objectifying thought which guides Bultmann's theologizing indicates that he is still very much bound by objectifying thought, so that he has not gone beyond it but has rather accepted its laws and remains trapped in the artificial dilemmas which it engenders. He is a prisoner of an idealism that is powerless to contact the substance of things.[51]

38. Remarks. Recourse to the "poetic sense of mystery" does not defend the realities of the object of faith from the onslaught of Bultmann's demythologizing.

---

48 Marlé, "Demythologizing Assessed," 47.

49 R. Marlé, *Bultmann et la foi chrétienne* (Paris, 1967 [henceforth referred to as *MBFC*]; Engl. trans., *Bultmann and Christian Faith* (Westminster, Md.: Newman Press, 1968 [henceforth referred to as *MBCF*]).

50 Marlé, *MBFC*, 79–80 (*MBCF*, 52).

51 Marlé, *MBFC*, 81–82 (*MBCF*, 53—54).

39. Exposition. Marlé sees himself as being neither an enthusiastic follower nor a bitter adversary of Bultmann's program of demythologizing, but rather as being one of Bultmann's moderate followers, who recognize in his program a justified concern, but reject the radicalism with which he has defined it and brought it into operation.[52] Marlé admits, however, that Bultmann has shown courage in presenting the program and that the radical character of the proposals contained therein is an incentive to theologians of every persuasion to renew their contact with the very foundations of the faith they profess.[53] Marlé admits also that Bultmann has himself pointed out the superficiality of those who criticize only the practical application of his principles or who simply reproach him for having gone too far, ignoring his claim that all of the elements of the program depend upon one another.[54] Marlé feels that the current revival of interest in tradition, in the Church, and in sacramental symbolism stems from anxiety to recover realities lost sight of in the last few centuries because of excessive zeal for evangelical purity on the one side and of a dogmatic lack of flexibility on the other, or to the immoderate development of critical reason. The rediscovery of the value of images, symbols, and "myths" is an important aspect of this modern movement. The re-evaluation of the imagination will enable us to rediscover the value of the "images" through which divine revelation is given to us. If there is a historical revelation, and if salvation has actually been realized in the world, this revelation and this salvation will always be communicated to us in the world of images. These images are reality itself, because they have been formed by the Spirit of God.[55]

40. Remarks. "Demythologizing" needs to be totally rejected. Bultmann's promotion of a rationalist interpretation of the New Testament is not an example of Christian courage. The re-evaluation of the imagination is

---

52 Marlé, *MBFC*, 77 (*MBCF*, 51).

53 Marlé, *MBFC*, 154–155 (*MBCF*, 106). "Aussi bien ne pouvons-nous nous contenter de voir en Bultmann un péril dont il faudrait exorciser le monde chrétien. Ce théologien intrépide nous a alertés sur l'urgence de problèmes que nous ne pouvons pas éluder. Par le caractère radical des solutions qu'il propose, et qui présentent au moins le mérite d'être des solutions réfléchies, il provoque en outre chaque confession à rejoindre les fondements mêmes de la foi dont elle se réclame. C'est pourquoi la ?crise' de conscience chrétienne qu'il a très largement contribué à formuler, voire à précipiter, ne devrait pas seulement, selon nous, être stérilement déplorée. Elle doit plutôt convaincre toutes les Eglises de l'urgence renouvelée de la tâche théologique" (ibid.).

54 Marlé, *MBFC*, 77–78 (*MBCF*, 51).

55 Marlé, *MBFC*, 84–85 (*MBCF*, 55–56).

no argument in face of someone who claims to have reduced the Gospel accounts to sheer religious fantasy.

41. Exposition. Marlé attributes the great interest shown by people in Bultmann's work to the fact that modern criticism has made us more demanding, so that the man of today has difficulty in understanding ancient religious language and can no longer be content with literal repetition of the biblical formulas. If the world of today is in continuity with the world of the first Christians, contrary to Bultmann's view, and if the fundamental biblical images do contain in themselves all reality (*realité*), so that our faith should let itself be formed and nourished by them, then the only way in which we can establish contact with the world of the Apostles is in terms of the exigencies that we have as twentieth-century men. In other words, it would be an empty illusion to try to recover an ingenuousness forever lost. But the instrument of research should not be the questionable criteria borrowed by Bultmann from a narrow concept of existence, but rather theological work based on history.[56] Bultmann, it is true, is in accord with the "intrinsic logic" of Protestantism, when he detaches faith from the historical and psychological elements in which it is rooted and transmitted. But those on the Catholic side who unilaterally develop a certain "Catholic logic" marked especially by its anti-Protestantism, also arrive at deficient and disputable positions. It is an error to try to reduce the faith of the various Churches to "logics" (*logiques*) of this kind.[57]

42. Remarks. Modern criticism is not sufficiently demanding of its own thought processes. The "Catholic logic" which is most needed here is not so much anti-Protestantism as anti-rationalism.

43. Conclusion. René Marlé bases his criticism of demythologizing on the following points:

a) For the Catholic theologian the Word of God is focused essentially in the Person of the Word Incarnate, who is at one and the same time truly God and truly man.

b) In addition to the corporal Resurrection of Jesus, the Ascension and the gift of the Spirit have also an essential significance for our faith.

c) In order to be faithful to the apostolic witness in all its realism, we must not begin to accuse it of myths.

d) It is the very same Jesus whom the disciples saw living after his death.

e) It is a world of extra-conceptual realities that is expressed in religion.

---

56 Marlé, *MBFC*, 85–87 (*MBCF*, 56–57).

57 Marlé, *MBFC*, 154 (*MBCF*, 106).

44. But Marlé includes another series of statements which weaken or contradict these points:

a) Bultmann has a very pure and very demanding theology of paradox; the ideal Catholic theologian is the moderate follower of Bultmann who recognizes in Bultmann's program a justified concern, but rejects the radicalism with which he has defined it and brought it into operation.

b) The guiding viewpoint of Bultmann's theology is that of a resolute believer, although the idols of New Testament mythology that he has marked out for destruction do seem artificial and contrived.

c) The imaged and symbolic language of myth could be the proper language of religion.

d) What Bultmann calls "myth" we call "mystery"; whatever may be the obscurity in which the Resurrection is enwrapped in the New Testament narratives, the humanity of Our Lord and Savior is not for us merely the expression of a speculation concerning the metaphysical nature of Christ; the dogmatic lack of flexibility in the Church has given way to the rediscovery of the value of images, symbols and myths; this re-evaluation of the imagination will enable us to rediscover the value of the images through which the divine revelation is given to us; revelation and salvation will always be communicated to us in the world of images; these images are reality itself, because they have been formed by the Spirit of God.

e) The man of today can no longer be content with literal repetition of the biblical formulas; if the fundamental biblical images contain in themselves all reality, then the only way to establish contact with the world of the Apostles is to recognize our needs as twentieth-century men and abandon the attempt to recover an ingenuousness forever lost.

45. In making these second affirmations, Marlé plays into Bultmann's hands:

a) Since Bultmann totally rejects the truth of the Incarnation of the Second Person of the Blessed Trinity, and categorically excludes the entire object of Catholic faith, a Catholic theologian cannot reasonably be a moderate follower of Bultmann.

b) Bultmann flatly and totally denies the Incarnation, the corporal Resurrection, the Ascension, and the gift of the Holy Spirit, all of which Marlé admits to be essential for faith. If Marlé seriously thinks this, it is conceding too much to say that the guiding viewpoint of Bultmann's theology is that of a resolute believer, with the soft qualification that it does seem artificial and contrived for Bultmann to have eliminated these elements from his faith. How can this "guiding viewpoint" of Bultmann's theology, which does not contain at all these essential elements of faith, be the viewpoint of a "resolute believer"?

c) Marlé has more than begun to accuse the apostolic witness of myths; he makes myth the proper language of the apostolic witness.

d) Bultmann opposes the creation by preachers and theologians of "improvised mysteries" like the Trinity and the bodily Resurrection. But Bultmann does not reduce the Resurrection to a speculation concerning "the metaphysical nature of Christ"; he gives it the status of an "eschatological event." And has Marlé reflected deeply on what he is saying when he affirms that the images are the reality? Is the Person of the Word Incarnate, whom according to Marlé we encounter in faith, an image which is the reality? The Fathers of the Church did indeed see various biblical images as reflecting deeper realities, but they did not maintain that the images were the realities. Marlé seems here to be attempting to enunciate an important truth, but he expresses it confusedly.

e) In the conflict with Jaspers, Ellwein, Künneth, Kinder, and Barth over the question of symbols of revelation and supernatural reality, the theory of Bultmann attained a subtlety of which Marlé seems largely unaware. Marlé does not expound his notion of "extra-conceptual realities" or clarify what they could be, and he aggravates this lack by his attack on conceptual realities. Faith, he says, cannot be reduced to Bultmannian logic, Catholic logic, or any logic. But we must ask whether any theology can get along without logic. It may be that opposition to logic is the cause of Marlé's confusion. How can he logically say, for instance, that Catholic theologians object only to Bultmann's premises, and not to his conclusions except to the extent that they illustrate the weakness of the premises? Are not the conclusions just as offensive as the premises? But which *are* the premises and which are the conclusions? Marlé tells us himself that in Bultmann's writings it is futile to try to distinguish the premises from the conclusions, and that he has never succeeded in doing so at all. Without the use of logic, he never will. When Marlé calls for the processing of the text of the Bible in order to produce a formulation that is acceptable to "modern man," he has virtually conceded the debate to Bultmann.

The Response of Joseph Cahill

46. Exposition. Joseph Cahill[58] undertakes to "examine some radical problems and solutions that are present and operative, though oftentimes not

---

58   P. J. Cahill, "(Notes concerning John Macquarrie's) *The Scope of Demythologizing*, in *Theological Studies*, 23 (1962), 79–92 [henceforth referred to as *JCSD*].

explicitly considered, in an assessment of Bultmann's theological approach." His intention is to "make explicit the beginnings at least of a systematic dialectic from which there is hope of progress in the understanding, if not the resolution, of mutual problems."[59] Cahill thinks that Bultmann's writings may have greater speculative value than those of exegetes like Oscar Cullmann, who, for example, "with commendable clarity and insight, restores the biblical teaching and categories," but is also constrained to affirm that all subsequent speculation in terms of explanatory categories and those of the absolute, such as the doctrine of the two natures of Christ, is useless and improper.[60] Bultmann has the merit of attempting to make the revelation contained in the Bible relevant for modern man through theological speculation and pertinent interpretation that have modern significance; he preserves the biblical categories while interpreting them in existentialist terms and in the thought patterns of modern man. Cahill does not agree with the modality of this twofold interpretation, but he welcomes Bultmann's attempt to bridge the gaps between the rich, modern interpretation of Scripture, speculative theology, and concrete "existential" man. "Criticisms of his total system should not obscure his grasp of the problem; and his projected solution with its twofold interpretation could be carefully studied by all theologians who must be concerned with the problem of theological relevance...."[61]

47. Remarks. Bultmann's theological speculation is of no use whatsoever for achieving an understanding of the biblical categories. Bultmann's "modern man" is that segment of contemporary men who believe in secular humanism and have no openness to divine revelation. In trying to make the New Testament relevant to his idea of modern man, Bultmann has denatured the Christian proclamation. Bultmann's interpretation of the New Testament writings has no objective or subjective richness.

48. Exposition. Cahill observes that Bultmann eliminates from his theology the objective consideration of God. This omission is common to all theologians who operate exclusively in existentialist categories.[62] "The result of

---

59 Cahill, *JCSD*, 79.

60 Cahill, *JCSD*, 86. "The Logos is the self-revealing, self-giving God—God in action. This action only is the subject of the New Testament. Therefore, all abstract speculation about the 'natures' of Christ is not only a useless undertaking, but actually an improper one" (O. Cullmann, *The Christology of the New Testament*, 266).

61 Cahill, *JCSD*, 86. Cf. Charles Davis, "The Danger of Irrelevance," in *The Downside Review* 79 (1961), 100; K. Rahner, "The Prospects for Dogmatic Theology," in *Theological Investigations* (Engl. trans., Baltimore: 1961), 2–37.

62 Cahill, *JCSD*, 89.

the exclusively existentialist emphasis is possibly suitable for the revivalist but hardly adequate for the theologian, who feels he must think about the entire deposit of faith, not simply one or other aspect of the faith."[63] It is Cahill's studied opinion that even to preserve the *existentiell* (I-thou) relationship with Scripture it is necessary to try, through reflective, essentialist theology, to understand the objective event in itself.[64] Despite Bultmann's rejection of all natural revelation, Cahill sees a striking possibility of natural revelation in the Bultmannian notion of pre-understanding. "Here one senses very definite echoes of Thomas' natural desire as well as Augustine's knowledge of divine Truth in the existential judgment."[65]

49. Remarks. Whoever eliminates the objective consideration of God from his theology has no theology left. Bultmann's notion of "pre-understanding" is based upon the idealist philosophy of Robin Collingwood and bears no resemblance to the speculation either of Thomas Aquinas or of Augustine of Hippo.

50. Exposition. From Bultmann's use of the term "presence" it does not appear to Cahill that Christ is present in the preached Word as God is present in the Word. It is not clear that "Word" has the univocal meaning that Bultmann claims for it. Some writers[66] have undertaken to develop the idea of Christ as a speech-event, but their presentations do not transcend the level of description, and they, therefore, do not even begin to explain the phenomena in question, since a description is not an explanation. Descriptive nomenclature simply tolerates the problem; it does not solve it.[67] Cahill agrees with Paul Althaus's judgment that Bultmann virtually reincarnates Ritschl's practice of supplanting historical facts with value-judgments; for Bultmann the only Christ is the Christ for us. Faith, therefore, becomes centered on a religious value-judgment. Using Robin Collingwood's distinctions, Cahill says that, in terms of Bultmann's principle, it is no longer clear that the "outside" of the religious experience (for instance, of the Person of the Jesus of history) "is anything more than a secular and profane, though sanguine, incident, with no intrinsic and permanent relation to the experiential grasp of the divine revelation."[68] Bultmann admits that his existential encounter cannot defend

---

63 Cahill, *JCSD*, 90.

64 Cahill, *JCSD*, 89.

65 Cahill, *JCSD*, 80, note 4.

66 See Carl Michalson, in *Christian Century* (1961), 553.

67 Cahill, *JCSD*, 85.

68 Cahill, *JCSD*, 84. Cf. Ian Henderson, *Myth in the New Testament* (London, 1952), 49.

itself against the charge of illusion, and he attempts no rational justification for it. The subjective encounter, as a subjective experience, is essentially incommunicable and could therefore easily be a mere personality projection. But the categories of religious experience must be capable of objective as well as intersubjective presentation, because man is a psychosomatic unity.[69] While the "inside" of strictly supernatural events may transcend direct historical investigation, "the validity and necessity of the strictly historical method for a reconstruction of certain past outer events which the believer apprehends with a new magnitude and dimension as revelation cannot be minimized or distinguished out of existence." The possibility of faith is offered because God has intervened in history. Since by "theology" is meant thinking about the faith, it follows that accurate historical investigation must always be a part of theology, so that "no amount of subjective *a priori* speculation or postulation can substitute for or replace critical investigation of the divine events as well as enlightened examination of the later understanding of the divine events manifested in the theological sources."[70]

51. Remarks. Bultmann glories in the fact that, as a "modern man," he has supplanted what naive Christians believe to be the Gospel facts with existentialist value-judgments. He admits that what, in Collingwood's terminology, constitutes the "outside" of the event of Christ is nothing more than a secular and profane incident. It is, therefore, incumbent upon those who would differ with Bultmann to refute his exegesis of the Gospels and to demonstrate that his conclusions about the purely imaginary character of the supernatural side of the life of Christ are false, or at least to refer to others who have already done so. Bultmann admits that his "existential encounter" cannot defend itself against illusion, because he believes that he is simply exchanging an ancient fantasy for a modern one. He is a modern sophist, and it is indeed surprising how far he has gotten with his sophistic argumentation.

52. Exposition. Cahill draws attention to the fact that Bultmann, theologizing from systematic premises taken from the Kantian separation of faith and knowledge and the Lutheran dichotomy between corruptive works of the intellect and the absolute status of faith, to which he has added the refinements of Heideggerian existentialism, dismisses the dogmatic formulations of the early ecumenical councils (as products of an objectivizing Hellenistic ontology) and reverts to Scriptural categories as the only legitimate understanding of revelation.

---

69 Cahill, *JCSD*, 82, note 7.

70 Cahill, *JCSD*, 83–84.

Bultmann fails to realize that dogma is the terminus of a transit from the descriptive to the explanatory.[71]

53. Remarks. Cahill's recognition that Bultmann reasons from Lutheran, Kantian, and Heideggerian systematic premises is a correct approach to the problem of demythologizing. In order to become effective, this manner of reply needs to be based upon a developed idea of the validity of "objectivizing Hellenistic ontology" and, in particular, upon the validity and importance of Thomist philosophy for contemporary believers.

54. Conclusion. Joseph Cahill's contribution to the demythologizing debate is in the form of a review of Macquarrie's book. Cahill's intention is to make explicit at least the beginnings of a systematic dialectic, and a scant beginning it is. Among the points briefly presented are the following:

a) Bultmann eliminates from his theology the objective consideration of God.

b) The categories of religious experience must be capable of objective presentation, because man is a psychosomatic unity.

c) Bultmann fails to realize that dogma is the terminus of a transit from the descriptive to the explanatory.

55. But Cahill weakens these points with other affirmations:

a) Bultmann preserves the biblical categories while interpreting them existentially in the thought-patterns of modern man.

b) There is a striking possibility of natural revelation in Bultmann's notion of pre-understanding. While the inside of strictly supernatural events may transcend directly historical investigation, "the validity and necessity of the strictly historical method for a reconstruction of certain past outer events which the believer apprehends with a new magnitude and dimension as revelation cannot be minimized or distinguished out of existence."

c) Since theology means thinking about the faith, accurate historical investigations must always be a part of theology: no amount of subjective *a priori* speculation or postulation can substitute for critical investigation of the divine events in the theological sources.

56. By not clarifying these affirmations Cahill plays into Bultmann's hands.

a) Once Cahill admits that Bultmannian existentialism accords with the thought-patterns of modern man, the burden of proof is on him to show that the elimination of the objective consideration of God and of his revelation is an error. Bultmann has provided false arguments of considerable length for this elimination.

---

71 Cahill, *JCSD*, 87–89.

b) Bultmann makes much of the fact that man is a unity. If it follows from man's psychosomatic unity that the categories of religious experience must be capable of objective presentation, it would be interesting to see how the convincing argument for this is constructed. Nevertheless, Bultmann admits that the categories of religious experience are capable of objective presentation. He calls this presentation "myth." Again, Cahill sees in Bultmann's notion of pre-understanding a "striking" possibility of natural revelation which Bultmann excludes. Cahill claims to see in Bultmann's notion what Bultmann denies is in it. It is incumbent upon Cahill to show clearly that this possibility is there. Furthermore, Cahill accepts Collingwood's thesis of the "inside" and the "outside" of events, a distinction which has served Bultmann's existentialism well. Cahill does not spell out how, on the basis of Collingwood's philosophy of history, he can legitimately speak of the "inside" of "strictly supernatural events" which may transcend direct historical investigation. Has Cahill meditated on the meaning of these terms in the philosophy of Collingwood? Finally, is Cahill admitting that revelation is not itself a historical event, but just a magnitude and dimension that is seen by the believer in certain past ("outer") events? This would seem to be a fatal concession to Bultmann.

c) Bultmann makes the results of a certain kind of so-called "historical investigation" a presupposition of his theologizing. He is a master of this kind of work. What Bultmann rejects is, to use Cahill's own words, the "new magnitude and dimension" that is said to have been "projected," or "objectified" by the primitive Christian believer into supernatural events that "critical historical investigation" finds to be a product of purely subjective speculation. And Bultmann does not deny that dogma is a transit from the descriptive to the explanatory; he simply repudiates dogma as being a false and uncritical explanation derived from speculation upon fanciful ideas that modern man can no longer accept. Cahill, in the admittedly short space of his review, does not give a convincing reply to Bultmann's basic contentions.

Part III. The Response of Xavier Léon-Dufour
(as translated and edited by John McHugh)

Living Tradition 82 (July 1999)

57. Bultmann's historical presuppositions. Catholic historical critics are wont to distinguish the form-critical method of Bultmann from his

philosophical and theological presuppositions, saying that they accept in large part his form-critical method but they reject his presuppositions, such as his Heideggerian existentialism and his exaggerated Lutheran notion of the "total fall of man." But Catholic historical critics, in taking this approach, often do not clearly recognize that, on the one hand, the method of form-criticism has presuppositions of its own that generate and control the method and, on the other hand, that the results of Bultmann's historical critical research are one of the principal presuppositions of his theology. Bultmann did not begin to expound his interpretation of the Christian proclamation until he had already himself proclaimed in his *History of the Synoptic Tradition* that the whole supernatural fabric of the Gospels is the result of the sheer religious fantasy of the early Christian community. In making this proclamation, Bultmann had a phalanx of other rationalist thinkers behind him and around him: the long succession of preceding rationalist interpreters of the Gospels and his fellow rationalist colleagues, such as Martin Dibelius, Karl Schmidt, M. Albertz, and D. Bertram. After Bultmann had eliminated in his own mind the entire supernatural object of Christian faith, he began to search for reasons why the modern person should any longer believe in the Gospel message and why the modern preacher should preach the Gospel message, and he came up with his existentialist interpretation of the kerygma. Now, this enormous presupposition of Bultmann's demythologizing, namely, the proclaimed results of his New Testament historical critical research, has never been substantially rebutted by Catholic exegetes, in the sense that they have never systematically taken up and refuted his imposing analysis of the "Synoptic tradition," with the result that these conclusions have come more and more to be accepted by Catholic exegetes, in the absence of available arguments on the contrary, and this has tended to leave a vacuum also in the opposition of Catholic theologians to his call for demythologizing. In the following discussion a thing to be noted is the extent to which the negative results of form-critical analysis of the text of the Gospels have affected the interpretation that Catholic historical critics are inclined to give to the inspired word.

58. Introduction. In 1963 Xavier Léon-Dufour published his highly influential work on the historical truth of the Gospels, *Les évangiles et l'histoire de Jésus*,[72] in which he does not deal *ex professo* with demythologizing as such, but he skirts the issue constantly as he develops his exegetical theme in keeping with the purpose of his book, which is "to give a fair hearing to the

---

72   X. Léon-Dufour, *Les évangiles et l'histoire de Jésus* (Paris: Éditions du Seuil, 1963 [henceforth referred to as *EHJ*]).

new set of questions [raised by Bultmann and others] without at the same time adopting the presuppositions which have prejudiced the results of an inquiry that was intended to be scientific (*sans pour autant adopter les préjugés qui ont compromis les résultats d'une enquête qui se voulait scientifique*)."[73] Léon-Dufour's book was translated into English by John McHugh and published under the title of *The Gospels and the Jesus of History*, in an abridgment that is about half the length of the original French text.[74] McHugh made efforts to keep all of the original thoughts and to render them faithfully into English, but the wording of the condensed version is not, of course, exactly the same. However, McHugh does note in his "Translator's Preface" that the final text was submitted to Father Léon-Dufour for his approval. In the following discussion it is the text of the English translation that will be cited, and the references will, therefore, be to Léon-Dufour (McHugh), meaning Léon-Dufour as translated by McHugh. The following quotations are arranged to show that Léon-Dufour (McHugh) presents one series of statements that reflect the traditional interpretation of the Fathers of the Church, and a second series of statements that sets this traditional meaning in a new and problematic context. The emphasis given in the quotations is intended to show the contrast and is entirely mine.

59. Exposition. The aim of Léon-Dufour (McHugh)'s book is "to find out, by using the critical methods of historical scholarship, the full and objective truth (as far as it can be known) about the life of Jesus of Nazareth."[75] However: "The aim [of this book] has been to rediscover, as far as possible, the 'objective truth' about Jesus of Nazareth; and the objective truth about him is that he confronts all mankind with a question demanding an answer. And the answer cannot be given except by faith."[76]

60. Remarks. In making these second affirmations Léon-Dufour (McHugh) plays into Bultmann's hands. Léon-Dufour (McHugh)'s form-critical research, like that of Bultmann, results only in *human* historical facts about the life of Jesus and to *a question to be answered*, not by the knowledge of any objective historical fact about Jesus, but only by the subjective response of the Christian believer. Now, Bultmann has expounded this answer to Léon-Dufour (McHugh)'s question in his

---

73 Léon-Dufour, *EHJ*, 8.

74 Xavier Léon-Dufour, *The Gospels and the Jesus of History* (translated and edited in abridged form by John McHugh, London: Collins 1968 [henceforth referred to as Léon-Dufour (McHugh)]).

75 Léon-Dufour (McHugh), 14.

76 Léon-Dufour (McHugh), 274–275.

extensive theological works, making full use of the method of demythologizing and of the existentialism of Martin Heidegger. Bultmann admits
that "the historical Jesus" is profitable for "salvation," but only in the
purely existentialist sense of providing the occasion for the believer to
take hold of his own subjective being as an act of "self-authenticity" or
self-realized "historicity." Jesus is thus thought to form some kind of
"historical model" for the modern believer's own act of faith. Léon-Dufour
(McHugh) does not intend to be a Bultmannian in that sense, but, since
Bultmann's explanation is already "in possession" in that area, by not
presenting any effective refutation of Bultmann's notion of the "event
of Christ," or any solid distinction showing how his view differs from
that of Bultmann, he virtually surrenders the field. Like the Gospel of
Mark in the form-critical version, Léon-Dufour (McHugh)'s theological
exposition ends with the question posed by the empty tomb, leaving it
to the reader and the Church to supply the answer. Where is the reader
to find this answer? If he turns to the existentialism accommodated by
Léon-Dufour (McHugh), he will find that for existentialists there is no
real answer, but only an ever-repeated question.

61. Exposition. Léon-Dufour (McHugh) points out that "Theology
(the study of God) becomes mere anthropology (the study of man)
when it despises the objective fact which is the transcendent element
in existential knowledge. And it is only because the faith of the early
Church was based on an objective fact that we can say Christianity
is more than mythology. ... The kerygma which is accepted by faith
derives from Jesus, and the full meaning of his life can be known only
through the "pattern of apostolic preaching."[77] However: "Towards
the end of the eighteenth century many writers began to attack the
historical value of the four gospels. ...These books were all written with
one purpose: to get back with real certainty to the unadorned facts,
and to reconstruct what actually happened in the past. What other
authors did in their day, we have to do again for our own generation."[78]
And further on: "Moreover, we must not see the past simply as events
which once took place, for in those events there is a message. The
contemporaries of Jesus did not grasp the full meaning of those events,
but the believer who lives in the present (the 'today') of the Church
can do so, for he sees the past, historical, objective event as a demand

---

77 Léon-Dufour (McHugh), 275.

78 Léon-Doufour (McHugh), 7.

addressed to himself."[79] And finally: "History provides the facts, and a question; faith provides the interpretation of those facts, and the answer to the question."[80]

62. Remarks. In making these affirmations Léon-Dufour (McHugh) plays into Bultmann's hands. On the level of historical science, there is no valid distinction between the "Jesus of history" and the "Christ of faith," since they are one single object of historical observation and there is nothing "adorned" about it. Bultmann minimizes the historical aspect of Christian faith for the reason that he falsely presupposes a radical separation between faith and reason. But Christian faith is more than a mere loving trust in God to the exclusion of the objective truth of dogma and historical fact. That for the early Christians the real historical fact of the Resurrection of Jesus was an object of their faith is clear from the obvious reading of 1 Cor. 15:13–14: "But if there be no resurrection of the dead, then Christ is not risen again. And if Christ be not raised again, then vain is our preaching, and vain also is your faith." To interpret this, as Bultmann has done, to mean that it doesn't matter to Christian faith whether or not there is *really* a resurrection from the dead or whether or not Christ *really* rose from the tomb, but rather that Christian faith can disbelieve the real objective historical factualness of the Resurrection and still be Christian faith is a total violation of the rules of literary interpretation.

63. Exposition. "Christians who read the gospel story in the light of their faith penetrate into the minds of the four evangelists and find no difficulty in believing that in the person of Jesus they have the key to the history of the world."[81] However: "The spirit of total commitment to God which has been described as a spirit of detachment and childlike simplicity is called, in technical theological language, faith. The word 'faith,' when it occurs in the gospels, does not mean primarily an acceptance of some proposition as true, or even obedience to divine revelation (though either of these meanings may be implied); the primary meaning of the word in the gospels is a total entrusting of oneself to God, as a child trusts his father."[82] Again: "The only faithful interpretation of the gospels, therefore, is that which reveals Jesus as a living person, speaking not only to his own generation, but to all future ages. Our inquiry has shown that the factual events of his life—even though

---

79 Léon-Dufour (McHugh), 88.

80 Léon-Dufour (McHugh), 275.

81 Léon-Dufour (McHugh), 267.

82 Léon-Dufour (McHugh), 242.

they include the answer which becomes evident only in the light of the Holy Spirit—are, first and foremost, a question addressed to mankind; "And you—who do you say that I am?"[83]

64. Remarks. Here again Léon-Dufour (McHugh) plays into Bultmann's hands. For the faithful to accept Jesus as a Person means first to let the objective truth of His historical words and deeds fill their minds with light so as to develop into a knowledge of His historical personality as it is manifested in His miraculous conception, His humble and miraculous life on earth, His providential death with its salvific consequences, and His glorious Resurrection in the same physical body, really and physically present in the Blessed Sacrament of the altar. To accept Him means also to receive Him into their hearts by corresponding in love to the objective meaning of His divine Person and thus allowing the Three Divine Persons of the Most Holy Trinity to dwell in them. Of course, accepting Jesus is more important than merely knowing objective facts, but the issue here is the denial, in the form-critical conclusions that Léon-Dufour (McHugh) defends, of objective facts stated in the Gospels. So the primary meaning of faith in this context does mean acceptance of the objective truths recounted in the Gospels and set down in propositions by the Church. The objective truth of Christ has a subjective phase of realization within the hearts of the faithful, without which the salvation brought by Christ is of no avail, but faith is fundamentally an affirmation of the objective truth.

65. Exposition. "More than anyone else, Jesus of Nazareth has been the subject of charges and counter-charges: when Christians are accused of falsifying history by idealizing His life, they may legitimately reply that history is falsified if his life is reduced to merely human proportions not because of the evidence but because of philosophical objections to anything which reason cannot explain as a natural phenomenon."[84] However: "All four gospels claim to record history, but they do not conceal the theological purpose which underlies the historical record, and some modern readers will no doubt wonder whether it is possible to write history with a theological purpose without thereby falsifying the narrative."[85]

66. Remarks. Léon-Dufour (McHugh) is playing into Bultmann's hands. Here he makes the big mistake of not distinguishing between the *finis operis* (purpose of the thing itself) and the *finis operantis* (purpose of the maker of

---

83 Léon-Dufour (McHugh), 276.

84 Léon-Dufour (McHugh), 19.

85 Léon-Dufour (McHugh), 23.

the thing). The purpose of a historical work as a thing in itself is primarily to present a record of historical events in some chronological sequence, and secondarily to provide some interpretation of those events. The fact that the narrator of history has some further purpose in mind which leads him to select or emphasize certain facts does not affect the historical truth of his account as long as he honestly recounts those facts. Thus, no reader of the New Testament should doubt that it is possible to write a true historical narrative while having a theological purpose in mind.

67. Exposition. "(T)he gospels do contain a wealth of trustworthy historical information."[86] However: "(The early Christians) did turn their attention to the past, but not in order to study it as an "objective fact"; rather, they sought to find in it guidance about the way in which they themselves ought to respond to the teaching of their Master. In modern language, we should say that they had an existentialist, rather than a positivist, attitude to history."[87]

68. Remarks. This is Bultmannian double-talk. The "trustworthy information" of the Gospels is here said to lack objective factualness but, nevertheless, to be "trustworthy" in that the existentialist believer trusts in it as an occasion for his ever-repeated decision to become his own authentic self.

69. Exposition. "The various forms of literature found in the gospel arose quite naturally from what we may label the "theological" and "historical" preoccupations of the Church."[88] However: "There are in the gospels certain short phrases which we can be absolutely sure were spoken by our Lord....It must be admitted, however, that these phrases are not numerous, and are rarely of importance."[89]

70. Remarks. Bultmann had already misused historical method back in 1921 to conclude that only a few short expressions in the Gospels can with any confidence be traced back to the lips of Jesus. It is a pity that Catholic historical critics have not been able to recognize the fallacies inscribed into Bultmann's form-critical method. We are absolutely certain, on the basis of faith and also on the basis of historical research, that the divine Word of God became incarnate in the womb of the Blessed Virgin Mary, worked many nature-miracles during His life on earth, rose from the dead, and ascended

---

86 Léon-Dufour (McHugh), 14.

87 Léon-Dufour (McHugh), 187.

88 Léon-Dufour (McHugh), ibid.

89 Léon-Dufour (McHugh), 207.

bodily into Heaven. The "historical and theological preoccupations" apparent in the Gospel accounts pertain to the level of historical explanation and do not thereby exclude factuality on the level of chronology. If the Gospel genre presents the mystery of man's union with God, it does so first by narrating the objectively true and historical words and deeds of the God-Man Jesus Christ. This objective truth has also its subjective phase in the first question with which the Person of Jesus confronts all men, namely, whether or not they will accept the objective truth of the Gospel.

71. Exposition. "The continuity of the disciples' faith before and after the Resurrection, and the identity of the Risen Christ with Jesus of Nazareth can be denied only on *a priori* grounds, because of philosophical or theological presuppositions, not because there is *historical* evidence to the contrary."[90] However: "This is the fundamental fact about the Resurrection: that the Risen Christ founded a Church. This was the cardinal belief of the early Christians, that the Church they knew and loved was founded by the Risen Christ: 'if Christ has not risen, then our preaching is worthless, and our faith is worthless' (1 Cor 15:14). This conviction they held by faith, but there were two observable facts to justify that faith: the tomb of Jesus had been found empty, and the timid apostles had been transformed in character. The empty tomb poses a question; the transformation of the apostles gives a clue to the answer. That is all history can provide: a question, and a hint or indication of where to look for the answer. Historical study cannot 'prove' the fact of the Resurrection, because the essence of the doctrine is that Jesus is enthroned at the right hand of the Father; and there can be no apodictic proof of contingent fact which belongs to another world."[91]

72. Remarks. In reducing the issue to these terms, Léon-Dufour (McHugh) plays into Bultmann's hands. Long before Léon-Dufour (McHugh) wrote this, it was Bultmann who announced to the modern believer that history provides the facts and a question, while faith provides the interpretation of the facts and the answer to that question. Léon-Dufour (McHugh) may disagree with Bultmann's answer to the question, but the fact remains that he makes no strong effort to formulate and express the scientific reasons for disagreeing with or refuting the false interpretation that Bultmann has made. Nor does he give his readers the means of doing so. Bultmann's theological conclusions follow with stunning logic from the historical conclusions of the form-criticism of the Gospels largely created by him. It is a formidable task to oppose Bult- mann's reasoning

---

90 Léon-Dufour (McHugh), 274.

91 Léon-Dufour (McHugh), 258.

on a technical level; Léon-Dufour (McHugh) does not undertake it. His endeavor is rather "to demonstrate that a thoroughgoing application of the principles of historical criticism does not weaken but rather strengthens the conviction that the gospels are historically reliable." Bultmann had already "demonstrated" this on a pseudoscientific level, except for certain subjective additions that the post-Bultmannians would later contribute. Léon-Dufour (McHugh) should have made it his task to show that true history provides an answer to the questions that it raises—an answer taking the form of historical science. By failing to recognize the historical challenge presented by the Gospels, Léon-Dufour (McHugh) misses the terms of the fundamental questions that he seeks to answer.

73. Exposition. "The whole life of Jesus is a proclamation of the mystery of man's union with God in him at the end of time." However (in context): "Mark's Gospel ends with the finding of the empty tomb. ... The women "had a promise from the angel that Jesus would meet his disciples in Galilee, and here Mark ends, on a note of interrogation, leaving the reader in suspense, wondering when Jesus will appear. The whole life of Jesus is a proclamation of the mystery of man's union with God in him at the end of time."[92]

74. Remarks. The folding up of the whole significance of the life of Jesus, as presented in the Gospels, into the proclamation of the mystery of man's union with God is Bultmannian. Certainly, on the level of the anagogical sense, the Gospels proclaim the final union of the elect with God and in some places on the level of the literal sense as well, but the literal sense first and foremost records the historical facts regarding the life of Jesus. The nature-miracles, the prophecies, the sublime teachings of Jesus are real and objective historical facts which are just as biographical as anything in the life of Caesar Augustus or Napoleon Bonaparte. The fundamental fact about the Resurrection is that Jesus of Nazareth rose physically from the dead, leaving an empty tomb behind. There were many witnesses to the appearances of the Risen Christ. Historical study "proves" the fact of the Resurrection by the testimony of reliable witnesses. Part of this proof consists in a systematic refutation of the fallacies excogitated by Bultmann and others as a pretext for rejecting the historical reliability of these witnesses.

75. Exposition. "[Matthew] has captured the lessons of the past; the object of his work is to be a "remembrance" of the union that God brought about—and still brings about with men. Matthew is the historian of God's fulfillment of his promises."[93] However: "It is quite clear that Matthew

---

92 Léon-Dufour (McHugh), 263.

93 Léon-Dufour (McHugh), 263.

did not attempt to write a biography of Jesus of Nazareth as an impartial non-Christian observer might have written it. ...By the way in which he groups events and teachings, by the hieratic style of his narratives and by his adaptation of traditions to serve a catechetical purpose, he shows the meaning of Jesus' life on earth. But if this is the type of writing in the first gospel, one may legitimately ask what its historical value is." On the other hand, "not only does Matthew retain untouched a certain number of bald historical data in his setting of events, but it is often possible to work out the broad lines of what happened, and this for two reasons. First, Matthew betrays a certain naivety in the way he groups and interprets the material he used as sources, and it is often possible for the scholar to detect what actually happened before Easter Day; secondly, a comparison with the parallel passages in Mark and Luke enables the scholar to get a firmer grasp of the life story of Jesus as an event in the past."[94]

76. Remarks. No rationalist has ever written impartially about the life of Jesus. The fact that Christians love Jesus does not mean that they cannot recount his history with great objectivity. Form-critics of the Gospels argue in a circle: they splinter the text into small units according to what they assume to have been the *finis operantis* of the composers of these units and then they show the *finis operantis* from the ways in which they imagine the text to have been sewn together. It is a noteworthy historical fact that Catholic historical critics have never produced a serious critique of the mountain of errors contained in Bultmann's *History of the Synoptic Tradition*, wherein he initiated many of the techniques upon which Léon-Dufour (McHugh) relies for his form-critical work. In this way Léon-Dufour (McHugh) plays into Bultmann's hands. The best way to detect what happened before Easter Day is not to listen to the conclusions of historical critics, but rather to read about it directly in the Four Gospels themselves.

77. Exposition. "This was the purpose of Mark's Gospel—to reveal to the pagan world the Good News that Jesus was the Son of God. ...Mark intended to give a faithful account of what happened before Easter Day."[95] For Mark "the gospel is not a book to be appreciated or criticized, but an event to be broadcast to the world. And the event is the arrival among men of the person of Jesus Christ, the Son of God. More accurately, the event is the ultimate triumph of God through the earthly life of Jesus."[96] Hence,

---

94 Léon-Dufour (McHugh), 124–125.

95 Léon-Dufour (McHugh), 134.

96 Léon-Dufour (McHugh), 136.

"the Gospel of Mark is the Good News of the victory of Jesus over the forces of evil."[97] However: "Mark does not attempt to write the biography of a man, even of a God-Man."[98] Mark's account of the life of Jesus is always subordinated to doctrinal interests and catechetical themes. "It is impossible, therefore, to use St. Mark's Gospel for a reconstruction of the life of Jesus without taking into account all the re-arrangement which has taken place for doctrinal or catechetical reasons."[99]

78. Remarks. Mark's intention, as the *finis operis* of his account, was to write down the real historical events that took place during the public life of Jesus. His intention, as the *finis operantis* of his account, was to reveal to all men the Good News that Jesus the God-Man had come to save them from their sins and to open to them the gates of Heaven.

79. Exposition. "[Luke] composed a book about the teaching of the Church concerning the life of Jesus." However: He did not consider it necessary to check the truth of what his eyewitnesses had said. "His sole concern was to demonstrate that the current teaching of the Church was in complete accord with apostolic tradition."[100] And so "his work must be examined very critically before it may be used as a source for the life of Jesus. This critical assessment of Luke's writing is all the more necessary since Luke was not just writing a straightforward biography of Jesus, but expounding a theological theme."[101]

80. Remarks. The idea that apostolic tradition was not interested in preserving the facts about the life of Jesus is based on the false accusations of rationalists and anti-clericals. St. Luke indicates great concern for checking the truth and the historical justification of what he wrote, and he was aided by the inspiration of the Holy Spirit. The pity is that Catholic historical critics have never examined very critically the false conclusions of Bultmann and of the other rationalists from whom they have derived many of their methodological beliefs.

81. Exposition. "For John, real facts had historical value, but they also showed him that God had intervened in history, and had thereby brought things to life by conferring on them a spiritual and symbolic value which could not be grasped by reason alone."[102] There are many

---

97 Léon-Dufour (McHugh), 137.

98 Léon-Dufour (McHugh), 136.

99 Léon-Dufour (McHugh), 138.

100 Léon-Dufour (McHugh), 141.

101 Léon-Dufour (McHugh), 147.

102 Léon-Dufour (McHugh), 106.

gaps in the narrative, but the biographical details given do indicate "that the author intended not just to set out the essential points of the Easter kerygma, but to give a factual account of the earthly life and teaching of Jesus."[103] However: "The work does not pretend to be an impartial record of events drawn up by a neutral and detached observer, but is meant to be a book of history relating the life-story of Jesus of Naza-reth.[104] ...John was not so much recounting what had happened in the past as broadcasting live a message to which he was himself listening; by transmitting this message to the men of his own time, he hoped to make them, like himself, true contemporaries of the Lord.[105] ...John the Evangelist...took the historical events themselves (which the historian can and must discover) and interpreted them. Historical research cannot exhaust the meaning of these events which it discovers, for the person whom the historian meets is Christ the Lord, whom the faith of John confesses in Jesus of Nazareth."[106]

82. Remarks. Léon-Dufour (McHugh) thinks that existentialists and form-critics are neutral and detached observers, but they are not. St. John the Evangelist, as a serious historian with the intention of writing real history, first and foremost recounted what had really happened in the past, much of it with himself as a witness, and, since he was writing under the influence of divine inspiration, he also inscribed a deep spiritual sense into the same words. St. John was indeed listening to the Holy Spirit as he wrote his Gospel, in a way that existentialists and form-critics studiously fail to understand, but he was certainly not listening to a message in the sense of a call merely to choose, by an ever-repeated decision, his own self-authenticity, divorced from any objective supernatural grace of Christ. Thus, the fact that St. John was filled with love for his Lord did not weaken or dilute his intention to recount the facts as they really took place.

---

103 Léon-Dufour (McHugh), 81.

104 Léon-Dufour (McHugh), ibid.

105 Léon-Dufour (McHugh), 85.

106 Léon-Dufour (McHugh), 107. "Once the *genre littéraire* of the fourth gospel is recognized, one can see why those who limit their aim to knowing the historical Jesus find it of little use for their purpose. John wanted to be both a witness of Jesus of Nazareth (by telling what he remembered of him) and a witness of Christ the Lord (by trying to make us share his faith in Christ). John's gospel is therefore a challenge thrown down against the positivist idea of history, and positivist historians are only logical in refusing to accept that such a book can be historical. But John had a different idea in mind: he never considered a bald fact without looking at it in the light of the Spirit, to see its significance" (Léon-Dufour (McHugh), 105–106).

83. Exposition. "The present book will endeavor to demonstrate that a thoroughgoing application of the principles of historical criticism does not weaken, but rather strengthens the conviction that the gospels are historically reliable."[107] However: "These, then, are the broad lines of Jesus' life. He began his ministry alongside the Baptist, beside the Jordan, and then preached in Galilee about the coming of the kingdom. His preaching provoked hostility among the Jews and from Herod, and the ordinary folk failed to grasp his spiritual message. He therefore ceased to preach in public, and after a period on the borders of Galilee (during which he concentrated on the formation of his closest disciples) went to Jerusalem, where he stayed three months. Finally, after spending some time in Transjordan, he returned to Jerusalem a few days before the Passover. ...With this framework of the Lord's life before us, we may now turn to the central question in our inquiry: what should men think of Jesus Christ? ...From the last few pages it is clear that only the broadest chronological pattern of Jesus' life can be known. ...But even though (the historian) cannot descend into details, and even though many questions remain unanswered (and perhaps unanswerable), it is certainly possible to make a valid synthesis of the teaching of Jesus, and to give a true account of his earthly life. We shall thereby see the originality of the Christian faith in all its splendor."[108]

84. Conclusion. The results of Xavier Léon-Dufour (McHugh)'s scholarly aim of finding out "the full and objective truth" concerning the little that he feels can be historically known of the life of Jesus of Nazareth do not substantially differ from the results of Rudolf Bultmann's pseudo-historical research. According to these results: Only the "broad lines" of Jesus' life can be known with any historical probability, and these lines do not rise above the limits of the merely human. As far as ascertainable historical events are concerned, there is no Incarnation, Virginal Conception, bodily Resurrection, or Ascension of Jesus into Heaven. Gone are the miracles, the real prophecies of future events, and the supernatural features attributed to the objective events themselves by the Gospel writers. While Léon-Dufour (McHugh)'s understanding of the results of this historical critical research is undoubtedly very different from how Bultmann had earlier understood them, it leaves the work of scientifically processing Bultmann's work still to be done. His adherence to the Catholic Faith is not in question, but, with such a small historical base on which to stand, it is not surprising that he offers no solid grounds to oppose the demythologizing of Rudolf Bultmann.

---

107 Léon-Dufour (McHugh), 14.

108 Léon-Dufour (McHugh), 222–224.

Part IV. Anton Vögtle and Ugo Lattanzi

Living Tradition 83 (September 1999)

85. The element of mental frameworks. As we reviewed in the first three parts of this study the responses of five Catholic writers to the call of Rudolf Bultmann for the demythologizing of the New Testament proclamation, the reader may have noted the recurring inability of these writers to produce a well-rounded reply or even to visualize the problem with adequate clarity. This may seem surprising, considering that Bultmann's challenge to Catholic belief is total: he calls "mythical" the entire supernatural object of Catholic faith. Among the causes of this weakness of response on the level of reason I would suggest a lack of sufficiently differentiated ideas in such areas as logic and theory of knowledge and the perennial absence of an adequate conception of historical science. Under the aspect of the relationship of faith to reason, the lack of full ability to respond can be traced in part to the modern separation between exegetes and theologians, according to which exegetes tend to lose sight of the full theological picture and theologians do not feel competent to examine the results of exegesis. And Catholic exegetes have never responded adequately to the outrageous results of the form-criticism of Bultmann and his many co-workers. As a result, both exegetes and theologians tend to address the notion of demythologizing with much more sympathy than it could ever deserve, and we have seen this sympathy spelled out in imperfectly formulated responses. The two writers who follow in the present part, Anton Vögtle and Ugo Lattanzi, were aware of this problem, and they attempted to fill in the gaps by better organized replies. As we review their analyses, we should especially keep in mind the need of an adequate mental framework, not only the assumed framework of this or that sacred writer, as historical critics do, but also the consciously formed and self-appropriated mental framework of the interpreter himself, which historical critics tend to overlook. It is Bultmann's mental framework that these two writers have especially in view, but the basic underlying problem kept in the background is how Bultmann's mental framework, the Evangelists' mental frameworks, the mental frameworks of Bultmann's critics, and, in general, every mental framework can be fitted into a general theory of biblical interpretation. We are searching for a clear idea of historical science and of how it functions in the interpretation of Sacred Scripture.

The Response of Anton Vögtle

86. Exposition. Anton Vögtle[109] is of the opinion that the program of demythologizing announced by Bultmann in 1941 is but the concentrated synthesis of an overall theological labor that had been oriented in this determinate direction from its very beginning. Vögtle agrees with the Lutheran theologian, Heinrich Ott, and the Catholic theologian, Heinrich Fries, that it is necessary to deduce the basic premises of Bultmann's demythologizing from the entire corpus of his theological production.[110] Following indications given by Heinrich Ott in his book on demythologizing,[111] Vögtle too sees the program to be based upon a series of purely philosophical postulates regarding time, history, reality, and the very notion of meaning itself. But he keeps in mind that Bultmann develops here and there in his writings premises of different kinds and of varying provenance, taking them from the schools of the "history of religions" and of "historical criticism," from rationalist liberalism with its view of reality, of man, and of the modern world, from existentialist philosophy, from dialectical theology and from Luther himself, bringing them together finally into a compact interior unity which is so imposing that to some critics it seems almost terrifying.[112]

87. Remarks. The answer to the imposing and almost terrifying unity into which Bultmann has molded the premises of his thought can be adequately answered only on the basis of a more imposing unity, namely, the unity of a new Catholic synthesis of theology, loyal to the existing syntheses of the great Fathers of the Church, of Thomas Aquinas and other great theologians of the past, and the employment in this new synthesis of the results of the neo-patristic exegesis of Sacred Scripture. The raw material for the expansion of the new synthesis is precisely the refutation of the kind of presuppositions, heretofore not fully dealt with by Catholic thinkers, that Bultmann and other rationalist critics use in their writings.

---

109 Antonio Vögtle, "Rivelazione e mito," in *Problemi e orientamenti di teologia dogmatica,* vol. I (Milan, 1957), 827–960 [henceforth referred to as *AVRM*].

110 Vögtle, *AVRM*, 830–831.

111 Heinrich Ott, *Geschichte und Heilsgeschichte in der Theologie Rudolf Bultmanns* (Tübingen, 1955). Ott proposed a systematic analysis of Bultmann's theology, but only in later works did he attempt to develop the general indications he had given in this book.

112 Vögtle, *AVRM*, 831–832.

88. Exposition. Vögtle sees Bultmann's program to be based upon four systematic and three historical premises.[113] The systematic premises include the following:

a) A radical dualism between "non-world" and "world." Bultmann's concept of myth as signifying something that cannot have taken place in space and time postulates an "appropriate dissociation"[114] of Christian belief from the world, a goal that Bultmann attempts to accomplish through the use of existentialist interpretation. But Bultmann's purely formal definition of myth will stand only to the extent that the fundamental dualism of world and ultraworld is accepted as a logical premise.[115]

b) A double concept of history and of historical knowledge. Bultmann posits a fundamental difference between nature and history, and thus also between the knowledge of nature and the knowledge of history. Then he distinguishes two heterogeneous levels of historical knowledge, calling the lower level *Historie* and the higher level *Geschichte*. He locates the true essence of history in that "historicity" which is "the existential structure of the being which exists necessarily in history," namely, *Dasein*, following the theory of Martin Heidegger.[116] Thus, Bultmann restricts the word "historicity" (*Geschichtlichkeit*) to what he calls "the essential character of historical being," which is the existentialist notion of existence, so that for him "true existence" means "being in the state of decision, in deciding and being able ever to decide anew." Thus, for Bultmann, "the encounter and the 'comprehending decision' (*verstehende Entscheidung*) derived from it form the essence of every historical being." But, in order to arrive at this conception of true existence, Bultmann has to divide objectivizing-cosmological thought and existential thought into two fields which he makes mutually exclusive on the ontological level. He thus reduces the thesis of the divinity of Christ to the following alternative: it can be interpreted either cosmologically in the objectivizing sense or soteriologically in the existential sense. The implication is: *Tertium non datur!*[117] *Vögtle, following Ott, distinguishes between the vertical unity of history (that in which man is found in the individual historical moment) and the horizontal unity of history (the unity of the meaning of the historical development as such), and he concludes that Bultmann's theory destroys both. In*

---

113 Vögtle, *AVRM*, 833.

114 Ott, *Geschichte und Heilsgeschichte*, 26.

115 Vögtle, *AVRM*, 837.

116 Vögtle, *AVRM*, 838–839.

117 Vögtle, *AVRM*, 839–841.

the sphere of history (Geschichte) things have meaning only to the extent that they are real (*wirklich*).[118]

c) The hermeneutical principle of "pre-understanding." Bultmann's conception of understanding is divided between the correlative notions of "pre-understanding" and "self-understanding," both understood in terms of the existentialism of Heidegger. By force of this distinction the historical event of Christ is reduced to an abstract and groundless "that"—namely, that Jesus lived and was crucified. Vögtle thinks that the jump from pre-understanding to understanding in the theory of Bultmann is unexplainable.[119]

d) A double concept of time. According to Vögtle the detailed research of Heinrich Ott has shown that Bultmann's double concept of time is the key idea of all of his systematic premises.[120] Bultmann makes a fundamental distinction between time as flux (*Verlaufzeit*) and time as now (*Jetztzeit*). He means that the flux of worldly time comes to an end every time that there is a "now" of decision in faith, for this "now" is a point without dimensions, not pertaining to linear time and not to be conceived as an infinitesimal portion of the line of time. In similar fashion, the future in its eschatological sense as proposed by Bultmann does not pertain to what will take place in the course of time. For Bultmann, to open oneself to the future means simply to live "authentically" in the Heideggerian sense. Nor does the past mean simply that which once was; in Bultmann's eminently historical (*geschichtlich*) and existential sense it signifies "that which is subjected to the law of the past." Therefore, in Bultmannian terminology, things which will take place in worldly time are already past, for anything is "past" that is disposable, objective, and ascertainable. In this way the unexplainable jump from pre-understanding to understanding actually becomes part of the theory: since the eschatological "now" stands just at the dividing line between past and future in the existentialist sense, the decision to open oneself to the future is so properly an *existentiell* experience that it in no way can be *explained* on the level of existentialist (*existential*) analysis.[121] In this way Bultmann limits the history of salvation to his notion of the kerygmatic situation, namely, to the encounter of the individual believer with the eschatological summons of the message of Christ.[122]

---

118 Vögtle, *AVRM*, 842–843.

119 Vögtle, *AVRM*, 851–852.

120 Vögtle, *AVRM*, 852.

121 Vögtle, *AVRM*, 854–855.

122 Vögtle, *AVRM*, 858.

89. Remarks. Vögtle is absolutely correct in observing that Bultmann's definition of myth will stand up only to the extent that his distinction between "non-world" and "world" is accepted as a logical premise. To carry this point further, Bultmann's "non-world" is just a euphemism for "imaginary world," as far as objectivity is concerned, and for "my awareness of my own subjectivity," as far as the believer is concerned. Bultmann's definition of historicity as "being in the state of decision, of deciding and of being able ever to decide anew," where the decision involved is merely the choosing of one's own "self-authenticity," amounts to a continual denial of the reality of the object of Christian faith and to a continual affirmation of one's own empty subjectivity. Bultmann's jump from "pre-understanding" to the "understanding" attributed to the "*existentiell* decision" is not a jump to any kind of real understanding; it is merely a turning away from reality to egoistic fantasy, it is a conversion away from the contemplation of the object of Christian faith to a preoccupation with one's own subjectivity as such; and thus, it does not seem to be conceptually distinct from the studious cultivation of the act of pride.

90. Exposition. Vögtle lists also three fountainheads of Bultmann's historical premises:

a) The story of Jesus. As a historian Bultmann carries forward the work of the liberal historical critical school and of the history-of-religions school, ending up with an extremely negative picture of the origin of Christianity.[123]

b) The origin of Christology. Through the use of form-criticism, Bultmann came to the conclusion that the life of Jesus as it actually took place was not messianic: in the most ancient layer of the Gospel tradition (Rom. 1:4; Acts 2:36; Phil 2:6–11) the life of Jesus is not presented as messianic, and the suspicion which this fact raises is confirmed by Mark's introduction of the literary device of the "messianic secret" to explain the absence of this messianic feature. Therefore, according to Bultmann, Jesus became the Messiah, the Son of Man, only in the interpretation of the primitive Christian community, and the interpretation of Jesus as a divine being was added even later in the Hellenistic milieu.[124]

c) The reciprocal relationship between historical criticism and Bultmann's total systematic outlook. In Bultmann's theology true faith cannot be damaged by even the most radical historical criticism, because faith is not based upon real and objective facts.[125]

---

123 Vögtle, *AVRM*, 859.

124 Vögtle, *AVRM*, 861–863.

125 Vögtle, *AVRM*, 865.

91. Remarks. Bultmann's "extremely negative picture" of the origin of Christianity results from a fallacious interpretation of the inspired text of the Gospels, and, therefore, merits full refutation. And Bultmann's notion of faith is immune to historical criticism, as Vögtle points out, inasmuch as it is merely a state of mind not based upon real objective facts. To all appearances, Bultmann's "faith" is nothing but his creation of a modern egoistic fantasy to substitute for genuine Christian faith, with the result that Bultmann's own theological writings present themselves in the category of poetic fantasy.[126]

92. Exposition. Vögtle lists as follows the principal arguments used against Bultmann's program of demythologizing.

a) The absence of conceptual exactness. There is a lack of sufficient distinction between the hermeneutic, homiletic, and apologetic problems presented by Bultmann. He does not distinguish the exegetical-historical problem of the thought of primitive Christianity from the philosophical-theological problem, and he is constrained to accord to the latter an unquestioned priority in the act of understanding the true intention of the texts.[127]

b) The abiding value of myth in the language of religion. In the teaching of Bultmann, mythology is taken to be a definite form of thought and expression which is always valid in the midst of evolving conceptions of the world and which is absolutely necessary and legitimate for religion as the means of expressing a certain non-mythical and actually existing transcendent reality (realtà).[128]

c) The explanation of the rise of the New Testament kerygma. Bultmann's account of the rise of the kerygma is untenable, because in order to sustain it he has to deny documented events. The faith-testimony of tradition has as its object history (Historie) itself, when it affirms that Jesus of Nazareth is the Christ of Israel.[129]

d) The groundlessness of the alleged need for demythologizing the New Testament. Bultmann bases this need upon the presupposition that a divine intervention into nature and history is impossible from the viewpoint of present-day natural science, upon a radically dualistic separation of God from the world, based probably upon the Lutheran principle that sin has produced a total break between the world and the

---

126 Cf. my article, "A Tentative Characterization of the Genre of Bultmann's Theological Writing," in *The Science of Historical Theology*, pp.155–164.

127 Vögtle, *AVRM*, 918.

128 Vögtle, *AVRM*, 921.

129 Vögtle, *AVRM*, 924–926.

activity of God, upon the validity of the existentialist interpretation of myth and of man, and upon the conviction that various accounts in the New Testament contradict one another.[130] The fact is, remarks Vögtle, that the kerygma and faith make intimate reference to the objective and *historisch* factor in the New Testament accounts. The value attributed to the first testimonies presupposes a personally lived history; the vigor attributed to the proof based upon the fulfillment in the coming of Christ of the expectation contained in the prophecies of the Old Testament illustrates the supremely historical character of the history of salvation. Within the horizon of Bultmann's theory, this promise-fulfillment proportion cannot be included.[131]

93. Remarks. Bultmann's theology thrives on sophistic arguments. What has enabled its impact upon Catholic theologians and exegetes is their lack of conceptual organization and exactness in analyzing his system. Vögtle is certainly on the right track in attempting to organize the question in terms of the premises of Bultmann's thought. The next step should be to organize a full response in terms of a mental framework that expresses and organizes the premises of Catholic thought. These premises are contained in large part in the Catholic exegetical and theological tradition, but they need to be expressed in terms of the new questions that have been raised especially during the last two centuries. The truly historical character of the Four Gospels is brought out in great splendor when they are interpreted according to a truly scientific method of exegesis.

94. Exposition. Vögtle points out that even from the Catholic side it is expressly admitted by some of the more recent writers that the Easter message is something more than a simple assertion of historical fact. Rudolf Schnackenburg, for instance, sees a grain of truth in Bultmann's assertion that the Resurrection cannot be established as an objective fact, even in the presence of so many testimonies, for the reason that it is *per se* an object of faith and therefore only the faith of the witnesses can be directly demonstrated. Nevertheless, Catholic critics have reached the conclusion that the reality of the fact of the Resurrection can be rendered "obviously believable."[132] Bultmann's existentialist interpretation does not take into account that salvation becomes actual for us in the sacraments as well as through preaching; his interpretation leaves no room for anything more than a purely

---

130 Vögtle, *AVRM*, 928–935.

131 Vögtle, *AVRM*, 941–942.

132 Vögtle, *AVRM*, 945.

formalistic ethic. Heinrich Ott sees as significant the fact that Bultmann was not ready to reply to Fritz Buri's proposal to carry demythologizing to its logical conclusion of dekerygmatization of the Christian viewpoint. Vögtle adds that Bultmann's exposition becomes particularly forced, obscure, and unconvincing precisely in those places where he tries to demonstrate the need of an act of divine love for the attainment of "authentic existence."[133]

95. Remarks. Schnackenburg's observation that the Resurrection of Jesus cannot be established as an objective fact for the reason that it is *per se* an object of faith confuses the issue. Scientific history is, for the most part, constructed on the testimony of reliable witnesses. The witnesses in this case are reliable. The *supernatural significance* of the Resurrection is a *per se* object of faith, but the *historical fact* of the Resurrection is a matter of history. The reliability of the witnesses to the Resurrected Jesus and of the Gospel writers themselves depends upon the consistent absence of error in the text of the Gospels, and this fact illustrates the extent of the disaster produced by the many Catholic historical critics who have adopted Bultmann's method of exegesis with its devastating conclusions. In this connection, it is important to note that the *per se* objects of faith pertain to the one continuum of reality recognized by those who are using the concept of reality in its authentic sense, and not in the sophistic sense suggested by Bultmann with his false distinction between *Wirklichkeit* and *Historität*. The probable reason for which Bultmann readily admitted that his notion of faith could not be defended against the charge of illusion was his awareness that his faith was, in fact, just a well-elaborated fancy. For this reason he was not ready to reply to Buri's proposal to eliminate the kerygma as well from the faith of modern man. But this refusal illustrates the apologetic weakness of demythologizing and of the form-critical method in general, namely, that historical critics, wherever they may be located on the spectrum of form-critical conclusions, glory in their denials of historical truth in the biblical text, but run for cover whenever they are challenged to defend any of the Gospel truths that they have not themselves eliminated. In other words, believing historical critics are notably inept at defending against attack the "core" of historical truth in the Gospels that they presume not to have been eliminated.

96. Conclusion. Anton Vögtle presents a well-written summary of the method of demythologizing, organized around the formulation of four systematic and three historical premises of Bultmann's thought. These premises are taken from the undeveloped indications given by Heinrich Ott. Vögtle uses the idea of these premises to organize his exposition,

---

133 Vögtle, *AVRM*, 949–951.

and he thus makes a good start on an adequate reply to Bultmann's proposal, but he does not develop his article in such wise as to provide a complete response. The main thrust of Vögtle's long article remains the presentation of Bultmann's thought rather than the incorporation of an answer to Bultmann's challenge into an independent synthesis of his own. Of the four chief arguments against demythologizing that Vögtle lists, the first (absence of conceptual precision) could have provided the basis of an independent interpretation. If, according to Vögtle, Bultmann's seven premises are the result of conceptual inexactness, then what are the exact definitions which Bultmann's inexact definitions represent? Vögtle does not undertake to tell us.

The Response of Ugo Lattanzi

97. Exposition. Just as primitive peoples grouped the conspicuous stars of the sky into configurations named and visualized according to their cosmogonic or cosmographic religious conceptions, so also, observes Ugo Lattanzi,[134] form-critics have cut up the living Gospels into constellations of texts in keeping with their own metaphysical conception of reality. This conception consists of a set of principles which Lattanzi calls *postulates* to the extent that they are expressly assumed as the basis of theoretical constructions and *presuppositions* to the extent that they are more or less consciously used as premises but kept implicit, perhaps for reasons of prudence. In terms of this distinction, it seems to Lattanzi that there are at the basis of Bultmann's thought three postulates and two presuppositions. Bultmann's thought has as its point of departure three postulates: a theological postulate, an exegetical postulate, and a sociological postulate.[135]

98. Remarks. Lattanzi follows the lead of Heinrich Ott and Anton Vögtle in undertaking to bring out the premises of Bultmann's thought, which he goes on to divide into postulates and presuppositions. Thus, the focus of attention is drawn, not simply to the supposed mentality of the writers of the Gospels, but also and more immediately to the mental framework of a critic of the Gospels, namely, Rudolf Bultmann.

99. Exposition. a) Bultmann's theological postulate. For Bultmann the relation of the world to God is based, not upon the analogy of

---

134 Ugo Lattanzi, "I sinottici e la Chiesa secondo R. Bultmann" in *Miscellanea Antonio Piolanti*, vol. I (Rome, 1963 [*Lateranum*, n.s., 29th year], 141–169, henceforth referred to as *ULSC*]).

135 Lattanzi, *ULSC*, 150.

being, but rather upon an essential antinomy and radical opposition of the two. Lattanzi comments that this basic dualism postulated by Bultmann does not admit of any relationship of causality that could be recognized by reason, since the world is taken to be an absolutely closed and autonomous system.[136] This postulate of Bultmann excludes any reasonable doctrine about God, and it excludes *a fortiori* any doctrine revealed by God. Consequently, the entire content of the Christian creed has to be considered a creation of the early Church, and the New Testament narratives which contain this creed have to be relegated to the status of myths, because they express in terms of the world what in itself does not pertain to the world. Similarly, Bultmann, by reason of this postulate, is constrained to speak of the act of God as completely hidden and undiscoverable by reason. Miracles are excluded by the same principle, for, as evident phenomena, they would contradict the essentially hidden nature of the act of God.[137] The theological postulate requires that faith be conceived, not as adherence of any kind by the human intellect to truth revealed by God, but rather as "the decision, achieved in the overcoming of the offense, *against the world* for God."[138] So faith is a leap into "non-world" and, hence, does not need to be rendered legitimate on a historical basis.[139] Lattanzi asks how Bultmann can deem it possible to rise above his own absolute separation of world and "non-world" to affirm the existence of "non-world" (God) and of his "mysterious acting." Bultmann stands between Scylla and Charybdis: any talk of an "act of God" either is mythological in the Bultmannian sense or it is a mere linguistic means of describing experiences of one's own consciousness referring to nothing outside of it. This is not a paradoxical identity of the objective event with the action of God; it is pure subjectivity. The same dilemma arises from the Protestant notion underlying Bultmann's notion of faith: faith is considered to be either an act of salvation worked by God *in* man, in which case it must be categorized as mythical, or an act of the man who decides "for God," as Bultmann says, in which case it has no reasonable and historically justifiable motivation and must, therefore, be categorized as purely subjective.[140]

---

136 Lattanzi, *ULSC*, 150.

137 Lattanzi, *ULSC*, 151. Cf. Bultmann, in *KuM* II, 198 (*KaM* I, 199).

138 Bultmann, *Theology of the New Testament* (New York: Scribner's, 1955), 76.

139 Lattanzi, *ULSC*, 153.

140 Lattanzi, *ULSC*, 156–158.

100. Remarks. As Lattanzi points out, Bultmann excludes any relationship of causality between the world and God and any reasonable doctrine about God. For Bultmann the "act of God" is not merely hidden, it is nonexistent. Lattanzi's basic charge against Bultmann's conception of the "act of God" is that it is unreasonable, and Bultmann has no answer to that charge except that for him faith does not depend upon reason. Bultmann calls "myth" any bringing over to "this side" of acts belonging to "the other side," but where is "the other side"? It seems that the "other side" is the world of fancy and religious imagination, and that is where, for Bultmann, any objective idea of God or of divine acts is located.

101. Exposition. Bultmann's exegetical postulate. Bultmann bases his thought on the principle that the message of Jesus was exclusively eschatological. From among all of the words attributed to Jesus in the Gospels, he selects as authentic precisely those which would show that the early Church considered itself to be the eschatological community having no interest in history in the sense of *Historie*.[141] Lattanzi maintains that it cannot be shown that the message of Jesus was exclusively eschatological and ethical in the Bultmannian sense. Nor can it be shown that the primitive Christian community had no faith-interest in *Historie*. On the contrary, it is easy to show that the Apostles and the "primitive Christian community" had the greatest interest in the historical truth of the words and deeds of Jesus, and above all in the fact of his Resurrection from the dead. The irrefutable proof of this interest is the early catechesis contained in 1 Cor. 15:3–8, in which it is clearly stated that five hundred of the disciples saw the resurrected Jesus at the same time and could give impressive witness to the fact that the Apostles were not deceiving them on this score.[142] "There is no need to say that this text of Paul annihilates the entire theory of *Formgeschichte* in general and the thought of Bultmann in particular." Hence, Bultmann[143] has reason to describe as "fatal" this kind of Pauline argumentation—fatal in the sense that St. Paul adduces proof for the credibility of the kerygma. But Bultmann confuses the fact of the Resurrection with the mysterious reality (Phil. 3:10) and sanctifying effects (Rom. 4:25) of its power, and he confuses the visible and historical aspect of the fact of the Resurrection with its invisible and soteriological aspect. Bultmann admits that St. Luke set out

---

141 Lattanzi, *ULSC*, 154–155.

142 Lattanzi, *ULSC*, 158–160.

143 R. Bultmann, *Offenbarung und Heilsgeschehen* (Munich, 1941), 64.

to write his Gospel from the viewpoint of a "scrupulous historian."[144] He should, therefore, have allowed the conclusion that Luke guarantees the historical truth of all of the verses in his Gospel, not just of the 541 verses that are proper to his Gospel. Bultmann, furthermore, has to assume a colossal stupidity on the part of the Church to have gone to such trouble to create sayings and stories to substantiate its claim historically and yet to have left lying around in its Gospels so many eschatological texts which belied the claim. Why also, if the Gospels were composed after the Epistles of St. Paul, are the more developed formulations of the kerygma in the Epistles of St. Paul not included in the Gospel accounts? The only answer that can be given to this question is that the Evangelists were concerned to narrate the historical past faithfully and objectively, without letting their accounts be influenced by subsequent developments of the apostolic kerygma.[145]

102. Remarks. Lattanzi here maintains that what St. Paul says in ICor. 15:3–8 in itself "annihilates the entire theory of *Formgeschichte* in general and the thought of Bultmann in particular." This is true for those who have an integrated understanding of the context of St. Paul's testimony, or even of the context of Lattanzi's observation. However, since the results of form-criticism have gained so much acceptance even among Catholic exegetes and theologians, it has become necessary to reinforce St. Paul's testimony by refuting point by point and line by line the false conclusions that the form-criticism of Bultmann has bestowed upon us.

103. Exposition. Bultmann's sociological postulate. According to Bultmann, an anonymous primitive Christian community "created" the kerygma and handed it down; it did not receive the kerygma from some historical person of the past, for instance, from St. Peter or from St. Paul.[146] Lattanzi declares that not a single definite and uncontestable instance can be pointed to in the whole New Testament of a poetic or religious myth created and inserted by the early Church. Nor can the transforming power of the Gospels and the ardor with which the Apostles and first disciples gave their lives for what the Gospels promise in the next life, be reconciled with the theory of the "creative Christian community."[147]

---

144 "... Luke, as a historian, undertakes to represent the life of Christ. He assures us in his preface that he endeavoured, as a scrupulous historian, to use trustworthy sources for his report" (R. Bultmann, *History and Eschatology* [New York: Harper and Row, 1957], 38.

145 Lattanzi, *ULSC*, 160–162.

146 Lattanzi, *ULSC*, 155.

147 Lattanzi, *ULSC*, 162.

104. Remarks. Here the urgency of the work remaining to be completed is highlighted. While there is not a single clear example in the whole of the New Testament of a myth, a miracle story, an event, or a prophecy after the event having been invented by Christian believers, form-critics maintain that the text of the Gospels is woven of such inventions. And sad to say, Catholic exegetes, most of whom belong to the historical critical school, have not only sat back and let many of those false conclusions stand, but they have added to them many false form-critical conclusions of their own, instead of plunging into the urgent work of producing in detail a better and more correct method.

105. Exposition. Lattanzi discerns two principles which stand at the base of Bultmann's thought and which may be called *presuppositions*, because they are passed over more or less in silence:

a) For his presupposition of the spontaneous generation of the Church, Bultmann is completely indebted to Alfred Loisy, who had earlier declared that the great mystical society of the Church sprang from the Gospel unexpectedly, emerging from the labors of the first missionaries "in a spontaneous manner as from an irresistible pressure of faith that produced something entirely different from what the believers had hoped for to achieve." The other presupposition assumes that the Church recovered from its initial shock at the failure of the expected *parousia* and allowed its transformation into a historical community.[148] Bultmann does not spend much time trying to explain why the Church, the "creative Christian community," was itself in its turn "created," or by whom or when, an omission which is all the more telling when Jesus, according to the same theory, is supposed to have appealed only to individual persons and never with the idea of gathering a community around him. What Lattanzi means is that an eschatological community, having no interest in the history of this world, would have had no motivation to unite itself into a society.[149]

b) Bultmann's difficulty regarding a presupposed spontaneous generation of the Church is increased by the decided implausibility of his second presupposition, that of the will of the Church to endure as a historical phenomenon, because the primitive community, once it saw that its hopes for an imminent return of Jesus were unfulfilled, would simply have had no reason to want to endure as an established Church. Bultmann says that the eschatological community "could not fail to recognize that it had become a historical phenomenon and that the Christian faith had

---

148 Lattanzi, *ULSC*, 155–156.

149 Lattanzi, *ULSC*, 163–164.

taken on the shape of a new religion."[150] Since hope for the imminent return of Jesus is presumed to have been the only bond of union among the disciples, there was no reason why they would not have disbanded immediately upon the rise of their disappointment and withdrawn their act of faith in the Resurrection. The fact that the Church did not dissolve implies two basic facts: that hope for an immediate parousia was not shared by the entire membership (cf. 2 Thess. 2:2–3) and that the chief basis of the Christian hope was the factuality of the words and deeds of Jesus, particularly of his Resurrection from the dead. Bultmann speaks of the primitive community as though the Apostles had vanished completely from the scene.[151] Perhaps Bultmann's reason for isolating Jesus from the Apostles and the Apostles from the primitive Church is to preserve Jesus and the Apostles from the accusation of fraud. But this reason is refuted by St. Paul himself in 1 Cor. 15:15. Consequently, Bultmann's demythologizing bolsters Hermann Reimarus' theory of fraud, but it is also torn apart from within by its contradictory efforts to present faith to man and to subtract from faith all rational validity and credibility.[152]

106. Summary. Ugo Lattanzi's article is aimed directly at Bultmann's overall interpretation of the Gospels and at his understanding of the origin of the Church rather than at demythologizing in itself. He presents five principal arguments against Bultmann's approach:

a) Bultmann's theological postulate of the radical opposition between God and the world does not lead to the paradoxical identity which Bultmann claims, but only to pure subjectivity.

b) Bultmann's exegetical postulate that the original message of Jesus was eschatological and in no way historical (*historisch*) in the interest it had for Him and for the first disciples is completely annihilated by the testimony of 1 Cor. 15:3–8; Bultmann's exclusion of a faith-interest of the first disciples in *Historie* assumes a colossal stupidity on the part of the Gospel writers which is not borne out.

c) Bultmann's sociological postulate that an anonymous primitive Christian community "created" the kerygma ignores the fact that there is not a single clear and uncontestable instance in the whole New Testament of a poetic or religious myth created and inserted by the early Church; nor can it account for the transforming power of the Gospels.

---

150 Bultmann, *History and Eschatology*, 38.

151 Lattanzi, *ULSC*, 164–166. Cf. V. Taylor, *The Formation of the Gospel Tradition* (London, 1933), 41.

152 Lattanzi, *ULSC*, 166–168.

d) Bultmann's first presupposition that the Church sprang spontaneously from the faith of the first believers does not explain why the Church was created, by whom, or when; a purely eschatological community would have no motivation for uniting itself into a society.

e) Bultmann's second presupposition that the eschatological community chose to endure as a historical phenomenon and as an established Church is implausible, since hope for the imminent return of Jesus would have been their only bond of unity. Rather, says Lattanzi, their Christian hope was based on the factuality of the words and deeds of Jesus, and particularly of his having arisen from the dead.

107. General conclusion of this series. We have now reviewed the responses of seven Catholic theologians to Rudolf Bultmann's program of demythologizing. Some of these responses appear to be no more than random comments of varying value not based upon a clear synthesis of principles in the commentator himself and often weakened by an acceptance of some of Bultmann's false conclusions. Lattanzi's arguments are powerful, penetrating, and well organized, inasmuch as he speaks from an impressive theological synthesis and utilizes the incisive analyses begun by Heinrich Ott and Anton Vögtle in order to advance to a broader and deeper picture of Bultmann's postulates and presuppositions. The essays especially of Vögtle and Lattanzi deserve to be developed into a full response to Bultmann's program of demythologizing. How can Bultmann's false paradox of faith be expressed in a sound theological synthesis? How can Catholic exegesis bring out, in a way that refutes Bultmann's form-critical interpretations, the historical solidity of the Gospel texts and the deeper meaning that lies within it? The neo-patristic method has the means to take up the challenge and provide these answers. A full critique of Bultmann's postulates and presuppositions does require a prior formulation of the critic's own principles of interpretation, a task which neo-patristic exegesis undertakes in making explicit its own frame of reference. The neo-patristic approach is challenged to take up the problems raised but not answered by the historical critical school, and, utilizing the treasury of wisdom left by the Fathers of the Church and the great Catholic commentators, to put straight the twisted conclusions of modern rationalist exegetes and their non-rationalist followers, so as to arrive at a renewed understanding of what the Scriptures have to tell us.

Chapter 11

Toward a Fuller Catholic Response to the Demythologizing Method of Rudolf Bultmann

Part I. Leopold Malevez, Heinrich Fries, and Joseph Cahill

Living Tradition 113 (September 2004)

1. In chapter 10 I have reviewed the responses of seven Catholic theologians to the challenge made by Rudolf Bultmann with his program of "demythologizing the New Testament mythology," published in 1941. Soon after the Second World War short articles by Catholic writers began to appear and then longer studies, some of which I have reviewed in the previous chapter with critical comments of my own. My conclusion was that the challenge demanded a fuller response, and I return to this argument now, because the challenge is still there and so is the opportunity to take a step forward in our understanding of the sacred text by analyzing the problems that Bultmann has raised and fitting the answers into an updated framework of neo-patristic interpretation. In the preceding chapter (*Living Tradition* 112), I tried to point out the incidence of Modernism in the demythologizing of Bultmann, as a means of tying this program to an erroneous approach that was condemned by Pope Pius X in 1907, and, therefore, as a way to indicate to Catholics the dangers that lie in this system. The essential features of Modernism show up explicitly in Bultmann's program, and that should be enough to warn Catholics to be wary of it. Pope Pius X noted in his encyclical *Pascendi* that some Catholics had already

adhered to the false doctrine of Modernism, and that many others were in danger of falling into it due to a certain "poisoned atmosphere" that had invaded the Church. It is my belief that this poisoned atmosphere continues to surround Catholic believers, especially Catholic students and teachers, and that part of this poison comes from the invitation to "demythologize" the Gospels and all of the objects of Catholic faith. For instance, Bultmann did not, to the best of my knowledge, declare explicitly that all religious ideas arise from a pre-conceptual religious instinct that lies invisible in the subconsciousness of men, but he did maintain that all of the imagery in the Gospels and, in general, in the whole of the Bible was derived from the fictitious imagination of the sacred writers and of the traditions that they recorded, and that they surrounded their subjects with this imagery in order to accomplish the religious needs that they were feeling at the time. This view of Bultmann not only implicitly fits the modernist idea of the religious instinct, but it also comes over into the background of many form-critical interpretations of the Gospels that Catholics read or hear about, and, in the absence of clear distinctions that would rule this background out, it tempts the Catholic to doubt the objective truth of one or another object of his faith. Thus, for this danger and for many similar challenges to Catholic faith, Catholics should have in mind an apologetic defense of the truths of their faith, including a defense of the historical truth of the Sacred Scriptures.

The Response of Leopold Malevez

2. The first of the responses to the demythologizing of Rudolf Bultmann[1] that I reviewed in 1999 was that of Leopold Malevez in his book, *The Christian Message and Myth*.[2] Early in his book Malevez makes

---

1 For the essay which touched off the "demythologizing debate" see Rudolf Bultmann, "Neues Testament und Mythologie," in *Offenbarung und Heilsgeschehen*: Beiträge zur evangelischen Theologie, VII/2 (Munich, 1941); reprinted in H.W. Bartsch, ed., *Kerygma und Mythos* (Hamburg, 1948 [henceforth referred to as *KuM*]); Engl. trans., H.W. Bartsch, ed., *Kerygma and Myth: A Theological Debate*, vol. I (London: SPCK, 1962 [henceforth referred to as *KaM*]). For a brief summary of the demythologizing debate, especially among Protestant theologians, with the relevant bibliography, see J.F. McCarthy, *The Science of Historical Theology* (2d printing, Rockford: TAN, 1991), pp. 1–5. For a brief presentation of the meaning and goal of the program of demythologizing, see McCarthy, ibid., pp. 5–14.

2 L. Malevez, *Le message chrétien et le mythe. La théologie de Rudolf Bultmann* (Brussels-Bruges-Paris, 1954 [henceforth referred to as *MCM*]); Engl. trans., *The Christian Message*

the important point that Bultmann's program of demythologizing "has taken away my Lord," since the *kerygma,* or Christian message, as proposed by Bultmann, cannot replace the Christian mystery of the God-Man, which Bultmann relegates to the realm of the mythological in his denial of the Incarnation as a historical fact.[3] Jesus, God and Man, is the prime object of Christian faith, but Bultmann, in his demythologizing, has eliminated, not only this object of faith, but every other object of Christian faith in maintaining that there are no longer any objects at all of Christian faith, since for him the only religious act remaining to modern man is the subjective experience of being and becoming one's own authentic self.[4] Gone in his demythologizing is all belief in the objective existence of God and of the Most Holy Trinity, of Heaven and Hell, of life after death, of Redemption, of sanctifying and actual grace, of miracles and prophecies, and of every other object of traditional Christian faith. Malevez notes that the Christian message does need to have an existential impact upon the believer, but not according to the existentialism of Martin Heidegger, with its reduction of authentic human existence to the experience of one's own self, which Bultmann uses for this purpose.[5] In fact, the Catholic understanding of faith in the message of Christ has its own great existential meaning and impact in that it places the believer in direct contact with the presence and the power of God, especially through prayer and virtuous acts. What Bultmann forgets, says Malevez, is that what he calls our "objective ideas" about God are the fruit of intelligence in love with God.[6] Malevez makes the observation that Bultmann's demythologizing act of faith is very much like a mythological act of faith,[7] and I have developed this judgment at length in discussing the literary genre of Bultmann's theological writing.[8] After Bultmann has negated the entire objective idea of God, the "act of God" in his existential encounter becomes purely fictitious.

---

and Myth: The Theology of Rudolf Bultmann (London: SCM Press, 1958 [henceforth referred to as *CMM*]).

3 Cf. Malevez *MCM*, p. 121; *CMM*, pp. 123–124.

4 See *Living Tradition* 112 (July 2004), paragraph 10.

5 Cf. Malevez, *MCM*, pp. 118–119; *CMM*, pp. 120–121.

6 Cf. Malevez, *MCM*, pp. 153–156; *CMM*, pp. 155–158.

7 Cf. Malevez, *MCM*, pp. 153–156; *CMM*, pp. 155–158.

8 J.F. McCarthy, "A Tentative Characterization of the Genre of Bultmann's Theological Writing," in *The Science of Historical Theology,* pp. 143–164.

3. The Sacred Scriptures, read in a spirit of faith, constantly call upon the believer to open his mind to the understanding of divine revelation and to open his heart to the grace that is made available therein. The quality of human existence made possible by true faith is one which leads to a complete conversion of the mind of the believer, fills his heart with authentic love for God and for his fellow man, and elevates his whole life onto a higher plane, but always in accordance with the reality of the objects of that faith. Hence, the first Catholic response to demythologizing is to affirm over and over again in thought and in prayer the reality of the objects of faith, beginning with the abiding reality of Jesus Christ, our Lord and Redeemer.

4. But accompanying this personal response on the part of everyone is the need for some Catholic thinkers to learn and make available to others the solid arguments needed to refute and put away forever the philosophical existentialism of Martin Heidegger and the theological existentialism of Rudolf Bultmann. They must realize that Bultmann has taken away every possibility of Christian prayer and contemplation by collapsing the entire objectivity of the Christian faith into the emptiness of the knowing subject as such. And even as regards the anointing by the Holy Spirit of the soul and heart of the believer, Bultmann takes that away too where he says that his "biological man cannot see how a supernatural entity like the πνεῦμα [Spirit] can penetrate within the close texture of the natural powers and set to work within him."[9] To restore the objectivity of faith missing from the Bultmannian scenario, the first step is for the scholar to get down on his knees and pray fervently to the Holy Spirit to illuminate his mind and enkindle his will to know and to savor the truth that in demythologizing has been erased. The opponent of demythologizing must employ the gift of humility before the eyes of God and the realization that of himself he can do nothing against the pride and arrogance inherent in the temptation to imagine that "we now know" that the traditional God of the Hebrews and of the early Christians has never really existed.[10]

5. Malevez points out that, while Bultmann's reason for excluding any intervention of God in the world is that every philosophical consideration of an act of God is limited to the sphere of the existential encounter in faith, this reason is unfounded, because neither Heidegger nor Bultmann has

---

9 Bultmann, in *KaM*, vol. I, p. 6

10 Cf. "The real *skandalon* of faith in God *vis-à-vis* modern technology can become clear only when we have abandoned the false view of God which that technology has exploded" (Bultmann, in *KaM*, vol. I, p. 120.

disproved the essentialist ontology which they oppose. Malevez does not feel constrained to accept the nihilistic approach of Heidegger's *Being and Time*.[11] In fact, it is essentialist ontology that disproves the existentialism of Heidegger and Bultmann. And so, I believe that what is needed for a full response to demythologizing is the use of contemporary Scholastic philosophy and theology, based upon the wisdom of the masters of old and updated to meet the problems of today. From Scholastic philosophy, and, in particular, from Thomistic philosophy, we know that there is a hierarchy of sciences, of which empirical science is just one. If "science" is defined merely to coincide with empirical science, there results a false concept of science and an impoverished idea of reality. Technical science, as distinguished from common sense, is "certified knowledge," and Bultmann, in his demythologizing, assumes that only the knowledge gained from empirical science is really certified, into which he might throw historical knowledge in a broader sense. But there are other areas and levels of technical science that also give certified knowledge. Not only is there true historical science, but, in the midst of the widespread confusion and misunderstanding in the field known today as "modern philosophy," there is still an area of true philosophical science, if one can manage to find it, and it resides in Scholastic philosophy. Again, there is still an area of theological science, and it resides today especially in Scholastic theology, and the knowledge presented in these latter two sciences is also objectively true and real. Hence, Catholic intellectuals who want to escape the dangers of Bultmannian demythologizing will do well to turn to Scholastic philosophy and theology and update it in their own minds to the best of their ability. A revival of Scholasticism—along the lines of neo-Scholasticism—is needed, and workers in the field are now urgently being sought.

6. An element of belief that Bultmann does not seem to have rejected as mythological is the fall of man into sin, and he sees this according to the Lutheran doctrine of the total corruption of the human intellect and will. He says: "*It is only because man is a fallen being, only because he knows he is not what he really ought to be, that he can be aware of his plight.*" (Even the philosophers agree that) "*man's authentic nature has to be apprehended by a deliberate resolve. […] Why then has the fall destroyed this actual possibility? The answer is that in his present plight every impulse of man is the impulse of a fallen being.*"[12] Malevez does not accept the idea of the total corruption of the mind and will of man, and he advances that it is the interior action

---

11 Cf. Malevez, *MCM*, pp. 139–145; *CMM*, 142–147.

12 Bultmann, in *KaM*, vol. I, p. 29.

and grace of the Holy Spirit that gives light to the intellect and strength to the will in order to enable a man to be converted and move toward holiness. The exercise of free will is a reality of human life, and this fact disproves the idea that human action is limited to the closed functioning of material forces.[13] In my estimation, many Protestants today are open to the idea that Luther's doctrine of the total corruption of the human mind and will is not true, and Catholics in fraternal dialogue with them should help them to know of the interior action of the Holy Spirit and the possibility of having sanctifying grace in their souls. And, as far as ecumenical dialogue goes, hitherto the discussion has been almost exclusively between liberal Catholics and liberal non-Catholics. The time may have arrived to begin a fruitful combined effort of traditional Catholics with fervent non-Catholic Christians to defend the historical truth of the Scriptures.

The Response of Heinrich Fries

7. The response of Heinrich Fries to the demythologizing of Rudolf Bultmann takes the form of a list of short arguments against the main features of the program.[14] On the positive side, he avers that Catholic theologians cannot be grateful enough for the impetus that Bultmann has given to theology by his emphasis upon its existential character.[15] One of Fries' objections is that Bultmann makes man's pre-understanding the measure of all understanding, so that Bultmann's "act of God" in the existential encounter is actually only an act of man, since it limits man's understanding of God to man's pre-understanding of himself, and it cuts the size of God down to the size of man, thus turning theology into anthropology.[16] In my opinion Bultmann has contributed almost nothing to the understanding of the Christian message except to have posed a challenging set of problems whose correct solution could effect in some areas a development of Catholic theology, not in existentialist terms, but

---

13 Cf. Malevez, *MCM*, pp. 149–152; *CMM*, pp. 151–153.

14 H. Fries, *Bultmann-Barth und die katholische Theologie* (Stuttgart, 1955 [henceforth referred to as *BBKT*]); Engl. trans., *Bultmann-Barth and Catholic Theology* (Pittsburgh: Duquesne Univ. Press, 1967 [henceforth referred to as *BBCT*]). See my review in *Living Tradition* 80 (March 1999), in the archive of articles at www.rtfourm.org and in chapter 10 above.

15 Fries, *BBKT*, pp. 137–138; *BBCT*, pp. 149–150.

16 Fries, *BBKT*, pp. 129–139; *BBCT*, pp. 141–150.

on the basis of Catholic theological tradition. If understanding is defined as "the knowledge of something true in relation to another truth," then all understanding does involve the pre-knowledge of something else. If all pre-knowledge were to be limited to what man can know by the light of his natural reason alone, as in the Rationalism of Bultmann's program, then no understanding of the supernatural would be possible. But pre-knowledge of the supernatural is possible from divine revelation, and so, for instance, a man can understand something about the objects of faith and even about himself in the light of truths revealed by God, and we call this kind of pre-understanding the light of faith. This function of pre-understanding can be illustrated in the moderate realism of Scholastic philosophy. In contemporary non-Scholastic philosophy and theology we often hear mention of the "subject-object link-up," usually with emphasis upon the subject of an "I-thou" relationship, while Bultmann suppresses it entirely in his demythologizing act of faith and of "authentic existence." What is missing in both cases in this common subject-object paradigm is the medium of the mind. Actually, what one is always dealing with in every act of understanding is a) the knowing subject, b) the remote object that is being understood, and c) the mental framework intermediate between the subject and the remote object being understood. Understanding comes from seeing the remote object in the light of the intervening proximate object, which is, therefore, the pre-understanding referred to by Bultmann in his own way. Hence, in responding to the demythologizing method of Bultmann, attention needs to be paid to the mental framework of understanding, in which the right philosophy provides many of the middle terms, and the right philosophy is the moderate realism of Scholastic philosophy, but some further development of Scholastic philosophy would be very useful in the area of theory of knowledge, seeing that some of the precise middle terms for a complete response to Bultmann's use of "pre-understanding" still need to be refined, as I have suggested at length where I treated the problem of the origin of intellectual knowledge.[17]

8. Fries sees the program of demythologizing as an attempt to carry the Reformation principle of "justification by faith alone" even into the sphere of knowledge, by forgetting that man is still made in the image and likeness of God and by emptying the act of faith of its real relationship to the real God.[18] We have noted elsewhere Bultmann's play on the word

---

17 See chapter 5 above.

18 Fries, *BBKT*, p. 141, 158–160; *BBCT*, pp. 152–153, 168–170.

"reality" and his negation of the reality of God.[19] This position traces back to another Reformation principle, the radical separation of faith and reason and the consequent setting up of an alternate world of religious belief, which Bultmann conceives of as "non-world." The rebuttal of this idea of the total separation of faith and reason amounts to a demonstration, as Fries points out, that Christian faith has sufficient grounds of credibility in human reason and does not need to flee from *Historie* into an existentialist *Geschichte*,[20] that is, from the real world into some kind of aesthetic dream-world, where the dreamer may imagine and believe anything he pleases during his times of recreation. We know that the true religion is much more than that and we need to prove it more decisively.

9. Another point made by Fries is that the Catholic Church correctly recognizes a multiple level of meaning in the text of the Sacred Scriptures, and a deeper spiritual meaning behind the direct literal meaning of the words.[21] And from this understanding come the theological concepts of the supernatural and of the sanctifying grace which elevates a human person to a present and future participation in the divine nature. This Catholic concept of supernatural grace contains what is lacking in Bultmann's demythologized notions of grace, redemption, and salvation.[22] Of course, Bultmann's rejection of the deeper spiritual sense of the Sacred Scriptures follows a general Protestant aversion to recognizing the spiritual senses, and also reflects the classical Lutheran denial of the reality of sanctifying grace. Catholic historical critics, following the lead of their liberal Protestant mentors, for a long time tended to look for only one meaning, what they saw as *the* meaning, of any given biblical text, and that was the literal meaning, except that they would manage to find a "fuller sense" (*sensus plenior*) in places where a deeper meaning had been officially proclaimed by the Church, but more recently they have begun to consider that a text can have more than one meaning.[23] Actually, the literal sense of many

---

19 See *Living Tradition* 112 (July 2004), paragraph 7.

20 Cf. Fries, *BBKT*, pp. 133–135; *BBCT*, pp. 145–147.

21 Cf. Fries, *BBKT*, p. 144; *BBCT*, p. 155.

22 Cf. Fries, *BBKT*, pp. 149–150; *BBCT*, pp. 160–161.

23 "In reaction to this multiplicity of senses, historical critical exegesis adopted, more or less overtly, the thesis of the one single meaning: a text cannot have at the same time more than one meaning. All the effort of historical critical exegesis goes into defining "the" precise sense of this or that biblical text seen within the circumstances in which it was produced. But this thesis has now run aground on the conclusions of theories of language and of philosophical hermeneutics, both of which affirm that written texts are

texts of Sacred Scripture cannot be fully understood unless there is some perception of the spiritual senses that lie behind them, and this is why a full response to the program of demythologizing cannot be given without a prior return to the traditional Catholic approach to Sacred Scripture, the method of the Four Senses, which is recommended by the *Catechism of the Catholic Church* as the proper way to interpret the Bible.[24] This approach in an updated way is being pursued by neo-patristic scholars.

10. A final point made by Fries is that biblical revelation does not present unhistorical ideas in the guise of history, and that the *kerygma* and faith of the New Testament are grounded in what actually happened.[25] This is true, but here we come to the question of the historicity of the events reported in the Bible, and particularly in the four Gospels. Now, Bultmann is heavily armed in this area. He published his scathing attack on the historicity of the Synoptic Gospels in 1921, and an even more scathing attack on the historicity of the Gospel according to John in 1943. To my knowledge no effective general answer on an organized critical level to these attacks has ever been published by any one of the Catholic form-critics who use his method, nor has any one of them advanced an alternative form-critical method that would effectively and explicitly distance itself from the Rationalism that underlies his conclusions. Hence, a complete answer to Bultmann's program of demythologizing urgently requires also a technical refutation of the arguments he presented in these two books to demonstrate the form-critical conclusions upon which this program is based.

The Response of René Marlé

11. René Marlé, in an article published in 1956, gave a rather indulgent appraisal of Rudolf Bultmann's program of "demythologizing the New Testament." Marlé found the program to be basically constructive and drawn up from the viewpoint of a resolute believer, while the demythologizing is intended only to clear the way for a rigorous "theology of paradox," even though the "idols" of New Testament mythology marked out for destruction do seem artificial and contrived.[26] But he does find it defective

---

open to a plurality of meaning" (The [reconstituted] Pontifical Biblical Commission, *The Interpretation of the Bible in the Church* (Libreria Editrice Vaticana, 1993), p.78.

24 Cf. *Catechism of the Catholic Church*, nos. 115–119.

25 Fries, *BBKT*, pp. 167–170; *BBCT*, pp. 176–179.

26 R. Marlé, *Bultmann et l'interprétation du Nouveau Testament* (Paris, 1956 [henceforth

to accuse the Apostolic witness to the Resurrection and Ascension of Jesus of being "mythological" and thus to deprive it of all of its objective reality and intrinsic meaning.[27] And he doubts whether the New Testament world view presented by Bultmann coincides with what these ancients thought.[28] As I have said above, it is my opinion that the demythologizing of Rudolf Bultmann is totally destructive of all of the objective reality of faith and has no redeeming feature, because his project aims at a purely imaginary goal, namely, to validate the now collapsed "fiction" of the biblical narratives by immersing it in the supposed authenticity of one's own being. There is no true paradox here. Marlé opines that there may be a world of realities not accessible to conceptual thought that are expressed in religion through the imaged and symbolic language of what Bultmann calls myth and we call mystery.[29] Now, there may be a world of realities not accessible to human conceptual thought, but the mysteries of the New Testament are contained in a narrative of real events. Certainly, those with mystical insight see realities that Bultmann could not even suspect of being there, but these realities have no relation to myth. The language of the New Testament is adapted to the expression of metaphors and allegories that pertain to the mysteries of the accounts, but these spiritual senses are based on the historical reality of the literal sense. The world-view of the New Testament is revealed and is based on the world-view of Genesis. The imagery in the world-view of Sacred Scripture conveys realities that go beyond the ability of human minds to confine them. The fact that these mysteries often go beyond human ability fully to comprehend them is no excuse for calling them myths. The challenge is to find the right framework in which to understand them as completely as possible, and that is the framework of the Four Senses of Sacred Scripture begun by the Fathers of the Church.

12. Bultmann has pointed out the superficiality of those who object to his conclusions but ignore the fact that the conclusions logically follow from the premises that he uses and that all of the elements of his program depend upon one another. In an article published in English in 1961 Marlé speaks of "the fatal outcome to which Bultmann's premises would normally lead," and he points out that, when Catholic theologians object

---

referred to as *MBI*]) pp. 174–175. See my review of Marlé's interventions in *Living Tradition* 81 (May 1999), in the archive of articles at www.rtforum.org.

27 Marlé, *MBI*, pp. 171–172.

28 Marlé, *MBI*, pp. 62–63.

29 Marlé, *MBI*, pp. 66–69; 180–181.

to the weakness or hollowness of his conclusions, it is only to bring out the fundamental weaknesses of his premises.[30] Yet Marlé also seems to admit that he cannot distinguish with any degree of success which are Bultmann's premises and which are his conclusions.[31] Actually, whoever denies the premises of an argument has to deny the conclusions, and the conclusions of Bultmann's reasonings are outrageous, and many of his conclusions are premises for further conclusions. Thus, his turning to the existentialism of Martin Heidegger was a resort to save something Christian from a New Testament message whose historical truth he seemed to have totally wiped out in his earlier exegesis, as laid out in his *History of the Synoptic Tradition*. And Catholic Scripture scholars who have been attracted to Bultmann's exegetical method have provided little in the way of refutation of the errors of method contained in this book.

13. As the years went by, one would have hoped that Marlé's opposition to Bultmann's theology would have strengthened and solidified. However, in another analysis published in 1967,[32] while he still maintains that Bultmann's conceptual instruments are too rigid to support a true theology, Marlé goes so far as to declare himself a moderate follower of this "intrepid theologian," who recognizes in his program of demythologizing a justified concern, but also who rejects the radicalism with which Bultmann has defined it and put it into operation,[33] even though Bultmann's proposals do contain an incentive to theologians of every persuasion to renew their own contact with the foundations of the faith that they profess.[34] Marlé feels that the current revival of interest in sacramental symbolism, among other things, reflects an anxiety to recover realities that have been lost sight of over the last few centuries. Hence, he says, the rediscovery of images, symbols, and "myths" with the re-evaluation of the imagination is an important aspect of the modern movement, since revelation will always be communicated to us in the world of images.[35] On the contrary, I maintain that there are no myths in the New Testament. Certainly, the Holy Spirit

---

30 Cf. R. Marlé, "Demythologizing Assessed," in *The Heythrop Journal* (1961), pp. 45–46.

31 Cf. Marlé, *MBI*, p. 176, note 5.

32 R. Marlé, *Bultmann et la foi chrétienne* (Paris, 1967 [henceforth referred to as *MBFC*]); Engl. trans., *Bultmann and Christian Faith* (Westminster, Md.: Newman Press, 1968 [henceforth referred to as *MBCF*]).

33 Marlé, *MBFC*, p. 77; *MBCF*, p. 51.

34 Marlé, *MBFC*, pp. 154–155; *MBCF*, p. 106.

35 Marlé, *MBFC*, pp. 84–85; *MBCF*, pp. 55–56.

uses imagery and parable to convey deeper truths, but these have no relation to mythology. What is truly unfortunate is that during the past several centuries Catholic exegetes have largely lost sight of the allegorical significance of much of the imagery in the Bible, thus leaving the door open to false interpretations like that of Bultmann. The answer is to forget about the "modern" movement and return to the solid approach of the medieval exegetes and the Fathers of the Church. In the restoration of the method of the Four Senses of Sacred Scripture, a clear distinction will be kept in mind between the literal and spiritual senses, with the result that the truth of the literal sense will become more apparent, and the deeper meanings of the spiritual senses will come into view. Bultmann's program does not represent a justified concern; it merely awakens a justified concern to refute his erroneous approach to the interpretation of the New Testament and, in the process, to discover additional meanings in the sacred text.

14. Marlé is being uncritical himself where he says that modern criticism has made us more demanding and that the only way in which we can establish contact with the world of the Apostles is in terms of the exigencies that we have as twentieth-century men, since it would be an empty illusion to try to recover a naivety that is forever lost. Marlé says that to this extent he agrees with Bultmann, but he disagrees with Bultmann's narrow concept of existence and favors instead theological work based upon history.[36] On the contrary, since Bultmann not only presupposes the Lutheran doctrine of the total corruption of the intellect and will of man, but also excludes all of the objects of Catholic faith, a Catholic theologian cannot reasonably be a "moderate follower" of his. Furthermore, the contact of twentieth or twenty-first-century men with the world of the Apostles has not been lost, because Bultmann's notion of modern man is totally mistaken. The naivety involved here does not involve an acceptance of the world of the Apostles, but rather the acceptance of the conclusions of Bultmann and many others of his historical critical followers that the events regarding Jesus that are recorded in the New Testament are unhistorical and mythological. Rather, they are historically real events. Hence, the needed theological work based on history must aim at refuting the form-criticism of Bultmann et al. and securing the historical truth of the Gospel events. This work includes the development of an adequate theory of history and its application to the problems presented by historical criticism.

---

36 Marlé, *MBFC*, pp. 85–87; *MBCF*, pp. 56–57.

The Response of Joseph Cahill

15. Joseph Cahill, like René Marlé, feels that Bultmann has the merit of trying to make biblical revelation relevant to modern man, and he welcomes Bultmann's attempt to bridge the gaps between what he calls the rich, modern interpretation of Sacred Scripture, speculative theology, and concrete "existential" man. Cahill thus shows a lack of understanding for what Bultmann has done to the concept of modern man and also a certain fascination for Bultmann's method of form-criticism, which leads him to underestimate the devastating effects of Bultmann's form-critical conclusions in *The History of the Synoptic Tradition*. Cahill rejects Bultmann's denial of the objective existence of God, but he sees in the Bultmannian doctrine of pre-understanding "very definite echoes" of the natural desire for God expressed in the writings of St. Thomas Aquinas and St. Augustine of Hippo.[37] I think that a closer look at the program of demythologizing would have shown that Bultmann's "modern man" embraces only those contemporary men who believe in secular humanism and have no openness to divine revelation or to any influence of divine grace in their lives. Bultmann's interpretation of the New Testament has no richness, either objective or subjective. His view of the Christian message is the view of a Modernist whose subjective pride of modern place obstructs any clear view or hearing of what that message is saying to him and of how it seeks to elevate his concrete existence here and now. In fact, Bultmann's method of form-criticism shuts out the whole moral impact of the Gospel message, which can take its effect only in a mind and heart that seeks it in an attitude of humility and prayer.

16. Cahill avers that, for Bultmann, the only Christ is the Christ for us, so that Christian faith becomes centered on a value judgment, and the Person of the Jesus of history has no intrinsic and permanent relation to the experiential grasp of divine revelation.[38] Cahill notes Bultmann's admission that his "existential encounter" cannot defend itself against the charge of illusion and could, therefore, easily be a mere personality projection, while "the validity and necessity of the strictly historical method for a reconstruction of certain past outer events which the believer apprehends with a new magnitude and dimension as revelation

---

37 P. J. Cahill, "(Notes concerning John Macquarrie's) *The Scope of Demythologizing*," in *Theological Studies*, 23 (1962), pp. 79–92 [henceforth referred to as *JCSD*]), pp. 86–90 and p. 80, note 4.

38 Cahill, *JCSD*, p. 84.

cannot be minimized or distinguished out of existence." In sum, he adds, the possibility of faith is made available because God has intervened in history, and "no amount of subjective *a priori* speculation or postulation can substitute for or replace critical investigation of the divine events as well as enlightened examination of the later understanding of the divine events manifested in the theological sources."[39] To my mind there is no doubt that the "outer events" of divine revelation cannot be minimized or distinguished out of existence, but the problem here is that Bultmann did not begin to make his existential distinctions until after he had already, in his estimation, destroyed the historicity of those events through the use of his historical critical method. And it is to the discredit of Catholic historical critics that they have never laid to rest the enormous concatenation of fallacies and non-factual statements enshrined in Bultmann's classic historical critical work, *The History of the Synoptic Tradition*. The "strictly historical method" that Catholics need is not the form-criticism instituted by Rudolf Bultmann and now followed by most Catholic biblical scholars. Rather, it is the method of the Fathers of the Church and of Catholic exegetical tradition, updated to meet the challenges posed by historical criticism. The sooner that the majority of Catholic scholars turn to this needed task, the more quickly will the Rationalism and the Modernism inherent in the exegesis of Bultmann cease to threaten Catholic faith and Catholic biblical studies.

17. In projecting the need of a fuller response to the demythologizing of Rudolf Bultmann, I have stressed the need of clear apologetic arguments to counter the invitation to Modernism implied in the Bultmannian concept of "modern man" with a greater recourse to prayer and to affirming over and over the supernatural objects of Catholic faith, above all the divinity of Jesus. I have mentioned the need of a return to the method and insights of Catholic exegetical tradition with all of the answers that it can provide, and of an effort to develop that tradition with the use of contemporary historical methods properly defined and refined. In my reviews of 1999 I tried to point out how each of the four Catholic theologians mentioned above in this article, while they had many good things to say, in some ways played into the hands of Bultmann by conceding things that they were in no position to concede, and which did not deserve to be conceded, and I think that they made these mistakes because they had not sufficiently thought out the debate that they were in and did not come to the discussion sufficiently prepared

---

39 Cahill, *JCSD*, pp. 82–84.

for the defense of their own side. In the continuation of this article, I shall present the responses of three other theologians reviewed in the series of the year 1999, to see how much they contributed to the challenge of a fuller response to the program of "demythologizing" by which Rudolf Bultmann gained world-wide fame and notoriety.

PART II. The Response of Xavier Léon-Dufour
(as translated and edited by John McHugh)

Living Tradition 114 (November 2004)

18. *The call for demythologizing.* In his celebrated essay of 1941, "New Testament and Mythology," calling for the "demythologizing" of the New Testament proclamation, Rudolf Bultmann began with the claim that "the New Testament is essentially mythical in character," seeing that it projects a mythical viewpoint of the world as a three-leveled structure composed of Heaven, Earth, and Hell, and a belief in "the supernatural activity of God and his angels on the one hand, and of Satan and his demons on the other," an outlook in which "miracles are by no means rare" and "man is not in control of his own life" (*KaM*, 1). Bultmann then declared that Christian preachers cannot expect modern man to accept as true this mythical view of the world (*KaM*, 3). Even the eschatology of the New Testament is untenable, he said, "for the simple reason that the parousia of Christ never took place as the New Testament expected" (*KaM*, 5). And "the biblical doctrine that *death is the punishment of sin* is equally abhorrent to naturalism and idealism, since both regard death as a simple and necessary process of nature." Regarding the death of Christ on the Cross, Bultmann asked, "How can the guilt of one man be expiated by the death of another who is sinless—if indeed one may speak of a sinless man at all?" To Bultmann this very thought implied very primitive notions of guilt and righteousness and "a primitive idea of God." And he was led to exclaim, "(W)hat a primitive mythology it is, that a divine Being should become incarnate and atone for the sins of men through his own blood!" Bultmann went on to say, "(T)he resurrection of Jesus is just as difficult for modern man, if it means an event whereby a living supernatural power is released which can henceforth be appropriated through the sacraments." It was, he averred, "Gnostic influence" that introduced the idea that "this Christ, who died and rose again, was not a mere human being but a

God-man" (*KaM*, 7–8). *What should be done* about this problem? Well, Bultmann explained, we cannot save the kerygma (proclamation) for modern man by rejecting some features of the New Testament mythology and keeping others, and it is the duty in all honesty of the theologian and of the priest not to keep their hearers in the dark about what they themselves have quietly eliminated. It is rather a matter of reinterpreting the mythology. "The real purpose of myth is not to present an objective picture of the world as it is, but to express man's understanding of himself in the world in which he lives" (*KaM*, 9–10). The event and the person of Jesus, he continued, can and must be interpreted apart from this mythology; *they must be interpreted existentially*. The New Testament offers man an understanding of himself which will challenge him to a genuine existential decision ((*KaM*, 15–16). The New Testament "regards the fall as total" and sees that man has lost the actual possibility to grasp his authentic nature by a decision, because "in his present plight every impulse of man is the impulse of a fallen being" (*KaM*, 29). For Bultmann, "to talk of sin ceases to be mere mythology when the love of God meets man as a power which embraces and sustains him even in his fallen, self-assertive state." The event of Jesus Christ is "the revelation of the love of God," and it is "faith in the love of God revealed in Christ" (*KaM*, 31–32). The event of Christ presents "a unique combination of history and myth." The New Testament is mythological to the extent that it presents Jesus Christ as the Son of God, as a pre-existent divine being, but it presents him also as a concrete figure of history—Jesus of Nazareth. Is not the mythological language "simply an attempt to express the meaning of the historical figure of Jesus and the events of his life"? If it is, then "we can dispense with the objective form in which they are cast" (*KaM*, 34–35). To believe in the cross of Christ means "to undergo crucifixion with him." The redemptive cross of Christ is not the mythical event but "the judgment and deliverance of man" (*KaM*, 36–37). And the resurrection is not a past event of history or a miraculous proof, since cross and resurrection "form a single, indivisible cosmic event which brings judgment to the world and opens up for men the possibility of authentic life." The resuscitation of the dead Jesus is impossible to believe, except as an "article of faith," and, as an article of faith, it is "the eschatological event" (*KaM*, 39–40). Hence, *"faith in the resurrection is really the same thing as faith in the saving efficacy of the cross,"* and so, "to believe in Christ means to believe in the cross as the cross of Christ." And the real Easter faith is "the rise of faith in the risen Lord," with the result that "all that historical criticism can establish is the fact that the first disciples came to believe in the resurrection" (*KaM*, 41–42). *In conclusion*, the redemption "is not a miraculous supernatural event, but a historical event wrought out in time and space," while the word of God "is not some mysterious oracle, but a sober, factual account of a human life, of Jesus of Nazareth, possessing saving efficacy for man," and the transcendence of God "is not as in myth reduced to immanence" but is "present and active in history: the Word became flesh'" (*KaM*, 43–44). This is the "decisive act of God in Christ proclaimed as the event of redemption" (*KaM*, 15).[40]

19. In 1963 Xavier Léon-Dufour published his work on the historical truth of the Gospels, *Les évangiles et l'histoire de Jésus*, the purpose of which, he says, is "to give a fair hearing to the new set of questions [raised by Bultmann and others] without at the same time adopting presuppositions which have prejudiced the results of an inquiry that was intended to be scientific (*sans pour autant adopter les préjugés qui ont compromis les résultats d'une enquête qui se voulait scientifique*)"[41] Again, the aim of his book is "to find out, by using the critical methods of historical scholarship, the full and objective truth (as far as it can be known) about the life of Jesus of Nazareth."[42] Léon-Dufour maintains throughout his book that the Four Gospels do not present the full and objective truth. He points out that "Towards the end of the eighteenth century many writers began to attack the historical value of the four gospels. ...These books were all written with one purpose: to get back with real certainty to the unadorned facts, and to reconstruct what actually happened in the past. What other authors did in their day, we have to do again for our own generation."[43] Léon-Dufour notes that some historians, such as Rudolf Bultmann, having been deeply influenced by existentialism, claim that we can know practically nothing about the historical Jesus. On the contrary, Léon-Dufour feels that conclusions of this kind seem to be unjustified and in contradiction, not only to traditional faith, but also

---

40 The description of the "demythologizing" of Rudolf Bultmann in this paragraph has been reprinted from *Living Tradition* 81 (May 1999), p. 1. For the abbreviation *KaM*, see above, part 1, footnote 581, of this chapter.

41 X. Léon-Dufour, *Les évangiles et l'histoire de Jésus* (Paris: Éditions du Seuil, 1963), p. 8. Cf. "At the same time there can be no question of accepting philosophical presuppositions which determine the outcome of any inquiry from the start" (Léon-Dufour [McHugh]), p. 14.

42 Léon-Dufour (McHugh), p. 14.

43 Léon-Dufour (McHugh), p. 7.

to the historical evidence.[44] However, we find as his book goes along that Léon-Dufour, as a historian, doesn't find much more certified about the facts of Jesus' life than did Bultmann, for he ends up with the conclusion that "*only the broadest chronological pattern of Jesus' life can be known,*" and what is that pattern? "These, then, are the broad lines of Jesus' life. He began his ministry alongside the Baptist, beside the Jordan, and then preached in Galilee about the coming of the kingdom. His preaching provoked hostility among the Jews and from Herod, and the ordinary folk failed to grasp his spiritual message. He therefore ceased to preach in public, and after a period on the borders of Galilee (during which he concentrated on the formation of his closest disciples) went to Jerusalem, where he stayed three months. Finally, after spending some time in Transjordan, he returned to Jerusalem a few days before the Passover. ... With this framework of the Lord's life before us, we may now turn to the central question in our inquiry: what should men think of Jesus Christ? [...] But even though (the historian) cannot descend into details, and even though many questions remain unanswered (and perhaps unanswerable), it is certainly possible to make a valid synthesis of the teaching of Jesus, and to give a true account of his earthly life. We shall thereby see the originality of the Christian faith in all its splendour."[45]

20. These meager results of Léon-Dufour's historical investigations might seem impressive until one comes to realize that they are virtually the same as the results of Bultmann's investigations, published in 1921 in *The History of the Synoptic Tradition*.[46] Everything in the resulting pattern is merely human. Following this basic conclusion, Léon-Dufour will discuss many things about the life and ministry of Jesus, but he will not conclude that any of the supernatural events reported in the Gospels are verified historical happenings, even though they are meaningful for his faith and for the faith of believers. Bultmann made the same distinction, although, in his program of demythologizing, he eliminated all of the supernatural objects even from faith. In my analysis of 1999 I tried to show that the arguments of Léon-Dufour played repeatedly into Bultmann's hands. Bultmann was ready to admit most of the human results of Léon-Dufour's research; he had concluded this himself. It

---

44 Léon-Dufour (McHugh), p. 14.

45 Léon-Dufour (McHugh), pp. 222–224.

46 R. Bultmann, *Die Geschichte der synoptischen Tradition* (8th ed., Göttingen, 1970); Eng. trans. by J. Marsh: *The History of the Synoptic Tradition* (Oxford: Blackwell, 1963).

was the supernatural elements that Bultmann denied. And Bultmann retained the "event of Christ" as an existential stimulus for Christian faith, while denying the historical truth of practically all of the words and deeds of Jesus recorded in the Gospels. Similarly, Léon-Dufour plays down the importance of the words and deeds of Jesus, reducing faith essentially to the existential act of a trusting acceptance of the Person of Jesus. But who is Jesus, apart from the extraordinary words and deeds ascribed to Him in the Gospels, such as His Incarnation in the womb of the Blessed Virgin Mary, His Resurrection from the dead, and His Ascension into Heaven?

21. As a believer, Léon-Dufour professes all of these things. He says, for instance, "and just as the co-eternal Word of God took human flesh at a particular date and in a particular place..."[47] Again he says: "The person of Jesus, the Son of God incarnate and our Saviour, ensures that our faith is firmly anchored to this earth... ."[48] He goes on to say that "the earthly life of Jesus cannot be reduced to that of an ordinary man."[49] But, as a historian, he sees problems in this. For instance, that God became man has been the constant teaching of the Church, but "assertions like these, which are of their nature incapable of empirical verification, present the historian with problems of a unique kind."[50] The Church asserts that in the Church the risen Christ is present today, but "This belief ... too raises a problem for the historian."[51] Regarding the fulfillment of prophecies recorded in the Gospels, the critical historian can retort that "they made up episodes to illustrate the fulfillment."[52] With regard to the fulfillment of prophecies recorded in the Passion story, "a host of problems arises."[53] In St. John's Gospel, "the historian who is looking for an unadorned account of the original event, or for the *ipsissima verba Jesu*, finds himself completely disconcerted." But he goes on to add that "this, however, should lead him to wonder whether he himself is asking the right questions,"[54] and one does

---

47 Léon-Dufour (McHugh), p. 26.

48 Léon-Dufour (McHugh), p. 65.

49 Léon-Dufour (McHugh), p. 106.

50 Léon-Dufour (McHugh), p. 18.

51 Léon-Dufour (McHugh), p. 19.

52 Léon-Dufour (McHugh), p. 24.

53 Léon-Dufour (McHugh), p. 26.

54 Léon-Dufour (McHugh), p. 105.

wonder whether Léon-Dufour has asked himself the right questions. For
him, as a critical observer looking at St. John's Gospel, "it becomes obvious
that the problem of historicity is here very acute."[55] He notes that "one
must not uncritically accept an event or speech simply because it is related
in the gospel," and, indeed, "once the literary genre of the fourth gospel
is recognized, one can see why those who limit their aim to knowing the
historical Jesus find it of little use for their purpose."[56] Léon-Dufour finds it
very reasonable to ask whether some episodes in John "have not been made
up to illustrate a doctrine," and he finds it clearly legitimate to ask whether
Mark's Gospel "is an exact record of what really happened, or whether it is
the result of theological reflection."[57] Similarly, since the author of the third
gospel admits that he did not witness the events that he has recorded, "his
work must be examined very critically before it may be used as a source for
the life of Jesus," also because "Luke was not just writing a straightforward
biography of Jesus, but was expounding a theological theme."[58] In fact,
says Léon-Dufour, while all four Gospels claim that they are recording
history, they do not conceal "the theological purpose which underlies the
historical record."[59]

22. There are two rules of scientific historical method of which Léon-
Dufour seems not to be fully aware. The first is the distinction between
the purpose of the work (*finis operis*) and the purpose of the worker (*finis
operantis*). The fact that a Gospel has been written for a "theological purpose,"
which is the purpose of the writer, in no way diminishes the historical
truth of the account, as long as the immediate purpose of presenting the
historical facts (the *finis operis*) is honestly served. And there is no reason to
doubt that the four evangelists honestly presented what they knew to be the
historical facts. The second rule of solid historical method is the distinction
between chronology and historical explanation. A historical work, in order
to remain perfectly objective, is not limited strictly to chronology, that is,
to listing the facts in some kind of chronological order, without stating
or even implying what the writer considers to be the underlying meaning
of those facts. Historical explanation goes along with chronology, as long
as facts are not suppressed or altered to fit the explanation that the writer

55 Léon-Dufour (McHugh), p, 97.

56 Léon-Dufour (McHugh), p. 105.

57 Léon-Dufour (McHugh), p. 23.

58 Léon-Dufour (McHugh), p. 147.

59 Léon-Dufour (McHugh), p. 23.

has in mind. Now, the scientific historian of today has no good reason to assume that the four evangelists suppressed or altered facts in order to adjust them to the meanings that he saw in those facts, and, therefore, their supposed "theological themes" or "theological purposes" do not subtract from the historical truth of the events that they have recorded.

23. Let us take, for example, the Incarnation of the Divine Word in Jesus of Nazareth. It does not help for Léon-Dufour to say that in the Synoptic Gospels "there is scarcely a word about the pre-existence of Jesus or about his relation to the Father."[60] Of course, both St. Matthew and St. Luke talk about it very graphically in the Infancy Narratives at the beginning of their Gospels, but Léon-Dufour, as a historian, avers that "a critical reader may well wonder whether they are to be taken as history in the same sense as the narratives of the public life," because "it must be clearly stated that neither Matthew nor Luke makes an attempt to conceal the doctrinal purpose of his writing," and also because in the Infancy Narratives "it is not miracles but 'marvels' (the 'supernatural') which continually come before our eyes." Léon-Dufour is referring especially to the appearance of angels to Zachary, Mary, Joseph, the Magi, and the shepherds, that is, the repeated intervention of the "invisible world" in a "most extraordinary manner." The employment of angels indicates to Léon-Dufour the use in Matthew of a fictitious literary device. Now, the appearances of angels are listed by Bultmann in his *History of the Synoptic Tradition* as one of the so-called biblical "literary forms," and he says that these appearances are always fictitious. Léon-Dufour has here accepted Bultmann's listing, but with the following distinction: ""One is not justified in concluding, on the ground of the literary form, that no real event underlies the infancy narratives; and one is not justified in saying that the literary form had no influence on the way in which Matthew and Luke presented their story."[61] Léon-Dufour is saying that the Infancy Narratives cannot simply be taken at face value, and so, once he has accepted Bultmann's designation of the appearance of angels and the recounting of other "marvels" as being a "literary," that is, in Bultmann's terminology, a fictional, form, the burden of proof is on Léon-Dufour to demonstrate that there is any real event underlying it. The main underlying event would be the Virginal Conception and the Incarnation of God the Son in Jesus, and Catholic historical critics do tend to avoid denying the presence of a real underlying event when the event concerned is a dogma of the Church, but, as Bultmann rejoins, "once you

---

60 Léon-Dufour (McHugh), p. 72.

61 Léon-Dufour (McHugh), pp. 215–216.

have begun to use the form-critical method, where can you logically draw the line?" Léon-Dufour, having accepted the fictitious form of the "angelic appearance," gives only weak reasons to support a real underlying event. Bultmann had said that the idea of a virginal conception was most probably suggested from pagan mythology after the early Palestinian Church was transformed into the Hellenic Church,[62] even though it could have been taken over from pre-Christian Judaism.[63] Léon-Dufour counters that it could not have been introduced from pagan sources, because here there is depicted no carnal union of a god with a human, but only a "new creation by the Holy Spirit." But, in either case, the same theme of conception from on high is there. And Léon-Dufour finds it "very doubtful" that it was suggested by Isaiah 7:14, even though the prophecy was well known and Matthew 1:23 cites it in narrating the event. As far as historical investigation is concerned, where a fictional literary form is encountered, any underlying real event has to be verified from outside sources, and Léon-Dufour has no outside source to cite. The proof of the real event of the Incarnation lies in the fact that the appearance of the angel Gabriel to the Blessed Virgin Mary is itself a real historical event which has no fictional element to it at all. It is the form-critical presupposition that angelic appearances are always fictitious that is itself a fictitious idea.

24. In his exegetical work, Bultmann claims that the Gospels are basically a fictitious creation of the Christian community.[64] Léon-Dufour notes that the form-criticism of Bultmann has this presupposition, namely, that the early Christians were so dazzled by the idea of the Resurrection that they quickly began to idealize the figure of Jesus and to adorn it with stories. He rejoins that Bultmann's principle represents a false conception of the attitude of the early Christians toward Jesus, and, "if this presupposition is false, then the whole theory falls."[65] How, then, does Léon-Dufour present the attitude of the early Christians? He says, regarding the Gospel according to St. John: "The Church, though never once mentioned by name, is present on every page, and its presence can be detected by a number of literary clues."[66] Again he

---

62 R. Bultmann, *The History of the Synoptic Tradition,* English trans. (Oxford: Basil Blackwell, 1963), pp. 291–292.

63 Bultmann, *The History of the Synoptic Tradition,* p. 304.

64 Bultmann, *The History of the Synoptic Tradition,* p. 4.

65 Léon-Dufour (McHugh), p. 168.

66 Léon-Dufour (McHugh), p. 83.

says that "It would have been surprising if the regular worship of the Church had not had deep influence on the presentation of the gospel."[67] Léon-Dufour does find that "a close literary analysis of the gospel tradition leads us to conclude that it records trustworthy historical fact, precisely because the early Christians were interested in the life of their Master,"[68] but he also finds that, in those parables of Jesus which concern the kingdom of God, "It is quite certain that many of these texts have been cast into their present form by the catechetical practice of the early Church."[69] Now, since this last point about the formative influence of the catechetical practice of the early Church is what Bultmann claims for the whole of the Gospels, Léon-Dufour's prior acceptance of Bultmann's novel list of fictitious "literary forms," puts him on weak grounds to defend their underlying historicity, especially as regards what Bultmann calls the "mythology" in the Gospels, such as the Incarnation, the Resurrection, the Ascension into Heaven, and the miracles of Jesus, and it is of these things that Léon-Dufour's defense is weakest.[70]

25. Bultmann did not just deduce the fictional character of the Gospels from the general presupposition that the Christian community had made them up. He claimed to prove this from a detailed and thoroughgoing form-critical analysis of each and every passage of the Gospels, and it is the failure of Léon-Dufour and of all of his historical critical colleagues to disprove the mountain of fallacies underlying Bultmann's claim by providing a detailed and thoroughgoing refutation of Bultmann's form-critical analysis that constitutes the main weakness of Léon-Dufour's book. Once Léon-Dufour has accepted Bultmann's exegetical method, he is assumed to accept Bultmann's exegetical conclusions, except where he effectively establishes differing results, especially as regards the supernatural elements of the Gospel accounts, and this he does not do. Bultmann, already in 1921 as a historical critic, had denied the objective reality of every supernatural event recorded in the Gospels, even to the extent of denying the objective existence of God, and Léon-Dufour

---

67 Léon-Dufour (McHugh), p. 182.

68 Léon-Dufour (McHugh), p 189.

69 Léon-Dufour (McHugh), pp. 234–235.

70 Léon-Dufour follows the form-critical method of breaking the Gospel accounts into the small "literary forms" listed by Bultmann in his *History of the Synoptic Tradition,* such as "pronouncement stories," "controversy stories," "stories about Jesus," and "miracle stories" (Léon-Dufour (McHugh), pp. 164–165.

cannot effectively counter Bultmann's conclusions by praising him as a "theological giant."[71]

26. Regarding the objective truth and reality of the miracles of Jesus recounted in the Gospels, Léon-Dufour observes that "miracle stories" in the Gospels "do not stress the extraordinary—i.e., the strictly miraculous—side of the occurrences, but the faith or astonishment of those who witnessed the event: the evangelists were concerned not primarily with the material fact," and "in certain groups of miracle stories, a theological intention can be perceived."[72] Léon-Dufour feels that several of the miracle stories are probably authentic versions of happenings that took place before the Resurrection,[73] but these happenings did not provide "irrefutable proof" that the claims of Jesus were true."[74] As regards the words quoted in the Gospels, Léon-Dufour avers that the speeches of Jesus in the Gospel of St. John and similar speeches presented in the earlier Gospels were composed by the evangelists themselves from sayings uttered by Jesus in varying circumstances, but "in the fourth Gospel the style of the writer seems to be one with that of Jesus himself, though it is not always impossible to distinguish one from the other."[75] And Matthew "has no scruples about placing on the lips of the disciples terms and phrases like 'Lord' and 'Son of God,' even though these had not been applied to Jesus before the Resurrection."[76] Of course, he adds, Jesus is called "Son of God" at his baptism and at his transfiguration, but these texts must be left aside, because "Christian belief may well have influenced the expression here."[77] Léon-Dufour is confident that "certain short phrases" were actually spoken by Our Lord, but these "are not numerous and are rarely of importance." Hence, rational criticism of the Gospels is "indispensable" in order to comprehend "the religious teaching of Jesus."[78] What kind of answer is this to the demythologizing of Bultmann?

---

71 Léon-Dufour (McHugh), p. 273. "By using those literary methods of Form-criticism which Bultmann has developed so splendidly, (many of his former pupils) seek to advance from a knowledge of the religion of the early Christians to a knowledge of Jesus himself, because he must surely have been a greater figure than anyone in the early Church" (Léon-Dufour [McHugh], p. 274]).

72 Léon-Dufour (McHugh), p. 185.

73 Léon-Dufour (McHugh), p. 201.

74 Léon-Dufour (McHugh), p. 233.

75 Léon-Dufour (McHugh), p. 103.

76 Léon-Dufour (McHugh), p. 183.

77 Léon-Dufour (McHugh), p. 244.

78 Léon-Dufour (McHugh), pp. 207, 209.

27. While Léon-Dufour affirms that for St. Paul the Christian faith is epitomized in the death and resurrection of Jesus, and that St. Paul appealed for evidence of the Resurrection to the witness of those who had seen Jesus risen from the dead,[79] he hastens to point out that the "real triumph" of Jesus was not in His Resurrection from the dead, but rather in His being enthroned forever at the right hand of the Father.[80] Léon-Dufour is of the opinion that, if there could be proof beyond all doubt that Jesus rose from the grave, there would be "no mystery left, nor any freedom of belief,"[81] and he insists that there could not be the same kind of proof for the Resurrection as for the death of Jesus, because death is a natural and observable happening to a man, but the Resurrection is not natural and, "in the strict theological sense, is not physically observable," because one cannot observe with the senses "that this living man is sharing the glory of God the Father, and that is the principal assertion in the doctrine of the Resurrection."[82] Léon-Dufour's appeal to "the strict theological sense" as a reason for excluding historical proof of the Resurrection of Jesus may seem a bit mysterious, and I think that he is here making another mistake in historical method. From a historical point of view, the Resurrection is to be studied as an event in itself, and honest witnesses who saw the risen Jesus are a source of historical evidence. Léon-Dufour is looking at the Resurrection as a *theologoumenon*, that is, as an episode imagined to express a religious idea, namely, the idea that Christ has been seated at the right hand of God the Father, and this seems very much like a Bultmannian approach. In fact, Bultmann, who, as a complete Rationalist, denied even the possibility of a resurrection from the dead, denied the Resurrection of Jesus, and said that the idea of the lifting up of Jesus on the Cross gave birth to the fictitious events of his Resurrection from the dead and his Ascension into Heaven. Léon-Dufour is certainly presenting no defense against this error of Bultmann by trying to identify in some theological way the event of the Resurrection with the event of the seating of Jesus at the right hand of the Father. Léon-Dufour notes that, in 1Cor. 15:1–11, St. Paul mentions the post-Resurrection appearances of Jesus, not out of concern to prove the truth of Christ's Resurrection,

---

79 Léon-Dufour (McHugh), pp. 55–56.

80 Léon-Dufour (McHugh), p. 60.

81 Léon-Dufour (McHugh), p. 44.

82 Léon-Dufour (McHugh), p. 255.

but out of anxiety to convince his hearers that all men will rise from the dead, that is, he concentrates all of his attention "on the mystery rather than the history."[83] Actually the whole passage in 1 Corinthians extends to verse 19, and it is in the latter part that St. Paul insists on the historical fact of the Resurrection: "If Christ has not been raised, then our preaching is in vain and your faith is in vain. We are even found to be misrepresenting God, because we testified of God that he raised Christ, whom he did not raise if it is true that the dead are not raised. For if the dead are not raised, then Christ has not been raised (1Cor. 15:14–16). While this text is more directly opposing those like Rudolf Bultmann who say that there is no such thing as a resurrection from the dead, it is also opposing those like Xavier Léon-Dufour who say that St. Paul was not concerned to prove the truth of the Resurrection of Jesus. Faith in the Resurrection is an affirmation of the historical fact of the Resurrection and a conviction that this historical fact has been confirmed by reliable witnesses.

28. Léon-Dufour claims that Luke and Matthew tell conflicting stories about the post-Resurrection appearances of Jesus, inasmuch as in Luke 24:49 Jesus ordered the disciples to remain in Jerusalem until Pentecost, while in Matt. 28:7 Jesus told them that he would see them in Galilee. Léon-Dufour maintains that this conflict cannot be resolved except by recourse to the literary form of the respective passage. He finds that, as a literary work, Luke 24 is an artificial composition in which several stories have been combined around the idea that the salvation of the world was to come from Jerusalem.[84] In other words, his form-critical analysis concludes that Jesus may never have told the disciples to remain in Jerusalem; it was Luke who put these words on the lips of Jesus. But is this conflict really so otherwise irresolvable? I think that in Luke Jesus is saying that the Apostles were soon to be sent out individually as missionaries to all nations, but that they should keep their common headquarters and residence in Jerusalem until the Holy Spirit would descend upon them and give them their mission to move out. This command did not mean that none of them was permitted for any reason to go away on visit to Galilee.

29. According to John's Gospel, the mystery of Jesus resides in his Incarnation, his Redemption of mankind, and his Ascension into Heaven.[85]

---

83 Léon-Dufour (McHugh), p. 256.

84 Léon-Dufour (McHugh), p. 257.

85 Léon-Dufour (McHugh), p. 91.

This mystery confronts Christians day by day with a choice.[86] "The historical theme that one must make a choice for or against Jesus recurs on every page of (John's) Gospel."[87] During the preaching of Jesus, his hearers were bound to ask themselves, "Who, then, is this man?"[88] In his historical studies, Léon-Dufour has found that Jesus, before his trial, "made no explicit claim to be the Son of God," but he did use words that implied that "he was conscious of a unique relation to the Father," and he "thought of himself as being in a quite unique sense the Son of God.[89] But from the time that He was asked by the high priest, "Are you the Christ, the Son of the Blessed One," Jesus made no secret of his claims."[90] In his Gospel John constantly invites the reader to believe in Jesus as a man who "really is the incarnation of God," yet this recognition "is, of course, only possible to those who accept an interior enlightenment from the Father."[91] For Léon-Dufour the primary meaning of faith is "a total entrusting of oneself to God," and "Jesus demanded that men should show this same unbounded trust towards himself."[92] The final conclusion of Léon-Dufour's search for the historical Jesus is this: "The objective truth about him is that he confronts all mankind with a question demanding an answer. And the answer cannot be given except by faith."[93]

30. Was, then, Bultmann right after all in claiming that historical inquiry removes from reality the supernatural objects of Christian faith? On the level of theology, Léon-Dufour finds Bultmann's error to lie in his having adopted the totally subjectivist philosophy of Martin Heidegger as his way of making the Gospel message relevant to modern man, whereas, for Léon-Dufour, "it is only because the faith of the early Church was based on an objective fact that we can say Christianity is more than mythology." This is true, but Léon-Dufour's defense of the historical facts is weak, inasmuch as he follows Bultmann's so-called "historical method" to historical conclusions that seem to admit only

---

86 Léon-Dufour (McHugh), p. 93.

87 Léon-Dufour (McHugh), p. 97.

88 Léon-Dufour (McHugh), p. 234.

89 Léon-Dufour (McHugh), pp. 243, 245.

90 Léon-Dufour (McHugh), p. 262.

91 Léon-Dufour (McHugh), p. 270.

92 Léon-Dufour (McHugh), p. 242.

93 Léon-Dufour (McHugh), pp. 274–275.

natural historical facts about the life of Jesus, leaving faith to provide the rest. Léon-Dufour concludes: "History provides the facts and a question; faith provides the interpretation of these facts and the answer to the question."[94] Bultmann claimed that none of the supernatural happenings reported in the Gospels are historical facts; Léon-Dufour, in his book, does not find any of the supernatural happenings to be verifiable historically. By using the historical method of Bultmann, he comes largely to the historical conclusions of Bultmann. He does stop before concluding with Bultmann that the supernatural events are entirely fictitious, but he can offer no historical evidence that any of the reported supernatural happenings ever took place. Bultmann, in his exegetical work and in his later program of demythologizing, asked historical critics to reject what he considered the fictitious cate-chetical adornments of the gospels as being the mythology that they are, and to turn to the real existence of their own subjectivity as the way to be honest Christians today. Léon-Dufour does not turn to his own subjectivity; rather he gives his readers the choice of embracing or not embracing Jesus in faith. But who is Jesus? If Jesus is the merely human figure resulting from the "unadorned facts" of Léon-Dufour's inquiry, what is there in Him to attract the faith of a critical observer? And, if a person is disposed to believe the supernatural facts about Jesus, what need does he have of Léon-Dufour's critical research, especially when this research only raises doubts with regard to what he is asked to believe? Bultmann claims that for a critically informed modern man to embrace the adorned Christ of faith would be to follow a primitive pre-conceptual instinct and to revert to an obsolete world-view. Léon-Dufour does not address this problem. Léon-Dufour certainly does not draw the devastating conclusions of the demythologizing epitomized in paragraph 18 above, but, while he raises many of the same historical questions that Bultmann has raised, he provides at best weak answers to these questions. Solid answers there are, but they are to be found largely in the traditional teaching of the Church and in the works of traditional Catholic theologians and exegetes, of whom not one is quoted or referred to in the whole of Léon-Dufour's book. And the answers still lacking to the array of new questions created by historical critical research are waiting to be found too by the use of a sounder historical method than that now in use by Léon-Dufour and other Catholic historical critics.

---

94 Léon-Dufour (McHugh), p. 275.

Part III. Anton Vögtle, and Ugo Lattanzi

Living Tradition 115 (January 2005 abridged)

31. Anton Vögtle is of the opinion that Rudolf Bultmann's program of demythologizing is a concentrated synthesis of an overall theological labor oriented in this determinate direction from the very beginning.[95] Following indications given earlier by Heinrich Ott,[96] he sees this program as being based mainly upon four philosophical and three historical presuppositions, but also upon other secondary premises of different kinds and of varying origin, such as historical criticism, existentialism, and Lutheran theology. The four philosophical premises which he systematically uses are: a) *a radical dualism of non-world and world;* b) *a double concept of history and historical knowledge;* c) *a particular notion of "pre-understanding" and "self-understanding;,"* and d) *a double concept of time.* Bultmann's three historical premises have to do with *a) the Jesus of history; b) the origin of Christianity;* and *c) the way to offset the results of historical criticism.*

32. *A radical dualism of non-world and world.* Bultmann maintains that the true meaning of the New Testament mythology does not pertain to any of the mental objects and images in which it is presented. He defines mythology as "the conception which makes the non-worldly and divine seem worldly and human, that which pertains to the other side seem to be on this side."[97] Vögtle points out that Bultmann's concept of myth as being false in imagery but true in existential meaning can stand up only to the extent that one accepts his existentialist premises and his radical distinction between "world" and "non-world."[98] For instance, Bultmann says, if we postulate an "act of God" happening in this world, we are illicitly trying to bring "the other side" over to "this side," but we are left to wonder what exactly he means by "the other side." I believe that what he means is "the

---

95 Antonio Vögtle, "Rivelazione e mito," in *Problemi e orientamenti di teologia dogmatica,* vol. I (Milan, 1957), 827–960 [henceforth referred to as *AVRM*], pp. 830–831.

96 Heinrich Ott, *Geschichte und Heilsgeschichte in der Theologie* Rudolf Bultmanns (Tübingen, 1955). Ott proposed a systematic analysis of Bultmann's theology, but only in later works did he attempt to develop the general indications he had given in this book.

97 Bultmann, in H.W. Bartsch, ed., *Kerygma and Myth,* vol. 1 (London: SPCK, 1953), p. 10.

98 Vögtle, *AVRM,* p. 837.

other side of reality," that is, of what we commonly conceive of as being real, and this is why he has divided the Gospel accounts into literary genres, that is, into genres of fiction. Bultmann is arguing from the modernist viewpoint that all of the objects of religion are imaginary, and he is arguing against the tendency of religious people to ascribe reality to fictitious ideas, such as the idea of an act of God. But if the recorded acts of God really took place and are part of what we know as reality, then Bultmann's application of non-world to the Gospel accounts falls.

33. Entering into the background of Bultmann's idea of non-world is the historic total separation of faith and reason in Lutheran theology, which gave rise, on the one hand, to the Rationalism in the liberal Lutheran tradition, and, on the other hand, to the Fideism by which one believes contrary to and in spite of what one considers to be the results of science and the dictates of human reason. Lutheran fideism has spawned belief in a religious world totally different from the real world of science, history, and common sense, and it is against this belief that Bultmann is reacting in his appeal to modern man, not by rejecting it entirely but by transposing it into the existentialist experience of one's own authentic being. And to accomplish this Bultmann advances a radical distinction between two kinds of reality, the *Realität* of science, history, and common sense, and the *Wirklichkeit* of the existential encounter. Thus, in taking away all that is supernatural and miraculous in the Gospel accounts, he clothes the existentialist experience with a substitute reality of its own. Hence, it is obvious that, to restore Christian faith to its normal state, it is necessary to affirm the real existence of the supernatural events in the Gospel narratives and to refute the alleged reality of Bultmann's existential experience. Catholics of today are surrounded by modernist invitations to doubt the reality of the objects of faith. Our first reaction to these doubts should be to reaffirm over and over again in thought and in prayer the reality of the existence of God, the living presence of Jesus in Heaven and in the Holy Eucharist, the knowledge that our prayers can be heard, that we have well-founded hope of reaching Heaven, our rational fear of falling into Hell, if we flag in our efforts, and all the other objects of faith. Then, to the best of our time and ability, we should look and pray for the answers to these questions.

34. *A double concept of history and historical knowledge.* Vögtle notes that Bultmann first distinguishes the knowledge of history from the knowledge of nature. Then he makes a radical distinction between a lower level of

historical knowledge, which he calls in German *Historie*, and a higher level, which he calls *Geschichte*. Following the philosophy of Martin Heidegger, he restricts "true historicity" to the existentialist notion of "authentic existence," which is "being in the state of decision, deciding and being able ever to decide anew."[99] Bultmann thus divides objectivizing-cosmological thought and existential thought into two mutually exclusive fields.[100] He applies this division of historical knowledge in a preeminent way to the objective figure of Jesus and to the subjective state of the individual believer. Vögtle reasons, following Ott, that objective historical events can have meaning only to the extent that they are real (*wirklich*), and, therefore, that Bultmann's distinction of two opposing kinds of historical knowledge, the simple and inauthentic knowledge of past events and the authentic act of existential decision, does not hold up.[101]

35. Bultmann's incorrect way of distinguishing two radically different kinds of history and historicity is a challenge to the rest of us to make the correct distinctions regarding historical knowledge, and it is the lack of correct distinctions that has both helped to hinder a full response to demythologizing and has enabled Bultmann's program to gain such great notoriety. Catholic historical critics seldom work with a complete set of historical concepts or even with a precise definition of history or of what they call "scientific exegesis." Thus, for instance, it is inadequate for David Stanley, following C.H. Dodd, to define history as (something) "consisting of events which are of the nature of occurrences *plus* meaning."[102] This is obviously not an essential definition. To examine scientifically Bultmann's double concept of history, it is necessary to work from a framework of the true genera and species of history, beginning from the definition of history as "the past as such," and proceeding from a first distinction between real history and fictional history through a second distinction of human history from natural history to a further distinction of historical chronology from historical explanation, and then we come to see where "occurrences plus meaning" comes into view.[103] If we take "science," in its essential definition,

---

99 Vögtle, *AVRM*, pp. 838–839.

100 Vögtle, *AVRM*, pp. 839–841.

101 Vögtle, *AVRM*, pp. 842–843.

102 D. Stanley, "The Gospel as Salvation History," in John J. Heaney, ed., *Faith, Reason, and the Gospels* (Westminster, MD: The Newman Press, 1965), p. 254, quoting C.H. Dodd, *History and the Gospel* (London, 1938), p. 36.

103 See Article 6, "The First Dichotomies of Historical Science," in J.F. McCarthy, *The*

to be "the knowledge of the real as such," then "historical science" has to do with the real past as real, and it must keep the use of the concept of reality constantly in mind as it examines the past as such.[104] And this is why Bultmann's definition of historicity as "being in a state of decision" cannot be correct, since it excludes by definition the past. Being in a state of decision has its importance, not because it is true historicity, but inasmuch as it is the act of love for God and neighbor, as objects of our will, exercised over and over again.

36. *A particular notion of "pre-understanding" and "self-understanding."* Bultmann observes that every interpretation is guided by a certain "putting of the question," in accordance with the particular interest of the interpreter, and that this putting of the question is in itself a kind of *pre-understanding*.[105] Bultmann agrees with Robin Collingwood in saying that the object of historical knowledge is not a mere object outside of the mind that knows it, but is rather "an activity of thought which can be known only in so far as the knowing mind re-enacts it and knows itself as so doing."[106] Vögtle points out that Bultmann divides human understanding into "pre-understanding" and "self-understanding" in terms of the Existentialism of Martin Heidegger, and he thinks that the jump from pre-understanding to understanding in the theory of Bultmann is unexplainable.[107] I think that the factor which must be brought into sight here is that of the mental framework necessary for all understanding. If we define "understanding" as "the knowledge of one reality in relation to another reality," then, to understand a remote object, we must see it in the framework of a proximate, or intermediate, mental object. Where both Bultmann and Collingwood go wrong is in failing to see the objectivity of the intervening mental framework and in thus dissolving understanding of the object into "understanding" of one's own subjective self.

37. *A double concept of time.* In Vögtle's estimation, Heinrich Ott has found the key idea of all of Bultmann's philosophical principles to be his

---

Science of Historical Theology (Rockford, IL: TAN Books and Publishers, 2nd printing, 1991), pp. 83–86.

104 See "The Locus of Specialized Science in Human Consciousness" and "The Locus of Historical Science in Scientific Consciousness," in *The Science of Historical Theology,*" pp. 46–56 and 60–63.

105 R. Bultmann, *History and Eschatology,* (New York: Harper Torchbooks, 1957), p. 113.

106 Bultmann, *History and Eschatology,* p. 119.

107 Vögtle, *AVRM,* pp. 851–852.

double concept of time.[108] Bultmann reduces everything that has taken place or will take place in worldly time to "that which is subjected to the law of the past," and he accordingly makes a fundamental distinction between "time as flux" and "time as now": worldly time comes to an end in the now of the decision in faith. And Bultmann admits that this decision to open oneself to one's existential future is a pure experience that cannot be explained even on the level of existentialist analysis. I believe that this kind of existential decision is not a jump to any real understanding, but is simply a turning away from reality into egoistic fantasy of a nihilist bent. In this existential "decision in faith," no event ever takes place, because, according to Bultmann's own explanation, the grasping for one's authentic self-existence never takes effect, but must be repeated unsuccessfully over and over again. I think that this is an existentialist dream to which has been added the Lutheran principle that the human will, being totally corrupt, is incapable of any good act and yet, through faith and faith alone, its state of sin can be disregarded by God, although it can never be removed. Hence, part of the solution to this problem of Bultmann is to put straight the Lutheran doctrine of justification by faith alone. The true "now" of Christian faith is the act of turning in repentance to the love of God, which is repeated over and over and with the effect of purification and growth in holiness. Then, the ultimate "now" of Christian existence is the eternity of beatitude in Heaven.

38. *Three historical premises.* Vögtle remarks that Bultmann's demythologizing depends in part upon the results of his historical critical interpretation of the Synoptic Gospels and the Gospel of John. From this research came forth a *Jesus of history* stripped of all of his supernatural attributes and works. This same research led Bultmann to postulate *the rise of Christianity*, not from a founding by Jesus, but from the faith of the primitive Christian community. Bultmann both presumed and concluded that Jesus first became the Messiah in the faith of the early Palestinian Christian community, and then was elevated to the level of the divine in the subsequent Hellenistic Christian community.[109] Finally, Bultmann maintains that these negative findings about Jesus cannot harm Christian faith, because *authentic Christian faith* is not based upon belief in anything historically objective but only upon the decision to choose one's own authentic existence.[110] Among the principal defects in the program of

---

108 Vögtle, *AVRM*, p. 852.

109 Vögtle, *AVRM*, pp. 861–863.

110 Vögtle, *AVRM*, p. 865.

demythologizing, Vögtle notes Bultmann's lack of conceptual exactness, his idea that mythology, properly understood, is necessary and legitimate for religion, his denial of the historical documentation regarding the life of Jesus on earth, his idea that sin has produced a total break between this world and any acts of God, and his faulty use of exegetical method. Vögtle adds that Bultmann's exposition becomes particularly forced, obscure, and unconvincing precisely in those places where he tries to demonstrate the need of an act of divine love for the attainment of "authentic existence."[111] I agree with Vögtle and I contend that the way to remedy these defects is to turn away from the use of historical criticism and revert to the Catholic exegetical tradition, updated in terms of the neo-patristic method. As I remarked in my longer review of Anton Vögtle's article, Catholic historical critics are notoriously inept at defending attacks against the "core" of dogmatic truth underlying the Gospels that they say abides the stripping process of their historical method.

The Response of Ugo Lattanzi

39. In his analysis of the demythologizing of Rudolf Bultmann, Ugo Lattanzi distinguishes two sets of controlling principles: *postulates* which are expressly assumed as the basis of theoretical constructions, and *presuppositions* which are used only implicitly. He says that Bultmann expressly uses *a theological postulate, an exegetical postulate, and a sociological postulate.*

40. As a *theological postulate,* Lattanzi observes, Bultmann bases the relation of the world to God, not upon the analogy of being, but upon *a radical opposition between the world and God,* not admitting of any causal relationship that could be recognized by reason, and so, the world is taken to be an absolutely closed and autonomous system.[112] With this postulate, Bultmann excludes any reasonable doctrine about God and any doctrine revealed by God. In addition, he is obliged to speak of the "act of God" as being completely hidden and undiscoverable by human reason, and Christian faith is conceived, not as an adherence of any kind to truth revealed by God, but rather as a leap into "non-world" having no need for

---

111 Vögtle, *AVRM*, p. 949–951.

112 U. Lattanzi, "I sinottici e la Chiesa secondo R. Bultmann" in *Miscellanea Antonio Piolanti,* vol. I (Rome, 1963 [*Lateranum,* n.s., 29th year], 141–169, henceforth referred to as *ULSC*]), p. 150.

justification on a historical basis.[113] Lattanzi notes that Bultmann's leap of faith is merely an act of pure subjectivity referring to nothing outside of itself.[114] We have noted this postulate earlier (cf. chapter 10 above, paragraphs 99–100).

41. Lattanzi finds that Bultmann reasons from an *exegetical postulate* that the message of Jesus was exclusively eschatological, that is, "of the occurrences with which our known world comes to its end."[115] From this principle Bultmann, in his form-critical analyses, selects as historically authentic only those words attributed to Jesus which point to the future, and he assumes that the early Christian community, immersed in the same eschatological preoccupations, had no interest in narrating the historical facts about Jesus. But, as Lattanzi points out, the historical evidence is against this assumption of Bultmann, as is clear from what is said in 1Cor. 15:3–8.[116] And, to me, this *is* clear, but today, because so many of the conclusions of Bultmann's form-critical analyses have gained acceptance among Catholic exegetes and theologians, it has now become necessary to reinforce St. Paul's testimony by undertaking a point-by-point and line-by-line refutation of the false exegetical conclusions that Bultmann has bestowed upon contemporary readers of the Bible.

42. Lattanzi ascribes to the influence of a *sociological postulate* Bultmann's tracing of the accounts presented in the Gospels to the fertile imagination of the anonymous Christian community, and he points out that there is not, in fact, a single clear instance in the whole of the Gospels of a myth created by the early Church and inserted into the Gospel tradition. But the sad fact is that, while there cannot be demonstrated in the whole of the Gospels a single fictitious miracle story, event, or prophecy after the event, form-critics are claiming today that the Gospels are woven of such fabrications. Hence the urgent need to challenge the results of form-critical analysis and to produce a better interpretation of the Gospels by the use of a better and more correct method.

---

113 Lattanzi, *ULSC*, p. 153.

114 Lattanzi, *ULSC*, pp. 156–158.

115 Bultmann, *History and Eschatology*, p. 23. "Today it is commonly accepted that the reign of God which Jesus proclaimed is the eschatological reign. The only point in dispute is whether Jesus thought that the reign of God was immediately imminent, indeed already dawning in his exorcisms, or whether he thought that it was already present in his person—what today is called 'realized eschatology'" (ibid., p. 31.)

116 Lattanzi, *ULSC*, pp. 158–160.

43. According to Lattanzi, the first of Bultmann's presuppositions is his assumption of *the spontaneous consolidation of the followers of Jesus into the Church as an eschatological community* after his death. Lattanzi claims that for this Bultmann is entirely indebted to Alfred Loisy, one of the founders of the Modernism that was rampant in the Catholic Church at the beginning of the twentieth century. And the second of Bultmann's presuppositions is his assumption that *only later came the decision of the eschatological community to endure as a historical phenomenon.*[117] For this assumption Bultmann depends upon his other postulate that the early Christians were at first so engrossed in the idea of the coming end of the world that they had no interest in establishing an enduring Church. It is Lattanzi's conclusion that Bultmann merely assumes but does not prove any of his postulates or presuppositions, and that a more faithful study of the Gospels would have shown that the hope of the early Christians was based, not on their hope for the immediate return of Jesus on the clouds of heaven, but on their awareness of the historical truth of the words and deeds of Jesus and of his bodily Resurrection from the dead.[118]

44. The time has come for a new deal in methods of interpreting Sacred Scripture. Writers like Anton Vögtle and Ugo Lattanzi have led the way in the task of providing a full response to the demythologizing of Rudolf Bultmann by critically analyzing the results of form-criticism so as to produce a neo-patristic interpretation that is consistent with Catholic exegetical tradition and at the same time makes room for new insights into the meanings of the sacred text. The questions raised by Bultmann deserve a better answer than what we have been hearing from Catholic form-critical exegetes and theologians. Bultmann has called upon proclaimers of the Gospel message to ask the right questions of the inspired text, that is, to examine and be aware of the principles that they use as their mental frame of reference, an exercise that has been egregiously lacking in most modern Catholic biblical scholarship. The first step, then, in a fuller response of Catholics to the challenges of Bultmann should be a clarification of the Catholic frame of reference and a refutation of those other frames of reference that do not lead to correct conclusions. Take, for

---

117 "The problem of eschatology grew out of the fact that the expected end of the world failed to arrive, that the Son of Man did not appear in the clouds of heaven, that history went on, and that the eschatological community could not fail to recognize that it had become a historical phenomenon and that the Christian faith had taken on the shape of a new religion" (Bultmann, *History and Eschatology*, p. 38).

118 Lattanzi, *ULSC*, pp. 163–166.

instance, the "existential encounter" proposed by Bultmann as the modern man's act of faith. Since by very definition it has no object, it is not an encounter at all, but it challenges us to ascertain what is the object of a true encounter reaching down to the very core of our existence, and this is the encounter in prayer with the objects of faith. It is an encounter with God as He has revealed Himself to us; it is an encounter with God as the essential object of our prayer, and it is an encounter with other things that are objects related to God, such as the humanity of Jesus, the Blessed Virgin Mary, and all the saints. So a full response to the demythologizing of Bultmann requires a firm understanding that prayer to God is possible, because God has placed Himself at our disposal for this purpose. We locate the true existential encounter of faith in the tropological sense of Sacred Scripture, inasmuch as the impact of the inspired word upon the believer is the subjective result of the objective truth and power that resides in the inspired word itself.

45. A fuller response to the demythologizing of the New Testament requires also a more consistent defense of the historical truth of the Gospels, in keeping with the tradition of the Fathers of the Church and of all Catholic exegetes and theologians before the ingress of historical criticism in the 1890s. In this renewed apologetic must be included more exact definitions of historical science and historical method. The New Testament literary genres proposed by Bultmann and followed by all form-critics do not meet the standards of historical science, because they are not based on a proper employment of the concept of reality or of the rules for exegetes laid down by Pope Pius XII in his encyclical *Divino afflante Spiritu*. One can read whole treatises of literary analysis of the Gospels by Catholic writers without there ever being expressed the question of whether the accounts they are considering are real or fictitious, whereas for scientific study this question should pervade the whole discussion. The form-critical literary genres, as used by Catholic writers, are not analytic in that they are not the result of proper distinctions of categories from the broader to the narrower. Catholic historical critics have persistently claimed that Pope Pius XII approved of their forms in *Divino afflante Spiritu*, where he says: "For the ancient peoples of the East, in order to express their ideas, did not always employ those forms or kinds of speech which we use today; but rather those used by the men of their times and countries. [...] The investigation carried out on this point during the past forty or fifty years with greater care and diligence than ever before has more clearly shown what forms of expression were used in those far-off times, whether in poetic description

or in the formulation of laws and rules of life or in recording the facts and events of history."[119] But note that the literary forms mentioned here are the analytical categories used by the Fathers of the Church and not any of the novel literary forms assumed by form-critics, such as "myths," "legends," "miracle stories," "I-sayings," "conflict and didactic sayings," "prophetic and apocalyptic sayings," "angelic appearances," etc. There is no doubt that the Sacred Scriptures contain literary categories in the classical sense, and that they also contain "certain fixed ways of expounding and narrating, certain definite idioms, especially of a kind peculiar to the Semitic tongues," of which "none is excluded from the Sacred Books, provided the way of speaking adopted in no wise contradicts the holiness and truth of God."[120] To say that the Sacred Scriptures present fiction as though it were truth would be to contradict the truth of God, and that is what the special literary forms of Bultmann and company presume to do.

46. Over the past century Catholic historical critics have assiduously looked for *the* meaning of respective verses and passages of Sacred Scripture, and only recently have they begun to realize that these texts could have and probably do have more than one meaning. What has been neglected throughout is the genuine spiritual sense of the inspired writings, even though Pope Pius XII asked that it be brought out where he said: "Let Catholic exegetes, then, disclose and expound this spiritual significance, intended and ordained by God, with the care which the dignity of the divine word demands; but let them scrupulously refrain from proposing as the genuine meaning of Sacred Scripture other figurative senses."[121] Thus, Pope Pius XII warned against the proposing of figurative meanings that are not really in the text, but at the same time he also asked for attention to the figurative meanings that are in the text. The task still remains of systematically discerning throughout the whole text of the Bible, in keeping with the tradition of the Fathers of the Church and of the great medieval theologians, first the literal sense of each respective verse or passage and then of going on to determine the spiritual sense or senses of the same verse or passage, in the light of the Four Senses as an adequate framework of study, and as required

---

119 Pope Pius XII, *Divino afflante Spiritu, (Enchiridion Biblicum 558): in Rome and the Study of Scripture,* 7th ed., Abbey Press, St. Meinrad, Indiana, 1964), p. 98. Or in Claudia Carlen, ed., *The Papal Encyclicals, Divino afflante Spiritu,* no. 36.

120 *Divino afflante Spiritu,* in *Rome and the Study of Scripture* (EB 559), or in Carlen, ibid.

121 *Divino afflante Spiritu,* in *Rome and the Study of Scripture* (EB 553), or in Carlen, loc. cit., no. 27.

by the *Catechism of the Catholic Church*.[122] The neo-patristic method is the effective way to make the proper distinctions, by its use of an adequate theory of history and of the best of exegetical tools. There is much to be gained by a reversion to the traditional Catholic approach to the interpretation of Sacred Scripture. *First of all*, it will end the vain search for a fully Catholic version of a historical critical approach that grew up outside of the Church and is replete with rationalist postulates and presuppositions that Catholic historical critics have never succeeded in eliminating so as completely to reconcile the method with the fullness of Catholic faith and devotion. *Secondly*, the attention that the neo-patristic method pays to the results of the historical critical method, both inside and outside of the Catholic community, will itself result in new positive insights into the Sacred Scriptures and in an integrating of these insights into the treasury of understanding contained in the writings of the Fathers and Doctors of the Church, in the liturgy, and in the traditional spirituality of the Church. *In the third place*, it will reinstate Catholic biblical scholarship in the position of the leading academic witness to the historic message of the Gospels, in place of being, as it is now, a minority group of scholars trying, on the one hand, to catch up with the thought and conclusions of some liberal non-Catholic scholars, and, on the other hand, striving, inconsistently with the historical critical method, to avoid logical conclusions that contradict the doctrinal tradition and dogmas of the Catholic Church.

47. Historical critics call "scientific" their method of exegesis, but they do not have a clear idea of what the word "scientific" means. A neo-patristic critique of the historical critical method must begin from a definition of the words "science" and "scientific." Natural scientists are notoriously poor at defining their own subject, and logicians, too, usually fall short of their aim. Common attempts to define the word "science," such as "*a body of universally applicable truths, formulated by the intellect as the result and expression of innumerable inductions and deductions*" or as "*a definite body of truths, derived from reasoned demonstrations of causes and reduced to a system.*"[123] are workable for many purposes, but they are not sufficient to resolve the unanswered questions raised by Bultmann and his followers. They don't provide for a science of history or for what may truly be termed "scientific exegesis." Certainly the science of history is, in some way, a definite body of truths, but how are these truths universally applicable in

---

122 See the *Catechism of the Catholic Church*, nos. 115–119.

123 Celestine Bittle, *Reality and the Mind* (New York: Bruce, 1936), p. 10.

historical science or resulting from innumerable inductions and deductions? Or does historical science even result from innumerable inductions and deductions or from reasoned demonstrations of causes? In order to be able to call a historical method "scientific," it is necessary first to determine clearly whether the things mentioned in common definitions of science are everything that is essentially characteristic of all science and then what is specifically characteristic of historical science. I believe that the needed fuller Catholic answer to the demythologizing of Rudolf Bultmann must begin from adequate definitions of these elements and then must proceed logically step by step to the many other concepts and techniques in a valid and reliable historical method.

Chapter 12

Critique of a Form-Critical
Reading of Matthew One

Living Tradition 130 (July 2007)

Jean Daniélou, The Infancy Narratives, translated by Rosemary Sheed (New York: Herder and Herder, 1968) – (original edition: Les Evangiles de l'Enfance (Paris: Editions de Seuil, 1967)

1. The neo-patristic approach to the interpretation of Sacred Scripture does not ignore existing form-critical interpretations of the same; it reads them critically. In undertaking a neo-patristic interpretation of the first chapter of the Gospel according to St. Matthew, I have chosen to begin with a critique of Jean Daniélou's widely circulated analysis, because it is typical of Catholic form-critical renditions and it serves to illustrate the difference between the two approaches. Matthew 1 has two basic parts: the Matthaean genealogy and the angelic appearance to Joseph. In Daniélou's view, the announcement by the angel to Joseph in Matt. 1:21 "was not intended to inform him that Mary had conceived virginally – that he already knew," but that he should assume legal paternity for Jesus (p. 40). Daniélou finds that these two parts thus present a perfect historical parallelism and a perfect theological parallelism. Historically, they narrate that Joseph, by his adoption of Jesus, made Him a legal member of the family of David, and that Joseph was persuaded to adopt Jesus, even though he felt unworthy to become the step-father of the Messiah. The problem of the chapter, according to Daniélou, must be to explain how Jesus could be of the family of David, even though He was not actually Joseph's son, and so Joseph's adoption of Jesus *in spite of the Virginal Conception* "is in fact the point of the account" (p. 41). Daniélou had been convinced

by Xavier Léon- Dufour (*Etudes d'Evangile*, p. 79) that Jesus was not the son of David through Mary, seeing that "we have no proof that Mary was descended from David, despite all the many efforts of well-intentioned critics" (p. 16—see a reply to this statement below, no. 11.) And then Daniélou says that he is indebted to Anton Vögtle for the observation that also theologically Matthew presents a parallelism between the creation of Adam and the Incarnation of the divine Word as follows: the first part of the chapter shows Jesus as having come at the end of the Old Testament to inaugurate a new humanity, while the second part shows how the genesis of the new Adam is the work of the Holy Spirit (pp. 12–13).

2. Daniélou makes a methodological distinction between "what is historical fact" in the Gospel text and "those elements whose purpose is to interpret the significance of these facts" (p. 7). To show that events in the life of Jesus had a divine content, he says, the New Testament writers used literary forms such as "the *midrash*, which recalled the lives of the major Old Testament figures, the *pesher*, which showed the events of the present as a fulfillment of past prophecies, and the *apocalypse*, which showed them as pre-existing in God's eternal design" (p. 8). In comparing the annunciation to Joseph in Matt. 1:18–25 with the annunciation to Mary in Luke 1:26–38, he says, we must distinguish between the historical fact of the revelation given to Mary and the way in which the evangelist presents it in terms of Mary's faith, which faith is also one of the most basic elements in the account. And, he adds, there are in the account "certain features borrowed from earlier biblical stories" (pp. 23–24).

3. The scene of the annunciation to Mary, Daniélou points out, seems in general most likely to be a *midrash* of Isaiah 9, dating back to the early Christian community. "That certainly is what Bultmann seems to prove" (p. 34). *Midrashim* are amplifications of historical fact in which acts of God are presented in the guise of extraordinary phenomena. Among the fictitious elements in Luke's story of the annunciation to Mary, Daniélou notes the following (pp. 33–37):

the appearance of an angel (*always an invention and here largely taken from the Book of Daniel*);

"Hail, full of grace ... (*borrowed from an Old Testament passage, such as Zeph. 3:14–17 or Dan. 9:21–27, and here put onto the lips of an angel*);

Fear not, Mary ... (*probably borrowed from Dan. 9:23 and presented here as words of an angel, but based on the actual revelation to Mary*);

"He will be great and will be called the Son of the most High" (*invented by Luke*);

"and the Lord God will give to him the throne of David his father ..."
(*a midrash invented on the basis especially of Isaiah 9:6–7*);

"The Holy Spirit will come upon you" (*a midrash derived perhaps from Gen. 1:2 and Isa. 32:15 to depict the Christian belief that this child was the new Adam and his birth was the beginning of the new creation*);

"and the power of the most High will overshadow you" (*a midrash based on Ex. 40:32–36 and adapted here to show the belief that Yahweh was present in the child*);

"and therefore the child to be born will be called holy, the Son of God" (*a title placed here on the lips of the angel by Christian circles of Luke's time to express their belief in the divinity of Christ*).

4. Daniélou observes, once again, that the point of the episode in Matthew 1 is not to tell of a Virginal Conception. Truly, he allows, in verse 23, Matthew does cite the prophecy in Isa. 7:14: "Behold, a virgin shall be with child ..."—but, he adds, Matthew's words are just an adaptation of the original statement, which referred to the birth of Hezekiah and not to a Virginal Conception at all. The opening words of the passage are "Hear then, O house of David," showing that the purpose of the prophecy was simply to foretell the birth of someone from the house of David. So, he reasons, this quote in Matthew is a free manipulation of an Old Testament text by early Jewish Christians who felt it was their right to project onto the Old Testament affirmations of the New Testament (pp. 47–52). (Let me interject that, while the birth of Hezekiah may have some secondary relation to the text, it was not a "sign.") It is Daniélou's studied opinion that Joseph, being a "just man," when he found that Mary was with child before they had come together, in his great esteem for her holiness, realized spontaneously that this had to be a Virginal Conception through the power of the Holy Spirit (cf. p. 40).[1] Matthew, he says, adorns this realization by placing appropriate words on the lips of a fictitious angel. And "You shall call his name Jesus" is then Matthew's expression of the fact that Joseph did legally adopt Jesus, while the words "for he shall save his people from their sins," are Matthew's theological reflection on the meaning of the name Jesus (p. 47)

5. Did then Mary in historical fact virginally conceive the Messiah, and, if so, how could we know that it happened? Daniélou accepts as a

---

1 Jerome and Origen thought that Joseph wanted to "put Mary away quietly" because he had read Isa. 7:14 and he now felt unworthy to cohabit with her sanctity and divinely instilled pregnancy. But this is a minor opinion. Augustine, Chrysostom, Rabanus Maurus, and others say that Joseph feared that Mary had sinned and wanted to deal with the situation in as kind a manner as possible, and this is the more obvious reading of the text. See Aquinas, *Super Evangelium S. Matthaei Lectura,* at Matt. 1:19.

fact of nature what is only an unproven assumption of rationalist form-critics, namely, that angelic appearances are a fictional genre, because, they say, angels do not exist. And this assumption is contrary to the teaching of the Catholic Church (*Catechism of the Catholic Church* 328, 333). Earlier Daniélou had published a book on angels in the writings of the Fathers,[2] but in this book he simply presented statements of the Fathers without ever addressing the question of whether the objects of their belief were real or not. Revealingly, in his Introduction to this earlier work, Daniélou remarks: "There came a time, however, when ... the attention of churchmen was centered elsewhere and a lively interest in the world of created spirits was no longer either possible or necessary. Thus, much of what the Fathers treated with special attention later theological developments have bypassed."[3] And in his *Infancy Narratives* it is painfully evident that the Angel Gabriel is for him of little theological interest. He defends the belief that the idea of the Virginal Conception of Jesus is based upon historical fact, but the form-critical method that he uses obscures and nullifies the point that he is making, because the method *presupposes* fiction where he would like to discover fact. Daniélou maintains that the Virginal Conception "was accepted from the first as incontestable fact," because otherwise the whole episode of the annunciation to Joseph in Matthew 1 would lose its point, namely, "how Jesus can be a descendant of David *despite* the virgin birth.... Nor," he adds, "is there any reason to doubt that the episode rests on a historical basis" (p. 41).

6. But in keeping with what Daniélou has eliminated in the angelic appearances in Matthew 1 and Luke 1, there *is* great reason to doubt whether the Virginal Conception ever took place. The form-critical method comes from a rationalistic and naturalistic tradition which excludes in principle any supernatural happening, and it is on this principle that the angelic appearances have been relegated to the sphere of fiction. It is certainly difficult to imagine how the revelation of the Virginal Conception and the Incarnation could have occurred, if it did not take place as described in Matthew and Luke. Daniélou avers that the early Christians believed in it, but, for the founders of form-criticism, such as Hermann Gunkel and Rudolf Bultmann, Christian belief is just the imaginary product of a primitive and pre-conceptual believing community. Hence, when Daniélou uses the form-critical method to analyze these passages of the Gospels, the

---

2 J. Daniélou, Eng. translation, *The Angels and Their Mission* (Westminster, MD: Newman, 1957).

3 Daniélou, *The Angels*, p. ix.

burden of proof is on him to show that the Virginal Conception really and historically took place, and even more so, the Incarnation of the eternal Son of God. But Daniélou does not attempt to do so. As any realistic thinker will admit, if the angelic appearances in the accounts are imaginary, if all the words were invented and placed on the lips of an imaginary angel, if the prophecy in Isaiah was twisted to fit a belief, and if all of this is to be considered an *honest and legitimate* means of expressing Christian faith, then there was nothing to prevent Christian believers from inventing the Virginal Conception as well. As a believing Catholic, Daniélou accepts the dogma of the Incarnation, but, as a teacher, he is forced to depend on the solid and pre-form-critical faith of his Catholic readership to accept the historicity of these two physical facts in spite of the damage that he is doing here to the evidence. To say this does not suggest doubt regarding Daniélou's Catholic faith, but there is something seriously missing in the kind of scholarship that he here presents.

7. If, as Daniélou avers, Rudolf Bultmann has "proved" that the scene of the Annunciation to Mary in Luke is a *midrash* of Isaiah 9, Bultmann has also "proved" that the idea of the Virginal Conception is a Hellenistic fantasy that was added later to an originally Palestinian report, according to which an angel simply promised to Joseph that his son would be the Messiah. Again, according to Bultmann, the Annunciation to Mary in Luke is a Hellenistic elaboration of an older story which had it that an angel appeared to Mary and simply told her that she would be the mother of the Messiah. By using Bultmann as an authority and then not attempting to refute Bultmann's denial of the historical truth of the Virginal Conception and the Incarnation, Daniélou loses his argument that either of these ever really took place. It is a pity that Catholic form-critics have spent so much time adapting Bultmann's methods to their scholarship and so little time refuting the obvious fallacies in his reasoning.[4]

8. The idea of the impossibility of miracles and the consequent impossibility of any objectively real miraculous accounts is a naturalistic presupposition of Bultmann's form-critical method. Also presupposed is the idea, following along the lines of Émil Durkheim's theory of the basic difference between primitive societies and modern societies, that the early Christian community was a primitive society whose instinctive faith-responses and stories were always dependent upon ideas already traditional in their milieu. Hence, Bultmann looked for ideas existing in

---

4 Cf. R. Bultmann, *History of the Synoptic Tradition* (English translation, Oxford: Blackwell, 1963), pp. 291–292, 295–296.

their Old Testament tradition as sources for the unoriginal stories that they would have gone on to elaborate and adapt to their new faith. Now, this presupposition is not in keeping with good historical theory, because true and valid historical method takes the facts as it finds them, miraculous events included, if they come along, without presuming to determine in advance on a naturalistic basis what the facts could or could not have been. And the idea that the early Christians were intellectually incapable of originating their own stories and could not even distinguish clearly between the real and the imaginary is contrary to historical fact. Not only does an unbiased reading of the biblical text show the constant presence of a distinction between fact and fancy, but this can also be shown from sources outside of the Scriptures. And authentic Christian faith is a faith whose objects are historical facts.

9. Since facts are the bedrock of real meaning, historical science validly distinguishes between the basic chronology of an account and the historical explanation that accompanies it. Because biblical history is an inspired object of faith, it is necessary for faith seeking understanding to presume the historical truth of a Scriptural account unless the sacred writer explicitly or implicitly indicates that it is not his intention to express historical truth. Doubts do arise when apparent contradictions are encountered, and these do need to be resolved, but by correct logical and historical analysis. The *midrash*-theory of Gospel interpretation excludes in advance the intention of the Gospel writers to record the historical facts in the accounts that they give, and it turns historiographic art into fictional fantasy. It assumes a novelistic approach of the Gospel writers without first having analyzed on the level of historical science whether this novelistic approach is scientifically justified and without assessing (especially on the part of Catholic scholars) the damage that such an approach will do to their faith and ours. An important distinction ignored by Daniélou and by all form-critics is the difference between the *finis operis* and the *finis operantis* of a work produced. The *finis operis* is the purpose of the work, while the *finis operantis* is the purpose of the worker. The *finis operis* of St. Matthew and St. Luke was to record the historical facts that took place. The *finis operantis* of the same was to instruct the faith of believers. God the Holy Spirit was fully capable of presenting through the inspired writers deep patterns of meaning embedded in a series of true historical facts in order to convey the truths that He wished to communicate.[5]

---

5 Daniélou published a book about history, titled *Essai sur le Mystère de l'Histoire* (Editions du Seuil—Eng. trans., *The Lord of History. Reflections on the Inner Meaning of History*

10. Two crucial historical facts narrated by Matthew and Luke in the annunciations to Joseph and to Mary are the assuming of a human nature by the Word of God to form the God-Man and his Virginal Conception as the mode of this divine intervention. They are real concrete happenings integrated into the process of universal history and known as such in the retrospective consciousness of man. While Daniélou seeks to retain these two events, his method obstructs him from doing so. He does not save the *fact*, because he includes it within an allegedly fictitious story, and he does not save the *content*, because he reduces the historical content of the episodes to the merely human event of Joseph's having legally adopted Jesus. The real content of the revelation to Mary was that she was historically to become the Mother of God Incarnate, who would also be the Messiah, and it was also revealed to Mary that this incarnation would take place by way of the historical event of a virginal conception. Mary experienced the Virginal Conception to be historically true. Joseph came to know of the Virginal Conception through his belief in the message of an angel.

11. Daniélou claims that Jesus was not a descendant of David through Mary, for the reason that Mary was not a descendant of David (p. 16), but there are powerful arguments to the contrary. St. Jerome affirms that Mary was a close relative of Joseph, and, therefore, a member of the tribe of Judah and of the family of David.[6] This testimony is reinforced by St. Ambrose, Tertullian, St. John Chrysostom, and St. John Damascene.[7] The Fathers of the Church almost unanimously defend the Davidic descent of Mary, and the same conclusion is in keeping with contemporary research.[8]

(New York: Longmans Green, 1958). But in his reflections on the "inner meaning of history," he shows a lack of prior reflection on the nature of history as a science. He treats such questions as "Sacred and Profane History," "A Biblical Interpretation of Modern History," and "The Development of History" in the absence of precise definitions of such important analytical elements of the science of history as *historical fact, historical meaning,* and *historical method.*

6 St. Jerome, *Commentary on Matthew* (in Latin), at Matt. 1:18, in PL, vol. 26, col. 24.

7 See H. Didon, *Jésus Christ* (Paris, 1891), p. 416.

8 See Jacques Masson, *Jésus, Fils de David dans les Généalogies de Saint Matieu et di Saint Luc* (Paris: Téqui, 1982). This is the publication of a doctoral thesis presented at the University of St. Thomas in Rome in 1979. The massive and painstaking research that Masson here presents on the two genealogies of Jesus, carried out according to the methods of modern genealogical inquiry, so expands the data and is so carefully put together that it should be considered essential for any further development of the discussion. Masson's research concludes that Mary was a descendant of King David. See also J.F. McCarthy, "New Light on the Genealogies of Jesus," in Chapter 13 below and in *Living Tradition* 11

12. A problem that lurks in this discussion is how a character in a dream can be regarded as a witness to an extraordinary historical event. If Joseph was a "just man" only in the form-critical sense of being a naïve observer of the Mosaic Law, he could easily have allowed his credulity to convince himself that his dream of hearing an angel speak gave the explanation of Mary's pregnancy. Such hypotheses have been advanced by the enemies of Christianity since the earliest years. Now, obviously a mere dream is a fictional mode of knowledge, but Matthew's account of the revelation to Joseph means that, amidst the quiet induced by natural sleep, an angel really spoke to the objectivity of Joseph's intellect, which was not itself asleep, and addressed his words to Joseph's understanding in such a manner that their meaning was impressed upon it. The comprehension and acceptance of these words by Joseph embodied an act of Christian faith in this objective historical reality.

13. Joseph's legal adoption of Jesus in Matthew 1 is not, as Daniélou maintains, "the point of the account" (p. 41). Although it is an element in the account, a more careful reading of the chapter will bring out that, in the genealogy, Matthew uses over and over again the verb *egennēsen* ("begot") to indicate and stress the carnal passage of the male seed from Abraham to David to Joseph, but not from Joseph to Jesus. The second part of the chapter then explains why the male seed of Abraham and of David did not pass from Joseph to Jesus. The explanation given by Matthew is that Mary had conceived of the power of the Holy Spirit (1:18) and without the intervention of any male seed, because she had virginally conceived (1:23).

14. The background of this miraculous intervention of the Holy Spirit is given in the prophecy taken from Isaiah 1:14: "*Behold a virgin shall be with child and shall bring forth a son, and they shall call his name Emmanuel, which being interpreted is 'God with us.'*" The point of this proof from prophecy and why Matthew quotes the word *virgin* from the Septuagint translation is better understood in the wider context of the quotation. King Ahaz was an evildoer in the eyes of the Lord, as had been several of his predecessors, all descendants of the royal seed of David. So the Lord said to Ahaz: "*Ask a sign of the Lord your God, from the depths below or the heights above.*" And Ahaz would not ask for a sign. So the Lord said through Isaiah: "*Hear then, O house of David! Is it too little for you to weary men, that you weary my God also? Therefore, the Lord himself will give you a sign. Behold a virgin shall conceive and bear a son, and shall call his name Emmanuel*" (Isa. 7:10–14). The point of this episode with King Ahaz is that

(May 1987), on the Internet at www.rtforum.org—archive of articles.

God would perform a miracle ("a sign") according to which a virgin would conceive without the use of male seed, and the implication is that the Messiah, the great "seed" of the house of David, would not be conceived from the male seed of these evil kings of the house of David. And this miraculous conception would embody an even greater miracle and the greatest of all miracles: the combination of the heights above with the depths below in the hypostatic union of the divine Word of God with a human nature in Jesus of Nazareth. So in this surprising way was the promise of God to David fulfilled, where it is written: "The Lord has sworn truth to David, and he will not make it void: *of the fruit of thy womb* I will set upon thy throne" (Ps. 131 [132]:11 [cf. the *neo-Vulgate* version]). It turned out for this prophesy that David's womb was Mary's womb. Again it was prophesied: "I have made a covenant with my elect: I have sworn to David my servant: thy seed will I confirm forever. And I will build up thy throne unto generation and generation" (Ps. 88 [89]:4–5). Again it turned out, as Matthew's inspired text reports, the seed of David confirmed was not the male seed as such passed down from king to king, but the womb of Mary, a female descendant of David. Hence, Daniélou's reading that Jesus was made a descendant of David only by the fiction of legal adoption does not do justice to the text of Matthew. And the inspired word of St. Paul also tells us that legal adoption was not the only way in which Jesus was a descendant of David, where it speaks of what God had promised "by his prophets in the holy Scriptures concerning his Son, who was made to him of the seed of David *according to the flesh* (Rom. 1:2–3).

15. To summarize and conclude this discussion. Matthew 1 presents historical chronology, historical explanation, and theological explanation. The facts contained in the historical chronology include, not only the legal adoption of Jesus by Joseph when he took Mary and Jesus into his home, but also the facts that the male seed of David did not generate the Savior of the World, that Mary conceived Him virginally by the power of the Holy Spirit, that God became man in this conception, that Joseph was troubled by the pregnancy of Mary, that he came to know of the Virginal Conception through the message of an angel, and that he believed this message, that Joseph and Mary named the child Jesus, and that both Mary and Joseph adored Jesus as Emmanuel, the God-Man. In the historical explanation of the chapter are included, among other things, the judgment of God against the male seed of the house of David because of the evil of these men, and the providential encouragement to Joseph to become the foster-father of Jesus. All of these constitute the *finis operis* of the account.

The theological explanation embodies the *finis operantis* of the account. Daniélou sees in the chapter a parallelism between the creation of Adam and the Incarnation of the divine Word of God, in that Jesus comes at the end of the Old Testament to inaugurate a new humanity generated by the work of the Holy Spirit (no. 1 above). But Daniélou shows no frame of reference for this observation, and form-criticism will never find one. Neither Adam nor the new humanity is mentioned in this chapter, but the Fathers of the Church have provided the proper frame of reference for finding them in the method of the Four Senses of Sacred Scripture. The contrast between Adam and Jesus, between the old humanity and the new, as observed in this chapter, fits under the category of the allegorical sense of Sacred Scripture, and specifically here, under the Christological sense.

16. The prophecy in Isa. 7:14 was addressed to the house of David, but David was just a prefigurement of Jesus, and Jesus came to establish his Church as the new and eternal house of David. Who first called Jesus "Emmanuel"? The original text of Isa. 7:14 says that "*she*" will call Him Emmanuel, while the citation of this prophecy in Matthew 1:23 says that *they* will call Him Emmanuel, but the theological meaning of this citation is that *all true believers* in the new house of David will call Him Emmanuel, because they will all adore Him as the God-Man. Mary believed and she adored Him. Joseph believed and he adored Him, and thereby he also became an adopted child of God and a member of the new house of David. But there is much more than this to the theological meaning of Matthew 1, as comes to light under the analysis of the Four Senses of Sacred Scripture. The names in the genealogy all refer allegorically to Jesus and they all, or at least many, have also a tropological meaning, as is brought out in the notes taken from the lectures of St. Thomas Aquinas on this Gospel.[9] Contemporary research according to the neo-patristic method can do much to increase and refine the deep insights of earlier Catholic commentators on the Gospel of Matthew and on the other Gospels, as well as to correct the many confusions that form-criticism has brought to the understanding of the same.

---

9 Aquinas, *Super Evangelium S. Matthaei Lectura,* chapter 1.

Chapter 13

New Light on the Genealogies of Jesus

Living Tradition 11 (May 1987)
The Problem of the Genealogies

1. Seeming contradictions loom large in the genealogies of Jesus in Matthew and Luke. Throughout the history of the Church these apparent errors have been an object of apologetic concern on the part of many believers, of curious and sometimes condescending interest on the part of others, and of triumphant delight on the part of some unbelievers. In modern times historical criticism has found more inconsistencies in these two genealogies than ever before, and yet by the goodness of God the pristine historicity of the Gospel accounts has also in our day begun to manifest itself with new vigor and clarity.

2. In *The Birth of the Messiah* Raymond Brown advises his readers that "the Lucan genealogy is no less theological in purpose than Matthew's and no freer of historical difficulties."[1] He observes that "the Lucan list, while in some ways more plausible than Matthew's list, scarcely constitutes an exact record of Jesus' biological ancestry." He finds that "(w)hat one may say with surety of Luke's list is that, in part, it is artificially arranged in numerical patterns of seven and that it contains enough inaccuracies and confusions to suggest a popular provenance (rather than an archival provenance) among Greek-speaking Jews." His final conclusion is: "Luke adopted this list and adapted it for theological purposes by placing it between the baptism of Jesus and his temptations. This means that, while the two NT genealogies tell us how to evaluate Jesus, they tell us nothing certain about his grandparents or his great-grand-parents. The message

---

1 Raymond E. Brown, *The Birth of the Messiah* (Doubleday, 1977), p. 90.

about Jesus, son of Joseph, is not that factually he is also (grand)son of either Jacob (Matthew) or of Eli (Luke) but that theologically he is 'son of David, son of Abraham' (Matthew), and 'Son of God' (Luke)."[2]

3. Brown's obviously nuanced conclusion raises certain questions of historical method. Does a theological purpose need to conflict with an accurate historical presentation? Can the cautious historian be *sure* that the seeming inaccuracies and confusions in the genealogies of Matthew and Luke are really what they seem? Can the careful historian be *certain* that these two genealogies tell us nothing about the grandparents or great-grandparents of Jesus? How can non-historical genealogies convey how to evaluate Jesus in a way that serious historians can take seriously? What is the value of a theological message that is not based on historical facts? Questions such as these might well be kept in mind as we review the age-old problem of the two genealogies of Jesus, arising from the fact that St. Joseph appears as the son of Jacob in the genealogy of Matthew and as the son of Eli in the genealogy of Luke, and subsequently that the names in Matthew's list differ almost entirely from those in Luke's list going as far back as King David.

Five Proposed Solutions to the Problem of the Genealogies

4. To the problem of the historicity of the genealogies of Our Lord in Matthew and Luke, five solutions may be considered. The two classic solutions are the theory of Levirate marriage and the theory of Marian genealogy.

5. Levirate Marriage. The Law of the Levirate states: "If brothers dwell together, and one of them dies and has no son, the wife of the dead shall not be married outside the family to a stranger; her husband's brother shall go in to her, and take her as his wife, and perform the duty of a husband's brother to her. And the first son whom she bears shall succeed to the name of his brother who is dead, that his name may not be blotted out of Israel."[3]

6. According to an explanation going back in essence at least to Julius Africanus in the first half of the third century A.D. (who claimed to have heard it as handed down by the relatives of Jesus), Joseph's grandmother

---

2 Ibid., pp. 93–94.

3 *"When brothers dwell together, and one of them dies without children, the wife of the deceased shall not marry another, but his brother shall take her and raise up seed for his brother. And the first son he shall have of her he shall call by his name, that his name be not abolished out of Israel"* (Deut. 25:5–6 – *Revised Standard Version*).

(Estha) bore Jacob to one husband (Matthan) and Eli to a second (Matthat). Joseph's mother married Eli, who died without children; then she married his uterine brother Jacob, who raised up Joseph as seed to Eli. Thus Joseph had Eli as his legal father and Jacob as his biological father. The genealogy of Matthew shows the biological ancestry of Jesus, and that of Luke the legal ancestry.[4]

7. This solution is excluded by Raymond Brown, who says: "The theory of a Levirate marriage solves so little and has so many difficulties that it should be abandoned as a solution in the problem of the two genealogies, and even in the more restricted problem of Jesus' overabundance of grandfathers."[5]

8. The difficulties as seen by Brown are four in number:

Matthan and Matthat are similar names. Thus one is faced with the "dubious coincidence" that the mother of Jacob and Eli married two men who had almost the same names. But similarity of first names is not unheard of in the case of successive husbands or in the case of brothers. Hence, no historian can *exclude* this explanation, handed down from early times, on the mere ground that the names of the two husbands are similar.

"We are not certain how widely Levirate marriage was practiced in Jesus' time." But it was probably practiced, as Brown himself admits. Therefore, no historian can *exclude* this explanation on the ground that it couldn't have happened. It would have taken only one instance to make it happen, and history abounds with unique happenings.

If Joseph were the issue of a Levirate marriage, it would be "very strange" to have a genealogical list going back through his biological father. It would not be strange at all, it seems to me, especially if Matthew had a particular purpose for doing so, such as tracing the more direct line of royal descent, which, in fact, he does. A prominent example of a known Levirate marriage in the same list of names, Obed, has his ancestry traced back through Boaz, his biological father (Ruth 4). And in the case of Matthew and Luke *both* ancestries are preserved. Hence, the explanation of a Levirate marriage cannot be *logically excluded* on this ground.

"Why does Matthew trace descent through David's son Solomon, while Luke traces it through David's son Nathan?" The answer to this is obvious:

---

4 Julius Africanus, Letter to Aristides, in Migne, *Patrologia Graeca*, vol. 10, col. 64. Cf. Eusebius of Caesarea, in Migne, PG, vol. 20, col. 93; PC, vol. 22, col. 901. Julius Africanus has Eli as the son of Melchi, rather than of Matthat. See the *Catholic Encyclopedia*, (1913 edition) p. 411.

5 Brown, *The Birth of the Messiah*, p. 504.

because two different lines of ancestry go back to David, one from Matthan through Solomon, the other from Matthat through Nathan. Hence, the Levirate explanation cannot be *excluded* on the ground of this divergence.

9. The conclusion would seem to be that Brown does not present cogent grounds for *abandoning the possibility* of a solution through Levirate marriage, since four flimsy reasons do not add up to one good reason. Difficulties and improbabilities do, indeed, lead one to be wary of accepting this solution as proven historical fact, but the historian needs real historical evidence in order to exclude it as a possible historical fact. The historian can recognize beneath the problem of the two genealogies a unique historical background created by the Law of the Levirate, whereby Levirate marriage was not merely permitted, but was legally imposed with a force that is clearly expressed in Deut. 25:5–10. With that background in mind, he may question, he may doubt, but he may not exclude, pending actual historical evidence to the contrary.

10. In a monumental piece of research, published in French in 1982,[6] Jacques Masson reviews the ancient argument of a Levirate marriage of Joseph's mother. To deepen his analysis of the last few generations in the two genealogies, he first presents a study of all the preceding generations. The wealth of material that he brings to bear on the question and the painstaking care with which he has sifted and arranged the data make his book a classic work on the subject. Masson does not prove that there was in this case a Levirate marriage, but he so increases the area of discussion and so challenges the reader to continue sifting the data that his work cannot be ignored in any serious treatment of the question. Not only does this book make clear the complexity of the question, it also brings the reader closer up to the history behind the Gospel text and behind the discussion of the text that has gone on now for nineteen centuries.

11. The possibility of a Levirate marriage as presented by Julius Africanus was questioned by Jacques-Paul Migne, [7] Urban Holzmeister,[8] and others on the ground that the Law of the Levirate did not apply to uterine brothers, seeing that neither did a uterine brother carry the same male seed nor would he keep the heredity within the same family. Masson sees general validity in this objection, but he finds high probability in a Levirate marriage of Joseph's mother with a relative of her deceased husband who

---

6 Jacques Masson, *Jésus, Fils de David dans les Généalogies de Saint Mathieu et de Saint Luc* (Paris: Téqui, 1982).

7 Note by J.-P. Migne in PG, vol. 20, cols. 98–100.

8 U. Holzmeister, "Genealogia S. Lucae," in *Verbum Domini* (1943), [pp. 9–18], pp. 11–12.

had a common ancestor with him. Such a common ancestor, according to the two genealogies, would obviously be David, but more proximately he finds Salathiel and even more proximately Eliud/Esli.

12. Masson argues as follows. Jechonias, having no son, adopted Salathiel, husband of his daughter and son of Neri, who was descended from David through Nathan. Salathiel thus became the *legal son* and *successor* of Jechonias. By the Law of the Levirate, the name of Salathiel's biological father disappears from the genealogy and the name of Jechonias appears. Salathiel becomes a common ancestor of both Jacob and Eli.

13. More proximately, both Jacob and Eli are descendants of Eliud/Esli. Achim of Matthew's genealogy died without children, and Naggai of Luke's genealogy begot Eliud/Esli as Achim's legal son. Matthew's Eleazar was the eldest son of Eliud/Esli. Naum was a younger son. Thus a Levirate adoption by Jechonias and later Levirate marriages raising up seed to Achim and to Jacob, the legal. father of Joseph, solve the contradiction of the two fathers of Joseph and the disparate lines of descent from David to Joseph.[9]

14. Masson's careful argumentation leading up to these conclusions should not be lightly dismissed.[10] The data that he presents can indeed be interpreted in different ways, but there is a substratum of truth that should not be ignored. The question, however, broadens at this point from an elementary base into issues related to the second solution, that of a possible genealogy of Mary, which Masson takes up in lesser depth.

15. Marian Geneaology The theory of a Marian genealogy in its simplest form is based on a reading of Matthew and Luke such that Matthew presents the ancestry of Joseph and Luke presents the ancestry of Mary. The theory is based on the fact of the Virginal Conception, which both Matthew and Luke clearly present, and on the reasoning that, because of

---

9 Masson, op. cit., (p. 456), sees a probability that Eli was the biological father of Joseph, and Jacob was the legal father. For this he relies on his genealogical analysis and especially on the general assumption that Matthew shows the legal descent of Joseph in relation to the monarchy.

10 Raymond Brown ("Gospel Infancy Narrative Research from 1976 to 1986: Part I" in the *Catholic Biblical Quarterly,* July, 1986, p. 479) finds that Masson's research displays a "passion for demonstrating scriptural accuracy" and is "largely futile." Brown wonders "what theological difference it would make if the lists are not reconcilable," or "what historical difference so long as Jesus is the (legal) son of Joseph who was a Davidid (on which both genealogies agree)." But Jacques Masson's work will not be futile, if the results of his research are properly taken up and developed. A passion for demonstrating Scriptural accuracy is a better attribute than a passion for demonstrating questionable Scriptural inaccuracies. Theological interest of the Evangelists does not eliminate the need of a historical base, or at least the need of a historical context, relating to what they write.

this fact, the real biological descent of Jesus is only through his mother. If Matthew gives the legal descent of Jesus, and if Luke gives the real descent, then Luke gives the genealogy of Mary.

16. Raymond Brown excludes this theory completely: "What influences this suggestion is the centrality of Joseph in Matthew's infancy narrative, as compared with the spotlighting of Mary in Luke's. Even at first glance, however, this solution cannot be taken seriously: a genealogy traced through the mother is not normal in Judaism, and Luke makes it clear that he is tracing Jesus' descent *through Joseph*. Moreover, Luke's genealogy traces Davidic descent and despite later Christian speculation, we really do not know that Mary was a Davidic." [11]

17. Brown's reasons for excluding this theory are questionable. What, indeed, may be called *normal* Jewish genealogical practice in the case of a virginal conception, which Luke clearly presents? There is simply no precedent for this. [12] Again, since Luke says "as was supposed," it is too much to affirm that Luke "makes it clear" that he is tracing the descent of Jesus through Joseph, except in some possibly secondary or superficial sense. Again, "we do not know" (that Mary was a Davidid) cannot be used as an argument for exclusion, since ignorance of the facts has very limited probative value.

18. René Laurentin, in *The Truth of Christmas*, [13] maintains that "the hypothesis of a Davidic filiation with regard to Mary is foreign to the two evangelists." Laurentin affirms: "Nothing is lost in Mary's not being biologically the daughter of David. The rigor with which the evangelists have avoided this easy solution gives a new indication of their exactitude. They do not invent in order to appease current expectations, as those who came after them did. On the contrary, they accepted the paradoxes which caused the difficulty. This honesty led them to a great theological profundity."

19. Great theological profundity there is in the accounts of the two Evangelists, but here the question is one of historical truth, and it is a

---

11 Brown, *The Birth of the Messiah*, p. 89.

12 Apart from the singularity of the Virginal Conception, there are some precedents for the tracing of the genealogy of a woman. Thus, in Judith 8:1 the genealogy of Judith is given. Compare this with Lk. 2:36: "Anna the prophetess, daughter of Phanuel of the tribe of Aser."

13 R. Laurentin, *The Truth of Christmas beyond the Myths* (St. Bede's Publications: Petersham, Massachusetts, 1986), pp. 342–345 (French original: *Les Evangiles de l'Enfance du Christ*, pp. 403–404).

mistake to suppose that an actual biological descent of Mary from David would somehow lessen the theological depth. Basically, where the history fails, the theology fails, unless the theology is clearly independent of history. As far as some aspects of the theology are concerned, nothing would be lost if Mary's biological father were an Egyptian. That could better explain why the Holy Family fled into Egypt. But such tampering with the historical facts would cause other aspects of the theology to suffer.

20. Jesus was born "from the seed (*ek spermatos*) of David according to the flesh" (Rom. 1:3). "Remember this: the Lord Jesus Christ rose from the dead from the seed (*ek spermatos*) of David according to my gospel" (2 Tim. 2:8). Laurentin avers that in these passages the Greek word *sperma* (usually translated as *seed*) does not mean *sperm* in the restricted biological sense that this word has in French (and in English), but rather means posterity, lineage, or descent in a very broad sense. Thus, he says, according to the Law of the Levirate, a man was to marry his brother's widow to raise up *seed*, that is, posterity, for his brother, not for himself. "The meaning is juridical and not biological."

21. Laurentin's exclusion of the biological meaning of the word *sperma* (seed) in these passages is not logical, because it is not an either/or situation. The extended legal or social meaning has an original and fundamental biological meaning as well. The reason especially why a brother was ordered in Deuteronomy to "raise up seed" is because brothers were carrying the same biological male seed as did their father. St. Paul says "according to the flesh," and Laurentin excludes any biological meaning; St. Paul says "rose from the dead," and Laurentin excludes any biological meaning from the seed of David. It is a question not of whether the word *sperma* has other meanings as well, but rather of how one can justifiably exclude the biological meaning in a context such as this.

22. Again, in Acts 2:30, Peter teaches that the Prophet David spoke of Jesus as "the fruit of his loins," with reference to the Resurrection of Jesus and to the fact that "his flesh did not see corruption." According to Laurentin, this and other texts "in no way focus on the biological connections, nor on the virginal modality." But in some way they certainly do. St. Peter is explicitly speaking about the flesh of Jesus, and St. Paul is speaking about the origin of Jesus "according to the flesh."

23. It is a mistake to imagine that in a given passage there must be only one meaning of a word. The fact that a word has wider implications does not exclude the particular meaning. Laurentin rules out the explicit reference to bodily processes in these passages and assumes an exclusively

transferred sense of the word *seed*. There is no way that Peter or Paul could get a biologically focused message through the barrier of this kind of interpretation, which impedes rather than produces knowledge.

24. St. Augustine and other Church Fathers saw a biological meaning in these passages. Augustine reasoned that Mary had to be of the family of David, because Jesus was born "from the seed of David," and no male seed was involved in Jesus' conception.[14] Laurentin observes that any such deduction "was foreign to the Apostle Paul," who "confined himself to quoting an ancient profession of faith." Paul was a sharp thinker. To assume (without evidence) that he mindlessly repeated an ancient expression without logical reflection on his own part does not do full justice either to the mind of the Apostle or to the rules of literary interpretation.

25. Laurentin "will not discuss the hypothesis of Annus [sic] of Viterbo (c. 1490), who made the Lucan genealogy apply to Mary," because "it is not maintained by anyone today." Having disposed of the theory with no discussion and no argument, Laurentin goes on to affirm: "Mt. 1 and Lk. 1 are silent regarding Mary's lineage, and this seems to be because they were not able to call her a descendant of David." But, according to this undiscussed theory, Luke is not silent; he need not have spoken about Mary's lineage in chapter one, if he was going to present it fully in chapter three. And reasons for the silence of Matthew can also be suggested, if, indeed, Matthew was as silent as Laurentin thinks.

26. That Mary was a direct physical descendant of King David is a teaching of the Fathers of the Church.[15] Whether this fact is illustrated in the genealogies of Luke and Matthew is a more particular question, but the idea that Mary's descent can be traced directly from David has been held since ancient times. A.J. Maas testifies as follows:

---

14 St. Augustine, *Contra Faustum,* Patrologia Latina 42, cols. 471–472.

15 "There is little doubt that the Savior's Davidic descent was part of the primitive *kerygma*, and it was eventually incorporated into the written gospel.... (On the supposition that Luke's genealogy is that of Mary) we should read Lk. 3:23 as follows: 'And Jesus Himself, when He began His work, was about thirty years of age, being—as was supposed—the son of Joseph [but in reality the grand-] son of Heli....' The real difficulty with the Marian hypothesis, as with that of Africanus, is that neither explains how Salathiel and Zorobabel appear as descendants of David in Luke's genealogy. It is useless to invoke the solution of a levirate marriage again, for we know the names of all the sons of Jechonia and none of them is called Neri (cf. 1Chr. 3:17–18)" (J. Edgar Bruns, "Genealogy of Jesus," in the *New Catholic Encyclopedia,* vol. 6, pp. 319–321). Masson and others have presented solutions to this "real difficulty." See above.

27. "Tradition tells us that Mary too was a descendant of David. According to Num. 36:6–12, an only daughter had to marry within her own family so as to secure the right of inheritance. After St. Justin (*Adv. Tryph.* 100) and St. Ignatius (*Eph.* 18), the Fathers generally agree in maintaining Mary's Davidic descent, whether they knew this from an oral tradition or inferred it from Scripture, e.g., Rom. 1:3; 2 Tim. 2:8. St. John Damascene (*De Fide Orthodoxa* IV:14) states that Mary's great-grandfather, Barpanther, was Heli's cousin; and her father, Joachim, was a cousin of Joseph, Heli's Levirate son. …At any rate, tradition presents the Blessed Virgin as descending from David through Nathan."[16]

28. St. Ignatius, second successor of St. Peter to the See of Antioch, martyred in the Colosseum of Rome about 110 A.D., declared: "I offer my life's breath for the sake of the Cross, which is a stumbling block to unbelievers, but to us is salvation and eternal life. What has become of the philosopher? What of the controversialist? What of the vaunting of so-called intellectuals? The fact is, our God Jesus Christ was indeed conceived by Mary according to God's dispensation *of the seed of David*, but also of the Holy Spirit."[17]

29. St. Justin, martyred in Rome about 165 A.D., in his *Dialogue with Trypho the Jew*, asserts time and again that Jesus was born of the Virgin Mary, who was physically descended from King David. In one place (No. 100) he is more specific: "Therefore (Christ) revealed to us all that we have perceived by his grace out of the Scriptures, so that we know Him to be the first-begotten of God, and to be before all creatures; likewise to be the Son of the patriarchs, since He became flesh from the Virgin descended from them, and submitted to become a man without comeliness, dishonoured, and subject to suffering. …He said that He was the Son of man, either because He had been born from the Virgin, who was, as I said, descended from the stock of David and Jacob and Isaac and Abraham: or because Abraham was the father both of Himself and of those whom I have enumerated, from whom Mary derives her descent. For we know that the fathers of women are the fathers likewise of those children whom their daughters bear."[18]

---

16 A. J. Maas, "Genealogy of Christ," in the *Catholic Encyclopedia* (1913 ed.), vol. 6, p. 411.

17 Ignatius Martyr, *Letter to the Ephesians,* ch. 18, in PG 5, col. 660. Trans.: James A. Kleist, ed., *Ancient Christian Writers,* vol. 1, p. 67.

18 Justin Martyr, *Dialogue with Trypho the Jew,* in PG, vol. 6, col. 709. Cf. Alexander Roberts-James Donaldson eds., *The Ante-Nicene Fathers* (Grand Rapids: Eerdmans, 1979), p. 249.

30. St. Irenaeus (ca. 140–202 A.D.), in his work *Against Heretics*, speaks of Jesus, "Who was of a virgin who was of the stock of David." Irenaeus, after reasoning that Jesus could not properly have inherited the promises through Joseph, because in the genealogy of Joseph (Mt. 1:2–16) his ancestor Jechonias had been prophetically deprived of the Messianic inheritance, turns to the genealogy of Luke and speaks of the Virgin Mary.[19]

31. The Greek philosopher Celsus, a great opponent of Christianity, in his so-titled *True Discourse*, written about 178 A.D., accuses Christians of insolence for having drawn up a genealogy of Jesus that traces his descent through the kings of the Jews all the way back to the first man and declares: "And so the wife of a carpenter would not have been unaware that she arose from such great ancestry!" Thus, the pagan Celsus in the second century saw the genealogy of Luke, and possibly that of Matthew, as pertaining to the Virgin Mary, and he attacked Christians for believing that this was the descent of Mary. Origen, writing *Against Celsus* in about 246 A.D., does not deny that Christians believe this about Mary. Rather he says: "So what? Say that she was not unaware. What does that do to us? Say that she was unaware. Does it follow from this that she was not descended from the first man or that her lineage does not pertain to the kings of the Jews? Does Celsus think that poor people are always born from poor people and kings from kings? It seems useless, therefore, to tarry longer over these things, since it is clear even in our age that some who are poorer than Mary have been born of rich and illustrious parents, and potentates and kings born of the least noble."[20] The point to be drawn from this exchange is that in the second and third centuries Christians were attributing to Mary a genealogical descent identical in at least some elements with the genealogies of Matthew and Luke.

32. St. Hilary of Poitiers (ca. 315–367 A.D.) testifies in the fourth century: "Many are of the opinion that the genealogy which Matthew lists is to be ascribed to Joseph and the genealogy listed by Luke is to be ascribed to Mary, in that, since the man is called the head of the *woman*, her generation is also named for the man. But this does not fit the rule or the question treated above [by Hilary], namely where the character of the genealogies is demonstrated and most truthfully solved."[21] Hence, according to Hilary,

---

19 Irenaeus, *Adversus Haereses,* in PG, vol. 7, cols. 951–958.

20 Origen, *Contra Celsum,* in PG, vol. II, col. 852.

21 Hilary of Poitiers, in Angelo Mai, ed., *Novae Patrum Bibliothecae* (Rome: Propaganda Fide, 1852), pp. 477–478. The editor notes that the text in which Hilary claims to have refuted the Marian theory is not extant.

by his time "many" had maintained that Luke's genealogy presents the ancestry of the Blessed Virgin Mary.

33. St. Epiphanius (315–402 A.D.) notes that Luke, in his genealogy, brings the line of descent back through Abraham and Noah all the way to Adam "in order that he who first of all (men) had been formed was sought unto salvation by Him who had been begotten from his (Adam's) substance, namely, from the Blessed Virgin. …But finally he goes beyond Adam and says 'who was of God.' And thus it is quite clear that He was the Son of God, who came from the seed of Adam, endowed with flesh by an unbroken succession."[22]

34. St. John Damascene (ca. 645–750 A.D.) sees the ancestry of Mary represented in Luke's genealogy: Mary was descended from David through his son Nathan. Mary's father Joachim was the son of Barpanther and the grandson of Panther. Panther was the brother of Melchi and the son of Levi in Luke's genealogy. Therefore, all of the names in Luke's genealogy from Melchi to Adam are direct ancestors of Mary.[23]

35. Cornelius aLapide, in his linear commentary, interprets Lk. 3:23 as saying that Jesus was only "supposed to be" the son of Joseph, but was really the son of Eli.[24] He notes that an extra-biblical tradition identifies the parents of the Virgin Mary as Joachim and Anne.[25] How then could the father of Mary have been "Eli"? ALapide explains that Joseph (Lk. 3:23) is called the son, that is, the son-in-law, of Eli, and Eli by apocope is short for Eliachim, which is an alternative name for Joachim. To be sure, we read in 4Kg. (2Kg.) 23:34 that "Pharao Nechao made Eliakim,

---

22 Epiphanius, *Adversus Haereses,* bk. 2, Tome 1, Heresy 51, No. 11; in PG, vol. 41, col. 908.

23 John Damascene, *De Fide Orthodoxa,* in PG, vol. 15, cols. 1155–1157.

24 Cornelius aLapide (Cornelius van den Steen: 1567–1637 A.D.), *Great Commentary,* commenting on Lk. 3:23. Among those who have held or at least have been open to the possibility that Luke gives the genealogy of Mary, aLapide lists Augustine of Hippo, Denis the Carthusian, Cajetan, Peter Canisius, Melchior Cano, Dominic Soto, Francis Suarez, and others. Holzmeister, op. cit., pp. 10 and 14, adds the names of six ancient writers (Justin Martyr, Celsus, Origen, Irenaeus, Epiphanius, and John Damascene) and eleven twentieth-century writers up to that time (1943) who held the theory: p. Vogt, J.M. Heer, V. Hartl, J. Pfättish, E. Mangenot, p. Pous, R. Riezler, Th. Innitzer, Simon-Prado, J. Geslin, and E. Ruffini. Jacques-H. Vosté, in *De Conceptione Virginali Jesu Christi* (Rome: Collegio Angelico, 1933), p. 100, lists nine late nineteenth and twentieth-century writers who hold the theory, including B. Weiss, A. Capecelatro, P.H. Didon, and E. Le Camus.

25 Joachim and Anne are presented as the parents of the Blessed virgin Mary in the *Protoevangelion of James* (second century A.D.).

the son of Josias, king in place of Josias his father, and he changed his name to Joakim" (cf. 2Chron. 36:4). Again, in Judith 4 the high priest is called Joakim in the Septuagint and Eliachim in the Vulgate and in some other manuscripts; in fact, the same man is called by the Vulgate "Eliachim" in Judith 4 and "Joachim" in Judith 15:9. The etymological basis for the interchangeability is that the syllables 'Jo' (Jehova) and 'El' (Elohim) are both names of God and that both names mean "God makes firm" or "God raises up."

36. Francis Xavier Patrizzi, in an elaborate treatise on the genealogies of Matthew and Luke published in 1853, claims that Annius of Viterbo was the first writer who attempted to show that Eli of Lk. 3:23 was the biological father of the Virgin Mary and the biological grandfather of Jesus. [26] Subsequently, many Catholic and Protestant exegetes adopted the theory, including Cornelius aLapide, as stated above. In his treatise, Patrizzi severely criticizes this hypothesis, not for seeing the ancestry of Mary within Luke's genealogy, which Patrizzi himself upholds along with many before him beginning in ancient times, but solely and simply as understanding Eli to be the Father of the Virgin Mary.

37. Patrizzi claims that this is an unacceptable reading of the text:

Patrizzi claims that there is no example in Sacred Scripture to illustrate the shortening of Eliachim (or Eliakim) to Eli; in fact, he points out, the 'E' in 'Eli' is actually a different vowel in the Greek from the 'E' in 'Eliachim,' and, in the Hebrew 'Eli' comes from a different root altogether.

Again, he says, there was no other way that a man could be called the 'son' of another man who was not his biological father except by way of Levirate marriage. Joseph could not have been the adopted 'son' of Eli. The Fathers of the Church saw both genealogies as those of Joseph, and never did one writer before Annius of Viterbo seek to solve the problem by attributing Luke's genealogy to the Virgin Mary.

---

26 Francis Xavier Patrizzi, *De Evangeliis* (Freiburg in Breisgau, 1853), vol. 2, pp. 82–105. Regarding Annius of Viterbo: pp. 84–91. 26. Annius of Viterbo (Giovanni Nanni: born in Viterbo in 1432 and died in Rome in 1502) wrote *Antiquitatum variarum volumina XVII*, a collection in seventeen volumes of fragments of ancient writings, all of which are apocryphal according to the *Grande Dizionario Encyclopedico Utet* (1967), art. "Annio." It is not known whether Annius was himself a falsifier or accepted these documents in good faith. In any case, he does not make a very reputable "founder" of the theory of Marian genealogy, and Patrizzi tears his historical references to shreds. But did Annius originate this theory? According to the indications given above in this article, he did not. Annius presents his theory about the genealogy of Mary in his commentary on the *Breviarium de Temporibus* of Philo the Jew.

Again, he says, Luke would not have made a parenthesis like this: "Jesus... (as was thought, the son of Joseph), who was of Eli." Would not the sacred writer rather have said: "Jesus ...who (although he was thought the son of Joseph) was of Heli"?

Again, he says, the name of Mary would have had to be mentioned by Luke. If Matthew broke the Jewish custom of mentioning Joseph, who did not beget Jesus, how much the more would not Luke have broken the Jewish custom by mentioning Mary? And yet there was no such fixed custom among the sacred writers. Matthew, a Jew writing to Jews, mentions several women in his genealogy. Why would Luke, a non-Jew writing to non-Jews, have been more careful not to mention the woman who brought forth Jesus by virginal conception? And, in fact, the Jews did trace genealogies through women (Judith, Sarvia, Abigail, Rebecca, and the daughter of Sesan).

Again, grammatically, the Greeks did not write genealogies in this manner, and no early translation of the Gospels brings out a reading that links Jesus to Eli.

38. Patrizzi's arguments batter the idea of a Marian link to Eli, but they do not destroy it:

a) Vowels and consonants often get changed in the popular shortening of names. In English, John (Johann) becomes Jack, Charles becomes Chuck, William becomes Will or Bill, James becomes Jim, Robert becomes Bob. Therefore, Eliachim could possibly have become Eli.

b) A man could in Jewish custom be called the son of another man also by adoption (see below).

c) The word order of Lk. 3:23 is somewhat unusual by any reading. Most translations rearrange or add words, such as "the son" or "who was" in continuing the genealogy. Patrizzi himself, in discussing the alleged parenthesis, does not present the word order correctly, which in the Greek is as follows: "... Jesus... being son (as was thought of Joseph) of Eli, of Matthat...." By the correct order of the words (which the Vulgate gives) the parenthetical phrase is awkward but not quite as strange as Patrizzi claims.

d) Luke was not prohibited by custom from mentioning the name of Mary, but he would not have been obliged to mention her if he had a reason for not doing so.

e) Nor did the Greeks write genealogies exactly in the manner that Luke writes this one. A feature in the Greek text not to be ignored is the fact that Joseph is set off from Eli and the following names by not having the definite article before his name. Is this difference suggestive of a parenthesis? St. Jerome may have left this possibility open in his translation of the passage, even though he did not follow the Marian theory himself.

39. What seems to follow from Patrizzi's analysis of the Marian theory is that the genealogy of Luke belongs to Joseph in the plain and simple reading of the text, but that there could be a connection with Mary in a deeper historical reading of the text, especially if a historical reason could be suggested to explain the actual manner of expression used by Luke.

40. Can one correctly surmise the following from the accounts of Matthew and Luke? When Joseph went down to Bethlehem with Mary his espoused wife, who was with child, to register for the census (Lk. 2:1–5), he could well have registered his ancestry more or less according to the genealogy reported in Matthew 1:2–16a. In view of the attempt shortly afterwards by Herod to murder Jesus as a possible claimant to the throne, this genealogy became a dangerous credential. Is it out of question to suppose that, in the process of returning from exile in Egypt, Joseph decided to adopt and adapt the genealogy of Mary as a new credential for himself, thus transferring it from her real ancestry to his supposed ancestry? It would have been necessary to make Mary's ancestry look like that of Joseph. If they were cousins, the two lists might have joined anyhow a certain way back. Joseph might have substituted for the name of Mary's father, Joachim, the equivalent name Eliachim, and shortened it to Eli. This would not have been a falsification, but it would have been enough of a change to throw suspicious outsiders off the track. And it is not inconceivable that one or two other immediate ancestors of Mary (Matthat and Levi) might have been dropped from this legal credential or listed according to their substitute names.

41. There is no actual evidence that such an adaptation was made by Joseph, but the real and established threat to the life of Jesus as a descendant of the Davidic monarchs might have constituted a motive for doing this over and above the concealing to outsiders of the fact of the Virginal Conception. If the adaptation was made by Joseph, then Luke is presenting the adapted and merely supposed genealogy of Joseph, and beneath the adapted genealogy, concealed for historical reasons, is the real genealogy of Mary.

42. Legal Adoption. Urban Holzmeister transforms aLapide's theory into a theory of adoption. The reading of Lk. 3:23 as directly presenting a biological bond of Jesus with Eli, to the exclusion of Joseph, he finds to

be unconvincing and in violence to the text. But, he says, if Mary was an only child, as we have every reason to believe, it would have been entirely in keeping with Old Testament law and custom for her father to adopt her husband and transfer to him all of his rights and possessions. If this happened, then the genealogy of Luke could well be materially the genealogy of Mary, but *formally* (and grammatically) the genealogy of Joseph, who had inherited Mary's ancestry from her father by way of adoption. Hence, all of the names in Luke's genealogy beginning with Eli are ancestors of Mary, but she is not named. He finds a precedent for this kind of adoption in 1Chron. 2:34. Sesan had no sons, so he gave his daughter (unnamed) in marriage to his Egyptian servant Jeraa, and she brought forth to him (Sesan) a son named Ethei. Thus Ethei was the son of Sesan through his unnamed daughter and his adopted (and named) Egyptian son-in-law.

43. The theory of "special adoption" proposed by Holzmeister and others replaces the theory of "generic adoption" held for a time by St. Augustine of Hippo which contemplated the (childhood) adoption of Joseph by Eli. St. Augustine withdrew this theory in favor of the theory of Levirate marriage after he had seen and studied the solution of Julius Africanus.[27]

44. Jacques Masson rejects Holzmeister's theory of the adoption of St. Joseph by the father of the Blessed Virgin Mary on the ground that Holzmeister resorted to this to save the historicity of the text, since he was convinced that the Law of the Levirate could not have applied to uterine brothers. Masson resolves Holzmeister's problem with the provision of Jewish law that the two successive husbands of Joseph's mother need not have been uterine brothers but rather could have been close relatives descended from a common male ancestor. Nevertheless, Masson does not really exclude the legal adoption of Joseph as a possibility. In fact, Masson readily admits the possibility in general of the adoption of a son-in-law in the Jewish law and customs of the times, and he includes an instance of it (Salathiel) in his own explanation.[28]

---

27 Holzmeister, op. cit., pp. 15–18. Holzmeister maintains that the theory of general adoption is very weak, but the special adoption of one's son-in-law by a man without sons is highly tenable. Holzmeister points out indications of such special adoption also in Esd. 7:63 and in Num. 32:41 (taken together with 1Chron. 2:21 and Gen. 50:22). Augustine discusses the problem of the two genealogies in nine different places. See Holzmeister, in *Zeitschrift fur Katholische Theologie* 47 (1923), pp. 205–209. Augustine presents the theory of general adoption in PL, vol. 34, cols. 1072–1073; he withdraws the theory in his *Retractationes* PL, vol. 32, cols. 632–633.

28 Masson, op. cit., pp. 437–439, 347.

45. Holzmeister's idea that Joseph was adopted by Eli, the father of Mary, is untenable in Masson's estimation, because, according to St. John Damascene, Joachim (son of Barpanther, son of Panther, son of Levi) was Mary's father. But Patrizzi, studying the same testimony of John Damascene, concluded that Joseph was Mary's uncle;[29] and Masson does not refute Patrizzi's reasoning. The data can be interpreted differently, and Eli may even be Joachim.

46. If Mary was an only child, Masson cannot logically exclude that her father might have arranged her marriage to her cousin Joseph and then adopted him in keeping with Jewish law and custom. But that would make the genealogy in Luke the real ancestry of the Blessed Virgin Mary, as Holzmeister maintains. The two theories tend to merge in the sense that even for Masson the names in Luke's genealogy from Levi, father of Matthat, all the way back to Adam are also the ancestors of Mary. Only Eli and Matthat are exclusive ancestors of Joseph in the theory of Masson.

47. Here, again, the idea of Levirate marriage appears in a more sublime way. Mary conceived without male seed by the intervention of the Holy Spirit. Thus was raised up a descendant to Eli (Joachim), to David, and to Abraham, Isaac, and Jacob according to the promises. Joseph appears as adopted son-in-law of Eli (Joachim) and as servant of the Holy Spirit, inheriting the promises in a spiritual way.

48. Consanguinity. St. Jerome affirms that Mary was a close relative of Joseph, and, therefore, a member of the tribe of Judah and of the family of David. This testimony is reinforced by St. Ambrose, Tertullian, St. John Chrysostom, and St. John Damascene. The Fathers of the Church almost unanimously defend the Davidic descent of Mary.[30]

49. Cornelius aLapide expounds an elaboration of the Marian theory whereby both genealogies present the ancestry of Mary. Still commenting on Lk. 3:23, he affirms that, while Eli (of Luke's list) was the father of Mary, Matthan (of Matthew's list) was the biological grandfather of both

---

29 Patrizzi, op. cit., p. 98.

30 Jerome (345–420 A.D.), *Super Matthaeum,* commentary on Mt. 1:18: (in PL, vol. 26, col. 24): "Since Joseph is not the father of Our Lord and Savior, how does a genealogy coming down to Joseph pertain in any way to Our Lord? To this we reply, first, that it is not the custom of the Scriptures that the category of women be woven into genealogies; secondly, that Joseph and Mary were from one tribe: whence by law he was obliged to receive her as a near relative, and they were registered together in the census in Bethlehem, as having sprung from one tribe." So also, for testimonies of Irenaeus, Ambrose, and Tertullian regarding the consanguinity of Mary and Joseph, see H. Didon, (Paris, 1891), p. 416.

Joseph and Mary, because Jacob was the brother of Anne, the mother of Mary. By aLapide's theory, Matthew gives the ancestry of Mary through her mother Anne, but Anne's brother Jacob is mentioned in the list instead of Anne, just as Joseph is mentioned instead of Mary. Thus the customary male genealogical tenor is observed and the maternal ancestry of Mary is retained. In this way, concludes aLapide, both genealogies express the real (biological) ancestry of Jesus.

50. In defense of the idea that Mary and Joseph could have been cousins, aLapide notes that according to Num. 36:6–10 women who are heiresses of their parents are ordered to marry, not only within the same tribe, but also within the same kindred and closely-related family, lest the inheritance pass to outsiders. Mary seemingly was an only child.

51. ALapide maintains that, by their respective genealogies, Matthew and Luke show that Jesus was son and heir of David by a double title, by descent from Solomon, who reigned after David, and by descent from Nathan, who was next to Solomon in order to the throne. He cites Ambrose, Jerome, Theodoretus, Jeremiah, Bernard, and Suarez as holding that the Blessed Virgin Mary was a descendant of David through Solomon and therefore, he says, through the genealogy of her mother, as presented by Matthew.

52. Patrizzi maintains that both genealogies are those of Joseph by Levirate marriage; yet they both reflect the ancestry of Mary and the biological descent of Jesus from King David because of the blood-relationship between Mary and Joseph. St. John Damascene, Andrew of Crete, Hugo Grotius, and others had presented explanations to show this which Patrizzi finds to be inexact. He prefers the explanation of Possini, Zaccaria, and others according to which Joseph was actually the paternal uncle of Mary and the brother of her father Joachim. He finds this explanation to be in conformity with the data on Mary's family provided by St. Epiphanius and also with the testimony of Julius Africanus, who says that Joseph was the third son of Jacob, and with some very early Christian records. Thus Joachim, Cleophas, and Joseph were the three sons of the last Jacob in Matthew's genealogy. Marriage of an uncle with his niece would seem to have been forbidden by Jewish law, but Patrizzi maintains that some exceptions were made, especially by way of the Law of the Levirate, since Joachim and Joseph were brothers. He cites also the case of Aristobulus, King of the Jews, whose uncle Absalom became his son-in-law.[31]

---

31 Patrizzi, op. cit., pp. 99–103. See Josephus, *Jewish Antiquities*, bk. 14, ch. 4.

53. Fillion in the early twentieth century agreed with aLapide that St. Anne, the mother of the Virgin Mary, was the sister of Jacob and the aunt of St. Joseph. Masson, after further genealogical studies, concludes that Mary and Joseph were second cousins on her father Joachim's side, inasmuch as Levi in Luke's genealogy was the great-grandfather of Joseph and the great-great grandfather of Mary. But Masson also agrees with aLapide that St. Anne was the sister of Jacob and the aunt of St. Joseph. Therefore, according to Masson, Mary and Joseph were first cousins on her mother's side.[32]

54. Historical reservation. A fifth possible solution to the problem of the two genealogies stems from the laws of historiography as related to the text of Matthew and Luke:

Mt. 1:1–17. Matthew presents his genealogy with the words, "book of the generation (*biblos geneseós*) of Jesus Christ, son of David, son of Abraham" (Mt. 1:1). The Greek word *biblos* means a *written* tablet (as does the corresponding Hebrew word *sepér*). Therefore, the "book of the generation" referred to by Matthew seems to be a written genealogical record to which he is referring—a document that he is quoting. This is therefore an explicit citation of a document.

According to the laws of historiography, a historian has diminished personal responsibility for the historical accuracy of an account which he explicitly quotes, and he has no responsibility if he dissociates himself from the veracity of its contents. Now Matthew in chapter one sets up an explicit contrast between the record of the generation of Jesus that he is quoting (Mt. 1:2–16a) (which, he says, does not really link up with Jesus) and the way in which the generation of Jesus really took place (Mt. 1:18–25). Therefore, it is possible that Matthew did not intend to guarantee the historical accuracy of the genealogy or that he even implies that it is inaccurate.

Lk. 3:23–38. Luke begins his genealogical presentation with the words, "as was supposed." Now, it is clear that Luke is saying that Jesus was only supposed to be the son of Joseph, whereas in biological fact he was not. But it is possible that the phrase "as was supposed" applies as well to other links in the genealogy, or even to the whole genealogy. Thus, Luke may not be guaranteeing the historical accuracy of the genealogy which he presents; in fact, he may be implying that the genealogy is not historically accurate.

---

32 Masson, op. cit., pp. 494 and 498. Cf. C. Fillion, *Vita di Gesù Cristo* (11th ed. Turin, 1940), pp. 105 ff.

55. From these indications regarding Matthew and Luke, it is possible to retain the complete historical accuracy of the two inspired writers according to their express intention, and at the same time to consider possible or probable inaccuracies and confusions in the lists of names themselves. Analysis of the texts of Matthew and Luke according to the principles of true historiography does not, on the one hand, exclude the possibility that one or both of these sacred writers, in presenting a genealogical list, intended to present doubtful or erroneous names to contrast with what they were really affirming about the origin of Jesus. On the other hand, textual analysis does not show unambiguously that either Evangelist did in fact intend not to guarantee his list or that either list is in fact to some degree historically inaccurate.

Convergences of the Five Solutions

56. Pending more conclusive evidence to the contrary on the part of exegetes, all of the following appear to be historically viable possibilities regarding the relationship of the two genealogies of Jesus in Matthew and Luke:

Both Matthew and Luke give true historical genealogies of Joseph (by Levirate marriage or by legal adoption).

Matthew gives the true historical genealogy of Joseph and Luke gives the true historical genealogy of Mary (by bracketing Joseph in Luke's genealogy).

Matthew gives the true historical genealogy of Joseph and Luke gives the true historical genealogy of both Joseph and Mary (by Levirate marriage or legal adoption together with consanguinity).

Both Matthew and Luke give the true historical genealogies of both Joseph and Mary (by Levirate marriage or legal adoption together with consanguinity).

Matthew gives the true historical genealogy of Joseph and Luke gives a non-historical genealogy of Joseph (by historical reservation).

Luke gives the true historical genealogy of Joseph and Matthew gives a non-historical genealogy of Joseph (by historical reservation).

Both Matthew and Luke give non-historical genealogies of Joseph (by historical reservation).

57. In the various solutions proposed to the problems of the two genealogies of Our Lord, there seems to be a certain underlying tendency towards convergence. Both the theory of Levirate marriage and the theory

of special adoption have tended to include the factor of consanguinity between Mary and Joseph. Joseph, the son of a Levirate marriage, could later have been adopted by the father (Joachim) of the Blessed Virgin Mary, his spouse.

58. The Marian reading of Luke's genealogy is weak in the plain reading of the text, but it converges with the Levirate and the adoption theories after two or three generations, because of the factor of consanguinity. Therefore, there probably is a deeper Marian meaning beneath the genealogy of Luke and possibly also of Matthew. The first four theories are all saying ultimately that the genealogies of both Matthew and Luke are presenting the ancestry of Mary. The idea that the genealogy of Jesus in Luke is a genealogy "doctored" for good historical reasons is also a possibility not to be ignored.

What comes forth from a consideration of all of the theories is the split-level meaning of the genealogies, even in their literal sense. The fact that the genealogies are of Joseph does not mean that they are not also of Mary. The solution by historical reservation is important in the study of the purpose of the genealogies, because it gives a certain freedom to the sacred writers in the way in which they have selected the names and arranged the lists. But the mass of historical evidence prevents the interpreter from depending too much on an *a priori* exclusion of historical accuracy. As the purposes of the genealogies are examined, the five solutions may present themselves in a fuller light.

Chapter 14

The Historical Meaning of the Forty-two Generations in Matthew 1:17

Living Tradition 13 (September 1987)

Introduction

1. For those who study deeply into the Gospel text, Matthew's prologue, contained in his first two chapters, is one of the most masterful pieces of writing ever presented to human eyes. The genealogy with which this prologue begins displays its full share of wondrous artistry, but so subtle is its turn that many commentators have failed to grasp the logic that it implies.

2. Raymond Brown, in *The Birth of the Messiah* (p. 68), observes that, from the opening verse of his Gospel, "Matthew" (not the apostle) presents Jesus to both the Jewish and the Gentile Christians of the community that he is addressing: "Jesus is heir to the promises made to David and kept alive in Judaism; he is also heir to the wider promise of blessings to the Gentiles made through Abraham." Matthew thus stresses by his genealogy "Jesus' insertion into a history and a people" (p. 69).

3. The genealogy of Matthew, Brown points out, is intended to show "that the coming of the Messiah marks the end of God's carefully delineated plan" (p. 81). How does Matthew show this? Brown explains: "Matthew drew upon two genealogical lists already in existence in Greek," one covering the period from Abraham to David, and the other (a popular genealogy containing errors and omissions) covering the monarchical and early post-monarchical period. Matthew noted that there were fourteen

names in the first list, and then he noticed that in the second (accidentally abbreviated) list there were fourteen more names down to the Babylonian Exile, and, by adding himself the names of Joseph and Jesus, a third set of fourteen emerged. "Giving rein to a predilection for numerical patterns, Matthew thought that he had discovered the key to God's plan of salvation, a 3 x 14 pattern" (p. 70). And thus was devised the message of Mt. 1:17:

Therefore, all the generations from Abraham to David (are) fourteen generations, and from David to the Babylonian Transmigration fourteen generations, and from the Babylonian Transmigration to Christ fourteen generations.

4. Actually, Brown avers, there are only thirteen generations in the first set, but Matthew may have intended the unmentioned generation of Abraham as the fourteenth. In the second set four known historical generations have been left out, and in the third set there are only thirteen generations. Brown thinks that four generations in the second set had been accidentally omitted earlier by a copyist of Matthew's source, and Matthew did not realize this in making his count (p. 75). The third set, according to Brown, is plainly one of thirteen generations, but Matthew may have implicitly intended the omitted generation of Jechoniah (and Joakim begot Joachin [Jechoniah]) at the end of the second set.

5. Could Matthew count? Raymond Brown, reading Matthew's genealogy from the viewpoint of a modern reader, does not plainly see fourteen generations in each of the three sets of names, but by using ingenuity he can "salvage Matthew's reputation as a mathematician." He cautions, for one thing, that we should not expect too much logic in Matthew's reasoning, since omissions are frequently made in tribal genealogies "for reasons that do not seem logical to the Western scientific mind" (pp. 82–84).[1]

6. Brown's reasoning leaves a big problem. In the light of the deficiencies that he sees in Matthew's counting, how can one seriously believe that Matthew really shows by his 3 x 14 pattern that "God planned from the beginning and with precision the Messiah's origins" (p. 80)? What kind of precision is this? And what could the number fourteen seriously mean in the message of Matthew? Brown believes that for Matthew fourteen was, indeed, "the magic number" (p. 74), but he cannot surmise what that number was supposed to mean. He knows of no special symbolism

---

1 Cf. M. D. Johnson, *The Purpose of the Biblical Genealogies with Special Reference to the Setting of the Genealogies of Jesus,* in New Testament Studies Monograph Series, No. 8 (Cambridge University, 1969), p. 166.

attached to the number fourteen, and, therefore, he cannot grasp at all the point that Matthew is trying to make. So, rather than "salvage" Matthew's reputation as a theologian, Brown leaves Matthew's theology of 3 x 14 generations in a very precarious state.

7. Now, in order to appreciate what the numbers of Mt. 1:17 are saying, it is necessary first to realize that the text is saying something on a literal and historical level and something additional on a symbolic level. The literal level has itself a plain meaning and, probably, a more subtle meaning as well that requires study in order to be perceived. The purpose of the plain literal meaning is to provide a general, although somewhat imprecise, idea of the data in which the spiritual message resides. The purpose of the more subtle literal meaning is to provide an implicit but precise historical statement of the facts in conformity with the spiritual message of the text. In this article I am addressing the literal meaning of Mt. 1:17 on its plain and subtle levels, leaving the allegorical meaning for a subsequent writing.

A. The Plain Literal Meaning of Mt. 1:17

8. Let us look at the plain message of the text of Mt. 1:17. Matthew states that from Abraham to King David there were fourteen generations. Commentators contend that there were more than fourteen generations. Thus, Raymond Brown (op. cit., p. 74) maintains that "even God did not arrange things so nicely that exactly fourteen biological generations separated such crucial moments in salvation history as the call of Abraham, the accession of David, the Babylonian Exile, and the coming of the Messiah." The spans of time, he continues, "are too great to have contained only fourteen generations each, since some 750 years separated Abraham from David, some 400 years separated David from the Babylonian Exile, and some 600 years separated the Babylonian Exile from Jesus' birth." But, we would respond, Matthew is not plainly saying that there were fourteen *immediate* biological generations in each period. In fact, when in his opening verse Matthew speaks of Jesus as "Son of David, son of Abraham," he is setting up a definition of terms which enlarges the notion of a generation. Just as Matthew can use the word *son* to mean any descendant in the direct line, so can he use the word *begot* to mean any ancestor in the direct line. Therefore, he does not err in saying in the second set of names that "Joram begot Oziah" (Mt. 1:8), even though there were three immediate biological generations in between. Matthew is saying that there were fourteen un-disqualified generations in each period of time, and his point has force as

long as there is a discernible reason for omitting some of the immediate generations in keeping with the purpose of his writing. But how is there any cogency in first omitting three immediate generations between Joram and Oziah (also called Azariah) and then saying that *all* of the generations were fourteen? I think that the answer lies in the special meaning of a generation in the plain purpose of Matthew's writing. A generation signifies the passing on of the seed of Abraham, of Isaac, of Jacob, and of David, together with the promises that were given to this seed. There is a fulfillment aspect and a polemic aspect in Matthew's purpose regarding this seed. There was a feeling abroad among the Jews that the Messiah to come would save and vindicate all of the descendants of Abraham, of Isaac, and of Jacob, for the one and only reason that they were the descendants of Abraham, of Isaac, and of Jacob, *because God had promised so*. Matthew intends to show that God fulfilled his promises, but not in the way that many were expecting. To show this, Matthew (1:23) recalls with slight variation the prophecy in Isaiah 7:14 ("Behold, the virgin shall be with child and shall bring forth a son, and you will name him Emmanuel") with the historical setting that it implies.

9. Basically, the prophecy was delivered by Isaiah to Achaz, son of Joatham and grandson of Oziah, mentioned above. The burden of the prophecy is this: You kings of Judah, you kingly descendants of David, have caused a lot of annoyance to people who matter. You presume that you can do anything you please, because God promised to Abraham and to David that in you, in the seed of Abraham and of David, will all the nations be blessed. But I want to tell you something, King Achaz. In the seed of Abraham and of David will all the nations be blessed. But it won't be your seed, passed down from David to you, and from you to your descendants that will produce the Savior. Rather, a *virgin* will conceive and bear a child without the concourse of any male seed, and you, the House of David, will name the child and will call Him, "God with us."

10. The principal purpose of Matthew's first chapter is to show that this prophecy was completely fulfilled in the actual historical event of the coming of the Savior. The male seed was passed down from Abraham to David, from David to the last king, Jechoniah, and from Jechoniah to Joseph, in whom the prophecy was fulfilled. Joseph discovered ("behold") that the Virgin was with child, and he learned from God through an angel that this had happened by the miraculous intervention of the Holy Spirit. Joseph, son of David, representing the House of David, accepted the Savior, accepted his Virgin Mother, and adored Jesus as "God with

us." And Joseph named the Child, as Isaiah had prophesied he would do. Matthew's account of the generation of Jesus ends with the naming of Jesus by Joseph (Mt. 1:25). Many commentators have missed the importance of this conclusion and the relationship that it has to Isa. 7:14.

11. How does Matthew stress by his genealogy "Jesus' insertion into a history and a people"? He does so basically in two different ways, first by the way in which he traces the descent of the seed of Abraham to David and then to Joseph, and secondly by his use of the number fourteen. These two devices are employed to show that God is the Lord of history, that the Messiah came at the time appointed by God, and that the promises of God to Abraham and to David were kept exactly.

12. It is Matthew's use of the number fourteen that concerns us here. From the earliest times commentators have remarked that some immediate generations were omitted by Matthew, and the reason that they ascribe has to do with wickedness. Thus, the wickedness of Her and Onan (Gen. 38) led to the elimination by God of one generation in the descent of the seed of Abraham to Joseph. Otherwise, the first set would have had fifteen names.

13. Regarding the second set of "fourteen" generations, we read that "Joram begot Oziah" (Mt. 1:18). But we know that Joram was actually the great-great-grandfather of Oziah, because Oziah is another name for Azariah (cf. 2Chr. 26:1; 2 Kg. [4Kg.] 14:21), and in 1Chr. 3:11–12 we read: "and Joram begot Ochoziah, from whom sprang Joas, and his son Amasiah begot Azariah." Hence, Matthew omits the generations of Ochoziah, Joas, and Amasiah from his list, and the judgments given in the Old Testament upon these people may tell us why.

14. St. Jerome[2] sees a reason in the fact that Joram married Athalia, the daughter of Jezebel of Sidon, who drew him deeper and deeper into the practices of idolatry, and that the three generations of sons succeeding him continued in the worship of idols. In the very first of the Ten Commandments given by God through Moses on Mount Sinai it was stated: "Thou shalt not have foreign gods before me. …Thou shalt not adore or serve them. I am the Lord thy God, powerful and jealous, visiting the iniquity of fathers upon their children unto the third and fourth generation of those that hate me, and showing mercy unto thousands to those that love me and

---

2 The following discussion from the Fathers of the Church is based principally upon the presentation given by Thomas Aquinas in his linear commentaries: *Readings on the Gospel of St. Matthew* and *Catena Aurea: Matthew*, especially verses 8, 11, and 17 of Matthew's chapter 1.

keep my commandments" (Ex. 20:3–6). Now Solomon was a sinner and an idolater (1Kg. [3Kg.] 11: 7–8), but he had a good man for his father and was therefore not punished in his own generation (1Kg. [3Kg.] 11:12).

15. St. Augustine[3] points out that the same was true of Joram, who had Josaphat for his father, and therefore did not have his name removed from Matthew's genealogy (cf. 2Chr. 21:7).

16. St. John Chrysostom[4] adds the further reason that the Lord had ordered the house of Ahab to be extirpated from the face of the earth (2Kg. [4Kg.] 9:8), and the three kings eliminated by Matthew were, as descendants of Athalia, of the seed of Ahab. Jehu eradicated the worship of Baal from Israel, but he did not forsake the golden calves in Bethel and Dan. Nevertheless, the Lord said to him: "Because you have diligently performed what was right and pleasing in my eyes and have done to the house of Ahab in keeping with everything that was in my heart, your children shall sit upon the throne of Israel unto the fourth generation (2Kg. [4Kg.] 10:28–31). So it is interesting to note that while these generations of Jehu were inserted into the royal lineage of Israel, the three generations of Ahab were taken out of the genealogy of Jesus by the judgment of God through the inspired pen of St. Matthew.

17. In concluding his second set of fourteen generations, Matthew says (Mt. 1:11): "And Josiah begot Jechoniah and his brothers at the time of the deportation to Babylon." This statement seems erroneous. Critics have from the earliest times pointed out that the Old Testament (e.g., 1Chr. 3:15–16) tells a different story: "And the sons of Josiah were, the firstborn Johanan, the second Joakim, the third Sedekiah, the fourth Sellum. Of Joakim were born Jechoniah, and Sedekiah." So Matthew 1:11 should read: "And Josiah begot Joakim and his brothers. And Joakim begot Joachin (Jechoniah) just before the deportation to Babylon." The pagan philosopher Porphyry claimed that this confusion of persons proves the existence of historical errors in the Gospels.

18. Two basic solutions to this problem of "confusion of persons" in Jechoniah have been proposed:

A) St. Augustine[5] takes the 'Jechoniah' of Mt. 1:11 and Mt. 1:12 (who begot Salathiel) to be Joachin, the son of Joakim. He thinks that Matthew may have omitted the name of Joakim deliberately in order to

---

3 Augustine of Hippo, *De quaestionibus novi et veteris testamenti,* question 85.

4 John Chrysostom, *Commentary on Matthew,* homily 1.

5 Augustine of Hippo, *De consensu evangelistarum* libri 4, in PL, vol. 34, col. 1076. So also John Chrysostom, *Commentary, on Matthew.*

show that Joakim ruled, not by divine right, but by the will of Pharao
Nechao, as well as to arrive at the number of fourteen generations for
the second set. This makes fourteen generations for the third set also,
if Jechoniah is counted twice: once as the son of Josiah and again as
the father of Salathiel; that is, once as concluding the royal descent of
the seed of David and again as beginning the generations of private
individuals. This solution has some reasonability. Jeremiah's prescription,
"Write this man barren, a man that shall not prosper in his days, for
there shall not be a man of his seed that shall sit upon the throne of
David and have power in Judah any more" (Jer. 22:30), referring to this
Jechoniah, could have been taken by Matthew as an editorial directive
for himself. The royal seed ran out with the capture of Jechoniah by
Nebuchadnezzar, but after thirty-seven years of imprisonment the same
Jechoniah was given a new lease on life as a private citizen and was able
to have children (Jer. 52:31–34). Just as Abraham and his nephew Lot
are called brothers (Gen. 13:11) and just as the sons of Joseph were
adopted by Jacob and made brothers of their uncles (Gen. 48:5), so
could Joachin have been reputed the son of Josiah and the brother of
his uncles. Just as Abraham in this genealogy is counted as a generation
even though his begetting is not recorded here, so could Jechoniah
the captive conceivably be counted as a generation, even though he
is already counted in the preceding set: the descent of the seed turns
a corner with Jechoniah, and the promise passes to more chastened
children of Abraham and of David; as a humble citizen and expatriate,
Jechoniah is able to begin the descent of the fourteen final generations
to the birth of the Savior.

B) St. Jerome[6] takes the Jechoniah of Mt. 1:11 to be Joakim and the
Jechoniah of Mt. 1:12 to be his son Joachim. Since the names Joakim
and Joachin are almost alike, they could have been confused by a copyist
or a translator.[7] By linguistic analogy the appellation *Jekoniah* could be
applied to Joakim, or even, according to Cornelius aLapide, with the
spelling Jechoniah by linguistic assimilation. Thus the Jechoniahs in
verses 11 and 12 could refer to father and son.

---

6 St. Jerome, *Linear Commentary,* on Dan. 1:1.

7 The opinion that a copyist of Matthew's text inadvertently omitted three names in
the second set because of the resemblance of Ochoziah and Oziah was later defended by
Gaspar Sanchez (1553–1628) in his commentary on 2Kg. [4Kg.] 14:18. Again, Sanchez
held that the copyist had also accidentally skipped "Jeconiah begot Jechoniah" because of
the similarity of names.

19. St. Ambrose[8] says that the connecting link, "Jekoniah begot Jechoniah," was not expressed by Matthew because he wanted to stress the separation produced by the deportation to Babylon. Epiphanius[9] says that Matthew did express it, but a later copyist left it out, and some Greek and

---

8 St. Ambrose, *Commentary on Luke,* ch. 2. Another possibility is that the chain of generations is not broken by the exile, but the two generations of Joakim and Joachin have been condensed into one. The generation of Joachin may have been editorially absorbed into that of his father as a means of "writing him barren" (Jer. 22:30); linguistic license would enable Matthew to impose the name Jechoniah upon Joakim to fulfill the prophecy of Jeremiah regarding the latter: "They shall not mourn for him" (Jer. 22:18). With an adroit stroke of the pen Matthew could have wiped out the memory of Joakim and the generation of Joachin, while retaining the memory of Joachin and the generation of Joakim and his brothers, with all the infamy that it brings to mind and all the strictures against it that are recorded in the Book of Jeremiah. By this reading Josiah begot *Jechoniah* (Joakim) and his brothers, and Jechoniah (Joakim) begot Salathiel through Joachin (Jechoniah), whose begetting is not expressed. The name Jechoniah means "the Lord has put right," and Matthew would be saying that the Lord put the royal seed right by bringing on the Babylonian captivity and ending the royal succession.

9 St. Epiphanius, *On the Sect of the Epicureans.* Cf. Jacques Masson, *Jésus, Fils de David dans les Généalogies de Saint Matthieu et de Saint Luc* (Paris: Téqui, 1982), pp. 49–63, who also holds that a copyist omitted the link "and Joakim begot Jechoniah (Joachin) in the Babylonian Transmigration."

Raymond Brown's idea that 'Matthew' unwittingly used a Greek genealogy damaged by the errors of an earlier translator from the Hebrew seems untenable in the light of all the data, taking into consideration especially the reasons that Matthew had for omitting some of the names. But the possibility that Matthew wittingly took a defective genealogical record with four names missing and used it to contrast with the true story that he had to tell (Mt. 1:18-25) cannot be entirely excluded in view of the principle of historical reservation.

The theory of Epiphanius, taken up in our day by Jacques Masson and others, is that a translator from Hebrew to Greek of Matthew's genealogy inadvertently confused the generations of Joakim and Joachin. Masson argues that verse 11 of the genealogy must in the Hebrew originally have read as follows: "And Josiah begot Joakim and his brothers; and Joakim begot Joachin...." The translator into Greek must have written the verse in this way: "And Josiah begot Joakim and his brothers; and Joakim begot Joakim...." A copyist would then have dropped as redundant the clause "and Joakim begot Joakim," while a later copyist in order to bring the remaining part of the verse into consonance with verse 12, changed it to read: "And Josiah begot Jechoniah and his brothers."

While this is a carefully-thought-out explanation, it has several weaknesses. It supposes a series of errors of transcription with no checking either by the scribes involved or by those around them, and there is no documentary evidence for such a happening. Conceptually, this explanation assumes that there were fifteen generations in the second set, since Joachin (Jechoniah) was born before the Babylonian Transmigration, and that is excluded by verse 17. Finally, it ignores the possibility that Matthew used the name *Jechoniah* precisely to avoid confusion with the name of his father Joakim.

Latin codices do have it in. The explanation of Epiphanius would make fifteen generations in the second set, since Joachin was begotten before the deportation to Babylon, whereas that of Ambrose preserves the fourteen generations by positing a tacit link in the chain of generations.

20. We thus begin to see a point that Matthew is making with his three sets of fourteen generations. The Messiah came, and the promise was fulfilled in the forty-second generation from Abraham. Some generations had not been qualified to be included in the count because of absolute wickedness: Her and Onan, Ochoziah, Joas, Amasiah, and Joakim/Joachin (one or the other, since both had been extremely wicked). Perhaps other generations have been omitted as well for the same reason. But God was merciful. Many other persons in the chain of generations were admitted into the count, even though they were involved in evil themselves. Thus, Judah begot Phares as an intended act of adultery and with no thought of the passing on of the seed of Abraham (Gen. 38); David sinned grievously in taking to wife Bathsheba, the mother of Solomon (2Sam. [2Kg.] 11); Solomon fell into idolatry (1Kg. [3Kg.] 11:1–4); Roboam was a cruel and idolatrous king (1Kg. [3Kg.] 12 and 14); Abia "walked in all the sins of his father" (1Kg. [3Kg.] 15:3); Joram was an evil king (2Chron. 21); Achaz (to whose face Isaiah foretold the Virginal Conception of Jesus) cast statues to Baal and "sacrificed to pagan gods in the high places and on the hills and under every green tree" (2Kg. [4Kg.] 16). Yet God allowed these generations to be included in the count. The resulting generations are 3 x 14, a long period of time, to be sure, but God could have waited for 7 x 14 generations, or even for 70 x 14 generations, and mankind would still not have received more punishment than it deserved. The lesson that Matthew is teaching actually illustrates the mercy of God.

B. A Possible Subtle Literal Meaning of Mt 1:17

21. Is there a subtle historical message contained in the seemingly rude mathematics of Matthew's genealogy? If there is such a meaning, it will necessarily remain elusive and ambiguous, but it will also correspond in a rewarding manner to penetrating scientific inquiry, even though it may not teach or express scientific truth in a plain and pedagogical manner. Let us look again at Matthew's number pattern.

22. To begin with, Matthew's three sets of fourteen generations appear to be divided according to the notion of a primitive 28-day month. From the new moon of Abraham, Jewish history waxes to the full moon of David;

then it wanes to the blackout of the Babylonian Deportation; and finally it waxes again to the full moon of the coming of the Messiah. Such an image would convey a messianic meaning as well as illustrate the unfolding of the Providence of God, and I think that this lunar image is suggested to some extent by the 14 x 3 generations, [10] but the full historical meaning seems much more refined than that. Looking at the lunar image, we find that David was in some sense the greatest king of the Jews: Jewish history waxed from Abraham to David. The Babylonian Captivity was perhaps the greatest catastrophe of the Jews before the time of Christ: Jewish history waned from David to the Captivity. And the coming of the Messiah was the culmination of the ancestral expectations: Jewish history waxed from the Captivity to Jesus. In this sense the lunar image fits the text of Mt. 1:17.

23. In biblical imagery the moon often represents the beauty and stability of nature. Thus the Spouse of Christ is described in Cant. 6:9: "Who is she that comes forth as the morning rising, fair as the moon, bright as the sun, terrible as an army set in battle array?" But the moon in Sacred Scripture is also a witness to the fickleness of human endeavors and the futility of human events transpiring in an atmosphere of moral iniquity. Thus, the paschal lamb was sacrificed under the full noon of the first Hebrew month, in the evening of the fourteenth day (Ex. 12:6), because this act symbolized the merciful intervention of God, but also because this day symbolized the plenitude of the iniquity of men. Christ, the true Paschal Lamb, died under the full moon of the same first month of the Hebrew year, not only as the supreme act of divine mercy, but also because iniquity was seen to have reached its height at that moment (cf. Lk. 22:53).

24. The phases of Hebrew history can therefore be read in an opposite sense. David, a prototype of Jesus Christ, was given to the Hebrew people in the fourteenth generation from Abraham as an act of divine mercy, but the true Savior did not come at that time because of the evilness of the people. In fact, it was out of inordinate desire for worldly glory and power that the Hebrew people clamored to have a king, and they were given kings, not unto their happiness and prosperity, but rather unto their punishment and oppression (1Sam. [1Kg.] 8:11–20). Again, the Savior could have come in the fourteenth generation of the second set, but

---

10 "The two Hebrew words for month are *yéráh* and *hodésh*, whose primitive meaning, moon, or new moon, points to the dependence of the Jewish month on the phases of the moon. As a matter of fact, the Hebrew months have always been lunar, and extended from one new moon to another" (Francis E. Gigot, "Calendar, Jewish," in the *Catholic Encyclopedia*, 1908 edition).

because the people were evil, and their kings were exceedingly evil, they received instead the Deportation to Babylon. But the Savior was born in the fourteenth generation of the third set (although mankind did not yet deserve Him), because the fullness of time had come according to God's Providence, and a truly good man, St. Joseph, had arisen from the seed of David, able to appreciate the Virginal Conception and to adore the Divine Child as his God. This *Sitz-im-Leben* (life situation) of good and evil seems to be implied in Matthew's Infancy Narrative and in the Old Testament imagery which forms its background.

25. We can see in Psalm 88 (89) a possible backdrop to the lunar imagery of Matthew's genealogy. "I have made a covenant with my elect; I have sworn to David my servant: thy seed I will set up forever. And I will build up thy throne unto generation and generation. The heavens shall confess thy wonders, O Lord, and thy truth in the church of the saints. ... Once have I sworn by my holiness; I will not lie to David: his seed shall endure forever. And his throne as the sun before me, and as the moon perfect forever, and a faithful witness in heaven" (Ps. 88:4–6; 36–38; cf. Ps. 71 [72]: 1–7).

26. But even more directly does the message of Matthew 1:17 reflect the Book of Isaiah, which opens with somber words about the moon and the wicked royal descendants of David, and which concludes in the joyful vision of the months and festivals of the Jews and Gentiles converted to the blessed seed of David, Jesus Christ: "The vision of Isaiah the son of Amos, which he saw concerning Judah and Jerusalem in the days of Oziah, Joathan, Achaz, and Ezechiah, kings of Judah. ...Woe to the sinful nation, a people laden with iniquity, a wicked seed, delinquent children: they have forsaken the Lord, they have blasphemed the Holy One of Israel, they are gone away backwards. ...Offer sacrifice no more in vain; incense is an abomination to me. The new moons, and the Sabbaths, and other festivals I will not abide; your assemblies are wicked. My soul hates your new moons and your solemnities; they are troublesome to me, I am weary of bearing them" (Isa. 1:1, 4, 13–14). This opening of Isaiah contrasts with its conclusion: "For as the new heavens and the new earth, which I will make stand before me, says the Lord, so shall your seed stand, and your name. And there shall be month after month, and Sabbath after Sabbath, (and) all flesh shall come to adore before my face, says the Lord" (Isa. 66:22–23).

27. Let us now take a closer look at Matthew's calendar. A month of 28 days (4 seven-day weeks) is not as primitive as it sounds. In fact, a year of thirteen 28–day months (which equal 364 days) plus one more day at

the end of each year and an additional day in the same leap years as on the Gregorian calendar would be as accurate a calendar as is the Gregorian. In ancient times, of course, men did not have the means of computing the exact length of the solar year except by observation. But the length of the thirteen 28–day-month calendar described above could have been accurately determined by observing the heliacal rising of a bright star like Sirius[11] and adjusting the new year accordingly. Two advantages of such a calendar are that dates of a month always fall on the same day of the week, and each month has an even four weeks.

28. Yet, the moon has tended to impose itself conspicuously upon the measurement of time, and months related to the phases of the moon have become units of almost every calendar. It was early recognized, however, that the lunar month is longer than twenty-eight days, and it was also discovered that the cycles of the moon vary in length; what is more, these cycles do not coincide with the solar year. The average length of a lunar (synodic) month, during which the moon goes through all of its phases, is 29.53059 days, that is, slightly more than 29.5 days; it actually varies in irregular succession from 29.26 days to 29.80 days. A further perennial problem of lunar calendars is that the solar year is not evenly divisible into lunar months. In fact, the solar (tropical) year is 365.2422 days in length, while twelve lunar months are only 354.3670 days in length. Therefore, the year of twelve lunar months is about eleven days (10.8752 days) shorter than the solar year. This shortfall has to be corrected by the intercalation (insertion) of an extra lunar month in a cycle of years. For instance, in a cycle of eight years, three years would have thirteen months and the other five years would have twelve. The resulting eight-year cycle would be just 1.5906 days longer than eight exact solar years.

29. As late as the seventh century A.D. the Moslem Arabs adopted a calendar of twelve lunar months with no intercalary corrections; it is still in use today. Since this calendar is about eleven days (10.8752 days) shorter than the true solar year, it slips gradually through the seasons and around the solar year until it comes back to its original position about once every 33.6 years.

30. A look at the article *Calendar* in any standard encyclopedia will show how complex and complicated has been the effort to produce accurate

---

11 As a bright star moves away from vicinity to the sun in the annual revolution of the heavens, it pops back into sight with an unaided visual regularity accurate to within a few hours.

calendars composed of lunar months.[12] In Babylonia, three centuries of careful lunar observations enabled the framing of a calendar set up on a fixed 19-year cycle containing 235 lunar months, divided in such a way that twelve of the nineteen years had twelve months and the other interspersed seven years had thirteen months. This calendar deviated from true solar time by only about two hours in nineteen years, or less than one day in two centuries. It was in use in Babylonia by 367 B.C., and it has been in continuous use in some parts of the world ever since. The year began originally, as in the Hebrew calendar, with the new moon following the vernal equinox, but after 312 B.C., in the Seleucid Empire in Mesopotamia and Syria, the new year was set to begin with the new moon following the autumnal equinox. This 19-year cycle was adopted by the Hebrews for their religious calendar and is still basically in use by them; it is also used by Christians for determining the date of Easter.[13]

31. In Egypt the primitive lunar calendar was replaced by a solar calendar as early as 2773 B.C. This solar calendar consisted of twelve 30-day months followed by an intercalary period of five days to make a year of 365 days; it began in coincidence with the heliacal rising of Sirius (Sothis), i.e., if I am not mistaken, on July 19 of the Gregorian calendar. But since this Sothic year was about a fourth of a day shorter than the true solar year (exactly 0.242199 days) it ran ahead of true solar time at a rate of about one day every four years, and this deviation was not corrected, so that each respective day and season of the calendar slipped all around the solar year in a period of 1507 true solar years, at the end of which time the first day of the year once again coincided with the heliacal rising of Sirius. The inconvenience and confusion of such slippage can easily be imagined, as well as the complexity of determining the true season and date of a happening in the past.

32. Some of these efforts to construct an accurate chronological system seem to be implicit in the background of Matthew's numbering of the generations. But even more so is the crucial intervention made by Julius Caesar in 46 B.C., when he proclaimed the Julian calendar and made it official for the Roman Empire. Caesar intervened to abolish the lunar calendar then in use in Rome, with its intercalary month, and based the civil year entirely on the sun.

---

12 Cf., for example, the articles "Calendar" ("Calendario") in the *Encyclopedia Americana,* the *Encyclopaedia Britannica,* the *Enciclopedia Cattolica,* and the *Enciclopedia Italiana.*

13 Cf. "Calendar," in the *Encyclopedia Americana* (vol. 19, 1967, pg. 191; Herbert Thurston, "Calendar," in the *Catholic Encyclopedia* (vol. 3, 1908, pgs. 158–160).

33. Those who say that Matthew miscounted his third set of generations, calling fourteen what are only thirteen, may be missing the fact that Matthew has actually set up two cycles of generations, one of forty generations from Abraham to Joseph, and a second of two generations, those of Mary and Jesus. Matthew's counting would be correct, for, according to his system, the first person in a cycle counts as a generation. Just as Abraham is the first generation of the first cycle, so Mary is the first generation of the second cycle. The two cycles are simultaneous rather than successive: a) the seed of Abraham does not pass from Joseph to Jesus; b) the second cycle could have occurred biologically at any point in the forty-generation cycle.

34. Let us compare Matthew's mathematics with the Julian calendar. An interesting thing about the Julian calendar is that it sets up a "perpetual calendar" of fourteen months in a cycle of twenty-eight years.[14] The characteristic numbers of this cycle are, therefore, fourteen, and twenty-eight. Another curious thing about this calendar is that it does have a month of twenty-eight days, February, which becomes twenty-nine days in the final year of each 4-year cycle. These facts could be mathematical clues to a subtle chronological message that Matthew is giving to us: the exact date of the Birth of the Messiah.

35. The Julian Reform of the old Roman Calendar went into effect early in the year 46 B.C. (of the Gregorian calendar) with regard to the filling in of the ninety days or so that the old Roman calendar was by that time running ahead of the true solar year. Then the new Julian calendar went into effect on January 1, 45 B.C. This was Julian Year 1. In ancient times it was the priests who traditionally determined when the new month and when the New Year began. So it was among the Jews, and so it was among the Romans. In fact, it was as pontifex maximus, or high priest, that Julius Caesar proclaimed his reform of the Roman calendar. Now, pagan Roman priests had been responsible for the great deviation of the old Roman calendar, and pagan Roman priests proceeded to cause errors in the new Julian calendar. In fact, Caesar's plan called for a 29th day in February (doubling the 24th day) in every *fourth* year, but the priests mistakenly provided the extra day in every third year, beginning with Julian Year 3. Thus, by Julian Year 36, there had been twelve leap years instead of nine, with the result that the Julian calendar had slipped

---

14 See "Perpetual Calendar" in *The World Almanac* or in any comparable source. The term is taken, not in the sense of a calendar of thirteen fixed 28-day months, but in the sense of the pattern of 14 different day-of-the-week and date-of-the-month relationships set up by the Julian Calendar.

about three days behind solar time. Augustus Caesar then intervened to proclaim a period of twelve years with no leap years included in order to bring the Julian calendar back to solar time.[15] Thus there was no leap year (officially) in or near the year of the Birth of the Savior. We are left with the curious historical fact that, at the time of the Birth of the Savior, the erroneous Julian calendar, as implemented by the pagan priests, was running about two days behind the correct solar time, but the true Julian calendar, as projected by Julius Caesar, had not by then deviated as much as a single day from the correct solar time. [16] The background material on ancient calendars is challenging; it invites the further investigation of those who are able to look into the question with an open mind and in an orderly manner. The seeming mathematical inaccuracy in the inspired text of Mt. 1:17 may actually be a subtle invitation to ponder the verse for deeper meaning. We know that the Church has traditionally celebrated the anniversary of the naming of Jesus on January first. Could this be an implicit adherence to history that is based in part on the same tradition that is reflected in the Gospel of Matthew?

36. While such a correlation is conjectural and by no means an established fact or a plain reading of the text of Matthew, I do propose it for the further study of competent scholars, because it is not only coherent with Christian faith but also potentially satisfying to the scientific mind. That Jesus Christ would have come in the forty-second year after Julius Caesar subjected the "whole world" to his new framework of time—a framework which became the chronological instrument of Western civilization and of the Christian Church down to the present day—is not out of keeping with the biblical approach, which emphasizes the contrast between the interventions of the powers of this world and the subtle unfolding of the Providence of God.

37. Isaiah 7:14 predicted that the House of David would adore and name the Infant Savior, virginally conceived. St. Joseph, the 40th generation of the seed of Abraham, adored and named the Infant Jesus, conceived of the Virgin Mary, whose generation became the 41st by reason of her espousal to Joseph. The naming of the Savior is important in the prophecy of Isaiah,

---

15 See the *Encyclopedia Italiana*, art. "Calendario," vol. VIII, pp. 399–400.

16 It is true that, because the 28 year cycle of the Julian Calendar ran slightly slower than the true solar year (taking about 11 minutes and 14 seconds longer than the solar year), it fell behind true solar time by about one day in 128 years. This error was corrected by the Gregorian Reform in 1582, which eliminated three leap years at the turn of every four centuries, thus reducing the excess to 26 seconds a year, or one day in 3,323 years. But the fact is that, at the time of Jesus' birth and naming, the true Julian Calendar (as projected by Julius Caesar) had not deviated from true solar time by as much as a single day.

and it is doubly important in Matthew's description of Jesus' birth, which ends precisely with the naming of Jesus by Joseph (Mt. 1:25). Jesus was thus probably named on the first day of the 42nd Julian year, January 1, 4 B.C., having been born seven days earlier, on December 25, 5 B.C.

38. It might seem more symmetrical according to Matthew's numbers for the *fulfillment* of Isaiah 7:14 to have taken place at the *end* of the 42nd Julian year rather than at the beginning. But the biblical period of waiting for a fruitful result lies especially in the number 40, and this number was fulfilled in the generation of Joseph. Then began the supernatural cycle, with the Annunciation to Mary occurring in the 41st Julian year. The symbolism of the number 42 could, of course, rest in the completion of 42 years from the decree of Julius Caesar early in 46 B.C., inaugurating the Julian Reform, but it seems more in keeping with the tenor of Matthew's mathematics to locate the climactic moment at the exact beginning of the 42nd year of the new Julian calendar.

39. While the number 14 has special symbolic reference to the allegorical sense of Mt. 1:17, we might consider some historical implications of Matthew's implicit "month" of twenty-eight generations. Julian Year 28, by Julius Caesar's projection, should have been a leap year; that is, February should have had 29 days. By human historical error, February of Julian Year 28 had only 28 days. Comparing this fact with Mt. 1:17, we find that, by modern historical accuracy, Matthew's 28th generation should have been doubled (Joakim / Joachin), but Matthew fuses the two generations into one. Is there subtle irony in this fusion?

40. Furthermore, in the plan of Julius Caesar, the extra day in a leap year was to be inserted immediately after February 24. Looking at Matthew's genealogy we find that the 24th generation from Abraham was Ezekiah, son of Achaz, which son had just been born when Isaiah delivered the prophecy in Isaiah 7:14 to Achaz. The subtle message in Matthew 1:17 could be that the Messiah was not born to Ezekiah but to a virgin; that is, the divine intervention did not come upon the 24th generation, but rather it came entirely apart from the whole biological succession of male seed and at the time decreed by the Providence of God, namely, at the time of the fortieth generation (since the number forty symbolizes the end of a fruitful period of waiting) and as the forty-second generation (40 + 2), which is the second generation of the supernatural cycle.

41. The proposal of a deep mathematical meaning beneath the simple numbers of Matthew's 3 x 14 generations does not change in any way the plain reading of the text, but it does aim to provide a possible deeper under-

standing of the historicity of this verse and of the exactness of Matthew's mathematics. I leave this for the study of more qualified scholars.

Chapter 15

Called by the Prophets a Nazorean
(Matthew 2:23)

Part I. A Long-Standing Question

Living Tradition 84 (November 1999)

1. The text and context of Matt. 2:23. The second chapter of the Gospel according to St. Matthew ends with the return of the Holy Family to Nazareth. Matthew records that, after King Herod had died, an angel instructed St. Joseph to return with Mary and the Child Jesus to the land of Israel, and this Joseph did. But, when he heard that Archelaus was ruling in place of his father Herod, he was afraid to settle in Judea, (Matt. 2:23). Some English versions, such as the *Revised Standard Version* or the *New American Bible*, render the final words of this verse as a direct quotation: e.g., "that what was spoken by the prophets might be fulfilled, 'He shall be called a Nazarene,'" basing this translation upon the fact that in classical Greek the word *hoti* is often used (pleonastically) to set off a direct citation. But the same Greek word is equally used to introduce an indirect citation, as a glance at any classical Greek dictionary will show, and that is what seems to be the case here, because Matthew is not citing, as in other verses, "the prophet," but rather "the prophets," which does not appear to be referring to any particular one.

2. A doubt about Matthew's inerrancy. Some have doubted the inerrancy of Matthew's claim that a prophecy had here been fulfilled, namely, that Jesus would be called a Nazorean (Nazarene), on the ground that no such word as Nazareth, Nazarene, or Nazorean, appears anywhere

in the canonical books of the Old Testament, leading them to conclude that no bona fide prophet ever predicted this. Now, granted that the name Nazareth, either in itself or in its adjectival forms, does not appear in the Old Testament, it is, nevertheless, our contention that a more complete analysis will indicate that true prophecy was fulfilled, and it is my purpose in the present article to indicate how.

3. The word 'Nazorean.' Two Greek words used in the New Testament have often been translated into English by the one word 'Nazarene.' The word *Nazoraios* (Nazorean) appears exactly thirteen times in Matthew, John, Luke, and Acts, while its counterpart *Nazarenos* (Nazarene) appears six times in Mark and Luke. The two designations do seem to have been used interchangeably, at least on the level of popular parlance. Thus, in Matt. 26:71, a maidservant of the high priest is quoted as saying: "This (man) was with Jesus the Nazorean (*Nazoraios*)," while, in Mark 14:67, the same maidservant in the same incident is quoted as saying to Peter: "You also were with Jesus the Nazarene (*Nazarenos*)." Now, it is obvious that in that one historical statement she used one word or the other, and that, in doing so, she was using it as a place-name for the town of Nazareth, because she went on to say, "for your accent gives you away," and, therefore, we must assume that the two words were used equivalently, at least on a popular level, to refer to being from Nazareth.[1] Hence, I shall not argue that the designation *Nazoraios* has a special meaning in itself that *Nazarenos* does not have, but rather that it may have a special meaning from the context in which it is presented in Matt. 2:23.

4. What prophets foretold that Jesus would be a Nazorean? Speculation on this question has gone in two principal directions: either it was literally prophesied in one or more statements that do not appear in the canonical books of the Old Testament, or it is figuratively implied in one or more Old Testament statements taken as a whole. The first of these two possibilities was never greatly investigated, but the second was taken up by the Fathers of the Church and is succinctly epitomized by Thomas Aquinas where he says: "'*that he will be called a Nazaraean (Nazaraeus).*' This is not found written, but it can be said that it is gathered from many places. Nazarene, therefore, is translated 'holy': and, since Christ is called holy in Dan. 9:24, '*that the holy one be anointed,*' therefore, it is

---

1 It follows that versions of the Bible such as the *Douay Rheims* and the *Revised Standard Version,* which always render the Greek words *Nazoraios* and *Nazarenos* as 'Nazarene' or 'of Nazareth,' are not incorrect, but they may not be reflecting some more subtle differences of the two designations.

expressly said by a prophet. Or it can be said that by Nazarene is meant 'flowering': and this occurs in Isa. 11:1, '*there shall go forth a branch from the root of Jesse, and a flower will ascend from his root ....*' And this fits in with what is said in Cant. 2:1, '*I am the flower of the field and the lily of the valleys.*'[2] To the objection that Jesus should have been named from his birthplace (Bethlehem), Aquinas replies that Nazareth means "a flower," and Jesus preferred to be named from the place where his virtuous manners flowered than from the place where he was physically born.[3] What St. Thomas is stressing here is the presence of a meaning based metaphorically upon the etymology, that is, the possible root or roots, of the words Nazarene and Nazorean. And in his approach he is using a mental framework in which a distinct metaphorical sense is understood to be present in the verse, whether by intent of the human author, or, at least, by intent of the Holy Spirit, the divine Author of the text. And Matthew is challenging his readers to search for that sense. Since our neo-patristic approach accepts the framework of Aquinas, we will keep ever in mind the distinction between the literal and the spiritual sense as we proceed with this study, allowing also for the possibility that the spiritual meaning is the literal sense, as sometimes occurs in Sacred Scripture.

5. The origin of the name Nazareth. As noted in the previous paragraph, Thomas Aquinas, following the speculations of the Fathers of the Church, considers two possible origins of the name Nazareth. One possibility is that it comes from the Hebrew root *nzr* in the form of the noun *nazir*, meaning someone "set apart," "consecrated," and, therefore, "holy," or in the form of the noun *nezer*, meaning "crown." A second possibility is that it comes from the Hebrew noun *netser*, meaning "branch" or "flower." And it is not clear which of the two is the original etymon or even which of the two is intended by the divine Author as the spiritual sense of the text. As Cornelius aLapide pointed out more than three centuries ago, while the Greek text of Matthew seems to have been translated from a Hebrew or Aramaic original, the Greek words *Nazoraios* and *Nazarenos* do not indicate the answer, since the Greek consonant zeta (pronounced like the dz in adze) would be the same for both *nazir* (with *zayin*) and *netser* (with *tsade*). And William Albright, in his penetrating research into the possible origin of the name Nazareth, concluded that, in view of the linguistic phenomenon of "consonant shift," either word could be the root

---

2 T. Aquinas, *Super evangelium S. Matthaei*, at Matt. 2:23.

3 Aquinas, *Summa Theologiae*, III, q. 35, art. 7, ad 24. Cf. W.F. Albright, The names 'Nazareth' and 'Nazoraean,' in the *Journal of Biblical Literature* 65 (1946), pp. 399–400.

of Nazareth. Albright, in fact, favored the root *netser* and thought that the original name of Nazareth was probably *Notseret*. Bargil Pixner maintains that the Greek word *nazoraios* in Matt. 2:23 "certainly" comes from *netser*, because a Hebrew inscription found in Caesarea in 1962 and dating back to the third or fourth century A.D., spells Nazareth with *tsade* and not with *zayin*. And this discovery, he says, "eliminates the supposition that the appellation Natzoraios/Nazarene was linked to the name Nazirite.[4] But this conclusion ignores the linguistic phenomenon of "consonant shift" as well as the possibility that the spelling of the name Nazareth may have been ambiguous back in the first century A.D. Pixner claims also that the title "Natzorean/Nazarene" denotes especially the royal status of Jesus as a descendant of King David, basing this assumption on the supposition that a "Davidic clan" resettled the deserted area of Nazareth around 100 B.C. and the conjecture that they then became known as "Natzoreans," that is, as a kinship planted by God.[5] However, this last conjecture is weakly based and is challenged by the remark of Nathanael in John 1:46. Moreover, Pixner does not seem to distinguish clearly enough between the literal and the spiritual meanings of the word as it is used in Matt. 2:23.

6. Behold a virgin shall conceive. That the reader is being challenged to find the spiritual meaning of the prophecy about the Nazorean in Matt. 2:23 can be seen by the way in which the four preceding prophecies are quoted in these two chapters. Matthew first quotes Isa. 7:14, where he says: *"Behold a virgin shall conceive and bring forth a son, and they shall call his name Emmanuel,* which is translated 'God with us.'" Matt. 1:23 says that this prophecy in Isaiah has been literally fulfilled in the conception and birth of Jesus. It says that Jesus was miraculously conceived in that he was conceived by the power of the Holy Spirit without any male intercourse (Matt. 1:20). But, in addition to this miracle in nature, Matthew is conveying a spiritual message: Jesus, in not having been generated from the male seed of David, has been "set apart" from the political and cultural milieu of the House of David. Spiritually, the Virgin Mary has become the new "House of David." Jesus will be called, that is, He will be "God-with-us." In the conception and birth of Jesus, God is with us in a new and greater way: not insofar as a distant God has helped his people to win battles, to occupy lands, to gain prosperity, but by actually taking flesh in this man, Jesus. Matthew is saying that the fact of this incarnation is confirmed by the miracle of the

---

4 B. Pixner, Eng. trans., *With Jesus through Galilee according to the Fifth Gospel* [the biblical landscape] (Corazin: Rosh Pina, Israel, 1992), p. 15.

5 B. Pixner, ibid., pp. 14, 16, 17.

Virginal Conception, and that the Virginal Conception is confirmed by its prediction in Isaiah 7:14.

7. *And you, Bethlehem, in the land of Judah, are by no means least among the rulers of Judah, for out of you shall come a leader who shall rule my people Israel* (Micah [Micheas] 5:2, as quoted in Matt. 2:6). Matthew is affirming that this prophecy of Micah was literally fulfilled by the birth of Jesus at Bethlehem. As Matthew will show in the course of his Gospel, Jesus was not called to be a political or a military leader of Israel, but rather a spiritual leader in a new and better way, that is, of a spiritually constituted people, of the Kingdom of God on earth and in Heaven, of the new Israel established in his blood and conceptually distinguished from the Israelite race and society as such. Matthew is developing a different idea of holiness, centered in and around the holiness of Jesus.

8. *Out of Egypt I have called my son* (Hosea [Osee] 11:1, as quoted in Matt. 2:15). Thomas Aquinas and many others have seen this statement in Hosea as a prophecy *de praeterito*, that is, as an affirmation about the past that refers literally to the Exodus of the Chosen People out of Egypt under Moses.[6] The fuller quotation is as follows: *when Israel was a child, I loved him, and out of Egypt I called my son. The more I called them, the more they went from me; they kept sacrificing to the Baals and burning incense to idols* (Hosea 11:1–2). Hence, the statement refers literally to the people of Israel who went out from Egypt in the Exodus and then did not live up to their vocation. But Matthew takes the Exodus as a figure of the return of Jesus from Egypt to Palestine, applying to Jesus the calling from Egypt, but not the idolatry of the Israelites. We note in particular that Matthew sees the prophecy fulfilled, not in a literal, but in a figurative way, based upon the understanding that the original Israel (Jacob) was himself a prototype of Jesus and that the promise of God to Israel and to his seed was fulfilled literally in Jesus (cf. Gal. 3:16).

9. Rachel bewailing her children. Matthew's fourth citation is taken from Jeremiah, whom he quotes as follows: *A voice was heard in Ramah, wailing and loud lamentation: Rachel weeping for her children and would not be comforted, because they are not* (Jer. 31:15, as quoted in Matt. 2:18). Many have agreed with Thomas Aquinas in seeing this description also as a prophecy *de praeterito*, referring directly and literally to some misfortune of the tribe of Benjamin prior to the proclamation of Jeremiah, such as the slaughter of the Benjaminites recorded in Judges 20, when twenty-five thousand men of the tribe were slain and only six hundred survived. For

---

6 Cf. Aquinas, *Super evangelium S. Matthaei,* at Matt. 2:15.

Rachel was the mother of Joseph and Benjamin. Or in seeing this as being literally a prophecy regarding the Babylonian captivity of Benjamin and all the other tribes of Israel. But Aquinas goes on to show that Matthew interprets the prophecy as prefiguring the slaughter of the Innocents by Herod. The Hebrew word *ramah* means "height," and thus, in the prophecy the affirmation that "a voice was heard in Ramah" means figuratively that "a voice was heard on high," that is, by God in Heaven. The prophecy mentions Rachel as weeping in Ramah, which is, weeping from the place of her burial, but the expression is metaphorical, because it is not saying that the sound of loud weeping was sensibly heard from her grave. And so, even literally, Rachel is taken symbolically as the mother of all of the tribes of Israel, inasmuch as she was the principal and predilect wife of Jacob. Now, Bethlehem is in the territory of Judah about one or two miles from the border with Benjamin, and the soldiers of Herod killed the male infants "that were in Bethlehem and in all the borders thereof" (Matt. 2:16), so that they probably killed some infants also in the territory of Benjamin. In any case, all of the mothers of the infants slain were figuratively "little Rachels," and thus, in my opinion, the prophecy of Jeremiah was literally fulfilled in their weeping. But the prophecy was to be spiritually fulfilled, since it goes on to say: *Thus says the Lord: 'Let your voice cease from weeping, and your eyes from tears, for there is a reward for your work,' says the Lord; 'and they shall return out of the land of the enemy. And there is hope for your last end,' says the Lord, 'and your children shall return to their own borders.'* As a race, as a people, the Benjaminites and other Israelites did return from Babylon to their own borders, but the slain individuals would never again literally walk on this earth, and yet the Holy Innocents would return to life within the Church in Heaven. Hence, figuratively, Rachel weeping represents the Church weeping for her slain children but comforted by hope in their future resurrection. Jeremiah, further in the same chapter, states the basis of this hope: *a woman shall encompass a man* (Jer. 31:22), that is, the Virgin Mary shall conceive the God-man without the use of male seed, and He will bring the grace of justification and of eternal resurrection.[7] Rachel

---

7 That this verse of Jeremiah is a prophecy referring literally to the Virginal Conception of Jesus is amply discussed and defended by Cornelius aLapide in his *Great Commentary on Sacred Scripture* (*Commentaria in Scripturam Sacram*, Paris, 1874–1876) at Jer. 31:22. ALapide bases this interpretation upon the common opinion of the Fathers and Doctors of the Church, and in particular upon the teaching of Jerome, Cyprian, Augustine, Nicholas of Lyra, Rabanus Maurus, Hugo of St.Victor, and Thomas Aquinas. In a footnote at this place (vol. 12, p. 230), Joseph Peronne, the editor of the volume, observes that this has been the constant opinion of the Fathers of the Church and of Catholic exegetes, and he

is also a figure of Mary, Mother of the Church, who once wept on this earth for the slain children of Bethlehem and who is now comforted by the knowledge of their future resurrection and their eternal happiness in Heaven. Let us note, finally, that Ramah, in this prophecy of Jeremiah, is a place-name having also the obvious metaphorical meaning of "on high," and this may be another clue to the existence of a metaphorical meaning in the names Nazareth and Nazorean.

10. *That he would be called a Nazorean.* Matthew's four preceding citations from the Old Testament are taken in a different spirit of fulfillment than was understood in the Old Testament as such. Jesus is "God-with-us" in the sense of a physical incarnation of God in this man, and Jesus thus becomes the supreme example of holiness in a man. The fact of the Incarnation is confirmed by the prophecy in Isaiah and by the miracle of the Virginal Conception. The Virgin Mary is presented as the second greatest example of Christian holiness. The prophecy in Micah of the birth of the Savior at Bethlehem is interpreted in Matthew's Gospel as the birth of an other-worldly King who had come to establish the Kingdom of God on earth. The prophecy in Hosea is interpreted as referring to Jesus, who came back from Egypt to dwell in Israel and then to establish the Kingdom of God. The prophecy in Jeremiah of Rachel weeping has the same other-worldly sense: Rachel, representing literally the mothers of the Holy Innocents and figuratively the Church and the Blessed Virgin Mary, weeps at the slaughter of these children but is consoled by the fact that they will rise again in glory, not in this world, but in the next.

11. The allegory in Matt. 2:23. Now, this spiritual interpretation of the Old Testament prophecies in Matt. 1–2 gives some indication as to how the prophecy about Jesus the Nazorean is to be interpreted. If Jesus is the supreme example of holiness, then He is the Nazirite, the "holy man," *par excellence*, with the result that the Nazirites of the Old Testament were only faint reflections of what perfect holiness really is. It is true that Jesus would not abstain from drinking wine, as the Nazirites did, but his humanity was consecrated from his mother's womb in a higher and holier way than was Samson or John the Baptist. And the Virgin Mary is also a high-level Nazirite in the sense of a person "consecrated to the Lord" (cf. Num. 6:2). She too was consecrated to the Lord from her mother's womb, and both she and her divine Son were "set apart" from all the other descendants of Adam

---

cites the words of St. Jerome: *"The Lord has created a new thing upon the earth: without the seed of man, without that coitus and conception, a woman will encompass a man in the bosom of her womb...."*

and Eve in that they were conceived free from Original Sin. Jesus will be the King of Heaven and of the New Israel, while Mary will be the Queen Mother. Both were called out of Egypt to lead lives of perfect sanctity in the land of Israel. Mary, Mother of the Church, weeps for the injustice of the slaughter of the Innocents, but Jesus will console her by raising them again in glory. Behind this whole infancy narrative is the allegory of Christ and of his Church, an extended metaphor which is not a fictitious analogy but is rather another dimension that has been instilled into the history of the events and the meaning of the prophecies. This allegorical pattern lies also behind the prophecy that Jesus would be called a Nazorean, that is, an inhabitant of Nazareth who exemplifies and fulfills the etymological meaning of the name. Jesus is a Nazirite, because He is "set apart" from this world in his divine origin, in his virginal conception, in his hypostatic union, in his heavenward vocation, in his supreme holiness. And Jesus is "from the root," because He is divinely from God the Father, because he was conceived of the Holy Spirit, the source of all holiness, because he was conceived virginally from the holiest of all pure creatures. To find how these qualities of Jesus are reflected in the words *nazir* and *netser* in the Old Testament is to recognize the spiritual sense of the prophecy in Matt. 2:23. And this spiritual sense may also be the literal sense, but we shall now consider briefly whether or not there might be something more implied on the level of history, even though the inerrancy of the text does not depend upon this further speculation.

12. *And he went and dwelt in a city called Nazareth.* Historical critics tend to believe that the final versions of the infancy narratives in Matthew and Luke depend at least in part upon an earlier story that was common to both, even though developed differently. But mainline historical critics also tend to conclude that both infancy narratives are fictional and that all of the episodes are imaginary.[8] Neo-patristic interpreters, on the other hand, recognize the common antecedent to the two infancy narratives to consist in the real history that lies behind them, probably in two different antecedent reports regarding that real history. A question, then, that occurs here is: Did Matthew add the reference to the prophets in Matt. 2:23, or is he saying rather that Joseph went to Nazareth because Joseph saw the reference to the prophets? Matthew's narrative tells us that Joseph, in

---

8 Historical critics would not agree with the interpretation that I am presenting here, and it is characteristic of the neo-Patristic method critically to examine their critical theories and objections. However, in order to avoid overly long digressions, I have postponed this treatment to the following part.

coming back from Egypt, had the intention of settling in Judea, but *hearing that Archelaus reigned in Judea in the place of Herod his father, he was afraid to go there, and being warned in a dream he withdrew to the district of Galilee* (Matt. 2:22). *And he went and dwelt in a city called Nazareth that what was spoken by the prophets might be fulfilled....* Luke tells us that Joseph and Mary had come from Nazareth to Bethlehem. Why, then, was Joseph intending to settle in Judea? It seems that it was to fulfill the prophecy in Mic. 5:2 that the Messiah would be from Bethlehem, but, after being warned about Archelaus and having learned of the continuing danger to the life of the Infant in Judea, he thought about the prophecies regarding Nazareth. And in this reflection he was probably aided by the Virgin Mary, who had herself reflected much on the same subject. In fact, Mary may have been the original interpreter of these prophecies, since she was used to meditating upon prophecies and events and to seeing their spiritual implications (Lk. 2:19, 51).

13. A possible connection with the Annunciation to Mary. Just before the Incarnation of Jesus, Mary asked the angel: *'How shall this be done, because I know not man?'* And the angel, answering, said to her: *'the Holy Spirit will come upon you and the power of the Most High will overshadow you. And, therefore, the Holy to be engendered will be called Son of God'* (Lk. 1:34–35). The Greek word used here for "Holy" is *hagion*; what was the Hebrew or Aramaic equivalent used by the Angel Gabriel in speaking to the Virgin Mary? If the word was *nazir* or some derivative of *nazir*, then we have here the prophecy referred to in Matt. 2:23, given literally and historically by the angel and contained figuratively in the Scriptures of the Old Testament. And if the word spoken by the angel to Mary was something else, such as *qadosh* ("holy" or "set apart"), it would still relate conceptually to *nazir* for prophetic purposes. And so in either case the literal meaning of Matt. 2:23 may well be that Joseph went and settled in Nazareth, not simply because this was where he and Mary had been living earlier, but especially because he was convinced that it had been prophesied that Jesus would be a Nazorean, that is, a greater and holier Nazirite than all of the others, or a Natsorean, that is, a mystical "branch" or "blossom" of royal Davidic descent.

14. What was the source of Matthew's infancy narrative? It is my opinion that the one ultimate source of the infancy narratives both in Matthew and in Luke is the Blessed Virgin Mary, who was an eye-witness or immediate ear-witness to all of the events narrated. Some critics say that Mary could not be the source of the infancy narrative in

Matthew, inasmuch as the story is centered on the figure of Joseph, but this objection does not hold. Mary could have deliberately told the story as highlighting Joseph both as a function of her own humility and for the following historical reason. It is very likely that Mary narrated two separate accounts of the infancy of Jesus. The one related to events that could be told safely within her family milieu; the other contained events that were never divulged to anyone until after the death of Jesus, because He would have been in immediate danger of arrest and execution by the political authorities had they known about these events. Mary could easily have recounted these dramatic events either directly to Matthew in answer to his questions, or he could have learned about them indirectly from other sources. And Mary could have shown at any time after the Resurrection the scroll of the genealogy in Matthew which she very likely had kept hidden for the reason that it could well have been the genealogy with which Joseph had registered himself and Jesus in the census at Bethlehem. On the other hand, the genealogy in Luke seems to have been the genealogy of Mary, artfully adjusted by Joseph in returning from Egypt in order to be able to conceal his own genealogy and yet have some ancestry to show, to which he would also have had legal claim if he was the adopted son of Mary's father, as Urban Holzmeister suggested. [9] This may be fanciful, but the adjustment could have happened in this way. Joseph changed the name of Mary's father Joakim to its equivalent Eliakim (cf. 2Kg. [4Kg.] 23:34; 2Chron. 36:4) and then shortened it to Eli, while leaving the rest of the names in Mary's ancestry unchanged. Joseph, to use a modern term, traveled with two "passports" in the form of two genealogies. [10]

15. The figurative application of *nazir* to Jesus. It has been indicated above that three possible figurative antecedents of the name Nazareth in Matt. 2:23 are the Hebrew words *nazir*, *nezer*, and *netser*. A selection of texts that could provide a wider background of the figurative meaning of these three words is as follows. With regard to the figurative dimension of *nazir*, in the sense of someone "set apart," "consecrated from the womb" or "holy," as prophetically intended for Jesus by the Holy Spirit in either the literal or the allegorical sense of the text, I suggest the following related possibilities. [11].

---

9 Cf. U. Holzmeister, "Genealogia S. Lucae," in *Verbum Domini* (1943), pp. 15–18.

10 The idea of the "two passports of Joseph" is just a conjecture, but to me it is a better conjecture than those offered by historical critics in their endeavors to go back beyond the letter of the inspired text.

11 I am not here presenting texts that refer more directly to the Mystical Body of Christ.

Where the word *nazir* itself is used: Gen. 49:26: ... *may they* (the blessings of Heaven) *be on the head of Joseph and on the brow of the separated one (nazir) among his brothers.* Compare also Judg. 13:7; Judg. 16:17.

Where the *idea* of being "set apart," consecrated from the womb," or "holy" may be figuratively related to Jesus. Ps. 39 (40):8–9: *Then said I, 'Behold, I come. In the roll of the book it is written of me that I should desire to do your will, my God, and your law is in my heart.* (The divine Word became incarnate to do the will of the Father.) Compare also Deut 4:39; Ps. 109 (110):3; Isa. 11:2; Isa. 12:6; Isa. 47:4; Isa. 54:5; Jer. 1:5; Jer. 23:6; Ezek. 37:28; Ezek. 37:28;

16. The figurative application of *nezer* to Jesus. The noun *nezer* ("crown") is seen by some as having a figurative relation to the name Nazareth in its use as a priestly crown or a royal crown: Ex. 29:6: *And you shall put the miter on his head, and you shall put the holy crown (nezer) on the miter.* Compare also Ex. 39:30; Lev. 8:9; Lev. 21:10–12; Ps. 131 (132):17–18.

17. The figurative application of *netser* to Jesus. We know that Jesus is "the root and the offspring of David" (Apoc. 22:16). It has been indicated above (no. 5) that a second possible root of the name Nazareth in Matt. 2:23 is the Hebrew noun *netser*. With regard to the figurative dimension of *netser* in the sense of "blossom," "flower," "branch," or "from the root," as prophetically intended for Jesus by the Holy Spirit in either the literal or the allegorical sense of the text of the Old Testament, I suggest the following related possibilities.

Where the word *netser* itself is used: Isa. 11:1–2a;

Where the *idea* of "flower," "branch," or "from the root" may be figuratively related to Jesus: Gen. 1:9 [cf. Jn. 15:5]; Ps. 84 (85):12; Cant. 2:1; Isa. 11:10; Isa. 45:8; Isa. 61:11; Jer. 23:5–6; Jer. 33:14–15; Ezek. 29:21; Ezek. 34:23, 29; Hosea 14:6–7.

18. An abbreviated neo-patristic interpretation of Matt. 2:23. The literal sense. The neo-Patristic method uses the framework of the Four Senses of Sacred Scripture. Since no text of the Old Testament says literally "He will be called a Nazorean (or Natsorean)," and since the name Nazareth does not appear at all in the Old Testament, it is reasonable to suppose that Matt. 2:23 is appealing to a figurative relationship of one or more texts of the Old Testament to the root-meaning of the word Nazareth. This appeal may have originated from the insight of Matthew into the figurative sense of one or more Old Testament verses (what some scholars refer to as the *sensus plenior*), but Matthew could also be recounting the insight of Joseph himself, who had thought of resettling in Judea because of the prophecies

regarding the Messiah (e.g., Mic. 5:2), but saw afterwards this prophetic relationship to Nazareth. In either case, if the name Nazareth was seen to derive from the root *nzr* by way of *nazir* ("consecrated") or *nezer* ("crown"), then the emphasis of the verse is either upon the supreme holiness of Jesus the Nazorean or upon his priestly and royal status. Relative to this message, among others, are the Old Testament prophecies: *may they* (the blessings of Heaven) *be on the head of Joseph and on the brow of the separated one (nazir) among his brothers*; the idea that *the Saint of saints may be anointed* (Dan. 9:24), and the prophecy that *his crown (nezer) shall flourish* (Ps. 131 [132]:18). But even more pertinent may be the New Testament prophecy of the Angel Gabriel in Luke 1:35: *He will be called Holy*, especially if the word used for "holy" was *nazir*. But if the name Nazareth was seen to derive from the root *ntsr* ("branch" or "flower"), then the emphasis of the verse is on the humanity of Jesus the Natsorean as having sprung forth and flowered from the root of Jesse and the royal lineage of David, as in Isa. 11:1: *and a branch (netser) shall grow out of his root*. These two possible derivations tend to merge in concept, so that it is entirely possible that both meanings are intended in the message of Matt. 2:23.

19. The allegorical sense of Matt. 2:23. Behind the literal sense is to be sought in figurative fashion the allegory of Christ and his Church. The humanity of Christ is reflected in Jesus the Nazorean (*nazir* and *nezer*). The idea of consecration to God (*nazir*) even from the womb in the Nazirites of the Old Testament is fulfilled and elevated in Jesus, as is the very notion of personal holiness. We take for example, limiting ourselves to some of the Old Testament texts that have been referred to above, how the humanity of Jesus brings to completion such ideas as: consecration to the will of the Father (cf. Ps. 39[40]:8–9, saturation with the grace of the Holy Spirit (cf. Isa. 11:2), hypostatic union (cf. Isa. 47:4; 54:5), and being the sanctuary of God on earth (cf. Ezek. 37:28). Furthermore, the humanity of Jesus elevates and fulfills the priestly and royal character implied in the word *nezer*, for instance as presented in Ex. 29:6; 39:30; Lev. 8:9; 21:10–12; Ps. 131 (132):17–18. And the humanity of Christ is reflected in Jesus the Natsorean (*netser*). Jesus is "the root and offspring of David" (Apoc. 22:16). Jesus is in a metaphorical way, which is also a higher and more real way, the "tree of life" (cf. Gen. 1:9; Jn. 15:5); He is the "flower of the field" (cf. Cant. 2:1; Isa. 61:11; Jer. 33:14–15; Hosea 14:6–7), having sprung like a flower from the virginal womb of Mary to become the choicest "flower" of all creation (cf. Ps. 84 [85]:12; Isa. 45:8; Ezek. 29:21); He

is the "just branch" of David, of Jesse, of Jacob, of Abraham, of Adam (cf. Jer. 23:5–6). The Church, as the Mystical Body of Christ, shares in this fulfillment as reflected also in the figurative character of the name Israel.[12] Thus, for instance, in the prophecy that, when the "just branch" of David shall reign, *Israel will dwell securely* (Jer. 23:5–7), the word "Israel" refers figuratively to the Church of Christ.

20. The anagogical sense of Matt. 2:23. In the anagogy of the Most Holy Trinity, the *holiness* of the body and soul of Jesus (*nazir*) is seen to have arisen from the sanctifying presence of God the Holy Spirit, just as the supreme *flowering (netser)* of virtue in the life of Jesus stems from the saturation of his human nature with the plenitude of the grace of the Holy Spirit. Many references to God and to the Son of God in the Old Testament refer literally or figuratively to Jesus: on the lower allegorical level to Jesus the God-man as the Son of God, and on the higher allegorical level to Jesus, the Word of God, as the eternal Son of the eternal Father. Thus, e.g., the words "before the day star I begot you" of Ps. 109 (110):3 refer literally to the divine Person of Jesus, eternally begotten of the Father and eternally willed to become incarnate. Again, the words "Behold, I come" of Ps. 39 (40):8 refer to the Incarnation. Similarly, in Isa. 12:6, the "Holy One" who is "in the midst of you" is, on the higher level, the Triune God, and, on the lower level, God incarnate in Jesus. In Ps. 84 (85):12, the words "truth will sprout from the ground" refer to the truth of the Eternal Word which will sprout from the sacred womb of the Virgin Mary, while the following words "and holiness will look down from the sky" refer to the action of the Father, the Son, and the Holy Spirit in the miraculous production of the incarnation of the Eternal Word in Jesus.

21. In the anagogy of the Four Last Things one can see the fruition of the prophecy in Matt. 2:23. In Gen. 49:26, the blessings of Heaven are pronounced by the patriarch Jacob upon the head of the patriarch Joseph "and on the brow of the separated one (*nazir*) among his brothers." The patriarch Joseph was separated geographically from his brothers in the literal sense of this blessing, but Jesus was separated in a fuller and more real way in the spiritual sense of this verse. By assuming the nature of Adam, the Divine Word entered into solidarity with his fellow Adamites, but he remained "separated" above all in being both God and man. He reigns now and forever as the King of

---

12 In this article I have not cited for the most part Old Testament texts that refer to the Church as the New Israel.

Heaven and the Head of his Mystical Body. All of the blessed in Heaven are "consecrated" forever to God and "separated" from natural life on earth and from the damned in Hell. Literally, in the beatific vision, they see "God in Heaven above," while He is perpetually embraced in their hearts as in "the earth below" (Deut. 4:39). They also see and embrace God in Jesus. "The Spirit of the Lord" (Isa. 11:2) rests upon them and warms their hearts for all eternity. The Holy Spirit is the "sanctuary" that "will be in the midst of them forever (Ezek. 37:28). This is the "everlasting justice" (Dan. 9:24) that was brought to them by Jesus and is now being fulfilled in Heaven.

22. The tropological sense of Matt. 2:23. The tropology represents the appropriation of the allegory to the soul of the sanctified believer. In the case of Matt. 2:23, it is the appropriation of the truth and holiness of Jesus the Nazorean/Natsorean to the minds and hearts of his followers. The "blessings of Heaven" (Gen. 49:26) are extended by Jesus through Baptism and all the other sacraments of the New Covenant as well as by every other act of sanctification. The "Holy One of Israel" is "in their midst" (cf. Isa. 12:6) in that Jesus is in the midst of the members of the Church and dynamically present to make them holy (*nazir*) in the sanctifying grace that lives in their hearts. The Cross of Jesus is "an ensign to the peoples" (Isa. 11:10), and his sepulchre is glorious, because He has risen from the dead, and now reigns forever in Heaven as the King of Glory. Tropologically, his followers carry their crosses after Him on their way to heavenly glory. The figure of the flower (*netser*) appears tropologically in the supernatural virtues that spring up in the souls of the baptized (cf. Isa. 45:8; 61:11; Hosea 14:6–7). There is also the special tropology of the Blessed Virgin Mary. She is, after Jesus and in total dependence upon his grace, a "holy person" (*nazir*) in the highest and fullest sense of term. She is the offspring of David, and, in the fertility of her virginal soul, the fullness of virtue sprang forth, so that she both physically and spiritually gave birth to the Savior of mankind. And she is the Mother of the Church who spiritually gives birth to all those who enter Heaven through the portal of the humanity of Jesus. To the extent that these things reflect the personal sanctity of Mary, constituted by the grace of God within her, they represent also the special tropology of the Blessed Virgin Mary.

Part II. In Answer to the Form-Critical Analyses of Martin Dibelius and Rudolf Bultmann

Living Tradition 85 (January 2000)

1. The background of this article. In the November 1999 issue of *Living Tradition*, I presented a neo-patristic interpretation of what is said about St. Joseph in Matt. 2:23, the text of which reads as follows: *And he went and dwelt in a city called Nazareth that what was spoken by the prophets might be fulfilled that he would be called a Nazorean.* My interpretation used a contemporary neo-patristic framework, based upon the teaching of the Fathers of the Church and upon Catholic exegetical tradition, especially upon the interpretation of Thomas Aquinas. This interpretation defends the historical truth of the verse and of the entire Infancy Narratives of Matthew and Luke in terms of the Four Senses of Sacred Scripture. I recognized a certain ambiguity in the literal sense, inasmuch as Matthew may be affirming either that Joseph went and dwelt in Nazareth because Joseph saw this to be a fulfillment of prophecy concerning Jesus, or that Matthew himself saw the settling in Nazareth as a fulfillment of a prophecy. In that article I offered evidence in favor of the possible historical truth of either alternative, and I presented different ways, on the levels of the Four Senses, in which this verse of Matthew indicates a fulfillment of prophecy. The conclusion of that study was that there is no error of logic or of fact in Matt. 2:23 either on the level of the literal sense or on the levels of the three spiritual senses. I noted that historical critics would not agree with this conclusion, but, in order to avoid an inopportune digression, I postponed the problems they raise to a subsequent writing, which problems pertain almost entirely to the literal sense of the text. I now take up an analysis of some of these difficulties, but, for the sake of brevity, I limit this discussion to the form-critical phase of historical critical interpretation.

2. The form-critical approach of Martin Dibelius. The form-criticism of the Gospels arose in Germany just after the First World War, centered mainly around two critical works, *Die Formgeschichte des Evangeliums*, published in 1919 by Martin Dibelius, whose English translation, *From Tradition to Gospel (FTG)*, will be quoted in this article,[13] and *Die Geschichte*

---

13 Martin Dibelius, *Die Formgeschichte des Evangeliums* (first published in 1919, second revised edition, 1933); English translation by Bertram Lee Woolf of the revised edition: *From Tradition to Gospel* (Cambridge, England, The Library of Theological Translations, 1971, hereafter to be referred to as *FTG*).

der Synoptischen Tradition, published in 1921 by Rudolf Bultmann, whose English translation, *The History of the Synoptic Tradition* (*HST*), will be quoted here.[14] Dibelius expressed the aim of his study as "a research in the history of the Form of the Gospels," in particular of the Synoptic Gospels, beginning from "the recognition that they are collections of material" which was chosen, limited, and finally shaped by the evangelists but not given by them their "original molding" (*FTG*, pp. 2–3). The objective of his book is to defend "the right to read the Gospels from the standpoint of the development of their form" (*FTG*, 6). He sees the study of these Gospels as a study of popular writings not dependent upon individual writing ability and having no individual source of a personal and creative character, but expressing a mere "sociological result" in which the literary categories are determined "according to laws which are independent of the individual personality," so as to enable the form-critical researcher "to draw a conclusion regarding their *Sitz im Leben*, i.e., the historical and social stratum in which precisely these literary forms were developed" (*FTG*, 7). Characteristically, the form-critic pursues the question of "what categories are possible or probable in this sociological connection" (*FTG*, 8).

3. The form-critical approach of Rudolf Bultmann. The form-critical approach of Rudolf Bultmann does not differ essentially from that of Martin Dibelius. "The aim of form-criticism," according to Bultmann, "is to determine the original form of a piece of narrative, a dominical saying or a parable" (*HST*, p. 6). For this work he summarizes certain presuppositions, which are now to be taken for granted, such as the following. Mark is the oldest of the four Gospels, and even Mark "is the work of an author who is steeped in the theology of the early Church" (*HST*, 1)[15]; there is a "fundamental assumption that the [Synoptic] tradition consists of individual stories or groups of stories joined together in the Gospels by the work of the editors" (*HST*, 2); "the distinction between traditional and editorial material" in the Gospels is an established procedure (*HST*, 3); the respective "literary form" which the form-critic assigns to the respective Gospel units "is a sociological concept and not an aesthetic one," although "one piece of the tradition is seldom to be classified unambiguously in a single category"

---

14 Rudolf Bultmann, *Die Geschichte der Synoptischen Tradition* (1st ed., 1921; 8th rev. ed., Göttingen, 1970; Eng. trans. by J. Marsh, *The History of the Synoptic Tradition* (Oxford: Basil Blackwell, 1963, hereafter to be referred to as HST). Another important book in the launching of the form-criticism of the Gospels was K.L. Schmidt's *Der Rahmen der Geschichte Jesu*, published in 1919.

15 I shall not deal with the question of the oldest Gospel in this article.

(*HST*, 4); form-criticism "has to move in a circle," inasmuch as "the forms of the literary tradition must be used to establish the influences operating in the life of the community, and the life of the community must be used to render the forms themselves intelligible." What is more, in Bultmann's opinion, form-criticism not only "presupposes judgments of facts," but must also "lead to judgments about facts," such as "the genuineness of a saying, the historicity of a report and the like," gravitating around "the one chief problem of primitive Christianity, the relationship of the primitive Palestinian and Hellenistic Christianity" (*HST*, 5).

4. How does the form-criticism of Martin Dibelius and Rudolf Bultmann relate to the prophecy referred to in Matt. 2:23? Dibelius concludes that Matt. 2:22–23, narrating the decision of Joseph to go and settle in Nazareth, did not pertain to the original story of "the slaughter of the children," but expresses "remarks of the evangelist who wishes to introduce Nazareth as Jesus' home." Dibelius excludes that this element could have been original, because, "Otherwise we should have to ask why the angel said nothing of the renewed danger, or why Joseph under such an openly proclaimed divine protection, gave hearing to the voice of human fear" (*FTG*, 129). This is flimsy reasoning. Joseph had given hearing to human fear even earlier, when he fled with the Virgin and Child into Egypt, knowing that it would have been presumptuous on his part to count upon some not-promised extraordinary divine protection. Fear was more than justified on Joseph's part, according to all of the circumstances of the episode. And we don't have to ask why the Angel said nothing of the renewed danger: we are told in the text that Joseph was warned in a dream. Yet Bultmann concurs with this form-critical conclusion as he states: "Dibelius rightly says that verses 22f. [of Matt. 2] are not legendary, but were added by Matthew with the intention of introducing Nazareth as the home of Jesus (*HST*, 439). For Bultmann, this "awkward combination of the historical tradition of Nazareth as Jesus' home town with the messianic dogma of his birth at Bethlehem" is an idea, not based upon any prior happening, but invented by Matthew himself in order to give continuity to his account (*HST*, 294).

5. The immediate background of this form-critical interpretation. To address this question adequately, one must situate the brief remarks of Bultmann and Dibelius about Matt. 2:23 within the context of their treatment of the entire Infancy Narrative (Matt. 1–2). It is important to realize that both Bultmann and Dibelius take for granted that the separate units that they distinguish in the Gospel accounts have, in general, their

origin in human imagination, with some possible real basis in some cases. Thus, the Christian tradition that Jesus came from Nazareth is accorded more historical probability than the tradition that He was born in Bethlehem (which they consider to be a non-real story made up to show a fulfillment of the prophecy in Mic. 5:1). As a general procedure of the form-critical method, the presumed imaginary origin of the episodes recounted gives way only to evident realities gathered from outside sources, and, while these evident realities are accepted provisionally by the form-critic, they also undergo a continual probing in search of difficulties that could call into question their status as real. Furthermore, affirmations pertaining to supernatural events of any kind are systematically relegated to the category of the unreal and the unhistorical. Such processing is done in the name of historical science, but it is not scientific, because true historical science deals with unique events of the past, and it must seek to discover what actually happened; it cannot define in advance what could or could not have happened on the basis of assumed statistical laws. Neither Bultmann nor Dibelius ever demonstrated historically that Jesus was not born in Bethlehem; they simply reasoned from the assumption that the story of Jesus' birth in Bethlehem was concocted by Christians from meditation on the prophecy in Micah. Now, if the prophecy in Micah was inspired by God to predict the real historical birth of Jesus in Bethlehem, an idea that form-critics have excluded *a priori* but never refuted, then the tradition of the birth of Jesus relates a historical fact, and, consequently, its narration in Matthew is historical reality. In this case, the result is that Matthew's account of the decision of Joseph to go and settle in Nazareth is not an "awkward combination" of history with dogma; it is rather a true historical happening.

6. The more remote background of this form-critical interpretation of Martin Dibelius. Unfounded presuppositions form the basis of this form-critical conclusion. On the basis of uncertified and non-existent "sociological laws," both Dibelius and Bultmann assume that these Christian writers of the first century A.D. could neither have gathered historical facts with critical judgment regarding their reality nor could they have made up their alleged events with independent creativity. Rather they take for granted that the "laws" governing their sociological environment would necessarily have caused these narrators to copy ideas derived from outside of their Christian culture and shape them instinctively into stories that fitted their sociological compulsions. But, seeing that these Synoptic Gospel writers possessed intelligence and free will, no such "sociological laws" were

governing them; all of the historical evidence regarding their culture is against such an assumption. For Dibelius the "literary understanding of the Synoptics begins with the recognition that they are collections of material" and that the composers are principally "collectors, vehicles of tradition, editors" but "only to the smallest extent authors" (*FTG*, 3). One can recognize here some twisted logic. Historians are collectors of material; they judge concerning the reality of the material, but they are not authors of the material. The Synoptic evangelists, Matthew, Mark, and Luke, were collectors of material, they judged concerning the reality of the material that they collected, but they were not authors of the material. Dibelius has himself stepped away from this reality; he assumes without proof that the Synoptic Gospels are in the genre of "aesthetic" (imaginative) literature, not of reality-oriented literature, and then he reduces the evangelists to the level of "vehicles" having little creative influence of their own. It is this assumption of non-reality that invalidates his conclusion.

7. The concurrence of Rudolf Bultmann. The same can be said for Bultmann's method. In his form-critical apparatus, Bultmann agrees with Dibelius that each literary form that is unearthed in the Synoptic Gospels is "a sociological concept and not an aesthetic one." What he means is that the short pieces that he sees sewn together by the editors of the Synoptic Gospels do not arise from free human creativity but rather as an unfree reaction to the impulses of the sociological environment of the respective human instruments. There is no scientific basis for this assumption. Moreover, Bultmann admits that his conclusions have to "move in a circle," inasmuch as he judges what is factual according to his presuppositions and he adds presuppositions from facts that he has so adjudged. Is this science or pseudo-science?

8. Two form-critical views of the Virginal Conception of Jesus. Dibelius sees Matthew's Infancy Narrative as being basically "legendary" (*FTG*, 129–131), but he feels that Matthew's account of the Virginal Conception (Matt. 1:18–25) "can in no way be called a legend," because "it is not the miracle but its defense which is the center," and "the decisive proof-passage from the Old Testament about the virgin who should become a mother (Isa. 7:14) is not interwoven into the speech of the angel but given as a meditative quotation." So Dibelius concludes that the entire passage is "the work of this evangelist" (*FTG*, 128), meaning that this entire passage was phrased by the evangelist in defense of what Dibelius calls "the Legend of the Virgin," as it appears in Luke 1:26–38. Since this "legend," he says, "depends verbally on Isaiah 7:14," the prophecy "must be regarded as an

essential element of the whole legend" ((*FTG*, 124). And the response of the Virgin, "*How shall this come about, since I know not man,*" reveals to the form-critical eye of Dibelius that Joseph did not belong originally to the story, but was interpolated by the evangelist (*FTG*, 124). Bultmann, on the other hand, in his form-critical research, sees a likelihood that the conception and birth of Jesus reported in Matt. 1:18–25 was a Semitic report which "would not have contained the motif, unheard of in a Jewish environment, of a virgin birth." Bultmann concludes that the "Virgin Birth" motif "was first added in the transformation in Hellenism, where the idea of the generation of a king or a hero from a virgin by the godhead was widespread" (*HST*, 291). Believing that he has gone back into the history of this account, Bultmann reasons that "the old story had simply told how an angel promised Joseph that his son would be Messiah" (*HST*, 292), supporting his conclusion with the observation that in the story Joseph is expressly addressed as "son of David."

9. The weakness of this form-critical explanation. We already knew why Joseph, in Matt. 1:20, was addressed by the angel as "son of David." It was for him to represent the male seed of the House of David in an acceptance of the Virginal Conception of Jesus and in becoming a Christian. The carnal interpretation of Bultmann and Dibelius does not stand up in the light of the full spiritual meaning of the text. If one compares the reasoning in these two form-critical treatments of the Virginal Conception of Jesus, presented by the two principal founders of the form-criticism of the Gospels, the weakness and invalidity of the reasoning becomes apparent. Dibelius concludes that the prophecy in Isa. 7:14 is clearly essential to the story, inasmuch as, in his estimation, the story originated from pious meditation on Isa. 7:14 and the desire to make it apply to Jesus. Bultmann, using the same form-critical method, concludes that Isa. 7:14 clearly could not have belonged to the original story about the conception of Jesus. Since the conclusions flatly contradict one another, both could not be right, and, truth to tell, neither is right. If the Virginal Conception actually took place in history, and if an angel did speak to Mary as narrated in Luke 1:35 and to Joseph as narrated in Matt. 1:20, then the historical fact of the virginal conception of Jesus is the basis of the story. In this reading, the prediction of the Virginal Conception in Isa. 7:14 is a proof of the event but is not "essential" to the historical fact itself. Bultmann and Dibelius exclude in principle the historical fact, but they never deal adequately with the question of historical fact. Thus, Bultmann declares

to his readers: "The idea of a divine generation from a virgin is not only foreign to the O.T. and to Judaism, but is completely impossible" ((*HST*, 291). On historical grounds Bultmann cannot correctly begin from the presupposition that a virginal conception is "completely impossible," but it is this presupposition that underpins all the rest of his reasoning about it. He believes that the idea is "foreign to the Old Testament and to Judaism, while the truth is that the idea was initiated with the prophecy of Isaiah in the Old Testament. Bultmann sees himself forced to resort to an unhistorical distinction: not foreign to Hellenistic Judaism (which began in the fourth century B.C.), but to "Palestinian Judaism," as though there had been no cultural exchange between "Hellenistic Judaism" and "Palestinian Judaism," whereas Judaism of its very nature transcends such a cultural separation. Bultmann assumes that the Palestinian Jews of early Christian times had no acquaintance with the Septuagint and that the Septuagint translators of Isa. 7:14 were under the influence of "Egyptian ideas" (*HST*, 438). There is no evidence for this. With the method he is using, it seems futile for Bultmann to adduce his "parallels" of virginal conceptions from pagan literature without first having determined when those pagan stories arose. That any of these pagan stories dates from before the time of Isaiah he does not show. Form-critics like to assume that pagan parallels are older than they are. Almost inevitably they trace the biblical story to the pagan parallel, rather than ever considering that the pagan parallel may derive from the biblical source, Isaiah 7:14 being the case in point.

10. In relation to Luke 2:39. Form-critics think that they see a logical conflict between the episodes in Matt. 2 and what is said in Luke 2:39: *And when they had performed everything according to the law of the Lord, they returned into Galilee, to their own city, Nazareth.* How could the flight into Egypt have occurred, if the Holy Family returned to their home town of Nazareth immediately after the purification in the Temple? If, by "the law of the Lord" is meant "the law of Moses," then it is to be noted that the text does not say that they returned "immediately" after the purification. Or "the law of the Lord" could include the command to flee into Egypt and remain there for a time. In the previous article I speculated on the idea that the Blessed Virgin Mary was the principal source of the Infancy Narratives both in Matthew and in Luke, and that she had narrated these happenings at different times in two different sequences according to the indications of prudence.[16] In the sequence of events recounted in Luke,

---

16 See chapter 15, part I above, paragraph 14.

the chronology skipped over the happenings in Matthew 2, making use of a mental reservation according to which an *immediate* return to Nazareth was not really implied.

11. Bultmann's modernist idea of "Hellenistic Christianity." A novel idea of the "transformation" of "Palestinian Christianity" into "Hellenistic Christianity" is the characteristic instrument in Rudolf Bultmann's devastating interpretation of the Gospels. This alleged transformation, which goes against the very essence of Christian faith, has never been historically demonstrated to have taken place; it is just a belief of modernist anti-faith, and Bultmann has at times needed to stretch the plausibility of this belief to the utmost in order to maintain it. We have seen above how it required him to deny any possibility of the occurrence of the idea of a virginal conception in the imagination of early Palestinian Christians or of the fact of any such conception in the real world. It also forced him to downplay the fact that the Palestinian people had been in contact with the Hellenistic world from the fourth century B.C.; they did not first encounter it a generation after the death of Jesus. One cannot adequately survey the exegesis of Bultmann or Dibelius without taking into account their form-critical framework and the way in which this framework is controlled by modernist anti-belief to produce the results that they desire. Their system depends upon an initial acceptance of the world-view of Rationalism together with certain modernist presuppositions, and it progresses by meditation upon plausible arguments intended to show how these presuppositions apply to the Sacred Text. But the arguments are never more than plausible, and closer examination reveals in every case that the plausibility is not based upon objective truth but only upon the emotional satisfaction that it gives to the form-critic as he thinks that he is peeling away historical truth from the Gospel text.

12. Can the form-critical method of Bultmann and Dibelius be separated from their rationalist and modernist beliefs? One can always draw a theoretical distinction between the form-critical method itself and the system of rationalist/modernist presuppositions in which Bultmann and Dibelius believed. However, in order to pursue this theoretical distinction, one must also identify the presuppositions of the form-critical method itself. Now, in undertaking this work one will quickly discover that rationalist and modernist presuppositions underlie the form-critical method itself, at least as it is used by Bultmann and Dibelius and by any of their followers who have not completed the preliminary

task of eliminating such presuppositions. I know of no form-critic who has performed this task or who has shown objectively that such a task can be completed successfully. In our examination of the form-critical interpretation of Matt. 2:23 presented by Bultmann and Dibelius, we saw that Rationalism/Modernism was clearly functioning. Both of these writers exhibit modernist belief in assuming that the episodes in Matt. 1–2 and Luke 1–2 are products of the religious instinct of the early Christian community, and they exhibit rationalist belief in assuming that none of the supernatural elements in these narratives could possibly be true, on the ground that nothing beyond the natural can possibly take place. Without these beliefs their form-critical process could not go forward. Matt. 2:23 speaks about what was predicted by the prophets, but the Rationalism of Bultmann and Dibelius prohibits them from giving any consideration to the idea that this might really be so. Instead, they give flimsy arguments against the historical truth of the settling of the Holy Family in Nazareth, realizing that those many biblical scholars who share their rationalist/modernist beliefs will be predisposed to agree with them and will, therefore, be the more easily convinced. But such scholarly activity is not critical thinking in the true sense of the word. Added to this defect of method is the failure of form-criticism to give ear to the spiritual message of the Sacred Text. The method itself tells the operator to set his mind above the message and to let his presuppositions override both the historical truth and the moral impact of the text.

13. The first basic error of form-criticism is to assume that the Synoptic Gospels are products of a religious instinct functioning in a credulous people who did not have sufficient intellectual development to be able to think on their own but simply concocted stories under the influence of certain "sociological laws." This assumption is belied by overwhelming evidence on the contrary. All serious historical study of Palestinian Christians at the time of Christ shows that the Palestinian people of the time were perfectly capable of thinking on their own and of making up their own stories, if they had had any desire to do so. But there is no historical reason for affirming that they made up these stories. The text of the Gospels is simple and straightforward in the genre of real chronology; it has none of the characteristics of narrative fiction. And the "sociological laws" invented by Émile Durkheim and others to control the function of a society devoid of intelligence and free will is a mere figment of the rationalist imagination. Form-criticism assumes that those who formed the Gospel traditions had to copy their ideas from elsewhere,

whether it was to copy them from Old Testament texts or from current Jewish practices, from pagan traditions, or from one another, but they could not record what they saw happening in actual fact. And so the early Christians are assumed to have been dishonest people who spread lies in the name of truth and then often believed their own lies. There is no historical basis for this accusation. Form-criticism applies prevenient methodic doubt to the text of the Gospels, and this kind of doubt is anti-faith. Catholic form-critics try to exempt from such doubt the dogmas of the Church, but they are often under pressure from the method itself to doubt various teachings of the Church.

14. The second basic error of form-criticism lies in the way it understands its own tradition. Bultmann and Dibelius see their form-critical tradition as a vaguely scientific one, but in their expositions, the question of science is never clearly defined. In fact, whether they are attempting to present reality as reality is never clear in their exposition. They do (uncritically) limit all reality to the bounds of the natural, but their speculation in support of this position often goes beyond the presentations of logic and of natural reality. It is true that they are spokesmen for a historic school of exegesis, and of this they are aware. Dibelius tells his readers that Johann Gottfried Herder "was the pioneer" of movements to understand "the special character of religious popular literature," while Georg Heinrici distinguished the New Testament writings from literature proper, inasmuch as they were to him "the sources and the witnesses of a missionary activity." Then Hermann Gunkel made the analysis of the smallest details "an axiom of research" (*FTG*, 5). Bultmann, too, has his list of accepted results of the historical research of his predecessors. Thus, Wilhelm Wrede performed a "quite annihilating criticism" of the seemingly clear historical development in the Gospel according to St. Mark, and Julius Wellhausen showed "how the theology of the early Church has influenced the traditional material"; it was Wellhausen who "stated very clearly the fundamental assumption that the tradition consists of individual stories or groups of stories joined together in the Gospels by the work of the editors." Bultmann notes that Gunkel had shown how the methods of form-criticism could be applied to the Old Testament, and K.L. Schmidt presented a conclusive discussion of "the distinction of traditional from editorial material." Finally, Martin Dibelius has "brilliantly shown" the fruitfulness of form-criticism "for discovering the stages in the development of the tradition as well as for the Gospels as a whole" (*HST*, 1–3). Looking at these evaluations from

outside of the historical critical tradition, one is inclined to question how correct is the classification of the Gospels as "popular religious literature" with no appreciation of its inspired character, and to ask whether Gunkel's analysis of the "smallest details" of the text of Genesis did not actually lead him to miss the meaning, not only of the details, but even of the text as a whole. Would that there were available a consistent critique of these and other "accepted results" of historical critical research, but this important work still remains largely to be done. Wrede's notion of "historical development" does not meet the standards of serious historical research, while Wellhausen, in his work on the influence of the theology of the early Church upon the traditional material, doesn't even seem to have understood the distinction between the *finis operis* and the *finis operantis* of the respective sacred writer.

15. Conclusion. The neo-patristic method of biblical interpretation can present a full and a truly fulfilling commentary on the Gospels, as we have tried to demonstrate with regard to Matt. 2:23 and with other passages of the Sacred Text. But in the circumstances of contemporary biblical scholarship, the neo-patristic study of the Sacred Text requires also an analysis of the results of historical critical research. In the present article I have done some analysis of the form-critical conclusions of Rudolf Bultmann and Martin Dibelius regarding Matt. 2:23 and its background, which could serve as one more illustration of how form-critical interpretations of the Gospels can be objectively analyzed. Form-critics tend to assume that Gospel episodes do not recount real historical events. Since they have never demonstrated this assumption, they depend upon arguments which appear to be plausible, especially to those who have already to some degree been disposed to doubt the historicity. It is my conclusion that this kind of argumentation cannot stand up under neo-patristic criticism. In the case of Matt. 2:23, Bultmann and Dibelius dismiss the historicity of the Holy Family's going and settling in Nazareth for insufficient reasons, seeing that they present weak and questionable criticisms of a historical account in Matthew that is already logical and clear. But the use of something like the neo-patristic method is important for determining why their form-critical analysis is insufficient and how the account of Matthew can be regarded as logical and clear.

Part III. In Answer to the Form-Critical Analysis of Raymond Brown

Living Tradition 86 (March 2000)

1. The text of Matthew 2:23. In the November 1999 issue of *Living Tradition*, I presented a neo-patristic interpretation of what is said about St. Joseph in Matt. 2:23, the original Greek text of which I translated to read as follows: *And he went and dwelt in a city called Nazareth that what was spoken by the prophets might be fulfilled that he would be called a Nazorean.* This translation understands that the text is presenting an indirect citation from unidentified prophets. But Raymond Brown, in his well-known work, *The Birth of the Messiah*, follows another rendering in placing quotation marks around the reference so as to read: *There he went to dwell in a city called Nazareth, so that what was spoken by the prophets might be fulfilled: "He will be called a Nazorean."* Brown makes this choice for the reason that in Greek the use of *hoti* to introduce a direct quotation is "more normal" than its use as the conjunction *that*. But this reason is not cogent. The fact is that Matthew, in keeping with general Greek practice, commonly uses *hoti* in either of these two senses, with the result that there is no valid argument regarding which is "more normal." Brown adds as a second reason that for Matthew not to have introduced a direct quotation in Matt. 2:23 would have been against the "general pattern of the fulfillment formula," as though, by some non-existent natural law or scientific discovery, Matthew had been locked into a rigid mental pattern. Matthew does follow a method of showing the fulfillment of prophecies from the Old Testament, but this method does not always require verbatim citations, especially where there is a reason for not citing verbatim, as is the case here. The fact is that Matthew's verbatim quotes always refer to unique texts in the Old Testament, whereas in 2:23 he is referring to "the prophets," that is, to more than one prophetic text. Brown, of course, doesn't find any verbatim text in the Old Testament to fit this reference; he leaves Matthew "holding the bag."

2. Jesus the Nazorean. Brown presents an important fact when he notes that the Greek word *hagios* ("holy") has sometimes been used to translate the Hebrew word *Nazir*.[17] Thus, for example, in the *Codex Vaticanus* version

---

17 Cf. Raymond E. Brown, *The Birth of the Messiah* (Garden City: Doubleday, 1977), 211.

of the Septuagint, the *"Nazir Elohim"* of Judges 13:7 is translated *hagion theou* ("holy one of God"), and similarly in Judges 16:17. He adds that Jesus is called the "Holy One of God" in both Mark 1:24, and Luke 4:34 (by an unclean spirit) and in John 6:69 (by Simon Peter), thus indicating a Scriptural basis for saying that Jesus was regarded as a Nazir. But Brown does not advert to the use of *hagion* in Luke 1:35: *And therefore the Holy to be engendered will be called Son of God.* If the word used for "Holy" by the Angel Gabriel in the real historical event of the Annunciation to Mary was *Nazir* or a derivative thereof, then the prophecy referred to in Matt. 2:23 would have been literally given at least by an angel.[18]

3. Raymond Brown's form-critical conclusion regarding Matt. 2:22–23. Raymond Brown is of the opinion that the two verses in Matt. 1:22–23 represent Matthew's "own appended composition" to a narrative tradition that he was reporting.[19] Brown's form-critical analysis leads him to consider as "virtually confirmed" that "onto a tradition about Joseph being sent from Egypt to Israel, Matthew has tacked a specification about Galilee and Nazareth to prepare for the formula citation." Matthew had to invent this additional dream episode of Joseph, reasons Brown, because Matthew's nativity scene was located in Bethlehem, while it was "a commonplace of the Gospel tradition" that Jesus grew up in Nazareth. Matthew was "forced to explain how the family got to Nazareth," and this is how he did it.[20] Brown actually uses these two verses as a clear illustration of how the form-critical method works.[21] He lists three basic guides that "scholars have used" to distinguish what is Matthean from what is pre-Matthean. First of all, "If a passage in the infancy narrative is almost purely Matthean in vocabulary and style, it is more likely that Matthew has composed the passage himself." The second guide is "the presence of internal tensions or conflicts within a passage." The third guide is "the presence of parallels to other material." In terms of the first guide, Brown compares Matt. 2:22–23 with Matt. 4:12–16 and shows that the pattern, grammar, and vocabulary of the two passages are clearly the same. With reference to the second guide, Brown sees an "internal tension" in Matt. 2:22–23 inasmuch as Joseph is told, on the one hand, to take the child and his mother to the land of Israel, and, on

---

18   I have given some treatment above in this chapter, part I, paragraph 13, to the possibility that the *hagion* in Luke 1:35 comes from *nazir.*

19   Cf. Brown, *The Birth of the Messiah*, 217.

20   Cf. Brown, *The Birth of the Messiah*, 106–107.

21   Cf. Brown, *The Birth of the Messiah*, 109.

the other hand, to take them to Galilee. Brown form-critically reasons: "If this story were a unity, why would there be two different dreams? Why did not the angel tell Joseph in the first dream to 'go to the land of Galilee'?"[22]

4. The weakness of Brown's interpretation of Matt. 2:22–23. In his reasoning about the origin of Matt. 2:22–23, Brown follows the lead of Martin Dibelius and Rudolf Bultmann, the two principal founders of the form-criticism of the Gospels. In part II of this chapter I undertook to show how flimsy is the reasoning of Bultmann and Dibelius regarding the alleged "internal tension" within this text. Dibelius reasoned that the original story had been about "the slaughter of the children," and that the decision to go and settle in Nazareth could not have been part of it, because "otherwise we should have to ask why the angel said nothing [in his appearance to Joseph in Egypt] of the renewed danger [from Archelaus]."[23] But, if we do ask, we can easily discover that in the Sacred Scriptures the revelation of realities is often given gradually and not all at once. And, if it really happened in that way, it was correct on Matthew's part to describe it in that way. Bultmann concurs with Dibelius in concluding that these two verses "were added by Matthew with the intention of introducing Nazareth as the home of Jesus."[24] But Bultmann was a Modernist, and, according to his modernist belief, almost everything described in the Infancy Narratives of Matthew and Luke is assumed to have been invented by religious imagination proceeding from a religious instinct, allowing that some rare elements of reality may be contained beneath these scenes. Thus, Bultmann and Dibelius would readily concede that there was a man Jesus of Nazareth who grew up in Nazareth and was, therefore, probably born in Nazareth. This, according to them, would be an element of reality in the Narratives. But, by the same presuppositions, the other things stated in the Narratives are presumed to be fictitious unless there is overwhelming evidence to the contrary. Now, Raymond Brown is starting from the exegesis of form-critics like Bultmann and Dibelius and adapting it as he sees fit. In this case Brown's conclusion is practically the same as that of the originators of the method, namely, that Matthew "tacked on" (read "invented") this journey to Nazareth in order to explain how the Holy Family got there. And Brown reechoes the flimsy reasoning of Dibelius as he asks with Dibelius why, otherwise, the

---

22 Cf. Brown, *The Birth of the Messiah*, 105–107.

23 Cf. M. Dibelius, English translation, *From Tradition to Gospel* (Cambridge, England, 1971), 129.

24 Cf. R. Bultmann, English translation, *The History of the Synoptic Tradition* (Oxford, 1963), 439.

angel did not tell Joseph about going to Galilee in Joseph's earlier dream in Egypt. We can just as reasonably and even more justifiably reason that the angel had no need to tell Joseph everything at once. Brown thinks that he espies "internal tension" in the orders said to have been given by the angel to Joseph, namely, first to go to "the land of Israel" and later changed to go instead to Galilee, as if Galilee were not in the land of Israel and Judea were not on the way to Galilee. Brown seems to have understood that the first order of the angel was to take the Child and his Mother to Judea, but that was not the case. Actually there is no contradiction in the orders of the angel, but only a further specification that fits in very logically with the rest of the account.

5. Matthean vocabulary and style. Brown's comparison of Matt. 2:22–23 with Matt. 4:12–16 shows a similarity of vocabulary and style, but his point is not verified, because it involves circular reasoning. The fact is that, since any historian will write according to his own style, one can expect to find Matthew's style appearing time and again in his history. Brown's reasoning assumes without proof that Matthew didn't write his history but only copied imaginary stories and reports that were already stereotyped in their wording and style, while, nevertheless, making some editorial changes and remarks. We have no difficulty in accepting that the evangelist composed Matt. 2:22–23. What we deny are the unfounded assumptions that the material gathered by Matthew was imaginary and that, in his writing, he did not correctly express here a real historical fact.

6. Parallels to other material. Brown's third guideline for distinguishing what is "Matthean" from what is "pre-Matthean" is the presence of "parallels to other material." Brown sees a parallel to Matt. 2:22–23 in the divine command to Moses in Exodus 4:19: *Go to Egypt, for all those who were seeking your life are dead.* Linking this parallel with what he sees to be the "pattern of angelic dream appearances to Joseph," Brown is led to believe that this pattern is "pre-Matthean" and joins other probabilities to suggest that the origin of Matthew's Infancy Narrative is "a pre-Matthean narrative patterned on the infancy of Moses and built around angelic dream appearances to Joseph."[25] This conclusion means that Brown has subscribed to the theory of Bultmann and Dibelius that Matthew's Infancy Narrative is basically a product of the religious imagination of the early Christian community, put together and edited by an unknown writer who came to be identified with Matthew the Apostle. Form-critical theory assumes that the early Christians, following a Jewish practice of Old Testament times

---

25 Cf. Brown, *The Birth of the Messiah*, 107–108.

in which imaginary scenes had been invented for religious purposes, took ideas and scenes from the Old Testament and shaped them into their own stories about Jesus, while the unknown editor "Matthew" made up the additional story of Joseph's later instruction in a dream to take Mary and the Child to Nazareth.

7. Patterned on the story of the Patriarch Joseph and on the infancy of Moses. According to form-critical theory, these early Christians were not psychologically able to invent entirely new stories; they built upon stories already existing in Jewish midrashic tradition. Brown thinks that the idea of the angelic dream appearances to Joseph may have been taken from the Old Testament narrative of the Patriarch Joseph, who was himself a "man of dreams" (cf. Gen. 37:19) and a specialist in the interpretation of dreams. The Patriarch Joseph was taken down into Egypt and began a relationship with that Pharaoh which led centuries later to the command of another Pharaoh to kill all the male babies of the Israelites. Brown thinks that the similarity of the two names Joseph may have helped to suggest this parallel. But he goes on to say that the parallelism between Jesus and Moses is even more deeply rooted in early Christian thought, and this is the reason why our Matthew "has chosen an infancy narrative which fills out the parallelism more perfectly."[26] Brown brings out in detail how Matthew follows the pattern of Moses in Exodus: the Pharaoh gave orders that all the male babies of the Hebrews were to be killed; much later the Pharaoh sought the life of Moses, and so Moses fled out of Egypt; but after the Pharaoh had died the Lord said to Moses, *Go back to Egypt, for all the men who were seeking your life are dead.* Brown conjectures that, from this Old Testament material, early Christians invented the stories of the Massacre of the Innocents and the Flight into Egypt.[27]

8. The extra-biblical tradition. Brown is impressed by parallels in the Jewish midrashic tradition about the infancy of Moses, especially in what is reported by the historian Josephus in his *Antiquities of the Jews*. It is related in the *Antiquities of the Jews* that the Pharaoh at the time of the birth of Moses had been marvelously forewarned by a sacred scholar that a Hebrew leader was about to be born who would be a danger to his kingdom, and that this Pharaoh was alarmed upon hearing this. But, so narrates Josephus, the father of Moses, Amram, was told by God in a dream that his coming child would escape the death decreed by the Pharaoh. The parallelism here is indeed remarkable, and it continues in later stories of the Jewish midrashic tradition,

---

26 Cf. Brown, *The Birth of the Messiah*, 112.

27 Cf. Brown, *The Birth of the Messiah*, 112–113.

according to which the Pharaoh of the time was forewarned of the coming birth of a "deliverer" of the Hebrew people "from a dream that had to be interpreted by his magicians (magi)." Brown has learned that, according to these later stories, the Pharaoh was alarmed by his dream, and so he ordered the killing of all the forthcoming Hebrew baby boys. The similarity of these stories to what we now read in the first two chapters of Matthew fortifies for Brown the conclusion that the contents of Matthew's Infancy Narrative were suggested and shaped from earlier Hebrew stories about the infancy of Moses. Brown believes that the appearances to Joseph in dreams are products of a "dream motif" that was copied from dream visions narrated in stories about the life of Moses.[28] This idea presupposes that in either case the dreams never really took place but are part of imaginary religious literature. Brown notes, "A dream motif is widespread and may be original in the Moses legend." He points out that both the *Chronicle of Moses* and Pseudo-Philo recount a dream experienced by Miriam, the sister of Moses, in which an angel appeared to her and told her that the child to be born to her parents would be the savior of his people. Since Miriam is the Hebrew form of Mary, it was easy for some early Christian to reshape this story into the appearance of an angel to the mother of Jesus and thus start the New Testament tradition of the Annunciation to Mary.[29]

9. The weakness of Brown's parallel with midrashic tradition. Underlying Brown's conclusion that Matthew's Infancy Narrative was created imaginatively by Christians from parallel stories about Moses in the Jewish midrashic tradition there appears to be an error of anachronism. Brown, to be sure, is aware that, according to the historical evidence, "most" of these Jewish stories cannot be dated prior to the 80s, the time when he supposes that Matthew's Gospel was published,[30] but he is unaware that *all* of these Jewish stories appear to have been fashioned after the time when the episodes in Matthew 1–2 could already have been in circulation. The curious fact is that Brown, while he likes to examine all of the historical possibilities behind an episode, completely overlooks the idea that the Jewish stories may have been created imaginatively from the parallel accounts now recorded in the Gospels. And this kind of oversight is typical of form-critics. As I indicated above,[31] the episodes in Matt. 1–2

---

28 Cf. Brown, *The Birth of the Messiah*, 114–115.

29 Cf. Brown, *The Birth of the Messiah*, 114, note 42 and 116, note 45.

30 Cf. Brown, *The Birth of the Messiah*, 114.

31 See chapter 15, part I, paragraph 14,

were known by the Virgin Mary from the time that they took place, and she could easily have recounted these events to Matthew the Apostle as early as the gatherings in the Upper Room before the first Pentecost or at any time thereafter. Josephus wrote down the Jewish stories about the birth of Moses around the year 90 A.D., which would be up to sixty years after the time when some Christians and also some anti-Christian Jews could have known the episodes that Matthew has recorded. Brown goes along with Bultmann, Dibelius, and a host of other non-Catholic form-critical scholars, in believing that "no one of the four evangelists was an eyewitness of the ministry of Jesus," and that the Gospel of Matthew was composed by someone else in or near the 80s.[32] Form-critics readily grant that a complex tradition of imaginative Christian stories could have developed in less than sixty years, but they take no account of the same possibility for the Jewish tradition that Brown is citing here. Yet the Jews had a motive for creating these stories. We know from the Acts of the Apostles that a heated debate between Christians and Jews over the facts about Jesus took place beginning from the time of the Resurrection of Jesus, and this debate could have motivated some creative persons to counteract the true accounts of the Infancy of Jesus with parallel stories about the birth of Moses. In fact, form-critics do assume that the stories in the Jewish midrashic tradition were invented, but their method prevents them from realistically considering the hypothesis that the Jewish stories were taken from the Christian tradition.

10. The presence of rationalist and modernist presuppositions Let us take a serious look at Brown's manner of reasoning. He begins from a theory of interpretation put together by Rationalists who do not accept the possibility of any supernatural happenings in history and who, therefore, relegate all reports of such happenings to the realm of fantasy. He begins from a method elaborated by Modernists which assumes in advance that what is reported in the New Testament is merely the imaginary product of a subrational religious instinct. Brown, as a Catholic exegete, does not profess the rationalism and the modernism from which form-criticism

---

32 Cf. Brown, *The Birth of the Messiah*, 27. Again on page 45: "Most scholars today maintain that the Gospel [of Matthew] was written in Syria by an unknown Greek-speaking Jewish Christian, living in the 80s in a mixed community with converts of both Jewish and Gentile descent." I am not examining here the weakness of Brown's opinion about the late date of composition of St. Matthew's Gospel. The point that is rather being made here is that the episodes reported in Matthew's Infancy Narrative were known by Blessed Mary from the time of the Birth of Christ and could have been known by Matthew the Apostle and other members of the Church as early as about 30 A.D.

arose, but neither does he deal adequately with the way in which these false philosophies influence the method that he is using. His conclusion that the episodes recounted in Matthew's Infancy Narrative are imaginative adaptations of earlier Jewish stories is basically the same as the conclusion of Bultmann, Dibelius, and other rationalist scholars, and he admits that his conclusion follows from their method, but he assumes as a Catholic scholar that his method does not proceed from their rationalist presuppositions. Brown does present somewhat different evidence than they do for his similar conclusion. I commented earlier on the weak, flimsy, and false arguments made by Dibelius and Bultmann for denying the reality of some pertinent episodes in Matt. 1–2.[33] Now, Brown bases his arguments more upon an error of anachronism, but the result is the same, because it is presupposed by the method. If one takes away the modernist presupposition that the Gospels are imaginative fabrications, and if one takes away the false psychological presupposition that the early Christians had to copy fantasies from earlier non-Christian stories, such as those of the pagans and of the Jews, then this whole aspect of form-critical analysis falls to pieces. True historians do not assume in advance what could have taken place and what could not have taken place, using rationalism as the basis of their judgments. Rather they use the instruments of their profession to determine what did take place, and, if what took place was miraculous, they accept it as miraculous. Catholic form-critics do not deny categorically that miracles could have taken place, but their method tempts them to deny miracles wherever Catholic dogma does not forbid, and always to retain a measure of doubt regarding the rest. True historians do not, like form-critics, deny that Jesus was born in Bethlehem on the basis of an unproved assumption that Jesus must have been born in Nazareth. When true historians read a sober account like that of Matthew's Gospel, they do not assume, using weak plausibilities to justify their assumption that he made up events to smooth out his story; they need evidence which, in fact, is not there. A fundamental mistake that Catholic form-critics almost universally tend to make is that they do not attempt to show concretely and with respect to the particular passages that they are analyzing how their conclusions as Catholic form-critics do not carry with them the rationalist presuppositions of the method. If the first two chapters of Matthew are adjudged to present a complex of imaginative stories, what does this judgment do to Christian faith? How can a Catholic accept that these episodes regarding the early childhood of Jesus are imaginary, and that

---

33 See my comments in chapter 15, part I above, paragraphs 9–14.

Christians could blithely fabricate such accounts as though they were true without being liars and deceivers? Catholic form-critics like Brown do not say that the composers of these stories were liars and deceivers, but neither do they squarely face these implications and provide adequate answers.

11. Some studied contradictions between the Infancy Narratives of Matthew and Luke. Brown finds that the infancy accounts of Matthew and Luke "are contrary to each other in a number of details."[34] In Luke, Mary lives in Nazareth; in Matthew, she lives in Bethlehem, since Matthew gives no hint of a *coming* to Bethlehem. Thus, Matthew considers Joseph and Mary to be citizens of Bethlehem, while Luke considers them to be citizens of Nazareth.[35] Luke says that the Holy Family returned tranquilly to Nazareth after the birth of Jesus in Bethlehem; "this is irreconcilable with Matthew's implication (2:16) that the child was almost two years old when the family fled from Bethlehem to Egypt." Hence, reasons Brown, it must be "ruled out" that both accounts are "completely historical."[36] He reckons that "at most, only one of these two narratives can stem from family reminiscences," thus establishing the "tacit assumption that most of the other is not historical."[37] Brown seriously doubts that the episodes of the Massacre of the Innocents and the Flight into Egypt are historical. He finds no remembrance of the Flight into Egypt in the inspired accounts of the ministry of Jesus, and "a journey to Egypt is quite irreconcilable with Luke's account of an orderly and uneventful return from Bethlehem to Nazareth shortly after the birth of the child."[38] Brown notes that an attempt has been made to support an actual sojourn of the Holy Family in Egypt by the fact that some Jewish stories originating in the second century A.D. represent their presence there. But he is quick to point out that these stories were invented to discredit the Holy Family by having them flee to Egypt to avoid the censure of an illegitimate birth and to get themselves involved in black magic and occult practices, with the result that this "Jewish polemic against the Gospel picture of Jesus" does not provide "independent support" for the historicity of such an event.[39]

---

34 Cf. Brown, *The Birth of the Messiah*, 36.

35 Cf. Brown, *The Birth of the Messiah*, 207.

36 Cf. Brown, *The Birth of the Messiah*, 36.

37 Cf. Brown, *The Birth of the Messiah*, 35, note 25.

38 Cf. Brown, *The Birth of the Messiah*, 225.

39 Cf. Brown, *The Birth of the Messiah*, 225–226.

12. *A more realistic look at Brown's studied contradictions.* It is interesting to note how quickly Brown sees in these second-century A.D. Jewish stories a motive of discrediting the reputation of Jesus and his Mother, *as soon as these stories are used in some way to support the historicity of Matthew's Gospel,* and yet is prevented by his form-critical approach from even suspecting that the Jewish stories of the first century A.D. might have had the similar motive of raising the image of Moses by taking episodes in the history of Jesus that are now recorded in St. Matthew's Gospel and applying them to the infancy of Moses, *when such an alternative would support the historicity of St. Matthew's Gospel.* And the reason for this is that the progress of form-criticism, as it was authentically conceived and is still at least subconsciously practiced, is tied solely to doubting and denying the historicity of the Sacred Scriptures, so that residues of seemingly historical events that form-critics believe that they have not yet eliminated represent only delays on the way and work remaining to be done. But form-critics have never actually demonstrated that Matthew and Luke "are contrary to each other in a number of details," as Brown believes. Matthew doesn't say or imply that Mary and Joseph were fixed inhabitants of Bethlehem; Brown reads this into the account in order to enhance his theory. Nor does Matthew say or imply that "the child was almost two years old when the family fled from Bethlehem to Egypt." While Brown often tells his readers that he is examining all of the possibilities, he has not read carefully what Matt. 2:16 gives us to understand. Matthew narrates here that King Herod "sent [soldiers] and killed all of the boys who were in Bethlehem and in all of its surroundings from two years of age downwards, according to the time that he had found out from the Magi." This does not mean that the Child was almost two years old. It means that the Child Jesus may have been nearly one year old. It is obvious that the soldiers sent to kill these boys were not told to check birth certificates first to determine how old the babies were. Herod, as a cruel and cunning man, would assuredly have at least doubled the probable age of the Child, to make sure that, if He were a big baby for his age, He would not escape the massacre. Brown is persuaded by the fact that Josephus "never mentions a massacre of children at Bethlehem." But how would Josephus have known? There was no reporter covering the event, and it would not have been included in the annals of Herod's court. Massacres were common occurrences in those days and could easily escape the record. Hence, Jesus may have been close to a year old, but there is greater likelihood that He had more recently been born, if the star of

Bethlehem appeared to the Magi in the East, not at the time of his birth, but at the time of his conception, and they then took at least nine months to arrive. It is disappointing to see that Brown did not even think of this possibility. Nor is there any good reason why references to the Flight into Egypt would have to have been included in the inspired account of the ministry of Jesus, as Brown requires for its acceptance as historical.

13. The question of "family reminiscences." What Brown vaguely refers to as "family reminiscences" I have concretized in the reminiscences of the Blessed Virgin Mary. Luke tells us twice (2:19; 2:51) that Mary "kept all of these things, pondering them in her heart."[40] I have explained elsewhere how Mary could have been the principal source both of Matthew's and of Luke's accounts. The account in St. Luke would have been a narrative that Mary discreetly told to relatives during the life of Jesus, while the account in Matthew consists mainly of events that Mary would have kept hidden before the death of Jesus, because their telling could have put his life into immediate danger from the political authorities. Thus, one could conjecture that, as early as during the fifty days that Mary spent with the Apostles in the Upper Room before the descent of the Holy Spirit at Pentecost, she could have narrated these hidden events to an inquiring Matthew, or they could have come to him later, whether directly or indirectly. Brown does not consider these possibilities, and so he uncritically concludes that "at most, only one of these two narratives can stem from family reminiscences." And he assuredly fails to read "between the lines" when he assumes that Matthew's account cannot be reconciled historically with "Luke's account of an orderly and uneventful return from Bethlehem to Nazareth shortly after the birth of the child."[41] From what I have indicated in the preceding paragraph, it may not have been very long after the nativity of Jesus that the Holy Family fled into Egypt and returned to Nazareth. And Luke doesn't say that this was "an orderly and uneventful return"; he says that they returned to Galilee to their town Nazareth "after they had performed everything according to the law of the Lord" (Luke 2:39). Since Luke does not say "immediately after," nor does he say that nothing happened in

---

40 So affirms Pope Paul VI (*Insegnamenti di Paolo VI* [1972], p. 1325): "St. Luke, as if to indicate the authentic source of that night at Bethlehem, concludes it with this precious testimony: 'And Mary kept all these things, pondering them in her heart (Luke 2:19).'" Pope Paul VI again affirms (*Insegnamenti di Paolo VI* [1974], pp. 24–25): "Very probably Mary was the genuine and direct source of information for Luke, the evangelist who wrote this." Cf. Pope John Paul II, General Audience of 13 September 1995.

41 Cf. Brown, *The Birth of the Messiah*, 225.

between, and what did happen in between was dangerous to tell, we can easily see that the episodes in Matthew 2 may have been left out in an earlier telling by Luke's source (the Blessed Virgin Mary) as a legitimate omission, considering also that the Flight into Egypt did take place in obedience to a command of the Lord. Brown feels that there is "an *a priori* unlikelihood" that Mary was Matthew's source for the material in his Infancy Narrative, for the reason that Matthew's narrative "centers upon Joseph," while Mary "figures only on a secondary level."[42] But this reason lacks all likelihood. Why would Mary, in her perfect humility, have needed to make herself the center of the story? This is, indeed, a flimsy reason for excluding her testimony.

14. From the viewpoint of historical science. Raymond Brown's conclusion that the writer of Matthew 2:22–23 invented the journey of Mary, Joseph, and the Infant Jesus to Nazareth after a non-existent return from Egypt to Judea does not stand up under critical analysis. Brown's refusal to accord historical fact to this report of Matthew is based upon unproved assumptions, faulty reasoning, and anachronism. The "internal tensions" within Matthew's account and the conflicting affirmations that Brown espies between the first two chapters of Matthew and the first two chapters of Luke can be satisfactorily resolved with a little study. Historical scientists do make use of conflicting testimony to help them to ascertain the historical facts, but they first use their ingenuity and resourcefulness to see if the conflicts are really there. Form-critics often use what are only apparent conflicts or contradictions to build their system of conclusions. In this respect form-critics are not historical scientists.

---

42 Cf. Brown, *The Birth of the Messiah*, 33.

Chapter 16

A Brief Commentary on Matthew 2
According to the Four Senses of Sacred Scripture

Living Tradition 134 (March 2008)

1. For several centuries, and above all during the last hundred years, it has been the custom of scholars to comment on the literal sense alone of Sacred Scripture. As a result, the spiritual sense and spiritual sub-senses have fallen into obscurity except in such areas as spiritual writing and the sacred liturgy. An indication that an awakening to the spiritual sense of Scripture is now in order and is being called for is given in the *Catechism of the Catholic Church*, nos. 115 to 119, where the method of the Four Senses is described as the way in which the inspired word is to be read and interpreted. The present article is an attempt to show how this can be done, but it is necessarily sketchy and non-definitive, since so little work has been done by scholars along these lines for a long period of time. My approach here is to take the *Commentary* of St. Thomas Aquinas on the Gospel according to St. Matthew, along with the remarks and quotations from the Fathers of the Church and other approved writers in his *Catena Aurea*, in order to show how the beginning of a contemporary, that is, a neo-patristic, interpretation can be constructed from the work that he did, without presupposing a critical study on my part regarding the accuracy of the sources he quotes in these two books. An invitation to a critical re-working and expansion of the following brief exposition is hereby extended to other neo-patristic scholars.

2. The basic framework of the neo-patristic approach of the Four Senses of Sacred Scripture is explained by St. Thomas in the *Summa Theologiae*, part 1, question 1, article 10, together with his Quodlibet Seven, question 6, and his *Commentary on the Letter of St. Paul to the Galatians*. This

framework is based on the idea that given statements in Sacred Scripture often have more than one intended meaning, in such a way that some statements have only a literal meaning, while others have one, two, or even three additional meanings representing the spiritual sense of the text. The literal and historical sense is, then, the immediate and most obvious sense of the words (Quodlibet 7, q. 6, art. 3), while the spiritual sense is based upon things inasmuch as they are the figures of other things (Quodlibet 7, q. 6, art. 2). The spiritual sense is divided into three sub-senses: the allegorical (or typical) sense, in which events of the Old Testament are seen in relation to Christ and to his Church; the tropological (or moral) sense, in which one sees how to act righteously; and the anagogical (final, or eschatological) sense, in which the New and Old Testaments together signify the Church Triumphant (ibid.).[1]

3. I might add that the perception of the literal and historical sense requires an adequate use of historical method in the true meaning of the term, while the perception of the spiritual senses requires an effective use of the supernatural virtues of faith, hope and charity. The perception of the allegory of Christ and of his Church requires a use of the analogy of faith based upon solid belief in the historical truth of Sacred Scripture and an affirmation that the supernatural things and events presented in the Bible belong to the one continuum that we call reality. The tropology is the appropriation of the truth and holiness of Sacred Scripture to the souls of individual believers, and it is based upon a prior awareness of the pattern of supernatural virtues available to the sanctified Christian believer. The tropology presupposes an openness of the heart of the reader to the truth and holiness of the text and a willingness to let the moral truth impact upon his own consciousness. This is a function of the supernatural virtue of charity. The anagogy pertains to the Four Last Things of death, judgment, Heaven or Hell, and to the signature, or hallmark, of the Most Holy Trinity impressed here and there upon the sacred text. The perception of this final sense requires an exercise of the supernatural virtue of hope. Awareness of what is affirmed in Sacred Scripture pertains to the virtue of knowledge; awareness of the meaning of what is affirmed pertains to the virtue of understanding; and living the truth and holiness of what is affirmed in Sacred Scripture pertains to the virtue of wisdom.

---

1 For an exposition of the framework of the Four Senses according to St. Thomas Aquinas, see Thomas P. Kuffel, "St. Thomas' Method of Biblical Exegesis," in *Living Tradition* 38 (November 1991), at www.rtforum.org – archive of articles.

4. Matt. 2:1. *Now when Jesus was born in Bethlehem of Judea.* Literal sense. It pertains to the virtue of knowledge to realize that Jesus was in fact born in Bethlehem of Judea: "*there came wise men* (magi) *from the East to Jerusalem.*" Originally the word *magi* applied to Persian philosophers, and it came to apply in the Hellenistic world to wise men from that part of the world. It was also used in common parlance to mean wizards (Rabanus Maurus in the *Catena Aurea*[2]) or astrologers, but not here in the text of Matthew.

5. Matt. 2:2. *For we have seen his star in the East.* Literal sense. There is question as to whether "in the East" means that the star was in the East or that they were in the East when they began to see it (Ordinary Gloss in the *Catena*), but it seems more likely that they were in the East. How did they understand from the sight of this unusual "star" that the great King of the Jews had been born? According to St. Augustine (Aquinas, *Commentary*[3]) and St. Leo the Great (*Sermon 34, "On the Epiphany,"* in the *Catena*), the Magi were instructed by some revelation or interior enlightenment.[4] This was not a star in the usual sense of the word, because a star existing an immense distance away could not have guided them to Jerusalem and then to Bethlehem (John Chrysostom in the *Catena*). Rather, it was a small, luminous body situated a short distance above the surface of the earth. Speculation that this star was a supernova or something of that nature that rose in the eastern sky is based upon the presupposition that the visit of the Magi is a story made up later by Christian believers who were intellectually too dependent to have invented it all by themselves, and who, therefore, needed some previous story (such as the "star that shall rise out of Jacob" in Num. 24:17) to help them. It is based also on the naturalistic presupposition that it would have been impossible for a luminous body to have been miraculously created to guide the Magi. But there is no physical or historical evidence that this did not really happen, and our faith tells us that it did. However, several of the Fathers did affirm that the prediction

---

2 St. Thomas Aquinas, *Catena Aurea,* English translation, vol. I, part I (Albany, N.Y.: Preserving Christian Publications, 1993), p. 70.

3 St. Thomas Aquinas, *Super Evangelium sancti Matthaei lectura* (Turin: Marietti, 1951), no. 162; English translation by Paul M. Kimball: St. Thomas Aquinas, *Commentary on the Gospel of St. Matthew* (Dolorosa Press, from Amazon Books).

4 For some further speculations on the star of Bethlehem by the Fathers of the Church, see Robert A. Sungenis, *The Gospel According to St. Matthew,* in The Catholic Apologetics Study Bible, vol 1 (Queenship Publishing, P.O. Box 220, Goleta, California 93116, A.D. 2003), pp. 209-215).

of the star of Jacob helped the Magi to understand that the Savior had come (Cornelius aLapide, *Great Commentary*, vol. 15, p. 75A).[5] Others have conjectured that the luminous body was the Holy Spirit or an angel or was moved by an angel (Cornelius, p. 75B).

6. Matt. 2:1–2. Spiritual sense. The word "Bethlehem" means "house of bread," and, in the allegory of Christ and his Church, the name signifies the Church, in which dwells Jesus eucharistically under the appearance of bread (Gregory the Great in the *Catena*, p. 70), and spiritually, because He is the Bread of Life (Jn. 6:35) (Aquinas, *Commentary*, no. 162). The Magi were the first of the Gentiles to come to adore Jesus, and they represent tropologically the many Gentiles who have come and continue to come into the Church over the span of history. Christians adore in faith the body of Christ, and they seek in hope to see Him in his divinity face to face in the next life.

7. Matt. 2:3. *When King Herod heard this, he was troubled, and all Jerusalem with him.* Literal sense. Herod's worldly ambition and his focus solely upon the natural world and its allurements made him fear exceedingly any seeming threat to his throne and to confuse heavenly highness with earthly highness (Gregory the Great in Aquinas, *Commentary*, no. 179). The coming of a new kingdom had been prophesied: "But in the days of those kings the God of Heaven will set up a kingdom that shall never be destroyed ...." (Dan. 2:44). But this would be a spiritual kingdom, not a kingdom of this world (Jn. 18:36). The expression *all Jerusalem* here means those in Jerusalem who were closely around Herod. Herod feared, and the Devil, his master, feared even more (Jn. 12:31) (Aquinas, *Commentary*, no. 177). Thus, Pseudo-Chrysostom in the *Catena* (p. 70): The Devil instigated Herod. Allegorically, Herod represents the Devil, who was greatly grieved by the calling of the Gentiles and by this new threat to his power over the people of this world (Leo the Great, Sermon 36, in the *Catena*, p. 69). Again, Herod represents the Devil attacking and killing those who are new and weak in faith and virtue and having only the first inspirations and good thoughts in their minds before they grow and become strong (Leo the Great, Sermon 2 "On the Epiphany"). Tropologically, Herod represents every man acting under the influence of the world, the flesh, and the Devil (Gregory the Great, Homily 10, cited in Cornelius, p. 82A).

8. Matt. 2:6. *And you, Bethlehem, in the land of Judah ...* (Mic. 5:2). Literal sense. The prophecy actually reads as follows: *And you, Bethlehem*

---

5 Cornelius aLapide, *Commentaria in Scripturam Sacram,* edited by Augustinus Crampon (vol. 15, on Sts. Matthew and Mark, Paris: Vivès, 1877).

Ephrathah, are a little one among the thousands of Judah: out of you shall he come forth unto me who is to be the ruler in Israel; and his going forth (is) from ancient times, from the days of eternity. Thus, the prophecy does not regard a merely human ruler, and so Herod probably would not have become so concerned if his advisers had cited to him the whole prophecy (Pseudo-Chrysostom, in the *Catena*, p. 71). This prophecy does not literally regard the worldly state or kingdom of Israel, but the spiritual kingdom of Israel, composed of those Jews who would believe in Christ and of all Gentiles who would also adhere to Him (cf. Chrysostom in the *Catena*, p. 72). Aquinas points out that in this way the birth of Jesus the Messiah is confirmed by two witnesses, as required in Deut. 19:15: the star and the prophecy in Micheas (*Commentary*, no. 184).

9. Matthew 2:7: *...the time of the star.* Literal sense. There have been various guesses on the time when the star first appeared. Some say two years before the nativity of Jesus or at least a long time before, others say on the day of the nativity (*Catena*, p. 73). Cornelius aLapide holds that the star appeared on the day of the birth of Jesus, and that it took just thirteen days for the Magi to arrive in Bethlehem, probably from Arabia. Cornelius reasons that it would have taken Herod about fifteen months first to realize that the Magi had deluded him and then to set up the slaughter and get the permission of Caesar Augustus to carry it out (pp. 85B–86B). But it seems more likely that the star appeared on the day of the virginal conception of Jesus, and that it took about nine months for the Magi to arrive in Jerusalem. Nine months is vaguely close to a year, and Herod, in his vicious cruelty, would probably have doubled the one year to two for the slaughter of the innocents just to make sure that he did get the Infant King, although aLapide and others have conjectured that the mothers and their babies were actually called together beforehand, having birth certificates in hand (Cornelius, p. 86B).

10. Matt. 2:8. *...that I also may come and do him homage.* Literal sense. When the malicious are secretly intending to harm someone, they often pretend to be well-intentioned and affectionate toward him (Pseudo-Chrysostom in the *Catena*, p. 74).

11. Matt. 2:9. *...and behold the star which they had seen in the East went before them until it came and stood over where the child was.* Literal sense. The star was in the atmosphere, and came close above the house in which the divine child was (Ambrose in the *Catena*, p. 74). Allegorical sense. The star of the Magi, the star of Bethlehem, is a figure of Jesus, who arose out of Jacob through the Blessed Virgin Mary. Jesus says: *I am the root and stock of*

David, the bright and morning star (Apoc. 22:16). And it also represents the Virgin Mary, who is the Star of the Sea (St. Bernard of Clairvaux). The star leads the way to Jesus and to salvation, and the way is Jesus (cf. Ambrose, ibid.). "… *and nations that knew you not shall run to you*" (Isa. 55:5). The star is a figure of the light of grace in Jesus, and the house is a figure of the Church, while Herod is a figure of the Devil. Whoever turns to the Devil loses the light of grace, but, when he turns away from the Devil, he regains this light leading to Jesus in the Church (cf. Remigius in the *Catena*, p. 75). Tropologically, the star of the Magi prefigures the light of faith and divine inspiration leading those who are sincerely searching for Jesus to knowledge of the truth and to higher levels of goodness and holiness. Anagogically, the star represents the destiny of those who lead others to truth and holiness: *But they that are wise shall shine like the brightness of the firmament, and they that instruct many to justice like stars for ever and ever* (Dan. 12:3). "He who has a taste for the things that are above … is in a sense a heavenly light. And while he preserves the brightness of a holy life, he shows to many the way to the Lord like a star" (Leo the Great, Sermon 3 "On the Epiphany," quoted in Cornelius, p. 77A).

12. Matt. 2:11. *and entering into the house they found the child with Mary his mother, and falling down they adored him.* Literal sense. While seeing the child, they acknowledged Him as God (Pseudo-Chrysostom in the *Catena*, p. 76). Tropological sense. Those who truly find Jesus find Him in the house which is the true Church of Christ and always with Mary his mother. Those who truly adore Jesus also give special veneration to Mary his mother and the Mother of the Church. *…and opening their treasures, they offered him gifts: gold and frankincense and myrrh.* Prophetic sense. Isa. 60:6: *A multitude of camels shall cover you, the dromedaries of Midian and Ephah: all they from Sheba shall come, bringing gold and frankincense, and proclaiming praise to the Lord.* Allegorically. They brought gold as to a king (cf. Jer. 23:5), frankincense as a sacrifice to God, and myrrh as for the embalming of a dead person (Gregory the Great in the *Catena*, p. 76). Or they brought myrrh as to one who was to die for the sins of all (Augustine, ibid.). While the Magi may not have understood the mystical significance of the gifts they brought, the same grace that moved them to give the gifts brought about their mystical meaning as well (Chrysostom, ibid.). The three gifts represent Jesus, who offered on the Cross the gold of his love for God the Father and for his fellow men, the incense of his submission to the Father, and the myrrh of his suffering and death (Cornelius, p. 81B). Tropologically, the three gifts represent in the devout believer the

gold of an increase of wisdom and charity, the incense of prayer, and the myrrh of a mortified and uncorrupted life (Gregory the Great, Homily 10, in Cornelius, p. 80B). Again, the three gifts can represent the three principal kinds of good works: the gold represents the voluntary giving away of money and goods to the poor; the incense represents the prayer of those detached from the spirit of this world; and the myrrh represents the mortification of fasting and abstinence (Cornelius, p. 82A). Again, the gold may typify wisdom; the frankincense may typify the power of prayer; and the myrrh may typify the mortification of the flesh (Gregory the Great, ibid.). Anagogically, the gold represents the price given by Jesus for our redemption from the power of the Devil; the incense signifies the large-scale ending of Devil-worship on earth; and the myrrh suggests the restoration of our bodies in the final resurrection (Maximus, Homily 3 "On the Epiphany," cited in Cornelius, p. 82A). Again, the opening of their treasures may typify the profession from the hearts of believers of their faith in the Three Divine Persons of the Most Holy Trinity, or, for the verbal allegory, it may represent the three spiritual senses of Sacred Scripture (compare and contrast Anselm in the *Catena*, p. 77, and Aquinas, *Commentary*, no. 204).

14. Matt. 2:13. *Arise, and take the child and his mother, and flee into Egypt. ...* Tropologically. In order to flee successfully from sin, it is necessary to shake off laziness (Eph. 5:14) and have trust in the Virgin and her Child (Sirach 24:24) (cf. Aquinas, *Commentary*, no. 211). Trials and troubles are on the road to Heaven. God, as it were, weaves our failures and successes into a crown of glory (Chrysostom, in Cornelius, p. 84A).

15. Matt. 2:14. *Who arose and took the child and his mother by night and retired into Egypt. ...* Tropologically. The strong flee for a good reason, and not out of fear. Jesus was carried to Egypt also to teach us to take no account of exile, since we are pilgrims on our way to Heaven (Gregory Nazianzen, *Oration 28*, in Cornelius, p. 84A).

16. Matt. 2:15. *That it might be fulfilled which the Lord spoke by the prophet, saying: Out of Egypt I have called my son.* Literal sense. The prophecy is in Hosea 11:1: *When Israel was a child, I loved him: and out of Egypt I have called my son.* The prophecy in its literal sense applies to the children of Jacob, that is, of Israel, and is a statement made in reference to a past already accomplished, since the children of Jacob, the Israelites, had already long before been called out of Egypt. Compare this prophecy with that in Numbers 23:22. Allegorical sense. Jacob/Israel, called out of Egypt in the Exodus as represented by his descendants, is a type, or

prefigurement, of Jesus (Jerome in the *Catena*), who is by nature the only true and only-begotten Son of God, whereas his followers become children of God through adoption into his Mystical Body and only to the extent that they bear a likeness to Him (cf. Aquinas, *Commentary*, no. 216). In the Old Testament prophecies, the coming of Christ and the call of the Gentiles are foreshown in such wise that the thread of history is never broken (Jerome in the *Catena*, p. 81). John Chrysostom points out that this kind of fulfillment is not unusual, because Old Testament prophecies are often said of some and fulfilled in others, and he gives as another example the prophecy of Jacob in Gen. 49:7 regarding Simeon and Levi, which was fulfilled, not in them but in their descendants (Chrysostom in the *Catena*, p. 81).

17. Matt. 2:16. ...*and* (Herod) *sending, killed all the male children that were in Bethlehem and in all the borders thereof, from two years old and under.* ...Literal sense. This slaughter of the innocents really took place. Some historical critics have objected that such a massacre would not have escaped the attention of historians of that time, but actually mass killings were rather common in those times, especially in the case of certain peoples. This King Herod was noted for the frequency and magnitude of his killings. Of his six sons, he had three put to death, and, knowing that he was no object of love among the Jews, just before his death he tried to make sure that there would be weeping at the time of his funeral by leaving orders that many noble Jews should be captured and killed on that occasion (Aquinas, *Commentary*, nos. 235 and 238). Note also that people can become so accustomed to the mass killing of humans that it becomes no longer noteworthy, such as is the case with tens of millions of human infants in the womb that are in these days being slaughtered therapeutically with no notice from historians and the secular press. Tropologically, these Holy Innocents represent all of the martyrs killed in their humility and innocence of heart, who in their lifetimes had turned and become spiritually like little children (Matt. 18:3) (Bede in the *Catena*, p. 83), and, in the allegory of numbers, the age of two years of the infants may represent tropologically the supernatural virtues of love for God and neighbor (Aquinas, *Commentary*, no. 224), or anagogically, the intended attack of the Devil against the life of the incarnate Son of God, since the number two can represent the Second Person of the Blessed Trinity.

18. Matt. 2:18. *A voice was heard in Ramah, lamentation and great mourning: Rachel, bewailing her children, and she would not be comforted, because they are not.* Literal sense. This prophecy in Jeremiah 31:15 is again

a prophecy of the past, because it refers literally to the earlier massacre of virtually all of the able-bodied men of the tribe of Benjamin as narrated in Judges 20 (Aquinas, *Commentary*, no. 226). But, according to St. Thomas, the prophecy may have had a twofold future fulfillment. It may first have been fulfilled literally when the descendents of Benjamin and of the other tribes of Israel were being led away into the Babylonian captivity, because on the way they passed through Bethlehem near Ramah, where Rachel was buried (Gen. 35:19), and she is predicted here metaphorically to weep for them as they go by. More to the point, the prophecy, he says, refers to the slaughter of the innocents. The word Ramah means "on high," and the passage says that *a voice was heard on high*, namely, the voice of Rachel. But Leah, not Rachel, was the mother of Judah and his descendents, so why would Rachel be singled out as weeping? St. Jerome considers that the killing spilled over from Judah into the territory of Benjamin. Augustine suggests that Rachel wept for her sister at the loss of her sister's descendents, because the killers came from the territory of Benjamin, and they were thus incurring eternal damnation (Aquinas, *Commentary*, no. 227). Or perhaps Rachel is described as weeping because, in a true sense, she represents all Israelite women, since she was the principal and predilect wife of Jacob. In the allegorical sense, Rachel, whose name means "ewe," is the sheep who weeps over the slaughter of her little lambs.

19. Matt. 2:20–22. *...go into the land of Israel. ...But, hearing that Archelaus reigned in Judea in place of Herod his father, he was afraid to go there: and, being warned in sleep,* (he) *retired into the district of Galilee.* Literal sense. Form-critics question the reality of this event partly on the ground that an angel of God, if there were any such, would not logically have commanded Joseph first to go to Judea and then afterwards have changed the destination to Galilee. But the passage does not say that Joseph was ordered first to go to Judea and afterwards to Galilee. He was first ordered to go into the land of Israel, which, in the general sense, includes both Judea and Galilee, and then, more specifically, to go into Galilee (Augustine in the *Catena*, p. 89). On a more general level, mainline form-critics, using faulty historical methods, deny the existence of angels and call into question the historical truth of the whole second chapter of Matthew. Form-critics reason in a circle in the sense that they first assume that the supernatural events recorded in the Bible couldn't have taken place, and then they reason from this premise that they didn't take place.

20. Matt. 2:23. *and he went and dwelt in a city called Nazareth that what was spoken by the prophets might be fulfilled that he would be*

called a Nazorean. Literal sense. The literal meaning of this verse seems to depend upon the origin of the word Nazorean, which is treated at length above in chapter 15, part I.

21. Matt. 2:23. Spiritual sense. It seems that the reader of Matt. 2:23 is being challenged to find a profound spiritual meaning behind the surface of the text, and this is illustrated by the way in which the four preceding prophecies have been cited. In the prophecy from Isa. 7:14 in Matt. 1:23, Jesus, by reason of his virginal conception and by the presence of his divine person, is holy, not only in that He is saturated with the grace of the Holy Spirit, but also because He is consecrated and set apart from the sinfulness of his Adamite brothers and from the political and cultural milieu of the evil kings of Judah. And this is confirmed in the prophecy from Mic. 5:2 in Matt. 2:6, in that Jesus was not called to be a political or military leader of Israel, but rather a spiritual leader in a new and better way. The prophecy from Hosea 11:1 in Matt. 2:15 refers literally to the Exodus of the Chosen People out of Egypt, and it goes on to say: *The more I called them, the more they went from me; they kept sacrificing to the Baals and burning incense to idols*, but Matthew here sees it fulfilled figuratively in this sense that the original Israel (Jacob) was a prototype of Jesus, and the promise of God to Jacob and his seed was fulfilled in Jesus (cf. Gal. 3:16). The prophecy from Jeremiah 31:15, as mentioned above, applies literally to the biological mothers of these Holy Innocents of Bethlehem and its surroundings, but it has also a spiritual fulfillment, as is made clear by the continuing words of Jeremiah in verse 16: *Thus says the Lord: 'Let your voice cease from weeping, and your eyes from tears, for there is a reward for your work," says the Lord, 'and they shall return out of the land of the enemy. And there is hope for your last end,' says the Lord, 'and your children shall return to their own borders.'* Thus, in the allegory of Christ and his Church, Rachel weeping prefigures the Church weeping for these her slain children but comforted by hope in their future resurrection (Rabanus in the *Catena*). Then, there is the special allegory of the Blessed Virgin Mary as Mother of the Church. As Jeremiah goes on in verse 22 of the same chapter to predict that *a woman shall encompass a man*, so the Virgin Mary shall literally conceive without the use of male seed the God-Man who would become the Lamb of God, so that in the special allegory of Mary, Rachel, whose name means *ewe*, may well prefigure in this prophecy the Blessed Virgin Mary, Mother of the Lamb and Mother of the Church, the sheep who gave birth to the Lamb of God, and who wept, indeed, for her lost children during her earthly life but is now happily with them in Heaven.

22. The spiritual interpretation of these four preceding prophecies in Matt. 1–2 gives some indication of the spiritual sense of Matt. 2:23. In speculating on the possible Hebrew roots of the name Nazareth, the notion of 'holy' (from *nazir*) is paramount. Literally speaking, Jesus is a Nazarene, a man from Nazareth. Allegorically speaking, Jesus is a Nazorean, the "holy man," *par excellence*, in the sense that he has been preeminently "set aside," and "crowned with holiness" as well as "consecrated to the Lord" from his mother's womb in many ways, such as, in his divine origin, in his virginal conception, in his hypostatic union, in his heavenward vocation, in his sacrificial mission, and in his saturation with the holiness of the Holy Spirit. Behind Matt. 2:23 and behind the whole infancy narrative of Matthew is the allegory of Christ and of his Church. This is an extended metaphor which is not an analogy contrived after the fact, but is rather a spiritual dimension instilled by God from the beginning into the history of the events and into the meaning of the prophecies. Jesus was to be a man from Nazareth who fulfilled and exemplified the supposed (popular) origin of its name. Related to this fulfillment was the mission of Jesus to establish a spiritual Kingdom of God distinct from the common Jewish understanding of the same, which envisioned an earthly kingdom in which there was no distinction between the land, the people, and the religion.

23. The two more likely roots of the name Nazareth are complementary to one another, because whoever is detached from earthly pleasures is also flowering with virtue (Jerome, in Cornelius, p. 92B). Did Matthew add this prophetic reason for returning to Nazareth, or was this reason already in the story that Matthew received? Either case is possible. We do know that Nazareth was Mary's home town and that Jesus was conceived in Nazareth. We know also that Joseph, having been warned in a dream, went on from Judea to Nazareth. It is not out of the question that Joseph had been thinking of settling in Bethlehem or Jerusalem in view of the fact that Jesus was the Messiah, the great future King of the Jews, but, after having been advised in a dream by an angel and after discussing this matter with Mary, he came to see the prophetic value of bringing the Child to Nazareth as it is expressed in Matt. 2:23. Note in this regard that in Luke 1:35 the Angel Gabriel prophesied to the Virgin Mary concerning Jesus: *He will be called holy.* If the word used by the angel for "holy" was a derivative of *nazir*, then by this the reference to "the prophets" in Matt. 2:23 is doubly confirmed.

24. Matt. 2:23. The Tropological sense of this verse regards the appropriation of the truth and holiness of Jesus the Nazorean to the

minds and hearts of his followers, who carry their crosses after Him on their way to heavenly glory, and the supernatural virtues that flower in their souls. All of the members of the Kingdom of God and of the Mystical Body of Christ have been set apart from the spirit of this world by their vocation to eternal life, and so they are all called to be Nazoreans of the Holy Spirit, and this title belongs in a particular manner to those who dedicate themselves to a life of poverty, chastity, and obedience. "The word 'Galilee' means 'transmigration' and 'Nazareth' means *flower*, because the more the Church transmigrates to heavenly things, so much the more does she abound in the flower of virtues" (Rabanus, as quoted in Cornelius, p. 91A). Or the word "Galilee" means *circle* (*Young's Analytical Concordance*) or *turning of the wheel* (*Cruden's Complete Concordance*), because the more the faithful turn from earthly to heavenly things, so much the more do they abound in the flower of virtues. Again, the Virgin Mary is a descendant of David, and, in the supernatural fertility of her virginal soul, she is the Virgin of Virgins. The prophecy in Matt. 2:23 was also fulfilled in her in the sense, not only that the word Nazareth is feminine in gender, but especially that Mary too was "consecrated to the Lord" from her mother's womb (cf. Num. 6:2), and she was "set apart" by reason of her immaculate conception free from any taint of Original Sin. She lived a life full of grace and virtue in her vocation to prayer and virginal chastity. Thus, on a spiritual level, Jesus was a Nazorean also in the sense that He was "from the Virgin Mary," who received Him into her body and into her heart. This further relationship of the name Nazorean pertains to the special tropology of the Blessed Virgin Mary.

Chapter 17

A Neo-Patristic Return to the Calling of Nathanael

Living Tradition 42 (July 1992)

Part I. Regarding Two Form-Critical Evaluations

1. *The superiority everywhere verifiable of the neo-patristic method to the form-critical method of Scriptural interpretation is illustrated by the following interpretation of the episode of the calling of Nathaniel (Jn. 1:45–51). Please note that the use of allegory in this article may not be everywhere exact and is subject, as always, to the judgment of the Church and the review of other competent scholars.*

2. A form-critical analysis. Rudolf Bultmann, in his highly influential commentary, *The Gospel of John*, regards the narrative of the calling of Nathanael (Jn. 1:45–51), in the larger context of the calling of the first disciples (Jn. 1:35–51), as nonhistorical.[1] Bultmann observes that the Evangelist used an older literary source about the calling of these disciples which itself did not attend to historical details or have any interest in them.[2] According to Bultmann any attempt to harmonize this account with the true historical record "destroys the specific intention of the narrative."[3] Using form-critical analysis, Bultmann notes that the chronology of the

---

1 Rudolf Bultmann, *The Gospel of John: A Commentary,* Eng. trans. by G. R. Beasley-Murray (Oxford: Basil Blackwell, 1971, translated from the 1964 printing of *Das Evangelium des Johannes* with the Supplement of 1966), pp. 94–108.

2 Bultmann, ibid., p. 99.

3 Bultmann, ibid., p. 108.

passage, as narrated by the Evangelist, is obscure: on one day John the Baptist gave testimony to the priests and Levites from Jerusalem (v. 19); "the next day John saw Jesus coming to him" (v. 29); "the next day again John stood and two of his disciples" (v. 35); "the next day (Jesus) was going to Galilee" (v. 43). In his reconstruction, Bultmann reasons that the scene in vv. 29–34 was composed wholly from the imagination of the Evangelist, while vv. 35–51 reflect an earlier story that was in the source and may have had historical elements behind it, although even the source had not been composed with the intent to narrate history. The title "Lamb of God" was never pronounced by John the Baptist; it "must come from the Jewish-Christian tradition, perhaps from its liturgical vocabulary." The Evangelist took this simple title found in the source (v. 36), elaborated his own presentation (vv. 29–33), and, to make a link, added "the next day again" to v. 35.[4]

3. Regarding the chronology of vv. 35–50, Bultmann asks, "would it be possible to imagine the situation at all?" In v. 43 Jesus sets out for Galilee and finds Philip, meeting him, therefore, on the way. Then how would Philip have had the opportunity of finding Nathanael (v. 45)? "All becomes clear if the subject of *heuriskei* ("he finds") in v. 43 was originally one of the disciples who had already been called.... Thus v. 43 has been altered by the Evangelist...." Looking at the literary source he claims to see, Bultmann surmises that, since v. 41 ("he finds first his brother Simon") does not begin with "on the next day" after the two disciples had followed Jesus (v. 37), so also the words "on the next day" in v. 43 were probably added to the source by the Evangelist, as well as the words "now it was about the tenth hour" in v. 39, leaving the form-critic to conclude that logically "all the events recorded in vv. 35–50 would take place on *one* day; but there is no reason for this assumption."[5] In other words, the chronology makes no sense at all as far as serious history is concerned; it is just a confusion.

4. The analysis under criticism. Like all form-critical treatments, this analysis of Bultmann falls apart under careful examination. There is certainly something odd at first blush in the report in v. 29 that "the next day" John saw Jesus and said "Behold the Lamb of God," and then in vv. 35–36 "the next day again John stood and said 'Behold the Lamb of God.'" It looks like two different days, and many good commentators, like St. Thomas Aquinas, e.g., have read it that way with impressive reasoning. But here we seem rather to have a subtle historical meaning

---

4 Bultmann, ibid., pp. 95–98.

5 Bultmann, ibid., p. 98.

of the text. If the Greek word *pálin* in v. 35 means "again," not in the narrative sense of "on the next day again," but rather in the editorial sense of "going back again" to what was begun to be narrated in v. 29 and "repeating" more briefly those initial words, then the two scenes in vv. 29–30 and 35–36 are one and the same episode having taken place on one and the same day. And this seems to be the true exegesis of the word *pálin* on the historical level of the text. This reading shows explicit attention to the chronology on the part of the Evangelist, contrary to Bultmann's supposedly reasoned idea that this story has been told "without any attention to historical detail."[6] Rather, the Evangelist here explicitly distinguishes between the historical details of the calling of the first disciples of Jesus and the testimony of John the Baptist which was given at that time.

5. Similarly, while the understood subject of *heurískei* (he finds Philip) in v. 43 may be Jesus in the naive reading of the verse, it is certainly Andrew in its historical reading. On the level of chronology, Andrew *first* finds his brother Simon (v. 41), and then "on the following day he was setting out for Galilee, and he finds Philip" (v. 43). It is clear from the text that Andrew had decided to follow Jesus to Galilee, and so he went and found Philip to tell him, because Philip was from his town and might like to go with them. One can surmise that Peter, Andrew, and Philip had come down there to listen to John the Baptist, as had Nathanael, who was from Cana, and they were in contact with each other. Since John the Baptist had pointed out Jesus as the Messiah, it is reasonable that these Galileans (in the wide sense) might have been inclined to follow Jesus back to Galilee as a group. Bultmann claims that the Evangelist changed the subject of "he finds" in v. 43 from Andrew of the literary source to Jesus, but Bultmann errs, because the subject remains Andrew. It is only that, in a deeper sense, the subject is Jesus, inasmuch as Andrew was following the decision of Jesus.

6. Hence, the reasons given by Bultmann for excluding "any real interest" on the part of the Christian composer in "the external details" of the account simply do not stand up under criticism. Even his observation that the remark of the Evangelist in v. 39, "now it was about the tenth hour," has merely some symbolic significance such as that "the tenth hour is the hour of fulfilment"[7] does not stand up, because the actual words "about the tenth hour" convey chronological precision; there is no symbolism in the adverb "about."

---

6 Bultmann, ibid., p. 99.

7 Bultmann, ibid., p. 100.

7. After the invalid reasoning of the form-critic has been put straight, it becomes clear that Jn. 1:29–51 could very well be the faithful reproduction of an eyewitness report. Andrew could have related the whole story to John, as could Philip have done, especially if Philip is the other disciple mentioned in v. 35. Finally, John, son of Zebedee, author of this Gospel, could have been the other disciple mentioned in v. 35, as Thomas Aquinas and many other able commentators have conjectured, and, therefore, John could have been an eyewitness to the whole episode. In fact, in his Gospel, John out of humility habitually does not mention his own name, but rather refers to himself as "that other disciple" or something similar (cf. Jn. 13:23; 19:26–27; 20:2, 3, 4, 8; 21:7, 20, 23, 24). Interestingly, at the very conclusion of this Gospel, it is declared, referring to John, that "this is that disciple who gives testimony of these things," without mentioning John by name (Jn. 21:24). An additional reason, perhaps the initial reason, for not mentioning his name would be the confusion or emulation with the name of John the Baptist in v. 35 as well as the occurrence of the name of John, father of Simon, in v. 42.

8. Bultmann, for flimsy reasons, maintains regarding the Fourth Gospel that "the author remains unknown to us." He claims that the Gospel does not name the author, but to do so he must attribute the claim of John in 21:24 to a hypothetical redactor, and even then he admits that "the redactor holds the author to be an eyewitness to the life of Jesus" and "identifies him with the enigmatic figure of the Beloved Disciple." Relying only on a far-fetched inference from Mark 10:39 and on "several witnesses of the ancient Church" whom he does not name, Bultmann maintains that John "must have been killed by the Jews very early."[8] He needs to affirm this in order to be able to keep up his whole approach while admitting also that in historical fact "a part of the Baptist's following went over to the Christian community" and "it is probable that the Evangelist himself was among these disciples."[9] The fact that Jesus said to that disciple whom He loved "So will I have him remain till I come" (Jn. 21:22) already cancels Bultmann's facile assumption from Mark 10:39 that John "must have been killed by the Jews very early." One would have to want very badly not to see the truth in order to accept Bultmann's weakly defended hypothesis that John's declaration, "this is that disciple who is giving witness of these things"

---

8 Bultmann, ibid., pp. 11–12.

9 Bultmann, ibid., p. 108.

(21:24), must have been written by a redactor. No fact or testimony can survive the subjective plausibility test of a form-critic whose mind is made up to the contrary.[10]

9. The world and human existence. Bultmann's method of form-critical literary analysis, so seemingly rigorous and scientific in its presentation, is actually a fallacious application of mistaken presuppositions about the world. Bultmann followed from the beginning the idea that nothing miraculous can happen and that there can be no real intervention of God in this world.[11] He went on to declare that God does not exist in objective reality and cannot, therefore, be a real object of our thoughts.[12] On the basis of this total exclusion of the object of Christian faith, Bultmann gave a meaning to the Gospels which is diametrically opposed to what their authors intended and which reduced the Gospels to mere products of human subjectivity.[13] He excluded on principle that the Incarnation of God could really have occurred as well as the Resurrection of Jesus and every other miracle reported in the Gospels.[14] In excluding these things *a priori*, he was not acting as a true historian, because he was not open to consider what might actually have taken place inasmuch as it contradicted what he already supposed could not have taken place.[15] He did not really examine the reported facts objectively, but only sought plausible reasons to exclude them, if they did not accord with his presuppositions.

10. In applying unhistorically his presupposition about the world to the narrative in John 1:29–51, Bultmann sees illustrated the theme of the "divine man," or "man issuing from the gods," which, he says, was an idea "widespread in pagan and Christian Hellenism." Thus, for Bultmann, the origin of the idea of the divinity of Jesus is Hellenistic pagan mythology, and this idea penetrated into the story of Jesus after the Christian community had spread to the world of Greek culture. He sees the Gospels as a particular form of religious literature, reflecting some events surrounding the life of

---

10 For a summary of the solid arguments in favor of John the Apostle as the author of the Fourth Gospel, see John M. Steinmueller, *A Companion to Scripture Studies*, rev. ed. (Houston: Lumen Christi Press, 1969), vol. III, *Special Introduction to the New Testament*, pp. 137–147.

11 See J. F. McCarthy, *The Science of Historical Theology*, art. 8.0 (pp. 101–102).

12 Presented by McCarthy with critique, ibid., pp. 146–151.

13 Presented with critique, ibid., pp. 5–14.

14 Presented with critique, ibid., pp. 101–113.

15 Presented with critique, ibid., pp. 113–119.

Jesus, but expressed in the genre of pious fantasy according to the dictates of certain psychological laws that govern pre-conceptual thinking. All of this is nothing more than a calumny against Jesus and his followers, not based upon historical facts, but merely deduced from false presuppositions about human existence and the real world.[16]

11. For Bultmann the Gospel of John "fundamentally contains but a single theme: the Person of Jesus," with the result that "the detail no longer possesses worth on its own account." According to Bultmann "the source of the discourses which John takes over or to which he adheres is Gnostic in outlook. ... In John Jesus descends from heaven, like the Gnostic Redeemer, to bring to men the saving message, and he returns to the Father after completing his work." But, at the same time, "in his Gnostic form a pointed anti-Gnostic theology is expressed. John knows no cosmic dualism. ... John thus uses the language current in Gnostic circles to give expression to the Christian understanding of faith."[17]

12. What Bultmann means here by the "Christian understanding of faith" is Bultmann's own idea of Christian faith, which he discovers in John by peeling off the "mythology" in which he finds it encased. The divinity of Jesus is for him the center of that mythology. Thus, he says, the idea of omniscience, attributed to Jesus in this Gospel, "belongs to the mythological elaboration of the idea of revelation," and "the close connection between the omniscience of the Revealer, grounded in his unity with God, and his task of revelation can already be seen in Gnosticism."[18] Thus, in meeting Nathanael (v. 47), Jesus shows himself to be the divine man "because he knows the character of the man he meets." In v. 51 the Evangelist quotes Jesus as saying "you shall see heaven opened and the angels of God ascending and descending upon the Son of Man," but Bultmann credits the Evangelist with merely using the mythological idea of heaven opened and the angels of God ascending and descending to convey the more real idea, not of the vision of heavenly beings, but of the vision in faith of the glory of Jesus in the here and now, "as the vision which sees in him the Father." In Bultmann's reading, the source of vv. 45–51 showed Jesus as a divine being (a God-Man) whose miraculous knowledge overwhelms those who meet him, but the Evangelist transforms this into "the paradox of the glory of the Incarnate," in that his narrative "at once portrays the right

---

16 Presented with critique, ibid., pp. 126–135, 155–164.

17 Bultmann, *Gospel of John*, pp. 7–9.

18 Bultmann, ibid., p. 102.

way of seeking Jesus, the power of the word which proclaims him, and the right way of hearing this word—in the 'following' of discipleship. ... Thus faith in him is grounded in the fact that in the encounter with him the believer's own existence is uncovered. ... In the earthly presence of the Son of God the promise is fulfilled. Jesus is the Son of Man, not, as understood by Jewish and early Christian apocalyptic, as he who one day will come in the clouds of heaven, but in his earthly presence."[19] Thus Bultmann finds in John's account of the calling of Nathanael (vv. 45–51) his own impoverished idea of Christian faith, and he excludes, by the reductive process of his form-critical and existentialist method, all the richness of faith that John actually presents.

13. Bultmann's exegesis by no means presents "the right way of seeking Jesus" or "the right way of hearing" the Word of God written in the inspired text of the Gospels. His denial of the divinity of Jesus makes his outlook no longer Christian. He has, in fact, eliminated from his outlook the entire object of Christian faith. Once Bultmann had made the mistake of denying the historical fact of the Incarnation of God in Jesus, his corrupted imagination was able gradually to bring him to a denial of the entire historical truth of the Gospels. In ascribing to John's Gospel the theme of the "Gnostic Redeemer," Bultmann's intellectual appetite would not let him consider that the Gnostic Redeemer was only a corrupted interpretation of the true event of the Incarnation. Bultmann exulted in his exclusion, as a "modern man," of the "Gnostic view of the world," in which "the divine world of light and the demonic power of darkness stand over against one another,"[20] but, in closing his eyes to what the Gospel of John was telling him about the powers of darkness, he opened his mind to the influence of those demonic powers. As a form-critic he compared unfavorably the inspired word of God with the mythologies of surrounding cultures, but he never stopped to think that those mythologies were only corruptions of the true Revelation, created from the unbridled fantasy of men enslaved to Satan and falling further into sin. The two principal sources of Bultmann's thought could well have been his own unbridled imagination and the suggestion of devils seeking to empty the Scriptures of their meaning. Bultmann's thinking does not begin from prayer to the one true God or induce to prayer to the one true God. It is anti-Christian in the sense that it opposes faith in Jesus as the God-Man; it deprives Christians of hope in the sense that it denies the existence of heaven and

---

19 Bultmann, ibid., pp. 104–107.

20 Ibid., p. 7.

of God, whose triune life constitutes heaven; it is devoid of charity in the sense that the love for God evoked by the inspired Scriptures is falsified by form-critical analysis. Bultmann did not hesitate to place the "almost magical power of attraction" of the Person of Jesus as described by John the Evangelist in the category of a transposed "fairy-tale motif,"[21] not realizing that this attraction only appeared to be fanciful from the viewpoint of his own warped subjectivity.

14. A Catholic form-critic. Raymond E. Brown, a Catholic form-critic, in his well-known commentary, *The Gospel according to John*, conjectures that the Fourth Gospel was composed in five stages from one dominant source, with the second, third, and fourth stages put together by the same evangelist—not necessarily John the Apostle—and the fifth stage done by a redactor who was of the same bent of mind. Brown believes that the redactor added the final chapter to the Gospel and probably also the Prologue, which is "a once-independent hymn composed in Johannine circles."[22] While he quotes from a great variety of writers in this voluminous work, it is clear that Brown depends heavily upon Bultmann for his method of literary analysis and for many of the ideas that he considers. Brown does not express Bultmann's radical anti-Christian conclusions, and it may be assumed that he, as a Catholic, does not accept them, but his method does not enable him to pull clearly and decisively away from the rationalism that underlies Bultmann's thought.

15. Thus, regarding the historical truth of this Gospel, Brown observes: "If John is based on historical tradition and genuine theological insight, then one of the principal reasons for writing the Gospel may have been to preserve this tradition and insight."[23] This hypothetical statement is not an affirmation that historical tradition and genuine theological insight are in fact preserved in this Gospel, or even that there was an intention to preserve them. Brown comments on both possible elements as he goes along, but the expressions "historical tradition" and "genuine theological insight" remain undefined throughout his work. Bultmann, on the other hand, openly admits that there is historical tradition underlying the Gospel of John, such as that Jesus of Nazareth did live and preach to people in Palestine in the first century, and that some of the disciples of John the Baptist probably did adhere to Him. What Bultmann denies is that one

---

21 Ibid., p. 106.

22 R. E. Brown, *The Gospel according to John,* The Anchor Bible (Garden City: Doubleday, 1966), pp. XXXIV–XXXIX.

23 Brown, ibid., p. LXVII.

can take as historical at face value anything that is asserted in this Gospel, on the ground that it is not in the genre of sober historical narrative but rather of religious fantasy. And Brown does not ably defend the truth against this charge. Bultmann also sees "genuine theological insight" in this Gospel, especially inasmuch as it historicizes assumed mythological imagery and leads towards the uncovering of the believer's own existence. Brown presents no explicit idea of what "genuine theological insight" might mean, and his lack of definition seems to prevent him from arriving at a position that is clearly different from that of Bultmann.

16. Thus, Brown accepts Bultmann's basic reconstruction of Jn. 1:19–34, while questioning indecisively whether the material in these verses that has Synoptic parallels was added by the "Ecclesiastical Redactor," as Bultmann conjectures.[24] But if neither the Evangelist nor the conjectured "Ecclesiastical Redactor" was reporting the sober historical facts, what difference does it ultimately make, and what reason should people today have for putting any credence in it? This question Brown never addresses, nor does he oppose Bultmann's answer to the question, but he accepts Bultmann's working hypothesis that these are imaginary scenes used as a framework for the presentation of theological ideas. Brown sees the narrative in John of the calling of the disciples of Jesus as reorganization "under theological orientation" of whatever historical information might underlie the account, according to the theme of "a gradual deepening of insight and a profounder realization of who it is that the disciples are following." This insight "reaches a climax in 2:11, where Jesus has revealed his glory and the disciples believe in him." This is exactly what Bultmann has suggested with greater incisiveness.[25] St. John's Gospel quotes John the Baptist, Andrew, Peter, Philip, and Nathanael as expressing various titles of Jesus at the time of their calling. Bultmann sees this as the Church generations later placing these words on the lips of John the Baptist and of the disciples in imaginary scenes created for the purpose. Brown follows suit in saying: "What John has done is to gather these titles together into the scene of the calling of the first disciples. ... That the disciples did not attain such an insight in two or three days at the very beginning of the ministry is quite obvious from the evidence of the Synoptics. For instance, only halfway through Mark's account (8:29) does Peter proclaim Jesus as Messiah, and this is presented as a climax. Such a scene would be absolutely unintelligible if, as narrated in John, Peter knew that Jesus was the Messiah before he ever met him. ...

24 Brown, ibid., p. 70.

25 Bultmann, op. cit., pp. 106–107.

Thus, we cannot treat John 1:35–51 simply as a historical narrative. John may well be correct in preserving the memory, lost in the Synoptics, that the first disciples had been disciples of John the Baptist and were called in the Jordan valley just after Jesus' baptism. But John has placed on their lips at this moment a synopsis of the gradual increase of understanding that took place throughout the ministry of Jesus and after the resurrection. John has used the occasion of the call of the disciples to summarize discipleship in its whole development."[26] In v. 49 Nathanael is quoted by John as exclaiming: "Rabbi, you are the Son of God, you are the King of Israel." Looking at this exclamation as words placed upon the lips of Nathanael, Brown observes: "The former of the two titles, 'the Son of God,' was probably a messianic title.... In the theological progression indicated by the titles of ch. 1 which capsulizes the disciples' gradual growth in insight throughout the whole ministry of Jesus, John may well have wished to include in 'Son of God' a confession of the divinity of Jesus. ... Certainly, the readers of the Gospel in the late 1st century would have become accustomed to a more profound meaning for 'Son of God.'"[27]

17. Dependent thinking. In this appraisal, Brown does not succeed in distinguishing his position from the devastating conclusions of Bultmann. In fact, Bultmann's denial that the scenes of the calling of the disciples could possibly have taken place is based ultimately upon his failure to comprehend that Jesus really is the God-Man. For Bultmann, the notion of the divinity of Jesus first came into the Church in the Hellenistic period, many years after the death of Jesus. Hence, it was the Church that created from its own imagination the progression of titles leading up to belief in Jesus as the God-Man. With this presupposition, Bultmann falsely but logically argues that neither Jesus nor his first disciples could have spoken as they are quoted to have spoken in John's first chapter.

18. How should one read what Brown says about the historical truth of John's narrative? As a Catholic, he presumably knows that Jesus actually is the God-Man, and from this conviction it follows that Jesus could have said what He is quoted by John as having said at the calling of the first disciples. Brown's difficulty regarding the confession of Peter is paltry, because in Mark 8:29 Peter declares as his firm conviction what Andrew had claimed to him in a preliminary way in John 1:41. Such a scene is absolutely intelligible in harmony with John 1:41. Peter had discovered in the meanwhile, not only that Jesus really was the Messiah, but also that

---

26 Brown, op. cit., pp. 77–78.

27 Brown, ibid., pp. 87–88.

Jesus was God Incarnate (Matt. 16:16), and he had come to know this on a level that merely human insight could never attain (Matt. 16:17). Had Brown reached the same level of insight when he wrote these words?

19. Brown does not define even implicitly in any discernible way what he means by a gradual deepening of "genuine theological insight," or by a "profounder realization of who it is that the disciples are following," or by a "gradual increase of understanding." For Bultmann the progression towards the proclamation of Jesus as King, as Messiah, as Son of God was not an increase of understanding; it was a regression into religious fantasy. Brown offers no arguments against this accusation; the primary question for the exegete of whether Jesus is or is not really the Son of God seems to be completely outside of his focus of attention. But since reality is the necessary medium of all science,[28] this lack of focus takes Brown out of the field of scientific thinking.

20. Thus, when Brown (pp. 87–88) observes that "the readers of the Gospel in the late 1st century would have become accustomed to a more profound meaning for 'Son of God,'" he is presenting a mental confusion. According to the form-critical sources upon which Brown depends, the idea of the divinity of Jesus arose in the Church later in the 1st century, borrowed from Hellenistic pagan mythology, and was then retrojected into the Gospel accounts. If Brown accepts this presupposition, then his expression "more profound meaning" is itself meaningless for the historian, because such a retrojection is "more profound" only in a fanciful way. But, on the other hand, if the idea that Jesus was the "Son of God" arose, as it did, from the historical fact that He is the Son of God, then Peter could already have "become accustomed" to this more profound insight already during the ministry of Jesus, in which case Brown's appeal to readers of the Gospel in the late first century is seen to be a confusion.

21. Bultmann's position regarding this is both clear and clearly unacceptable to a Christian. He presupposes that Jesus was no more than an ordinary man of his time with highly limited capacities and insights, and from this (false) presupposition he logically concludes that everything illustrating the divinity of Jesus has been retrojected into his life-story after his death, beginning with his imagined resurrection. Brown does not affirm Bultmann's unbelief, but he lacks the apparatus to deal with it as he expounds his own conclusions. Thus, the attribution of divinity which Jesus makes of Himself in the Gospel and which the disciples make concerning Him, Brown, for no logical reason, assumes

---

28 Cf. McCarthy, *The Science...*, pp. 47–53.

could not have taken place in historical reality. He says, for instance: "We have spoken of the sequence of titles in ch. 1. Verse 51 introduces 'the Son of Man' (which is not found in the Genesis background of Jacob's dream). This is the only title in the chapter that Jesus uses of himself, a fact that may reflect a historical reminiscence that Jesus did use this title, as distinct from the titles given to him by the disciples after the resurrection, e.g., Son of God."[29] By this distinction Brown is implying that Peter, for instance, before the Resurrection could not have called Jesus the Son of God (Jn. 6:70; Matt. 16:16). But Brown has no historical evidence or logical reason for saying this. Bultmann's exclusion of the divinity of Jesus is essential to the coherency of his form-critical reasoning. In the absence of this presupposition, form-critical reasoning is seen to be confused and incoherent with the historical fact that Jesus is the divine Son of God.

Part II. The Historical Sense of John 1:45–51

22. A distinct historical sense. The neo-patristic interpretation of Sacred Scripture is emerging at this time in the Church both as a continuation of the valid exegetical tradition of the past and as a reaction against the invalid and often harmful exegetical results of form-criticism. It begins from the insight that form-criticism, in using a defective historical method, is falsifying the Scriptures on both the historical and the theological levels. Neo-patristic exegesis has already the use of a partially developed scientific historical framework of research by means of which it can discern the errors in form-critical method and, with the help of God's grace, arrive at new insights into the meaning of the sacred text.

23. The principal source of the neo-patristic method is the exegetical tradition of the Roman Catholic Church in the patristic, medieval, and modern periods, as contrasted with approaches that oppose this tradition. Other sources include wholesome contributions from Orthodox, Protestant, and Jewish writers who reflect in some way the Catholic tradition. Another important source for the development of the framework of research is the Catholic philosophical tradition, to which is added the valid speculation of philosophers of history and the work of scientific historians regarding the specific area of historical science.

---

29 Brown, op. cit., p. 91. For places in the Gospel according to John where Jesus calls Himself or others call him "Son of God" (apart from equivalent expressions such as in 1:14 and 1:18), compare 1:49; 3:16; 3:18; 6:70; 9:35; 11:4; 11:27; 19:7; and 20:31.

24. Neo-patristic exegesis distinguishes systematically between the literal sense and the spiritual sense of the sacred text.[30] On the level of the literal sense, it again distinguishes systematically between the "simple" literal sense and a "subtle" literal sense that frequently comes into focus under technical analysis. It is precisely by failing to see the subtle literal sense that form-critics find a basis for many of their arguments against the historicity of the Scriptures, and it is very often by resolving the historical problems raised by form-critics against the text that the subtle literal sense is found. We may, therefore, divide what was formerly called the "literal and historical sense" into two literal senses, the simple literal sense and the historical sense, and deal with them accordingly.

25. In commenting above on Jn. 1:29–51, I examined some chronological difficulties raised by form-critics against the text. I suggested that the Greek word *pálin* in v. 35 was explicitly editorial and thus brought the Evangelist's historical framework into view. I suggested also that the understood subject of "was setting out for Galilee" in v. 43 is Andrew and thus drew attention to a meaning that is not obvious to the simple reader, who will spontaneously assume that Jesus is the subject. And, in some way Jesus is the subject, so that the question of a double literal sense arises. Neo-patristic exegesis undertakes to treat this question, and much work remains to be done. In the case of the two instances in vv. 35 and 43, which I have just mentioned, either my suggested reading is the only true literal reading or there is an intended double literal meaning in the text.

26. Neo-patristic analysis often finds that the plain and simple literal meaning of a problematic passage is true but imprecise, while the subtle literal meaning that can be gathered without falsifying the wording is a precise statement that is completely in harmony with the demands of historical science. The simple meaning of a text is usually available to anyone who can recognize even the most naïve and slavish meaning of the words in the text, however technically inaccurate that meaning may be. That the Holy Spirit would present a text that is not technically correct in its simple reading can be explained as follows: a) so that persons not having technical education or a precise framework of knowledge can perceive the spiritual message within the text; b) so that readers may deepen their understanding of the message by finding answers to the historical problems that have been deliberately left in the text; c) so that the truth may remain hidden from those who are not honestly seeking for answers.

---

30 See chapter 3 above.

27. St. Thomas Aquinas, following St. Augustine, allows that there could be a multiple literal sense of words in Sacred Scripture, although he does not declare that there is.[31] One of the tasks of contemporary neo-patristic exegesis is to study various examples of the contrast between the simple and the subtle senses of passages in order to try to resolve the question as to whether they are instances of a double literal sense or vague versus clear understandings of a single literal sense. The example which we shall consider here is the description of the calling of Nathanael in Jn. 1:45–51.

28. Verses 45–46. In v. 46 Nathanael is quoted as saying to Philip: "Can anything good come from Nazareth?" Bultmann misses the subtle meaning as he comments: "It seems incredible to Nathanael that obscure Nazareth could be the home of the promised one. It makes no difference whether one takes the sentence as a question or an ironic statement. There is no need to suppose that Nazareth had a bad reputation; it is enough that it was an insignificant village."[32] Brown looks only at the naive sense as he suggests: "The saying may be a local proverb reflecting jealousy between Nathanael's town of Cana and nearby Nazareth."[33] Commentators of the Catholic tradition have also explained Nathanael's remark on the level of the plain and simple sense. Thus, St. Thomas quotes St. John Chrysostom as suggesting that Nathanael knew from the prophecy of Micheas 5:2 that the Messiah would come from Bethlehem,[34] and Cornelius aLapidé adds that Nathanael also knew that Nazareth was a homely little village despised by the Jews.[35]

29. But to understand with historical precision the expressions of Nathanael and Jesus in this penetrating conversation it is necessary to go beyond the naive sense of the words. Philip had said to Nathanael: "We have found him about whom Moses in the law and the prophets wrote, Jesus the son of Joseph of Nazareth" (v. 45). It needs to be understood that Nathanael was a student of the Scriptures and a conceited young man as well. In his

---

31 Aquinas, *Summa Theologiae*, I, q. 1, art. 10 corp. Cf. Augustine, *Confessions*, bk. 12, ch. 31, no. 42 (ML 32, 844); *De Genesi ad litteram*, bk. 1, ch. 19 (ML 34, 260f.). See also T.P. Kuffel, "St. Thomas' Method of Biblical Exegesis," in *Living Tradition*, No. 38 (Nov. 1991), p. 3. See also note b to *Summa Th.*, I, art. 10 in the Leonine edition (Marietti, 1952), Tome I, p. 561.

32 Bultmann, op. cit., p. 103.

33 Brown, op. cit., p. 83.

34 Aquinas, commentary on Jn. 1:46.

35 Cornelius aLapide, commentary on Jn. 1:46.

erudition was included an interest in the origin of words. Hence, he could easily infer that the name "Nazareth" came from the Hebrew word *nazir*, meaning "set apart," "consecrated," and, therefore, "holy."[36] Nathanael was thus making a witty remark to Philip as he said in effect: "Can anything *good* come from the holy?" And this quip was a humorous reflection upon the origin of Jesus, who was here being described as coming from Nazareth.

30. Verse 47. But Nathanael came to see. "Jesus saw Nathanael coming to him and he said to him: 'Behold a true Israelite in whom there is no guile'" (v. 47). According to Bultmann, with this greeting Jesus is being shown as the "divine man" in that he knows the character of the man he meets: one who is worthy of the name of Israel, because in him there is no guile.[37] Brown opines: "The proclamation of Nathanael as a genuine Israelite without guile is another example of the revelatory formula isolated by De Goedt" ("Look!" followed by a description "wherein the seer reveals the mystery of the person's mission").[38] St. Thomas says that Nathanael is here called "truly an Israelite," that is, one without guile, because the name "Israelite" in its etymology means either "very righteous" (cf. Isa. 44:2) or "a man seeing God," and Nathanael was very righteous as well as possessing the cleanness and simplicity of heart needed by those who see God.[39] Cornelius aLapide relates the interpretation of St. John Chrysostom that Jesus implied in this encomium that He was not offended by Nathanael's question to Philip about being from Nazareth, because He knew that Nathanael was of an open mind and was sincerely seeking the truth.[40]

31. However, there is obviously something enigmatic about these plain readings of the text. An Israelite is a descendent of Israel (Jacob), and Jacob was one of the most guileful individuals who ever lived, as exemplified by the way he acted towards his brother Esau (Gen. 25:25–34); towards his father Isaac (Gen. 27:11–29); towards his uncle Laban (Gen. 30:29–43); and in the "blessings" that he pronounced for his own sons at the time of his death (Gen. 49). The very name Jacob means "he grabs the heel," which is a trick used by wrestlers to overthrow their opponent. It is obvious, on the level of historical analysis, that the greeting of Jesus, "Here is a real Israelite, in whom there is no guile," is an ironical and witty riposte to

---

36 Cf. Cornelius aLapide, commentary on Matt. 2:23.

37 Bultmann, op. cit., p. 104.

38 Brown, op. cit., pp. 83, 87, 58.

39 Aquinas, commentary on Jn. 1:47.

40 Cornelius aLapide, on Jn. 1:47.

Nathanael's flippant question. In straight and prosaic words, Jesus could have said, "Behold a true Israelite, full of guile," but the ironical form meets Nathanael on his own terms and shows him that Jesus knows him for the cocky individual that he is.

32. Verse 48. This spirited opening by Jesus causes Nathanael to ask in surprise: "From where do you know me?" This sets up another witty reply from Jesus: "Before Philip called you, I saw you being under the fig tree," that is, "I saw you when you were under the fig tree" (v. 48). Now, Nathanael may have been standing or sitting under a fig tree before Philip called him. But this declaration of Jesus seems to have said much more than that to Nathanael, in the context of the quip that he had made about the hometown of Jesus. The play on words is about origins of words and of persons. It seems that, within the ambit of obvious Scriptural references, the allusion is to the Garden of Eden, so that it is as if Jesus is saying to Nathanael: "You joked about my supposed father and place of origin, but I saw you when you were only in potency in the procreative seed of Adam and Eve, your first parents, as they stood naked and ashamed under the fig tree from which they took leaves to make garments (Gen. 3:7). Therefore, I, Jesus of Nazareth, am the God who created you and your ancestors."

33. Verse 49. Nathanael understands this, and he exclaims: "Rabbi, you are the Son of God, you are the King of Israel" (v. 49). Bultmann's interpretation of this confession of faith excludes entirely the action of divine grace. On the metaphysical level he denies the existence of God as an objective Being who could in any way interject Himself or his action into the closed causal reality of this world.[41] Hence, he denies that the incarnation of God in a Man could really have taken place. And on the psychological level he holds that the imaginative instincts of these primitive people in Palestine, including Jesus and Nathanael, were so behaviorally conditioned by the culture in which they lived that they could not have imagined that Jesus was God Incarnate.[42] Thus, Bultmann believes that

---

41 In *The Science of Historical Theology*, I have summarized at length Bultmann's principle of the exclusion of God from this world (pp. 5-6 and 101–102) and presented a refutation (pp. 103–113).

42 Bultmann states his principle of cultural conditioning in *The History of the Synoptic Tradition*, Eng. trans. by John Marsh (Oxford: Blackwell, 1963), p. 4. He says: "The proper understanding of form-criticism rests upon the judgement that the literature in which the life of a given community, even the primitive Christian community, has taken shape, springs out of quite definite conditions and wants of life from which grows up a quite definite style and quite specific forms and categories. Thus every literary category has its 'life situation' (*Sitz im Leben*: Gunkel), whether it

the idea of Jesus as the Son of God had to have been taken from some pagan source in the Hellenistic period and placed on the lips of Nathanael by a writer of that time. His explanation is that the direct source of the idea of the divinity of Jesus is Gnosticism and that the writer of St. John's Gospel was a Christian Gnostic who historicized the Gnostic images that he used by applying them to the here-and-now rather than to some distant heaven.[43] Bultmann adopted this interpretation because it fit in with his own nonbelief in the existence of heaven, and he maintained this position even though he admitted that the form of the Gnostic "redeemer myth" that he took as a model did not develop until after the Gospel of John had been written.[44]

34. Brown does offer some arguments against Bultmann's notion of the meaning of Jesus. He notes that the expression "and the Word became flesh" in Jn. 1:14 "is a clear reference to the Incarnation" and "describes the Incarnation in strongly realistic language by stressing that the Word became *flesh*," a term which "seems to have been associated with the Incarnation from the earliest days of Christian theological expression." He feels certain that the theology of this Johannine expression "would not have been compatible to Gnostic or Docetic strains of thought".[45] "Thus," he adds, "in becoming flesh the Word does not cease to be the Word, but exercises his function as Word to the full." Bultmann also admits a contrast here with the Gnostic picture in that Jesus is presented as Wisdom incarnate or as revelation itself, "for Jesus brings no teaching and is not a guide to heavenly mysteries" as in Gnosticism. To this idea Brown asks, "But does not Bultmann make too much of a revealer without a revelation? ... If the fact that Jesus was sent is all important, this is in itself a tremendous revelation of 'the one thing that is necessary.' It is a revelation that the Creator is here present to his creatures; and the Creator does not come

---

be worship in its different forms, or work, or hunting, or war. The *Sitz im Leben* is not, however, an individual historical event, but a typical situation or occupation in the life of a community. In the same way, the literary 'category,' or 'form,' through which a particular item is classified is a sociological concept and not an aesthetic one, however much it may be possible by its subsequent development to use such forms as aesthetic media in some particular literary product. But in the literature of primitive Christianity, which is essentially 'popular' (Dibelius) in kind, this development has not yet taken place, and it is only possible to understand its forms and categories in connection with their 'life situation,' i.e. the influences at work in the life of the community."

43 Bultmann, *Gospel of John*, pp. 28, 106–107.

44 Bultmann, ibid., p. 27.

45 Brown, *Gospel according to John* p. 31.

with empty hands, for he gives light and life and love and resurrection."[46] To Bultmann's claim that the revealer is only a man, Brown counters: "Käsemann, writing against Bultmann, insists on the glorious character of the Word-become-flesh. The flesh is not simply an incognito through which men must see; rather the glory of the Word keeps breaking through the flesh in the miraculous works which can be seen."[47]

35. Brown's response to Bultmann lacks critical historical apparatus. An ambiguity hanging over Brown's commentary is whether the Word *did* become flesh in historical fact, or whether that is merely what is claimed in the theology of this Gospel. Bultmann admits that the writers of the Gospel *believed* that God had become man; the credit that he gives to this Gospel lies in his understanding it as reflecting historicized interpretations of full-blown mythology that are in the direction of "the right way" to understand Jesus. In Brown's argumentation the relationship of the "theology" of this Gospel to actual historical fact never becomes clear. Is Brown affirming as a critical exegete that the eternal Word of God exists in historical fact and that He became flesh in historical fact, in response to Bultmann's charge that this is mere religious fantasy? Brown's method does not seem able to address this question adequately. To say "If the fact that Jesus was sent is all important" remains hypothetical. The fact that Jesus *was sent* from God is all-important, not only for the theology of John, but also for the critical historian today. Is Brown saying unambiguously that the "vertical aspect" of the Gospel according to John *in historical fact* "expresses the uniqueness of the divine intervention in Jesus,"[48] seeing that he also says that "one cannot claim that the dependence of John on a postulated early Oriental Gnosticism has been disproved"?[49] Brown identifies the "founding fathers" of Gnosticism to have been "Simon Magus and Dositheus of Shechem,"[50] thus indicating the Satanic origin of this doctrine, but he cannot show with conviction that this inspired Gospel depends only on historical fact and not at all on the perversion of the historical truth of the Incarnation suggested by devils to the corrupt imaginations of these evil men. Brown agrees with Bultmann and others that "the main emphasis in the Gospel is on realized exchatology,"[51]

---

46 Brown, ibid., p. 32.

47 Brown, ibid., p. 35

48 Brown, ibid., p. cxvi.

49 Brown, ibid., p. lvi.

50 Brown, ibid., p. lxviii.

51 Brown, ibid., p. cxx.

but he does not show that John presents the *historical reality* of God, of heaven, and of life after death, without which this Gospel would become a mere religious fantasy, as Bultmann claims.

36. Verse 50. Jesus approves the fact that Nathanael believes because He had said to Nathanael "I saw you under the fig tree." Nathanael's pride in his learning had been shaken, he had repented of his vanity, and this had disposed him for the grace of having his eyes opened to catch a glimpse of the divine Person within the human figure of Jesus. Nathanael had seen a new and higher reality of God present in the man Jesus. "Greater things than these shall you see." Jesus promises to Nathanael that he will see more than this earthly power of the personality of Jesus; he will have more than a glimpse at the divinity of Jesus, because the clarity of his vision of supernatural things would increase.

37. Verse 51. Jesus turns to the group of the disciples and makes this promise: "You shall see heaven opened and the angels of God ascending and descending upon the Son of Man." This is a precise prediction of what was going to happen in historical fact. Those of the disciples who would remain faithful were going to see, after their death, the gate of heaven opened and the King of Heaven therein. St. Thomas points out that in heaven the angels are seen ascending and descending upon the Son of Man: ascending toward his divinity and descending upon his humanity.[52] This did take place in historical fact. It has been said erroneously by some that "history ends with death." This is a misstatement of the truth. With death certainly ends the series of changes visible on this earth. But life within the one continuum of reality goes on. To say that heaven exists in historical reality means that this enriched phase of life is in the one continuum of being that the historian knows as reality. The heaven promised by Jesus is not a religious fantasy, it is not a dream. Nor is Jesus in heaven a figment of the imagination. In v. 51 Jesus reveals with unshakeable authority that history does not end with death and that death is not itself the end of life.

Part III. The Spiritual Sense of John 1:45–51

38. A triple spiritual sense. The spiritual sense is a pattern of meaning, relating to the Person and the mission of Jesus the Messiah, which has been impressed upon the text of Sacred Scripture by the Holy Spirit, its principal Author. It centers on the allegory of Christ, a sustained analogy

---

52 Aquinas, commentary on Jn. 1:51.

which raises the mind from the merely visible and historical meaning of the words to a supernatural meaning that contains and illustrates some aspect of divine revelation. The simple allegory centers around Jesus as a Divine Person present on earth in the human nature which He has assumed. The higher allegory, called anagogy, centers around Jesus as the Word of God, existing from all eternity and present in Jesus as the King of Heaven, together with the Divine Persons of the Father and the Holy Spirit. The higher allegory includes both this Trinitary meaning and also the eschatological "last things" of death, judgment, Heaven, and Hell. In addition to the lower and the higher allegories of Christ, there is a moral allegory known as tropology, which presents itself as a pattern of application of the truth of Christ to the soul of the individual believer, especially as it moves from the state of sin to the state of virtue or as it advances to higher degrees of virtue. I shall attempt here to apply these distinctions to the narrative of the calling of Nathanael.

39. Regarding verse 45. Philip says to Nathanael: "We have found the one about whom Moses in the law and the prophets wrote, Jesus, the son of Joseph, from Nazareth." On the historical level, the Evangelist is not affirming that Jesus is the son of Joseph; rather, he is quoting Philip, who is reporting the common opinion of the people of Nazareth that Jesus was the son of Joseph (Lk. 3:23), although Jesus was in historical truth only the *adopted* son of Joseph.

40. Prominent among the keys to the allegory of Christ are the etymology of names and the typology, or figuration, by which persons, things, and events on the natural level, especially as recorded in the Old Testament, represent the reality of Christ and his Church. Etymologically, the name Jesus means "Yahweh saves" or "Yahweh has saved," and, therefore, "God saves." Jesus is the Savior. To recognize who Jesus is means to recognize that Jesus is the Second Divine Person, the Son of God, having become a man in order to save mankind from slavery to sin and death. The name Messiah means "anointed," as does its Greek translation *Christos* and the English word "Christ." The Messiah is the one anointed by God as the great prophet, priest, and king of Israel. Moses in the Pentateuch and the prophets of the Old Testament wrote about Jesus, partly in a directly prophetic way, but more often under the imagery of prototype and figure. Jesus is the Supreme Prophet, the King of Heaven, and the great High Priest sent as a Mediator between God and sinful men. His human nature was anointed with the grace of the Holy Spirit, the Third Divine Person, at the moment of his Virginal Conception.

41. The allegorical sense comes into sight with the recognition that Jesus is the Messiah. In v. 45 it is clear that Philip and the others had begun to realize this. But Philip is probably not thinking yet about the allegory of names when he presents Jesus as "the son of Joseph, from Nazareth." We are told that the name Joseph means "may God increase."[53] On the level of anagogy this may apply to any of the Three Divine Persons. Jesus is the "increaser," in the sense that He brought the increase of sanctifying grace to mankind enslaved by sin (Jn. 1:17). The Holy Spirit is the "increaser," in the sense that every increase of goodness and sanctifying grace is produced by the Holy Spirit. But above all, and by appropriation, God the Father is the "increaser," because He is the absolute origin of the increase of all things. On the level of divinity, God the Father is the origin by eternal generation of God the Son, and by eternal spiration, with the Son, of God the Holy Spirit, thus being the absolute "increaser" within the Blessed Trinity. On the level of natural creation, God the Father is the absolute origin and creator through the Son of all created things, angelic and corporal, invisible and visible, living and inanimate. On the level of grace, God the Father is the origin of every increase (1Cor. 3:7), because He sent his only-begotten Son to make the increase possible (Gal. 4:4–5). Cornelius aLapide points out that St. Joseph, in his role as foster father of Jesus, was a figure of God the Father.[54]

42. Regarding verse 46. "Can anything good come from Nazareth?" I have noted above the ironic nature of this question in the historical sense of the text. Cornelius aLapide observes that, since the name does not occur in the Hebrew text of the Old Testament, the Hebrew etymology of the name is uncertain. We cannot tell from the Greek transliteration whether it was written with *zain* (*Naz*), and derived from *nazir* or *nozeri*, meaning "set apart," "consecrated," and, thus, "holy," or rather written with *tsade* (*Nats*) and derived from *netser*, meaning "budding," "flowering," or "a shoot."[55] There is strong indication in Matt. 2:23 of a double etymological meaning of the name in the inspired text.[56] William Albright held that the original Hebrew name was probably *Notseret*, and

---

53 Cf. J.E. Steinmueller and K. Sullivan, *Catholic Biblical Encyclopedia, Old Testament*, "Joseph"; R. Young, *Analytical Concordance to the Bible*, "Joseph."

54 Cornelius aLapide, commentary on Matt. 1:18.

55 Cornelius aLapide, commentary on Matt. 2:23.

56 See Benedict Viviano on Matt. 2:23 in *The New Jerome Biblical Commentary*, p. 636; Henry Wansbrough on Matt. 2:23 in *A New Catholic Commentary on Holy Scripture*, p. 908.

that "since the Aramaic name had not been etymologically transferred into Aramaic as *Natserath* (Heb. nṣr, 'to protect,' appears in Aramaic after the shift of consonants as nṭr), there was nothing to keep the s between the two voiced (sonant) consonants from being changed by partial assimilation to z...."[57] Thus, the original consonant may have been tsade, as aLapide and other writers had suggested. Albright, in his use of modern "linguistic and philological orientation," presents solutions that contrast at least superficially with those of the Catholic exegetical tradition, but he also admits that, "in view of the numerous still unsolved puzzles of vocalization and ending with which the student of the Aramaic toponymy of Palestine is faced," he is only presenting "the most plausible solution."[58] In the case of Nathanael's query, the problem is not the historical origin of the name Nazareth; it is rather what an Aramaic speaking student of the Hebrew Scriptures would likely have assumed the etymology of "Nazareth" to be. And we can guess from the structure of his remark that he was associating it with *nazir* in the sense of "holy." Jesus does come from what is holy. God is all holy, and Jesus is from God. Jesus is God. The Holy Spirit is God, and the holiness of God is by appropriation ascribed to Him. Jesus was virginally conceived in the womb of the holiest of all pure creatures by the overshadowing of the Holy Spirit. The body and soul of Jesus are saturated with the holiness of the Holy Spirit. The perception that Jesus is from what is holy in the most absolute sense of the word is an insight that puts a man on the road to perfection and to union with God. Nathanael was asking in his conceited way for that insight, and Philip gave him the opportunity with the invitation, "Come and see."

43. Regarding verse 47. "Behold a true Israelite." For modern commentators, the etymology of the word Israel is uncertain. With reference to the changing of Jacob's name to Israel in Gen. 32: 28 (cf. Hosea 12:34), the name Israel is usually presented as me aning "may God rule,"[59] "ruling with God,"[60] "to strive with God,"[61] "wrestler with God,"[62] or something of this sort. The etymology "man sees God" (*ish-roe-el*), presented by some of

---

57 W.F. Albright, "The Names 'Nazareth' and 'Nazoraean,'" in the 65 (1946), pp. 399–400.

58 Albright, ibid., pp. 397, 400.

59 R.E. Murphy, in *The New Jerome Biblical Commentary*, on Gen. 32:28.

60 Young, *Analytical Concordance to the Bible*, "Israel."

61 Bruce Vawter, in *A New Catholic Commentary on Holy Scripture*, on Gen. 32:28.

62 Steinmueller-Sullivan, *Catholic Biblical Encyclopedia*, "Israel."

the early commentators (Philo, Nazianzen, Hilary, Eusebius, and Prosper) is now commonly rejected.

44. Cornelius aLapide rejected this interpretation to follow the Septuagint, Theodotion, Symmachus, Jerome, and Aquila in holding that the name means "ruling over God."[63] While all aspects of Jacob's encounter are not clear, it must be kept in mind that the "vision of God" is an important element of the episode: "I have seen God face to face and my life has been saved" (Gen. 32:30).

45. In this episode Jacob is a prototype of Jesus. The name Jacob ("he grabs the heel") suggests a wrestler. Jesus wrestled with Satan and supplanted him (St. Thomas). Historically, Jesus is the man who "saw God and lived" even during His sojourn on earth, and His human consciousness sees God forever in heaven. Anagogically, on the level of divinity, Jesus, the Word of God, "wrestles" eternally with the Father in the infinite dynamism of divine love, and they "overcome" each other in the spiration of the Holy Spirit. Thus, Jesus can say, "I am strong against God; how much more shall I prevail against men" (cf. Gen. 32:28), even though He is totally subject to the Father.

46. Tropologically, the follower of Jesus "wrestles with God" in the dynamism of grace given by the Holy Spirit. He sees God obscurely by the infused virtue of faith, especially by analogy with natural concepts and the images supplied by Sacred Scripture. He will be blessed with the clear vision of God in the life after death. Thus, Jacob is a figure of the true believer and of the Church. God is "overcome" by love for the living members of the Mystical Body of Jesus, and gives them the blessing of heaven, which they win by their prayers and sacrifices and by overcoming the world, the flesh, and the Devil.[64]

47. In vv. 46f. Nathanael is "wrestling" verbally with Jesus. In this he is a true follower of Jacob. Jesus confronts him with the guileful character of Jacob and challenges him to change his manner and become a "true Israelite" in the spiritual sense, that is a true follower of Himself. Implied here is the beginning of a deep conversion from a Jewish mentality, which sees no distinction between the secular and the sacred, to a Christian outlook in which both the Savior and his followers are "set apart" from the spirit of this world.

48. Regarding verse 48. "Nathanael said to him: 'From where do you know me?'" The question of origins underlies this whole exchange, and so

---

63 Cornelius aLapide, commentary on Gen. 32:28.

64 Cornelius aLapide, ibid.

the interrogative adverb "from where?" (*póthen*) is very important. Jesus replies: "Before Philip called you I saw you under the fig tree." Literally, "I saw you being under the fig tree." I have treated above under the historical sense the probable allusion to Adam and Eve in the Garden of Eden. On the level of tropology the allusion may go deeper, especially in relation to the allegory of names and to the question of who Nathanael really was.

49. It has long been disputed whether Nathanael is to be identified with Bartholomew the Apostle. In a thoroughgoing study of the issue, Urban Holzmeister reviewed the reasons for and against such an identity and concluded that the most probable opinion is in favor.[65] St. Augustine, followed by St. Gregory the Great, St. Thomas, and others held that Nathanael was not Bartholomew, largely for the reason put forward by St. Augustine, that Nathanael was learned in the Scriptures, while Jesus chose only unlettered men to be his apostles. Holzmeister finds this reason to be very unconvincing. In favor of the identity is the fact that Bartholomew is a patronymic meaning "son of Tolmai," and, therefore, could easily be the surname of Nathanael. The argument from the patronymic was first advanced only in the ninth century, but it fortifies other reasons often advanced in favor of the identity, as I shall try to explain on the level of tropological allegory.

50. The remark of Jesus to Nathanael, "Behold a true Israelite," is, as I have explained, a play on words. Now the name Nathanael, as Holzmeister points out, means "God has given" and is actually of Babylonian origin. Hence, in terms of the historical origin of the name, it does not represent a true Israelite at all. Nathanael himself was from Cana in Galilee, and Cana means *reed*, which is a tall grass growing usually in swampy waters. Thus, Cana symbolically indicates lowliness of birth, and the designation "from Cana" indicates allegorically a tall non-Israelite from low and swampy ground.

51. Similarly, the name Tolmai (or Tholmai) according to some means "covered with furrows," and Tolmai again is not an originally Hebrew name. In fact, the name is first encountered in the Old Testament in Num. 13:23, which speaks of Tolmai as one of a race of giants living in Canaan at the time of Moses. And the name Canaan means "low (ground)." Now, since furrows are conduits of water on the ground, the "son of Tolmai" is represented etymologically as a tall non-Israelite stemming from low and watery ground.

---

65 U. Holzmeister, "Nathanael fuitne idem ac S. Bartholomaeus Apostolus?" in *Biblica* 21 (1940), pp. 28–39.

52. Since I am not expert in philology, I leave it to those who are to examine these derivations and correct them where necessary. I think that a moral message was definitely given by Jesus and accepted by Nathanael. Tall in his estimate of himself and of his learning, proud of his Hebrew descent, Nathanael is confronted with the actual lowliness of his origin. "I saw you being under the fig tree" means, I think, that Jesus, a Divine Person with eternal knowledge, saw Nathanael when he was still in potency in the ground from which the human race has sprung. It is an invitation to Nathanael to make an act of humility in the recognition of the reality concerning himself. And this involves a change of focus, because Jesus is the true "Nathanael," the true "gift of God," and it is Jesus who gives the gift of grace to men, also to little Nathanael, if he asks for it with humility.

53. Regarding verse 49. Nathanael is struck by the response of Jesus, and he exclaims: "Rabbi, you are the Son of God, you are the King of Israel." We do not know how deeply he understood the words of Jesus, but this was certainly for him a moment of grace and of conversion, and he was definitely being helped to understand. In this experience Nathanael began to move away from pride in himself and pride in his race, and to recognize who Jesus is. The title Son of God expresses the divine origin of Jesus, while King of Israel means King of the true Israelites, of those who share in the dynamism of divine grace. Neither title is here understood as basically political in nature. Nathanael's motive is his realization of the highness of the origin of Jesus, and this recognition suggests many Scriptural allusions which we cannot take up here.

54. Regarding verses 50–51. "Greater things than these shall you see." Nathanael has seen the power of the intelligence of Jesus in its impact on himself, and he has begun to believe in Jesus as the Son of God and as the Messiah. Higher degrees of insight will be given to him. He will, in fact, as did Jacob allegorically in Gen. 32:30, "see God face to face" in the beatific vision. Just as the "man" in Gen. 32:29 blessed Jacob at the end of the struggle, so Jesus blesses Nathanael at the end of this verbal contest.

55. "You will see heaven opened, and the angels of God ascending and descending upon the Son of Man." The Son of Man is Jesus in His human nature. Jesus has turned to the group of the disciples as He makes this promise; the "you" is in the plural. To see heaven opened is to enter into heaven, where the good angels serve Jesus both as God and as man. This promise of Jesus is one of the literal and historical bases of the anagogical sense of Sacred Scripture. There is in this promise of Jesus an

obvious allegorical allusion to the dream of Jacob. The ladder extending from heaven to earth and from earth to heaven is Jesus in his humanity. The angels are seen ascending and descending upon this ladder. God is seen leaning upon this ladder and saying to Jacob: "…your seed will be like the dust of the earth, … and in you and your seed will all the tribes of the earth be blessed" (Gen. 28:14). The seed to which this prophecy refers is Jesus (cf. Gal. 3:16) and then those of every tribe of the earth who are sanctified in Jesus. Nathanael inherits this promise, not by being a physical descendent of Jacob, but by abandoning his pride of race and adhering to the other-worldly spirit of Jesus. In his pride, Nathanael is little more than "dust of the earth." But through humility the furrows of Nathanael's human soul become irrigated by water turned into the wine of divine grace, the "gift of God" given by Jesus, and the gates of heaven are opened for him.

Appendix

How Long Were the Six Days of Creation in Genesis 1?

1. In an official magisterial response to the question of this appendix, the original Pontifical Biblical Commission on June 30, 1909, replied as follows: "*Whether the word* Yom *(day), which is used in the first chapter of Genesis to describe and distinguish the six days, may be taken either in its strict sense as the natural day, or in a less strict sense as signifying a certain space of time; and whether free discussion of this question is permitted to interpreters. Answer: In the affirmative.*"[1]

Objection 1

2. According to the story of creation in Genesis 1, the world was created in six natural days of 24 hours each, but we know from natural science that the world is billions of years old. Therefore, the creation story in Genesis 1 is a myth, while to say that the six days of creation in Genesis 1 are not 24–hour days but rather are indefinite periods of time would not solve this problem, because that would not be a literal interpretation of the text.

Reply to Objection 1

3. Now, it seems rather that the indefinite periods of time reading of the days of creation in Genesis 1 is closer to a literal interpretation of the text than is the 24–hour-day reading. First of all, the text of Genesis 1 itself says that the natural day of 24 hours was established by God only on the fourth day of creation: "And God said: 'Let there be lights made in the firmament of heaven to divide the day and night, and let them be for

---

1 Rome and the *Study of Scripture,* 7th ed., Abbey Press, St. Meinrad, Indiana, 1964), p. 124.

signs and for seasons and for days and years – to shine in the firmament of heaven and to give light upon the earth'" (Gen. 1:14–15). Therefore, there were no natural days equaling natural days in our time during the first three days of creation. In fact, according to the text of Genesis, the very notion of the 24–hour-day did not exist during the first three days of creation except in the mind of God. The word "day" usually means a 24–hour period, but it has other meanings as well, for instance, in the expression, "He worked all day," where it means only the bright part of the day. Other intended meanings of the word "day" usually need to be ascertained by the context in which they appear. And the Genesis account seems to give a definition of these six days of creation where it repeats each time that it was "evening and morning," thus indicating that a "day" is darkness succeeded by light. And this inspired definition of a day of creation as the transition from a state of darkness to a state of light leaves undetermined the length of time involved.

4. On the first day of creation, the physical matter already created by God to become the universe was at first totally and absolutely dark, until God said: 'Let there be light" (Gen. 1:3). The original dark and almost formless matter which constituted "the abyss" was utter chaos and probably occupied very little space, which would increase as God later added new forms to the primal matter, just as on this first day He added the form of waves and particles of light.

5. On the second day of creation, God said: "Let there be a firmament made amidst the waters, and let it divide the waters from the waters" (Gen. 1:6 in the Vulgate and the Douay-Rheims Version). In contrast, the New American Bible says: "Let there be a dome in the middle of the waters," but the Hebrew word rāqîa seems not to mean "a dome," but rather to mean "something that hardened as it spread out," and so the Revised Standard Version of the King James Bible reasonably retains the translation: "Let there be a firmament in the midst of the waters," And another translation reads: "Let there be an expanse." The text of Genesis may here be literally saying that the tiny and chaotic mass of almost formless elemental matter and energy created "in the beginning" becomes now empowered to expand into a universe. This primal matter on the second day is called "waters," where the word "fluids" would seem to be more precise, comprising, as it seems, the firming-up of the expanding universe on the second day with the creation of the laws of physics and chemistry and the addition of such fluids as the elemental physical forces and elemental particles, and then the development of flaming balls of swirling gases (the stars, some of which

cooled to become planets), and H2O as well. Why the vagueness of the word "waters" in the inspired text of Genesis? It was not the purpose of the all-knowing God to teach people these natural facts that would not be known to human thinkers for thousands of years to come.

6. Supposing, then, that the heliocentric theory is correct, and in the scenario of the Big Bang, the "waters above the firmament" are the firmed-up contents of structured outer space, and the "waters below the firmament" are the swirling gases that became the globe of the Earth, with the focus of the Genesis account from here onward placed upon the Earth. The text of Genesis seems to be saying that God protected objects in inner space from being damaged by objects and forces from outer space. One thing that suggests itself in this scenario, of course, is the ozone screen, but more importantly is the creation of the laws of physics by which the Moon does not fall upon the Earth and the Earth does not fall into the Sun. As the tiny mass of shining matter of the first day expanded into the exterior darkness surrounding it to become the universe, the evening darkness of the second day passed into the growing lighted sky of the morning of the second day.

7. On the third day of creation, God said: "Let the earth bring forth the green herb," etc. (Gen. 1:11–13). Briefly, with the creation of the green herb and of vegetative life in general, creatures appeared that were photosensitive to light and using photosynthesis, thus representing a new movement of darkness to light. The evening of the third day of creation was the absence throughout physical creation of this living sensitivity to light, and the morning of the third day was the growing use of this living function.

8. On the fourth day of creation, God said: *Let there be lights in the firmament of heaven to divide the day and the night, and let them be for signs and for seasons and for days and years, to shine in the firmament of heaven and to give light upon the earth. And it was so done* (Gen. 1:14–15). This verse does not mean that God created the Sun, the Moon, and the stars on the fourth day of creation, but rather that God made them to be lights in the sky by positioning them to indicate signs and seasons and days and years. Here is presented a visual scene appearing in the sky from the surface of the Earth. The evening of the fourth day is the absence of these lights in the sky, and the morning is their appearance. Some have speculated also that up to a certain point the atmosphere of the Earth was too dark to display the sky. How God so positioned these lights in the sky is easy to explain, if the heliocentric theory is valid. To determine the length of a year, God needed only to fix permanently the speed of the rotation of the Earth

around the Sun; to determine the length of the seasons, God needed only to adjust permanently the speed of the angular movements of the Earth; and to determine the length of the natural day, God needed only to fix permanently the speed of the rotation of the Earth upon its axis.

9. On the fifth day of creation, God also said: "*Let the waters bring forth the creeping creature having life, and the fowl that may fly over the earth under the firmament of heaven*" (Gen 1:20). On the fifth day were created many living biological beings having physical sight, and, therefore, having the ability to see things physically. The evening of the fifth day was the time before there were biological creatures having the light of physical sight, and the morning was the coming of some biological creatures with physical sight.

10. On the sixth day of creation, God said: "Let the earth bring forth the living creature in its kind: cattle and creeping things, and beasts of the earth. And it was done. ...And he said: Let us make man to our image and likeness" (Gen. 1:24–26). It is especially important for our discussion here that on the sixth day of creation God created men and women to his image and likeness. The evening of the sixth day was the time before there were any biological creatures having the light of intelligence, and the morning was the living presence of that light.

Objection 2

11. *The idea of the six darkness-to-light days of creation is a unique interpretation of Genesis 1 by John F. McCarthy that has never been advanced before and which arouses the concern that it may never be accepted by anyone skilled in biblical interpretation.*

Reply to Objection 2

12. My explanation of six darkness-to-light days of creation is a new twist, but is not a new idea. Saint Augustine of Hippo proposed and expounded this idea in the early fifth century A.D., understanding the six days of creation as six enlightenments instilled by God into the minds of the good angels, as he explains at length in his *Letter of Genesis* and in other places. Augustine holds that God made "the heavens and the earth" (Gen. 1:1), that is, the whole world, out of nothing in the first instant of time, and he says that "the heavens" means the angelic spirits, and "the earth" means all of the primal matter in the universe, seen conceptually as totally formless in the beginning but ready to receive from God the forms

to become the universe.[2] Augustine does not maintain that the various things described as made by God during the six days of creation appeared full-blown in the first instant of time. Rather, he says, when God made all things together, He made them hidden in the secret recesses of nature, that is, potentially and causally, so as to become visible over the due course of time.[3] Thus was the earth given a certain power to produce, that is, an invisible inner potency to be unfolded over the ages, not without creative divine interventions and not without the guidance of God's providence.[4] He also says that the six days of creation are not necessarily in chronological order but are primarily in causal order as the effects of creation became known in the minds of the blessed angels at six revealed levels of understanding of the created world.

13. "*God is light*" (1 John 1:5). Augustine reasoned that the command of God "*Be light made*" (Gen. 1:3) means here especially the passage into the sanctified minds and hearts of the good angels of the Beatific Vision of God and of eternal wisdom, so that the evening of the first day of creation and of the other evenings was the absence of this higher supernatural light, and the mornings were the presence of this light.[5] But, says Augustine, in another sense evening could also mean the absence in a created material thing of a higher natural form, and morning could mean the presence of the higher natural form impressed upon it.[6] Thus, evening of the first day is the contemplation by the angels of their own created nature, while morning is their turning from self-contemplation to the praise and love of God. Evening of the second day is their knowledge of the firmament in itself, while morning is their referring this knowledge to the praise and love of God. Evening of the third day is their knowledge of the earth and the sea and all the things that grow out of the earth, while morning is their referring this knowledge to the praise and love of God. And so forth for the other three days.[7]

14. St. Thomas Aquinas examined the more common interpretation by St. Ambrose and other Fathers of the Church regarding the six days of creation as being composed of natural-day periods and compared it

---

2 Augustine, *Letter of Genesis*, I, 8.

3 Augustine, *Letter of Genesis*,, VI, 1–4.

4 Augustine, *Letter of Genesis*,, IV, 12; VII, 22; VIII, 3; VIII, 8.

5 Augustine, *Letter of Genesis*,, IV, 21; *City of God*, XI, 9.

6 Augustine, *Letter of Genesis*,, IV, 1.

7 Augustine, *City of God*, XI, 7.

with the interpretation of St. Augustine as being six levels of intellectual darkness followed by six levels of intellectual light, and he concluded that the more common opinion was "more in keeping with the surface of the literal sense," but that the opinion of St. Augustine was "more reasonable and defends Sacred Scripture more from the derision of non-believers," a fact that made it more pleasing to St. Thomas and led him to say in agreement with a point made by St. Augustine regarding the nature of the firmament that, where the text of Scripture admits of more than one explanation, "no one should adhere to some explanation so rigidly that if by conclusive reasoning it should have been shown to be false, he would rashly continue affirming it as the meaning of the text, lest the Scriptures on this account be laughed at by nonbelievers and thus the way to believing be closed to them." [8]

15. The reason for which St. Augustine felt constrained to develop his theory of darkness-to-light days is that he could not fathom how plants could have been created before the creation of the Sun, the Moon, and the stars. Following the lead of Thomas Aquinas, my reading of the fourth day as embracing, not the creation of these heavenly bodies, but their being placed, that is, positioned, visually in the sky to determine signs and seasons and (natural) days and years, would seem to remove St. Augustine's need for this recourse. It is, therefore, my recommendation that the darkness-to-light characterization of the days of creation given in Question 1 of this series be taken as the literal sense of the six days of creation, and that the six levels of enlightenment of St. Augustine be regarded as a tropological, or moral, reading of the text, where by "tropological" is meant the impression of the objective truth of the literal meaning of a passage into the mind and heart, faith and devotion, of believers, since it is clear that the meaning of the text of Genesis 1 presented by St. Augustine involves precisely the elevation of the understanding and love of the good angels to perfect knowledge and love for God. There is also in the creation account a tropological meaning reaching out to mankind, and that is the seven-day week, the idea of which is implicitly mandated for the observance of human believers and servants of God, and this is a reason for which the creation is presented by God on the surface of the letter of Genesis 1 as divided into seven seemingly natural days.

16. The creation account in Genesis 1 embodies the worldview not only of Catholic faith but of the entire Judeo-Christian culture. To call

---

8 Aquinas, II *Sent.*, dist. 12, q. 1, art. 2, corp.; *Summa Theologiae*, I, q. 68, art. 1, corp.; cf. Augustine, *Letter of Genesis*, I, 18–21.

this narrative a myth means to undermine this culture. The real concern is that the creation account in Genesis 1 is being presented today as a "creation myth" throughout the public school systems in the United States and elsewhere and in some Catholic schools as well, and even in some Catholic catechisms. Partly as a result of this, a huge percentage of Catholic and other Christian children are ceasing to believe and to practice their faith even before they graduate from high school, and heavily again among college students. It is clear, therefore, that effective defense of the historical truth of the creation account in Genesis 1 is badly needed, and an instrument of this is the alternative explanation provided here.

Bibliography

aLapide, Cornelius, *Commentarii in Scripturam sacram*, vol. 8, *Expositio in quatuor Evangelia* (Lyons, 1864); Eng. trans., *The Great Commentary of Cornelius aLapide* (John Hodges: London, 1887).

Albright, William F., *From the Stone Age to Christianity* (2nd ed., Baltimore: Johns Hopkins Press, 1957).

Yahweh and the Gods of Canaan (Athlone: London, 1968).

Ambrose, Saint, *Commentary on Luke.*

Aquinas, Thomas, *Summa Theologiae.*

Catena Aurea, English translation, (Preserving Christian Publications, Albany, N.Y. 1993).

Quaestiones Quodlibetales, Quodlibet Seven, quest. 6.

Commentary on the Epistle of St. Paul to the Galatians

Super Epistolas S. Pauli Lectura (Turin-Rome: Marietti, 1953);; Eng. trans. by F. R. Larcher, *Commentary on St. Paul's Epistle to the Galatians* (Magi Books: 33 Buckingham Dr., Albany, N.Y., 1966).

Super Evangelium S. Ioannis Lectura (Turin-Rome; Marietti, 1952), p. 49; Eng. trans. by J. A. Weisheipl and F. R. Larcher, *Commentary on the Gospel of St. John* (Magi Books: 33 Buckingham Dr., Albany, N.Y., 1980).

Super Evangelium S. Matthaei Lectura; English translation by Paul M. Kimball: *Commentary on the Gospel of St. Matthew* (Dolorosa Press – order from Amazon Books).

II *Sent.*, dist. 12, q. 1, art. 2, corp.

Posterior Analytics, bk. I, Lect. XVIII, number 9.

De Anima.

Truth (Chicago, 1953).

Augustine, Aurelius, *The Literal Meaning of Genesis* (trans. by J.H. Taylor, New York: Newman Press, 1982), (= *Ancient Christian Writers*, vol. 41).

The City of God, XI, 7.

Contra Faustum, Patrologia Latina 42, cols. 471–472.

De quaestionibus novi et veteris testamenti, question 85.

De consensu evangelistarum libri 4, in PL, vol. 34, col. 1076.

Confessions, bk. 12, ch. 31, no. 42 (ML 32, 844).

Aveling, F., "Rationalism," in *The Catholic Encyclopedia*, vol.12, 652.

Barnes, Henry Elmer., *New History and the Social Studies*.

"History, Its Rise and Development," in the *Encyclopedia Americana*, vol. 14.

Bartsch, H. W., ed., *Kerygma and Myth: A Theological Debate*, vol. I (London: SPCK, 1953).

Beck, W. David, "Agnosticism: Kant," in Norman L. Geisler, ed., *Biblical Errancy* (Grand Rapids, MI: Zondervan, 1981).

Benedict XV, Pope, Encyclical Letter *Spiritus Paraclitus* (September 15, 1920).

Bittle, Celestine N., O.F.M. Cap., *The Science of Correct Thinking* (Bruce Publishing Company, Fourteenth Printing, Milwaukee, 1948.

Reality and the Mind (New York: Bruce, 1936).

Blanshard, B., "Rationalism," in the *Encyclopedia Americana* (1967 international edition), vol. 23.

Bouyer, L., *Dictionary of Theology*, (Eng. ed., Desclée: New York, 1965).

Bradley, F. H., *Appearance and Reality* (Oxford, 1897).

Brown, Raymond, *The Virginal Conception and Bodily Resurrection of Jesus* (London: Geoffrey Chapman, 1973).

The Birth of the Messiah [Garden City: Doubleday, 1977], p. 529).

The Gospel according to John (New York: Doubleday, 1970 [= *The Anchor Bible*, vols. 29 and 29A])

("Gospel Infancy Narrative Research from 1976 to 1986: Part I" in the *Catholic Biblical Quarterly*, July, 1986,

Bruns, J. Edgar, "Genealogy of Jesus," in the *New Catholic Encyclopedia*, vol. 6, pp. 319–321).

Bultmann, Rudolf, *Die Geschichte der synoptischen Tradition* (1st ed., 1921; 8th rev. ed.: Gottingen, 1970); Eng. trans. by John Marsh, *The History of the Synoptic Tradition* (Oxford: Basil Blackwell, 1963).

Neues Testament und Mythologie," first published in German in 1941, and republished in English as "New Testament and Mythology" in H.W. Bartsch, ed., *Kerygma and Myth: A Theological Debate* (vol. 1, SPCK: London, 1953).

"Zum Problem der Entmythologisierung," in H. W. Bartsch et al., *Kerygma und Mythos* (Hamburg: Evangelischer Verlag), vol. VI-1. English Translation:
History and Eschatology (New York: Harper and Row, 1957).
The Gospel of John (Oxford: Basil Blackwell, 1971), translated from the 1964 printing of *Das Evangelium des Johannes* with the Supplement of 1966.
Essays Philosophical and Theological (trans. by J. C. Greig: London, 1955), p. 287.
R. Bultmann, Offenbarung und Heilsgeschehen (Munich, 1941).

Cahill, Joseph, "(Notes concerning John Macquarrie's) *The Scope of Demythologizing,"* in *Theological Studies*, 23 (1962), 79–92 [herein referred to as *JCSD*]).
Carlen, Claudia, ed., *The Papal Encyclicals 1740–1981* (in five volumes: McGrath Publishing Company, 1981).
Chrysostom, John, *Commentary on Matthew*, homily 1.
Clifford, Richard, "Genesis," in *The New Jerome Biblical Commentary*. Collins, Raymond, "Inspiration," in *The New Jerome Biblical Commentary*, R.E. Brown et al., editors (Englewood Cliffs: Prentice Hall, 1990),
Copleston, Frederick, *History of Philosophy,* vol. 6, *Modern Philosophy*, Part II, *Kant* (Image Books: Garden City, NY, 1964); vol. 4 (1963), p. 49.
Cornelius aLapide (Cornelius van den Steen: 1567–1637 A.D.), *Great Commentary*.
"Criticism," in L. Bouyer, *Dictionary of Theology*, (Eng. ed., Desclée: New York, 1965).
"Criticism," in *Webster's Third New International Dictionary* (1996).

Daniélou, Jean, *The Infancy Narratives*, translated by Rosemary Sheed (New York: Herder and Herder, 1968) – (original edition: *Les Evangiles de l'Enfance* (Paris: Editions de Seuil, 1967)
Eng. translation, *The Angels and Their Mission* (Westminster, MD: Newman, 1957).
Essai sur le Mystère de l'"Histoire (Editions du Seuil – Eng. trans., *The Lord of History. Reflections on the Inner Meanintg of History* (New York: Longmans Green, 1958).
Danto, Arthur, "Common Sense," in *Encyclopedia Americana* (1967), Vol. VII, p. 415

de Lubac, Henri, *Exégèse médiévale. Les quatre sens de l'Ecriture* (Paris: Aubier, 1959).

Descartes, René, *Principles of Philosophy* (1644).

Dibelius, Martin, *Die Formgeschichte des Evangeliums* (first published in 1919, second revised edition, 1933); English translation by Bertram Lee Woolf of the revised edition: *From Tradition to Gospel* (Cambridge, England, The Library of Theological Translations, 1971—hereafter to be referred to as *FTG*).

Didon, H., *Jésus Christ* (Paris, 1891).

Dyson, R.A. and R.F. MacKenzie, "Higher Criticism," in *A Catholic Commentary on Holy Scripture* (Thomas Nelson and Sons: London, 1953)

Encyclopedia Americana
Encyclopaedia Britannica
Enciclopedia Cattolica
Enciclopedia Italiana
Epiphanius, *Adversus Haereses*, bk. 2, Tome 1, Heresy 51, No. 11; in PG, vol. 41, col. 908.
On the Sect of the Epicureans

Fitzmyer, J.A., *The Biblical Commission's Document "The Interpretation of the Bible in the Church,"* (Pontifical Biblical Institute: Rome, 1995).

Fries, Heinrich *Bultmann-Barth und die katholische Theologie* (Stuttgart, 1955 [herein referred to as *BBKT*]); Engl. trans., *Bultmann-Barth and Catholic Theology* (Pittsburgh: Duquesne Univ. Press, 1967 [herein referred to as *BBCT*]).

Gigot, Francis E., "Calendar, Jewish," in the *Catholic Encyclopedia* (1908 edition).

Goering, John M., "Durkheim, Émil," in the *Encyclopedia Americana*, vol. 9 (Danbury: Americana Corp., 1980).

Gregory XVI, Pope, *Mirari vos*, in Claudia Carlen ed., The Papal Encyclicals (McGrath Publishing Co.), vol. 1.

Gunkel, Hermann, *Genesis* (Göttingen, 1901); Eng. trans. of the 3d revised edition (1910), *Genesis* (Mercer: Macon, Georgia, 1997). Gutwenger, E., "The Gospels and Non-Catholic Higher Criticism," in *A Catholic Commentary on Holy Scripture* (1953)

Hardon, John A., "Philosophy," in his *Modern Catholic Dictionary* (second printing, Bardstown, KY: Eternal Life, 2001).

Hilary of Poitiers, in Angelo Mai, ed., *Novae Patrum Bibliothecae* (Rome: Propaganda Fide, 1852), pp. 477–478.

Holy Bible: Nova Vulgata.

Douay-Rheims Version.

Revised Standard Version – Catholic Edition.

Holzmeister, Urban, "Genealogia S. Lucae," in *Verbum Domini* (1943).

Hutchins, R.M., et al., *Great Books of the Western World*, vol. 31, (Descartes).

Ignatius Martyr, *Letter to the Ephesians*, ch. 18, in PG 5, col. 660. Trans.: James A. Kleist, ed., *Ancient Christian Writers*, vol. 1, p. 67.

International Theological Commission, Eng. trans., "On the Interpretation of Dogmas," in *Origins* 20 (1990–1991),

Irenaeus, *Adversus Haereses*, in PG, vol. 7, cols. 951–958.

Jerome, Saint, *Commentary on Matthew* (in Latin).

John Damascene, *De Fide Orthodoxa*, in PG, vol. 15, cols. 1155–1157.

John Paul II, Pope, Address of 23 April 1993 to the members of the Pontifical Biblical Commission, no. 10.

Apostolic Constitution *Fidei depositum*, 11 October 1992.

Johnson, M. D., *The Purpose of the Biblical Genealogies with Special Reference to the Setting of the Genealogies of Jesus*, in New Testament Studies Monograph Series, No. 8 (Cambridge University, 1969), p. 166.

Josephus, *Jewish Antiquities*, in *Josephus* (Harvard Univ. Press: Cambridge, Mass., 1930).

Julius Africanus, Letter to Aristides, in Migne, *Patrologia Graeca*, vol. 10, col. 64.

Justin Martyr, *Dialogue with Trypho the Jew*, in PG, vol. 6, col. 709.

KaM and *KuM*: H.W. Bartsch, ed., *Kerygma und Mythos* (Hamburg, 1948 [henceforth referred to as *KuM*]); Engl. trans., H.W. Bartsch, ed., *Kerygma and Myth: A Theological Debate*, vol. I (London: SPCK, 1962 [henceforth referred to as *KaM*]).

Kant, Immanuel, *Critique of Practical Reason* (Indianapolis: Bobbs-Merrill, 1949).

Religion Within the Limits of Reason Alone.

Kselman, John, "Modern New Testament Criticism," in *The Jerome Biblical Commentary*

Kuffel Thomas, "St. Thomas's Method of Biblical Exegesis," in *Living Tradition*, No. 38 (November 1991).

Kwasniewski, Peter A. "A Brief Introduction to the Literal and Allegorical Senses of Scripture," in *The Latin Mass (Magazine)*, vol. 25, no. 2 – Summer 2016.

Lagrange, Marie-Joseph, *La méthode historique surtout à propos de l'Ancien Testament* (Paris, 1903)

Larcher, F.R., English translation of Thomas Aquinas'*Commentary on the Gospel of St. John* (Magi Books: 33 Buckingham Dr., Albany, N.Y., 1980).

English translation of Thomas Aquinas'*Commentary on St. Paul's Epistle to the Galatians* ((Magi Books: 33 Buckingham Dr., Albany, N.Y., 1966)

Lattanzi, Ugo, "*I Sinnottici e la Chiesa secondo R. Bultmann*," in *Miscellanea Antonio Piolanti*, vol. I (Rome, 1963) [= *Lateranum*, new series, 29th year], 141–169.

Laurentin, René, *The Truth of Christmas beyond the Myths* (St. Bede's Publications: Petersham, Massachusetts, 1986),

Leo XIII, Pope, *Providentissimus Deus*, no. 17. Quotations in English translation from the papal encyclicals are taken from Claudia Carlen, *The Papal Encyclicals*, unless otherwise specified.

Leon, W., and B. Orchard, "The Place of the Bible in the Church," in *A Catholic Commentary on Holy Scripture*, no. 3j.

Léon-Dufour, Xavier, *The Gospels and the Jesus of History* (translated and edited in abridged form by John McHugh, London: Collins 1968 [henceforth referred to as Léon-Dufour (McHugh)]).

Levie, Jean, *La Bible, parole humaine et message de Dieu* (Paris-Louvaine, 1958); English translation: *The Bible, Word of God in Words of Men* (London: Geoffrey Chapman, 1961) here *BWG*.

Living Tradition: on line at *rtforum.org*.

Lonergan, Bernard, *Method in Theology* (London: Darton, Longman & Todd, 1972).

Lyonnet, S., "Critica biblica," in the *Enciclopedia cattolica*, vol. 4 (Sansoni: Florence, 1950), 928–929.

Maas, A. J., "Genealogy of Christ," in the *Catholic Encyclopedia* (1913 ed.), vol. 6, p. 411.

L. Malevez, *Le message chrétien et le mythe. La théologie de Rudolf Bultmann*

(Brussels-Bruges-Paris, 1954 [here referred to as *MCM*]); Engl. trans., *The Christian Message and Myth: The Theology of Rudolf Bultmann* (London: SCM Press, 1958 [here referred to as *CMM*]).

R. Marlé, *Bultmann et l'interprétation du Nouveau Testament* (Paris, 1956 herein referred to as *MBI*]).

Masson, Jacques, *Jésus, Fils de David dans les Généalogies de Saint Matieu et di Saint Luc* (Paris: Téqui, 1982).

Meyer, Stephen C., *Signature in the Cell: DNA and the Evidence for Intelligent Design* (HarperCollins, 10 East 53rd St., New York, NY 10022).

Montagnes, Bernard OP, *The Story of Father Marie-Joseph Lagrange: Founder of Modern Catholic Biblical Study*, English translation by Benedict Viviano, OP, (Paulist Press, New York, 2006).

Moore, Thomas V., *The Driving Forces of Human Nature* (London: Heinemann, 1948).

Cognitive Psychology (Chicago, Lippincott, 1939).

Murphy, R.E., in *The New Jerome Biblical Commentary*, on Gen 32:28.

New Catholic Commentary on Holy Scripture (Nashville: Thomas Nelson, 1969).

New Jerome Biblical Commentary, R.E. Brown et al., editors (Englewood Cliffs: Prentice Hall, 1990).

Nicholson, "Foreword to the English Translation" of H. Gunkel, *Genesis*, p. [3].

Nisbet, R.A., "Durkheim, Émil," in the *New Catholic Encyclopedia*, vol. 4 (New York: McGraw-Hill, 1967).

Origen, *Contra Celsum*, in PG, vol. ll, col. 852.

Ott, Heinrich, *Geschichte und Heilsgeschichte in der Theologie Rudolf Bultmanns* (Tübingen, 1955).

Paul VI, Pope, (*Insegnamenti di Paolo VI* [1972], p. 1325) *Insegnamenti di Paolo VI* [1974], pp. 24–25)

Patrizzi, Francis Xavier, *De Evangeliis* (Freiburg in Breisgau, 1853).

Phillips, R.P. *Modern Thomistic Philosophy* (Westminster, Maryland: Newman Press, 1950), vol. I.

Pius X, Pope, *Pascendi dominici gregis*, no. 30.

Pius XII, Pope, *Humani Generis* (1950, in Claudia Carlen ed., *The Papal Encyclicals, 1939–1958* (McGrath Publishing Co).

Pixner, B., Eng. trans., *With Jesus through Galilee according to the Fifth*

Gospel [the biblical landscape] (Corazin: Rosh Pina, Israel, 1992), p. 15.

Pontifical Biblical Commission (reconstituted), *The Interpretation of the Bible in the Church* (Libreria Editrice Vaticana, Rome 1993)

Pontifical Biblical Commission (original), English translation: Instruction, *The Historicity of the Gospels* (Boston, MA: St. Paul Editions, 1964).

Ratzinger, Joseph (Pope Benedict XVI), *Jesus of Nazareth*, (Ignatius Press, 2011)

  Ratzinger, Joseph (Cardinal), "Biblical Interpretation in Crisis," in Richard J. Neuhaus, ed. same title (Grand Rapids: Eerdmans, 1989). *"L'interpretazione della Bibbia in conflitto,"* in Ignace de la Potterie, ed., *L'esegesi cristiana oggi* (Casale Monferrato, Italy: PIEMME, 1991), pp. 93–125; "Schriftauslegung im Widerstreit," in J. Ratzinger, ed., *Quaest. Disp.*, 117 (Freiburg: Herder, 1989).

Reid, Thomas (1710–1796), *Works* (1863 edition), p. 101 (quoted in William Turner, *History of Philosophy* [Boston: Ginn and Co., 1929), p. 593).

Reimarus, H.S., *Apologia for the Rational Worshippers of God*.

Ricciotti, Giuseppe, Eng. trans., *The Life of Christ* (unabridged edition, Bruce: Milwaukee, 1947).

Rizzi, Anthony, *The Science Before Science* (Baton Rouge, LA: IAP Press, 2004).

Roberts, Alexander, and James Donaldson, eds., *The Ante-Nicene Fathers* (Grand Rapids: Eerdmans, 1979), p. 249.

Rome and the Study of Scripture, seventh ed., (Abbey Press, St. Meinrad, Indiana, 1964).

Schmidt, Karl L., *Der Rahmen der Geschichte Jesu*, published in 1919.

Simon, Richard, *Critical History of the Old Testament*.

Suelzer, Alexa, "Modern Old Testament Criticism," in the *Jerome Biblical Commentary* (1968)

Slade, C.F., "History: Methodology," in the Encyclopaedia Britannica, vol. 11.

Smith, Vincent Edward: *The General Science of Nature* (Bruce Publishing Company, Milwaukee, WI, 1958).

Stanley, David, "The Conception of Our Gospels as Salvation History," in *Theological Studies*, vol. 20 (1959).

Steinmueller, John M., *A Companion to Scripture Studies*, revised (Lumen

Christi Press, 1969), vol. III, Special Introduction to the New Testament, pp. 137–147.

Steinmueller, J.E. and K. Sullivan, *Catholic Biblical Encyclopedia, Old Testament*, "Joseph" and "Israel."

Swain, Lionel, "The Inspiration of Scripture," in R.C. Fuller et al., editors, *A New Catholic Commentary on Holy Scripture* (Nashville: Thomas Nelson, 1969),

Thurston, Herbert, "Calendar," in the *Catholic Encyclopedia* (vol. 3, 1908, pg.158–160).

Turner, William, *History of Philosophy* (Ginn: Boston, 1929).

Vaganay, "Catholic Exegesis," in A. Robert - A. Tricot, *Guide to the Bible* (Desclée: New York, 1960), 738–743.

Vawter, Bruce, "Genesis," in the *New Catholic Commentary on Holy Scripture*.

Viviano, Benedict, on Matt. 2:23 in *The New Jerome Biblical Commentary*, p. 636

Vögtle, Anton, "*Rivelazione e mito*," in *Problemi e orientamenti di teologia dogmatica*, vol. I (Milan, 1957).

Waldstein, Michael M., "Analogia Verbi: The Truth of Scripture in Rudolf Bultmann and Raymond Brown," [in Scott W. Hahn, editor, Letter and Spirit (St. Paul Center for Biblical Theology, 2228 Sunset Boulevard, Suite 2A, Steubenville, OH 43952), p. 98.]

Walsh, William H., *An Introduction to Philosophy of History*, 3d rev. ed. (London: Hutchinson and Co., 1970), pp. 14–15.

Wansbrough, Henry, on Matt. 2:23 in *A New Catholic Commentary on Holy Scripture*, p. 908.

Webster's New College Dictionary (2007).

Wikipedia (on line).

Wood, F.J., "Scientific Method," in the Encyclopedia Americana.

World Almanac, "Perpetual Calendar."

Young, R., *Analytical Concordance to the Bible*.

Index

Albright, W.F.: introd. no. 34; chap. 2, nos. 9, 49; chap. 6, no. 39; chap. 15, no. 5; chap. 16, no. 20; chap. 17, no. 42

Allegory of the two testaments: chap. 3, nos. 28–36.

Baur, Ferdinand: chap. 6, no. 11.

Barnes, Henry: chap. 5, no. 13; chap. 6, nos. 25–26.

Beck, David: chap. 2, nos. 16, 42.

Benedict XV, Pope: chap. 2, no. 52 ; chap. 6, no. 8; chap. 7, no. 2E; chap. 8, nos. 4–6, 13D-13E; chap. 9, no. 23.

Benedict XVI, Pope: introd. nos. 3–4, 6; chap. 2, nos. 1–3, 5–6, 26; chap. 5, nos. 1, 40.

Bouyer, Louis: chap. 6, nos. 3, 24.

Brown, Raymond: chap. 2, no. 55; chap. 4, nos. 32–33, 37; chap. 13, nos. 2–3, 7–9; chap. 14, nos. 2–6; chap. 15, part III, nos. 1–14; chap. 17, nos. 14–21, 34–35.

Bultmann, Rudolf: introd. nos. 4, 5, 11, 15–17, 19, 21 23, 36–37, 42, 45; chap. 1, nos. 4, 6 16–18, 21–25; chap. 2, nos. 3–5, 7–8, 13, 16, 42, 44–50; chap. 3, nos. 1, 3, 5–6, 7–9, 11, 23–25, 27; chap. 4, nos. 1–40,; chap. 5, nos. 1, 37–38, 44, 52; chap. 6, nos. 2, 18, 29, 31, 40, 42; chap. 7, nos. 5–7, 11–13; chap. 8, nos. 1–2, 14–16; chap. 10, throughout; chap. 11 throughout; chap. 12, nos. 3, 6–8; chap. 15, part II, nos. 1–15; chap. 17, nos. 2–13.

Cahill, Joseph: chap. 10, nos. 46–56; chap. 11, nos. 15–17.

Catechism of the Catholic Church: chap. 4, no. 8.

Catholic form-critical exegetes: chap. 4, nos. 13, 15; chap. 6, nos. 36–42.

Catholic writers responding to demythologizing: chap. 4, nos. 22–24; whole chapters 10 and 11.

Chrysostom, chap. 3, no. 23; chap. 4, nos. 34, 39, 41; chap. 12, no. 11;

Rationalism: introd. nos. 2, 23, 30, 33, 35 38, 44; chap. 6, nos. 9–22; chap. 9, nos. 5–8, 20–22.

Ratzinger, Joseph: ch. 1, nos. 1–5, 17, 19–20; chap. 2: nos. 2–6, 17; chap. 4, nos. 6, 8; chap. 5, nos. 38, 44; chap. 7, nos. 11, 13.

Reality: chap. 1, nos. 11, 23–24; chap. 2, no. 48; chap. 3, nos. 5–6; chap. 4, nos. 18–19.

Reductive approach: chap. 1, no. 21; chap. 2, nos. 43–44, 52–53.

Reimarus, Hermann: chap. 9, nos. 5, 7; chap. 10, no. 105b.

Rizzi, Anthony: introd. nos. 25–26; chap. 5, nos. 34–36.

Schmidt, Karl L.: chap. 4, no. 10; chap. 6, no. 39; chap. 10, no. 57; chap. 15, part II, no. 14.

Science in general: introd. nos. 25, 27; chap. 2, nos. 11, 39; chap. 3, no. 6; chapter 5, nos. 1–8, 20–36.

Science of historical theology: chap. 5, nos. 51–59.

Second Vatican Council: chap. 4, no. 7.

Simon, Richard: chap. 6, nos. 2, 5, 8; chap. 9, nos. 2–3; chap. 9, no. 5; chap. 15, part III, no. 2.

Sitz im Leben: chap. 4, no. 25.

Slade, Cecil: chap. 6, no. 28.

Stanley, David: chap. 6, no. 17.

Strauss, David: chap. 6, no. 11.

Suelzer, Alexa: introd. no. 30; chap. 6, nos. 13, 38.

Swain, Lionel: introd. no. 32; chap. 7, nos. 1, 3–5, 11.

synthesis of exegetical method: introd. nos. 5, 6, 17, 18, 23, 24; chap. 1, no. 1; chap. 2, no. 12; chap. 3, nos. 1–3, 10–12; chap. 4, no. 16; chap. 5, nos. 40, 44; chap. 7, nos. 11–13; chap. 8, no. 11; chap. 10, nos. 87, 96, 107.

Theological science: chap. 5, nos. 45–51.

Unscientific procedures: introd. nos. 12, 16; chap. 2, nos. 9, 34, 47, 49–50, 55; chap. 3, no 8; chap. 6, nos. 20, 22; chap. 7, no. 12; chap. 8, no. 17; chap. 9, no. 16.

Vawter, Bruce: introd. no. 30, chap. 6, no. 37.

Vögtle, Anton: chap. 10, nos. 85–96; chap. 11, nos. 31–39.

Waldenstein, Michael M., introd. no. 37